Bison Books editions by David Lavender

Bent's Fort

The Fist in the Wilderness

One Man's West

Westward Vision: The Story of the Oregon Trail

CALIFORNIA

LAND OF NEW BEGINNINGS

DAVID LAVENDER

Afterword by the Author

University of Nebraska Press
Lincoln and London

First Bison Book printing: 1987
Most recent printing indicated by the first digit below:

        5   6   7   8   9   10

Library of Congress Cataloging-in-Publication Data
Lavender, David Sievert, 1910–
  California, land of new beginnings.
  Reprint. Originally published: New York: Harper &
Row, 1972.
  Bibliography: p.
  Includes index.
  1. California—History. I. Title.
F861.L38 1987   979.4   86-30929
ISBN 0-8032-2874-0
ISBN 0-8032-7924-8 (pbk.)

Reprinted by arrangement with David Lavender

For Mildred, with love

CONTENTS

Maps

CALIFORNIA: LAND OF NEW BEGINNINGS

Prologue to Giganticism

Patterns of Irony

About six miles west of downtown Los Angeles is an accidental jux-
taposition of landmarks, natural and man-made, that serves as an ironic
introduction to some of California's furious ambivalences. The site is
Hancock Park. Within the park's modest thirty-two acres are several ugly
black bogs, a few life-sized, fiberglass replicas of prehistoric mammals,
and a cluster of three spectacular buildings that were opened in March,
1965, as housing for the Los Angeles County Art Museum. Fronting both
the bogs and the buildings is the nervous energy of Wilshire Boulevard,
created during the 1920's to exploit the revolutionary shopping and living
patterns just then being created by the automobile.

All tour guides of the city mention these items in isolation. More might
be learned by pulling them together.

First, the black bogs. Fenced off by heavy gray wire from the public's
careless feet but not from the public's litter, they are a family of odorous
petroleum seeps known as the La Brea Tar Pits. Many similar upwellings
were once active throughout Southern California, and a few still remain.
As their viscous liquid oozed down the hillsides or collected in depressions, as at Hancock Park, the volatile components evaporated. The residue was, and is, a sticky black pitch.

For centuries the pitch served as a useful resource for humans. By
daubing it onto their reed baskets and letting it harden, Indians achieved
watertight utensils. They used it as a binding material when adding
patterns of colored seashells to various objects. Canoes caulked with the
pitch could be paddled across twenty or more miles of open ocean to the
islands of the Santa Barbara Channel.

The original settlers of Los Angeles also learned to utilize the stuff,
hauling congealed chunks into their pueblo, or town, softening it in

1

cauldrons, and smearing it as waterproofing onto the earthen roofs of their square adobe houses. It was a mixed blessing up there, however. Under a hot sun the tar liquefied and dripped in gooey stringers over the eaves onto passers-by careless enough to walk beneath.

But men are curious as well as pragmatic. In 1792, eleven years after the founding of Los Angeles, a visiting scientist, José Longinos Martínez, heard stories that led him to ride to the pits in search of nothing more tangible than information. Rain drainage, he had been told, collected on the shiny surface of the depressions, and when other sources of water dried up, the sheen of the liquid was fatally tempting to thirsty wildlife. True enough, Martínez found. "In hot weather animals have been seen to sink in it [the lake] and when they tried to escape they were unable to do so, because their feet were stuck and the lake swallowed them. After many years their bones have come up through the holes, as if petrified."

He collected several specimens, but the earth sciences were not far enough advanced in 1792 for him to realize how very old and petrified the bones really were. Another century passed before the La Brea Tar Pits were heralded as one of the stupendous paleontological treasure houses of the world.

For perhaps 40,000 years a succession of mammals (but no dinosaurs or other reptilians) had walked into that deceptive ooze, had bellowed their fright as it engulfed them, and had perished. Condors and great wolves came to feast on the carrion and were caught in their turn. Flesh gone, their bones sank with the others, to be preserved in the airless vaults of bitumen. Recovered, they have provided scientists with a panorama of endless changes in climate and of life adapting itself to the altering weather. There have been saber-toothed tigers and woolly mammoths, inured to cold; tapirs that throve in hot and humid swamps; desert peccaries, tall storks, a peacock; and primitive horses from herds that once ranged the grasslands of the entire continent and then vanished.

There were also human hunters among those mammals. In 1971, a fragment of skull from the pits was tentatively dated as being 23,000 years old. Its belated appearance there in the ooze represents a profound new spirit in the life flow. One manifestation of it later led José Martínez to reach gingerly out into the black gum for petrified bones that he could take home and study. Still later, the warmth of that same strange inner fire prompted the building of the nearby art museum, its slender colonnades rising beside those ancient pools of darkness like cords of solidified air—"one of the most magnificent buildings," declared historian T. H. Watkins of Oakland, an area not given to hyperbole about Los Angeles, "ever achieved by any civilization anywhere at any time."

And from out front comes the surging roar of Wilshire Boulevard.

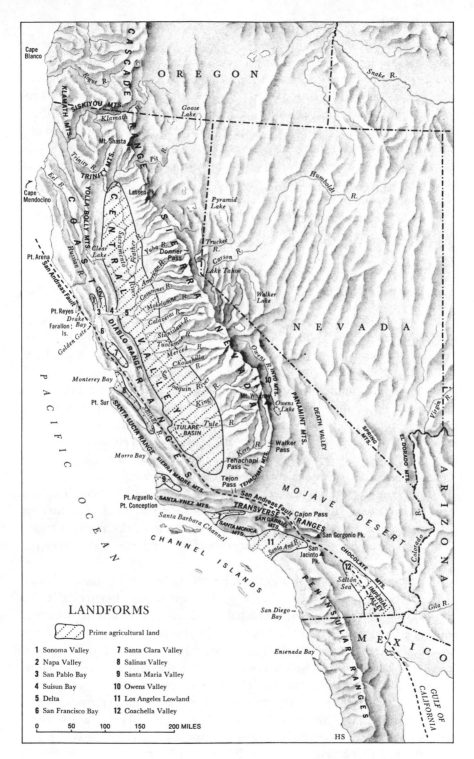

Cape Blanco

O R E G O N

Snake R.

C A S C A D E

KLAMATH MTS.
SISKIYOU MTS.

Rogue R.

Klamath

Goose Lake

Mt. Shasta

Pit R.

R A N G E

Pyramid Lake

Humboldt R.

Cape Mendocino

Eel R.

Trinity R.

TRINITY MTS.

YOLLA BOLLY MTS.

Lassen Pk.

C E N T R A L

Clear Lake

Sacramento R.

Feather R.

Yuba R.

Donner Pass

Truckee R.

Carson R.

Pt. Arena

Russian R.

San Andreas Fault

Pt. Reyes
Drake Bay
Farallon Is.

Golden Gate

3 4 5

6

DIABLO RANGE

C O A S T

American R.

Cosumnes R.

Mokelumne R.

Calaveras R.

Stanislaus R.

Tuolumne R.

Merced R.

V A L L E Y

S I E R R A

N E V A D A

Lake Tahoe

Walker Lake

N E V A D A

Monterey Bay

7

Chowchilla R.

San Joaquin River

Owens Rive Mts.

10

Owens Lake

Mt. Whitney

PANAMINT MTS.

DEATH VALLEY

SPRING MTS.

EL DORADO MTS.

Virgin R.

Pt. Sur

SANTA LUCIA RANGE

Salinas R.

8

R A N G E S

Kings R.

TULARE BASIN

Tule R.

Morro Bay

SIERRA MADRE MTS.

Kern R.

Tehachapi Pass

Walker Pass

Pt. Arguello
Pt. Conception

9

SANTA YNEZ MTS.

Tejon Pass

TEHACHAPI MTS.

M O J A V E   D E S E R T

A R I Z O N A

Colorado R.

Santa Barbara Channel

SANTA MONICA MTS.

TRANSVERSE RANGES

San Andreas Fault

Cajon Pass

SAN GABRIEL MTS.

San Gorgonio Pk.

C H A N N E L   I S L A N D S

P A C I F I C   O C E A N

11

Santa Ana R.

San Jacinto Pk.

CHOCOLATE MTS.

12

Salton Sea

IMPERIAL VALLEY

Gila R.

San Diego Bay

P E N I N S U L A R

Ensenada Bay

M E X I C O

GULF OF CALIFORNIA

R A N G E S

LANDFORMS

Prime agricultural land

1 Sonoma Valley
2 Napa Valley
3 San Pablo Bay
4 Suisun Bay
5 Delta
6 San Francisco Bay

7 Santa Clara Valley
8 Salinas Valley
9 Santa Maria Valley
10 Owens Valley
11 Los Angeles Lowland
12 Coachella Valley

0   50   100   150   200 MILES

HS

Opposing phalanxes of automobiles stream and stop, stream and stop, their motors agitated by complex refinements of the same substance that preserved, in the La Brea Pits, those petrified relics of vanished forms of life. It was on Wilshire Boulevard, one remembers idly, that synchronized traffic lights were used for the first time anywhere by any civilization. That, too, is a manifestation of the human spirit, making, like art, still another declaration of imposed order. And the cars stream and stop, stream and stop, and there are days when the huge depression known as the Los Angeles Basin is filled almost to its brim with another dark pool of hydrocarbons.

In some distant future will a member of a new species reach out for one of our relics and turn it in his hands, puzzling?

Stored Energy

We know—without really knowing, because the scope of the process stuns the imagination—that this continent, like all continents, has been shaped by incalculable forces working throughout almost incalculable stretches of time. It may even be that time does not exist within so boundless a happening. Still, there were rhythms. Oceans advanced and retreated. Mountains rose, were leveled, and stubbornly rose again. Valleys sank and were filled. One would hardly call it a plan of action. But as an inchoate experiment, a testing of methods . . . well, anyway, there came to the central section of the state-to-be a certain enduring pattern.

It was a four-part alignment: salt water, then a long mountain range bordered on part of its eastern side by a profound geosyncline, and beyond that depression a still greater line of mountains. Using current terminology and moving from west to east, we have the Pacific Ocean, the Coast Ranges, the Great Central Valley, and the Cascade-Sierra Nevada wall.

The heart of this sequence is the Central Valley, an elongated mountain-girt bowl shaped like a hot dog. Its curved northern rim is the Trinity Mountains, a heavily forested tangle of peaks and canyons that links the Coast Ranges to the Cascades. In the process these mountains create in the extreme northern part of the state an isolated, thinly populated region that is almost always ignored in the grand plans of politicians, economists, and historians of the western scene.

The Central Valley's southern rim is formed by an extension of the Sierra Nevada. Called the Tehachapi Range, this brushy uplift curls westward to meet, eventually, a series of precipitous ridges that run due east and west like corrugations in a tin roof. Called generically the Transverse Ranges, these ridges go by a multitude of local names. South of them is a subtropical entity known as Southern California, which no planner ever ignores for any reason, even though the region is as isolated geographically from the state's central core as is the extreme north.

One other anomaly might be noted. It is natural to think of the California coast as running due north and south. For a little distance below the Oregon border it does. But after the shoreline has passed Cape Mendocino, which is the westernmost bulge of the conterminous United States, it develops a southeasterly trend. From Point Conception in the Santa Barbara area on to Los Angeles there are stretches where the line strikes due east. Here the dominant mountains, the Transverse Ranges, also run east. When the coast dips southward again, the mountains continue stubbornly in their old direction, pushing as far inland as San Bernardino and climbing to more than 11,000 feet in elevation. Not until they have reached the San Bernardino area does another major line of north-south mountains appear, the San Jacintos, which wall off the Los Angeles Basin from the wastes of the Colorado desert.

Nimble geographers frequently win drinks in barrooms out of Southern California's insistent easterliness: Los Angeles, in spite of the stubborn disbelief of an ever-renewed crop of outlanders, really is east of Reno, Nevada; San Diego really is on a line with the western border of Idaho. One is even tempted to read cultural symbolism into this topographic slant. San Francisco, at least in the minds of its own inhabitants, is true West. Los Angeles is Midwest.

As noted earlier, the understructure of these geographic alignments was established eons ago. But though the skeleton has remained fairly constant, its flesh has not. And it has been this interplay of geologic change on top of relative stability that accounts in many ways for the quality of California living today.

For example: ocean floors heaved upward at various periods. Great sheets of polar ice inexplicably melted. When those phenomena occurred, the level of the sea (the great "invariable" by which we measure altitude) was lifted cataclysmically. Salt water rushed in through the low saddles of the Coast Range. Peaks became islands; probably they looked much like the islands that now parallel the coast of Southern California from Point Conception to the vicinity of San Diego. San Francisco Bay was enormously enlarged, and the Central Valley was inundated by waves rushing into it through the mouth of its combined rivers, the Sacramento and San Joaquin. Most of Southern California was awash. Farther inland, rampaging tides swept northward out of what we call the Gulf of California.

This invading water, like all water, nurtured hosts of microscopic, single-cell plants called diatoms. Diatoms reproduce by cell division—an awesome population explosion. Within one month a single parent can be the source of one billion descendants. Each has its own hard, siliceous cell. As these billions and billions of plants die, a tiny blizzard of cell coverings falls constantly onto the ocean floor (or lake floor, since there are also fresh-water diatoms). Thus when California's unstable ocean retreated after a few million years, it left behind, as part of its marine sediment, deposits of light-colored diatomaceous earth, some of them hundreds of feet thick.

Indians used suitable concentrations of this substance for painting white stripes on their bodies. Outsiders, arriving later, utilized diatomaceous earth in the manufacture of dynamite and soundproofing material. Those economic values were insignificant, however, compared to what was produced by the bodies of the dead diatoms. Certain concentrations of them turned, under favorable conditions of temperature and pressure, into petroleum.

Small quantities of that diatom-produced oil later welled up in the La Brea Tar Pits and elsewhere. Some of the wealth gained from deeper lakes of petroleum helped build the nearby art museum. Wherever produced, this ancient energy provides the ambience of a thousand boulevards like Wilshire. Or, to put matters another way, the remnant of our lost oceans has been, for the past century, one of the principal dynamics of California history. We shall hear more of it.

More Treasure Troves

In those early times—early to our boggled imaginations but relatively late in geological spans—the easternmost of the California's geologic staples, the Sierra Nevada, was relatively low—almost flat enough, indeed, to be called a peneplain. Underneath it and responsible, in part, for the original uplift was a giant mass of igneous rock. Mostly granite, this huge block measured approximately 400 miles in length and 40 to 80 miles in width. The convulsion of its first rising had produced cracks that filled with molten quartz. Through some still-obscure set of circumstances, the veins of quartz in the west-central section of the mass chanced to be freighted with stringers of gold. Though not the only deposits of gold in what became California, those in the western Sierra were by all odds the most important.

Erosion broke bits of the quartz loose from the surrounding rock. Later the gold was eroded out of the quartz. Because it was heavy, the fragments of metal settled quickly to the bottoms of the still-gentle streams.

Distribution probably was not widespread.

Matters changed when a series of deep-seated paroxysms cracked the eastern part of the Sierra loose from the adjacent land and tilted it upward several thousand feet, not all at once but in widely spaced stages. During the same period the Owens Valley, a trough to the east of the mountains, dropped abysmally. The result was a towering escarpment. Somewhat modified now by erosion, this jagged, 400-mile wall reaches its apex near its center. The highest point is Mount Whitney, 14,495 feet in elevation, the loftiest peak in the United States outside of Alaska.

Such violent mountain forming creates geologic echoes. One sounded a century ago (at 2:00 A.M., March 26, 1872) near the little town of Lone Pine in the Owens Valley at Whitney's eastern toes. The land along the old fault slipped a little. That is, it moved a few feet, not thousands. The roar of the displacement was heard as far away as Sacramento on the other side of the range. Rock avalanches crashed down Whitney's flanks; lakes vanished; streams burst from their channels. Two dozen people, perhaps more, died in the wreckage of the village. If such a blow were to strike a crowded city . . . well, California would learn about that, too. But this is a digression.

The tilting of the Sierra placed its ridgetop very near the eastern escarpment. Ninety percent of the mountain block sloped west. No escarpment marked that descent. The one-time peneplain still looked much like a rolling plateau, densely forested. After the upheaval, however, the total drop from ridgetop to valley was far greater than it had been before. The major streams now plunged boisterously, carving canyons of great depth and carrying vast amounts of alluvial material into the Central Valley. There it added deep bands of soil to the layers of sediment deposited much earlier during the influx of the sea.

Nor was the carving of the Sierra yet finished. During Pleistocene times—the geologic period nearest our own—huge ice sheets crept south from the Arctic, shrank, then inched south again. These repeated glacial flows did not touch the Sierra, but they cooled the air enough so that abnormal quantities of snow fell along the main ridge. There it compacted into local glaciers. As the ice slipped downward, it chiseled out basins for today's exquisite alpine lakes and polished the pale granite of the high country to such a sheen that John Muir, enthralled by it, named the Sierra "the range of light."

In a few places, where unusually thick accumulations of ice had gathered, long glacial fingers were squeezed down the stream channels. Relentlessly grinding, they widened and flattened the canyon bottoms and scoured the walls into giant precipices. Tributary streams, flowing in from the sides, came to the brinks of these cliffs and dropped over in lacy falls. Most famous example of these ice-sculptured valleys is Yosemite.

As the streams along the western slope of the Sierra deepened and quickened, the gold they wore out of the veins of quartz became more widely distributed. At flood times especially, roils of gravel swept the bits of metal farther downstream before allowing them to settle in eddies created by curves or behind boulders and ledges of rock. New blockades appeared, either the moraines left by the ice or blankets and dikes of lava produced by volcanic eruptions that occurred in scattered places throughout Pleistocene times. In finding ways around these interrupters, the rivers sometimes shifted their beds erratically. Often an old streambed would be left high and dry, to turn into a forested flat or even a hillside. Later it was discovered that the gold in these former streambeds still remained in its original resting places, unlikely though the new sites at first appeared.

This widespread dispersal of gold in stream channels and on hillsides throughout a long reach of the Sierra's western foothills created another powerful set of dynamics for emergent California. There was room along the scattered gravel bars for tens of thousands of men to work. Many found gold in sufficient concentrations for them to remove it with simple devices that needed very little capital and only a few helpers for successful operation. The result was ready money in many hands and a quick demand for a dazzling variety of goods—this in a land far removed from most sources of supply. Entrepreneurs of all sorts leaped to fill the vacuums. What followed was a wild economic upsurge in a region that, as the Spanish and Mexicans well knew, had hitherto been highly resistant to material development.

Unearned Increment

The Pleistocene glaciers, whose chill breath created the ice fields of the Sierra Nevada, also drew to themselves so much water that the level of the ocean dropped dramatically—from 75 to as much, during one epoch, as 300 feet. San Francisco Bay turned into a dry plain, and the Golden Gate, the outlet for the united rivers of the Central Valley, became a rocky canyon.

In the far north these sinkings exposed a broad stretch of land between Alaska and Siberia. Calling that union of continents a land bridge, as is generally done, stirs inaccurate connotations. The span may have been as wide, at one era, as 1,000 miles. No one wandering through such a stretch of country would have any feeling of being on a "bridge."

Wanderers were there. Perhaps because of slight snowfall, the western rim of the continent escaped, except along the mountaintops, the glacial blankets that covered so much of the earth farther east. Nor was the exposed land as barren as one might think. The currents of the Pacific tempered the pervading chill. Soon, geologically speaking, scrub willows, thick moss, and coarse grass softened the surface of the emergent plain. Hordes of mammals adapted to such forage grazed back and forth between the continents, followed by huge flesh eaters. Inevitably some of these random herds drifted south through the open valleys. In time they reached the Great Plains at the eastern base of the Rockies, from which reservoir of life further scatterings took place. Behind the animals came scattered little bands of big-game hunters, armed with stone-tipped spears, from the Asian steppes, the ancestors, perhaps, of the American Indian.

There is no agreement among archaeologists as to when the migrations occurred or how many waves there may have been. Conservative estimates date them at from 12,000 to 35,000 years ago. One body of opinion also questions whether these Paleo-Indians, as the first-comers are named, actually reached what we now call California. The Far West, theorists suggest, was not settled until after cultures had already begun to change from a hunting to a food-gathering economy.

But any discussion of origins, as Will Durant has remarked, is little better than educated guesswork. Consider, for instance, this recent find. In 1964, diggers began excavating a hearth in a dry gully about ten miles outside the town of Barstow in California's Mojave Desert. After spending six years, on and off, sifting through 23 feet of overburden, the patient searchers retrieved, early in 1970, artifacts which were then subjected to rigorous carbon dating and magnetic examinations. In the opinion of archaeologist S. B. Leaky (who has found, in Africa, traces of a manlike creature dating back perhaps 2.6 million years) these tests indicate that humankind of some sort inhabited the Mojave area at least 50,000 years ago "and more probably 100,000 years ago."

Where did these hominoids come from? What is their relationship, if any, to California's Indians?

Millennia past, the Mojave was very different from what it is now. Meadows rustled; streams abounded. A wealth of animal life beyond our conception roamed everywhere. Then, for some unknown reason—say 10,000 years or more ago—the last of the glaciers began its retreat. Cold air warmed, cloud covers thinned, evaporation quickened. California's two north-south lines of mountains milked moisture from Pacific storms, and scant rainfall reached the interior. As aridity increased, the herds of grass eaters began to disappear. It was a frightening extinction. Thirty-five kinds of mammals who left their bones in the dark pitch of the La Brea Tar Pits no longer survive in North America. Many have vanished entirely from the earth.

Man, whatever the place of his origin, proved more resilient. It is not likely that his adaptations were conscious, panicked, or hurried. Probably the groups who inhabited the slowly drying Great Basin and Southwest had already experimented, between feasts on mammoth meat, with other foods: seeds, pine nuts, rabbits, the small deer of the brushlands, lizards, locusts, and even the larvae of certain flies that collected in masses on the sedge around the shrinking lakes. As big game grew scarce, reliance on these substitutes increased until at last the methods of obtaining and preparing them seemed as old as time. The new life styles that accompanied the changes were sanctified meanwhile by a fresh corpus of myth and ritual handed down from generation to generation until this too seemed part of eternity. It is so with all evolving cultures, including our own.

As has already been suggested, the first groups to arrive in California may have been hunters whose origins are lost in dimness. Or, possibly, the land really was empty of humankind until after the shift from a hunting to a food-gathering culture had begun. Whenever immigration developed, it was not a concerted flow. The wide diversity of tongues spoken within historic times—more than a hundred dialects of five basic language stocks—suggests a varied influx over a long period from many starting points, until at last the area sustained more native Americans than any other region north of tropical Mexico—as many, according to such noted anthropologists as S. F. Cook and A. L. Kroeber, as 250,000 persons. Villages appeared in every part of the state-to-be except the High Sierra—and even its delicious meadows became refuges, then as now, for dwellers in the Central Valley who were eager to escape the heat of the rainless summers.

The magnet during the centuries was California's profusion of foods. Successive runs of salmon filled the northern rivers, including the Sacramento system, throughout most of the summer. The coast furnished an abundance of shellfish. A variety of seeds, among them acorns and mesquite beans, grew in the valleys and on the hillsides. Between harvests these could be stored in big baskets on platforms out of reach of rodents. Ground into flour with stones (and the acorn meal leached of its bitter tannic acid with hot water), they were boiled into mush or baked into cakes. Meat came from a skittering of small game that could be killed with curved throwing-sticks. There were numerous bear, elk, and deer. Though hard to stalk down and kill with the weapons available, these furnished both variety and challenge.

Distributing this cornucopia brought about a unique social system. The unit was not the sort of tribe found farther east (the Sioux or Iroquois, for instance) but a small cluster of people related by blood lines or marriage. In the arid sections of Southern California and in the foothills of the northern Sierra, where nature was more grudging, this cluster was a clan of fifty to seventy people—enough for self-defense but not so many that they would deplete local food stocks. Though the clans lived part of the time in villages of fragile brush houses, the sparse harvest of their land made them more nomadic than the Indians of the rest of California.

Where foods were abundant, the people clustered in more permanent villages called rancherías by the Spanish. A ranchería—there might be related "suburbs" nearby—was the center of what Kroeber has denominated as a tribelet. A tribelet's population varied from one hundred to five hundred men, women, and children. The average was perhaps two hundred and fifty. Scores upon scores of these rancherías were scattered throughout the area of the present state. Several neighboring tribelets might speak dialects of the same language, and ethnologists have used this bond to link the Indians of California into twenty-one "nationalities." In ancient times, however, language bonds created no sense of common purpose, such as we associate with the word "nation" today. It was the tribelet that considered itself one people. Neighbors beyond the next hill were outsiders, even though languages were similar. (An exception to this generality were the Yumans who lived along the Colorado River in the extreme southeast. There, several villages, each speaking the same language, considered themselves a unit. Perhaps because of their numbers, the Yumans were more warlike than the small California tribelets, and looked on battle as a way to prestige.)

Each tribelet had its hereditary chief. If this leader proved incompetent, he could be replaced by a relative. He had little authority, but was an adviser, an arbiter, and the one who welcomed trading parties from another group or visitors attending a festival.

According to the demands of the seasons—the maturing of the plants, the fattening of the animals, the migrations of the fish—the people of each ranchería moved in a set pattern through a carefully delineated block of territory. The area was, in our eyes, quite small. A day's walk would often take a man from one side of it to the other. Within this unit, every natural resource was known, and the inhabitants were, of necessity, instinctive conservationists. If the number of rabbits in a stand of scrubland showed signs of diminishing, the covert most likely was let alone until it recuperated.

Herbs for oral contraception, sexual abstinence at certain periods, coitus interruptus, occasional abortion, and even infanticide all helped, in the opinion of some scholars, to maintain the delicate adjustment between population and the natural carrying capacity of the territory. Aggression for the sake of more living space was rare. If a group suffered "crop failure," it might ask and receive permission to hunt and gather food for a limited time in the territory of a neighboring tribelet. Unauthorized trespass, however, swiftly brought about one of the small wars that from time to time disturbed the normally peaceful societies. In our view, the battles were hardly serious. After a little long-range shooting with bow and arrow had resulted in a few minor casualties, the chiefs, who had watched from the background, arranged a truce and the old ways returned. Yet there were exceptions. A death in one of these encounters—or a raid for the sake of stealing wives—might bring about retaliatory attacks from which long feuds were born.

A powerful sense of place developed among the members of each small group. Stories of tribal migrations, common to most of the other native races of North America, disappeared. Each villager believed that his group had always lived where it currently ranged. Society became patrilocal; that is, the boys stayed with their fathers, who taught them every minute detail concerning the land and the utilization of its products.

The coming of manhood was the time for sanctifying this training. Until then a youth had been strongly influenced by his mother. Because of the demands of exogamy, a custom that may have had its source in the need to cement alliances with neighboring groups, she was quite probably from outside the father's village. As an outsider, she was not the inheritor of local lore and local ritual. Thus when the time arrived for a boy to take his place in the group as a hunter and provider, he was subjected to an initiation that would solemnly and forcefully link him to the beliefs and customs of his father's group.

Initiation was by means of song, story, dance, the handling of sacred objects, and the study, in certain areas, of fragile sand paintings. To make sure that attention did not wander and that the occasion would be remembered, powerful mnemonic devices were employed. The priests in charge of the rites wore fanciful masks and striking costumes. Hallucinatory drinks were used in some locales. Ordeals were frequent. The Yuki of the north thrust an obsidian knife so violently into the pupil's throat that he bled; the Luiseño of the south required their initiates to lie on ant heaps. All this, too, became bound up with the meaning that place held for most California Indians.

To the restless denizens of today's paths of concrete, so profound a territorial attachment is difficult to grasp. And yet the lingering effects of that ancient cultural fact are still with us, most noticeably in certain land patterns bequeathed by the Indians through the Spanish missions.

When the first Franciscan proselytizers came into the coastal strip between San Diego and San Francisco, they sought out building sites close to unfailing water, good timber, and fertile soil. Indian rancherías generally occupied the better sites. The patient padres settled nearby and in ways to be noted later made themselves acceptable. Gradually their buildings became the core of each district, much as the tribelet's central village of reed-thatched huts had been. The land that the missionaries used for their livestock was, in the beginning, the same stretch of valley or coastal terrace that made up the heart of the tribelet's territory. Thus an ambivalent hate-love attached itself to the new establishment. Though each mission was an intruder and a destroyer of ancient ways, it was also a provider and, in part, a cultural replacement of the old village.

Once rooted, the missionary holdings spread rapidly. Within half a century each station's pasture lands sprawled across territory once ranged by several tribelets—a total area, eventually, of some 9 million desirable acres. On the breakup of the missions during the 1830's and 1840's, the bulk of these lands was not returned to the Christianized Indians for whom they had supposedly been held in trust or even divided among colonists whom the Mexican government occasionally tried to lure into California. Rather the vast estates, whose hearts were solid blocks of erstwhile ranchería territory, became private cattle ranches controlled by very few owners—a system that was extended during the chaotic 1840's throughout the lower San Joaquin and Sacramento valleys.

It was the beginning of California's cancerous system of land monopoly. Its evils carried swiftly over into the gold-rush era. Many Americans who had stampeded to the coast in search of instant riches decided to stay. The normal method for those inclined toward farming would have been to settle on small freeholds of the sort that the government of the United States was offering settlers farther east. When the newcomers tried to take up small farms in California, however, they found themselves frustrated not just by the difficult climate but, more exasperatingly, by baronies greater than they were willing to concede to any man within their country's bounds. There were violent riots of protest in Sacramento, bitter legal battles in the San Francisco courts. Alarmed by title uncertainties, farmers who might otherwise have migrated from the east stayed away in droves—at least 250,000 families during the 1850's alone, in the opinion of early-day historian John S. Hittell.

Many of these ranchos, most of them mission-derived, passed undiminished into the hands of a few absorptive Americans. Additional landed empires were patched together from railroad grant lands and from the corrupt manipulation of public domain acres originally given to the state by the federal government. Thus the agrarian ideal of small subsistence farms supporting the bulk of the country's population—an uncertain chimera at best—never had the least chance of taking hold in California. Henry George saw the truth very early here; his brooding on it resulted in one of the most widely read books of economics ever printed, *Progress and Poverty.*

The missions had long since showed that these huge holdings could be worked with Indian labor paid the merest of pittances. The system continued. Farming in California became (and continues to be in many areas) a corporate exercise dependent on the development of massive irrigation projects and the exploitation of vulnerable seasonal help—Indians first, then Chinese, Filipinos, Mexicans, and the Okies and Arkies of the depression period. Not all the tensions rising from this system of agricultural bondage have been solved.

As urbanization spread, strategically located land often became valued more for its unearned increment than for its produce. As one noteworthy example, consider the brand-new city of Irvine, southeast of Los Angeles. It has been waved into being on a ranch compounded originally out of old Spanish rancho grants and part of the holdings of the mission of San Juan Capistrano.

In 1960 the Irvine Company decided to start farming people instead of cattle and other crops. As part of its planting program it donated 1,000 acres to the University of California. The university in turn was to build on that acquisition a branch campus which would serve as the nucleus for a community of 100,000 population. Under the terms of the agreement there were to be no major alterations in the basic plan. Company concepts changed, however. A larger city was envisioned, realigned in such a way that the university campus, already under construction, would stand not in the center but on the periphery of the development.

Certain regents of the University of California, who felt that it was not their function to instruct the Irvine Company about its business, were willing to go along. After all, its land had been a free donation. Others, believing that the proposed alterations would amount to the university's condoning an allegedly unjust enrichment to the company of $430 million, protested. Matters were not helped by the fact that a few of the regents had, as private citizens, certain somewhat nebulous business connections with the company.

Tempers flared during the discussions. At one public meeting on October 16, 1970, while reporters scribbled busily, Governor Ronald Reagan —all governors of the state are automatically members of the university's Board of Regents—became vexed enough that he audibly called a fellow board member a "lying son of a bitch." When millionaire Norton Simon, another regent and one-time candidate for the United States Senate, sought to intervene, Reagan pushed him aside, an episode that became a momentary national scandal—and an outflowing, in part, of land patterns that came into being nearly two centuries since. And so it is not quite correct to say, as famed philosopher Josiah Royce of Harvard said nearly a hundred years ago and as some contemporary observers continue to say, that "the missions have meant, for American California, little more than a memory." Rather, the effects of their land policies, born originally of the territorial attachments of the Indians, are still very much with us, however obscure the chain of title may seem to the impatient developers of modern suburbia.

Or to return to our original metaphor, land has been another of the powerful dynamics shaping the course of California's history.

The Way to Go

Geography also spawned cancerous monopolies in transportation. No matter from what direction a would-be trader or colonist approached California, he ran into difficulties. Winds that blew with dismaying regularity out of the northwest buffeted sailing ships coming up from Mexico. Long expanses of aridity shriveled the spirits of those traveling by land. And even after a traveler had survived the long approaches, he found that there were few natural gateways into California itself.

The geographical restrictions first became evident along the seacoast. To borrow the translated words of the first European to report on it (Bartoloméo Ferrelo of the Cabrillo expedition of 1542–43), most of the littoral is made up of mountains "that rise to the sky, and against which the sea beats and which appear as if they would fall on the ships."

This stern coastline is, moreover, relatively straight—1,264 miles from border to border in comparison to a crow-flight distance, north to south, of 780 miles. In other words the barrier is scalloped by few natural harbors and estuaries.* Of true landlocked refuges there are only three in California, and two of them were long prevented by topographical circumstances from engendering a competitive commerce.

To be more precise: the northernmost of these three ports, tree-girt Humboldt Bay, flourished during the gold-rush era and intermittently thereafter as an entry into lucrative timberlands, especially coastal red-

---

*The equivalent stretch of the Atlantic coastline runs from approximately Cape Cod, Massachusetts, to Charleston, South Carolina. Deeply indented by many commodious sounds and river mouths, that eastern littoral is much longer than the western, as even a superficial glance at the map will show.

woods, but there was little else in the rugged back country to attract traders. San Diego's rim of mountains created similar problems. Although the bay was large enough to shelter most of the United States Navy, its geographic isolation long frustrated efforts to develop a flourishing hinterland.

Only the central bay, San Francisco, furnished a true breach in the barrier. But what a breach! It is so generous and so unexpected (a scattering of Spanish mariners sailed by the Golden Gate intermittently for two hundred years without detecting it) that nature appears almost apologetic, as if trying to make up in this one spot for the commercial niggardliness she has shown everywhere else from the mouth of the Columbia River (whose bar has dangerous teeth) to the tip of Baja California. Just that one opening—nothing else. No wonder the sea merchants of New England and New York were solidly behind President Polk's determination to obtain California from Mexico—not for the great bay's value at the time, when only whalers and hide droghers were using it, but for the command they sensed it would eventually have as an American outlet to Asia.

Which shows how accurate people can be for the wrong reasons. For it was not Oriental commerce that swiftly justified Polk's acquisitiveness, but rather California's own gold fields.

The whole western slope of the Sierra Nevada, it will be recalled (and much of the southern Cascades as well), drains into the long depression that makes up the state's core. The waters of the northern valley gather in the Sacramento River and flow south. The San Joaquin collects most of the southern waters and carries them north.* The rivers meet in a confused, island-strewn delta midway between the cities of Stockton and Sacramento. Having joined, they push west into broad Suisun Bay, are constricted again at Carquinez Strait, and finally emerge in San Pablo Bay, the northern extension of San Francisco Bay. And the bay's only entrance is the Golden Gate.

Supplies for the foothill mines poured in along that water highway; bullion poured back. There was no way, at first, to divert it. Unchallenged by competition, the entrepreneurs of the cool white city beside the Golden Gate worked out their own fat distribution systems for handling it all: steamers, riverboats, express companies, stagelines, mule trains, freight wagons. They even began experimenting with little short-line railroads whose rails and locomotives were brought by ship around Cape

---

*The extreme southern section of the valley is a sink that has no outlet. In preirrigation days water from the Kern and other rivers collected there in broad, shallow lakes bordered by dense growths of tall rushes called tules. During unusually wet springs, the lakes overflowed through a tangle of meandering channels into the San Joaquin.

Horn. These first trains, it should be noted, remained completely sea-oriented. The merchandise they carried arrived by water, and they were used only as auxiliaries to what was essentially a water monopoly.

The system had its vulnerabilities, nevertheless. Waterborne freight from the East Coast either had to circle South America or else had to take a shortcut across the Isthmus of Panama on a dinky little railroad, completed January, 1855, whose charges were limited only by the competition of the Cape Horn steamers. Both routes were tedious and often dangerous. Dissatisfied shippers and travelers soon began clamoring for a transcontinental railroad that would link the East directly to the West.

Four Sacramento merchants (not seaside San Franciscans) responded. Underwritten by the federal government, they drove their Central Pacific across the Sierra to connect with the Union Pacific in Utah. In May, 1869, cross-country cargoes began rumbling down from Donner Pass into the Central Valley. For a long time no competitors appeared. Again geography explains why. There were few practicable routes over the mountains or across the deserts. Using a new corporate name, the Southern Pacific Company, the owners of the railroad—Charles Crocker, Mark Hopkins, Collis P. Huntington, and Leland Stanford—quickly plugged those openings with their own track.

Few other states ever received so wide a network of rails so rapidly—or so monopolistically. Resistance to the iron embrace stirred four decades of angry reverberations throughout the state. There were bitter novels of protest, fatal shootings, sly accommodations in every county courthouse and in the legislative halls at Sacramento. Some observers still contend that the present unstructured condition of California's politics dates back to the demoralization of those frantic days.

Now the din is shifting to the freeways controlled by a monopolistic state bureaucracy which, because of its mastery of gas-revenue money, is almost as unresponsive to popular clamor as was the railroad. That is to say, transportation has always been a major theme in the California story.

Irrigating the People Farms

And finally, the surprising patterns of precipitation. California, as stated earlier, is 780 miles long and from 150 to 350 miles wide. Altitudes range from below sea level to 14,495 feet. Rectilinear surveys, the standard American method for calculating area, yield a figure of 158,297 square miles, or something more than 100 million acres. If the landscape were pulled out flat, the way one smooths a rumpled bedspread, the area would be considerably greater—how much greater, I have no idea.

Spreading entirely across this big, bent parallelogram is one remarkable constant in climate, summer drought. The last showers have generally misted away by mid-April. By May the fields of poppies, lupine, and bright yellow mustard have gone to seed. The heavy-headed wild oats that nod on such flats and hillsides as are not clotted with housing developments turn as dun-colored as the hide of a cougar. By September a footstep crackles. If circumstances conspire, the backfire of a tractor suffices to set the grasslands ablaze.

Even more dangerous is the mixed brush, called chaparral, that cloaks the steeper mountainsides of central and southern California. In the early 1900's, when promoters were hunting out romantic terms for everything in the land, these widespread thickets were named "elfin forests." In the spring there is some appropriateness to the name. Thorny buckbrush shakes out its bridal white, sumac its dull red spikes; California's "wild lilac," *Ceanothus*, waves lacy plumes colored every shade of blue. By fall, though, the tight evergreen needles and the small leather leaves have puckered like wrinkled skin to resist the transpiration of moisture. Loaded with sap, they are ready to explode at the touch of a careless— or deliberate—match.

By now the hazard should be thoroughly known. Mission records a century and a half old speak of tornadoes of flame sweeping across the hillsides, of women and children running in terror to the beaches, of workers at the compounds wetting blankets and watching embers swirl onto the tile roofs. Tile, notice. The missionaries learned. Today many people are less wise. Forgetting how far wind can blow a brand, they cover their suburban houses with shakes that look properly rustic but are as dry as the chaparral. Each year fires devour dozens of carelessly placed homes. Later, when winter rains drench the denuded slopes, masses of muddy ash slip like black syrup down the hillsides and through the canyons.

As a preventative, huge bulldozers regularly and precariously scrape firebreaks along the tops of the ridges on whose lower slopes the reckless houses rise. The effort often fails. Flame leaps wildly, especially when Santa Ana winds roar in from the desert. The withering blasts, named for the Santa Ana canyon east of present Los Angeles, were first noticed by Spanish settlers nearly 200 years ago. Set in motion by changing barometric pressure, great masses of air cross the mountains from the desert and burst down the canyons toward the coast. Grown hotter still from compression, the winds suck away humidity and leave people feeling as shriveled as the chaparral.

In 1961 a single mad conflagration destroyed 400 plush estates in the wealthy Bel Air section of Los Angeles. The fall of 1970 was worse. An intermittent series of wind-driven fires howled across firebreaks by the hundreds, blackened more than half a million acres of brushland, killed several people, and consumed or damaged 1,500 buildings in scattered spots between Oakland and San Diego. The diffusing smoke from the holocaust drifted as far as Wyoming, where it spread a strange, diaphanous veil across the mountains.

Fire fighters pray then for a resumption of the normal inflow of humid air from the ocean. Sooner or later it comes, a benediction from the coastal fogs that prevail during most of the summer nights and in the early morning. The drip of it sustains the giant redwoods that once extended along the shoreline from the Oregon border south past Big Sur into the deep canyons of the Santa Lucia Mountains. Lima beans on the Oxnard plain seldom need any other moisture; the touch of its fingers invigorates lemon trees on the coastal terraces and in the seaside canyons of Ventura and Santa Barbara counties. When Santa Ana winds are not blowing, this misty inflow maintains, day in and day out, the soft, monotonous mildness of which old-timers in the Los Angeles Basin and at San Diego are so proud. Farther north, where the mists are thicker, human reactions vary. Some people, the long-legged girls of San Francisco and Monterey in particular, stride briskly, feeling stimulated. Others grumble at the damp rawness.

In November, when the smell of seven months of dust lies heavy on the leaves, the Pacific High begins to crack. Storms born in the Aleutian Islands thrust southward. During the subsequent twenty weeks or so the coastal mountains in northwestern California are turned sodden by as much as a hundred inches of rain. Farther south, amounts dwindle. San Diego's annual average is ten inches. Yet even in the south the mountaintops often receive three feet or more of rain, most of it during a few violent storms. Runoff cascades furiously through canyons that drop like narrow ladders down the steep hillsides. It is an awesome experience to stand, during a downpour, at the point where one of the lateral streams debouches into a main valley and listen to rampaging boulders crash together under the chocolate-colored surface. Unlike fires, these winter torrents have been partly harnessed. In populous sections, their channels have been straightened, lined with concrete, and aimed like rifles toward the sea, to the detriment of underground aquifers that the periodic runoffs once kept full.

The Coast Ranges, the Transverse Ranges, and the mountains that shut off the Los Angeles Lowlands from the Colorado Desert create dry rain shadows over the land to the east of them. So far as the Central Valley is concerned, this aridity is relieved by the Sierra. Its slowly rising western slope deflects storm currents upward. Moisture, turning to snow at high elevations, drenches a wide swath of the mountains. A total fall of 60 feet of snow during a winter is not abnormal; the record is 100 feet. Fed by the slow melting, streams flow steadily into the Central Valley throughout the parched months of summer.

These incredible tonnages of moisture are not concentrated where they are most needed—in the cities circling San Francisco Bay, the fertile lands of the southern San Joaquin and of the oven-like Imperial Valley in the Colorado Desert, in the Los Angeles Basin and the crowded coastal strip leading to San Diego. The result has been a monumental tampering, at astronomical cost, with the natural scheme of things. Water whisked from the Owens Valley east of the Sierra to Los Angeles destroyed several small communities for the sake of one Gargantua. Natural wonders have been drowned; ecological balances have been altered in ways not yet fully understood.

For a time economic results seemed to justify the alterations. Lettuce farmers in the Imperial Valley, cotton farmers in the San Joaquin Valley, and the creators of suburbs north and south throve as never before. Overnight cities, springing alive beside piped-in artificial lakes, boasted in various media of their country-style amenities and of their speculative possibilities: THIS LAND WILL GROW PEOPLE was one favorite slogan. Smog-weary parents, hunting a touch of soil and the excitement of rising property values, swarmed in. Blossoming with schoolyards and two- to three-car garages, the new creations were soon demanding freeways to connect them with still-newer "recreational communities" farther afield. Meanwhile the hearts of the original cities decay, spawning ghettos with their proliferating problems.

California's furious ambivalences: the following three things occurred during the same two-week period in October, 1970. Governor Ronald Reagan dedicated a huge new reservoir near Riverside, in Southern California. This reservoir is part of the gigantic California Water Plan for canaling northern precipitation into the south—it will be discussed in more detail further on—and is deemed necessary to provide for immediate increases in population. But what of more distant needs? Bemused by that persistent California question, President Nixon signed, almost simultaneously with the dam dedication, a bill that will provide funds for studying the feasibility of building yet another conduit from the wet north. This one, its planners hope—and the imagination staggers—will run beside the coast *underneath* the ocean, and beside atomic plants constructed to provide still more water by desalting part of the sea. Where is the end?

It may not be the end envisioned by the water harvesters. Within days of the time that Governor Reagan dedicated the dam near Riverside and President Nixon launched studies for an undersea pipeline, members of the State Air Resources Board took a long look at the smog levels projected for Southern California in 1990. On the basis of that (and in spite of recent census figures indicating a slowdown in growth rates) the board issued a warning that if California is to survive, life styles will have to change. There will have to be less consumption of electric power, fewer automobiles per capita, and increasing dependence on mass rapid transit. It may even come to pass, said board chairman Arie J. Haagen-Smit of the California Institute of Technology, that the state will impose limits on the number of people moving into the area—people who might innocently suppose that the proliferating dams amounted to an invitation that they come.

The remark is historic and sobering. For the first time a responsible public agency has officially questioned the goals of a state that grew to its present size by fostering immigration.

And out on Wilshire Boulevard, beside the tar pits that remind us of vanished worlds, past the museum's ringing affirmation of what has been, the opposing phalanxes of cars stream and stop, stream and stop. How many of the drivers, one wonders, could really say where it is they think they are going?

Water, then, is the fifth dynamic. There have been others, including the imponderable of consuming personal ambition, but those five—land, gold, oil, transportation, and water—are the primary themes in the following account of a beautiful state's reckless rise to giganticism.

part one

A TOUCH OF MADNESS

1. For Greater Glory

The man responsible for the long-delayed settlement of California, José de Gálvez, was a relentless worker, highly imaginative, vain, roughshod in his ambition, yet charming whenever he chose to be. He was also unstable. Not long after launching the California adventure, he went mad, proposing, among other things, to import six hundred apes from Guatemala, dress them as soldiers, and turn them loose to confound his enemies. None of these drawbacks interfered, however, with his extraordinary ability, when lucid, to recognize the tap of opportunity. In her time California has known many like José de Gálvez.

He was born January 2, 1720, son of one of the hundreds of petty noblemen, called hidalgos, who swarmed through Andalusia, in southern Spain. Because he had a nimble mind, a local priest pointed him out to a visiting bishop. The bishop in turn offered the lad a scholarship at the University of Malaga, evidently with the understanding that he would enter the priesthood. But the bishop went to his reward, and Gálvez became a lawyer.

At the age of thirty, his first wife having died, he married a French-woman. Through her he attached himself to the French diplomatic corps in Madrid. He rose steadily, attracting, in time, the attention of King Carlos III himself.

It was a time of bitter reassessment. The Seven Years' War had left Spain and her ally France totally humiliated. England had wrested Canada and the eastern part of the Mississippi Valley from France, the Floridas from Carlos. At that point the other nations of Europe, wanting to slow English expansion toward the Orient, transferred the western half of the Mississippi's drainage from French to Spanish suzerainty. Inasmuch as Spain also claimed, under the name California, the Pacific littoral of the continent, the blockade seemed complete—if Carlos could muster enough sinew to maintain it.

The last thing Carlos needed right then was more land to explore, organize, and defend. At home, trade had stagnated and the treasury was almost empty. Abroad, particularly in Mexico, an entrenched bureaucracy of colonial administrators had sunk into torpor, riddled with corruption. Tattered glories—yet Carlos, stimulated by the odds, was determined that Spain should rise again.

Not everyone shared his optimism. The first man he called on to oversee the revitalization of Mexico turned the job down. The second died before he could start overseas. As his third choice, Carlos finally turned, somewhat reluctantly, to José de Gálvez. Gálvez accepted because success in the New World might lead to munificent royal favor in the Old.

In order that the new administrator might have powers commensurate with his responsibilities, Carlos named him *visitador-general*. This meant that Gálvez, working in conjunction with Mexico's regular viceroy and court of nobles, could impose whatever programs he deemed necessary. His only restraints were laws that would have bound the monarch himself—and such practical briars as resentful local officials might try to put in his way.

Knowledge was one safeguard against opposition. During the summer of 1765, as the ship bearing him to Vera Cruz plowed heavily across the Atlantic, the *visitador* pored over such reports and books on Mexico as he had been able to resurrect from the archives. One of his concerns— the only one that concerns us—was the northern frontier. By what means could it be turned into a true bulwark?

The point became an obsession—so much so, historian Walton Bean suggests, that it was symptomatic: the touch of madness was already on him. Be that as it may, he looked deep into the ancient accounts he carried with him, and this is what he learned.

Following the trampling of the Aztecs (1519–21), Hernando Cortés had pushed, with his incredible energy, on across Mexico to the shores of the Pacific. There he had built ships and had sent them west toward China and north toward the Strait of Anian, a reputed shortcut around the top of North America. His men found neither place, but did learn that an enormous peninsula nearly 800 miles long, today's Baja, or Lower, California, lay opposite the coast of northwestern Mexico. (At first Baja was believed to be an island and so appeared on many European maps.) There were pearls along its inner shore, and in high excitement Cortés tried to develop the fisheries. He failed. The Indians were hostile, the land sterile, and the problem of supplying his settlement across the tempestuous Sea of Cortés (we call it the Gulf of California) all but insuperable. Beset additionally by enemies at home, he was forced to withdraw.

Shortly thereafter, in 1542, his successor, Viceroy Antonio de Mendoza, ordered two ships under a hired Portuguese navigator, Juan Rodríguez Cabrillo (or, in Portuguese, Joao Rodríguez Cabrilho), to follow the outside shore of the peninsula north to Anian, at the continent's end. Omens for the future: contrary winds turned the trip into a long misery. During the winter of 1542–43 Cabrillo died on San Miguel Island in the Santa Barbara Channel. His Levantine pilot, Bartoloméo Ferrelo, continued the northern thrust as far, possibly, as the present border between California and Oregon. In his mind, and in Mendoza's, results were negligible. The Indians whom the mariners visited at several points between San Diego Bay and Point Conception possessed neither gold nor jewels. And there was no sign of the Strait of Anian.

An uninteresting land: some scholars think that the name California was the product of derision, sprung from a medieval romance called *The Exploits of Esplandian*. One character in that freewheeling novel was a redoubtable female warrior, Queen Califía, ruler of California, an island "very near to the terrestrial paradise." Queen Califía's soldiers were beautiful black Amazons. Their weapons were gold, their allies enormous griffins trained to swoop up whatever men they encountered, soar high, and drop the victims to their deaths on the rocks below.

A fabled land. But what had the explorers found? In the south a gaunt peninsula whose Indians were so primitive, it was said, that they even dried and sifted their own excrement in order to recover the undigested seeds from one of their favorite foods, the juicy red fruit of the pitahaya cactus—a second harvest, as the tellers of the tale remarked. Nor, in the eyes of Cabrillo's and Ferrelo's scurvy-wracked mariners, were matters much more promising in the wind-tormented north. Paradise enow: or, as the disappointed searchers growled in mockery, California.

So far as the Pacific was concerned, effort centered next on developing the rich trade with the Philippine Islands, conquered by Miguel López de Lagazpi between 1565 and 1571. Each year thereafter crazy fleets of junks congregated in Manila, laden with silk, spice, porcelain, and fine furniture eagerly desired by the status-hungry, new-rich mine exploiters of central Mexico. Under the monopolistic eyes of the royally chartered Philippine Company, the exotic cargoes were transferred to ships recently arrived from Mexico with gleaming bars of silver.

Homeward bound, the vessels steered north past Japan to catch trade winds that would carry them east. Depending on the course set by the breezes, their first landfall might come anywhere from Cape Mendecino, north of present San Francisco, south to Baja California. By then the voyage had lasted six months. Many of the travelers were either dead or in desperate straits from scurvy, which the seafarers of the time did not understand, yet the profits were so great and so quick that each year more men took the risk.

In 1578–79, while the commerce was just developing, Francis Drake of England battered through the tempestuous Strait of Magellan into the Pacific. He raided the coastal towns of South America, captured a treasure ship loaded with silver ingots from Peru, picked up information about the Philippines, and disappeared to the north—perhaps intending, so the Spaniards feared, to return to England through the waterway of Anian.

It may be that Drake did carry secret orders from Queen Elizabeth to look for Anian's western outlet. If so, he hardly took the directions seriously. Somewhere off the coast of Oregon he let himself be turned back, according to his chaplain, by "many extreame gusts and flawes . . . most vile, thicke and stinking fogges"—hardly a terror, one would think, to sailors who had recently mastered the howling storms of the Strait of Magellan.

At Drake's Bay, now part of Point Reyes National Seashore a few miles north of San Francisco, the Englishman spent a month careening and repairing his *Golden Hind*, meanwhile talking at great length to the local Indians, whom he totally misunderstood. Then, having named the region New Albion and having set up a brass plate laying claim to it for his sovereign, he sailed home by way of the Cape of Good Hope, Africa's southern extremity.

Although he missed the ships from Manila, the respite was short. In 1587 another English buccaneer, Thomas Cavendish, followed Drake's route through the Strait of Magellan, surprised a laden vessel from the Philippines off the lower part of Baja California, and captured her after a furious battle. The dealers in Mexico City had barely absorbed that warning of the new dangers threatening their trade when a fresh blow fell. They had been making too much money, with the result that the merchants in Spain complained to the king. The mother country, the jealous ones said, was losing business to a mere colony—should not the silver miners be compelled to buy from them?—and they asked for restrictions on the Pacific commerce. The king responded in 1593 by limiting traffic from Manila to Mexico to a single 500-ton ship a year, carrying cargo worth no more than 250,000 pesos.

Bribery, lies, and favoritism were used to circumvent the restrictions. The result was the Manila galleon, a swollen tub of a ship, crammed with triple decks, its stem and stern built up, in the words of one contemporary, "like a castle." Every cranny was stuffed with merchandise, even at the expense of food and water and decent quarters for crew and passengers.

So plump a prize would be a dazzling temptation for pirates. Realizing this, the traders of Mexico began agitating for a thorough exploration of the California coast. The idea was to find a haven where the galleon could meet patrol ships whose captains would tell them whether foreign raiders were near and, if so, help them avoid the dangers. The men stationed at the wayside port could also grow fresh fruit and vegetables for the scurvy-ridden sailors.

The government agreed but tried to economize by ordering Sebastián Rodríguez Cermeño, commander of the 200-ton galleon *San Agustín* (gargantuism had not yet set in), to explore the coast during his 1595 trip from Manila to Acapulco. Cermeño, too, put into Drake's Bay. Unaware that anyone had been there before him, he let a Franciscan friar who happened to be aboard name the harbor San Francisco after his patron saint.

While the *San Agustín* was in the bay, unexpected winds slammed her ashore, broke her to pieces, and destroyed a cargo worth scores of thousands of pesos. The sailors improvised a launch and in that open craft set out for Acapulco. They clung close to land and at times stopped to explore and beg food from the Indians. Ironically they did not see the bay that we call San Francisco—and neither did other mariners before and after them. The gap leading into it was concealed either by persistent fogs or by the way the inner islands seem, from the sea, to be part of the coastline.

Obviously a laden galleon was not a proper ship for exploring a dangerous coast. The task was next assigned by the Viceroy de Monterrey to Sebastián Vizcaíno, who set out in 1602 with 200 men in three light, maneuverable craft. Once again California proved dreadfully hard to reach; contrary winds so delayed the expedition that before it ended fifty men died of scurvy.

Vizcaíno drove the survivors mercilessly, for if the venture succeeded he would be rewarded with the command of the oversized Manila galleon, which by then was starting its annual runs. He reached Drake's Bay (Cermeño's Puerto de San Francisco) but did not consider it suitable for a post. Like Cermeño, he missed our San Francisco Bay. Thus he was left with nothing to recommend but a wide indentation to the south. This he named Monterrey Bay (the second *r* was soon dropped) in honor of the viceroy. He extolled it to the skies, and then went home for his reward.

Alas for ambition. The Conde de Monterrey was replaced by a vindictive rival, and as part of the power struggle Vizcaíno was shunted into obscurity. His mapmaker, the only competent cartographer to visit the coast up to Gálvez's time, was hanged on spurious charges. The galleon merchants decided they did not need a refuge after all—it was better to press on without pause to the high profits at Acapulco—and interest in the north died. Knowledge retreated. Once again California was described in contemporary geographies as an island.

By this time settlement had reached the province of Sinaloa on Mexico's northwestern coast. From those remote towns hard-twisted adventurers occasionally sailed across the turbulent waters of the gulf to Baja California. There they traded with the Indians for pearls, a process often entwined with chicanery, torture, and the ravishment of the native women.

Partly to protect the Indians and partly to make sure that the king received the 20 percent tax assessed on all new pearls, Madrid ordered that colonies be established on the peninsula. For years the enmity of the Indians and the barrenness of the land blocked success. Finally, however, in 1697, a combined force of soldiers and Jesuit missionaries managed to sink roots at Loreto, about a third of the way up the peninsula from its southern extremity.

The sword and the cross—Gálvez's interest quickened. During the century preceding his arrival, those two forces, as represented by the frontier presidio and the mission, had proved indispensable in advancing settlement along the northern arc of Spain's possessions. Any extension he made would have to utilize both institutions. It was well to know how they operated.

Most of the men who came from Spain to Mexico were either soldiers or adventurers bent on exploitation. Humbler white colonists, women in particular, had little opportunity to share in the riches and accordingly declined to migrate to the new territory in numbers sufficient to populate it. Accordingly the government tried to fill the lack by transforming the Indians into ersatz Spaniards, a process that involved gathering them together under devoted priests, baptizing them as Roman Catholics, and teaching them a few useful mechanical and agricultural arts.

The training process had several variants. In the northwest it went like this. Presidios, or barracks, were established at strategic points from which mounted men equipped with awesome muskets could sally forth in the event of trouble with the "unreduced"—that is, unconverted—tribes. Meanwhile a pair of Jesuit missionaries accompanied by a guard of five or six soldiers built small stations in nearby locales. With kindness, free food, bright trinkets, and the wonders of music and pageantry they lured the natives to leave their own rancherías, as the Spaniards called the Indian villages, and settle in new huts beside the mission compounds, where workshops, gardens, and a church were laboriously brought into being.

As soon as the Indians became Spaniards—that is, as soon as they were capable of producing raw materials for Spanish traders, of buying Spanish goods, of working on ranches and in mines, of paying Spanish taxes and worshiping under Spanish priests—then the missions were secularized. This meant turning the Indian village at the mission into a pueblo, or town. The king or the local governor granted each pueblo four square leagues of land, about 17,500 acres. Within this area each resident was given a house lot and a farm plot and rights to graze his cattle in the communal pasture. The converted Indians were also given part of the tools and livestock of the erstwhile mission, which simultaneously became a regular parish church run by secular clergy.

It was fully expected that Mexican frontiersmen would settle in the pueblo with the Indians and by their precept add the final touches of civilization. The amalgamated groups, called mestizos, or mixed bloods (they were soon the dominant element of the Mexican frontier), thenceforth lived together under their own alcalde, a sort of combined mayor and justice of the peace, and their own *ayuntamiento*, or town council.

How long should the transformation of Indian to citizen take? The government, eager for manpower and sensitive to charges of abuse in the system, decreed that it must be accomplished within ten years—and then looked the other way as the time span stretched out, in most cases, to many times ten. There were several reasons. The arrival of enough outsiders to make acculturation possible was sometimes long delayed. More importantly, as the priestly citizen-makers gradually learned, the deep-seated beliefs which the culture of a race comprises are not easily altered.

It was embarrassing to have to explain why the Indians were so slow to embrace the joys that were offered them. Since a man disliked faulting his own civilization, the "savages" were blamed. They were not, it was propounded, fully human. Although they had souls worth saving, they were otherwise "irrational." The prejudice emerged clearly in the name non-Indians gave themselves. They were the *gente de razón*, the people of reason.* The Indians, being irrational, naturally progressed with painful slowness, and had to be supervised throughout their lives like children. Even after baptism and confirmation, grown converts were called neophytes, or novices, and treated as such.

A dilemma resulted. At some point a rational citizen had to emerge from the mission chrysalis, or else the program was, from a practical

---

*The term was protean. Toward the close of the Mexican era in California it apparently included only the social and governing elite. Elsewhere, one drop of white blood in a Catholic's veins was enough. Occasionally, in the case of converted Indians who managed to achieve financial equality with the local rulers, Christianity alone sufficed. One bar remained unalterable, however: no gentile (unconverted Indian) was ever classed as rational.

standpoint, merely quixotic. To avoid such accusations, the government and the missionaries evolved a tacit compromise. An Indian achieved rationality as soon as the dissolution of his mission became unavoidable. This generally happened after a number of would-be settlers had drifted into an area and began clamoring against mission land monopoly and mission agricultural competition. At that point secularization was ordered, and the mission Indians were turned loose to mingle with the newcomers.

The alkaline lands of Baja California proved particularly resistant. Few colonists appeared; the military tried to avoid assignment there. Acculturation appeared very unlikely, yet the Jesuits clung on, locating new stations wherever water was available. When government financing proved inadequate, they supported themselves by soliciting private donations to what was called their "Pious Fund." It was a precarious living, and one of continuing concern to the greatest of New Spain's far-ranging Jesuit proselytizers, Italian-born Eusebio Francisco Kino, trailblazer of the northwestern deserts. Having experienced failure himself in Baja, Kino watched with intense sympathy the struggles of his fellow Jesuits to turn their tiny adobe stations into viable establishments worthy of their order.

Extraordinary success was meanwhile attending Kino's own work in Alta Pimería, the land of the Pima Indians, today's northern Sonora and southern Arizona. In that starkly beautiful region Kino founded twenty-nine missions. One of his monuments, rebuilt since his time, is the ornately decorated church of San Xavier del Bac, still flourishing a few miles south of Tucson.

Eternally curious, Kino in 1702 managed to reach the Colorado River and follow it downstream almost to its delta. Thus he discovered, or rather rediscovered, that California was not an island.

To him the implications were staggering. At last supply boats for the missions in Baja California, several of which had been swallowed by the stormy gulf, could be replaced by laden pack trains circling the Colorado delta. Far more exciting was the possibility of opening a land route to Monterey. No expeditions had gone to that remote harbor since Vizcaíno's return in 1603. Why bother? A garrison could not be maintained there because of those contrary winds, and, anyway, where was the money to be found?

Kino had the answers now. Land travel to the north, quite feasible if California was not an island, would remove the need for ocean shipping. Money would come from the stimulation to commerce: while provisioning itself at Monterey, each Manila galleon could unload part of its cargo and send it directly by land to the rich mining communities in Sonora and Sinaloa. Think, too, of all the Indians in Alta California (Kino was the first to use that term) who could now be brought to salvation. To be sure, the way was long and the natives were numerous. Management from Mexico City would be difficult. Therefore let a powerful new administrative center be built among the big, genial, naked Yuma Indians, who lived where the Gila River of present-day Arizona flows into the Colorado.

The radical plans scarcely ruffled the inertia of the officials in Mexico City. A new administrative center to dilute their powers in the north? An endless desert to swallow their funds at a time when new missions were being called for in Texas? And what was Alta California anyway? A wasteland. After an effort to take a pack train around the head of the Gulf had collapsed in the wilderness, the whole notion was pushed aside.

The vision was too powerful to die. After Kino's death in 1711, a succession of men familiar with northwestern Mexico took up his crusade. The most eloquent among them was a border captain named Fernando de Sánchez. Sánchez advocated not just a new administrative center in the north, but an entire new viceroyalty made up of the provinces of New Mexico, Nueva Vizcaya (now Chihuahua), Sinaloa, Sonora, and both Californias. Why? Because the north was vulnerable. The Russians, led by Vitus Bering, had discovered Alaska in 1741. The English were pushing west across Canada from their stations beside Hudson Bay. If Spain did not fill the empty lands along her northern frontier someone else would, regardless of Spanish claims to title through discovery.

Mexico City shrugged. From the viceroy's snug offices the north still looked as unpromising as a bone. Nonetheless the dream persisted. In 1757 a man named Andrés Burriel, writing anonymously, gathered up half a century of arguments into a three-volume book entitled *Noticia de la California* and declared that eternal blame would attach to the governing bodies if through sheer negligence they allowed foreign powers to "erect colonies, forts, and presidios on the coast of the Californias." To Anglophobes in Madrid it hardly seemed chance that within two years a translation of the *Noticia* had appeared in England.

The *Noticia* was one of the books that José de Gálvez studied on his journey to Mexico City in the summer of 1765. Immediately he recognized the tap of opportunity. Circumstances had changed, as his own mission to Mexico showed. The king wanted Spain revitalized. He was ready to listen, as his predecessors on the throne had not been, to any sound proposal that would help show his ancient enemies that in spite of recent defeats the nation was still capable of rolling back the unknown. The proposed new viceroyalty in the north—Gálvez called it a commandancy-general—together with expansion into Alta California would be a long step in that direction. It would also prove to the king Gálvez's abilities as an organizer.

There was no rushing things, however. First, he must shake the sloth from Mexico's officialdom, weed out corruption, and institute harsh new government monopolies for raising revenue. Resistance was instant. The viceroy, the powerful Marquis de Cruíllas, fought bureaucratic reform, and the silver miners north of the capital, mostly mestizos, rioted against the new taxes. In the northwest, meanwhile, the Pima and Seri Indians declared war against the encroaching frontiersmen of Sonora and southern Arizona. Until they were subdued there could be no expansion northward.

Vigorously Gálvez struck down the rioters, executing, banishing, or imprisoning their leaders in wholesale lots—nearly 1,000 all told. He wrote directly to the king demanding Cruíllas' removal. He proposed raising a special army of 1,100 men for crushing the Indians of the northwest. To still criticism about expense he boldly offered to finance the Sonora campaign by personally soliciting contributions from private, patriotic donors.

At first all went smoothly. Cruíllas was replaced in the summer of 1766 by Carlos de Croix, a competent but complaisant administrator. Contributors in both Spain and Mexico pledged 200,000 pesos toward pacifying the northwest—reputedly it was very rich in minerals—and in November the king formally authorized the campaign. Troops began moving toward Sonora in April, 1767. Since roads were bad, Gálvez decided to build a new port, San Blas, on Mexico's west coast and dispatch matériel from there northward through the Gulf of California by ship. A clever solution, he thought—for as soon as Sonora was pacified, San Blas could be transformed into a civilian port for furthering expansion into his proposed new commandancy-general.

Before the military movement was well started Gálvez was jarred by royal orders that the Jesuits were to be expelled from the country as part of a concerted multination attack against the Society. The upheaval threatened to delay his northern dreams, for he had counted on using the services of the blackrobes in founding new missions in Alta California as precursors to settlement there. Now there would be monumental confusion while some new order stepped into the Jesuits' shoes.

Well, confusion could be overcome. A royal order could not. Resilient as always, Gálvez helped draw up plans to strike before the Jesuits could stir their neophytes to resistance or hide the gold and jewels they had reputedly hoarded in great quantities during the years. He himself led one of the companies that struck throughout central Mexico during the predawn hours of July 26, 1767. With swift and brutal efficiency the raiders dragged the priests, who proved to have few stored riches about them, to Vera Cruz for banishment abroad.

Continual pressure, continual uproar—yet through it all Gálvez managed to keep working on his plans for the north.

Together he and Viceroy Croix drew up a formal memorial listing the benefits of the proposed commandancy-general. The frontier, they said, was too far from Mexico City for vigorous administration. A new entity responsible only for those distant lands would bring greater efficiency and refreshed energy to areas already settled. In areas yet untouched it would open riches of many kinds. Souls would be saved, new citizens created, fresh mines and ranches developed. On the coast new presidios would be located to avert dangers "which now threaten us . . . from certain foreign powers who now have an opportunity and the most eager desire to establish some Colony at the Port of Monterrey."

They presented this memorial to Mexico's council of nobles, the Junta, for comment. As expected, the group endorsed the arguments and sent the paper to the king for his consideration. Gálvez then turned his attention to more immediate problems. The expulsion of the Jesuits from Baja California, assigned to a task force under a new provincial governor named Gaspar de Portolá, had created massive confusion on the peninsula. Meantime the campaign in Sonora had bogged down miserably, partly because of slow work on the new harbor at San Blas. All these matters cried for rectification, and since all were connected in one way or another with the proposed commandancy, Gálvez decided to take charge in person.

First he would shake up things at San Blas, then visit Baja California, and finally sail to Sonora to assume command of the campaign there.

He started for San Blas on April 9, 1768. While he was still on the road he received a dispatch from Viceroy Croix relaying garbled reports from Spanish secret agents in St. Petersburg. The Russians, it was said (incorrectly), were planning to establish colonies in North America, and Croix should be alert. Lacking any understanding of the continent's size, Croix forwarded the reports to Governor Gaspar de Portolá with a request that Portolá keep an eye on the Russians, "frustrating them if possible." Because Gálvez was already bound for Baja California, a copy of the dispatch was handed to him.

Again that tap of opportunity! Here was a way to expand into the north without waiting for royal approval of the commandancy. The feat accomplished, it in turn would furnish additional reason for Carlos to authorize a new administrative unit. The move would have to be made quickly, of course, and that ruled out an overland thrust from unpacified Sonora.

Instead Gálvez would have to launch the drive from Baja California.

There were risks. He would have to divert ships from the Sonora campaign, missionaries, colonists, and supplies from their work in the peninsula. Expenses would be heavy. To justify this he had only Croix's offhand instructions to Portolá about watching the Russians. Yet Gálvez, in his fierce ambition, never hesitated.

He was cautious enough still to cloak himself with the appearances of justification. He summoned four distinguished leaders to meet him at San Blas and discuss the methods of occupation. Obligingly this quartet authorized a two-pronged expedition. One group, composed of colonists drawn from the Baja pueblos, was to travel overland up the peninsula and on to the bay of Monterey with a herd of livestock and an escort of cavalry. The other was to transport bulky equipment, also drawn from the peninsula, aboard two ships detached from the Sonoran campaign. These vessels, the *San Antonio* and the *San Carlos*, were to rendezvous at the Bay of La Paz, on the inner coast of the peninsula, as soon as they had finished carrying a fresh contingent of troops to Sonora. As a final sign of approval, two of the planners also agreed to join the expedition. One was army engineer Miguel Costansó; the other, naval captain Vincente Vila.

The purity of his motives thus attested, Gálvez, in company with Costansó, boarded a wretched little vessel for what turned out to be a forty-day, storm-wracked journey into the lower Gulf. In July, 1768, they reached La Paz. There for the first time, probably, the *visitador* began to wonder about two key men on whose cooperation much of the success of the venture would depend. One was the new governor of Baja California, Gaspar de Portolá; he would be called on to furnish from his meager stores the soldiers and military supplies needed for the occupation. The other man was Father Junípero Serra, a Franciscan monk who, on behalf of the Apostolic College of San Fernando in Mexico City, had just taken charge of the fourteen peninsular missions recently administered by the Jesuits. Serra would be responsible for assigning to the expedition the missionary padres and religious equipment that were an automatic part of every colonizing venture.

From what little information he possessed about Baja California, Gálvez sensed that the resources of both men, whom he knew only through letters, would be sorely strained by his demands. Yet he was confident that he could prevail on them to do as he asked, even though the plan had no real sanction. For was he not *visitador*? And would not success redound to the greater glory of their church and nation, to their own exaltation—and to the triumph of José de Gálvez? Of course they would cooperate.

2. First Plantings

Gaspar de Portolá, the records insist, entered the Spanish army as an ensign at the age of eleven. Thirty-three years later, still unmarried, he was a captain, two grades up from where he had begun. Under the circumstances his appointment to be military governor of Baja California may have looked to him like an advance.

He soon learned better. His headquarters, the presidio of Loreto some 150 miles north of La Paz, was a cluster of small mud buildings crouched under a smothering sun; there was not one tree for shade. Aside from Indians, soldiers, and priests, the population of his entire domain amounted to about 400 *gente de razón*—a scattering of miners and pearl fishers, of roustabouts for handling pack trains, cattle ranchers and farmers scratching at the grudging soil.

His first assignment was to cripple this stunted economy still further by expelling the Jesuits from their fourteen missions, scattered at wide intervals along the lower two-thirds of the peninsula's 800-mile length. Kindly by nature, Portolá did not send out guards to fetch them in but let them assemble at Loreto under their own recognizance. As they made ready to leave the peninsula with their shabby possessions, he treated them with as much respect for their dignity as circumstances allowed. Then, following instructions, he sent out squads of his soldiers to take charge of the vacated stations.

Conditions were abysmal. Many of the missions had been located, during excesses of fervor, in stark valleys where irrigating water sometimes failed or where there was not enough arable land to support the Indians whom the priests gathered around them. The natives were in no better shape than the stations. Syphilis introduced among them years earlier by the soldiers of the presidios and the mule skinners of the supply trains, and typhoid lurking in contaminated wells, had reduced their numbers from an estimated 40,000 to 7,000. Apathetic already, they were completely demoralized by the abrupt removal of their mentors.

The soldiers Portolá sent among them intensified the trouble. Believing that the Jesuits had secreted treasures in pearls around the missions, they tore the places apart. Finding nothing, they turned vindictive. They abused the Indians, who fled into the mountains, slaughtered cattle out of spite, and disdained the labor of maintaining fields and workshops.

The inheritors of this chaos, sixteen Franciscan monks for fourteen missions, reached Loreto on April 1, 1768. Their hands were tied, for they had been granted only spiritual control of the stations, while the military remained in charge of the temporalities. Nevertheless their leader, Junípero Serra, sent them out, one priest to a mission (the normal rule was two), with a bubbling show of enthusiasm—he was a master of that. After they had gone, he settled down at Loreto with a single secretary, hoping that through divine help he might somehow find energy, wisdom, and money enough to solve his problems. He was fifty-five years old and in poor health.

Into this desolation, in July, came a letter from Gálvez at La Paz, announcing his intention of drawing on the impoverished missions for help in occupying the north. Serra answered politely and then went on a tour of inspection among some of his stations. October was at hand before he finally went to Loreto to consult with the *visitador*.

It is next to unbelievable that Gálvez still clung to his plans. He knew by then that he could not recruit colonists for Alta California from the underpopulated hamlets of the peninsula; rather he was going to have to strengthen Baja by luring in settlers from outside. This meant that for an indeterminate time there would be no pueblos in Alta California to help feed and clothe the new garrisons. Both they and the embryo missions would have to depend on supply ships from Mexico, at least until the missions became self-supporting, and one could predict with assurance that the government would not like this unexpected expense. Moreover, there were not enough soldiers available in Baja California to support the venture; additional men would have to be drawn from the already frustrated army in Sonora. Finally, the disorganized missions on the peninsula were in no shape to provide either priests or material for the new establishments. And yet Gálvez persisted, either out of incipient madness or an unshakable belief in what he was doing.

Serra had no such motives. Suddenly, however, he volunteered to accompany the expedition and personally launch the new missions. Why? An opportunity for greater service to his God? Or a subconscious desire to escape from the hopelessness of Baja? There is no way to be sure. He has been encysted for so long in the Romance of the Missions that reality is dimmed by the amber carapaces of sentiment.

This much can be recovered. He was 5 feet 2 inches tall and very intense. Born to peasants on the Mediterranean island of Majorca, he had risen through church schools to a brilliant career as a professor in the island's leading Franciscan college. Intellectualism palling, he had sought appointment, at the age of thirty-seven, as a missionary. For eight difficult years he had served fearlessly and well in the Sierra Gordo Mountains north of Mexico City and then had been transferred to the Apostolic College of San Fernando in Mexico City. There he had won a reputation as an able administrator and fervent preacher.

Often he dramatized his sermons by scourging himself with chains, pounding his chest with heavy stones, searing his skin with tapers. For years he was handicapped by a suppurating sore in one leg, the result of an infected insect bite. He refused to seek a cure for the wound. Pain was a delight—a reaction that perhaps was not shared by recalcitrant Indian neophytes whom, when he was in the field, he occasionally flogged for the good of the system that was carrying them toward redemption.

It is a dark picture in many ways, and an incomplete one. For there was also an uninhibited joy in Junípero Serra that flowed out to embrace the natural beauties of the world, and a personal sweetness, welling up in his moments of repose, that stirred intense devotion among his followers.

Excitement over Alta California did not make him forget the peninsula. He soon persuaded Gálvez to turn full control of the missions over to the friars. Shocked by the conditions, the *visitador* went even further, closing the more marginal stations and ordering that their neophytes be moved to other establishments. Later this impulsive shifting of home-loving Indians from region to region would prove to have been a mistake, but at the time it seemed sound. For one thing, the consolidations released priests for work in the north.

Portolá, too, was kept busy, discussing plans for bringing new colonists to the peninsula, and reorganizing the mines and the pearl fisheries. He disliked the northern project, fearing that it would undercut his work in Baja. Nonetheless Gálvez placed Alta California under his jurisdiction and then astounded the reluctant governor by ordering him to take command of the expedition. Good soldier that he was, Portolá acquiesced.

The land-sea thrusts that Gálvez had first envisioned during the conference at San Blas were elaborately amplified. Two parties were to go by ship and two by land, so that failure by any one group would not cripple the work. Although Monterey remained the main goal, the leaders agreed that the four parties should rendezvous first at San Diego Bay and found a mission and presidio there before pushing farther north. If circumstance allowed, an intermediate station, to be called San Buenaventura, was to be built at some desirable location between the other two. Eventually, if all worked out, a fourth mission-presidio complex would be placed north of Monterey at Drake's Bay, which the mariners of New Spain were still calling San Francisco.

In order to equip these four groups, the planners laid heavy demands on the only convenient source of supply, the missions of Baja. They asked for dozens of horses, scores of mules, hundreds of cattle. They would need untold bushels of grain and dried fruit, slabs of cheese, sacks of coal, flour, and sugar, quantities of tools, saddles, rope, and seed. Hoping to make the new missions shine in the eyes of the benighted Indians of Alta California, they ordered bales of brightly colored altar cloths and vestments, glowing silver chalices, censers, and candlesticks, and eighteen church bells of varying sizes.

The officials of the College of San Fernando in Mexico City were appalled. These requisitions were little better than looting, they whispered angrily to each other, but Gálvez was *visitador*. How could they, one wrote in dismay, "resist him who commands us with power absolute, admitting neither supplication or argument?" And how could the friars in Baja deny their father-president, Junípero Serra, the things that he insisted he must have?

The first to start north was Captain Fernando Rivera y Moncada, who had been in charge of the garrison at Loreto for the past twelve years. With a company of hard-bitten soldiers, he moved slowly from mission to mission, picking up cattle and pack animals. The ultimate gathering ground for these and for his supplies, sent to him through the stormy Gulf in four lighters, was supposed to be the most northern of the old Jesuit stations, Santa María de los Ángeles. Pasturage there proved inadequate, however, and he moved on another 50 miles to certain broad, uninhabited meadows called Velicatá, within 150 miles of what eventually became the international border between the United States and Mexico. At Velicatá his advance party—twenty-five soldiers, one priest, a few mule skinners, and forty-two Christianized Indian laborers—settled down to wait until word arrived that the ships had started. The marchers would then slant northwest across the peninsula to the vicinity of the bay of Todos Santos (we call it Ensenada) and follow the coast from there to San Diego.

Time passed slowly. The expedition's ships, the *San Carlos* and the *San Antonio*, reached La Paz later and in worse condition than anticipated. Extensive repairs were necessary before the *San Carlos*, commanded by Vincente Vila and carrying sixty-two sailors, soldiers, artisans, and friars, started for San Diego on January 9, 1769. The *San Antonio* followed on February 15 with a crew of twenty-eight and an unknown number of passengers. Her captain, Juan Pérez, former commander of the Manila galleon, was perhaps the ablest Spanish naval man on the Pacific. We will hear more of him later.

Both vessels, neither more than 80 feet long, had dreadful trips against the contrary winds that for most of the year blow steadily down the California coast. Hoping to avoid the obstacle, the *San Carlos* swung far out into the Pacific, overshot her mark, picked up the coast well north of San Diego, and had to turn back. The circular voyage ate up 110 days. When the ship at last nosed into the landlocked harbor on April 29, Pérez's *San Antonio* was already there, having spent only half as much time on the way.

Scurvy—discoloration of the skin, swollen limbs, hardened joints, puffy gums, and agonizing pain—had swept through both vessels. So many seamen, soldiers, and officers were incapacitated that the ambulatory were barely able to drop anchor and move the invalids to a camp near good water. There they built a crude fortification of earth and spread awnings of sailcloth to protect the sick from the weather. In spite of the heroic efforts of surgeon Pedro Prat, the disease continued until thirty-four men were dead.

Rivera meanwhile had started his trip from Velicatá on March 24. It was moving pandemonium. One hundred and forty-four mules had to be packed and unpacked each day, more than 200 stubborn cattle had to be grazed as they went, and the whole had to be guarded each night against frenzied stampedes. The Christian Indians bore the brunt of the labor. Overworked, some died. Others ran away. Without those who remained faithful, the journey could hardly have been finished.

The confused caravan spent 52 days covering some 230 miles. Supplies dwindled. The men were on half rations when finally, May 14, they reached the desolate camp at San Diego. All they had to offer the invalids in the way of help were pack animals. With these they moved the pestilential bivouac to a healthier location on the hilly northeastern curve of the bay. Laboriously they then unloaded the *San Antonio*, intending to send her to San Blas with a question: Would it not be foolish to risk pressing on to Monterey, even after Portolá had arrived with reinforcements?

Back at Loreto, Serra, who was ill, had himself lifted onto a mule and set out to overtake Portolá and the slowly moving second column. Gálvez waved the priest farewell, gave orders for a third little ship, the *San José*, to deliver additional supplies to the pioneers during the summer, and then sailed to Sonora to take charge of the Indian campaign. Success achieved, he would complete his great dream, so he thought, by opening a land thoroughfare from northwestern Mexico to Monterey. He would put an administrative center for the new commandancy-general some-where near the junction of the Gila and Colorado rivers. Colonists would then march through to California with their families and livestock, Spain's enemies would be thwarted, and José de Gálvez would deserve, most surely, the tangible thanks of his grateful king.

At Velicatá, Serra dedicated a new mission, the only one founded in Baja California by the Franciscans. Then, on May 15, the day after Rivera had reached San Diego, he and Portolá started the second land contingent toward San Diego. Except for his swollen, oozing leg, the padre's health had improved. Another blessing came when a mule skinner alleviated the pain in the leg by smearing on a concoction of herbs and grease normally used for healing saddle galls. After that Serra kept up more easily, rejoic-ing in the unsullied sky and the spangles of wild flowers. Because the way was known and the party had fewer animals to contend with, they cov-ered the miles faster than Rivera had. Even so, the days were toilsome enough that thirty-two of their forty-four Indian helpers either died or deserted, a serious loss.

Conditions at San Diego had not improved. Only eight of the expedi-tion's sailors were on their feet. They were not enough for taking either the *San Antonio* or the *San Carlos* against contrary winds to Monterey Bay. Yet Portolá, hating the job though he did, refused to give up. Enough soldiers and Indians were still ambulatory for him to occupy the area and build the presidio as ordered—if the third ship, the *San José*, were sent to him as soon as she appeared. Meanwhile Pérez and the eight hale mariners should take advantage of the favoring winds to return to San Blas for sailors and workers to replace those who had died.

He carried his point. Those who were well built a low earthen redoubt to protect the sick. Pérez weighed anchor for the south on July 9. Leaving Serra at San Diego to help surgeon Prat care for the ailing, Portolá started north on July 14. With him he had, to use his own term, sixty-one "skeletons"—thirty-five soldiers and officers, two priests, two servants, seven mule skinners, and fifteen Christianized Indians.

The aristocrats of the party were the soldiers, uniformed in sleeveless leather jackets made of white deerskin. They carried swords, lances, short-barreled muskets, and round shields made of heavy bullhide. Though most were unable to read or write, they were patient, hardy, and well trained, the best horsemen, according to Miguel Costansó, in the world.

There was little need for spectacular riding. A hundred laden mules slowed travel to a plod. On top of that Portolá rested the caravan one day out of four lest the animals collapse before the journey was completed.

Each day's march had to be scouted in advance, gullies bridged, and trails improved with pickaxes and crowbars wherever necessary. Camps were spotted not where mileage quotas suggested but where grass and water were available.

At first the cavalcade kept close to the coast. Then, as the shoreline veered westward, they struck north along the thin sparkle of the Santa Ana River. Sharp earthquakes, more characteristic of the region than they had any way of knowing, startled but did not injure them. All along the route Indians came out to meet them, wide-eyed at the sight of such men and such animals but bold enough to stand their ground and hold out peace offerings of food. Portolá was careful to reassure them with small presents in return, and when the travelers rode on, a few of their new friends generally went along to show the way to the next ranchería, or village.

As the newcomers progressed they saw ahead of them an abrupt wall of mountains running east and west, harshly contoured, some of the peaks reaching elevations of 11,000 feet or more. This they named the Sierra Madre. It was the first of the Transverse Ranges. Impenetrable, it bent them west, past lovely oak groves where Pasadena now stands to a camp on the banks of a small, erratic stream to which Portolá gave a more famous name than he had any way of foreseeing—El Río de Nuestra Señora la Reina de los Ángeles de Porciúncula. From there they went on past the extraordinary lakes of pitch later named La Brea Tar Pits and then swung north across Sepulveda Pass, route now of the San Diego freeway, into the San Fernando Valley, brown and simmering with summer's heat. Still thrusting due north, they managed to gain the Santa Clara Valley of the south. Faced there by another impenetrable range, they swung west again toward the ocean, hoping to find sandy beaches that would let them skirt the toes of the barrier.

As they neared salt water, they encountered the largest and ablest tribe of Indians they had yet seen. These were the Chumash, whose homeland fronted the Santa Barbara Channel from below present-day Ventura to beyond Point Conception. They were superb craftsmen. With flint knives they carved beautifully finished bowls out of both wood and steatite, a soft soapstone. Their dome-shaped houses, Costansó reported, were as much as 60 feet in diameter and sheltered three or four families each. They built seagoing canoes 30 or so feet long by splitting planks out of driftwood with wedges of whalebone, stitching the boards together with thongs of deer sinew, and daubing them with asphaltum from the numerous oil seeps in the vicinity. No other boats like them were made by Indians anywhere in North America. Almost as unique were the magnificent abstract paintings that the Chumash drew on certain rock walls in the nearby mountains, but this display of artistry the pioneers seem not to have noticed.

The padres with the party were excited. Here surely was an unrivaled spot for San Buenaventura, the mission-presidio complex that Gálvez had authorized as midway station between San Diego and Monterey . . . if conditions warranted. But first they would have to find Monterey, build Monterey, and then prove that Monterey could be maintained.

On they went. Beyond Point Conception, where the coastline bent sharply north again, the land grew more difficult—huge sand dunes, occasional marshes, and then, north of Morro Bay, the Santa Lucia Mountains, a wild tumble of bold headlands, fog-wet brush, and impassable gorges. Unable to continue along the rocky beaches, the explorers turned upward. Not even goats could travel there, Padre Juan Crespí wrote in despair. But at a staggering toll in physical well-being, they fought the mules ahead, building trails as they went, until after several days they came down the eastern slope to the north-flowing Salinas River. Beyond the tawny valley were the sunny Gabilan hills that John Steinbeck would celebrate so eloquently nearly two centuries later.

Unfortunately, the maps they carried—maps made 166 years earlier by Vizcaíno's cartographer—led them to believe that they were on the Carmel River. Thus when the Salinas reached the sea, the travelers became confused. Hasty explorations north and south did nothing to reorient them. The exposed, 20-mile-wide coastal indentation they saw in front of them seemed in no way to fit the overblown description that Vizcaíno had penned aboard ship. Could this possibly be Monterey Bay?

Most unnerving of all, the supply ship *San José* was nowhere in sight. What if she were anchored in the real bay somewhere else, waiting for them?

Portolá called a council of his officers and the two friars. They voted to push on north, at least until the men collapsed or the situation became clearer.

Painfully, sometimes carrying the sickest of their comrades in litters swung between mules hitched in tandem, they passed the site of present Santa Cruz and moved slowly along lovely beaches at the foot of steep, north-running hills. The first rains of the year whipped them, and, miraculously, it seemed, the ailing began to recover. They plowed through thickets of laurel and madroño; they fought the mules in and out of steep ravines; they rode in awe beneath enormous trees whose thick red bark led Portolá to name them *palo colorado*, the first known report of the towering redwoods of the coast.

On October 29 they halted near Half Moon Bay, their progress blocked by cliffs. They rested a day, and then Portolá sent a party scrambling up the precipices to see what lay ahead. It must have been one of those gloriously clear days that come to the central coast after storms. Not a trace of mist was in the air; the sea was a blue radiance. The scouts were able to see, far out in the ocean, three rugged little islands laid down on the Vizcaíno chart as the Farallones. Forty miles northward was a line of white cliffs marking Point Reyes and Drake's (still called San Francisco) Bay. The implications were as clear as the weather. They had passed Monterey.

The misadventure was not without import. If the occupation of Alta California continued as originally planned in Baja, a fourth mission-presidio station would someday be built beside that bay, and now that they were so close it would be well at least to take a look. Portolá ordered a party of scouts under Sergeant José Ortega to ride ahead and work out a trail that the main party could follow through the rough countryside. While the scouts were gone he sent hunters into the hills above the camp in a search for deer.

Both groups returned with astounding reports. Ortega's scouts had been blocked by an unexpected inlet that John Charles Frémont of the United States army would name, nearly eighty years later, the Golden Gate. It opened into an enormous bay, as the hunters confirmed. From their hilltop they had glimpsed one of its arms running southeast almost as far as they could see. They were on a peninsula. To reach Drake's Bay they would have to retreat and then circle a gigantic body of water.

To Portolá it seemed quite impossible that so magnificent a harbor had never before been discovered. It must be, he decided, part of Cermeño's Puerto de San Francisco. Right then, however, his party was in no condition to make sure. After a half-hearted attempt to learn whether the *San José* might be waiting somewhere in those vast waters, he turned the group back south. Eleven weeks later, on January 24, 1770, they dragged into San Diego, having ravenously devoured during the closing stages of their march twelve of their mules.

His return compounded a desperate situation. Neither the *San Antonio* nor the *San José* had appeared with supplies. There had been a sharp fight with the Indians, who were so obsessed to have cloth that they had even tried to pull blankets out from under the sick and cut up the sails of the *San Carlos,* lying idle in the harbor. Peace would have brought a resumption in trade, except that the Indians wanted the very clothes off the Spaniards' backs in exchange for the food they offered. And now Portolá's return added sixty-three more men to feed.

To lighten the burden, Portolá sent Rivera, who had just completed the northern trip, to Velicatá for such supplies and cattle as the new mission there could spare. Before Rivera reappeared, however, the commander lost hope—at least according to Serra's biographers—and ordered the abandonment of the camp on March 19. That very day, as if in answer to the fervent prayers of the padres, the *San Antonio* appeared with new supplies and fresh men, and the unfortunate order was rescinded.

The *San José*, however, never arrived. Presumably she was lost at sea with all hands. Thus the cost in lives of the initial occupation of Alta California came to more than half of the 300 or so men who participated in the different phases.

In April the northern cast was resumed, this time by both sea and land. Because Portolá had decided by then that Monterey must be the bay into which the Salinas River flowed, rendezvous was set for there. The way being known now, Portolá's land group moved more rapidly than the *San Antonio*, tacking against contrary winds. The riders reached their destination in 37 days, as compared to 83 days on the first cast. A week later the *San Antonio* dropped anchor outside their camp.

On June 3, 1770, the mission and presidio—mere frames of posts as yet —were dedicated with hymns, a sprinkling of holy water, a High Mass. Then came symbolic acts of possession: a tearing up and scattering of grass and earth, a planting of flags, a shooting of muskets that terrified the watching Indians into flight. As far as Portolá was concerned, that was it; the midway station that he had been authorized to found if conditions warranted, San Buenaventura, was quite out of the question. On June 9, he turned the military command of Spain's newest province over to Pedro Fages and sailed with Pérez and Costansó in the *San Antonio* for Mexico.

At Tepic he paused for the rest that assuredly was due him. Pérez and Costansó continued to Mexico City with the news: Alta California had been occupied; Russia and England were forestalled. Relieved perhaps that the unauthorized venture had not ended in a failure for which he would have to share the blame, Viceroy Croix ordered the bells of the great cathedral tolled in a special paean of celebration. Soon the bells of all the other churches in the city were replying in kind.

To José de Gálvez the clangor must have been particularly gratifying. He had gone through an unfortunate year. Shortly after reaching Sonora from Baja California he had been stricken with fever. For months he was in and out of bed, quite mad much of the time, confusing himself on occasion with the king of Sweden and even with God Almighty, all the while roaring out impossible orders about the Indian campaign, including the use of Guatemalan apes as soldiers. Finally, in the spring of 1770, his harried secretaries managed to get him to Mexico City, where, it was reported, his health and sanity slowly returned.

Portolá may have had doubts on the latter point. In his opinion, and the tough old soldier bluntly said so in his report, it would be well to punish the Russians by letting them have California. Supply difficulties being what they were, it would not be possible to maintain the province from Mexico. Why throw good money after bad by trying?

Gálvez and, because of him, Viceroy Croix were not willing to admit they might have made a mistake. Off went letters to Serra and Fages promising reinforcements for the new stations at San Diego and Monterey and for the proposed midway mission-presidio complex of San Buenaventura. In addition, Fages was directed to explore the unexpected bay discovered by Portolá's men and, in consultation with Serra, to pinpoint somewhere on either its shores or those of Drake's Bay a site for a fourth presidio.

As for keeping the establishments alive, that would be the problem of Mexico's new viceroy, Antonio de Bucareli. Both Croix and Gálvez had been recalled. After turning over to Bucareli their reports and symbols of office, they sailed to Madrid, where the king rewarded their many accomplishments, including California, by elevating them to handsome new positions in his council.

California had served humbly born José de Gálvez well. Insane or not, he remembered. Even from halfway around the world the touch of his power would continue to brush across the fortunes of that isolated land that to so many other people was nothing but a toil and a trouble.

3. Bricks Without Straw

On October 20, 1772, sick and angry Junípero Serra boarded one of the returning supply ships for the long trip to Mexico, there to plead the case of the missions—in his mind it was the same as the case of all California —before the new viceroy, Antonio Bucareli.

Serra, the father-president, had just had a final, bitter confrontation with California's military comandante, Pedro Fages, over the latter's refusal to establish somewhere along the Santa Barbara Channel the midway mission and presidio of San Buenaventura. To Serra, it was a brazen defiance. From the beginning Gálvez had wanted a military and religious center there. Just before leaving Mexico in 1771 the *visitador* had sent enough priests north for that work and more besides—ten men all told, two for replacing retired padres, six for manning three new missions in the presidial districts of San Diego and Monterey, and two for San Buenaventura.* Fages let the new missions go ahead but balked at launching a new presidial district. He did not have enough soldiers, he said—a mere sixty men scattered between San Diego and Monterey—and that reality, not Gálvez, was the ultimate boss. San Buenaventura could wait.

Serra suspected the sincerity of the argument. What Fages was testing, in his opinion, was the question of who had ultimate authority in California affairs, the military or the church. Only Antonio de Bucareli, the new viceroy, could resolve the issue.

Other California crises also demanded the attention of the viceroy— an attention that so far he had been strangely remiss about giving. One was the stark matter of food enough to keep the missionary program

---

*The three new missions were San Gabriel, located about 9 miles west of present-day downtown Los Angeles; San Antonio de Padua in the western foothills of the Salinas Valley; and San Luis Obispo, on the site of today's city of the same name.

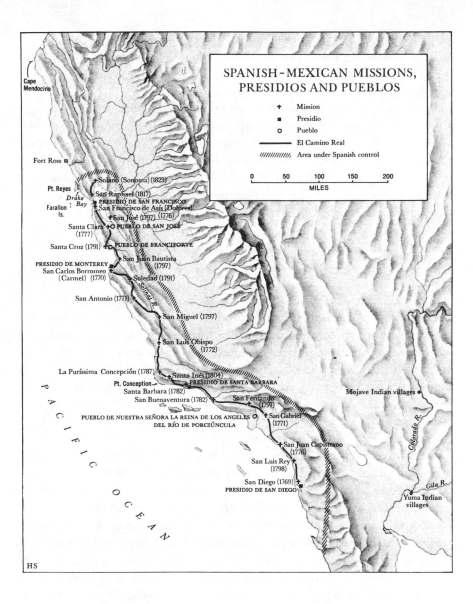

Cape
Mendocino

Fort Ross ■

Pt. Reyes
Drake
Bay
Farallon
Is.

Solano (Sonoma) (1823)
San Raphael (1817)
PRESIDIO DE SAN FRANCISCO
San Francisco de Asís (Dolores)
San José (1797) (1776)
Santa Clara ○ PUEBLO DE SAN JOSÉ
(1777)
Santa Cruz (1791) ○ PUEBLO DE BRANCIFORTE
PRESIDIO DE MONTEREY
San Carlos Borromeo
(Carmel) (1770)
San Juan Bautista
(1797)
Soledad (1791)

Salinas R.

San Antonio (1771)

San Miguel (1797)

San Luis Obispo
(1772)

La Puríssima Concepción (1787)
Pt. Conception
Santa Inés (1804)
PRESIDIO DE SANTA BARBARA
Santa Barbara (1782)
San Buenaventura (1782)
San Fernando
(1797)
PUEBLO DE NUESTRA SEÑORA LA REINA DE LOS ANGELES ○
DEL RÍO DE PORCIÚNCULA
San Gabriel
(1771)

Mojave Indian villages ●

P A C I F I C   O C E A N

San Juan Capistrano
(1776)
San Luis Rey
(1798)
San Diego (1769)
PRESIDIO DE SAN DIEGO

Colorado R.

Gila R.
Yuma Indian
villages

HS

moving. California's climate, on which self-sufficiency depended, had
proved treacherous. In the springs of 1770 and 1771 late rains had saved
the little fields of maize and wheat that the padres and soldiers had
planted at San Diego and Monterey. The Lord's favor, it had seemed, for
the Indians who had watched this miracle of controlled growth had been
impressed and delighted, especially after feasting on the results. Several
women and children and even a few husbands had let themselves be
baptized, a real triumph when one recalled that the padres at San Diego

had not achieved a single conversion during their first year there and that Serra himself had worked six months at Monterey to redeem his first soul, a child.

And then disaster. In 1772 the rains failed. Crops withered; the Indians wandered back to gathering seeds and acorns. The padres and the soldiers were reduced to living on herbs brought them by kindly natives and on niggardly dabs of milk from scrawny range cows that had been driven north by the land marchers in 1769. Nor was that the worst. During the year of famine, 1772, the annual supply ships, the *San Antonio* and the *San Carlos,* had been so buffeted by gales that Pérez had refused to go farther than San Diego. The people in the north, he had said, would have to wait for their sacks of grain and sugar and nonagricultural goods until pack trains could be assembled for carrying the material the rest of the way.

At least Fages had risen to the emergency. He had gone into the mountains with his soldiers and had killed enough grizzly bears so that the garrison at Monterey and the priests and the few neophytes at the missions had been able to live on dried bear meat until the pack trains arrived. But the crisis had also furnished additional proof of Fages' anti-missionary bias. He had declined to investigate charges that his packers had appropriated more of the mission mules than could be conveniently spared and that more than a fair share of the new supplies had somehow found their way into the barracks.

In any event, it was clear now that dependable harvests in Alta California would have to depend in large part, as they did in Baja California, on irrigation. That meant ditches, diversion dams, even reservoirs in places. In fact, there had to be buildings of many kinds. So far the mission compounds consisted of nothing more than chapels covered with boughs and poor little sheds of upright poles daubed with mud and roofed with reeds. Civilization—and weren't the Franciscans there to civilize?—de-manded proud churches, well-equipped workshops and dormitories, infirmaries for the neophytes, walled gardens, fenced grain fields, assured water—a monumental program. To date the padres' only help had come from the Christian Indians who had survived the march north from Baja. It was much—more than is generally noted—but it was not enough. Bucareli should be made to realize the crying need for skilled artisans to help the padres plan the work and for peon laborers to help the unskilled neophytes execute it.

Similarly, the presidios needed soldiers. But not any soldiers. New recruits should be married men accompanied by their families. Settled in pueblos close to the barracks, they would grow crops at first for them-selves and, after their retirement, for the presidio kitchens, thus helping preclude future clashes with the missions over the allocation of resources. More importantly, family men would end an explosive source of trouble with the Indians. Starved for women, the soldiers often escaped the surveillance of their officers by asking permission to hunt meat for their messes and then used their lassos to snag the human quarry they really wanted.

Hoping that distance would help avert such collisions, Serra had moved the Monterey mission (its formal name was San Carlos Borromeo) a few miles away from the presidio into the Carmel Valley, where better soil might improve agriculture. The San Diego mission had likewise moved to a new site up the San Diego River. But no isolation could be complete. There had to be a small guard at each station to help the padres control the neophytes, and the corporal in charge did not always watch the soldiers as he should. During the erection of the first stockade at San Gabriel a guard had openly lassoed and raped the wife of a neighborhood chief. When the aggrieved husband led a charge with bows and arrows, he was killed by a musket ball and his companions retreated in disorder. The soldiers then cut off the dead man's head and placed it, impaled on a pike, outside their camp as a warning against further attacks.

There had been no punishment. The only effect of the incident on Fages had been to give him another excuse for putting off San Buenaventura until reinforcements arrived. Throughout all the arguments over the matter he kept insisting that as military comandante of California he was in complete charge of the soldiers, even those at the missions; the padres could neither discipline nor remove a man without his consent. And because he felt, correctly, that the missionaries were muttering against him, he had the temerity to open and read their mail.

Now Serra, fighting the sickness that felled him for a time on the road from San Blas, was on his way to end all that—to demand that Bucareli remove Fages as commander and tell his successor without equivocation that in missionary affairs the priests were supreme. San Buenaventura, moreover, should be founded promptly, helpers should be sent to the missions and married soldiers to the presidios, and supply should be stabilized.

These were major demands, and Serra asked the viceroy's secretary for a personal interview with some diffidence. Bucareli's very name was awesome. Member of a powerful family of nobles in Spain, he had been lured to Mexico from Cuba, where he had been serving as governor, only by the offer of the highest salary ever yet attached to the viceregal position. Beset by the multiple problems of his vast new domain, he had ignored California. Moreover, as Serra knew, the head of the Apostolic College of San Fernando in Mexico City, which had charge of the California missions, was so discouraged about their prospects that he had openly questioned the advisability of continuing them. Did those doubts, rubbing off on the viceroy, account for Bucareli's silence? Would he even see anyone from California?

To his surprise and delight the secretary told the padre to present himself within the week, on February 13, 1773. The luck of timing was responsible for the warmth. Some months before, the minister of the Indies, administrative head of all Spanish colonial affairs, had written Bucareli concerning reports of continued British and Russian activity in the Pacific. (This was the same bugaboo that Gálvez had used to justify his northern push. Was it only coincidence that the former *visitador* was now a member of the Council of the Indies?) Under the circumstances, the letter to Bucareli went on, it might be well to strengthen those parts of the coast already settled and explore those that remained unknown.

Very little investigation had already shown Bucareli that a major problem in pushing settlement was one of the things that worried Serra, the difficulty of supply. Colonists, their families, and their livestock could not be tumbled like sacks of grain into some tiny ship and sent north on the sort of storm-tossed, scurvy-racked ordeal that so far had plagued every one of the annual supply trips to Alta California. Effective growth must depend on a land route.

Three alternatives presented themselves. One was the route the original settlers had followed—a treacherous crossing of the Gulf of California to Baja and then a long march up the peninsula. The other two possibilities had never been examined. One would originate in Sante Fe, New Mexico; that province, deemed to be on almost the same latitude as Monterey, was now producing agricultural surpluses, and offered an established mestizo population on which to draw. The third possibility was the long-advocated trail through Sonora, where the Indians had at last been quelled, more by a stampede of miners into the gold fields of the Altar Valley than by military action.

The Sonora route was receiving the most vocal support, largely because of a memorial from a hard-bitten, thirty-seven-year-old border captain, Juan Bautista Anza, who had fought under Gálvez, sane and insane, during the *visitador*'s Indian campaign. His interest was deeply personal. Anza's father and grandfather had both served in Sonora before him, and both had been advocates of Kino's old dream of an overland trail through the desert to Monterey Bay. Young Anza, who knew of Gálvez's intent to press ahead with that worn hope, was now fighting for it in his turn. Supporting him was an extraordinary Franciscan missionary named Francisco Garcés, as far-wandering as Kino had ever been.

In 1771 Garcés had followed Kino's almost forgotten trail to the villages of the Yuma Indians at the junction of the Gila and Colorado rivers. After winning the respect of the Yumas' splendidly muscled chief, Salvador Palma (a Hispanic name Garcés may have bestowed), he had crossed the Colorado and had zigzagged west through appalling deserts until he had glimpsed a far-off line of mountains, today's San Jacintos. Low saddles appeared in them; probably the gaps could be used as passes. And the Pacific, Garcés told Anza on his return to Sonora, was surely just beyond.

The lure caught Anza's throat. He wrote Bucareli, describing what Garcés had seen and offering to open the road to the coast. Counting perhaps on suitable rewards in the event of success, he even volunteered to meet out of his own pocket all expenses involved, save for the regular salaries of the soldiers he took with him.

Bucareli was still weighing the three routes against the whole problem of California when Serra appeared. Promptly the viceroy called the intense, short-statured padre into his presence and began picking his brain.

What about a permanent road for colonists through Baja California? Serra shook his head. The crossing of the gulf was too arduous and the peninsula too sterile to support the number of riding animals, pack mules, and cattle herds that would be involved. As for Sonora, he feared the Apaches and leaned therefore toward New Mexico. But any of those routes would be long and expensive. He urged, accordingly, that the harbor be improved and that ocean transport be continued for bulky goods.

Perhaps Monterey would not remain the end of the run. Bucareli was full of questions about the great bay farther north. Yes, Serra agreed, it was a strategic spot, and should be occupied before any other power could take it. Yes, Fages had made two attempts to circle it and thus reach Cermeño's Puerto de San Francisco (Drake's Bay) but had been blocked by an enormous river flowing into the bay's northern reaches. Because of these difficulties in travel, a fortification, if any, should be placed on the southern shore of the grand inlet, the Golden Gate, to which the Spanish referred simply as La Boca, the Mouth. Naturally, the padre added, if a presidio were located there, missions should follow.

Bucareli listened noncommittally and sent Serra off to write out his full list of suggestions and complaints in the form of a memorial. The project, which occupied the Franciscan for three weeks, resulted in an exhilarating triumph. A presidio and at least two missions were to be placed on the southern perimeter of the still-unnamed bay. As an adjunct to that defensive maneuver, Juan Pérez was to sail a new ship, the *Santiago*, as far north as the Arctic, watching for Russians and landing now and then to claim the empty lands for Spain by right of discovery.

Of more immediate joy to Serra was Bucareli's affirmation that the California padres were to have full control over soldiers stationed as guards at their missions. The military was not to meddle with mission mail, supplies, mules, or other property. Best of all, Fages was removed as comandante of Alta California, and his successor was instructed to take several married soldiers with him to the north, where they were to settle after they had fulfilled their enlistments.

There were disappointments, of course. The new military governor was not the man Serra recommended, but rather sulky old Rivera y Moncada—he was sixty-two then—who had led the first land party from the peninsula to San Diego. Because budgets allowed for only one new presidio, Bucareli again postponed San Buenaventura in favor of San Francisco. Serra was not granted the laborers he wanted for mission construction, but he was allowed to recruit a handful of carpenters, blacksmiths, tanners, and other artisans to help speed the training of the California converts.

As for supply, Bucareli temporized. He did rule out Baja California as a possibility, and he did order that San Blas be improved. But he wanted the other land routes examined before he committed himself about future supply programs. He sent messengers over the long trail to New Mexico, ordering that explorations be initiated from there—an effort that eventually bogged down in present-day Utah. Simultaneously he directed Anza to see what he could find by striking out with a small party northwestward from Sonora. Until the reports were in, the usual routines would have to suffice for the north. Yet after adding everything together, Serra was, by and large, content.

Of the various adventurers—Rivera, Pérez, the New Mexicans, even Serra—Anza and Garcés were the first to start for California, despite troubles with horse-stealing Apaches. They had thirty-four soldiers and mule skinners in their party. By good luck they picked up at the little mud hamlet of Caborca, in northwestern Sonora, a California Indian called El Peregrino, the Wanderer, who had fled all the way there from Mission San Gabriel, presumably with Yuma Indians. He might be useful as a guide.

With the Yumas helping, the explorers forded the Colorado River into the desolate sand dunes beyond. In that seared, glistening wasteland, neither El Peregrino nor Garcés proved helpful. After a week of thirsty wandering the party had to retreat to the river and reorganize. Leaving some of their baggage behind under a small guard, the rest, mounted on the best horses, found a way through the desert and crossed the San Jacinto Mountains by means of a wild canyon that looked, Anza said, as if it contained all the broken sweepings of the world. At sunset on March 22, 1774, they knocked at the gates of San Gabriel. The padres, astounded by the feat, set up a clangor of bells in celebration. A new contact with home!

The annual supply ship, on which Serra was returning to California, had not yet reached California, and all the missions were tiptoeing along the edges of hunger. To avoid burdening them further, Anza sent Garcés and most of the men back to the Yuma villages. He himself hurried on to Monterey with a small escort. That trail needed no exploration; he was driven over it by deeper needs. By dipping his scarred hand into the waters of the distant bay, he could fulfill at last a yearning that had been tugging at the desert wanderers of northern Mexico, his father and grandfather included, for three-quarters of a century. How could he have turned back at San Gabriel?

Delighted by the achievement, Bucareli promoted Anza to the rank of lieutenant colonel and ordered him to recruit soldier-colonists for the new presidio. As a supplement to that push, the viceroy directed naval surveyors to take a ship through La Boca into San Francisco Bay, as it was being more and more often named, and map its shoreline. Finally he sent two other ships toward Alaska to finish the examinations that an onslaught of scurvy—and of timidity—had kept Juan Pérez from completing. For now that understanding had at last come to him from Madrid, Antonio de Bucareli was determined to make all western North America a Spanish prize. These were the first steps.

Disturbing omens, not fully understood at the time, emerged during Anza's recruiting. He had been authorized to offer liberal inducements to California settlers. In addition to the men's salaries as soldiers, they and their families were to receive, free of charge, the clothing, pack animals, and equipment they needed for the trip, and free rations during their first five years in the north. But who wanted to go to California, end of nowhere? When it was time to leave, his recruiting agents had signed up, partly from Anza's own garrison at Tubac, only 40 poverty-stricken men. Their wives and children raised the count to 205. It was a paltry start toward occupying half a continent.

In addition to the soldier-settlers, Anza's column included José Moraga, two other officers, three missionaries, and several roustabouts for handling upwards of 1,000 horses, mules, and cattle. They began their march in October, 1775. They had no wagons. Every item had to be packed on muleback and unpacked each morning and night. The winds were cold and gritty with sand, and these were people accustomed to heat. They complained endlessly, but they kept creeping on, a few miles a day. Anza bickered just as endlessly with the ranking priest, Pedro

Font, who considered himself the true head of the flock. A principal cause of contention was the *aguardiente* that Anza doled out on the coldest nights to start fiddle playing and dancing beside the campfires as a boost to morale. Perhaps it helped. In any event, he brought more people into California than he had started with. Eight babies were born along the way. Except for one mother who died early in the trip, all concerned survived and reached San Gabriel on January 4, 1776.

No one was happier to see them than California's new military governor, Fernando Rivera. Two months earlier, 800 Indians had attacked the relocated mission in the valley of the San Diego River, six miles from the presidio. Before being driven off by the fearsome thundering of the muskets, they had killed a priest and one other man, and had wounded several, one of whom later died.

Fear of a general uprising swept the south. Messengers rushed to Monterey to bring back Rivera and reinforcements. By chance the comandante's party reached San Gabriel just one day ahead of the colonists.

Rivera was nervous and unhappy, filled with the aches of his long winter ride through cold rains. Prior to Anza's arrival, he had had only seventy soldiers for defending all California, and who could say how far this trouble might spread? Remember Sonora: the Indians there had held off Gálvez's army of 1,100 men for years. Anza's appearance under such circumstances was like a miracle. Rivera prevailed on the weary desert commander to join him with seventeen men. Together they rode on to San Diego.

All was quiet. The stout resistance of the defenders of the mission, the guns and horses of the soldiers from the presidio, and the opportune arrival of a supply vessel had discouraged the Indians and they had melted away. To impress them still more, Rivera and Anza marshaled their men in battle array, pennants fluttering, and rode through the unresisting rancherías in a bold show of strength. A reassuring opinion of California's Indians emerged. Their basic unit was a very small tribelet centered on one or two villages. Beyond that there was no social cohesion, and it was highly unlikely that a widespread, Sonora-type uprising would ever take place.

Less comforting was the dilemma in which Anza found himself. He had been instructed to cooperate with Rivera in building the new presidio at San Francisco Bay, but the comandante refused to countenance the project. In spite of Bucareli's orders to select a site, he had sat tight at Monterey for several months before riding the hundred miles to La Boca to look over the land. By then winter rains had been sluicing down, and after a miserable examination of the peninsula he returned with his prejudices confirmed. Settlements, either military or religious, that depended on agriculture could never survive in that fog-shrouded cluster of sandhills.

He refused to change his mind. When Bucareli's naval surveyors paused at Monterey and invited him to join their explorations of the bay, he grumpily declined. Wasting money up there would be folly. The colonists who were coming should be used for developing the presidial pueblos at San Diego and Monterey. He had written as much to Bucareli, and now he told Anza so. There was to be no San Francisco.

Part of the trouble was jealousy. Though twenty-five years younger than Rivera, Anza was already a lieutenant colonel—merely because he had found a way across the desert. Well, Rivera had found a way up the Baja peninsula for the first land column ever to reach Alta California; later, when moving north to assume the governorship, he had brought fifty-one soldier-settlers with him over the same route—this before Anza had even started his recruiting. Yet he was still a captain. But in California he was comandante. There was to be no San Francisco.

While the two were arguing, an urgent message came from San Gabriel. The mission was running out of food. The colonists waiting there must move on.

His hand forced, Anza told Rivera that he was going to take his people at least as far north as Monterey. He got them there through drenching rains that felled him with pleurisy. Before he was fully recovered, he was riding again. With José Moraga, Padre Font, and a few others, he went to La Boca and located a site for the presidio high above the glittering waters "on," Font wrote, "a flowering tableland abounding with wild violets. From it the view is *deliciocisima.*" The next day they crossed a low hill covered with flowering manzanita to a creek that they named, in honor of the Virgin, Laguna de Nuestra Señora de los Dolores, Our Lady of Sorrows. There they staked out the bounds of the mission of San Francisco de Asís. (Because of the creek it would be more generally called Mission Dolores.) Riding another 18 miles to a spot close to the southern tip of the bay, they located a second station, to be named Mission Santa Clara.

Anza then washed his hands of the affair. He had brought his people to the coast, and now it was up to Serra and Moraga to decide whether or not to defy Rivera by going ahead with the building. Back at Monterey he assembled his cavalcade in the plaza, bade them an emotional farewell, and rode south, to be rewarded for his success with the governorship of distant New Mexico.

Many signs indicated that Rivera's opposition to San Francisco would be overruled in Mexico. Confidently Moraga and Serra took 193 people to La Boca. (They reached their destination in June, a few days before the American colonists beside the Atlantic declared themselves independent of Great Britain.) They cleared off the site of the forbidden presidio and dedicated it on September 17, 1776. The mission of San Francisco de Asís was dedicated on October 9; Santa Clara on January 13, 1777. In recognition of Alta California's new importance, Bucareli named Monterey the governmental seat of both it and Baja California. A new governor, Felipe de Neve, was sent north, and Rivera was transferred back to Loreto as his subordinate.

The old soldier had made a valid point, however. San Francisco might be justifiable as a guard for the great bay, but the garrison there would never survive if it had to depend on vegetables grown in that sandy, wind-whipped soil. Rivera was so insistent on the point—and, indeed, on the whole problem of supplies for the presidios—that Neve, the new governor, decided to conduct a personal survey of the province's agricultural resources.

He soon found that Rivera was right: real difficulties loomed. Because the soldiers could spend little time farming, the presidios were not likely to be self-sustaining for years, if ever. Scant help could be expected from the missions. True, they were making great strides in conquering California's rainless summers by means of little irrigation projects, and they were slowly adding fruit trees, grape vines, and garden produce to the original staples of beef, maize, and wheat. Success, however, was quite literally feeding on itself. As each establishment grew more crops and cattle, more Indians came in from the rancherías, ready to abandon their seminomadic freedom and laborious food gathering in exchange for three sure meals a day. No provender was left over. The presidios still had to depend on the annual supply ships for sustenance, and as their population grew this would place excessive demands, both physical and financial, on that uncertain source.

The solution, Neve wrote Bucareli, was the establishment of farming pueblos to grow supplies for the presidios. He had already chosen two sites on which to start. One lay beside Gaudalupe Creek at the southern tip of San Francisco Bay, near the new mission of Santa Clara. The other was in the south, nine miles west of San Gabriel on the banks of the little stream to which Portolá had given so sonorous a name in 1769: El Río de Nuestra Señora de los Ángeles de Porciúncula.

The letter mailed, Neve plunged straight ahead with the founding of the first of the towns, San José de Guadalupe. He was not acting blindly. He knew, and told prospective townspeople in Monterey and San Francisco, the terms under which government-sponsored pueblos could be established. Each village would receive four square leagues of land, roughly 17,500 acres. Within this area the head of each family would receive, close to the central plaza, one lot for his home and one for his garden, plus the right to graze his cattle and horses (they too were gifts from the government) on the outlying communal pasture. While the town was getting established, each settler would be paid a small salary for his service and be granted an allowance toward his family's daily rations. The pueblo would be governed in local matters by an elected alcalde, or mayor, and an *ayuntamiento*, or council, both closely supervised by the governor and removable at his will. In return for these benefits, the colonist agreed not to sell his land to outsiders without permission, to work on such community projects as irrigating ditches, and to deliver to the nearest presidio, at prices fixed by the government, any surplus food he raised.

Fourteen families, sixty-eight persons all told, agreed to the terms and on November 29, 1777, launched California's first civil community, San Jose. Nearly seven months later, Neve received Bucareli's permission to go ahead with the job.

Interruptions brought about by José de Gálvez delayed the second town. In 1776, the founder of California had become chief Minister of the Indies in Madrid, one of Spain's topmost governmental positions. Almost his first move after being inducted was to wave into existence the northern commandancy-general that he had first envisioned while serving as *visitador* in Mexico. He named as governor of this huge new domain, which now stretched out to include Texas as well as the other northern provinces, young Teodoro de Croix, nephew of Gálvez's complaisant friend of Mexico days, the retired viceroy, Carlos de Croix. Teodoro's headquarters were to be in Arispe, Sonora, rather than among the Yuma Indians, as first planned. The Yumas were not forgotten, however. Missions and farming towns for easing the way of settlers bound for California were to be established among them as soon as possible.

Trouble with Apache Indians absorbed Teodoro's energies. As a result neither Neve's plans for California (which now included the long-delayed presidio beside the Santa Barbara Channel as well as the agricultural town in the south) nor the Yuma establishments began to roll until 1780. There were two of the latter—mongrel affairs, part mission, part presidio, and part pueblo. They stood about nine miles apart on the west bank of the Colorado River, opposite the mouth of the Gila. The Indians hated them. The first colonists—sixteen soldiers, sixteen civilian families, and four friars headed by Francisco Garcés—gave them fewer gifts than they had been led to expect. Worse, the newcomers elbowed the Yumas away from certain mud flats where Indians had been growing squash, beans, corn, and melons longer than anyone remembered. Angrily the natives began making what the settlers considered exorbitant demands for restitution. Within the year tempers on both sides were ripe for a collision.

Meanwhile Rivera had been charged with recruiting fifty-nine soldiers for the channel presidio, thirty-four of them married, and twenty-four farm families for the agricultural town in southern California. His overtures met the same kind of unwillingness to go to California that Anza's had. Though he eventually scratched together the soldiers, he had to be content with eleven farm families—forty-four persons, counting wives and children, or fewer than half as many as Neve wanted. The husbands were a mixed lot: two who claimed Spanish blood, four Christian Indians, two blacks, one mestizo, one mulatto, and one mix of Indian and black called a chino. Their wives were either Indians or mulattoes. This polyglot mixture Rivera sent north through Baja California with an escort of seventeen of his newly recruited soldiers, four of them with wives.

Governor Neve met the eleven families at San Gabriel and led them to the site of the new town. There, borrowing the name of the little stream, he launched, on the evening of September 4, 1781, with a minimum of ceremony, El Pueblo de Nuestra Señora la Reina de los Ángeles de Porciúncula. (Six weeks later at Yorktown beside the Atlantic Lord Cornwallis surrendered to George Washington.) For a time the new town went by the shortened name of Porciúncula. Fortunately for a host of yet unborn spellers, the designation did not last. Instead it became Los Angeles.

While the Los Angeles settlers were still marching through Baja California, Rivera and the remaining forty-two soldiers pushed across the desert from Sonora, driving with them 1,000 head of cattle, horses, and mules. The dry, hot trip exhausted about half the stock—and Rivera, too; he was seventy-one now and worn by too many rides like this. Sending the married soldiers ahead with the soundest part of the herd, the gray old captain and the unmarried men halted at the Yuma villages to recruit the trail-weary animals.

Like the dwellers in the new settlements, Rivera was parsimonious with his gifts. His herdsmen let the stock feed in the Indian gardens. Some of the soldiers ran loose among the Indian women. The outrages triggered an attack already well planned. On the night of July 18, 1791, Yuma warriors fell on the military camp and both settlements. Every man died, Rivera and Garcés included. The women and children were, in accord with Indian practice, made prisoners. It was by far the bloodiest massacre of non-Indians in California's pioneering history.

In time the captives were ransomed by Pedro Fages, marching up out of Sonora, where he had been serving since his removal from California at Serra's request. No effective punitive campaign was waged, however, and the overland trail stayed closed. Once again California's reliance would have to be on the sea and on the products of her own husbandry.

There was nothing to do but go ahead. Using the military families that had escaped the disaster, Neve in 1782 launched the presidio beside the Santa Barbara Channel. He named the fortress Santa Barbara; the original designation, San Buenaventura, was switched to a mission, forerunner of today's Ventura, located twenty-seven miles down the coast toward Los Angeles. Serra himself, old and frail now, rode down from Monterey to dedicate the stations he had so long hoped for. He planned another mission near the presidio, but a bitter jurisdictional quarrel with Neve interrupted, and the famed Santa Barbara mission, the only one that has ever been used continuously for religious purposes from Spanish times until now, was not started until 1786.

To complete Serra's discomfiture, Neve was replaced as governor by, incredibly enough, Pedro Fages. The two found each other as stiff-necked as ever, but no time remained for a new confrontation. On August 29, 1784, fifteen years after his arrival at San Diego, Junípero Serra died and was buried at San Carlos Borromeo in the Carmel Valley. He was seventy years old.

It had been a remarkable fifteen years. During them two towns, four presidios, and nine missions had been founded. To review them chronologically: the towns were San Jose and Los Angeles; the presidios, San Diego, Monterey, San Francisco, and Santa Barbara; the missions, San Diego, San Carlos Borromeo (originally at Monterey), San Antonio de Padua, San Gabriel, San Luis Obispo, San Juan Capistrano, San Francisco de Asís (Dolores), Santa Clara, and San Buenaventura.

Attached to those nine missions were some 5,000 Indian neophytes, an astounding acceleration. But in that very momentum lay the seeds of trouble. Spanish colonial policy was firmly based on an amalgamation of races, yet there were hardly 500 non-Indians—one-tenth of 5,000—in the entire province. Unless immigration quickened enough to force secularization and make true acculturation possible—with the one road closed and prospects reluctant anyhow!—a serious imbalance threatened. Let that come to pass, and there was little question who then would be carrying all Spanish California on their bowed shoulders: the Christianized Indians.

One is tempted to read a kind of cosmic symbolism into the matter. Madness, too, is an imbalance, as men associated with José de Gálvez well knew. So perhaps it was inevitable, in the strange ways of destiny, that an incongruous founding should leave its demonic mark on the far coast for decades—even for centuries—to come.

part two

THE ADVENT
OF THE AMERICANS

4. Illegal Entry

During the last years of the century, the old specters of foreign encroachment on the northwest coast solidified into frightening reality. Russian fur traders, questing for downy otter skins that could be sold at astronomical profits to Chinese mandarins, began leapfrogging island by island along the Aleutian chain toward Alaska. British traders, belatedly alerted to the possibilities of the commerce by James Cook's explorations, began steering toward Vancouver Island off the southwestern coast of present-day Canada. Even a pair of ships from Boston soon joined the rush. In reacting to the emergency, as it seemed in Mexico City, the Spanish government at last faced up to the serious population and defense problems confronting California. Unfortunately for Spain, the net result of the agonizing was a series of blunders.

The first inkling of what was afoot reached Monterey in 1786, when two French warships under Admiral Jean François de Galaup, Comte de La Pérouse, hove to in Monterey. Governor Pedro Fages was suspicious of the visitors—with reason. The admiral had been prowling the North Pacific to evaluate commercial and colonial prospects for his own government. France and Spain were then allies, however, and so Fages received the newcomers (they were the first non-Spanish whites ever to touch California) with such pomp as he could muster. During the exchange of civilities La Pérouse told the governor that Russian fur hunters had recently built outposts on Kodiak and Unalaska islands. Fages thanked him politely for the information and straightway wrote a warning to Mexico's new viceroy, Manuel Flores.

Two years later—exchanging dispatches with Madrid took time— Flores sent two ships under Esteban José Martínez and Gonzalo López de Haro northward to learn just what was going on. They returned to San Blas boiling with excitement. They had not only found the Russian otter hunters, but had listened to them boast (with little basis in fact, actually) that their government planned to build a military stronghold at Nootka Sound on Vancouver Island, in order to eject the British fur traders who were using that harbor as a base.

Juan Pérez had visited Nootka in 1774; Martínez had been there with him as a junior officer. The north, Martínez now declared belligerently, belonged to Spain by right of discovery, and the government should defend its title by erecting a presidio at Nootka. "To prove the feasibility of it," he wrote the viceroy, "I will sacrifice my last breath."

This time Flores did not wait to consult with Madrid. Early in 1789 he ordered soldiers and priests aboard Martínez' and Haro's ships and sent them to Nootka to establish a colony. He promised that a supply vessel would follow and—confidence of ignorance!—that a land force would march north from Monterey as soon as possible.

Shortly thereafter Flores received startling new information from the remote island of Más-a-Tierra, one of the Juan Fernández group west of Valparaíso, Chile. On May 24, 1788, the 212-ton *Columbia Rediviva*, eight months out of Boston, had put into the island's harbor in search of relief after a terrible battering received while rounding Cape Horn. Her captain was forty-seven-year-old John Kendrick, who had served as a privateer in the West Indies during the American Revolution. Associated with Kendrick but currently separated from him by the storms was thirty-two-year-old Robert Gray, in command of the 90-ton sloop *Lady Washington*. Their backers were six Boston merchants eager to develop a triangular trade with the Orient based on otter fur. The two captains were to trade Yankee notions to the Indians of the Northwest Coast for pelts, swap the skins in China for porcelain, tea, and silk, and bring the new cargo home by way of southern Africa.

Gales off Cape Horn drove the two ships apart. Assuming that if Gray stayed afloat he would continue to their assigned rendezvous at Nootka Sound, Kendrick steered the *Columbia* toward Más-a-Tierra, hoping to make repairs. Ignoring Spanish prohibitions about intercourse with foreigners, the island's lonely comandante received the Americans graciously and sent them on refreshed. He then wrote Flores about what he had done. For his hospitality, he was demoted.

Afterward, in reporting to Madrid on the affair, the viceroy mused with remarkable prescience, "We ought not to be surprised that the English colonies of America, being now an independent republic, should carry out designs of finding a safe port in the Pacific and of attempting to sustain it by crossing that immense country of the continent. . . . It is indeed an enterprise for many years, but I firmly believe that from now on we ought to employ tactics to forestall the results."

No such foresight troubled Martínez. On reaching Nootka, he found the two American ships and more English vessels than he had bargained for. To strengthen his position, he decided to make common cause with the Bostonians. After all, had not their countries been allied against Britain during the American Revolution?

Personal ambition was involved. Martínez hoped that if he succeeded in driving off the English and asserting Spanish control over the northwest, he would be rewarded with an otter-trading monopoly, wherein he would pick up, at the California missions, skins collected by Indian hunters and carry the pelts to the Philippines for trade. Somehow (the details are unclear) Kendrick figured in the scheme. In any event, Robert Gray and he exchanged shipboard banquets with the Spanish captains and watched unmolested during Martínez' ceremony of occupation. Priests, soldiers, and sailors marched onto the beach, erected a cross, and sang *Te Deum Laudamus*. With his sword Martínez touched trees and stones while crying out, "I take and I have taken, I seize and I have seized possession of this soil . . . for all time to come." He then began building a barracks for his men and setting up a battery on a little island that commanded the main entrance to the harbor.

The groundwork laid, he pounced on the next few British ships that entered the sound. Two he manned with his own sailors and sent them to San Blas with their crews imprisoned inside the holds. He raised Spanish colors above the third vessel, intending to use her on trading expeditions along the northern coast. When the British crew refused to cooperate, he sent them to China with Robert Gray, who was not involved in the scheme, and thereafter operated the captured schooner with help from Kendrick's men.

In due time the Spaniard went eagerly back to Mexico to receive his reward. Instead he was stripped of his command, ostensibly because of his wife's complaint of nonsupport. The failure cut Kendrick adrift from his hopes, too. For the next few years he floated aimlessly around, met Gray on the latter's return from Boston, whither he had gone from China, but never worked in harmony with his fellow countryman and never rendered any accounting of his trade profits to his backers in Boston. In 1794 he was killed in an accident in Hawaii. Gray worked more effectively. In 1792, during his second trip to the Northwest Coast, he entered the mouth of the Columbia River, giving the United States her first thin claim to a piece of the Pacific coast.

Meanwhile, in the early part of 1790, three more ships sailed from Mexico to Nootka laden with livestock, soldiers, and priests. They established a presidio at Nootka and a smaller settlement at Neah Bay on the south side of Juan de Fuca Strait in present-day Washington state—all to no avail. Britain responded to the seizure of her citizens' ships by mobilizing and threatening war. Madrid backed down and in October, 1790, granted British subjects the right to settle or trade at any point in the Pacific not already occupied by Spanish colonists. In return Britain agreed to keep her subjects from trading at Spanish ports except as Spain allowed, and from hunting otter within "ten maritime leagues from any part of the coast already occupied by Spain."

Obviously these provisions had no effect on the Russians or the Americans. Unless the Spaniards somehow found ways to shackle them, their hands were free.

Shackle? How? The whole world was learning of California's nakedness. At the conclusion of the Nootka agreement, the English Admiralty sent one of Britain's most capable navigators, George Vancouver, to the Pacific to see that every picayune detail of the treaty was carried out as stipulated. He and the Spanish commander at Nootka disagreed on certain points, and while waiting for instructions from London, Vancouver visited California three times between November, 1792, and November, 1794. He was not impressed by what he saw. In particular he scorned the feebleness of the presidios, and with raised eyebrows wondered rhetorically in his report why on earth Spain had gone to so much expense and labor in colonizing the coast, only to let the effort sag "into no account whatsoever."

Spanish administrators in Mexico, humiliated by Nootka and fearful of what Vancouver's nosiness might lead to, began agitated discussions about California's defenses. Among the men called into consultation was engineer Miguel Costansó of the pioneering Portolá-Serra expedition. He recommended the obvious: a beefing up of the presidios and, more importantly, intensified efforts to spread a self-reliant citizenry throughout the coastal regions. For, as he wrote to the new viceroy, the Marquis de Branciforte, "Of what value are immense areas of territory if we do not populate them?"

A great bustle began. The presidio at Nootka and the settlement at Neah Bay were withdrawn in favor of concentrating energies farther south. An able new military governor, Diego de Borica, was entrusted with levitating the corpse there. To help him, Miguel Costansó drew up plans for erecting *castillos*, or batteries, where their little cannon could command the harbor entrances at San Francisco, Monterey, Santa Barbara, and San Diego. (The presidios, being barracks rather than forts, were too far from the inlets to control them directly.) Out from Mexico sailed seventy-five veteran soldiers to man the guns and reinforce the garrisons.

Costansó's plan for stimulating immigration did not fare as well. He urged the government to give livestock, tools, daily rations, and monthly pay to qualified families who would settle in the Indian villages that were growing up beside the missions. These newcomers would teach the neophytes by precept rather than by paternalistic edict from above. True acculturation would result; a sturdy body of mestizos would be hurried into existence.

The missionaries opposed the idea, fearing that the settlers would corrupt their charges. The government shied away from its expenses. The result was a compromise. A score of artisans were sent north to serve temporarily, under the padres, as instructors in agriculture and handicrafts. Further stimulation to farming was to come from a single new agricultural town, to be located at the north end of Monterey Bay and called Branciforte in honor of the viceroy. Meantime the Franciscans were to fill the blank areas between San Francisco Bay and San Diego with five new missions.

Recruits for Branciforte proved even more reluctant to leave home than they had been during Anza's time. Why should they move? Immigrants were not pouring into Mexico as they were into the United States, and hence there was little competition for available jobs. If a farmer did go to California, he would have to sell his produce to the presidios at rigidly controlled prices. A merchant who did dream up an independent pursuit, as Martínez had in connection with otter fur, was crippled by jealousies and restrictions. A man might as well stay home with his friends.

In order to obtain a full quota of settlers, the government finally had to send along a small batch of convicts, foundlings, and prostitutes. Four retired soldiers joined the party in California—and that was Branciforte, California's third civil pueblo, designed during critical times to attract some of the non-Indian population deemed necessary for creating a viable citizenry.

In contrast the missions throve. Since Serra's day, four more, including Santa Barbara and Santa Cruz, had been added to the original nine. In one year, June 11, 1797, through June 13, 1798, Fermín Lasuén, Serra's successor as father-president of the Alta California religious establishments, launched another five. They reached from Mission San José on the southeastern side of San Francisco Bay to San Luis Rey, about 25 miles north of San Diego. Although Lasuén was seventy-seven years old at the time, he rode horseback to each one to hold the dedicatory services and then visited the established stations as well.

By the end of the century, 13,000 Indians were clustered within the eighteen missions. (There were 1,800 *gente de razón* living at the four presidios and in the three pueblos.) Under the leadership of the imported artisans, construction programs spurted, and the compounds began to take on the appearance associated with them today—arched colonnades, fountains plashing in cool courtyards, stone churches, soft red roof tiles, impressive bell towers. Wheatfields, orchards, and vineyards flourished; prolific herds of cattle grazed across literally millions of acres of tall grass.

There were mutterings. The comandantes of the bedraggled little presidios, traditionally jealous of the power of the priests, pointed accusing fingers at the bulging warehouses and asked whether such riches accorded with Franciscan vows of poverty. Retiring soldiers and ambitious townspeople who had accumulated a few head of cattle and wanted land on which to start ranches of their own complained that the priests blocked their petitions—and, indeed, during the entire Spanish period only 25 or so grants were issued to private individuals.* Resenting the system in general, the disappointed applicants cried out, often with exaggeration, against its particular faults.

There were faults. Size had bred an iron regimentation. During the early days of any mission, when living space and food had been limited, even baptized Indians had been allowed to spend much of their time in their home rancherías, living in accustomed ways. As the missions grew, however, the neophytes were brought into tightly clustered villages close beside the mission walls. Although the padres allowed some native customs to persist—sweat baths, dances, games, and occasional "vacation" trips to the home villages—the cultural shock attending the transfer was severe.

Families were separated. To check the casual sexuality normal among the young, the padres each night locked adolescent girls into crowded, ill-lighted, unsanitary barracks called *monjerios*. There and in the filthy villages outside, diseases introduced by the whites flared into epidemics. Despite the vigilance of the priests syphilis spread like wildfire. The death rate soared, and with it fear.

Ancient work habits were turned topsy-turvy. Although the Indians had not minded strenuous exertion when circumstances demanded—when the salmon ran or when the acorns were ripe and had to be gathered

---

*It should be noted that although grazing in early California required little work—mild winters did away with the need of shelter and hay—it absorbed enormous acreages. The grasses were annuals, not the deep-sodded perennials of the Great Plains. They reseeded themselves each year. As the pods shattered and the sun of the dry season withered the stems, nutrient values shrank and stock had to wander far to find enough to eat. Meantime the soft climate let the animals multiply prodigiously. As a result the ripples of the enterprise spread and spread. Eventually, for example, cattle belonging to Mission San Gabriel were grazed, of necessity, as far east as San Gorgonio, 60 miles away.

Little of this far-flung land was granted specifically to any mission. Spanish law said, however, that private land grants must not encroach on ranges used by pueblos or religious establishments. It was easy, consequently, for the padres to insist that a proposed grant would interfere with some part of their domain and by that means block the allotment.

and pulverized—they detested routine, even though the tasks involved might not be onerous. In the missions routine was rigid. Bells were forever summoning them to worship, to work, to meals, where they had to stand in line with their bowls to receive mush or stew ladeled out of bubbling iron cauldrons in the courtyard.

In their home villages strong totemistic attachments had kept the clans homogeneous, but at the missions the increasing numbers of converts led to a willy-nilly mixture of strange groups speaking different tongues. Jealousies led to maneuverings for favor and then to suspicion and unhappiness. Although flogging and confinement in stocks seemed natural punishments to the fathers—they were customary in all European navies, schools, and prisons of the time—the physical indignity horrified the Indians. Yet they could not escape. Once a person had voluntarily joined the system, he was never allowed to withdraw. If he tried to run away, as many did, he was pursued by soldiers riding swift horses and armed with irresistible guns.

The priests denied charges of overwork and overpunishment. They built infirmaries for the sick. They pointed out that the bulging warehouses at each mission had to feed several hundred Indians three times a day until the next harvest. As for the land used by the mission cattle and sheep, it was being held in trust for the Indians because the neophytes needed its output. Eventually secularization would come and the areas would be opened wide. In the meantime one must not be impatient. It took time, to use Lasuén's words, to "denaturalize" the Indians . . . "To make them realize that they are men."

Northward, the victors at Nootka were being driven off the stormy seas by their own country's mercantilistic policies. The South Sea Company, which held a royal monopoly over British commerce on the west coast of the Americas, demanded that the otter hunters buy licenses from them. The East Indian Company imposed further restraints in China. Disgusted, the British traders withdrew, leaving the field for the Americans and Russians to fight over among themselves.

American ships on their way to the North Pacific occasionally put into California ports for food and water. There they somehow learned—who can say through what whispers illicit commerce begins?—that Indian hunters were capturing several hundred otter a year. Some pelts they kept. More they turned over to the padres for baubles. Still others they gambled away with the soldiers at the presidios or with ranchers like José Ortega at isolated Refugio Canyon on the coast above Santa Barbara.

Although it was not legal for a Spaniard to swap fur or anything else with foreigners, the temptation was irresistible. Two tiny supply ships each year still supplied California, as they had from the beginning. It was physically impossible for them to bring into the province everything that was wanted, luxuries especially, or to take back to Mexico all the tallow, hemp, cowhides, and otter skins that the eighteen missions (nineteen after the founding of Santa Inés in 1804) relied on for creating credit. About 1800, American smugglers began filling the gaps by slipping along the coast offering bright cloth, satin shoes, costume jewelry, fine hunting knives, household utensils, furniture, altar pieces, and choice candles for otter pelts. According to William Shaler, one of the few contraband traders who left records, $25,000 in illegal fur was carried out of the province each year during the first decade of the century.

Though scornful of California's defenses, Shaler admitted that trouble sometimes occurred. In February, 1803, the comandante at San Diego, Manuel Rodríguez, an honest little martinet, seized 491 contraband skins that had been gathered by a certain Bostonian, John Brown of the *Alexander*, and peremptorily ordered him out of the harbor. Two weeks later along came the *Lelia Byrd* of Salem, Massachusetts. William Shaler, her captain, and Richard Cleveland, her supercargo, tried to bribe Rodríguez into selling them the confiscated skins, whereupon the comandante also ordered them to be off at dawn the next morning. That night he prowled the beach in person and arrested four American sailors red-handed as they were dickering with some of his soldiers. It was a short triumph. Cleveland rushed up with drawn pistols and rescued the men. The *Lelia Byrd* then fled from the bay under a furious but largely ineffective cannonading from the little guns of the *castillo*.

Besides being dangerous at times, smuggling was slow work, involving long night rides and interminable haggling. The same year, 1803, that Shaler was being bombarded, an impatient New Englander named Joseph O'Cain decided to experiment with swifter ways. Since California lacked any sort of naval patrol, he would hunt the offshore waters himself, using Aleut Indians from the north to do the actual work.

The Aleuts were experts. They built swift ocean-going bidarkas by stretching the skins of sea lions completely over long, narrow frames of driftwood and whalebone. The only openings in the lightweight craft were two rimmed holes in which a pair of hunters sat, one behind the other, their legs outstretched on the flat bottoms. Waterproof jackets made of the intestines of sea lions protected the upper parts of the navigators' bodies from spray and storm. They hunted in packs. After exhausting their diving quarry, they killed it with short spears hurled with devastating accuracy from wooden throwing slings. Because there would be no effective competitors along the California coast, they should do well.

O'Cain carried his proposal to Alexander Baranov, the short-statured, flaxen-haired, hard-drinking, hard-working governor of the Russian-American Fur Company. Would the Russian provide bidarkas, Aleuts, and whale oil and dried whale meat for feeding the hunters? In return O'Cain would transport the Aleuts in his ship to the coasts of Alta and Baja California, supervise their hunting, and split the proceeds with the fur company.

Baranov did not like the idea. He was intensely ambitious for himself and for Russia, which he envisioned as the leading power of the Pacific, with colonies stretching south along the coasts of both Asia and North America. Expansion should be spearheaded by his own countrymen, not by these persistent and opportunistic Americans. But what could he do? He had no vessels capable of such a trip; supply ships had not reached him that year; he desperately needed O'Cain's cargo in order to recapture Sitka from the Kolosh Indians who had recently seized the new post and had massacred most of its inhabitants.

Reluctantly he yielded to necessity, vowing to end the business as soon as possible. O'Cain reaped marvelously, returning from his first trip south in time to watch the costly retaking of Sitka. Other Americans, learning of his success and of Baranov's needs, likewise pressed for California share-hunting contracts. Baranov complied but kept brooding on his own plans, even in destitution.

He was soon given a boost by the arrival in Sitka of the Imperial Chamberlain himself, Nikolai Rezenov, one of the principal directors of the Russian-American Fur Company. Fully as ambitious for Russia as Baranov, Rezenov agreed that thrusts southward were desirable—when the time came. Right then, however, Sitka was starving and food was the first requirement.

In the last nick of time, in February, 1806, an American ship, the *Juno*, appeared through the sleet with a cargo of trade knickknacks. Rezenov bought her outright and steered for San Francisco to trade her goods for grain and beef. While he was on the errand, he told Baranov, he would investigate opportunities for Russian penetration of the south.

The Spanish received him politely—the shifting alliances against Napoleon had now brought Spain and Russia into uneasy amity—but they would not sell him so much as a sack of wheat. Seething with frustration, Rezenov chanced to look again at the charms of Concepción Argüello, daughter of the presidio's comandante. The Russian was nearly fifty years old and widowed not long since. Concepción was fifteen and completely bored with life in her father's little earth-floored, whitewashed headquarters.

The romance that blossomed has been embalmed since then in endless

California tales. By some magic Rezenov had learned, it would seem, enough Spanish to enthrall the naïve child of the frontier with tales of St. Petersburg's glittering court. (Official communications were carried on either in French between Rezenov and Governor Arrillaga, who had arrived on the scene, or in Latin between a scientist in the Russian's entourage and one of the mission padres.) When this astounding visitor from outer space suddenly proposed, Concepción accepted. Her parents objected, mostly to his Greek Orthodox religion, for, in Rezenov's words, they "had been raised in fanaticism," that is, Roman Catholicism. Concepción defied them and the priests they sent to instruct her in filial duty. To calm the tempest, Rezenov offered to appeal both to the czar and to the pope himself for sanctification of the marriage. To the governor he added that he would also travel in person to Madrid and arrange a treaty allowing free intercourse between California and Russian America. The parents thereupon allowed a formal betrothal, though not, until the pope had spoken, a marriage. And Arrillaga granted Rezenov permission to trade the *Juno*'s cargo of woolen cloth, tools, and kitchen hardware to the nearby missions for a boatload of food.

Back in Sitka, Rezenov authorized the founding of Russian colonies north of San Francisco Bay, at the mouth of the Columbia River, and in the Sandwich Islands. He then crossed to Siberia and started on horseback for Moscow. Was he on his way to or from Concepción? No one can say. His horse stumbled in an icy stream, fell, and killed him. Concepción waited thirty-six years for his return and then, learning of his death, entered a convent—or so the tale goes.

For various reasons nothing came of the projected Russian settlements beside the Columbia River, which Lewis and Clark had recently visited, or in the Sandwich Islands. In 1812, however, following careful preliminary surveys and treaties of friendship with the local Indians, the Russians built a stout wooden stockade, called Fort Ross, on a seaside bluff some 80 miles north of San Francisco Bay. They planted fields, which did not thrive well enough to help the food problems in Sitka very much, canceled the hunting contracts with the Americans, and, using Ross as a base, sent their Aleuts into Spanish waters.

Mexico City ordered the trespassers removed, even though Russia and Spain were still allied in Europe. But how go about it? Revolutions were shaking Latin America. Warships and sufficient numbers of troops for storming a fortified bluff were not available on the frontier. Even the annual supply ships ceased to run.

As substitutes for force, Governor Arrillaga and his successor, testy Pablo Vincente de Solá, issued pronouncements and made gestures. In a show of sword-rattling, Gabriel Moraga and a squad of ill-equipped soldiers rode overland to deliver stern messages to the offenders. On one occasion Russian traders were arrested at San Luis Obispo and sent to Mexico. A group of Aleut hunters who brazenly invaded San Francisco Bay were ambushed and killed when they landed to dry their water-logged bidarkas.

None of this had any real significance. The Spanish, bereft of other sources, had to have the manufactured goods that the Russians obtained from Yankee ship captains. On their part the Russians badly wanted the foodstuffs grown at the missions. And so the two outposts sparred with their right hands while trading with their left in another of the ambiva-lent, half-mad complications that California's remoteness seemed ever to inflict upon her.

South of San Francisco, sources of supply were even more unreliable. The War of 1812 kept most Yankee ships out of the Pacific. When the *Mercury*, commanded by George Washington Eayrs, did appear in the spring of 1813, she was promptly set upon by a tallow trader coming up from Lima in search of fat to be used in making candles for the silver mines of Peru. On the grounds that he had a trading permit whereas the Americans did not, the Peruvian made prisoners of Eayrs, his Indian consort, their month-old baby, and the fifteen-man crew. The Yankee protested righteously: "I have clothed many naked. . . . My dealings have not been clandestine. . . . Let Fray Marcos Amestoy at Santa Barbara be questioned." It was no use. Though his wife and child were sheltered at the Santa Barbara mission, Eayrs languished for two years in prison. Meanwhile, the triumphant Peruvian used the confiscated *Mercury* as if it were his own ship.

As revolutions against Spain spread throughout South America, even contacts with Peru were ended. Destitution in California grew so wide-spread that in February, 1816, the head of the missions urged Governor Solá to ignore his own country's laws against outside commerce, promis-ing that if he did, "the officials and all the missionaries in California will readily sign a statement in your favor, testifying to the reality of the difficulties confronting you." Thus buffeted, Solá let the government itself become an open participant in the contraband trade.

Now the presidios needed provisions to trade as well as to eat. Because neither their own gardens nor cattle ranches—*Los Ranchos del Rey*, they were called—nor the demoralized little towns of San Jose, Los Angeles, and Branciforte were able to supply what was required, Solá turned to the missions. During the next several years the government obtained from the padres food and labor billed at upwards of half a million pesos. None of the debt was ever paid. This meant, in effect, that the Indians footed the bill, for they were the producers.

Keeping the missions shipshape demanded ceaseless work. Timber had to be brought down from the hills for firewood and construction. Tiles and adobe bricks were tamped into endless molds. Stones for houses, walls, dams, and aqueducts had to be gathered and shaped. Inside the compounds male workers turned out rough tools, saddles, and other leather products. Women carded wool, spun thread, and wove coarse cloth for blankets and serapes. Cattle were slaughtered and skinned; the tallow was rendered out in huge pots, the hides scraped clean, and the lean meat dried into jerky. Grain was laboriously ground into flour, often by hand but sometimes in big stone mortars under a boulder dragged around and around by a plodding horse.

Always there were fields to clear, plant, irrigate, hoe, and harvest. Methods were Biblical. The Indians, hatless and shoeless under the fierce sun, chopping down weeds and brush with heavy machetes and grubbing hoes. Plows were forked tree branches tipped with iron. After seed had been broadcast by hand or, in the case of vegetables, dropped into holes made with pointed sticks, it was covered by dragging pieces of brush across the ground. When the yellow grain was ripe, a small, half-naked army attacked it with sickles, knife blades, even bare hands. The harvest was then heaped in a large enclosure, and three or four hundred frenzied horses were hazed back and forth across it to break the kernels loose from the heads. The grain was winnowed by tossing it overhead on windy days so that the chaff would blow away.

Living conditions grew steadily worse. In 1810 death rates from disease had amounted to 50 percent of baptisms (baptisms of adults as well as of children); ten years later it was 86 percent. Unhappy wives silently opposed the system with abortion and infanticide. Men were more likely to run away into the wilds.

The padres fought these drains on population as best they could. When detected, child slayers and abortionists were severely punished. In 1817 Mission San Rafael was established in a sunny valley north of San Francisco Bay as a recuperating station for the ailing Indians of fog-shrouded San Francisco Asís (Mission Dolores). Fugitives were pursued by soldiers from the presidios or, at times, by roughneck mission neophytes who welcomed this excuse to show their muscle among ancient tribal enemies and seize women as booty.

Since rewards were offered for bringing back "converts" as well as fugitives, neither the soldiers nor the neophyte auxiliaries were overly scrupulous about the persons they herded into the compounds. The overworked padres, beset by growing demands for labor, seldom asked searching questions. Thus the soaring death rates were counteracted and mission population slowly rose until by 1820 it had reached 20,000—a multitude whose devotions and labors were managed, be it noted, by 40 earnest padres assisted by a few soldier foremen and hand-picked Indian alcaldes. Non-Indian population, supposedly the basis for acculturation, stood at 3,270, including 150 convicts exiled from Mexico.

Except for forcing California into this primitive self-sufficiency, the revolutions against Spain touched the province only once. In 1818 two shiploads of insurgents from South America landed at Monterey in an effort to win the support of the people there. Governor Solá and his officers, ardent loyalists (as were the padres), disdainfully refused. The rebels thereupon looted and burned the capital city, sailed south, attacked a ranch near Santa Barbara, and ravaged the mission at San Juan Capistrano before vanishing over the horizon.

Nearly four years later, in March, 1822, word came across that same horizon that a Mexican general, Agustín Iturbide, had at last defeated the Spanish forces in his country and had proclaimed a temporary regency with himself at its head. As one sign of the new times, Iturbide announced that henceforth the California ports of San Diego and Monterey would be open to foreign trade.

To knowledgeable merchants in the Pacific, commerce meant, at that particular moment, cowhides. The continuing warfare in South America had dried up the sources of leather on which many shoe factories of the British Isles and New England depended. California just might prove to be a lucrative substitute, even though the untended cattle there were very small, tipping the scales at no more than 600 to 800 pounds each.

The first exploiters reached Monterey in July, 1822. They were young Lima-based Englishmen, William Hartnell and Hugh McCulloch. Talking fast, they persuaded Governor Solá to grant them special privileges for three years, the contract to take effect on January 1, 1823. Nudged by Solá, the father-president of the missions next sent a circular letter among the padres, urging them to receive the Englishmen courteously. By horseback the smiling newcomers confidently followed the letter from mission to mission, McCulloch in the south and Hartnell in the north. (By that time there were twenty missions. The twenty-first and last, San Francisco Solano, generally called Sonoma, would be founded in 1823 in the Sonoma Valley north of San Francisco Bay.)

Strangers in the land, Hartnell and McCulloch were neither fast enough nor adroit enough to press their advantage. Hardly thirty days behind them came two vigorous Yankees, Henry Gyzelaar and William Gale, financed by the Boston merchandising firm of Bryant and Sturgis. From years of smuggling and otter hunting along the California coast, both men knew the needs of the missions and were acquainted with several of the padres. Splitting north and south, they set about undercutting their favored rivals. Priests whom the English had not yet approached were soft-talked into ignoring the urgings of the governor and of their own father-president. Some of those who had already signed contracts were persuaded by offers of higher prices to violate the agreements. It was the beginning of the dominant position that Bryant and Sturgis would maintain in the California hide trade throughout the Mexican era.

As yet no one could guess what that era might bring. Mexican politics were zigzagging down a frantic course. Iturbide abandoned the regency and had himself crowned emperor. Liberal revolutionists thereupon deposed him and proclaimed a republic.

Only dim echoes of the upheavals reached California, but they were enough to rub festering jealousies and awaken long-suppressed ambitions. Ragged soldiers, their pay long in arrears, began saying that it was time to break up the overly rich missions and let others have a share of the land and the trained labor. Townspeople in Los Angeles and San Jose began to think that they too might pull away from their enforced ties with the presidios and participate in the new markets. The mission Indians caught the word *freedom* and stirred restively. When a soldier flogged a neophyte with unnecessary severity at Mission Santa Inés in the south, his fellows attacked the guards and burned several buildings.

The revolt soon spread to La Purísima Concepción, another mission in the Santa Inés Valley, which the Indians managed to seize and hold, and Santa Barbara. During the scuffles at Santa Barbara and Santa Inés, more Indians than soldiers were killed. Unable to cope with guns, hundreds of the ill-armed insurgents fled through the mountains into the reed-choked southern part of the San Joaquin Valley near present Bakersfield. For years the area had been a favorite haunt of fugitives—"a republic of hell," one exasperated padre had written, "and a diabolic union of apostates." Because of their familiarity with the missions, these runaways had often led bands of gentile (unconverted) Indians in raids on the padres' horse herds, to seize animals for eating rather than for riding. A fresh influx of rebels there could create serious problems.

The priests were stunned. Why had this happened? Unwilling to blame conditions at the missions, they insisted that the extra work occasioned by the demands of the presidios was the cause—as in part it was. But whatever the reason, the rebellion could not go unchecked. Troops gathered from as far away as Monterey. After retaking Purísima, they marched into the San Joaquin Valley, accompanied by several priests. The show of force, the difficulties that some of the mission-raised neophytes had experienced in adjusting to the wilderness, the promises of amnesty, and the blandishments of the padres, many of whom the Indians liked personally, prompted scores to return to their stations. Many others eluded pursuit, however, and became the nuclei of growing gangs of raiders who would plague California well into gold-rush times.

The urprising quelled, routines along the coast returned to their established patterns, at least on the surface. Underneath, however, doubt and uncertainty mounted. When the new republican regime was at last established in Mexico—if ever it was—what would it bring to the province, as isolated there at the edge of the continent as if it really were the half-mythical island that ancient geographers had once supposed it to be?

5. By Land as Well as by Sea

José María Echeandía, the first duly appointed governor of Mexican California, was tall, gaunt, courtly, strangely blue-eyed for a Latin, and ineffective. He resisted the job when it was handed him, and during his first years in office he begged passionately to be relieved. But when at last he was free to go home, he changed his mind, helped precipitate a revolution, and had to be nudged back to Mexico by threats of force.

No symbols commemorate his stewardship. Towns, streets, mountains and canyons have been named for other bumbling Mexican governors, even some whose California regimes collapsed within months; yet so far as I am aware, nothing has ever been called Echeandía. A historical wraith: yet in view of the highly volatile and often significant events that swirled about him for half a dozen years, it does seem that his likeness ought to be stamped onto a little adobe plaque somewhere, just out of respect for his troubles if nothing else.

From the outset his ideological position was as fuzzy as a mad cat's back. He came to California as a burning liberal and anticleric. He held office under a constitution that had created a loose federation of states wherein all Mexican Catholics, white, black, red, and mestizo, were theoretically entitled to political and civil freedom. He was charged with harnessing California's Spanish-born padres by demanding oaths of allegiance from them—and at the same time he was to undercut their work by launching the long-delayed secularization of the missions. On the side he was to stimulate foreign trade and foster home agriculture. So that he could bring these blessings of liberty into being, he was clad in autocratic powers.

He was both the civil governor of the territory and the commander of the troops stationed there. No effective checks against possible tyrannies existed. Although the native residents, the Californios, were entitled under the constitution to elect a *diputación*, or legislature, its members could not meet unless the governor called them into session, and then their function was advisory only. The Californios could send a representative to the Mexican Congress, but he had no vote there. The number of citizens entitled to participate in the balloting was also severely limited, for in spite of the high-sounding theory that emanated from Mexico City, no one actually on the scene pretended that either the mission Indians or the Californios had reached political maturity. How could they have? They possessed no experience in self-government to guide them, and little book learning. Fewer than 5 percent of the so-called *gente de razón*, the rational ones, could read or write, and the Indian who had been tutored to do so at the missions was rare indeed.

The handicaps did not produce meekness. Years of neglect by Spain had implanted in the Californios truculent feelings of apartness. They regarded outside appointees with suspicion. Their touchiness was increased by sectional envies. The provinces' most populous towns, Los Angeles and the presidial pueblo of Santa Barbara, were in the south. The greatest number of privately owned ranchos—there were still only thirty or so in the entire territory—also lay in the south. Yet governmental headquarters, including the lucrative new customs house that collected high import duties from all foreign ships, remained stubbornly at Monterey. Southerners, glimpsing private advancement in the control of public money, fulminated furiously in an early-day manifestation of the sectional infighting that still rumples California politics.

Echeandía, riding glumly north from Loreto in October, 1825, inflamed the situation by halting at San Diego. His stated reason was logical. He was political chief of Baja California as well as the political and military governor of Alta California, and San Diego was centrally located for both jobs. Other considerations were involved, however. The reluctant governor, an acute hypochondriac, feared Monterey's fogs. Still more to the point, he had glimpsed the charms of a dazzling San Diego belle, Josefa Carrillo. Stopping dead in his tracks, he laid suit, only to be outdone by a New Hampshireman—a Protestant, too—named Henry Fitch. One dark night Henry rowed Josefa out to a waiting vessel, sailed to Lima, embraced Catholicism, and married the unresistant abductee. Returning to California, the newlyweds did penance by providing a large bell for the new church then being erected in Los Angeles.

Call it a portent. Americans were intruding everywhere. As Echeandía sat nursing his hurt pride in San Diego—the territorial treasurer, José María Herrera, was simultaneously anchoring himself in Monterey—the exclusive contract that Solá had given the Englishmen Hartnell and McCulloch expired. The privilege never had proved very effective, and now that it was officially terminated, ships appeared from all sides—from

Russian Alaska, the British fur trading posts on the Columbia River, the Sandwich (Hawaiian) Islands, Peru, and, most especially, from the eastern coast of the United States.

One must not visualize fleets. The vessels were numerous only in respect to what had been the case, and many were very small. Weeks would pass after one had slid along the coast, lonesome as a ghost, before another appeared. To Californios, however, who for three-quarters of a century had been almost totally removed from the rest of the world, it was like a dawn at sunset. Most of them had never before seen anything like those factory-made shawls, ribbons, combs, mirrors, and sateen shirts; they had seldom tasted such sugar, coffee, wine, and pure, bolted flour. And with those things came new ideas. It was Echeandía's job to control it all.

Patterns emerged quickly. First was the haggling over import duties. Except for continued levies by the presidios on the missions for foodstuffs, no other form of government revenue existed. As a result duties were high and arguments inevitable. Words failing, the next resort was smuggling. Often false floors and false partitions hid valuable articles. Sometimes merchandise was hidden in a remote cove or on one of the islands off the southern coast and retrieved after the ship captain had piously shown the inspectors what remained aboard. At times bribery of venal inspectors was substituted for sleight of hand.

Licenses procured, the captains cruised along the coast to visit harbors authorized by the government as hide-collecting depots. The principal ones were San Francisco Bay, San Diego, Santa Cruz, Morro Bay, Santa Barbara, San Juan Capistrano, and, notably, San Pedro, inlet to the missions of San Fernando and San Gabriel and the pueblo of Los Angeles.

During this time the supercargo was riding horseback from mission to mission, with side jaunts to the few ranchos. He took a list of his wares with him, plus such samples as were easily packed, and told the missionaries when his ship was expected at the nearest authorized landing place. The padres, hungry for new faces, entertained the visitor as royally as circumstances allowed, then provided him with fresh horses and a vaquero to attend him on his way to the next stop, all without charge. It sounds delightful today when we envision the untouched countryside, but Alfred Robinson, who became one of the best-known of the traders, declared in his *Life in California* that the long rides were monotonous and tiring in the extreme.

Preparation of the hides and tallow threw the missions into turmoil. The slaughtering, the *manteza*, generally took place in the early summer, when the cattle were fattest. First a number of animals were gathered on some handy flat. Those selected for butchering were called "black" cattle.

Actually, colors ranged the spectrum: black, red with a white stripe down the back, dun, spotted. By modern standards they were small, but they had enormous horns, were as wild as coyotes and as fierce as bears. Occasionally the hard-riding vaqueros—and there were no better horsemen anywhere—would kill them by riding close and stabbing them. More commonly they lassoed each condemned animal by its neck and hind legs, threw it, and slit its throat.

Indians swarmed about the carcasses. Some stripped off the hide, scraped away the bits of clinging flesh and fat that would spoil if allowed to remain, and then stretched the skin out flat between pegs to dry. Other workers divested the flayed carcass of its tallow. The best suet was saved for the mission kitchen. The rest was liquefied in huge iron cauldrons and dumped, full of hair and dirt, into *botas*, big hide bags resting on the ground and held open by four stakes. Some of the lean meat and the tongues were smoked for later consumption, but most of the carcasses were left to rot. As soon as the pegged skins scattered about the flat were dry, they were folded lengthwise, hair inside, and taken to the ranch or mission storehouse to await the arrival of the ship.

As the collection date neared, the hides were loaded into little *carretas*, or carts, that looked somewhat like topless birdcages mounted on a single pair of solid wooden wheels. Off they jolted, dry hubs shrieking, Indian boys strolling beside to goad the oxen. In summer, when grass lay lifeless and yellow, the approach of a caravan was heralded from miles away by its slowly floating plume of dust. In winter, especially in the north, rain sometimes made roads impassable. Then, according to Mariano Vallejo, Indians did the carrying, each with a single stiff hide atop his head, long lines of half-naked men "trotting over the unfenced land through the wild mustard to the embarcadero."

At the shore the sailors took over. At Santa Barbara, San Pedro, and other shallow, exposed roadsteads, the ships anchored a mile or more out, partly so that they could slip anchor and run for the open sea in case of a storm. Oar-propelled launches brought the workers, many of them Kanakas hired in Hawaii, to the edge of the surf. There everyone except the boat tenders jumped barefooted into the water and waded ashore, often over sharp and slippery stones. Indian-like, each man lifted a single hide atop his head. While gulls wheeled and screamed above, they waded back through the surf to the launch, hopeful that a gust of wind would not catch their burdens and tumble them into the water. After two hundred or so hides had been collected in this way, the oarsmen rowed the cargo back to the ship, then returned for another load.

The launches also carried out to the ship such people as could afford individual purchases. Only gradually, as traders' representatives began to establish permanent headquarters in the larger settlements, did retail outlets appear on land. Even then a ship with its specially fitted showroom was more exciting, particularly to the women. They flocked to the landing places. Sailors carried them through the surf, a duty less arduous than packing hides, perhaps, and rowed them to the vessel to look, to yearn, sometimes to buy.

Competition was keen and the production of hides slow. Sometimes a ship had to cruise back and forth along the coast for eighteen months or so before obtaining a full cargo. Those collected on each run were stored in odorous warehouses at San Diego, Monterey, and, later, at San Pedro. Just prior to being loaded for the trip to England or Boston, they were soaked in brine, scraped to remove whatever grease the mission Indians had overlooked, dried, flailed to remove dust, and stowed away by means of winches until scarcely a paper's width of space remained in the ship's hold. Such a cargo—some 30,000 to 40,000 hides and tons of tallow—might net the owners of a vessel $50,000, thanks in large part to the outrageous markup placed on the goods used in barter.

In spite of intermittent smuggling and occasional girl-snatching, there was nothing difficult about overseeing such a trade. Echeandía had the hang of it within a year. He enjoyed the polite visits paid him by the ship captains who put into San Diego Bay and called on him with little gifts. Best of all, the regulations were very clear. Everyone, including the governor, knew exactly where he stood, and to Echeandía that was important.

He was sorely jarred, accordingly, to receive late in 1826 a message from San Gabriel stating that fifteen heavily armed American horsemen under a captain named Jedediah Smith had just reached the mission after crossing the appalling deserts beyond the mountains. Although Smith carried U.S. passports signed by General William Clark, formerly of the Lewis and Clark expedition, none of the party could produce a valid Mexican document. They were a rough-looking lot. They had two of the mission's runaway neophytes with them, and some of the horses they rode bore the mission brand, a large "T", and had been stolen not long since. According to the adventurers' account of themselves, they were beaver trappers, whatever that meant, but they might be spies. They had asked to buy enough food and fresh horses so that they could continue north through the coastal valleys until they reached the Columbia River. What should be done?

The law was clear. The intruders were operating outside the system and were subject to arrest and deportation to Mexico City. Echeandía, however, was not decisive by nature. Another letter, just arrived from Smith himself, sounded as if the American felt he had every right to be in California. And perhaps he had, since he bore papers signed by no less a personage than a general. After shilly-shallying for several days, the governor sent out a guard to bring Smith to San Diego for an interview. No more than one man should accompany the leader. To have all the hunters appear in a body might be too much like inviting in a cyclone.

The American turned out to be almost as tall as Echeandía. He was twenty-seven years old, sunbaked and hawk-nosed. Although his buckskins looked shabby beside the governor's resplendent uniform, he showed no diffidence. He told a remarkable tale.

The westering blood was strong in his veins—another portent, if Echeandía had realized it. His restless parents had moved after their marriage from Connecticut to New York, then to the shores of Lake Erie, and on to the Western Reserve of Ohio. Since 1822 young Jedediah had been in the forefront of General William Ashley's Rocky Mountain beaver trappers. In 1824 he had crossed the Continental Divide and had startled the traders of the Hudson's Bay Company by prowling as far as one of their posts in what is now western Montana. In 1826, he and two friends, David Jackson and William Sublette, had bought out General Ashley and had formed their own trapping concern. Their base—Jedediah called it a rendezvous—was at Bear Lake, north of much bigger Great Salt Lake, of which Echeandía may have heard. (He hadn't.) Among the company's assets were passports for fifty-four men, issued originally by William Clark to General Ashley just in case some of the hunters happened to stray across the unsurveyed 42nd parallel into Mexican territory.

Smith's partners and their men were currently trapping along the western base of the Rockies. Jedediah and several others had gone into the unknown country of the Southwest, hoping to find fresh supplies of beaver. No luck. The few streams in the dry land were entrenched in abysmal red canyons. Many of the party's horses had died, and the men had been uncomfortably close to real trouble when they had reached the territory of the Mohave Indians, who lived beside the Colorado River in villages much like those occupied by their relatives, the Yumas, 200 miles farther downstream.

One of the Mohaves knew a smattering of Spanish. So did one of Jedediah's men. Out of the stumbling conversations, Jedediah got the notion that Mission San Gabriel lay only a short distance west. Because a return trip to Great Salt Lake by his original route would have been impossible (Smith said), he had decided to cross the desert to San Gabriel, procure supplies, and travel north from there in order to circle the desert. Yes, he had seen the T brand on the few horses they had been able to buy from the Mohaves, but he had no way of knowing that the animals had been stolen from the mission. Yes, his men had found two coastal Indians who had agreed for a price to guide them through the desert, but how could he have told that they were fugitives?

It had been a ferocious crossing. Until the party reached the Mojave River (a series of puddles that Jedediah named the Inconstant), they'd had to carry their water in containers made of the greasy intestines of animals. Often they had traveled at night to avoid the sun, merciless even in November. Bare mountains whose dark rocks look charred; simmering dry lakebeds called playas; the spindly branches of vile-smelling creosote brush; the twisted, blade-leafed Joshua trees, branches akimbo like tortured arms—it was not a country a man would willingly risk twice. It was essential that he be allowed to go to the Columbia. Up there he would find country he knew and would be able to return to the Great Salt Lake area in time for the rendezvous with his partners.

All true—so far as it went. What Jedediah did not discuss was his hope of finding, in addition to beaver, the mighty Buenaventura River, which hypothetical geography insisted flowed from the interior of the continent through California to the Pacific. If so, it might furnish a cheaper, easier route for supplying trappers in the Rocky Mountains than did the long land trails from Missouri. Easy supplies in turn would enable Smith's group to meet the challenge of Hudson's Bay Company trappers based in the Northwest.

Admitting this to Echeandía would be folly, because the governor quite naturally would oppose foreigners coming into California in search of a Mexican river to exploit. Accordingly Jedediah confined himself to denying that he was a spy and to polemics about his rights as a trapper in distress. Were not hungry ship captains entitled to put into closed ports for help? Was his emergency any less?

Echeandía was not persuaded, even after Smith had shown him a beaver skin. An outdated, blanket American passport was not an adequate substitute for current Mexican papers covering each individual visitor in detail. Moreover, suppose beaver did live in the interior rivers of California. Suppose the Americans found and trapped them as they moved north. Might this not result in a further rush of hunters from the outside—hunters who, unlike the ship traders, would bring nothing of value with them and would slip away over the unguarded trails with their catches untaxed? His superiors would not like that one bit . . . and yet how roughly did he dare deal with a man who seemed so confident and who spoke of generals as his friends? The best solution, the governor decided after days of vacillation, was to send Smith to Mexico City and let the high brass there decide on policy.

Fuming, Jedediah wrote a letter of protest to the American minister in Mexico. Echeandía was fretting over that when the captains and supercargoes of three American ships that happened to be in the harbor came to him and signed a testimonial on Smith's behalf. The governor, whose mind could be changed by almost any show of vigor, thereupon relented. The trappers, he decreed, could reoutfit at San Gabriel, but they must leave the province immediately over the same harsh trail by which they had entered.

On January 18, 1827, the disgruntled group, the first Americans ever to reach California by land, started east. They clung obediently to their original trail until they had crossed the San Bernardino Mountains. They then veered northwest through Tehachapi Pass into the San Joaquin Valley. Either Smith considered that California was limited to the inhabited areas near the coast or he was ignoring the governor's terms.

They found beaver. Joyfully trapping as they went, they pushed north as far as the junction of the Sacramento and American rivers. (The latter name stems from their penetration there.) By then April was at hand. They had seen no Buenaventura River (none existed), but they had taken 1,500 pounds of choice fur, and it was time to think of getting the catch back to the company's summer rendezvous north of Great Salt Lake. Even more important, Smith wanted to tell his partners of his experiences, for the information would help determine next year's activities.

An attempt to cross the Sierra at the headwaters of the South Fork of the American bogged down in deep snow. After five horses had starved to death, the party retreated. Turning south along the San Joaquin, they came to a Sierra-born stream that soon would be named the Stanislaus. There, after a sharp tussle with local Indians, they went into camp. Immediately they were blamed with inciting trouble among the neophytes at Mission San José, 70 miles to the southwest.

Led by their able native alcalde Estanislao (hence the Stanislaus River), four hundred Christian Indians had run away from the mission during the night of May 15–16. When Narciso Durán, the priest in charge of the station, began an impassioned investigation, he was told by one of the remaining Indians that the Anglo-American hunters in the valley had triggered the exodus by promising to help the fugitives resist pursuit. A subsequent check by the military indicated that the Indian was making up the tale to protect the real plotters, but at the time it was easier for the padres to blame outside agitation rather than inside discontent. Durán rushed a letter to the authorities demanding military action against the Americans.

Somehow word of what was going on reached Jedediah Smith. On May 19 he wrote Durán, identifying himself and stating falsely that he had received a passport from Echeandía authorizing him to ride through the area on his way to the Columbia. Soothingly he concluded, "I am, Reverend Father, your strange, but real friend and Christian brother."

Durán sent the letter to Echeandía, who had recently journeyed to Monterey to investigate the affairs of his insubordinate treasurer, José María Herrera. A passport! The governor penned an angry order for Smith either to move out of the province at once or to submit to arrest. When soldiers carrying this message reached the American camp, they discovered that Jedediah and two men had disappeared into the mountains, hoping that a small party unburdened by excess livestock could cross the Sierra in time to reach the company rendezvous. On leaving, Smith had directed the remainder of his group to sit tight with their 1,500 pounds of beaver. He would return in four months, he said, with supplies and reinforcements. Presumably they would then resume trapping California beaver.

After looking over the stockade that the Americans had erected and at the long rifle each carried in the crook of his arm, the Mexican soldiers decided that their orders about arresting intruders extended only to Jedediah Smith, who was gone. Back they went to report that all was quiet.

Faced by the more immediate problem of his rebellious treasurer, Echeandía let the matter slide. Secretly he collected what seemed to him ample evidence of Herrera's scheming and dishonesty, summoned the territorial legislature to meet for the first time since his arrival in California, and stampeded that body into declaring the treasurer deposed. Then, fearing that if Herrera reached Mexico City he would start counterattacks among influential people there, Echeandía ordered the angry victim to remain in Monterey under technical arrest. Immediately Herrera started fomenting trouble among northerners who feared that Echeandía's next move would be the shifting of all governmental activities, including the customs house, away from Monterey to San Diego.

At that point Jedediah Smith stunned the governor by appearing once again. After a grueling, almost fatal trip in the Sierra and the grisly deserts farther east, the hunter and his two companions had reached their company rendezvous. Two weeks later Smith started back to California to pick up his stranded party and their beaver. With him were eighteen fresh trappers and the Indian wives of two of them.

Rather than risk the deserts that had nearly swallowed him on his way to the rendezvous, the American followed the first trail he had blazed, counting on refreshments at the Mohave villages beside the Colorado River. What he had no way of knowing was that a recent battle with trappers from New Mexico had turned the once-amiable Mohaves hostile toward all whites.

The Indians struck Smith's group as they were ferrying their equipment across the Colorado River on rafts improvised from reeds. Ten men died. The two women, the horses, and most of the baggage were seized. Smith and eight other survivors, with five rifles among them, held off the charging Mohaves and then fled on foot across the blistered wastes, traveling at night to avoid the August sun. Near the site of the sandy little neon strip now known as Baker, they found a camp of friendly Indians. From them they acquired a few horses for the trifles they had carried with them that frightful distance, and rode on into the San Bernardino Valley. There they butchered several mission cattle, dried the meat, sent a letter of explanation to San Gabriel, and headed for the camp on the Stanislaus. They arrived September 18, 1827.

Jedediah had promised the men waiting there supplies and reinforcements. Instead he was destitute. Of necessity he risked going with three of his men to Mission San José and begging Narciso Durán for help. The priest, blaming him still for the escape of Estanislao's neophytes, ordered the mission guard to clap the Americans into the mission jail. He then sent to the San Francisco presidio for help. The comandante himself appeared and took Smith and his three men under arrest to Echeandía in Monterey.

As usual the governor vacillated. He had a perfect right to imprison Smith for what amounted to violation of parole, yet the move might bring the rest of the trappers on the Stanislaus, and perhaps some American sailors, too, swarming into Monterey just when excitement and resentment over the Herrera affair were at a height. So now what?

Again American ship captains solved the dilemma. Four of them offered to give bond guaranteeing Smith's withdrawal from California if he were freed. Vastly relieved, the governor agreed.

To raise money for reoutfitting his party—save for two or three who astounded him by saying they would like to stay in California—Smith sold his beaver pelts at bargain rates to Captain John Bradshaw of the Boston ship *Franklin*. Obeying orders this time, he floundered north through the icy rains of January (1828), eager on his own part to leave California once and for all. On the Umpqua River in Oregon, Indians struck him again. Only Smith and three others survived that debacle— not for long. Three years later Jedediah fell to Comanche arrows on the Santa Fe Trail.

But if Smith was through with the coast, others weren't. Echeandía had scarcely returned to San Diego, wisely leaving the customs house undisturbed in Monterey, when guards from a mission in Baja California brought him eight more American fur hunters. Leaders of the group were Sylvester Pattie, gravely ill from exposure, and Sylvester's grown son, James Ohio Pattie. They told a tale as remarkable as Jedediah Smith's. Echeandía, indeed, found certain resemblances quite startling.

Natives of Kentucky, the Patties had been trapping the southwestern streams and mining copper in New Mexico since 1824. Running into hard luck at the mine in 1827, they had sought to recoup their fortunes by leading a large party of beaver hunters down the Gila River of today's Arizona. Dissension caused most of the group to turn back. The truculence of the Yuma Indians at the mouth of the Gila forced the others to flee down the Colorado River in two canoes contrived from cottonwood logs. Near the gulf a tidal bore almost overwhelmed them. Unable to pole back up the flooded stream, the men cached their furs in a pit in the riverbank and struck west on foot across the deserts of Baja California. The ordeal ended with their arrest and transfer to San Diego.

Beaver, Indian trouble beside the Colorado, hardship in the desert—to Echeandía it sounded too much like the tale told by Jedediah Smith. Curdled by that experience, he clapped the new group into the presidio's small, dank cells. Worn out by his earlier sufferings, the elder Pattie perished there.

Once again a ship trader appeared in the role of rescuer. Captain Bradshaw of the *Franklin*, who had purchased Jedediah's furs and perhaps scented another bargain here, persuaded Echeandía to let all the captives save James Pattie travel to the Colorado River with Indian helpers in search of their cached pelts. Pattie stayed in jail as a hostage for the men's return.

Everything went wrong. High water had destroyed the furs. Disgusted, some of the men kept on going east, and Echeandía was not placated by the few who returned. Meantime Bradshaw was implicated in smuggling and fled San Diego Bay under a hail of little cannonballs from the *castillo*. Pattie seemed destined to languish in prison.

A smallpox epidemic that swept the northern settlements in 1828 saved him, at least according to the *Narrative* that he later wrote about his adventures. By chance he had with him some vaccine left over from a supply his father had used for inoculating their workers at the copper mine. Promptly he offered to immunize all California for a dollar a person, plus freedom for himself and for those of his men who had returned loyally from the Colorado.

Harrowed by the wails of the terrified populace, Echeandía finally agreed. Replenishing his supplies by the pus of his patients, Pattie moved industriously north, inoculating by his own count in the *Narrative* 22,000 Californios and mission Indians. For good measure he let the Russians talk him into visiting Fort Ross, where he immunized another 1,500 persons for $100 in cash.

While he was in the north, he got mixed up in California's first revolution. Herrera, the deposed treasurer, sent the ill-paid troops of the Monterey and San Francisco presidios south under a cat's-paw, Joaquín Solís, an exiled convict from Mexico, to overthrow the government. Echeandía met the rebels at Santa Barbara.

What followed set the pattern for subsequent California civil wars. The adversaries bombarded each other with letters, issued proclamations to the people, and exchanged shots at long range. This routine completed, Solís suddenly decamped at dusk on January 15, 1830. His explanation: "Having taken a position between the Presidio and the Mission, I found it impossible to enter either the one or the other, the first because it was fortified and the second because of the walls pierced with loopholes for musket fire . . . so I knew we were going to lose, and this was the motive for not exposing the troops by entering."

With a few exceptions, this would be the ritual from then on. The adversaries sparred until they had decided who would win if a fight did take place. They then reacted accordingly, without the need of hurting anyone. In the long run it probably settled disputes as effectively as did the far deadlier revolutions in Mexico.

Herrera was arrested in Monterey. James Ohio Pattie personally ran down and captured Solís (he says) as the rebel leader was fleeing toward San Francisco. He sailed with the prisoners on the ship that took them to Mexico for trial. There they were released by the new conservative government that had just seized power from the liberals, but Pattie was not so fortunate. Instead of the cash that he says he had been promised for vaccinating 22,000 people, he was offered land and livestock, but only if he became a Roman Catholic and a Mexican citizen. He rejected the terms. Next he asked that he be compensated for the furs lost to high water on the Colorado, arguing that if he had not been unjustly jailed he could have gone back to the river in time to save the pelts. No one, not even the American minister in Mexico City, heeded him, and he returned empty-handed to the United States.

Despite Smith's and Pattie's misfortunes, outsiders kept pushing in, uncontrollably, by land. Down from Fort Vancouver on the Columbia came the powerful brigades of the Hudson's Bay Company; a district near present Stockton is still known as French Camp because of the winter rendezvous that the company's French-Canadian voyageurs regularly held there. No one could compete with them for beaver, as Ewing Young learned in 1830, after he had succeeded in crossing the deserts from New Mexico with teen-age Kit Carson in his train. They trapped the length of the Central Valley, helped capture some runaway neophytes for Narciso Durán, brawled in Los Angeles, and then went home again with little fur for their pains.

Three years later, another group of American trappers led by Joseph R. Walker forced a difficult way across the Sierra near Yosemite, only to fail, as Young had, to produce enough fur to pay for their efforts. If profits were to result from land contacts with California, they would have to be based, as the ship trade was, on commerce. This in turn meant finding land trails that would avoid both the fearsome passes of the High Sierra and the equally dreaded Apache Indians who lurked along the upper reaches of the Gila River in Arizona.

Searching for a safe slot, Antonio Armijo of New Mexico and after him William Wolfskill of the United States worked out a route that looped from Santa Fe far north into present-day Utah, then slanted back past meadows even then called Las Vegas, crossed the desert to the Mojave River, and entered southern California by means of Cajon Pass near today's San Bernardino. Soon the way was being used by regular winter caravans bringing silver coin, American cloth and metal, and fine New Mexican serapes to swap for horses, mules, and even bales of silk offered by ships that had touched at the Orient on their way to California. At about this same time, also, gypsy-like wanderers out of Sonora reopened Anza's trail through the land of the Yuma Indians. Thus by 1832 Los Angeles and Mission San Gabriel were in regular, if tenuous, contact with both St. Louis and the cities of northwestern Mexico.

Nearly every one of these far-ranging groups lost men to California's lotus land. So did the trading ships. After avoiding capture, these desert-ers settled down to hunting sea otter in little round boats built out of hide, opening inns, farming, building grist mills, and cutting lumber in the redwood forests near Branciforte on Monterey Bay. Salesmen for the ship traders settled in the principal towns, adopted the dress and customs of the more influential Californios, and married local girls. Whaling vessels took to stopping in San Francisco Bay to make repairs and load on supplies of fresh water and food. As a result of all this, Californians throughout the province were becoming used to outsiders, Americans especially. Concurrently American businessmen beside the Atlantic were hearing more and more about California and the two magnificent ports, San Diego and San Francisco, that faced temptingly west toward the Orient.

Except for the carefully regulated trade by sea, these intrusions by outsiders having neither Mexican passports nor licenses to trap were quite illegal and should have been looked into by Governor Echeandía. He was no longer paying much attention, however. For one thing, he lacked the resources for chasing down the will-o'-the-wisp land parties. For another, he had finally plunged, because of the eloquent proddings of his own protégé, José María Padrés, into a crash program to free the mission Indians. Compared to that overwhelming problem, the outlaw activities of a handful of wanderers from the other side of the continent seemed of minor significance.

6. What Do You Do with a Tame Indian?

The California missions presented Mexican liberals with a hard dilemma. Law and theory demanded immediate secularization. Practicality, as seen by the friars, the sea merchants, and the revenue collectors, forbade it. The result for Governor Echeandía, until José María Padrés laid hold of him, was several years of walking on eggshells.

By 1830, the oldest of the missions had been in existence for sixty-one years. Except for San Rafael, founded in 1817, and San Francisco Solano, or Sonoma, founded in 1823, their average age was forty-five years. Yet in 1813 the briefly liberal parliament of Spain had once again decreed—and again without result—that any mission more than ten years old was to be converted straightaway into a civil pueblo. The new nation of Mexico, her leaders exalted still by revolutionary slogans of human equality, was determined to do better. In 1829, her Congress stepped beyond its model, the Congress of the United States, and abolished slavery. Even before then Echeandía had forbidden the selling of Indian children, captured during punitive attacks on gentile rancherías, as domestics to wealthy civilian and military families. Did not the Indians at the missions have equal rights?

The Franciscans hotly denied the implication in the query. Their Indians were not slaves but trainees—apprentices to civilization. They had progressed mightily. Under the supervision of the padres, they tended hundreds of thousands of cattle, scores of thousands of sheep. They cultivated 10,000 acres of grain and other staple foods. Their shops turned out a surplus of basketware, blankets, leather goods, soap, and candles. Nor were their accomplishments limited to labor. A few could read and write—so few, however, that Echeandía ordered the immediate institution of schools to remedy the deficiencies. Indian artists decorated the mission churches with bright colors and bold designs. Indian choirs sang at the services; Indian orchestras played with gusto at fiestas and on holy days.

Many couples had spent their entire lives at their missions. The priests married them, baptized their children, buried their dead. All were fed and clothed. Ingrained propensities toward gambling, improvidence, and premarital sex—did not Latin families chaperone their daughters?—were checked. Ambitious neophytes earned pocket money by raising gardens and chickens beside their homes in the mission villages. Was this life style, the only one they knew, to be destroyed for the sake of hastily conceived theory? True freedom would come as the Indians mastered civilized living.

Foes of the system insisted that the life style was not as joyous as pictured. Modern statistical support of their arguments has been produced by S. F. Cook, anthropologist of the University of California, from his study of mission records. Between 1779 and 1833, Cook reports, there were 29,100 births at the missions. Additional population was provided during the same period by roughly 53,000 conversions, a half-century inflow of 82,100 people. The normal number of deaths in this group, so Cook believes, should not have exceeded 40,000. Actually, 62,600 deaths occurred, 22,600 beyond expectations. Most were attributable to white diseases, which of course neither the friars nor the soldiers introduced deliberately, though sometimes the Indians believed so. Syphilis in particular was so rampant, both in and out of the missions, that occasional observers, including an American immigrant, Edwin Bryant, speculated that the widespread debility and physical softness of the coastal Indians in later days was perhaps attributable to the taint of venereal disease in nearly every bloodstream.

There were side effects to the problem. The unmarried females, chaperoned by being locked each night in unsanitary *monjerios*, died at a more rapid rate than did the males outside. The result was an imbalance between men and women, with accompanying sexual frustrations for the males and a desire on their part to join raids on the wild rancherías for the sake of capturing female "converts." And finally there were the fugitives. Of the unknown thousands who ran away from the missions during the period that Cook surveyed, at least 4,250 made permanent escapes in spite of regular pursuit by armed soldiers. As for training in Christianity, the liberals demanded, what of the floggings? What of the priest at San Gabriel who persuaded Jedediah Smith's blacksmith to make him a bear trap so that he could catch the neophyte who was stealing forbidden fruit from his orange trees?

Would matters be improved by turning the missions into civil pueblos and letting the Indians manage their own affairs with as much freedom as Mexican law allowed to other villages? The Franciscans, most of them very old by then and reluctant to see their lives' work go for naught, denied the likelihood. The mission Indians had been tamed, but because of stunted aptitudes, as the priests interpreted their charges' listlessness, they had not yet learned the self-disciplines demanded by citizenship. Turning them loose prematurely would result only in disaster.

As evidence they pointed to the non-Christian Indians who hung around the civil towns of Los Angeles, San Jose, and Branciforte and the military villages attached to the four presidios. There were many such Indians. They had followed their tribesmen to the mission compounds and, although avoiding conversion, had picked up a smattering of Spanish and the rudiments of manual skills. Then, lured by drink and tawdry trinkets, they had taken to working for the townspeople. A large portion of these villagers were a feckless, poverty-stricken, uneducated class called *cholos*, or mongrels. Among them were several exiled convicts, for every year or so, until incensed protests from California stopped the practice, the Mexican government dumped a shipload of its undesired and resentful outcasts onto the province.

The chief interest of these *cholos*, according to the padres, was to trick Indians into working for them while they spent their own time gambling, racing horses, fighting cocks, drinking, and riding off to the native rancherías in search of young girls to seduce. When the Indian's work was done, he was turned out to scrounge a living however he could between drinks. For his vagrancy and his drunkenness he was often tied to the little ceremonial cannon rusting in each town plaza, publicly flogged, and kicked aside to begin the weary round again. Was this the sort of fate the idealists wanted for the mission Indians?

The liberals retorted that continuing a paternalistic watch over the Indians at the missions would not prepare them for self-reliance in the future any more than it had in the past. They would learn citizenship best by being allowed to live pridefully in their own pueblos. To say that they were incapable of doing this was to use a racist argument wholly repugnant to the new revolutionary theories about the perfectability of mankind.

Thus the recriminations. Echeandía heard them all. He had fought during the revolution against Spain as one of the principal officers in the Corps of Engineers, and he had brought with him to California the liberal theories that had led him into the army in the first place. Turn the Indians free!—and then he learned how completely the presidios depended on the mission fields for food and how impossible the maintenance of the territorial government would be without the revenues produced by the mission trade in hides and tallow.

The discoveries shook him badly. He could not even force the Franciscans, most of whom were Spanish by birth and sympathies, to take oaths of allegiance to Mexico. When he tried, more than half declined. By law he should have deported them. But, he wrote his superiors, he could not. No replacements were available in California to take over their work, and if the Indians were deprived of guidance, they would either revert to savagery in the wilds or become a burden on the towns. Industry would cease; "for lack of sustenance . . . the rest of the inhabitants and the troops would perish." Yet his orders and his desires were to end this essential system!

Defeated by the paradox, he floated off into unreality, putting onto paper idealistic plans that he hoped never to have to execute in person. The program that emerged was this. Beginning with the four missions nearest the presidios, each station was to surrender all its temporalities and become an ordinary parish church. Its adjoining village would be recognized as a chartered pueblo governed in local affairs by its own alcalde and *ayuntamiento*. Non-Indians would be welcomed; amalgamation had always been a fundamental part of the citizen-making theory.*

(Amalgamation how? he must have wondered in passing. Although mission population had declined since 1820 from 20,000 to 18,000—an ominous reversal in trends—the count of non-Indians had risen to only 4,200, hardly sufficient for true acculturation. But on paper one did not have to look too closely at such inconveniences. On he went.)

Every Indian family in a secularized village would be given two plots of land. One was to be a homesite of approximately an acre within the village itself. The other, a farmsite of seven acres, was to lie as close to the town as the availability of irrigation water allowed. The town would be granted four square leagues of communal grazing ground (about 17,500 acres) for each 500 homesites. In addition to land, every householder would receive, on the breaking up of the mission, prescribed amounts of equipment, tools, and livestock. What remained after the distribution— animals, vineyards, grain fields, workshops, and so on—would be managed by government-appointed administrators and the profits devoted to each pueblo's school, hospital, jail, and other municipal needs.

The plan was published December 11, 1828. Immediately the Indians at the missions grew restive—freedom! wheat fields and tasty beef!—and the priests suspicious. In their minds Echeandía was trying to circum-

---

*The non-Indians, it should be remembered, were almost always males, who mingled readily with Indian women. In theory, non-Indian women were also welcome, but there was a chronic shortage of these on the frontiers of Latin America.

vent the new Mexican laws regulating the passing out of land to private individuals. Those laws clearly stated that mission holdings were not to be granted to non-Indians until an accurate determination of the needs of the neophytes had been made. Echeandía was trying to make that determination himself by arbitrarily limiting the acreage that could go to each neophyte and to each Indian pueblo—by saying, in effect, that what he specified was all that the Indians needed. The rest of the pastures grazed by the mission herds (it came to some 9 million acres after the Indians had been "satisfied") would be opened to private individuals greedy for a share of the new profits resulting from the hide and tallow trade. Consider, too, the patronage plums Echeandía was harvesting in the form of administratorships for undistributed mission property. Was this liberal humanitarianism—or was it naked theft?

For Echeandía the uproar marked the end of a distressing year. First the friars had censured him furiously when the officers he sent against Estanislao's fugitives in the San Joaquin had burned and shot and hanged them in a merciless massacre. Then there had been the troubles with James Pattie and the smuggling ship captains, the smallpox epidemic and the Herrera-Solís revolt. Well, at least he had obeyed orders about the missions by preparing a plan. Now let someone else execute it. Wearily he sent the papers off to Mexico City for approval and followed them with a letter urgently requesting that his successor be hurried to California as soon as possible.

Torn by dissension, the central government paid no heed to the secularization papers. But it did name a new governor for Alta California, José María Padrés, formerly a brilliant young lieutenant under Echeandía in the Corps of Engineers. Intensely ambitious and something of a libertine, too—he suffered all his life from chronic syphilis incurred during his youth—Padrés was a lean, short, very dark, very handsome spellbinder who struck fire from the young liberals who thronged to hear him. Of equal importance, he had influential friends.

Through some carelessness this eager young man missed the ship that was to have carried him north. Before another was available, a right-wing revolution toppled from power the liberal federalists under whom he and Echeandía held their appointments and their hopes of future advancement. Padrés was demoted to inspector general of troops for California. Named to serve as governor in his place was a dour, autocratic mestizo, Manuel Victoria.

Completely disgruntled by his demotion and by the revolution, Padrés reached California in the summer of 1830, well ahead of Victoria. Quickly he ensnared Echeandía with his electric charisma. Putting their heads together in Monterey, the two erstwhile engineers decided to create tumult for Victoria by signing into law, with the approval of the California *diputación*, Echeandía's still unauthorized secularization plan of December, 1828.

The result was a year of utter confusion. Victoria reached California in January, 1831, just as the friars were being directed, by courier, to turn control of the twenty-one missions over to civil administrators. Furiously the new governor canceled the edict and ordered a return to the status quo, at least until the government had spoken. Brusquely he told Echeandía to report without delay to his army unit in Mexico. He sent Inspector General Padrés to the decaying presidio at San Francisco with stern instructions that he confine himself strictly to military matters.

Neither man obeyed. Echeandía, who once had been impatient to leave California but who now saw no future for himself in Mexico, halted at San Diego and set up a rebel cell. Padrés kept holding clandestine interviews with young liberals (and hopeful rancheros, too) who slipped into San Francisco to see him. Busy orienting himself to his new job, Victoria did not react until summer. He then clapped Padrés aboard a southbound ship and sent him to Mexico. Later, in November, he started toward San Diego to force a showdown with Echeandía.

Their ill-armed troops met in the San Fernando Valley at the foot of Cahuenga Pass, route now of the Hollywood Freeway. During a melee uncharacteristic of California revolutions, one of Echeandía's men and one of Victoria's principal officers were killed. Victoria himself was wounded painfully by a lance and later captured at Mission San Gabriel, where he had himself carried for medical treatment. Thoroughly tired of California by that time, the new governor agreed to return to Mexico as soon as he was well enough to travel. And he did.

His defection did not end the civil war. Urged onward by priests and traders who feared disruptive new efforts at secularization if Echeandía recovered power, Victoria's territorial secretary, Agustín Zamorano, declared himself provisional governor and began gathering a fresh army of a few dozen men. Echeandía retorted by summoning into session at Los Angeles a rump legislature of southern Californios who obligingly elected him governor. (Most of the electors foresaw land grants in the event of victory.) Clad in that dubious legality, the rebel leader then called on all mission Indians—he would free them if he won—to rally to his cause.

More than a thousand responded, pawns in a struggle for the control of California's grasslands that very few of them could possibly have understood. Echeandía mounted as many as were able to ride (another California paradox; fearing fugitivism, the friars had discouraged horsemanship among the Indians except for a few carefully selected vaqueros), distributed 300 lances among them, and put his regulars to drilling the disorderly throng. According to trader Alfred Robinson, no friend of Echeandía's, discipline collapsed completely. There were murders and robberies at San Diego, and continued brawls at the missions of San Luis Rey and San Juan Capistrano, where Echeandía quartered his troops. Everywhere, Robinson clucked, rose the drunken Indian cry of *"Soy libre!"* "I am free!"

Petitions showered on Echeandía, begging him to disband the unruly force. By the time he had brought it, in massive confusion, as far as San Gabriel, he too began to doubt his control if ever the mob tasted blood. Meantime Zamorano, sitting nervously in Santa Barbara while his small army hovered near Los Angeles, was wondering whether he could possibly snatch victory from a battle with such a horde. And so, since neither general could envision triumph, they reached in true California style, without fighting, the only reasonable solution—a draw.

According to the terms of the peace, Echeandía was to govern as far north as San Gabriel, Zamorano as far south as San Fernando, with the narrow strip of territory between serving as a buffer zone. The division was to last until Mexico City appointed a new governor. Each contestant hoped to be tapped, Echeandía because of his election by the *diputación*, Zamorano because of his defense of legitimacy.

The Indians were told that while they waited for this decision, which obviously would have much to do with their immediate fates, they should return to their missions. Most obeyed. The wilderness was an unknown quantity, and at their old stations they would have food and a familiar place in which to sleep. Besides, they had been led to believe that the missions would soon be theirs to do with as they chose. And so they returned, but not, in most cases, to work. *Soy libre!* As the padres of the southernmost establishments looked across their disordered shops and fields, they must have felt despair: could Humpty Dumpty ever be put together again?

To the shocked disappointment of co-governors Zamorano and Echeandía, the man chosen to try was Brigadier General José Figueroa, for the past six years comandante of turbulent Sonora. Figueroa was stocky, swart, and proud of his Aztec blood. His private life was not exemplary. He had deserted his wife, had fathered at least two illegitimate children, and gambled heavily. But he was a moderate in politics, something that divided California badly needed, he could not be bluffed, and he had a reputation, rare among the unruly partisans of revolutionary Mexico, for obeying orders. His chief drawback was poor health.

Like the liberals, the new conservative central government wanted secularization—national policy committed them to that—but not in a way that would bring credit to their predecessors. Figueroa was instructed to discard Echeandía's proposals, restore order to the missions, and then work out a brand-new plan for secularization. There was no hurry about it. He was even directed to take ten new missionaries to California with him to fill vacancies created during the past years by resignations and deaths.

At first the new governor's path in California was smooth. He sent his tough second-in-command, Nicolas Gutiérrez, south to make sure that Echeandía returned to Mexico. With surprising meekness, Echeandía complied. Meantime Figueroa quieted Zamorano by reappointing him territorial secretary, and California was reunited. The new friars leaped to their tasks with zealousness—so much so that some of them had to be reprimanded for overuse of the lash. *Soy libre?* Not yet: the Indians, dismayed by and uncomprehending of these whirling changes, slipped sullenly back into their old routines.

Smooth enough . . . but the ailing Figueroa disliked Monterey's fog and isolation as much as Echeandía had. In March, 1833, two months after his arrival, he wrote Mexico City asking to be replaced. And that brings us back to José María Padrés, who all this time had been plotting new ways either to free the mission Indians or to lay hold of the mission lands, depending on how one reads his motives. In either event, he did not intend for José María Padrés to suffer in the process.

The jig of factional politics was tormenting Mexico again, and times were ripe for men like Padrés. That notable chameleon, General Antonio López de Santa Anna, soon to win notoriety at an abandoned mission in Texas called the Alamo, had overthrown the conservatives and had lifted himself into the presidency as a liberal. Unlike his associates, however, Santa Anna had sensitive antennae. Once the fever of victory had cooled, he realized that the basic mood of the country was still conservative and that his government was not likely to endure. Abruptly he turned the affairs of the nation over to his vice-president, Valentín Gómez Farías, and retired to his country estate, ready to reappear, when the call came, as the new hope of conservatism. Meantime his erstwhile liberal associates pushed their programs ahead with little awareness of what portended.

Through his influential friends, Padrés gained the ear of Vice-President Farías and poured out a tale of California's woes under the mission system. The neophytes, he declared, were virtual slaves. Excessive amounts of land were closed to settlement, and colonizing as envisioned by the liberal land laws of 1824 and 1828 was at a standstill. The time had come to strike.

At that point Figueroa's request for replacement reached the capital.

Enthralled by Padrés' seeming earnestness, Farías asked him whether he would rather succeed Figueroa as civil governor or as military commander of California; enlightened theory was now demanding a separation of the powers. Padrés chose the military post and recommended a wealthy friend, José María Híjar, as governor. He also suggested that Híjar be named director of colonization. The two of them, Padrés and Híjar, would then recruit several hundred colonists, take them to California, and settle them (at Farías' suggestion) north of San Francisco Bay as a bulwark against the Russian establishment at·Fort Ross, for that old bugbear still troubled the government. Additional colonies would locate later on at other strategic spots formerly controlled by the missions, and at last California would begin to realize her potential.

Farías bought it all. Híjar was named governor of California and director of colonization. On August 17, 1833, the Mexican Congress passed a bill ordering the immediate transformation of the missions into civil parishes. Their demise as missions completed, they obviously would not need to draw for support on their principal endowment, a million-dollar account called the Pious Fund. Therefore Híjar could use part of the money to subsidize the movement of his colonists onto erstwhile mission land. It was something like borrowing a man's rope in order to hang him.

No unmixed Indian villages were to be allowed. "Especial care," Híjar's instructions read, "will be taken to bring the Indians into the [new colony] towns, mixing them with the other inhabitants." Beyond that insistence on integration little was said concerning the actual processes by which secularization was to be accomplished. As events turned out, the silence was fatal.

It may well be that cynical motives were at the root of the colonizing scheme. For one instance, it drew unto itself a commercial organization called the Cosmopolitan Company; this group, in which both Híjar and Padrés were interested, hoped to obtain government favors in return for stimulating trade in colony products. Even so, Padrés' determination to start a flow of capable settlers northward was the first energetic attempt since Anza's day to make something of California. Though the story is one of hard luck and failure, it deserves to be better known than it is.

During the winter of 1833–34 recruiters enlisted more than 300 men, women, and children. Most of the males were skilled workers—farmers, butchers, blacksmiths, shoemakers, tailors, schoolteachers, a doctor, and the like, a far cry from California's usual importation of soldiers and convicts. They assembled in Mexico City and in April, 1834, started their long trip by cart and horseback to San Blas, where two ships were scheduled to pick them up for the sea voyage to California. Very few were prepared by experience for the frontier challenges that lay ahead.

Their ships were delayed. During the wait at San Blas, courage oozed away and more than a hundred of the colonists withdrew. When the two transports at last stood out to sea on August 1, 1834, only 204 pioneers —99 men, 55 women, and 50 children, nearly half of them less than four years old—were aboard. (The usual shortage of women, notice. But in the new towns, it was promised, trained, Christian Indian females would serve as housewives and mothers of sturdy new citizens.)

Just before the colonists sailed, President Santa Anna waved himself into view again as the savior of reaction. He arrested Vice-President Farías, barred Congress from meeting, and as part of his sweeping attack on all the doings of his predecessors ordered the California project canceled. Informed that it was too late to halt the emigrants at San Blas, he summoned a notable scout, Rafael Amador, and handed him a dispatch addressed to Figueroa. The governor was not to turn over any of his functions to either Híjar or Padrés; he was not to surrender any mission land to the colonists. If Amador reached Monterey with that message ahead of the colony ships—2,200 miles on horseback: jungles, sterile plateaus, mountains, deserts, rivers, hostile Indians—he would receive 3,000 pesos. The scout said that he would try.

While the colonists were being recruited, news of what was afoot trickled into California by ships' mail. Resentment swept the territory. Ever since cattle raising had become profitable, Californios had been dreaming of the day when secularization would open land to private ranching. Now at last the missions were legally obliterated, but look what was happening. Locusts from Mexico were about to seize the land for themselves.

Liberals who had once sat entranced at Padrés' feet leaped to check him. In decreeing secularization the Mexican Congress had said nothing about specific steps. California's territorial *diputación* was therefore free, its members argued, to suggest the proper means. Meeting in Monterey in early August, 1834, while the colonists were still on the high seas, they dusted off Echeandía's old plan, modified it for the still greater benefit of would-be ranchers, and submitted it to Figueroa for consideration.

Under their plan, the territorial government, acting through commissioners appointed by the governor, would assume charge of all mission temporalities. As in Echeandía's scheme, the Indians would receive, in villages of their own governance, house lots, farm plots, and grazing rights in community pastures. Half of each mission's cattle, seed, farming implements, and the like would be distributed among them. The other half would be managed by the administrators for the benefit of the new municipalities. Because the towns would profit from that income, the

Indians could be called on at any time to do the necessary work of maintaining the undistributed property. *Soy libre?* Well, maybe, if the administrators were honest. Few restraints were written into the law, however. If a commissioner decided to cheat the Indians during the distribution of property or to overwork them on the community projects, the only recourse would be a direct appeal to the governor. And bureaucracy generally learns how to clog channels of that kind.

Figueroa, who had the power to reject the plan out of hand, surely must have wondered about the wisdom of sandbagging his own government's colonizing program. On the other hand, he had been an appointee of conservatives, and the oncoming colony was a liberal innovation. Moreover, part Aztec himself, he sympathized with the Indians and their desire for independence. The *diputación*'s plan allowed turning the mission villages into pueblos composed only of Indians, whereas the Híjar-Padrés program demanded integration. Perhaps the governor thought that unmixed Indian villages—he had recently authorized three small ones in the southernmost part of the territory—were the only realistic solution in a land where a perpetual shortage of non-Indian settlers made true acculturation impossible.

Or perhaps he felt, for an exhilarating moment, a touch of that mad independence that California's isolation seemed sooner or later to bring to all her residents. In any event, he ran contrary to his own reputation for faithful obedience and accepted the *diputación*'s plan, adding only one modification. It would be impossible, he said, to find on the instant twenty-one qualified administrators for the stations.

Therefore, he would move more slowly, secularizing ten of the missions during the remaining months of 1834, six in 1835, and the rest in 1836. And then, the barricades neatly erected, he sat back to wait for his two successors.

The confrontation that many Californios eagerly anticipated never came about. In one of the great courier feats of all time, Rafael Amador traveled the 2,200 miles from Mexico City to the environs of Monterey in 45 days—this in spite of losing his horse to Yuma Indians at the mouth of the Gila River and crossing the Colorado Desert on foot in summertime, living on a handful of withered berries and enduring one three-day period without a swallow of water. Thus California learned that Santa Anna was again calling the tunes, that Figueroa was still governor and military comandante. When Padrés sailed into Monterey harbor on September 11, 1834 (Híjar arrived a month later by land from San Diego), the burly little Aztec declined to surrender a single scrap of authority.

Although Híjar and Padrés blustered with angry shock, their colonists were the true sufferers. They had listened, as few others had up until then, to the siren song of California. They had clung to the dream after the faint of heart had given up at San Blas. But then the troubles had come. Those sailing with Híjar had landed at San Diego so battered by storms that they had refused to reboard their ship for the rest of their journey north and had tried to continue overland in disorganized groups. Many, held back by sick women and frightened children, never finished the journey but collapsed wherever townspeople or missionaries would give them refuge.

Those who reached Monterey went on eventually to the exquisite valley of Sonoma on the north side of San Francisco Bay. There Mariano Vallejo, stirred by fear of the Russians, was building a new presidio to replace crumbling San Francisco as the military bulwark of the north. He gave work to many of the colonists, but supplies were short. Because the pioneers had been promised rations for their first winter, Híjar asked Figueroa to have pity on them. The governor passed the requests on to the northern missions. They professed, perhaps truthfully, an inability to meet the unexpected demands.

It was a miserable winter. Quarrels turned into shrill recriminations. Convinced that the colony leaders were plotting against him, Figueroa found in a Los Angeles riot that involved a colonist or two a pretext for arresting Híjar, Padrés, and a handful of their leading supporters. Loading them and their families aboard a rented ship, he sent them back to Mexico. Like Echeandía, who had also rejected a successor, he then settled down to a love affair with the very territory that at the beginning of his sojourn he had detested.

So ended Mexico's one real effort to colonize California. With it died the last small hope of founding new towns where missionized Indians and non-Indians could mix on equal terms as citizens of a truly integrated province, such as had existed in other parts of Mexico. Eventually some of the unanchored colonists managed, after great privations, to lift themselves into positions of prominence. But for the mission Indians, who supposedly were to rise with them, it was a very different story.

On September 29, 1835, just as the secularization of the missions was rolling ahead at full speed, Figueroa died. His strong hand removed, rival factions began a confused struggle for power—northerners against southerners, conservative centralists who advocated close ties with Mexico City against liberal federalists who wanted home rule. Most of the battles, fought by sonorous proclamations issued against a boom of harmless cannonballs, were settled by compromise. Engrossed by the far bloodier upheavals in Texas, Mexico was unable to intervene. For a time California was, according to herself, an independent republic. For a time Los

Angeles was, according to herself, the capital city. After about three years of this, the leading revolutionist, a native-born northerner named Juan Bautista Alvarado, managed to seat himself firmly in the governor's chair at Monterey. Winning the blessings of Mexico City, he finally brought a pause to the chaotic struggle for political preferment.

A comparable halt in the looting of the missions proved impossible. Because of feeble laws and riotous conditions, the sequence of embattled governors who followed Figueroa had not even tried to control the dishonest and incompetent commissioners appointed to supervise the process of secularization. Although a few Indian pueblos were formed, mostly in southern California, the majority of the neophytes were never informed of their rights as newly emancipated citizens of the nation; very few ever received the property legally due them.

Alvarado made one gesture toward reform. He ordered the administrators to prepare their accounts for inspection and appointed the English trader William Hartnell, by then a naturalized Mexican and rancher, to be overseer of the erstwhile missions. It was a hopeless task; the despoilers were too deeply entrenched. Although Hartnell managed to replace a few bumblers, the more powerful men boldly defied him. Mariano Vallejo, administrator of San Francisco Solano in the Sonoma Valley, even arrested and jailed Hartnell as a trespasser! After a year of almost total frustration, the hapless inspector resigned.

Those of the Indians who did obtain property proved, for the most part, unable to hold onto it. They gambled it away, were befogged by drink and cheated, or simply robbed. Thousands of them migrated in deep bitterness to the interior, joined the unconverted tribes, and in several instances became the core of stock-raiding bands that would plague the outlying settlements of California well into gold-rush times. Less belligerent families who had known no other life than that at the missions clung forlornly to the new Indian pueblos or to the decaying stations, working for the commissioners and receiving comfort from those of the Franciscans who stayed loyally with them. Others wandered through the towns in abject poverty and degradation. The rest, some five thousand all told, went to work on the new ranches.

The speed of this transfer of economic power from the missionaries to the rancheros was extraordinary. Between 1784, when a retired soldier had received land from Pedro Fages, until the beginning of secularization in the final months of 1834, Spanish and Mexican governors had confirmed only 51 grants, an average of one a year. From 1834 through 1840, 309 titles were issued, an average of 44 a year—and the pace had not yet reached full stride.

Any native-born or naturalized Mexican Catholic without a criminal record was eligible to apply for unoccupied land in California—most of it land that formerly had been grazed by something like 400,000 mission cattle and lesser numbers of sheep and horses. First the petitioner de-scribed.what he wanted by reference to the area's topographical features, using a crude pictorial map, a *diseño*, to clarify his statements. If investiga-tion by local officials indicated that the would-be rancher was telling the truth about his status, was able to utilize the ground, and was not asking for land claimed in whole or in part by someone else, then the application would be forwarded to Monterey. After additional checking (in theory), the governor or legislature would issue provisional title. This would not become final (again in theory) until the petitioner had built a house on the property and had introduced livestock.

As soon as provisional title had been granted, the land was "surveyed." Measurement was by means of a rawhide riata, or lariat rope. Long stakes were tied to each of its ends. Mounted cowboys stretched out the rope between them, thrust the stakes into the ground, and then galloped ahead to repeat the process, guiding themselves haphazardly along what they thought was the boundary line of the property. From this came a rough estimate of the grant's dimensions. No single allotment could exceed 11 square leagues, or 48,700 acres. The same individual or members of his family could apply for additional grants, however, and so holdings as huge as a quarter of a million acres controlled by a single ranchero were not unheard of.

The carelessness that marked the surveying permeated the rest of the system. Such impermanent landmarks at trees, rocks, or even cow skulls served to designate corners. Claims overlapped without the petitioner's awareness or even concern. Sending applications to Monterey for con-firmation by a governor who might be unseated at any moment was a time-consuming bore and often omitted. Some men did not bother to erect houses on their property as required by law (from long habit many Spanish Mexicans preferred to live in towns and not on isolated ranches) but contented themselves with merely driving their animals out to the grant, turning them loose, and letting them wander until the next spring rodeo, or roundup.

Behind this casualness was an attitude toward land so different from the Anglo-American feeling that we still have difficulty really compre-hending it. Our ingrained idea of unearned increment, of holding real estate to sell on a rising market, scarcely brushed a Californio's mind. He regarded a pasture as one might regard a rough tool, almost valueless apart from its function—in this case the growing of wild cattle for the sake of hides worth from one to two dollars each. Everything was vast; everything cheap. A thousand acres *más o menos*—what is that, my friend?

So the problem was not one of finding land, but of obtaining breeding stock to put on the land. This too came from the missions. A ranchero would borrow a few thousand cows from the closest administrator, add a sweetener for the favor, and promise to return the parent animals as soon as he had his own herd under way. The repayment seldom occurred. The demand for exportable hides was high—upwards of 200,000 were shipped to Boston alone during the peak year of 1838—and a man seldom got far enough ahead to return the borrowed foundation stock to its source.

A very gay and fragile society resulted—as fragile as one of the hollowed eggshells (to borrow the description of trader William Heath Davis) that the wives and daughters of the rancheros "filled with fine scraps of pretty-colored silver and gold paper, or with cologne water," and broke over the heads of the men at one of their innumerable dances or fiestas. Life was good. As long as there were hides to be had, a man could buy dazzling clothes for himself and his women, bedeck his horses with silver-mounted saddles and bridles. Since most of the inhabitants were unable to read or write, they felt no need for libraries. They sang endlessly to their guitars and did not miss concerts. They ate well, if simply, and were healthy. Their families were enormous. William Hartnell's wife bore twenty sons and five daughters, not all of whom lived. There were no hospitals and few doctors; yet before another prolific housewife, Juana Cota, died, she could count five hundred living descendants.

A ranchero did no work that could not be accomplished on horseback. Children ran wild, riding half-broken mustangs and swinging lassos as soon as they were able to sit astride. Every ranch family, according to Charles Wilkes of a United States naval exploring expedition, lost young ones to horseback accidents. Perhaps it was compensation that those who survived developed phenomenal skill, even hunting grizzly bears for sport with only a lariat rope for a weapon. Meanwhile no one heeded the decline in all forms of economic activity from the days of the missions —in numbers of livestock, in handicrafts, in farm produce. Even the shoes that the ranchers wore came from New England and as often as not were made from hides they themselves had sent there around Cape Horn.

Supporting this carefree society were the newly freed, trained Indians of the secularized missions. They lived in cell-like barracks near the home of their *patrón*. They did not overstrain themselves at their tasks, and were not expected to. The ranchers, like the cotton planters of the American South, insisted that the workers were well off. They were fed, clothed, and administered to when sick. Unlike the slaves of the South, they could not be sold and, in theory at least, were free to leave when they chose. Almost always they came back. These were the ones who had been thoroughly tamed—that is, civilized—and neither the wilds nor drunkenness in the towns could wholly charm them.

A splendid idleness, one novelist described the ranchero period. Or, as the wife of Mariano Vallejo of Sonoma told one interviewer: "Each of my children, boy or girl, has a servant who has no other duty but to care for him or her. I have two servants for myself. Four or five grind corn for tortillas . . . six or seven serve in the kitchen. . . . Nearly a dozen are required to attend to the sewing and spinning." Outside, working in the fields and vineyards and tending the cattle, were six hundred more.

A romantic idleness, well exploited in California legend. Based on a shaky tripod of untaxed land, of scrub cattle that needed no care since only the hides were valuable, and of a liberal supply of cheap, pretrained labor, this fragile, charming, hospitable, thoughtless culture was able to endure only so long as it remained undisturbed. Those days were quickly numbered. Already other pioneers, conditioned to wholly different concepts of land use and land value, were edging westward along the dim trails of the mountain men.

7. The Schemers

Far in the van of land seekers from the East came two fugitives whose accomplishments during the next decades would be almost incredible even for California. One, Johann August Sutter, was from Switzerland. The other, John Marsh, was a disgraced alumnus of Harvard College. Both were obsessed with making fortunes big enough to wipe out the degradations of the past.

Sutter was the more imaginative of the two, once he had decided to seek salvation through his own wits. A native of the German side of the Rhine, he had moved as a youth to Switzerland and had taken up storekeeping. There he was forced into marriage with a woman for whose pregnancy he was responsible. Altogether he produced five children with her, stayed unhappy, floundered into debt, and finally, aged thirty-one, fled to sanctuary on the American frontier. Two dusty merchandising trips between Independence, Missouri, and Santa Fe brought him none of the fortune he desired, but in New Mexico he did learn that *empresarios* who agreed to settle colonists in California could obtain princely land grants.

Getting there in those days (the summer of 1838) took ingenuity. First he rode horseback with a strange mélange of Indians, beaver trappers, and Protestant missionaries to Fort Vancouver, a Hudson's Bay Company post on the Columbia River. Company trappers told him about the Sacramento Valley, and he decided that it was the very place for his colony. But he could not travel there by land in the dead of winter, and so he sailed restlessly on to the Sandwich Islands aboard a Hudson's Bay Company ship. After gathering more information from merchants in Honolulu, he boarded an 80-ton trading vessel bound for Monterey by way of Sitka, Alaska. Accompanying him on the zigzag trip were two Germans whom he had picked up during his travels, eight hired Kanaka (Hawaiian) laborers, and two Kanaka women, one of them his bedmate.

Despite a heavy German accent, Sutter had learned by this time to be persuasive in many languages. He was erect and graceful—later he would grow paunchy—and he enhanced his appearance by wearing a French military uniform that he had purchased for a beaver skin. He carried letters of introduction from important people he had met during his wanderings. Fortified by these assets, he told Governor Alvarado that if he were given a grant somewhere along the Sacramento River—naturally he would become a Mexican citizen and a Roman Catholic—he would found a colony of Swiss immigrants that would serve the Californios as a buffer against Indian raiders, Russian interlopers, English trappers, and American adventurers.

Those were grandiose promises, but Alvarado was impressed enough that he gave the newcomer permission to locate the land he wanted. A year later, if all went well, Sutter could make formal application for citizenship and 11 square leagues of land. That hope buttoned into his pocket, the fortune hunter next went to Yerba Buena cove in San Francisco Bay to start his preparations.

Changes of greater significance than Sutter was aware of were taking place in the little anchorage. Four years before his arrival, the old San Francisco presidio, located on the wrong (south) side of the still-unnamed Golden Gate to be effective against the Russians at Fort Ross, had been all but abandoned in favor of Mariano Vallejo's new fortress at Sonoma. Not all of the erstwhile presidial villagers had wanted to follow the soldiers north, however. Some thought it would be better to move eastward four or five miles across the sandhills at the tip of the peninsula and relocate their homes beside the sheltered cove on its inner side.

Called Yerba Buena after an aromatic plant that grew there, the hill-protected indentation had long been a favorite anchorage for whalers and trading ships having business to transact with the presidio. Sensing from the talk of the villagers that the place still might have a future in spite of Sonoma's competition, Governor Figueroa had decided to let the settlers move there and had directed a versatile Englishman, William A. Richardson, to lay out a pueblo for them. (In Hispanic America towns could be formed only with government permission.) In return for his efforts Richardson was to be captain of the port, with the right to collect pilot fees from ships nosing through the Golden Gate.

Richardson knew the bay well. He had deserted there from a British whaler in 1822 and afterward had married one of the daughters of the presidio's comandante. Using a homemade launch manned by Indians, he earned a living by ferrying goods and cowhides around the inland waters. While laying out the new town of Yerba Buena, he housed his wife and children in a tent on the bleak shore of the cove. They were not qualified pioneers. When their fire went out during one of Richardson's absences, the mother and her brood were unable to rekindle it. For two foggy days, until a rider chanced by with flint and steel, they could not cook their food. Still, they have their niche in local annals, for it can be argued that the tent at Yerba Buena and not the collapsed presidio above the wind-wracked entrance to the bay was the true beginning of the modern city of San Francisco.

Yerba Buena's next settler was a one-time American trapper named Jacob Leese who had wandered into Monterey after an overland trip from New Mexico. In Monterey he had joined the trading community and had boosted himself swiftly upward by marrying a sister of Mariano Vallejo. Hearing of the newly authorized town at Yerba Buena cove, Leese's partners sent him north to acquire a lot and build a long wooden cube of a store fronted by a deep veranda. After completing the building early in the summer of 1836, Leese decided to celebrate with a Fourth of July party. The captains and mates of three or four American ships in the harbor mingled with Mexican army officers from Sonoma and with gentry invited from the scattering of new ranches taking form around the periphery of the bay. The merriment lasted until July 6, by which time, according to trader William Heath Davis, "the ladies had become so exhausted that the festivities ceased." Throughout the celebration, an American flag floated overhead. If anyone remarked it, Leese probably replied that he had raised the banner as a gesture of international friendship, not as a prediction.

By the time Sutter reached Yerba Buena in 1839 several adobe huts stood haphazardly around those two original buildings. For California, the inhabitants were busy. The hide business was booming and a handful of lumbermen had begun cutting redwood a few miles down the peninsula at El Rancho de Las Plugas, the Ranch of the Fleas, today's Redwood City. Sutter had no trouble finding three vessels for moving his goods from the cove up through Carquinez Strait into the Sacramento River. One was a four-oared pinnace that he bought in order to maintain connections with the outside world; the others were chartered little sailing ships. Yerba Buena loungers, mostly American sailors who had jumped ship, agreed to man the little fleet. As its captain and pilot Sutter hired a garrulous young trader from Hawaii, William Heath Davis.

Devoured by whining clouds of mosquitoes, the wayfarers toiled as far upstream, perhaps, as the mouth of the Feather. There, crushed by the heat, the polyglot crew struck. No more! Yielding, Sutter dropped back to the flatlands where the American River, named for Jedediah Smith's trappers, flowed sluggishly into the Sacramento from the east. He wanted land that would be easy to plow, and this suited. However, the triangle of ground between the rivers, a tree-punctuated site where the city of

Sacramento would later take form, looked as if it might be inundated by spring floods. Hoping to escape the threat, Sutter turned the fleet up the American for a mile or so, until he saw a low knoll off to the south. That should do.

After unloading, he released the hired ships and their crews. As a gesture of defiance, perhaps, to the enormous solitude around him, he thrust powderbags into the little brass cannon he had brought from Hawaii and fired nine parting salutes. The racket terrified the Indians who had thronged about and set wolves howling and herds of elk galloping wildly across the plains. Then, as quiet returned, he put his Kanakas to work building little grass-topped shelters in which they could live while tackling the bolder structure he envisioned for the future—a private fort of a kind quite unknown in California and one so impregnable that he could never be dislodged. There he would root the colonists that he still intended to import from Switzerland; there he would rule like a benevolent and wholly independent emperor—he, Johann August Sutter, fugitive from ruin.

He lured in Indian workers, some trained originally at the distant missions, with cloth, beads, and the security of three meals a day. As their numbers increased, he poured their food into troughs and let them scoop it out with their hands—but there was no stinting on amounts. Like the Franciscans, he had only a half-dozen or so armed men for protection, but their rifles far outmatched the bows of the Indians. He used this minuscule force with restraint, but when he felt that reprisals were necessary, he struck unexpectedly and hard. Before long the tribes for miles around were walking gently in his presence.

He did not try to impose cultural changes, and he exacted punishment rarely. As long as his obsessions for wealth and power were not involved, he was kindly, generous, and without condescension. He was almost unbelievably plausible. During those early years he could talk his way to whatever he wanted, either Indian labor or cattle and other supplies that he wheedled on credit from ranchers scattered around the northern and eastern sides of San Francisco Bay.

Soon he discovered to his amazement that John Marsh, a hulking jack-of-many-trades whom he had known in Missouri, was already settled some 30 miles farther south on the west side of the lower San Joaquin River. In his solitary way, Marsh was as unique as Sutter. After graduating from Harvard in 1823, aged twenty-four, he had found a job tutoring, for $75 a year and board, the children of army officers stationed at Fort Snelling, Minnesota. He filled his spare time studying medicine under the post surgeon, carrying mail by canoe down the Mississippi River to Fort Crawford at Prairie du Chien, Wisconsin, and wooing the daughter of a Sioux Indian and a French-Canadian voyageur. Unwilling to take her east, he stayed on the frontier as an Indian agent and trader. She died, and shortly thereafter Marsh was indicted for selling guns to enemy Indians. He tried to escape both his grief and his pursuers by a summer trip to the Rockies with a party of trappers. Returning undetected in the fall of 1833, he opened a store in Independence, Missouri, where Sutter first encountered him. The business did not thrive. When he learned that the military police had relocated him, he decamped without regret for California by way of New Mexico.

In February, 1836, he reached Los Angeles. Having convinced the town council that his Harvard diploma, inscribed in Latin, was really a medical certificate, he was licensed as a doctor, the only one in the pueblo. After half a year's work he sold the hides and tallows he had collected in fees to a Boston trader for $500 in gold and started north in search of a ranch so isolated and undeveloped that he could afford to buy it.

He found what he wanted—11 square leagues for $500—between Mount Diablo and the lower reaches of the San Joaquin River.* He settled down to a morose, miserly existence, venturing away from his adobe hut only to treat patients in exchange for livestock. He won the good will of the Indians by treating their malaria with quinine. Their suspicions overcome, he hired them, in exchange for food and clothing, to work as vaqueros and to plant the fig, grape, pear, and olive cuttings that he obtained from the decaying orchards of Mission San José.

Convinced that his land would rise in value only if the United States acquired California, Marsh tried to foster immigration by writing boost-er-style letters to acquaintances in Missouri. He also sent along vague directions, gathered from trapper talk, about the best route to follow, notably the Humboldt River.

Discovered by Peter Skene Ogden of the Hudson's Bay Company in 1828, the thin trickle wound southwestward through the bleak deserts of Nevada, furnishing the only dependable source of grass and water for livestock. Three hundred and sixty miles from its starting point, the Humboldt vanished into saline swamps, about which Marsh probably knew nothing. His information about passes over the Sierra was little better. The only whites who so far had surmounted those formidable mountains from east to west were trappers under Joseph Reddeford

---

*Mt. Diablo, 3,896 feet in elevation, is the high point of the Contra Costa Range—Contra Costa, or "opposite coast," since that is what one sees from San Francisco. Winds rushing through the rocky gap in Diablo's double summit occasionally create whirling dust storms. These led to Indian and Mexican tales about monsters; hence the mountain's name. On a clear day the summit view of coastal mountains and valleys, the rivers, the distant sea, and the sparkling bay form one of California's superb sights. There is no record that John Marsh ever bothered to ride up and look at it.

Walker in 1833, and they'd had the devil's own time working their way along the brink of the precipices that border Yosemite Valley. Still, they had crossed; it could be done.

Partly because of Marsh's letters, fifty-some people gathered in May, 1841, at Sapling Grove, west of Independence, to make the trip. There were thirty-five or so men, five women, and ten or eleven children. (The number was augmented later by a scattering of other emigrants who overtook them on the trail.) They elected John Bartleson as captain, mostly because he and his seven or eight followers said they would not go unless he was. Bartleson's coterie proved unreliable and selfish during starving times. Accordingly historians tend to add the name of young John Bidwell, who later wrote the best-known memoirs of the trip, and call the group the Bidwell-Bartleson party.

They were a husky bunch. Except for an absconding banker, his peculation unknown to the others, they were farm people and had done considerable shifting in their time. They could handle wagons, livestock, and rough tools, but they knew nothing about travel on the dry, treeless plains that faced them. Quite possibly they were saved from disaster by the arrival of Thomas Fitzpatrick, one-time mountain man who in 1841 was shepherding three Jesuit priests and their eight lay helpers to a proposed mission in the Bitterroot Valley of Montana. Emigrants and missionaries joined forces. Although Fitzpatrick could say little about the Humboldt route, never having traveled that way, he did teach the party trail savvy as it moved slowly westward through South Pass to the Bear River in what is now southeastern Idaho.

There, where the trail forked, some of the party lost their nerve and decided to follow the known route to Oregon. The rest, thirty-one men and one woman with a year-old baby girl in her arms, determined to continue to California. The lone woman was Nancy Kelsey. Married at fifteen, she turned nineteen during the trip. Don't picture too much sunbonnet sweetness. Like her rough-and-tumble husband Benjamin and her lawless brother-in-law Andrew, Nancy Kelsey could swear the hide off a mule. She was cheerful, though, and kind, and she was the first American woman to follow what became known as the California Trail —though not quite the first to reach California by land, as will shortly become evident.

After separating from the Oregonians, the California-bound emigrants turned their nine wagons down Bear River to the northern edge of Great Salt Lake. There they bent west through skimpy grass so encrusted with salt that the hungry livestock could scarcely stomach it. The wheels lurched miserably over rocks and knotted sagebrush; the oxen collapsed. Before the party reached the Humboldt, they had to abandon the vehicles and transfer their most essential possessions to packsaddles made on the spot.

The short way to California from Humboldt Sink was southwest to the Truckee River and up that stream to Donner Pass. By steering too much south, the travelers missed the Truckee and reached the Walker instead, its mountain-born water so cold and sweet there in the desert that they called it the Balm. They followed it into the Sierra, a dreadful, starving trip. They crossed the divide somewhere north of today's Sonora Pass and floundered down the awesome canyons of the Stanislaus. On October 31, they reached the San Joaquin Valley and killed enough deer to satisfy their ravenous hunger. The next day one of John Marsh's vaqueros chanced on them and led them to his master's ranch. It was a shock. They had expected fine houses, prosperous fields, churches—or so one of them, Cheyenne Dawson, later wrote. What they found was a huddle of adobe huts without floors, doors, chimneys, or window glass. Though they did not know it, the cluster was typical of all but the grandest of the California ranchos.

Marsh was friendly at first, but a quarrel erupted when, out of ignorance, the immigrants killed and ate one of the few oxen that he had been able to break to plow. More hard feelings arose when Marsh charged them three dollars each for procuring passports for them from Comandante Vallejo. Resentfully they left him. Bidwell and a few others sloshed north through the flooded valley to work for Sutter. Others went to the north side of San Francisco Bay, where George Yount, an American trapper turned rancher, let them squat on his grant in the Napa Valley. Yet in spite of their defection, they had served Marsh's purpose. They had made the crossing, and if more followed, the unearned increment of his land would make him rich. On April 3, 1842, he wrote still another letter to Missouri. "A young woman with a child in her arms came in the company last fall and was about a month in my house. After this, the men ought to be ashamed to think of the difficulties."

Because the Bidwell-Bartleson group pioneered much of what became known as the California Trail, they are the most widely remembered of the land seekers of 1841. Several others were on the move that year, however. One group was composed of several American settlers of New Mexico who fled from their homes there because of a flare-up of antiforeign sentiment brought about by New Mexico's troubles with the Republic of Texas. Traveling with traders and driving sheep along for food, the refugees, their Mexican wives, and their children followed the looping caravan trail through southern Utah and Nevada and reached Los Angeles without incident. At least three of them, John Rowland, William Workman, and Benjamin (Don Benito) Wilson, soon became prominent in local affairs.

Northward, meanwhile, Navy Lieutenant Charles Wilkes of the United States' first official Pacific Exploring Expedition had been looking over the Oregon country, held jointly by his country and Great Britain. As Wilkes was preparing to move on to San Francisco Bay, he decided, without bothering to ask permission from Mexico, that it would be a fine idea to send a land party south past Mount Shasta to see what the interior was like. (One can imagine the stir if Mexico had sent armed explorers into Missouri without the permission of the United States.) Accompanying this inland party were a handful of immigrants who had reached the Columbia River by way of the Oregon Trail in 1840. Among them were Joel Walker, brother of mountain man Joseph Walker, his wife Mary, and their five children. They arrived at Sonoma shortly before the Bidwell-Bartleson group reached Marsh's ranch, and thus Mary Walker, not Nancy Kelsey, achieved the distinction of being the first woman to reach California overland from the United States. Nancy, however, made the trip directly and in a single summer.

During these years, the representatives of other nations were also showing a quickened interest in California. Eugene Duflot de Mofras, a commercial attaché of the French legation in Mexico, examined the coastal areas and Sutter's establishment during two visits in 1841–42. The Frenchman went into raptures over San Francisco Bay, wagged his head happily over the difficulties that Mexico would experience in holding the province against greedy outsiders, and proposed a French protectorate as the best way to forestall the designs of either Great Britain or the United States.

There was some reason for De Mofras to assume such designs. In 1839, Alexander Forbes, a British merchant in Mexico, published what purported to be a history of California—the first one written in English. Actually the book was a propaganda pitch for a colonizing proposal: let Britain accept the province on behalf of the English holders of repudiated bonds of the Mexican government and then foster colonies that would develop California's resources. Thus the bondholders could recover their investment. Shortly thereafter in what seemed to England-haters like a related move, the Hudson's Bay Company established, with Governor Alvarado's consent, a trading post at Yerba Buena cove.

Actually, as we now realize, Britain had no official interest in adding to her commitments south of the Oregon country. Yankee expansionists did not know this at the time, however, and looked on private stirrings as a sign of public policy. Suffused with a growing desire for continental wholeness and foreseeing a profitable trade in the future with the Orient, they began demanding that their government forestall England by acquiring both California and the Republic of Texas, through purchase if possible, by war if necessary. Offers to buy were indeed made. Mexico resisted angrily and found cause for indignation when one clumsy envoy from the United States tried to speed negotiations by offering bribes to Mexican officials.

Sitting uneasily in the governor's chair in distant Monterey, Juan Bautista Alvarado listened with sharp personal concern to warped echoes of all this. The focus of his suspicion was a gang of troublemakers scattered throughout the forests and valleys bordering Monterey Bay. As he well knew from personal experience, they were quite capable of creating incidents that might bring about uncomfortable international reaction, perhaps even foreign intervention.

Most of these hard cases, as Alvarado regarded them, were trappers who had dropped out of hunting parties or sailors who had jumped ship. Although several nationalities were represented, the majority were English and American. Because they declined to take out Mexican citizenship, they were not entitled to move freely around the countryside or to own land. For a living they felled redwood trees, laboriously whipsawed the logs into planks, and swapped the lumber for merchandise to Thomas Larkin, an American who had settled in Monterey in 1833 and by shrewd dealing and unremitting work had quickly risen to prominence. Larkin in turn marketed the wood in treeless southern California. Like the sawyers, as he called them, the merchant steadfastly refused to emulate his fellow traders in adopting Mexican citizenship.

Leader of the lumbermen was a former Kentuckian named Isaac Graham. In 1836 Alvarado had incautiously asked Graham and some of his woodsmen to support the revolution that had lifted the governor to power. Not receiving the reward to which they felt their services entitled them, the sawyers thereafter took to insulting Alvarado openly in the streets of Monterey. Worse, they began talking of a Texas-style uprising to take over the country—or so one of them, as he lay dying, told a priest who came to confess him.

The priest went to Alvarado, who professed to believe the tale. More probably, he saw in it a pretext for getting rid of a dangerous group who might join some other revolutionist in an effort to unseat him. In any event, he ordered his cousin José Castro, military comandante of California, to arrest all foreigners without passports and then determine which should be taken to Mexico for trial. About 120 were swept into the net—a considerable feat if the Californios were as inefficient and cowardly as the Anglo-Saxons liked to proclaim.

After peremptory questioning and rough handling in Monterey's overcrowded, ill-ventilated jail, all but forty-eight of the prisoners were released. Twenty-three were English; twenty-five, American. Larkin sent food to their miserable quarters and tried to interpose on their behalf, to no avail. Castro herded them aboard a small bark, paused in Santa Barbara to pick up twenty more, and carried the whole to prison in Tepic, Mexico.

Hot on Castro's heels came Thomas Jefferson Farnham, a lawyer from Peoria, Illinois, big with literary stirrings. Farnham had ridden overland to Oregon the year before—his companions on the trail later complained of his "low, intriguing disposition"—had not liked the country and had sailed on to California by way of the Sandwich Islands. Reaching Monterey just before the deportation of the prisoners, he appointed himself their counsel and followed them to Tepic. There he enlisted the support of the British consul and fortified his position by pouring out jingoist letters to the American press. Later he would use the effusions as the basis of a popular book extolling California's resources while decrying the shiftlessness, immorality, and treacherousness of the Californios. So inferior a people, he clearly implied, did not deserve so fair a land.

Eager to maintain British support during the maneuverings over Texas and disturbed by the uproar that Farnham's letters were causing in the United States, the Mexican government released the prisoners, promised them indemnity (it was never paid), dressed them in new clothes, and gave free passage to Graham and those of his cohorts who wished to return, swaggering in triumph, to California. A fiasco—or worse, because it persuaded many a roughneck outcast that Mexico could be easily bluffed and that the long arm of his government would protect him if ever he ran into trouble with California's unstable governors. The times, in short, were growing explosive, with arrogance, private greeds, and mutual suspicions. Mexico should have exerted control, but Mexico was far away and paralyzed by inner tumults of her own.

During this troubled period Sutter was industriously pushing his own forms of subversion. In August, 1840, thirteen months after his first visit to Alvarado, he returned to Monterey, took out citizenship papers, and presented the governor with a *diseño* of the land he wanted, nearly 50,000 acres stretching from a little south of the American River along the east side of the Sacramento to the Feather and beyond. He called the establishment he was building New Helvetia in contemplation of the stalwart colonists he would import from Switzerland, and he so bemused Alvarado that the governor not only gave him the land he asked for but in addition appointed him alcalde of the settlement, with jurisdictional powers over the entire Sacramento Valley.

More whites gathered around him, including young John Bidwell, who became his major-domo. Soon nearly a thousand Indians were building thick adobe walls 18 feet high around a rectangle of shops and barracks measuring 150 by 500 feet. When the Russian-American Fur Company decided late in 1841 to abandon Fort Ross, Sutter bought the establishment from under Vallejo's nose—the ruler of Sonoma was holding out for a lower price. The bill of 30,000 pesos was to be paid in three installments, mostly in the form of wheat grown at New Helvetia by Sutter's Indians. In addition to 5,000 animals, nearly half of which drowned while crossing the Sacramento River to their new pastures, the Swiss obtained through the transaction quantities of tools, lumber, and weapons, including several small cannon.

His growing power stirred suspicion and jealousy, particularly from Mariano Vallejo, who feared that his own barony at Sonoma would be overshadowed. Sutter sensed that trouble might be forthcoming. But he was not afraid, he wrote truculently to a friend. He had ten cannon and two fieldpieces in place and "50 faithful Indians which shoot their musquet very quick." If need be, he boasted wildly, he could summon reinforcements from the mountains, from Oregon, even from Missouri. "It is too late now to drive me aut of the country the first step they do against me is that I will make a Declaration of Independence and proclaim California for a Republique independent from Mexico."

A copy of this bombast fell into Vallejo's hands. He sent it to Mexico City and added information about the other foreigners—De Mofras, Charles Wilkes, the Hudson's Bay Company men. The government, he said, must send soldiers, rebuild the San Francisco presidio, and encourage colonization from Mexico. Above all, the province needed a strong new governor invested with both civil and military authority.

Conceivably Vallejo meant himself. If so, he was disappointed. Though he did arouse Mexico to action of sorts, the new governor was General Manuel Micheltorena. With him Micheltorena brought an "army" of three hundred *cholos* scoured for the most part from various prisons. Several of these soldier-colonists had families with them. Alfred Robinson, who watched them disembark at San Diego late in August, 1842, wrote that "not one individual among them possessed a jacket or pantaloon. . . . They concealed their nudity with dirty, miserable blankets. The females were not much better off; for the scantiness of their mean apparel was too apparent for modest observors. . . . Alas, poor California!"

Slowly Micheltorena marched northward, pausing now and then to drill his straggling column. In late October, 1842, while encamped at the half-tumbled buildings of Mission San Fernando, he received two astounding pieces of news. One had to do with a discovery of gold across the hills in rough canyons tributary to the upper Santa Clara River, about 35 miles north of Los Angeles. There the former administrator of the mission, Antonio de Valle, had carved out a huge land grant for himself.

After his death Valle's young widow rented part of the land as pasture to her uncle, Francisco López, who had once studied mining in Mexico City. While riding the range one March day, 1842, López and a single vaquero paused for lunch in what became known as Placerita Canyon. As the cowboy worked over the fire, López began digging wild onions with his hunting knife. Clinging to the roots of one plant were specks of gold.

Nearby Mexicans stampeded into the region. Their first year's take was about $10,000; the next year's, $42,000. After that the shallow placers failed, and California's first gold rush was almost forgotten.

Micheltorena had no time to investigate the unexpected resource. Couriers racing south from Monterey to San Fernando informed him that on October 18, 1842, a United States warship under Commodore Thomas Ap Catesby Jones had sailed into Monterey Bay and had seized the capital. After issuing a thunderous proclamation to the effect that he was about to hurl himself on the aggressors, Micheltorena inspected his *cholos*, reconsidered, and withdrew to Los Angeles.

Follow-up couriers soon reported that the attack had been triggered by inaccurate reports of an outbreak of hostilities between the United States and Mexico. Convinced by Thomas Larkin that the dispatches were mistaken, Jones reembarked his marines in red-faced good order and sailed south to tender formal apologies to Governor Micheltorena. Ceremonies were climaxed by a dazzling ball in El Palacio, the sprawling home that forty-one-year-old Abel Stearns, the wealthiest trader in Los Angeles, had recently built for his fourteen-year-old bride, Arcadia Bandini, reputedly the most beautiful woman in California.

Ceremony could not hide the hopelessness of Micheltorena's position, however. The treasury was empty, smuggling was rife, his *cholo* army uncontrollable. The south's most influential landholder, Pio Pico, whose family tree contained both black and Indian roots, began scheming to make Los Angeles the dominant city of California, with himself at the helm. In the north, Alvarado and Castro brooded over the best means of recovering the positions they had lost to the new governor.

Besides these internal schisms there were, on every hand, alarming numbers of new Americans. Ship arrivals increased. So did landsmen. Several of the immigrants of 1841, among them Joseph Chiles of the Bidwell-Bartleson party and John Rowland of the New Mexicans, liked California well enough that they returned east in 1842 for their families. These and many trail companions arrived in 1843. The following year the Stevens-Murphy party forced the first wagons up the Truckee River and over what would soon be named Donner Pass. Still others drifted down from Oregon, which in those days was a far more popular goal for settlers from America than was California, an exotic land with an unpredictable government.

The gravitational center of those entering northern California by land was Sutter's Fort. Intrigue simmered within the adobe walls. Boldest of the schemers was Lansford Hastings, who appeared from Oregon in 1842 with a wild plan of wresting California from Mexico and joining it to Oregon as the Pacific Republic, Lansford Hastings president. In order to recruit more strength he returned to the United States by way of Mexico in 1844. His intent was to stimulate immigration by writing a book that would describe how easily one could reach the coast and how simple it was to obtain bountiful estates. After enough settlers arrived, California would presumably fall into his hands like a plum. Dreaming so, he composed his infamous *The Emigrants' Guide*, in which he recklessly assured readers that there existed, in deserts he had never seen, an easy shortcut to the western paradise.

Unhinged by these developments, Sutter played both sides of the field. He assured Hastings of his cooperation and at the same time went out of his way to cultivate Manuel Micheltorena. He wrote the governor fulsome letters, visited him in Monterey in 1844, and promised the assistance of his Indians and of a company of American riflemen in the event of trouble. Impressed, Micheltorena made the Swiss an officer in the California militia.

Into this powder-keg situation stepped, quite without authorization, the still-enigmatic figure of John Charles Frémont, a lieutenant in the United States Army's Corps of Topographical Engineers. Illegitimately born, Frémont was brilliant in mathematics and surveying, an adept plainsman, and, by no means least, the husband of lovely Jessie Benton, daughter of bull-voiced Senator Benton of Missouri. In 1843 the Army had directed Frémont to examine the Oregon Trail for the benefit of travelers bound for the northwest. His orders were to return directly home from Fort Vancouver. Instead he struck south along the eastern side of the Cascade and Sierra Nevada ranges. His excuse was that he was looking for the San Buenaventura River, although by that time many people scattered between St. Louis and Vancouver could have told him that no such stream existed.

In Nevada he decided that his horses were too worn to carry his party eastward and that he must obtain fresh animals from Sutter's Fort. In February, 1844, led by Kit Carson and Tom Fitzpatrick, the men flogged their worn mounts toward the Sierra's white crest. It was a cruel, ill-conceived, almost fatal trip. Thirty-three of the animals died; even the party's pet dog went into the stew pot. But the lieutenant did make one of his few original discoveries. With his cartographer Charles Pruess, he climbed a wind-swept peak to look for an opening through the frozen ridges. From the icy summit the two men looked out in awe on another of California's scenic marvels, Lake Tahoe.

Agitated by this unexpected appearance of foreign soldiers in the dead of winter, Micheltorena sent an officer to Sutter's Fort to learn, if possible, what lay behind their extraordinary trespass. The investigators traveled too slowly. By the time they reached the fort, Frémont had gathered up the animals he needed and had ridden off through the San Joaquin Valley, to cross the southern Sierra by kindlier Walker Pass. On his return to Washington, he wrote, with his wife's skillful help, an official report on the ways west that did a great deal to fuel his countrymen's interest in the Pacific Coast still hotter.

While Hastings and Frémont were busily writing, Alvarado and Castro launched their revolution against Micheltorena. The governor at once called for help on Sutter, John Marsh, and, in his desperation, even on Isaac Graham. They responded with a ragbag collection of several hundred Indians and opportunistic riflemen. Outgunned, Alvarado and Castro retreated to Los Angeles. There they joined Pio Pico and with his help enlisted a foreign legion of their own, led by merchant Abel Stearns and Don Benito Wilson of the 1841 immigrant party from New Mexico. Unable to ride horseback because of hemorrhoids, General Micheltorena clambered unhappily into a covered carriage and advanced through one pelting rainstorm after another toward the southern dissidents. His poncho-clad horsemen, Sutter included, sloshed disconsolately beside him, their numbers shrinking a little more each day through desertion.

The climax came February 20–21, 1845, in the San Fernando Valley at the northern end of Cahuenga Pass. There Sutter underwent the acute humiliation of being captured by the enemy. With Sutter's voice stilled, John Marsh of Micheltorena's army and Don Benito Wilson of the rebels' were able to convince the Americans on both sides that this quarrel was not worth the bloodshed they were capable of causing. They all withdrew, and California's standard revolutionary procedures took over. The opposing generals fired off proclamations and long-range cannonballs. A mule or two perished, and through the mysterious computations used by California warriors, Micheltorena concluded that if a fight developed, he would lose. Capitulating, he agreed to return to Mexico with his *cholos*. Sutter was freed, peace reigned.

Torn by her own dissensions, Mexico had little choice but to accept the expulsion of her duly appointed officials and confirm the compromise of the California warriors. Pio Pico was named governor with headquarters at Los Angeles. José Castro was reinstated as comandante at Monterey.

Alvarado, dissipated and sluggish now, was placated by being sent as California's voteless delegate to the Mexican Congress. Once again the territory was afloat on the precarious seas of home rule.

The dangers were self-evident. Mexico was clearly incapable of governing the province—and yet California, which annually drew on the mother country for tens of thousands of pesos, could hardly exist as a separate entity. Almost immediately Pico and Castro began quarreling over the treasury, which was in Monterey, and over their rights in each other's zones of influence. The army melted away; Pico sold land grants at ridiculous sums in an effort to raise revenue.*

Obviously some new force would have to fill the vacuum. But what force? Should the Californios link their fortunes with Oregon and perhaps Texas as the Republic of the Pacific? What about annexation to the United States? Were strengthened ties with Mexico possible or even desirable? How would they fare as a protectorate under France or England?

For that matter, would their own wishes have very much to do with what developed?

---

*From the beginning of 1841 through the middle of 1846, Alvarado, Micheltorena, and Pico issued a total of 453 grants, an average of 82 a year. Several of these were in the Sacramento and San Joaquin valleys.

8. Sculpturing a War

Trapper James Clyman, who in the summer of 1845 came restlessly out of Oregon with a party composed of a lone widow, her three children, a dour carpenter named James Marshall, and thirty-eight other men, did not admire the immigrants he met in California. "The forigners which have found their way to this country," he scribbled in his diary, "are mostly a poor discontented set of inhabitants and but little education hunting for a place as they [want] to live easy."

The judgment was overly severe. The problem in 1845 was not living easy, though that has always been part of the California mirage, but living securely. To the American agriculturist of the pre-Civil War decades that meant a subsistence farm of 80 to 160 acres readily obtained from a government long since committed to dividing its wilderness among many independent farmers rather than concentrating it in a few baronial hands. Each recipient would clear his plot with his own labor, support himself on it until the neighborhood grew populous, and then, as a reward for his share in civilizing the frontier, would sell it on a rising market to later arrivals. The process had worked on successive frontiers from the Shenandoah Valley through Kentucky and Ohio into Missouri and Iowa, and newcomers to California expected it to work there, too. When they found the traditional channels blocked, they were angry and frightened. What now?

Self-delusion was part of the problem. Even though the Mexican minister to Washington published notices in several Eastern papers that only citizens of Mexico could own land in California, the migrants somehow convinced themselves that the authorities on the coast were so desperate for colonists that they would hand out homesteads to all askers. After pursuing that misconception into strangeness, the home seekers discovered that they were not saviors but, lacking passports, were trespassers. Unless they became Mexicans, they were barred not only from obtaining land by gift but even from buying or leasing it.

Unwilling to relinquish their American citizenship, some of the immigrants drifted sourly north to Oregon. (Sour Oregonians were simultaneously drifting south into California.) The rest hung around the lower Sacramento Valley, tantalized by what they saw. Towering Robert Semple—he stood 6 feet 8 inches tall and had arrived with Lansford Hastings in 1845—put the matter very bluntly in a letter home. A man outfitted "with sufficient teams and farming utensils," he wrote, "may employ as many Indians as he pleases for nothing but their victuals, and that very cheap, and about two shirts and pantaloons of the coarsest kind. He may keep them while he wants them, which is only at seed-time and harvest, and then send them to their villages again for the remainder of the year." That was better than a cotton plantation in the American South. Moreover, it was within even a poor man's reach—if only the Mexicans could be brought to see the light.

A man could defy the law, of course, by squatting on unoccupied land along the edges of the frontier or by making sub rosa agreements with the holders of isolated grants. There were many of those by 1846. Between them, governors Micheltorena and Pico gave away some 600,000 acres in the lower Sacramento and San Joaquin valleys alone, and naturally part of this wild land dribbled illegally into the hands of the newcomers. The subterfuge had its dangers, however. There was no telling when Mexican soldiers might appear with ejection orders.

Nor was that all. The Indians on the distant frontiers favored by the lawbreakers were growing increasingly hostile—and not just California Indians, either. Jim Clyman's immigrants from Oregon had brought along reports that the powerful Walla Walla tribe of the Columbia River country planned to wipe out the American colonies in California in revenge for the murder of their chief's son at Sutter's Fort during a quarrel over a mule. Could—would—California's military comandante, José Castro, help the trespassers if the attacks materialized?

What, indeed, could the outnumbered immigrants expect if war broke out between the United States and Mexico over the recent annexation of Texas? On top of that there were worries about England's intentions. Most Americans in California, including merchant Thomas Larkin, recently appointed as United States consul in Monterey, were convinced that the ancient foe was merely waiting for an excuse to pounce on the province, partly as a flank-protecting stratagem in case of war between Great Britain and the United States over Oregon. If that happened, what would be the situation of the American pioneers who had risked so much to reach California?

Inflaming these fears were deep-seated American antipathies toward

Mexicans in general: Protestants toward Catholics, Anglo-Saxons toward Latins, white backwoodsmen toward the part-Indian mestizos. Naturally many Californios, feeling themselves denigrated, returned the contempt in full measure—and they were the ones who, numerically and politically, held the whip hand. No, life did not seem easy or secure in California in 1845.

Like nervous people everywhere, the immigrants soon began reacting with more emotionalism than good sense. In October, 1845, for example, two prominent Americans in Yerba Buena foolishly interfered with a patrol of Californios who were searching for deserters from a whaling ship. The two meddlers were sorely beaten for their pains. Americans throughout the Bay area thereupon went into an uproar—partly, one suspects, because a United States warship, the *Levant*, happened to be available for showing its muscle. Consul Larkin rushed to Yerba Buena and with the ship at his back protested the incident with a peremptoriness that looked shabby compared to the restraint shown by the local officials—who, to be sure, were less interested in investigating the affair than in sweeping it under the rug.

While the ill will generated by the occasion was still simmering, word reached California that the government in Mexico City, reacting bitterly to the Texas situation, had ordered California's officials "to prevent the introduction of families from the Missouri and Columbia Rivers." Castro carried the decree to Sutter's Fort just as the year's immigrants were coming wearily down the Sierra. Seeing them, the comandante grew either wise or merciful. He could not drive those people back into the face of winter. If he tried, violence would inevitably follow. So he stalled. Foreigners without passports, he decreed, should locate where they could be found until a decision on their case was reached. He also offered to buy Sutter's Fort for a reputed $100,000.

The gestures bred wild alarm. Castro, the immigrants told each other, was simply waiting until he had a stronger army at his command. He would then transform Sutter's Fort from a haven into an obstacle and use it as a base for sweeping the interior valleys clean of Americans.

The immigrants feared that they could not resist, for they had been disappointed in their expectations that a large body of fellow pioneers would arrive in 1845.

Lansford Hastings, it will be recalled, had gone east the year before vowing to recruit 2,000 people. Hoping to add hundreds more to the figure, Sutter had employed Caleb Greenwood, a trapper said to be more than eighty years old, to ride with his half-Indian sons to the forks of the Oregon Trail and persuade emigrants bound for the Northwest to switch to California. It turned out, however, that Hastings recruited only ten people, Greenwood perhaps two hundred. Agitation caused by the failures reached such a pitch, so wrote newcomer W. F. Swasey, that the foreigners at Sutter's Fort formed a home militia and stood sentinel duty at night to prevent Castro's defeating them by a surprise attack.

At that point, December 10, back came John Charles Frémont of the U.S. Corps of Topographical Engineers, a captain now as a reward for his successes in 1843–44. With him were fifteen men, including Kit Carson. This year they were ahead of the snow and topped the Sierra by following the wheel tracks of the immigrants up the Truckee River. A larger division of their expedition, fifty-two men temporarily commanded by topographer Edward Kern and guided by Joseph Reddeford Walker, were still on the other side of the mountains, exploring Owens Valley. They were to cross the range at Walker's Pass and rejoin Frémont in the San Joaquin Valley.

The party's errand, the captain said, was a general survey of the Sierra passes for the benefit of California-bound immigrants. After that the explorers were to examine, at the Army's behest, the trail that ran north into Oregon. Also, Frémont wrote later in his *Memoirs*, he had become enthralled by California's lovely landscape and hoped to find in one of the coastal valleys a place where he could settle later on with his family. He certainly had no intention of raising anyone's hackles . . . he said.

Just how disingenuous was he being? Like the immigrants, he had no passports, and the very appearance of his party raised questions. Did mere mapmaking require a total of sixty-two heavily armed troopers, scientists, and mountain men, plus six tough Delaware Indian hunters—twice the size of the force that Lewis and Clark had led across the continent? Or was topography a pretense? No one, Frémont included, has ever produced satisfactory answers to the puzzle.

After missing Kern in the San Joaquin because of scrambled directions, Frémont returned impatiently to Sutter's Fort. Accompanied by William Ide, one of the more articulate and nervous of the newcomers of 1845, he next journeyed by launch to Yerba Buena. There he conferred with William Leidesdorff, a highly successful trader, son of a Danish seaman and a West Indies black, whom Larkin had appointed vice-consul during the turmoil occasioned by the assault on the two Americans. Thus when Frémont moved on to Monterey early in February, 1846, to visit Castro, he must have thoroughly understood the fears of the immigrants and the emotional responses that he, as the well-armed representative of their government's might, could evoke.

In Monterey, Larkin helped the engineer obtain from the Mexican comandante permission to winter in the Central Valley, provided that his party keep well away from any settlement. Promptly Frémont abused the courtesy. After he had brought his full party together, he camped with them on an abandoned ranch within 13 miles of San Jose. Then, having stirred up resentment there in a dispute over horses, he led his group straight toward Monterey. This was a completely egregious, probably intentional flouting of Castro's hospitality, yet from all Frémont says in his *Memoirs* one would suppose he rode that way merely to enjoy the scenery while looking over potential homesites for himself, his wife, and his mother.

At Hartnell's ranch in the lower Salinas Valley, hardly a morning's ride from the provincial capital, he was met by a messenger from Castro ordering him to be off. Taking umbrage at the rude wording of the dispatch, Frémont sent back ruder words of his own and then retreated to a wooded flat near the summit of Hawk's Peak in the Gabilan Mountains. There his sixty-eight men, as handy with axes as with rifles, threw up a stout breastwork of logs. Let the Mexicans come!

Castro obliged. Drumming together two hundred or more poorly armed but superbly mounted cavalry he rode toward the improvised fortress.

Excited rumor filled the northern settlements. "Great News! War! War!"—so wrote Charles Weber, who had reached California with the Bidwell-Bartleson party in 1841, to John Marsh at Mount Diablo. Farther north, Mariano Vallejo issued a midnight proclamation calling on his countrymen (so reported James Clyman in his diary) "to appear at Sonoma armed and Equiped . . . to defend the rights and priviledges of Mexican citizens."

Fortunately Larkin intervened. Sick of the instability wrought in California by self-serving revolutionaries, he was eager for an American takeover, but not for violence that might rend the province with racial hatreds and perhaps give his favorite bugaboo, Great Britain, an excuse for stepping in. "Caution!" he urged the antagonists—and simultaneously took precautions of his own: he rushed a message by the brig *Hannah* to an American naval squadron cruising off the coast of Mexico. Could a warship be sent to Monterey?

Both Castro and Frémont had been demonstrating partly for the sake of appearances, and now that a fight was at hand neither wanted it. The Mexicans could hardly hope to dislodge the barricaded sharpshooters with a frontal assault, nor could Frémont count on withstanding a long siege of his mountaintop. Perhaps, too, he was disappointed that more settlers did not rally to his cause. Anyway, he suddenly agreed with Larkin that it was not his business to compromise the United States any further. Withdrawing into the Central Valley, he turned north toward Oregon, as his original orders from Washington had told him to do. Castro made no effort to pursue.

Disturbed by the anticlimax, Weber and Marsh dispatched letters throughout the northern area proposing that a convention of "persons of foreign birth" meet in San Jose on July 4—significant date—to discuss ways of protecting their interests. Castro and Governor Pico exchanged heated letters about Castro's handling of the crisis, met grumpily to consider better methods, and ended up more at odds than ever. Castro, indeed, believing that Frémont was at last out of the way, began plotting a revolution to overthrow the governor.

Meantime the spring sun was drying out the land. The immigrants in the interior valleys, half their attention cocked for trouble, found such jobs and farm plots as were available and settled down to work. Sutter expanded like the trees with new plans. Although 1845 had been a disappointing year, '46 should be better. By then Hastings' book, *The Emigrants' Guide*, would have been out long enough to have real impact. On top of that, rumors persisted that 10,000 Mormons were planning to flee from their persecutors in the United States to sanctuary in California.

Why not make ready for the influx, Hastings suggested, by laying out, close to the fort, California's first American-style town, Sutterville? As soon as surveys for the streets and house lots were completed, Hastings would ride east, examine the shortcuts he had described so glibly in his guidebook, and, like Greenwood in '45, divert Oregon-bound travelers to the waiting townsite. They would arrive avid for lumber, flour, grain, beef, leather. . . . Sutter's imagination jumped. Trees suitable for commercial timber did not grow in the Sacramento Valley. Unless he intervened somehow, Larkin and other merchants from Monterey and Santa Cruz would supply the market by shipping in coastal redwood. No! He would find a rival spot in the pine belt along the American River, hew the wood there, and float it down to the fort on the spring rise. What he didn't sell to the settlers, he would use in his own building program. Afire with the prospects, he sent his major-domo, John Bidwell, into the foothills to locate a mill site.

All this while an extraordinary crisis was developing. On April 17, 1846, a hot-tempered, melodramatic young lieutenant named Archibald Gillespie arrived at Monterey after crossing Mexico disguised as an invalid in search of a spa. He had started from Washington in October with written dispatches for Consul Larkin, but had been so alarmed by anti-American demonstrations in Mexico that he had memorized the instructions and had destroyed the papers. In Monterey Gillespie repeated the orders orally. Larkin had been appointed confidential agent of the United

States charged with bringing about a Texas-style separation of California from Mexico. If the independent people of California should then "desire to unite their destiny with ours, they would be received as brethren." Meanwhile, beware of Great Britain!

Even as he talked, Gillespie must have been wondering whether circumstances had not outraced policy. Mexican resentment, stirred by rumors that President Polk of the United States had sent an emissary, John Slidell, to Mexico City with authority to pay up to $40 million for California, had helped touch off the demonstrations that Gillespie had witnessed, and it took no seer to guess that the purchase offer would be rejected. How calmly would Polk take that rebuff?

War was in the wind. As Gillespie knew, General Zachary Taylor's army was camped provocatively at Corpus Christi on ground that Mexico insisted belonged to her, not to Texas. (Actually Taylor had already advanced from Corpus Christi to the Rio Grande, but in April Gillespie was not yet aware of the movement.) In anticipation of a possible clash, Polk had sent orders to Commodore J. D. Sloat, one of whose ships had brought Gillespie from Mazatlán, that Sloat's Pacific Squadron was to occupy Monterey as soon as word arrived that hostilities had been declared. So how much chance was there, really, for a peaceful separation of California from Mexico, followed by voluntary annexation to the United States?

Larkin, who had been working unofficially for those ends ever since his appointment as consul two years before, was willing to try. It may be, too, that Gillespie did not tell him how taut circumstances really were. Obediently, and in all good faith, the consul began his campaign by writing circumspect letters to influential citizens in different parts of the territory, urging them to help prepare California for independence.

Gillespie started north. He had with him, for delivery to Frémont, letters from the captain's father-in-law, Senator Benton, and from Frémont's ambitious wife, Jessie. Whether Gillespie also carried secret messages—why else, his defenders ask, would he ride 600 miles through country filled with restive Indians?—is an enigma which has troubled California historians for more than a century. Let us guess along with the rest.

Two years later, when Frémont's entire conduct during the Mexican war was under scrutiny at an official court-martial, he stated that he received, partly by means of a secret family cipher in the epistles Gillespie delivered, firm instructions to abandon his surveys and return to the scene of probable conflict. There is no convincing documentary evidence of this. The statement, offered during a sensational trial, sounds defensive.

A more normal explanation (but one that would have involved admitting in public that he had disobeyed orders about surveying the trail to Oregon) is easier to swallow. Frémont's career was tied to the Army. Was it not natural for him to hover near the scene of impending action? Hover he did. He dawdled for nearly a month near Peter Lassen's ranch in the upper Sacramento Valley, waiting either for snow to leave the high country ahead of him—or for something to break behind. Late in April he at last moved slowly on, but he was still in the dark pine forests encircling Klamath Lake in southern Oregon when Gillespie overtook him on May 9, 1846.

Whatever else the messenger may have carried in addition to those family letters, he certainly bore with him the rumors of impending war that he had picked up in Mexico—plus one more item. During the Hawk's Peak affair, it will be remembered, Larkin had asked the Pacific Squadron for a warship. Commodore Sloat responded by sending the *Portsmouth*, under Captain John B. Montgomery, to Monterey. Montgomery dropped anchor just after Gillespie had left for the north. With him the captain brought word that Commodore Sloat had recently learned of Mexico's refusal to receive Polk's purchasing agent, John Slidell. Sloat expected to hear momentarily that as a result of the insult war had been declared. Larkin considered this information important enough that he relayed it to Gillespie by special courier.

One can imagine the discussion beside the surveyors' campfire. Would it not be wrong for Frémont to march essential manpower *away* from the crisis shaping up behind him? True, his turning back would be a technical violation of his original orders (unless secret directives had superseded them) and would agitate the Californios. It would disrupt Larkin's campaign to achieve peaceful independence, but wasn't that scheme already outdated? In any event, great opportunities demand great risks.

Fevered by their own speculations, the two young officers forgot to post sentinels when at last they went to bed. Indians crept into camp and killed three men before being driven off with the loss of a chief. Infuriated by the death of his friends, Kit Carson seized the slain Indian's half-ax and passionately chopped up his head with it. The grim party then searched out the village from which the raiders had come, killed fourteen of its inhabitants, and destroyed its huts. Vengeance satisfied, they moved back down the Sacramento Valley, halting finally near the Sutter Buttes, a volcanic mass humping high above the flat plains a little west of present Marysville.

Americans flocked to the camp. Their nerves had been tightened afresh by another of Castro's proclamations warning that foreigners could not hold land in California and by new rumors that an army was on its way to drive illegal settlers out of their homes. On top of that fear came another. Castro, it was said, was sending agents among the valley Indians, urging them to set fire to the settlers' fields of dry, ripe grain.

Convinced that the Indians might do just that, Frémont decided to strike first. One dawn he and most of his men swarmed down the west bank of the Sacramento and fell ferociously on a cluster of unprepared rancherías, burned the houses, and killed several inhabitants. From the immigrants' point of view, results were highly satisfactory. Their flanks were protected now, and they began to think that it might be a good idea to strike the Mexicans, too, by surprise.

Castro provided the opportunity. As the opening move in his campaign to overthrow Governor Pico, the comandante sent a company of troops to Sonoma to pick up 170 horses he needed for his army. Persuading themselves that the animals were to be used against the Americans in the valley, a group of frontiersmen suggested that Frémont lead them in an attack on the herd. He refused, but did nothing to check the raid.

The attackers triumphed without trouble and then proposed bolder action, again without Frémont's participation but certainly with his knowledge. Having picked up a few more reinforcements, they straggled off to Sonoma and at dawn on June 14 burst into the homes of the principal residents. Their bag included Mariano and Salvador Vallejo, both of whom had lately advocated annexation to the United States, Colonel Victor Prudon, and Mariano Vallejo's brother-in-law, Jacob Leese, one of the traders on whose help Larkin was relying in engineering a peaceful absorption of the province.

While some of the Americans regaled themselves with Vallejo's brandy, sobersided William Ide prepared a proclamation reciting the settlers' grievances and clothing their raid in the raiment of liberty. William Todd, a nephew of Mrs. Abraham Lincoln, manufactured a flag. His materials were a Mexican manta (a sheet of unbleached homespun), a red strip cut from his wife's flannel undergarments, and brown paint —or, according to some accounts, brown berry juice. He sewed the strip along the bottom of the rectangular sheet and with his coloring painted, in the upper left-hand corner, a large star reminiscent of the Lone Star of Texas. In the center of the field he drew an animal that he said was a grizzly bear and under it printed "California Republic." When the results were run up the flagpole in the Sonoma plaza, the watching Californios decided among themselves that the purported bear looked more like a hog.

The republic having been achieved by local effort, Frémont moved out from under his guise of neutrality. He appropriated Sutter's Fort, placed Kern in charge, and in spite of the Swiss's dismayed objections thrust

Vallejo and the other prisoners into flea-infested, cell-like rooms. When Castro sent an inadequate force across the bay to dislodge the Bear Flaggers, Frémont's troops joined the skirmishing.

During the scuffles, two noncombatant Americans were ambushed, killed, and, it was widely believed, gruesomely mutilated. In retaliation, Kit Carson's shore patrol shot down in cold blood an old man and his twin nephews as they stepped out of their rowboat after crossing the bay from Yerba Buena. Frémont, too, did some rowing, leading a commando force over the glossy waters one dark night to spike the useless little cannon of the abandoned presidio. But the foray did bring one result. During it the Great Romancer gave the entrance to the bay the name it still bears, the Golden Gate.

When Consul Larkin heard of the Bear Flag uprising, he was incredulous. Why would the government direct him to work for a peaceful acquisition of California and then, by the same messenger, order Frémont to provoke war—if, indeed, Frémont was acting under orders? The madness had destroyed his efforts and had bred hatred where there might yet have been a peaceful mingling of the two peoples—or so he thought at first.

Actually a shattering of his efforts was due in any event. On June 17, Commodore Sloat, cruising off Mazatlán, heard that Zachary Taylor's forces had clashed with the Mexicans beside the Rio Grande. Promptly Sloat sailed to Monterey and then froze with indecision. How could he be sure that the clash on the Rio Grande would necessarily be followed by war? He was unwell, sixty-six years old, and slated soon for retirement. A mistake could be fatal to his sunset years.

For five days he shilly-shallied. Finally, with Larkin pushing him on in hope of cutting ground from under Frémont's more aggressive feet, he consented to occupy the capital. Trying to be as conciliatory as possible, he composed, with Larkin's help, a proclamation fully in accord with international law concerning army-occupied lands but destined nevertheless to breed trouble in California. Until official treaties of peace settled the territory's fate—and how could either Sloat or Larkin foresee how long peace might be delayed?—until then, the proclamation decreed, Mexican laws would remain in force, local officials would continue in office, and titles to real estate would be guaranteed. Those promises solemnly made, Sloat on July 7, 1846, raised the American flag above Monterey. Two days later Yerba Buena and Sonoma were similarly occupied, and the Republic of California was out of business.

Ever resilient, Frémont formed what he called the California Battalion, enrolled his own men in it, and enlisted about a hundred more from the Sonoma and Sacramento areas. Many of the new recruits were former

Bear Flaggers. Although their three weeks' republic had produced little more than confusion and animosity before disappearing, they were proud of it and prevailed on the Battalion to adopt as its standard an improved rendition of their flag. Since then the state of California has accepted the filibusterers' own estimate of themselves. The Bear Flag is the state banner, and a forty-ton statue in Sonoma commemorates its first raising. Conceivably there are those among the million-plus Mexican Americans now living in California who would have preferred a different symbol.

Meantime Frémont had his war, though whether or not he deliberately helped manufacture the California phase of it is something no one is ever likely to learn.

9. The Impatient Conquerors

Sloat's regime in California lasted less than two weeks. On July 15, 1846, he was replaced by newly arrived Commodore Robert Stockton, an energetic strutter known behind his back as Gassy Bob. More proclamations flew. Then, although official notice of war with Mexico had not yet reached the Pacific, Stockton loaded his own men and Frémont's California Battalion aboard transports in the bay and carried the conquest to southern California.

Castro, who had fled to Los Angeles with his hundred-man army, breathed back defiance, also by proclamation. Pio Pico was quieter but more effective. By then the California governor understood the American immigrants' obsession with land and consequently undertook to keep huge acreages out of their hands by issuing grants in wholesale lots to friends, many of them naturalized traders, and to his relatives. He made one slip, however. Because these last bestowals followed the raising of the American flag in Monterey, he antedated the papers, an illegality that in time would cause considerable frustration to the recipients. By the time he had finished his hasty largess, there were more than 800 land grants in California, embracing between 12 million and 13 million acres. By public proclamation both Sloat and Stockton had promised that titles to real estate would be respected. So where did that leave the land-hungry immigrants?

Promising that they would soon return with a large army to dislodge the aggressors, Castro and Pico then fled into Mexico. Unresisted, Stockton and Frémont marched into the pueblos of the south. Kit Carson started east through southern Arizona with a small party to inform President Polk of the victories. Swollen with triumph, Gassy Bob contemplated sailing to Acapulco and winning the war (he had at last received official notice that a war was on) by striking a surprise blow at Mexico City from the west. But first he had to organize California as an occupied territory.

For administrative purposes he divided the inhabited areas into two military districts. Gillespie commanded the south from Los Angeles; Frémont, the north from Monterey. Stockton was the combined military commander and civil governor of the whole, but he promised that when he left for Acapulco he would make Frémont civil governor in his stead. Meantime local political customs were to continue with as little disruption as possible.

That last edict meant that until peace treaties between the nations were signed, the chief official of each California settlement would be the alcalde. Here were the seeds of more trouble, for this exotic functionary, the Mexican alcalde, combined in his single person the duties of mayor, sheriff, justice of the peace, and more besides, mingled in ways that were highly objectionable to American political theory.

As an administrative officer, the alcalde presided over the meetings of the town council, where there was one, and then made sure that its decrees were enforced. As a criminal officer, he could issue warrants, make arrests, sit in judgment, determine the sentence, and see that it was carried out. As a civil officer he held jurisdiction over disputes involving sums of a 100 pesos or less, and he sought to reach settlement not by weighing testimony but through compromise. He had no way, however, to execute writs, enforce the fulfillment of contracts, or assure the collection of debts. His jurisdiction generally extended far beyond the confines of the pueblo where he lived, and if the area was populous, relatively speaking, he was assisted by an alcalde of the second instance, over whom he exerted vague supervisory powers. No juries assisted these busy men. The only check on their law by whim, as American settlers contemptuously described the procedures, was the military governor, who could reverse decisions and remove alcaldes from office at will.

One of Sloat's first actions after raising the American flag had been to ask the Mexican alcaldes of the northern towns to continue in office. Sutter had agreed, of course, but the Mexican alcaldes of Monterey and Yerba Buena had refused to serve under the conquerors. Sloat had therefore appointed two of his own men to office. We shall soon hear more of both: naval Lieutenant Washington Bartlett in San Francisco and Walter D. Colton, chaplain of the battleship *Congress,* in Monterey. On assuming power, Stockton had gone one step further, announcing that on September 15, 1846, the inhabitants of each pueblo in California would be entitled to vote for their own alcalde, replacing, if they chose, those who had been appointed. Both Bartlett and Colton were returned to office by the voters.

This democratic concession did not quiet the protests of the American immigrants. They disliked the outlandish office even when it was held by elected Americans, and they did not—or would not—see why they had to tolerate it. They had won the war in California, hadn't they? A spade was a spade. Why shouldn't American customs take precedence, international law notwithstanding?

Obviously an awkward situation was developing wherein the American governor of occupied California would be obliged either to break the law or else to defy his own countrymen. Before Stockton had to face the issue, however, rebellion erupted in the south and a sharp question arose as to whether the war in California had really been won after all.

Southward, Lieutenant Archibald Gillespie had been ruling Los Angeles with unnecessary harshness. Several incidents rubbed tempers raw, and when he finally tried to arrest a group of half-drunk Mexican protestors, he precipitated an uprising. Striking with more efficiency than the complacent Americans expected, the rebels captured several settlers on outlying ranches, and besieged Gillespie's inadequate force of fifty-odd soldiers on a Los Angeles hillside. That night a messenger managed to slip through the attackers' guard and race north for help, but the spectacular five-day ride wasn't quite fast enough. Before reinforcements could arrive by sea, Gillespie was forced to capitulate.*

Generously the Californios allowed the lieutenant and his men to march south to the harbor at San Pedro on their promise to board a ship there and leave the province forthwith. Gillespie violated the parole by dawdling in the vicinity until Captain William Mervine, sailing rapidly down from the north with 300 sailors and marines, was able to extricate him.

Combining forces, the Americans then set out to retake Los Angeles. It was early autumn. Santa Ana winds were blowing, and heat lay on the plains like an anvil. At places the wild mustard grew taller than a man's head, shutting off such relief as even a hot wind might have brought. Dust fogged up from the marching feet.

The sixty Californios whom José Antonio Carrillo led out to meet the Americans were used to the weather. Moreover, they had with them a little cannon that once had been used in the plaza at Los Angeles for firing occasional salutes. At the time of the occupation an elderly woman had concealed the gun in her home. After the uprising she led Carrillo to it. Delighted, he instructed his best riders to mount the weapon on a stripped-down wagon. Hitching their horses to the vehicle with lariat ropes, they then whirled the little piece of ordnance with dazzling virtuosity through the mustard and across the plains, bewildering the

---

*The American garrison at Santa Barbara managed to flee through the dense chaparral of the Santa Inés Mountains and make their way, footsore and weary, to Monterey. The garrison at San Diego escaped by taking refuge aboard a handy whaling ship.

numerically superior Americans with lightning-like feints through the dust and terrifying them with bursts of grapeshot. After five men had been killed and several wounded, Mervine and Gillespie withdrew to their ships, joined Stockton, and contented themselves with occupying San Diego. The exuberant Mexicans elected José María Flores acting governor and determined to keep on harassing the Americans until Pico and Castro returned with an army to their relief.

In the north guerrillas captured both Lieutenant Washington Bartlett, alcalde of Yerba Buena, and Consul Larkin. After bloodying the only American patrol that managed to make contact with them, they took Larkin to Los Angeles for safekeeping. Frémont, the one American commander still unscathed, began to loom as the only man capable of salvaging the derailed conquest.

He started south, decided that he could not requisition as many horses during the march as he would need, and returned to Sutter's Fort for more animals and more men. The place had had its own alarms. In September, Piopiomoxmox, chief of the Walla Wallas, had stormed south from the Columbia River with 200 warriors to avenge the death of his son. Joseph Revere, Paul's grandson, a naval officer at Sonoma, rushed up marines to aid the defense. Farmers and local Indians joined them at the fort, and shortly thereafter the vanguard of the year's emigration creaked in from the Sierra. Faced by so formidable a gathering, Piopiomoxmox cooled off and even let some of his braves enlist under Frémont.

The recruiting for the reconquest lasted from October 20 through November 17, 1846. During that period Lansford Hastings, promoter of Sutterville, arrived at the fort with a train of wagons he had diverted from the Oregon Trail to his "shortcut" through the furnace-hot deserts south and west of Great Salt Lake. Although the folly had put his caravan well behind the immigrants who stuck to the longer route through southern Idaho, he was lucky and crossed the Sierra ahead of the first snow. The eighty-seven members of the Donner group, who also had listened to Hastings, and were dragging far behind, were less fortunate. Seven mule loads of food that Sutter sent to them in charge of two Indians proved inadequate, and snow trapped the worn, belated party near the lovely mountain lake that still bears their name. Before heroic rescuers managed to bring out the survivors, Sutter's two Indians and thirty-eight more men, women, and children had died. The bodies of many of them helped sustain some of the living.

Unaware of the disaster shaping up in the mountains, Frémont started south with 428 men and a long caravan of pack animals and extra riding horses. A torrential Christmas rainstorm struck the column as it was stumbling down steep San Marcos Pass behind Santa Barbara. A hundred or more horses died in the flooded ravines. The men all escaped, though there was discomfort enough that night in a fireless camp between sodden blankets, with "cold streams of water," wrote volunteer Edwin Bryant, "running through the tent and around our bodies."

By this time an unexpected squeeze was developing for the Californios. General Stephen Watts Kearny, having completed a bloodless conquest of New Mexico, was riding west with 300 dragoons to fulfill Polk's orders that he establish an American government in California. On meeting Kit Carson's dispatch carriers and learning that the coastal province had been subdued, as Carson believed, Kearny sent all but 100 of his men back to New Mexico. With the rest he continued over Arizona's difficult trails to the crossing of the Colorado River near the villages of the Yuma Indians. Plodding behind him, searching for a route suitable for wagons, came Philip St. George Cooke and a battalion of Mormons who had enlisted for the duration in order to send their pay to Brigham Young for furthering the exodus of their brethren to Utah.

Hearing of Kearny's approach, Stockton sent Gillespie and thirty-eight marines from San Diego to meet the newcomers. Andrés Pico, brother of the decamped governor, also rode toward them with an improvised cavalry regiment of superb riders equipped with little else than lances and lariat ropes. The attack came at dawn on December 6, a time of murky rain and fog, near little San Pascual, one of the few Indian pueblos Figueroa had managed to establish during the days of secularization. The Californios lured the vanguard of the Americans into a reckless charge —the damp weather had destroyed the priming of many of their guns— then turned and struck. Twenty-two of the invaders died. Seventeen were wounded, including both Kearny and Gillespie. Pico was unable to press his advantage, however, and when Stockton at last sent reinforcements, after a cruel delay, the march into San Diego was resumed.

Lacking adequate armament and disputing among themselves, the Californios fell back toward Los Angeles. After two fruitless skirmishes, they yielded the pueblo. Because many of their officers had violated the paroles given them earlier in the war on condition they not bear arms again, they feared death penalties if captured by either Kearny or Stockton. Frémont, however, had recently pardoned a cousin of Pico's for a similar offense. Accordingly the Californios fled across Cahuenga Pass to surrender to him on January 13, 1847. He responded with a generous amnesty, although technically he should not have accepted the capitulation when his superior officers were only a few miles away. Stockton approved, nevertheless, and, as promised, appointed Frémont civil governor of the reconquered province.

In a flush of euphoria, the new governor entrusted Larkin with $3,000 to buy a ranch for him on the peninsula south of San Francisco, where he and Jessie could make their home. Through an ambiguous "misunderstanding" as difficult to comprehend as are the other events in Frémont's California career, Larkin bought instead, from Juan Bautista Alvarado, a 45,000-acre grant called Las Mariposas, the Butterflies. Located where the distant Merced River wound through the foothills on the east side of the San Joaquin Valley, it was almost uninhabitable because of hostile Indians. Frémont was furious. Before he could rectify matters, however, he was caught in the middle of a splenetic quarrel between General Kearny and Commodore Stockton as to who was the supreme commander of the American forces in California.

Frémont naturally supported Stockton, who had first enrolled his California Battalion in the army and afterward had named him governor. Defiantly he established his headquarters in Los Angeles. Not quite daring to try dislodging him by force (together Stockton and Frémont controlled by far the greatest number of troops in California), General Kearny went sullenly to Monterey to take over the reins of government there.

Unhappily for himself, Frémont had picked the wrong man. Late in February, 1847, orders arrived in Washington confirming Kearny's top position in California. Stockton made a dignified withdrawal. As a Navy officer he was beyond Kearny's reach. A victim was available, however —Frémont. Kearny not only ended the explorer's brief governorship but also stripped him of his military prerogatives. That exercise in vindictiveness was hardly finished when, in the routine ways of the military merry-go-round, Kearny himself was replaced as California's civil governor and military commander by Colonel Richard B. Mason and was ordered to report to Washington for reassignment. He took Frémont across the Sierra with him under technical arrest.

To the Californios it was all very amusing. The Americans had been wont to mock them for political instability, but look at what was happening: the familiar, spiteful dissensions between rival officers, and the same dizzy sequence of appointed administrators. In eleven months they had been "governed" by five men—Sloat, Stockton, Frémont, Kearny, and Mason. Even the Californios' record of five in fourteen months (September, 1835, through November, 1836) was eclipsed by the parade.

In the East, Frémont was tried and, despite the roaring defense of his father-in-law, Senator Benton, was convicted of mutiny, disobedience, and misconduct to the prejudice of good order and discipline. Technically correct, the decision was nevertheless unnecessarily harsh. Seeking to calm Benton's resentment, Polk offered to reinstate the humiliated officer in the service. Neither the senator nor his son-in-law was placated.

In towering outrage, Frémont refused the gesture and as a civilian turned again toward California to restore the luster to his name—but more of that and of Benton's manipulations, later on.

Even while the insurgent Californios still held most of the south, immigrants in the north were hard at work Americanizing the territory. In August, 1846, a month before his position as alcalde of Monterey had been confirmed by the September elections, Walter Colton unearthed the ancient press on which Mexican officials had once printed their sonorous proclamations. Joining forces with long-shanked Robert Semple, he used it for producing the territory's first newspaper, the *Californian*. Three weeks later, when cantankerous Isaac Graham sued a French neighbor over the ownership of certain lumber, Colton was responsible for yet another innovation. He summoned a mixed jury of Californios and Americans to hear the testimony and was so pleased by their verdict (Graham won) that he wrote exultantly, "If there is anything on earth beside religion for which I would die, it is the right of trial by jury."

(He could be bizarre, nonetheless. When an outraged Mexican mother complained to him that her grown son had struck her, he allowed the woman to horsewhip the young man in the public square. Later, after deciding that Monterey needed a two-story municipal building to double as schoolhouse and meeting hall, he set about erecting it with yellow stone quarried and put into place by felons whom he himself had sentenced, not always through jury trial, to do the work.)

Washington Bartlett of Yerba Buena, who, like Colton, was confirmed in his alcaldeship by the September elections, thrust American ways into his Mexican town with equal vigor. The village by the cove was growing prodigiously, at least in terms of percentages. The single greatest increase came on July 31, 1846, when the miserable tub *Brooklyn*, six months out of New York by way of Cape Horn, dropped anchor with 238 quarrelsome Mormons aboard—70 men, 68 women, and 100 children—led by Sam Brannan, twenty-eight years old and a printer by trade. The contentious group had left the East Coast ahead of the declaration of war with Mexico, hoping to find a haven in foreign California where they would be joined by Brigham Young and several thousand more Mormons marching overland from Illinois. Instead, they discovered that they were back in American territory, and they did not know quite what to do—except sit down and wait for Young.

They inundated Yerba Buena. Some found shelter in the old adobe Mexican custom house near the shore. Some trooped southwest across the sandhills to the deserted remnants of Mission Dolores. Several lived in wind-whipped tents. Twenty went reluctantly, under Brannan's prodding, to the Central Valley. Where the Stanislaus River pours into the San Joaquin, they launched a colony named New Hope, projected nucleus of the new Mormon empire. Brannan, however, returned very soon to Yerba Buena. That magnificent bay—there was the future! Unlimbering a printing press he had brought with him, he issued, on January 9, 1847, the territory's second newspaper, the *California Star*. It simply was not possible, it would seem, for Americans to exist without newsprint.

As other hopefuls continued to drift into Yerba Buena, a demand arose for house and commercial lots. This placed an unfamiliar burden on Alcalde Bartlett. The village lay within the confines of the four square leagues originally granted by the Spanish government to the presidio of San Francisco. Titles to lots could be passed out only by the official alcaldes of the district, acting under prescribed conditions.

Bartlett, who had a tidy mind, wanted to make the distribution in orderly fashion. Accordingly he hired engineer Jasper O'Farrell to extend a modest early survey, made in 1839 by storekeeper Jean Jaquez Vioget, into a ground plan for a truly ambitious town, American style —ruler-straight streets intersecting at stiff right angles, even though this would eventually mean, to use the words of philosopher Josiah Royce, chewing "cruel stripes [into] the sturdy forms of the noble hills." But O'Farrell's instruments were precise, the plan was progressive, and a landowner knew exactly where his property lay in reference to every other square foot of ground in the town. Never mind the landscape.

Yerba Buena's success stirred rivalry. Why not build a competing town somewhere along the northern reaches of the bay, closer to the strait that opened into the great river highways of the Central Valley? Unfortunately, from an American view, the area there was embraced by land grants, and the Mexican owners seemed exceedingly lacking in imagination. They did not understand town promoting. Their government and the Spanish before them had always decreed where pueblos could be located. For an ordinary citizen simply to arrogate this right unto himself struck them as a dangerous presumption. *Mañana*, my friend, after we have seen what happens in other places.

Restless Robert Semple, drifting away from the Monterey newspaper in search of more profitable pursuits, was the one who broke the barrier. Backed by Thomas Larkin, he approached Mariano Vallejo, owner of broad reaches of land on the north side of Carquinez Strait. As the founder of government-authorized Sonoma, Vallejo had had some experience in founding towns. He listened carefully to Semple, even though the gigantic American, coonskin cap atop his shaggy head and stained buckskins clinging to his elongated shanks, had been one of the Bear Flaggers who had incarcerated him among the ravenous fleas of Sutter's Fort.

In the face of profit, why bear grudges? The new partners laid out, beside Carquinez Strait, a town named Francesca. This was Semple's compliment to Vallejo's wife, one of whose Christian names was Francesca, and it was also calculated to draw to the embryo city some of the fame associated with the name of the bay. But alas for cleverness. Alcalde Bartlett retorted by issuing an ordinance dated January 30, 1847, that changed the name of Yerba Buena to San Francisco, after the presidio. Because San Francisco was a going concern and Francesca was not, the promoters of the latter place substituted another of Doña Vallejo's Christian names, Benicia. Surely location favored them, they thought, and with that advantage on their side what then was in a name?

By this time it was evident that Pico and Castro were not going to return with an avenging army and that the war in California was over. Vociferously the Americans renewed their demands that they be allowed to live under their own forms of government. In February, 1847, Semple fired off a blast to his former newspaper at Monterey, calling for a convention that would prepare a set of laws in anticipation of Congress' admission of California as a territory of the United States. Promoter Lansford Hastings followed this with a proposal that the people elect a legislature whose primary duty would be the enactment of bills allowing home seekers to occupy vacant lands anywhere in California—with the legislature, which would be dominated by Americans, ruling on what was to be considered vacant. The devil take these monstrous land grants!

Kearny, who had not yet left for the East with Frémont in tow, quashed both proposals. As yet, he said, nothing had occurred to change the rules of the game. Until a formal peace treaty declared otherwise, it was his responsibility to make sure that Mexican law remained in force as promised by Sloat and Stockton.

Although his firmness temporarily dimmed the rumbles for legislative change, another challenge to his authority was raised by obstreperous John H. Nash, erstwhile Bear Flagger and the duly elected alcalde of Sonoma. Because of Nash's misdeeds in office, Kearny ordered him replaced by Lillburn Boggs, a former governor of Missouri and an immigrant of 1846. Nash defied ejection on the grounds that he had been elected and the power of the people under all circumstances transcended that of the military.

At that juncture Kearny was replaced by Colonel Richard B. Mason. Picking up the challenge, Mason ordered Captain Brackett of the Sonoma garrison to toss Nash out of office and install Boggs. Military tyranny! Rising in noisy demonstration, the American residents of Sonoma dared Brackett to try. The captain caved in and wrote Mason that inasmuch as he hoped to settle in Sonoma after his discharge from the Army, he would rather not stir up a hornet's nest right then.

Mason, tall, light-haired, and craggy-faced, was by nature gentle and accommodating. On reading Brackett's letter, however, he went livid and ordered his troops to prepare to march. His chief of staff, a young lieutenant named William Tecumseh Sherman, interposed then and suggested that they avoid civil strife (you can find irony anywhere) by the simple expedient of kidnapping the recalcitrant Nash. Mason told him to try. Borrowing a boat and a few marines from a ship in San Francisco Bay, Sherman rowed up twisting Sonoma Creek under the pretense of looking for suspected criminals. He pounced on Nash during the dark of the night, spirited him away, and gently persuaded him to resign in Boggs's favor. There were loud yowls of protest throughout the north, but the point had been made: until contrary orders came from Washington, the impatient conquerors would accept what international law said they must.

Thus squeezed, they settled down to business. California was growing mightily, thanks to military infusions. Philip St. George Cooke's famed Mormon Battalion marched into San Diego late in January, 1847, and then scattered out on garrison duty. Six weeks later four transports arrived on the West Coast laden with nearly 1,000 New York volunteers commanded by a Tammany politician, Colonel J. D. Stevenson. Like some Mexican soldiers before them, the New Yorkers had been recruited with the understanding that after their discharge they would settle in California.

Because the territory was pacified by the time they disembarked, they took over garrison duty from the Mormons, who were then free to rejoin their fellow saints. But join where? To his dismay Sam Brannan learned that instead of continuing to California, Brigham Young's people were halting at Great Salt Lake. As soon as the Sierra passes were open in the spring of '47, Sam made a desperate ride east to change the prophet's mind. Young refused. Wheeling stubbornly around, Sam returned that same summer to California. Let his own shipload of pioneers, including the founders of the forlorn New Hope Colony, and the members of the Battalion go to Utah if they wished—eventually many did—but he intended to stay. Opportunity, he hoarsely assured everyone who would listen, lay beside the Pacific.

Others thought so, too. Semple opened a ferry over Carquinez Strait, hoping to feed people into Benicia. Charles Weber laid out on his land grant beside the San Joaquin River a hamlet first called Tuleberg but soon rechristened Stockton. William Leidesdorff launched the first steam vessel on San Francisco Bay (only to see it sink three months later). Don Benito Wilson drove a pioneer trail herd of cattle north from Los Angeles County and made a fat profit selling breeding stock to ranchers who had depleted their own herds selling beef to the military. Sutter, whose grandiose plans had been interrupted by the war, grew more active than ever. Among other things he hired that dour carpenter, James Marshall, who had come south from Oregon with Jim Clyman in 1845, to resume Bidwell's abandoned search for a sawmill site somewhere along the South Fork of the American River. (Bidwell, who had never really believed in the project, had gone to ranching for himself farther north in the Sacramento Valley, near today's Chico.)

The Californios watched all this with mixed feelings. These strange Americans, who seemed to think that they had a divine mission to reform the world, were very brusque and assertive. Even so, the Californios felt entitled to their respect. During the past seventy-eight years they had created, out there on the farthest rim of the continent and with a minimum of help from Mexico City, a distinctive culture. They had shown, in the closing battles of the war, that they could fight with dash for the things they believed in. Although the Americans in the north equaled them in numbers, the north was not all of California. Southward, the Californios still held sway. During the September elections they had captured half the alcaldeships in the territory, including the important northern one of San Jose. They were still allied with the leading traders. They owned the vast bulk of the land. Given time, surely they could mingle, heads high, with these domineering yet vibrant and exciting newcomers.

Time for adjustment, for—but no. Not with James Marshall, riding beside his Indian guide into the foothills on a routine errand toward a hollow that the inland tribes called Coloma.

part three

LOST IN
A GOLDEN WILDERNESS

10. "It Made My Heart Thump"

Helped by his Indian guide, Marshall easily found, at the place called Coloma, the sawmill site that had eluded Bidwell. It was about 45 miles by trail from Sutter's Fort, on the floor of a basin whose pine-clad hills were gentle enough for wagons loaded with machinery to descend them. The south fork of the American River curved through the valley bottom in a big C, so that cutting a race across the flat for powering the mill's waterwheel would be no problem.

Pleased with the physical layout, Marshall returned to the fort and on August 27, 1847, signed a partnership agreement with Sutter whereby the Swiss would provide men, tools, livestock, and money for building the sawmill while Marshall furnished know-how and supervision. Sutter's grant did not include the basin, and so he had no legal right to cut timber there. But if the Indians didn't object, who would?

Manpower threatened to be the major problem. Fever had flattened the Indians on whom Sutter depended for most of his labor, and he feared he would not be able to harvest his wheat, let alone erect mills—plural, for he wanted to build a flour mill at the edge of the foothills as well as a sawmill. Then luck smiled. As mentioned earlier, the Mormon Battalion.had disbanded during the summer of 1847 and many of the soldiers started east to join their coreligionists beside Great Salt Lake. An emissary met them to collect their pay, which Brigham Young badly needed, and urged them to winter in California so that their needs for food and clothing would not place additional burdens on the new colony. Several of the disappointed men asked Sutter for jobs. Delighted, he put part of them to work around the fort. Others he sent, along with a few non-Mormons and Indians, up the river. Some were to build the flour mill where the stream foamed out of the foothills; the others were to continue on upstream to Coloma.

The sawmill was completed in January, 1848, but the millrace needed deepening before it would function properly. The workers chipped out the bottom and one evening turned river water into the channel to wash away the debris. Early the next morning—the date was sometime between January 19 and 24, 1848, with the 24th most likely—Marshall went out to inspect the work. The story he told afterward to artist Charles Gillespie contains the most famous sentences in California history:

"My eye was caught by something shining in the bottom of the ditch. . . . I reached my hand down and picked it up; it made my heart thump, for I was certain it was gold. The piece was about half the size and shape of a pea. Then I saw another. . . ."

What had happened, of course, was that the millrace had acted like a sluice box. The running water had tumbled the yellow fragments out of their resting place with the gravel and had started them rolling along the current. Being heavier than the other material, they had then settled to the bottom of the first quiet eddy, much as millions of other fragments would later settle behind riffles in the long toms and sluice boxes of tens of thousands of miners. But although the mechanics of the matter were ordinary, the results were not. Men's concepts of the possible would never again be quite the same.*

Sensing that he had stumbled onto something big, Marshall rode through a winter deluge to Sutter's Fort. Behind locked doors the two men tested the material (a tattered encyclopedia suggested ways), and after being convinced that the flecks really were gold Marshall returned to Coloma. Torn by ambivalences, Sutter soon followed. He wanted to be in on the discovery, if it really amounted to anything, but he also wanted the sawmill finished. With a persuasive show of fairness he told the workers that they could scratch into cracks in the bedrock for gold during their spare time—he even provided the knives—but in return he asked that they say nothing to outsiders about the discovery. And would they promise to stay on the job until the mill was running? They agreed.

To copper his bets Sutter then met with neighborhood Indians and leased from them ten square miles of land around the mill for $150 worth of shirts, hats, beads, flour, and dried peas. That ought to keep trespassers away—if the lease held up. To make sure it did, he sent one of his men,

---

*Soon after Marshall's discovery, tales began popping up about earlier finds in the Sierra Nevada. Walter Colton insists that a year before the discovery on the American River, an Indian told Colton's secretary, W. F. Swasey, of gold on the Stanislaus. Trader William Heath Davis belatedly recalled that on occasion Indians brought in shiny flakes to the mission fathers; fearing disaster if the word spread, the padres persuaded the Indians to say nothing. After talking to certain chiefs near Coloma, Editor E. C. Kemble of the *California Star* told a similar story. At this late date there seems no way either to prove or to disprove the yarns.

Charles Bennett, to Governor Mason in Monterey with a copy of the agreement and a six-ounce vial of yellow grains. Surely California's new government would protect honest enterprise of such moment.

Plans soon went awry. Marshall and the Mormons did stay on the job as promised, picking up occasional nuggets on Sundays and during the lengthening spring twilights. Secrecy was something else. Sutter himself talked. So did the children of the woman cook at the mill. So did Charles Bennett on his way to Monterey during the middle of February, 1848, and it chanced that one of the men who heard Bennett was Isaac Humphrey, a veteran miner from the gold fields of Georgia. As for the lease —no. Writing Sutter on behalf of Governor Mason, young Lieutenant William Tecumseh Sherman said that inasmuch as the United States did not officially own California, no representative of the American government could sanction such a lease; besides, American policy frowned on private land dealings between whites and Indians. With monumental lack of foresight, Sherman then added that since there was no settlement within 40 miles of the mill, Sutter was not likely to be disturbed by trespassers.

Because records are sparse, it is impossible to be sure of what happened next, but the sequence probably went like this. At the end of February, three Mormons working on the gristmill lower down the South Fork of the American River walked up to Coloma to visit friends at the sawmill and learn what the rumors of gold amounted to. On their return they noticed a topographical arrangement like the one at Coloma: a broad, C-shaped curve in the main riverbed and an overflow channel, resembling the millrace, that during high water created a kind of gravelly island in the valley bottom. Experimenting, the trio found gold. Sporadically thereafter they and their fellows from the gristmill scratched away in the bedrock with knives and spoons whittled from cow horns—the great horn spoon of folksay. This, apparently, was the first indication that the deposits at Coloma were not localized, as Lopez's 1842 discovery in southern California had been. By summer the new diggings were famous. Their name, Mormon Island, commemorates those who found them.

Meanwhile other discharged soldiers from the Mormon Battalion were gathering at Sutter's Fort to wait until enough snow melted in the high country to let them cross the mountains to Utah. They too heard of the gold and filled their time by journeying to Coloma, along with a few non-Mormons, to see the yellow harvest. By then enough information was floating around that they took tools with them—hoes, shovels, picks, and various scrapers made from wood. With these they could clear over-burden away from the bedrock whose pockets and crevices reputedly contained nuggets.

Their endless requests for guidance annoyed Marshall. He had sawed his first log on March 11, but there were still bugs to iron out of the operation, and these fevered visitors delayed matters deplorably. He waved them away, saying that they could find gold underneath any of the shallow gravel banks near the river and in the adjoining ravines. And they did.

During this same period Isaac Humphrey, the Georgia miner to whom Charles Bennett had talked, traveled up from San Francisco to see the source of Bennett's six-ounce vial of gold. The scrambling of the greenhorns amused him. Strutting a little, he showed them how things had been done in Georgia.

Somewhere he obtained a pan—an ordinary frying pan, most likely—and shoveled in earth from a selected spot. He picked the pebbles out of the mass and then, crouching beside the cold stream, dipped up water. Dexterously swirling the mixture about, he let the dirt slop bit by bit over the brim until only a little heavy sand remained, sparkling with pinpoints of gold. He put this into a container of some sort and worked another pan —how many one can't say. As a general matter, though, a man who had the hang of things could wash fifty pans a day. The take was then dried over the supper campfire, spread out on a flat surface, and the sand gently blown away from the gold with one's breath.

It was common in those early times to end the evening with at least two ounces of metal, and sometimes much more if luck had been good. In an era when clerks earned $50 a month and soldiers $7, those were dazzling, if uncertain, wages. At an Eastern mint one ounce of pure gold would bring $20.67. The East was a long way off, however, and some dross always clung to newly washed dust. Consequently neither Humphrey nor anyone else knew quite what to expect. But at least the handful of men in the valley learned from his demonstrations that there were quicker ways than clerking to grow rich. Swiftly they pressed all kinds of receptacles into service—cooking pans, bowls carved from wood, tightly woven Indian baskets, even shovel blades.

Satisfied that there really was considerable gold in the valley, Humphrey joined forces with one of the erstwhile mill builders and went to Sutter with a proposal: why not form a company to mine all Coloma? This was a bold concept and could hardly have been effected with knife blades and frying pans. Humphrey, however, had still another mechanical device in mind, again one he had used in Georgia—the cradle.

As its name suggests, a cradle was an oblong box on rockers, set in such a way as to slope from one end toward the other. One or more men dug and transported earth to a stockpile beside the machine, which had to be located close to water. Another shoveled the piled dirt into a hopper placed above the upper end of the cradle. A perforated sheet of wood or metal in the bottom of the hopper screened out pebbles. Water dipped vigorously into the hopper by still another worker carried the material down into the main box. As it cascaded in, the man who dipped the water kept shaking the cradle on its rockers so as to break up the mass. The jiggled stream then poured toward the lower end of the sloping box. Along the way the heavy particles of gold settled behind low riffles, or cleats, nailed at right angles to the flow.

As with panning, light particles of metal washed over the lip with the mud and were lost, but where gold was abundant the inefficiency was overlooked. A team of men working with a cradle could treat far more earth in a day than could a loner with a pan, but the total take would have to be divided among several partners—unless laborers could be employed at low rates. This was the hope that prompted Humphrey and his friend to approach Sutter: would the Swiss provide them with Indians and supplies enough for operating several cradles? It was an almost inevitable suggestion. California's pastoral economy had long depended on exploiting large acreages with cheap labor, and men familiar with the peonage naturally sought to adapt the system to the new industry.

Sutter signed the contract on, probably, April 3, 1848. Shortly thereafter, and well before the Indians could be gathered together and trained, a potentially unwelcome visitor appeared at the fort. He was Edward C. Kemble, not yet out of his teens but the editor nevertheless of Sam Brannan's *California Star*. He wanted to know exactly what was going on at Coloma.

He was not very excited. Rumors about gold in the foothills had been going around San Francisco for several weeks. Both Kemble and the editor of the rival *Californian* had mentioned the stories in little notices on the back pages of their papers. Reaction had consisted mostly of shrugs; if there was gold up there, it probably was as limited in scope as the placers that López had found in Southern California six years earlier. Still, there is that touch of magic in the very sound of the word. *Gold* . . . Kemble decided that he'd better take a look. Toward the beginning of April he sailed with two friends in a river sloop to Sutter's Fort, a seven-day trip. From there they rode to Coloma with the Swiss himself as a guide.

By digging a pit to bedrock and swirling mud from it in an Indian basket, the investigators managed to recover a few infinitesimal yellow flakes. This, a treasure! It was as meager as they had expected. Furthermore, Sutter made no effort to reassure them, perhaps because he wanted his new company established before a stampede of outsiders developed. Kemble returned to his paper convinced that the whole business was a

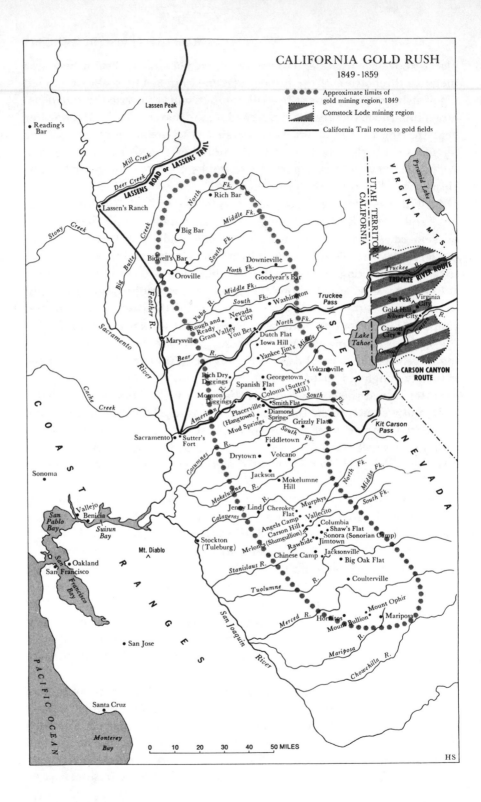

CALIFORNIA GOLD RUSH
1849 - 1859

●●●●● Approximate limits of gold mining region, 1849

Comstock Lode mining region

—— California Trail routes to gold fields

Lassen Peak
^

Reading's Bar

Mill Creek

Deer Creek

LASSENS ROAD or LASSENS TRAIL

North Fk.

Rich Bar

Middle Fk.

Big Bar

Lassen's Ranch

South Fk.

Butte Creek

Bidwell's Bar

Downieville

Oroville

North Fk.

Goodyear's Bar

Feather R.

Big

Middle Fk.

South Fk.

Washington

Truckee Pass

Yuba R.

Nevada City

Rough and Ready

Grass Valley

You Bet

Dutch Flat

North Fk.

Middle Fk.

Stony Creek

Marysville

Iowa Hill

Yankee Jim's

Sacramento River

Bear R.

Rich Dry Diggings

Volcanoville

Georgetown

Spanish Flat

Coloma (Sutter's Mill)

South Fk.

Cache Creek

Mormon Diggings

Smith Flat

Placerville (Hangtown)

Diamond Springs

Grizzly Flat

American R.

Mud Springs

Sacramento

Sutter's Fort

Fiddletown

South Fk.

Kit Carson Pass

Cosumnes R.

Drytown

Volcano

Sonoma

Jackson

Mokelumne Hill

North Fk.

Middle Fk.

Mokelumne R.

South Fk.

Vallejo

Benicia

San Pablo Bay

Suisun Bay

Jenny Lind

Cherokee Flat

Murphys

Calaveras R.

Angels Camp

Vallecito

Columbia

Shaw's Flat

Carson Hill

Sonora (Sonorian Camp)

Oakland

San Francisco

Mt. Diablo
^

Stockton (Tuleburg)

Melones (Slumgullion)

Jimtown

Rawhide

Jacksonville

San Francisco Bay

Chinese Camp

Big Oak Flat

Stanislaus R.

Coulterville

Tuolumne R.

Mount Ophir

Merced R.

Hornitos

Mount Bullion

Mariposa

San Joaquin River

Mariposa R.

Chowchilla R.

San Jose

COAST RANGES

PACIFIC OCEAN

Santa Cruz

Monterey Bay

SIERRA NEVADA

Truckee R.

TRUCKEE RIVER ROUTE

Sun Peak
^

Virginia City

Gold Hill

Silver City

Carson City

Carson R.

Genoa

Lake Tahoe

CARSON CANYON ROUTE

UTAH TERRITORY
CALIFORNIA

VIRGINIA MTS.

Pyramid Lake

0   10   20   30   40   50 MILES

HS

humbug. Farmers and mechanics, he wrote, should "stick to their calling and let the gold-mines severely alone."

Even stranger than Sutter's actions were those of Kemble's boss, Sam Brannan, owner of the *California Star*. The previous fall Sam and Charles Smith had opened a store in a rented room in Sutter's Fort. They had also built a little warehouse and boat landing on the tree-lined bank of the Sacramento River. Smith ran the store while Brannan returned to his other affairs in San Francisco. He shuttled back and forth quite often, and early in April he too went to Coloma and Mormon Island to investigate. He found gold, but he did not tell his editor so, even though they were in the district at the same time, though possibly without each other's knowledge.

Brannan was excitable by nature. Exuberance alone may have led him to stuff a quinine bottle with gold dust that he could show in San Francisco. But he was also a canny promoter, and it may have occurred to him that a rush of people into the area would benefit his and Charley Smith's store only insofar as they had merchandise on hand to sell. So he may have gained time for assembling some by letting Kemble print the discouraging report. In any event, people did stay away from the gold mines. May 12 had arrived—time enough for the partners to have done considerable buying on the sly if they wished—before Brannan strode along Montgomery Street in San Francisco waving his bottle and shouting at startled passers-by, "Gold! Gold! Gold in the American River!"

The strategy worked, if strategy it was. By the end of the month only old men, sick people, women, and children remained in San Francisco. The news leaped to other towns, and their excited inhabitants too headed for the American River by way of Sutter's Fort and the Brannan-Smith store. Indeed, the only people who did not succumb were those who had been first on the scene, the Mormons. As soon as the high country was open, most of them turned loyally away from the gold fields and chopped a new road over the Sierra Nevada south of Lake Tahoe, so that they could reach their friends and families in Utah. How much mineral they took with them is unknown, but it was enough to give a considerable boost to Brigham Young's struggling colony.

Brannan and Smith reaped well. In six weeks the store at Sutter's Fort grossed $36,000, and Sam bought out Charley Smith for another $50,000. By then so many men were in the hills that he decided to establish branch stores at both Coloma and Mormon Island.

Let's not give Sam too much credit for the rush, however. He simply triggered what was bound to have happened very soon, anyway. Throughout April and May ranchers from nearby valleys had been drifting in and out of Coloma, attracted by the same rumors Kemble had heard. They saw what Kemble didn't, however—the Sutter-Humphrey Indians at work. Because they too had peons at their disposal, they realized that opportunity was not merely knocking but battering. It was this amazing group of self-servers, not storekeeper Brannan, who showed the world how enormous the gold fields really were. Unfortunately their accomplishments—and the accomplishments of their Indians—have been dimmed by the later homage paid to the more numerous and far more vocal forty-niners who followed them.

Notable among the sharp-eyed pioneers of '48 were three of Sutter's ex-employees—John Sinclair, a Scot who had reached California in 1839; Pierson Reading, whose ranch far up the Sacramento River within sight of Mount Shasta's shimmering cone was the northernmost grant ever issued by the Mexicans; and John Bidwell, whom we have met before.

According to Sutter's diary, Sinclair looked over the region on April 11. Soon thereafter he brought fifty Indians to Coloma, trained them by imitating Humphrey's crew, then dropped down to the forks of the American, mined awhile, and afterward worked up the north branch. Results were spectacular. More significantly, the people pouring out of San Francisco soon knew that the whole drainage of the American offered promise.

Bidwell and Reading extended possibilities still further. Returning to his primitive ranch near today's Chico, Bidwell gathered up his Indians and marched them southeast to the Feather River, the Sacramento's principal tributary. There, on July 4, 1848, he made one of the great strikes of the gold rush, Bidwell's Bar. This meant that there was now an entire new river system to explore—one destined to produce hundreds of millions of dollars. For Bidwell, who quickly turned from mining back to farming, it meant riches enough to develop his Chico ranch into an agricultural showplace known throughout the world. Presidents came to visit him there; many years later, indeed, he himself was a presidential candidate.

During that same summer of 1848, Pierson Reading boldly turned his back on the Sierra Nevada and led his Indians northwest from his home between present Red Bluff and Redding to the Trinity River in the Trinity Mountains. He hit, too. As a result there was a whole new mountain chain to mine, a matter of moment to Oregon prospectors when they began streaming south later in the year to share the wealth.

Other ranchers with Indians at their beck and call followed comparable patterns. Jacob Leese and four friends from Sonoma unearthed $75,-000 on the Yuba, which flows into the Feather at today's Marysville. Nearby on the same stream, John Marsh's party, Indians included, found what later became famed as Park's Bar. Before Marsh fell so ill that he had to be carried home, he personally reaped $40,000, some of it at the rate of $50 an hour. Afterward he profited almost as much by sending beef, smoked ham, grain, and grapes from his Mount Diablo ranch to the diggings. Blossoming under the sun of those riches, the once miserly old misanthrope married the first American schoolmarm in San Jose, bedecked her in clusters of pearls that his fancy demanded be shaped like bunches of grapes, built her an astounding gimcrack mansion beside his old floorless adobe—and sat beside her bed as she died not long after they moved in.

Charles Weber of Tuleberg, a companion of Bidwell's on the pioneering 1841 trek across the continent, trained his Indians on a little stream that drains into the South Fork near Coloma (the tributary thereafter was known variously as Weaver and Weber Creek) and as an incident to this opened the way for William Daylor's discovery of the fabled Dry Diggings that later spawned the town of Placerville. Meantime Weber sent twenty-five of his trained Indians south to see whether or not there was more gold on either the Tuolumne River or the Stanislaus River. There was, especially in the Columbia-Sonora district. It, too, produced during its lifetime well over $100 million, a matter of considerable interest to the native Californians who were streaming north from Los Angeles and Santa Barbara with *their* Indians. Thus, by the fall of 1848, the known gold fields reached 300 miles north and south along the Sierra foothills and off into the Trinities, an extraordinary sweep by a handful of men whose locomotion was limited to their horses and their own feet.

In return for their part in the proliferating discoveries, the Indians were exploited mercilessly. Job Dye's party of seven whites, muscled by fifty Indians, gleaned 273 pounds of gold in less than two months; of this the Indians received about 13 pounds. The proportion is probably typical of most parties. Naturally the natives soon decided that they would be better off working for themselves. Both "tame" Indians and members of the foothill tribes began prowling through the ravines near the mountain rancherías, using wooden tools and wicker baskets of their own invention. Many reaped fabulously, but in the long run fruitlessly.

Far more Indians were involved than is generally recognized. Lieutenant Revere, who visited the American River during the summer of 1848, estimated that half the 4,000 miners working there were Indians. James Clyman, who had returned to California during that same summer, wrote a friend on December 25: "There are at this time not less than 2000 white men and more than double that number of Indians washing gold"—this at a time when the rainy season had driven many miners out of the mountains.

The gold that these native miners recovered meant little to them except in terms of what it would buy at the moment. Old California hands like Charles Weber, John Marsh, and James Savage, the latter of whom bore the journalistic-sounding nickname of "The White King of the Tulares Indians," knew well how to exploit this attitude. Marsh packed a few sacks of sugar into the mountains and sold it by the cup for an equivalent amount of gold dust. Similarly, Savage placed raisins and other delicacies on one pan of a scale and required the purchasers to balance the weight with gold. Weber found digging even with forced labor to be less profitable than staking traders with dabs of merchandise and telling them to follow the Indians to their camps. A certain Benito Perez from Los Angeles sold a year-old, nine-peso serape to one Indian for two pounds, three ounces of gold—and then topped off the bargain by surreptitiously following the fellow and his companions to the ravine where they went to replenish their supply. Afterward Perez led the rest of his company to the place. There they quickly elbowed the original discoverers aside.

That ravine was straight out of fantasy. One of Perez's companions was a *gambusino* from Sonora, "Chino" Tirador, who happened to be visiting in Los Angeles when news of the Coloma strikes started his party hurrying northward. The morning the group staked their claims in the ravine they appropriated from the Indians, Chino dug four feet down to bedrock and then spent the next seven hours picking up nuggets enough to fill a wooden *batea* (a Mexican gold panning bowl) so full that he could scarcely lift it. When darkness stopped him, Chino proved as careless of value as the Indians. He paid two pounds of gold dust for a bottle half full of *aguardiente* and then shopped around the camp for silver coins—pesos and reales—so that he could gamble. He obtained these by paying one ounce of gold for $2.50 in coin. By ten o'clock that night he was dead drunk and flat broke. Nor was Chino exceptional. A favorite form of ostentation among the lucky was to walk up to a bar, fill a glass to a certain level with gold, hand it to the grog seller, and ask for the same amount of wine or whiskey—which may explain why the first liquor vendors to reach the Stanislaus area are said to have reaped $1,000 a day, as long as their stocks held out.

Not everyone was so improvident. Another of Perez's companions was Antonio Coronel, a destitute schoolteacher who had reached California in 1834 with the Híjar-Padrés colony. Coronel and his two Indian servants, both of them mutes, dug up near Chino Tirador's claim a heap of earth from which they picked by hand during the first two days 83 ounces of gold. The third day they washed the heap and recovered another 51 ounces in smaller particles, or about 12½ pounds for three days' work. This was not comparable to Chino's harvest, and it is not known how much of it the Indians received. Coronel's share, however, fortified by

later gleanings, transformed his life. Four years later he was elected
mayor of Los Angeles and thereafter treasurer of the state of California.
Then there was John Sullivan, an Irish oxcart driver even poorer than
Coronel. During the summer of 1848 Sullivan dug up with his own hands
$26,000. With this he bought San Francisco real estate, prospered still
more, and founded the Hibernian Bank.

Ironically, neither Sutter nor Marshall benefited from the flood they
unleashed. They soon sold the Coloma sawmill, but Marshall tried to
keep the adjacent ground. The impatient stampeders turned him out.
When he sought to prospect, they dogged his footsteps. Badgered unmer-
cifully, he finally turned into a moody misanthrope, dependent on charity for his livelihood.

Sutter fared no better. Drunk much of the time, he split with his
partners and then proved unable to control his Indians, who sold what
metal they found to fly-by-night traders. His creditors, however, believed
that he was plated with gold and pressed him remorselessly. To avoid
bankruptcy, he deeded his property to his eldest son, twenty-one-year-old
John August, Jr., who arrived from Switzerland in the fall of 1848—
almost the only Swiss colonist ever to come to New Helvetia.

The lad did a heroic job of keeping the concern solvent until he ran
afoul of Sam Brannan. Slick-tongued Sam persuaded him that the old
man's dream town, Sutterville, was poorly located and that they should
start a rival, Sacramento City. At that Sutter interfered in drunken anger,
and soon both town sites were in confusion, overrun by squatters who
denied the validity of anyone's title and felt free meanwhile to take
whatever they could lift from the decaying fort. Finally August sold the
bastion. The rest of the family having arrived by then, they all moved
north in bickering unfriendliness to a second farm on the Feather River.

There were other miseries to richness. The sudden outpourings of so
much gold led to staggering inflation. Walter Colton, alcalde of Monterey, who visited the southern mines during the early fall of 1848, tells
of paying $400 for a barrel of flour, $4 for a pound of poor coffee, $26 for
a tasteless breakfast—all in terms of impure gold dust whose value during
those frenetic days had sunk to as little as $8 an ounce. Because sawn
lumber was a rarity except at Coloma, cradles rented for as much as $150
a day. In the towns laborers who once had worked for a dollar a day now
demanded a dollar an hour—if they would work at all. Anyone on a fixed
salary suffered. At Monterey, the governor of the province, the alcalde
of the town, and the commander of a U.S. warship in the harbor tried
to make ends meet by moving into a small house together and doing their
own cooking over the smoky fireplace in the kitchen.

In spite of the inconveniences, Colton waxed rhapsodic over the rush. The American dream had come true; the long-awaited elevation of the common man was at hand. When one patched and unshorn resident of Monterey returned from the mines with $15,000 worth of dust on his pack mule, Colton wrote ecstatically, "Clear out the way with your crests and crowns and let this democrat pass!"

From Governor Mason's viewpoint, however, altogether too many democrats were passing—right out of the barracks and into the foothills. "No time in our history," he wrote to his superiors, "has presented such temptations to desert as now exist in California. The danger of apprehension is small and the prospect of high wages certain." The commander of the Pacific Squadron, Thomas Ap Catesby Jones (he who had mistakenly seized Monterey in 1842), was even gloomier: "Nothing, sir, can exceed the deplorable state of things in all Upper California . . . this whirlwind of anarchy and confusion confounded."

Such law as existed was still Mexican law. To spread awareness of what it was, Mason ordered veteran trader William Hartnell to find a code, translate it, and publish it for the guidance of the tumultuous citizens. He announced sternly that order would be enforced and that if necessary he would march his remaining dragoons through the gold camps to arrest all deserters from the armed forces. He then rode with Lieutenant W. T. Sherman and a small party into the mountains to estimate exactly what faced him.

Although the July days were scorching hot, he found Mormon Island aswarm with men, several of whom readily gave him flakes of gold that he could send to Washington with his reports. He talked to Marshall at Coloma. At Weber Creek, Charles Weber carelessly handed him a "lump" of gold. When the governor returned to Monterey, he had a wealth of incidents for the documents he meant to prepare for his superiors and a stunning Exhibit A—about $3,000 in metal that he put in a tea caddy and entrusted to Lieutenant Lucien Loeser for delivery to the president of the United States. He was behind times. Commodore Jones had already sent Navy Lieutenant Edward Beale across Mexico with preliminary reports of the discovery.

On August 6, 1848, while Loeser was making ready for the trip, word reached Monterey that at long last the United States Senate had, on May 30, ratified the peace treaty of Guadalupe Hidalgo, signed by representatives of the two nations on February 2. California was now officially a part of the United States.

Hopeful that the maddening ambiguities of his position were at last ended, Mason on August 7 issued a jubilant proclamation stating that all Mexican residents of California would automatically become American citizens unless they elected otherwise within one year. He predicted that civil government for California would soon be a reality. When that happened, Mexican law would be inoperative, and he therefore canceled plans to publish the translations that Hartnell had made. He discharged Colonel J. D. Stevenson's unruly New York volunteers and abandoned plans for hunting down deserters, even those from the regular army.

By this time the frenzy of the rush was lapping back into San Francisco. Merchandise of many kinds was in high demand in the mountains. Almost simultaneously several men who either had found no gold or were repelled by the labor of producing it decided that supplying the miners was a surer way than digging to benefit from the excitement. Back to town they scurried, to cash in ahead of their fellows.

Available stocks were soon exhausted. Out went a flood of orders to the nearest source of replenishment, the Sandwich Islands, crossroads of the Pacific. Unable to meet all the requirements, the merchants there hurried the requisitions on to Oregon, Mexico, South America—anywhere that goods might be found. News of the fabulous discoveries traveled with the orders, and immediately the first truly international gold rush in history took shape, preparing California for the cosmopolitanism that ever since has been a characteristic of her population.

The first wave came from the Sandwich Islands; among the more prominent adventurers were many who brought along gangs of Kanaka workers to dig for them. Oregonians came next, riding south with pack trains (the first wagon caravan did not pull out of the Willamette Valley until September) or else paying outrageous prices for sleeping space between piles of boxes and stacks of lumber on sailing ships hurrying to the new markets. In northern Mexico, wealthy *patrónes* grubstaked hundreds of peons and sent them and their families, including babies in arms, north across the forbidding trails that Anza had pioneered through the desert three-quarters of a century earlier.

The meeting of these polyglot people in the gold fields was not going to be easy. When no authorization for launching a civil government came from Washington it gradually dawned on Mason that his uncertainties were increasing rather than diminishing. Now that California was part of the United States, the Americans would no longer accept Mexican law. This left only military law to control the situation, yet could he legally maintain army jurisdiction now that peace was an announced fact?

The questions were not mere sophistry. Already it was evident that California was going to be faced with monumental problems in persuading men to abide by the promises they gave each other. Merchant shipping furnished the most obvious example. Whenever a vessel put into one of the harbors, most of its crewmen ran away. What recourse did the owners and captains have? Was the military obliged to help them?

What of debts that were repudiated? Of contracts that were broken? Above all, what of land titles? By treaty, the United States government had promised to honor all land grants legally issued by California's governors and all town lots legally distributed by the various alcaldes. The key word was *legal*. Already settlers were challenging some of the holdings, and suits were inevitable. In order that the new territorial government, whenever it was founded, might have a sound basis on which to reach decisions, Mason ordered his chief of staff, young Lieutenant Henry W. Halleck, who knew both law and Spanish, to prepare a report on Mexican land grant procedures and history in California. Anything not legally embraced within the grants would become part of the American public domain and be subject to claim by citizens under the liberal new preemption laws of 1841.

Those laws embraced agricultural land only. Methods of obtaining mineral lands were vague and related to copper discoveries in Wisconsin and lead in Illinois and Iowa. To the few gold miners who bothered to think about the problem, those Eastern statutes were irrelevant. That being so, they ignored the law and openly took the land they wanted. Technically they were trespassers on the public domain. But who was to run them out? If Mason were to try with the inadequate force at his command, he would precipitate revolution. Yet sooner or later some sort of orderly process was going to have to be developed.

Nor was that the end of the mineral-land problem. Was the government to give away a resource worth incalculable millions without any return in the form of taxes of some sort? In Mason's opinion, the miners should be required to make some sort of payment on the gold they wrested from public land, but again he was in no position either to promulgate or to enforce such a decree.

Equally troublesome were considerations of law and order. At first the dangers were not immediate. Reminiscences in general support what later became a cliché about the Edenic year of '48: "It was easier to find gold than to steal it." To be sure, a man who had lived on salt pork and hard biscuits while standing in icy water under a broiling sun to wash out a ton of earth might not agree that he'd had an easy time, but at least he wasn't pressed. Most people still assumed that they could make the strike they dreamed of simply by wandering on to the next unoccupied bar. The search was still an adventure; good nature still prevailed. Theft was rare, and even under the compulsion of drink, crimes of passion were almost nonexistent . . . in the mountains. But would Eden last?

It had not lasted in the towns. By summer, Californios traveling to the gold fields through San Jose were brawling regularly with transient

Americans, and the Mexicans on the juries refused to convict such of their countrymen as were arrested. Who cured that problem—and how? The question took on urgency when a self-constituted posse at San Jose lynched two men suspected of robbing and murdering a pair of miners on their way home from the mountains. Was it the military's province, in the absence of any other form of government, to intervene in that kind of civil uprising? But why ask? Mason could not interfere, even if he thought he should.

As the days dragged by with no word from Washington, wild theories began to be advanced. Robert Semple declared that the military no longer had the right to collect custom duties on imported merchandise and that a merchant could bring in and land goods wherever he chose without having to pause at the customs house to pay its exactions. At a campfire in the Sierra Nevada, a Welshman out of Washington, D.C., James King of William (we will hear more of him), went still further, arguing that since there were no laws in California, not even murder could be punished.

Completely discouraged, Mason in November, 1848, wrote Washington asking to be relieved. Responsible citizens could not escape the problem that way, however. When the rainy season of 1848–49 washed some 6,000 miners out of the hills with a total harvest of perhaps $10 million and promises of more to come, they began to use part of their leisure time wondering how to regulate and safeguard their amazing fortune.

Their dilemma was acute, for in December the sloop *St. Mary* reached Monterey with news that Congress had adjourned for the summer without making any provisions for government in California. The reason, the disappointed Americans learned, was the North-South controversy over the admission of slavery in new territories carved out of the lands obtained from Mexico. Elsewhere no hitches had occurred. Oregon had won territorial government from Congress in August, 1848—surely an intolerable discrimination, Californians fumed. What did Oregon have to compare with a half-year harvest of gold worth $10 million?

Although the *St. Mary* brought no solution to California's governmental crisis, it did carry advice from prominent officials who at the time of writing had known nothing about the gold discoveries. Secretary of State Buchanan wrote a long, legalistic document urging the Californians to be patient and continue functioning under the government they had, since only Congress could bring about changes. (The de facto government they had? Mason must have smiled wryly at that.) By contrast, Senator Benton of Missouri, angry still at the administration over the court-martial of his son-in-law, assured the immigrants that their best hope was to take matters into their own hands and form their own government, since the power of the people transcended all else.

Form what kind of government? A few stump orators—reckless ones, most immigrants thought—advocated forming an independent nation. Others urged a mere provisional government to act as custodians until Congress moved. The majority, however, favored calling a convention that would establish, unilaterally and contrary to Buchanan's theorizing, an American-style government, either territorial or state, and then face Congress with a *fait accompli*: take us or leave us. What might happen if Congress did not take them no one seems seriously to have considered.

In order to stir up sentiment for the proposed conventions, the leading politicians of the northern settlements began summoning mass meetings (in San Jose on December 11, 1848; in San Francisco on December 21 and 23; in embryo Sacramento on January 6, 1849) to consider ways and means. A cosmic sense of destiny filled those who thronged the former Mexican plazas to listen to the speeches. For as they now realized from the fever of the stampeders who had already swarmed in on them, an unprecedented invasion of fortune hunters portended, and something had to be done.

Yet even in their wildest moments, they could hardly have envisioned the wave that was already rolling toward them.

11. The Deluge

The times were ripe for frenzy. Like so many American decades, the 1840's had been filled with uncertainty, fear, change, war, and wild speculation. Immigration was quickening as growing industrialism in England, political revolution in Germany, and crop failures in Ireland sent families pouring across the Atlantic. The cities that swallowed them were crowded and miserable and often wracked by antiforeign, anti-Catholic riots. Speculators battened on an unprecedented demand for land and on the capital requirements of a spreading network of canals and railroads. Underneath the swirling changes yawned the earthquake fissures of slavery, opened still wider by the clumsy victories of the Mexican War.

Into the tensions leaped the electric shock of the gold discoveries. As had been true in San Francisco, the first reaction was skepticism, until the stories were confirmed by President Polk in his State of the Union message to Congress on December 5, 1848: "The accounts of the abundance of gold in that territory are of such an extraordinary character as would scarcely command belief, were they not corroborated by the authentic reports of officers in the public service"—and by that $3,000 tea caddy carried safely across Mexico by Lieutenant Loeser and placed on display in the War Department.

Almost instantly something like 90,000 restless people here and abroad decided to go to California, scoop up the loose money, have fun, see the sights, and come home to a world that would perhaps look, through the perspective of golden lenses, a little more stable than it had. Comparable numbers continued to flow west during the next three years, so that in spite of unknown thousands of returnees the state's non-Indian population at the end of 1852 amounted to 224,435, as compared to 15,000 at the beginning of 1848.

The forty-niners in particular liked to look back on themselves as a special breed, educated scions of the most sterling families of the East:

ambitious, enterprising, persistent, generous, sympathetic, insistent on justice, and "knowing no distinctions of race," to borrow a sprinkling of terms from the buttery reminiscences of pioneer Edwin G. Waite. And, indeed, economics and the physical hardships of the journey west did impose some selectivity. The vast majority of the American stampeders were young, healthy, white, and Protestant. Except among the Sonorans of northern Mexico, many of whom brought families or mistresses with them, women and children were rare—probably no more than 5 percent of the total. Because few opportunities existed for working one's way to Golconda, the bulk of the migrants had to be prosperous enough to pay for the trip out of savings, mortgages on property, or loans from stay-at-homes who wanted to have at least a financial share in the great adventure. For the most part the fortune hunters were also abysmally ignorant of what they faced and completely careless about the social chaos that such sudden numbers of avowed transients was likely to bring to the distant territory. All they wanted was to get in, get rich, and get out.

Men close to the Atlantic turned naturally to ships as a way to travel. It let them start while winter still blocked wagon travel across the central reaches of the continent. Besides, theirs was a seafaring tradition, bolstered by traders and whalers already familiar with the West Coast. Between December 7, 1848 (two days after Polk's speech), and February 8, 1849, no less than 136 ships, some owned and manned by hastily formed companies of gold seekers, started from Atlantic ports for San Francisco, an average of more than two a day. By the end of the year 775 vessels, many from foreign lands, had passed through the Golden Gate, carrying perhaps 40,000 persons.

For most of those 40,000 it was a wretched experience compounded of discomfort, boredom, seasickness, and occasional moments of terror. Because adequate numbers of passenger ships were not available, a mélange of wallowing coastal freighters, coal ships, whalers, and even ferry boats were rounded up as substitutes, stripped of their old furnishings, and jammed full of tiered bunks. Traveling under sail, they heaved and tossed for six to eight months on their way to El Dorado. Winter storms in the Atlantic and muggy doldrums in the tropics were followed by fearful buffetings as the ships dodged the fog-shrouded cliffs in the Strait of Magellan or swung wide around Cape Horn. Galleys were inadequate, diets unbalanced; food and water frequently had to be rationed. Scurvy struck often, just as it had centuries before in the noisome little caravels of the Spanish explorers. Drained spiritually and physically by the experience, few of the argonauts reached California in shape for the strenuous demands of pioneer mining.

To theorists studying maps in comfort at home—and this included, in the main, residents of the Gulf Coast and of towns within reach of steamboats plying the Mississippi—it seemed possible to reduce the ordeal at sea by risking shortcuts across lower Mexico, Nicaragua, or Panama. Some improvident wayfarers sailed from New Orleans to Tampico or Vera Cruz in Mexico or to San Juan del Norte in Nicaragua. There they made such catch-as-catch-can arrangements as they could for crossing to the Pacific. Worrying about food shortages and tropical diseases, they then huddled in whatever coastal village they reached until some unscheduled ship chanced by to pick them up. During 1849, some 3,000 people reached California by those uncertain routes.

Panama seemed a safer bet. At the close of the Mexican War, two cooperating steamship companies had won government contracts for carrying mail from New York and New Orleans to San Francisco and Astoria, Oregon, by way of the Isthmus. Three steamers had been built for use on the Pacific end of the run, and it so happened that when the gold rush began they were traveling, at widely spaced intervals, around South America to their new locations. In spite of costly tickets and dismal tales about the Panamanian jungles, about 6,500 forty-niners decided to hurry to Chagres on the Atlantic side of the Isthmus, brave the fetid trails, and catch the steamers as they went by on their way to California.

It turned into a horrifying experience. The travelers landed in a palm-thatched jungle town utterly incapable of handling them. There they had to make arrangements for themselves and their baggage to be poled up the steamy, leaf-walled Chagres River in native dugouts. During the three-day trip to the head of navigation, they slept either on mudbanks or, more commonly, humped in their bongos. At Gorgona they changed to mules for a rough 20-mile ride through deep mud and over fallen trees to the ancient walled city of Panama. They soon filled accommodations there and overflowed into a shanty town created out of bamboo, canvas, India rubber ponchos, even blankets and overcoats stitched together.

Mud, mildew, and fungus oozed over everything. Sanitation was hopeless. Malaria, yellow fever, cholera, and dysentery swept the camps. The ships that appeared could not carry away the stranded hordes, even though they oversold space at speculative prices and then crammed far more people into their stinking holds than safety regulations allowed. Sick and dispirited, many an argonaut waited for months on the beaches at Panama before he could escape and rejoin the northward flow.

When at last ocean travelers passed through the Golden Gate and turned south around Clark's Point into Yerba Buena cove, tremendous anticipation shook them. Yet whatever they expected, they could hardly have been prepared for the reality that met them. A clot of lifeless ships abandoned by their crews filled the harbor. Although wharves, including one promoted by Sam Brannan, were beginning to reach toward deep water, unloading cargo and baggage throughout most of '49 proved to be a shattering experience, arrogantly mismanaged by stevedores demanding outrageous prices for their help. According to Howard C. Gardiner, who arrived on July 26, 1849, moving freight a few rods from ship to shore cost more than sending it 20,000 miles around the Horn.

The town itself was a shambles. "Went ashore," wrote Hiram Pierce, another July arrival, "& found such a wild state of things as almost to intoxicate a person without giveing 50 cts. a glass." The grid of streets inland from Montgomery, which then touched the cove, was choked by a heterogeneous collection of buildings in various stages of construction. Predominant were open-fronted sheds covered with canvas. Here and there an old hulk had been dragged ashore to serve as a warehouse, but as more and more vessels hove to, clamoring for attention, space ran out and merchandise was simply stacked in the open, either on the beach or in front of some dealer's overcrowded hut. Then as now, advertising signs competed stridently for attention. Amazingly, there was little theft, perhaps because people hurrying to reach the mines could not spare time for stealing.

Almost the only two-story buildings were the combined gambling houses and hotels that clustered around the old Mexican plaza, recently renamed Portsmouth Square. Inside—and the farm boys must have gawked—chandeliers glittered and "meritricious pictures" (Gardiner's words) adorned the walls. Brass bands played and barkeeps passed out free drinks to the gamblers in order to reduce their caution. Yet these oft-described dens of iniquity did fill a need for the insecure, homesick, womenless young men washing back and forth through the streets. They offered physical warmth and shelter and, more importantly, a sense of camaraderie in an environment that suddenly loomed far more strange and hostile than it had on the maps back in Lynn, Massachusetts, or Cincinnati, Ohio.

One could, if he had money enough, buy a hard bed in a crowded hotel or a surprisingly good meal in a number of restaurants, for already French, German, Italian, Chinese, Mexican, and American cooks were bringing to the city the international cuisine that has marked it ever since. Most transients, however, sought to economize by camping out. It may have been misguided thrift. Fleas, lice, and rats overran the litter-strewn grounds. Contaminated water from shallow wells spread a virulent dysentery whose effects plagued some sufferers for more than a year afterward. Lack of fruit and vegetables increased the onslaught of scurvy. Respiratory diseases flared. Dr. J. B. D. Stillman, one of the first physicians to reach California, estimated that 20 percent of the early argonauts died within six months of their arrival. The figure seems exaggerated; still the conditions that created the impression must have been staggering.

Even the climate assaulted the newcomers. Fog brooded over the conical hills until dissipated by the rising sun. As the day brightened, streets became thronged and noisy. Auctioneers selling merchandise and speculators offering town lots bawled their wares through the brisk air. Saws grated, hammers pounded. Carts rumbled toward the beach, many loaded with earth from freshly graded streets, to be used in filling the shallows of the bay so that the city could move closer to deep water. Toward afternoon rising sea winds lashed dust across the canvas roofs— the same dust that winter's rain would turn into bottomless mud. Men sought shelter then, and as dusk descended, lamps and candles transformed the hillside tents into dwellings of light, so that the city "gleams," wrote Bayard Taylor in September, 1849, "like an amphitheater of fire . . . unreal and fantastic."

Reaching the mines, the argonauts discovered, entailed yet another ordeal. Although small steamers brought around the Horn in sections began plying the bay late in 1849, the early adventurers either had to circle south through San Jose on horseback or push through the river delta aboard small sailing craft. The water journey appeared easier but often wasn't, for the vessels were frequently becalmed amid towering rushes in sweltering heat. The passengers had the choice then of being devoured by mosquitoes or going below decks into the furnace-hot holds, lighting a smudge, and suffocating.

Two main destinations beckoned—the northern mines, located on streams draining into the Sacramento River, and the southern mines, located on tributaries of the San Joaquin. Sacramento City was the doorway to the first, Stockton to the second. At first glance they seemed less overpowering than San Francisco. At Sacramento, ships could tie up snug against a riverbank shaded by tall sycamores and cottonwoods. Stockton lay on a peninsula between two huge, reed-bordered sloughs formed by the sluggish San Joaquin as it meandered toward the delta to join the Sacramento. Although neither town was as plagued during summers by wind and fog as was San Francisco, the change brought no relief to travelers: the Central Valley's heat was overpowering. In spite of it, men bustled about the dusty streets as frantically as they had in the city by the Golden Gate, and whatever impression of restfulness a newcomer had gained on first glimpsing the river towns soon boiled away.

After asking frenzied questions of local promoters and going through agonizing vacillations, the migrants decided which of the mountain canyons sounded most promising and started out. It proved to be the brutal end of a crushing journey.

Although occasional springless wagons equipped with plank seats and pulled by half-broken California broncos had already begun running as "stagecoaches" to the principal camps, most of the scrambling newcomers were lucky to find conveyance just for their baggage. With muscles flabby from six months on a cramped ship, they themselves walked, an unshaded, unwatered trudge of 30 miles or more across the baked red dust of the valley floor. Then slowly the foothills took shape through the haze and hearts lifted. Even the sunburned grass, one hopeful said, looked like gold. Trees, too, appeared—live oaks whose small, shiny leaves were prickled along the edges like holly; pink-barked madrono; towering pines. Chaparral crowded close. In some ravines poison oak was lush; allergic stampeders unlucky enough to blunder into it suffered unspeakable miseries.

Travel by and large was along the ridges. To the sides the canyons were deepening. Eventually each man came to the locale he had chosen and looked down the plunging slope past a jumble of brush and canvas shelters to a streambank warted with heaps of newly dug earth waiting to be washed. There the gold grew, it was said, and there, as the summer waned, the seafarers began meeting the advanced guard of the army of marchers who had been converging on the same goal by land.

The first landsmen to arrive were those who had been reckless enough and impatient enough—early come, early rich—to avoid the snows of the South Pass route in favor of the vaguely known deserts, Apache Indians, and possibly resentful Mexicans of the Southwest. More trails than can be described here wound through the area. One was the Old Spanish Trail, long used by horse traders and horse thiefs, that looped from Santa Fe, New Mexico, up through southern Utah, and then down through Las Vegas, Nevada, on its way to Los Angeles. It was likely to be snow-swept in places, however, and was not favored. More popular routes, none well known, struck southwest from Santa Fe, due west from El Paso, Texas, or northwest from Chihuahua City, Mexico. All of them aimed for the Gila River of southern Arizona. And all included dismaying encounters with deep, dry ravines, sterile ridges, sandhills, wide alkaline bolsóns, short grass, and, at the end, the blistered depths of what became known as the Imperial Valley.

By good luck many of the 10,000 stampeders who risked those trails were already preconditioned for survival. A significant percentage were veterans of the recent American campaigns in northeastern Mexico.

They had endured dry travel in the Army, and they were able to impose a military discipline of sorts on their companies. In addition to them there were a number of the Southwest's hard-twisted frontiersmen, including several famed Texas Rangers. Still, it is a wonder that most of those 10,000 not only reached the end of the trails but even managed to pull, push, haul, and lift a surprising number of wagons with them as they went.

Meanwhile a far more numerous and, in general, far less capable mass was preparing to leave the frontier towns of Missouri as soon as the spring grass of the plains was tall enough to support their livestock. These are the ones who, with their long lines of covered wagons, spring first to mind when one says "forty-niner." Most of the women and children who went to California that year—say 2,500 women and 1,000 children, though all estimates of gold-rush travel are subject to revision—accompanied this northern migration. Altogether some 30,000 people were involved, including 1,500 or so who eschewed wagons and in small groups jogged on ahead with pack animals.

A dismayingly large portion of the wagon people were townsmen. Unlike the farm folk of the earlier cross-country migrations, they did not know very much about handling livestock or tools or guns. Remedying the deficiencies through trial and error would cost them many a pain and some lives. That they learned as fast as they did says a great deal about the inherent American ability to make do when practicality demands.

Their start was chaotic. They overloaded their wagons. They assiduously studied guidebooks that had been patched together for quick sale, and they believed too much of what they read about equipment, shortcuts, and convenient campgrounds. Like stampeders using the other routes, they formed companies not only for the journey but also for cooperative work later on in the gold fields. The members gave their companies fancy names and sometimes designed snappy uniforms for themselves. They spent hours drawing up bylaws they could not enforce; as they learned in time, the only realistic punishment for a violater was exile from the company, and by that time he was ready to leave anyhow and join another group.

The dreadful specter of cholera followed them up the Platte Valley. A sufferer would be seized with violent stomach cramps and vomit so hard that he (or she) ruptured blood vessels in his face. He rattled with chills, burned with fever, turned blue, and died—or recovered almost as rapidly as he had sunk. How many perished? No one knows, but probably the figure was somewhere between 500 and 1,000, an awesome casualty rate for the friends who had to watch the deaths.

Fortunately the disease burned itself out in the dry air of present-day

Wyoming, and for the next several-score miles the chief cause of suffering was a mysterious "mountain fever," the result, probably, of tick bites. Dismal enough—yet there were compensations in the enormous vistas, the sense of freedom and growing self-competence, the adventure, the expectancy.

Incessant storms caused maddening delays at swollen river fords, created gummy mudholes, and dissolved the buffalo chips that on the eastern side of the Continental Divide were the migrants' chief campfire fuel. The wetness also brought out unusual stands of grass that postponed for precious weeks the slow starvation that was stalking their beasts of burden. The days of truth came in the Nevada deserts. An overworked oxen faltered, readjustments became mandatory. Out went surplus food, patented gold-washing machines that would not have worked anyhow, furniture, stoves, clothing, books: an incredible miscellany. Along the lower Humboldt River, scurvy began to appear, and it was with terror that the sufferers looked ahead at the strong blue lift of the Sierra Nevada.

For many those last miles were a friendless scramble. All along the way groups that had started with vows of everlasting solidarity had been breaking apart, to form new companies with the residue from other groups. On the final stretches of the trail the atomization of some of these chance amalgamations became complete. After that the little components struggled ahead by themselves however they could, often close to but not in company with others who happened to be traveling the same way at the same time.

Those who implored passers-by for help were often ignored by men who feared to kill themselves by being too generous with either their fading time or their dwindling supplies. In that extremity some destitute men stayed alive by cutting slabs of meat from the dead animals whose stench fouled the air for scores of miles through the final deserts. Yet tales are told of those who, on being forced by collapsing wagons to jettison extra food, either buried it or deliberately spoiled it so that no one else could benefit from their loss. Other tales tell of dying men being abandoned before they ceased breathing.

There is a brighter side, however. Many a friend stayed loyally beside an ailing comrade until they found some means of going on together. William Manly and John Lewis, whose chance companions became stranded in Death Valley, set out for help, walked twenty-six days with the meagerest of provisions, and stumbled finally onto the very ranch of the Santa Clara Valley in southern California where gold had first been discovered in 1842. Refreshed, they could have gone on and no one would have been the wiser. Instead they borrowed three scrawny horses (all of which soon died), one mule, and as many supplies as they could carry.

With this they returned with selfless heroism to their companions and brought them to safety.

Far to the north, on the mountainous Lassen Trail, an ill-judged "cut-off" that added 200 miles to the normal route, J. Goldsborough Bruff, wracked with rheumatism, agreed to stay with his companions' equipment (and his own now priceless journals and sketches) while they went ahead to Lassen's ranch for fresh livestock.* They never returned, and none of the many who passed by Bruff's camp offered to help.

Eventually two other derelicts joined the marooned man. Although the region is notorious for heavy snow, they managed to stay alive by hunting and, more rewarding, by scavenging through the heaps of litter discarded by desperate travelers. During their searchings they picked up a starving four-year-old boy who had been deserted by his own father. Until New Year's Day they kept the lad alive by giving him part of their meager supplies (a dozen or so beans one day), and when he died they chipped out a decent grave in the frozen earth.

Later, one of Bruff's companions disappeared while hunting. The others assumed he had frozen. In despair the second man decided on a wild effort to break out. Alone, in the spring of 1850, Bruff at last started down the mountain. Discovering an Indian's footprint in the soft earth, he decided ecstatically on cannibalism. But when he met the Indian he did not shoot—just as he had always refrained, at the last minute, from killing and eating a small dog, Nevada, that he had picked up along the way. Famished to stupefaction, he stumbled on until he met help.

During the fall of '49 untold hundreds of others were saved by the decisiveness of General Persifor F. Smith, who on February 23, 1849, had replaced Mason as commander of the Army's Department of the Pacific. The impetus came from some of the cross-country packing parties who had outsped the wagon trains. On their arrival in California they reported that enormous numbers of immigrants were lumbering along behind them, many with inadequate supplies. By September it was obvious that some of those people were not going to get across the mountains without help.

---

*Peter Lassen was a Dane who came to California in 1839, worked awhile for Sutter, and then obtained a land grant where Deer Creek flows into the Sacramento River near the present hamlet of Vina. Thinking to emulate Sutter by luring immigrants to his ranch, he had gone east by the regular trail in 1848 and had persuaded ten wagons to follow him west from the central part of Nevada's Humboldt River to what he said would be an easy crossing of the Sierra Nevada. Boxed in by the Black Rock Desert, he wandered almost as far north as Goose Lake near the Oregon border before turning south again along the headwaters of the Sacramento. Weirdly, a party of forty-niners saw Lassen's tracks the next year and swung after them, hoping for a shortcut. Sheeplike, 8,000 or more travelers fell in behind that first group! This saved grass for latecomers on the Humboldt route, but it sure was hell on the sheep.

On his own responsibility General Smith appropriated $100,000 for rescue work. San Franciscans contributed $12,000 more, and lesser amounts came from the residents of other communities—a considerable accomplishment when one recalls that there were no organizations whatsoever for soliciting and collecting charitable donations and only one small weekly paper in San Francisco (a merger of the original two) for stirring public opinion.

Major D. H. Rucker was put in charge of the field work. His chief assistant was a civilian, John H. Peoples, who only recently had reached California from Louisiana by way of the Gila River. They began operations in mid-September, when 10,000 weary travelers were still floundering through the mountains. They, their soldiers, and their hired civilians had three trails to cover: the Carson River route south of Lake Tahoe, opened in the spring of 1848 by the Mormon mill workers returning to Utah; the older Truckee River route north of Lake Tahoe, where the Donner party had disintegrated in 1846; and the roundabout Lassen Trail.

It was a heroic, understaffed effort by underequipped and underpaid men who might well have been off in the gold fields. Much of their effectiveness came from boosting morale, from letting stragglers who felt utterly forsaken know that their fellow men really were interested. Beyond that, the rescuers knit isolated parties together, gave the physical boost needed to start stranded wagons rolling again, made endless heartbreaking decisions on how best to allot the limited supplies they carried. They reached the far ends of their assigned territories in the thinnest nick of time. Snow and rain swept the mountains early that year. For half a month, Peoples reported, "not one of the party had a dry blanket, or dry clothes." But because of those dripping men, there was no repetition of the Donner tragedy. By the end of November everyone in the frayed horde, save for an occasional derelict like Bruff, had reached shelter either in the Central Valley or in one of the crude camps taking form in the canyons—the first considerable wave in the persistent, often unreasoning surges of population that have continued to flood into California.

Like the sea travelers, most of the throng were not in good shape for what lay ahead. Moreover, there was not one of them who did not realize, in some unhappy back part of his mind, that when he chose to return home with the riches he had come so far to seek, it would have to be by one of those dreadful routes. What psychological effect this awareness had on them during the coming months of frenzied fortune and frustration each reader will have to imagine for himself. One thing seems definite, however. Now that they had finally reached California, they were in no state of mind to be patient with anything that interfered with their desires.

12. "Wild, Free, Disorderly, and Grotesque"

The Boston and California Joint Stock Mining and Trading Company was a sturdy organization, well financed and glued together with a carefully drawn constitution. As one of the first groups to leave for the West, it attracted wide attention. Five different civic leaders—the United States secretary of state, the Massachusetts secretary of state, the president of Harvard College, and two Boston ministers—felt impelled, as satirist-member William Henry Thomes later spun the tale, to hand each argonaut a free Bible and a weighty adjuration:

"You are going to a strange country, and will meet many desperate people. You must overcome them. Take your Bible in one hand, and your great New England civilization in the other and always remember that you are Christians, and carry light into the darkness."

The torch, reports George R. Stewart in his biography of Thomes, soon flickered out. After two hard days in the placer mines, the company joints came unglued and the group disbanded, every man for himself. The last Thomes saw of the Bibles, they were stacked on a bar in Benicia, where they had been swapped, at a rate of 25 to 50 cents each, for whiskey.

Although the spoof was light-hearted as Thomes wrote it, it epitomized what to many observers was a shocking failure. The ideals of Manifest Destiny—America's self-generated mission to homogenize the continent with her vaunted Anglo-Saxon political, religious, and cultural institutions—had helped energize a war, but could they withstand the giant lottery in the Sierra foothills?

The collapse, as these doubters saw the situation, was both private and public. A dismaying number of stampeders abandoned long-held ethical values, while at the same time the public genius for government no longer seemed able to maintain customary guidelines and restraints.

175

Why? Was the chaos merely an intensified repetition of the old frontier struggle of barbarism against civilization? Or was it, asked Harvard's philosopher Josiah Royce, who had been born in a California mining camp during the gold rush, a kind of mystic ordeal from on high testing the worth of the American character?

Today we are not so inclined as Royce was to visualize a transcendent Spirit of Democracy demanding proper answers from the American community. Without question, however, individuals were tested, both in body and in spirit, far more severely and in far more insidious ways than they could have imagined on leaving home. The adjustments that followed, whether regarded as stark survival responses or as cosmic regeneration, were slow and painful. It can be argued that California still has not got over the effects, good and bad.

The first thing to remember, of course, is that practically no one in the mountains considered himself a citizen of an entity called California. He was a sojourner, intent primarily on getting rich and then going home, a motive not necessarily reprehensible. As miner Melvin Paden wrote his wife, "Jane i left you and them boys for no other reason than this to come here to procure a little property by the swet of my brow so that we could have a place of our own that i mite not be a dog for other people any longer."

Jane and the boys, however, were a long way off. Since few planned to stay in California, few brought their families with them. The census of 1850 indicated that throughout the state as a whole, the population was almost 93 percent male, and in the mining camps the ratio was even further out of balance.

One can easily grow excited, as Mark Twain did in *Roughing It*, about these "stalwart, muscular, dauntless young braves, brimful of push and energy, and royally endowed with every attribute that goes to make up a peerless and magnificent manhood. . . . But they were rough in those times! They fairly reveled in gold, whiskey, fights, and fandangoes, and were unspeakably happy. The honest miner raked in from a hundred to a thousand dollars out of his claim a day, and what with the gambling dens and other entertainments, he hadn't a cent the next morning if he had any sort of luck. They cooked their own bacon and beans, sewed on their own buttons, washed their own shirts—blue woolen ones; and if a man wanted a fight on his hands without any annoying delay, all he had to do was appear in public in a white shirt or a stovepipe hat, and he would be accommodated. . . . It was a wild, free, disorderly, grotesque society. . . . nothing juvenile, nothing feminine visible anywhere!"

All true—and untrue. Now and then some miner, honest or otherwise, did take a thousand dollars from his claim in a single day. Gamblers there certainly were, and long periods of monotonous work did bring on eruptions of high spirits. Whenever "good" women and small children appeared, they were treated with extraordinary deference. Meanwhile the San Francisco papers gave public notice of the arrival of cargoes of whores from Mexico and France. Wild, free, and grotesque—and none of it has suffered in the telling, either. It is an expected cliché of the times, endlessly repeated. But let us add a postcript by Louise Clappe, writing under the pseudonym Dame Shirley, who in one of her letters described a mass Christmas drunk at Indian Bar that lasted three days, until finally the celebrants could do nothing more than lie around on the floor amusing themselves with "a most unearthly howling; some barked like dogs, some roared like bulls, and others hissed like serpents. Many were too far gone to imitate anything but their own animalized selves."

All true, but it was not by roistering that some 20,000 or 30,000 working miners like Melvin Paden—*Jane, not to be a dog any longer*—took during the dry months of 1849 some $10 million in gold from the shallow placers, an average of between $330 and $500 each with which to face the long, wet winter.

Time was precious. After arriving in California a man had to go to the mountains, find a claim, acquire pick, shovel, and rocker, learn techniques, and begin a totally new mode of living within a matter of weeks. Many discovered to their dismay that a majority of the creeks went dry late in the summer. Faced by that contingency a miner either stockpiled his earth until rains renewed the streams—or else he sought to emulate the Mexicans, who could winnow the golden grains by first picking out the heaviest dross with their fingers and then tossing the fine material into the wind so that the light dust blew away. They caught the rest on a blanket, put it in a *batea*, or wooden bowl, and finished the separation by puffing the sand over the rim of the bowl with their own breath. It was not a quick way to great riches.

Or perhaps a man located himself where an ancient stream had deposited gold in gravel beds that lay several hundred yards from flowing water. In that event he packed his hopes to the creek in a leather sack on his own back or, if he could afford it, on a mule, which then had to be cared for when the owner was so tired he could hardly feed himself. The luckiest might even be able to hire a cart driven by some enterprising teamster—one successful driver was a quondam professor from Yale University—and then they were at last ready to get down to the real work of slowly washing the gold from their laboriously accumulated earth.

Perhaps thick layers of overburden covered rich deposits near bedrock. The miner reached those buried treasures—or maybe just barren stone —by sinking shafts from a few feet to as much as 30 or 40 feet deep. From the hole's bottom he radiated, foot by slow foot, horizontal tunnels like spokes. Then, using a primitive whim, he hand-cranked the earth in leather buckets to the surface. Such work was called "coyoting"—a grueling experience in bad air and wet surroundings, haunted by an ever-present likelihood of cave-ins.

And so we come to a soberer picture than Twain's. "The thirst for gold," wrote miner Theodore Johnson, "and the labor to produce it overruled all else, and absorbed every faculty. Complete silence reigned among the miners." Daniel Woods emerged from the wet winter of 1849–50 with an even bleaker recollecton. "In sunshine and rain, in warm and cold, in sickness and health, successful or not successful, early and late, it is work, *work*, WORK! *Work or perish!* . . . Cheerful words are seldom heard, more seldom the boisterous shout and laugh. . . . We have made [today, January 15, 1850] 50 cents each."

Probably the truth lies halfway between Twain's romance and Woods's glumness. By the end of 1850 there were about 50,000 miners in the hills, producing $41 million, or an average of a little more than $800 each. Naturally they did not all see the adventure in the same light. And there were blissful days, particularly in the spring when the water was still clear, the sun soft, and the hills a shimmer of wild oats spangled with wild flowers. The heat soon came, however—pessimist George Payson entitled his reminiscences *Golden Dreams and Leaden Realities*—and one has a feeling that Englishman Frank Marryat's insistence that "all was life, merriment, vigor, and determination" was perhaps mellowed just a bit by retrospect.

For one thing, living conditions did little to alleviate the hard labor. Diets were monotonous and ill-balanced, as one of the more famous of the folk songs of the period, "The Lousy Miner," clearly stated.

> I've lived on swine till I grunt and squeal
> No one can tell how my bowels feel,
>> With slapjacks swimming round in bacon grease
>> I'm a lousy miner,
> I'm a lousy miner; when will my troubles cease?

But at least they were able to laugh about it, most of the time.

Occasionally a packtrain arrived with fresh produce at high prices—50 cents for an egg, 6 bits for two apples. Now and then Mexican vaqueros, yelling and swinging their ropes, hazed a few half-wild cattle down the dusty hills into the camp, lassoed them, and butchered them on the spot. A tale is told of two Irishmen trudging into town with little bags of gold dust, the result of weeks of labor, and seeing a few potatoes on a box in front of a brush-roofed store booth. The sight was more than they could resist. Their gold, one remarked wistfully, looked mighty yeller, but them thar taters looked even yeller-er. And then there was the woman who reputedly earned $18,000 in a single season making dried-fruit pies in a frying pan held over a campfire.

California's rainless summers allowed men to sleep fairly comfortably outdoors without shelter. As the tired immigrants arrived in the fall, they saw the careless arrangements, and in their eagerness to be at work after their long journeys, they supposed that very little more would be necessary for winter, there where snow seldom fell. A weird conglomeration of hastily erected hutches appeared: holes in the ground roofed with pine boughs and earth, wigwams of branches, log frames covered with bark, canvas, and, especially among the Mexicans, green cowhides. These served during light showers. Unfortunately, the winter of 1849–50 turned out to be unusually wet and cold. Tent floors were churned by soggy boots into quagmires; pine boughs used as mattresses were trampled into the mud. It wasn't dramatic, just miserable. "My feet", wrote Ananias Rogers, mining that winter near Bidwell's Bar, "never felt like they were dry and frequently are so cold that I cannot sleep."

In heat or cold, disease flourished. Hugo Reid, a naturalized Scottish Mexican of southern California (and husband of an Indian woman raised at San Gabriel mission), wrote Abel Stearns in Los Angeles, "The diseases may be reckoned three in number, syphilis not counted: first, mountain fever or ague . . . carried out with great lassitude and dreadful stretching of the limbs. Second, a bastard pleurisy, with pain toward the region of the liver . . . terminating often fatally in a few hours. . . . Third, a compound patent nameless galvanic bilious fever, defying description, doing just as it pleases; in fact, a true republican democratic sickness, as stubborn as a mule and which kicks like a *macho*." To which he added, "Don't go to the mines on any account. . . . [They] are, moreover, loaded with vagabonds from every quarter of the globe."

More prosaically put, the common diseases were diarrhea, dysentery, generally called bloody flux, malaria, and acute rheumatism. Strangely, there were many doctors around. Along with lawyers, they were the most common of the professional men in California; merchant Daniel Coit of San Francisco even wondered in one letter how they were all going to make a living. They were not much help, however, for they were as intent as everyone else on digging as much gold as possible in the shortest time. Most invalids had to rely on quacks, who flocked to California as they did to all frontier towns in America, on partners, not all of whom had time for sympathy, or on self-prescribed quinine, laudanum, and patent medicine gulped at random.

For many so simple a thing as a tight roof would have been a salvation. After a solitary bout with fever, during which his weight dropped from 200 to 125 pounds, future railroad tycoon Collis P. Huntington remarked laconically that it was not pleasant to have to lie alone for weeks on the ground in a wet tent. Under the circumstances perhaps the most effective answers to the problem were the privately run, ill-equipped "Homes for the Sick" that sprang up in the distribution cities and the more populous mining camps. Their medical services were often rudimentary, but at least they let a man who could pay the bill lie down in a dry place and be fed regular meals, such as they were.

As the buffetings increased, a terrible sense of isolation gnawed at many of the sojourners. Always in the back of their minds was the memory of the fearful journeys they had endured to reach the shadowed canyons—a memory given particular poignancy by the knowledge that they could now reach China more easily and sooner than they could travel to New York City. Hungry for news from the states, they would pay as much as a dollar for a copy of the last outdated newspaper from New York or New Orleans. They yearned for mail, but for a long period San Francisco was the end of the run. The first express company in California developed because young Alexander Todd determined in his desperation to travel to the main post office and search personally for the letters he was sure were waiting for him. Hearing of his errand, neighboring miners offered him one dollar each to paw through the stacks for them and another three dollars for each letter he brought back. The venture proved so successful that Todd was soon carrying not just letters but papers, gold, and small packages of all kinds between San Francisco and the mines east of Stockton, a business quickly imitated by other men battening on the homesickness that surrounded them.

Time! Wisdom dictated that as soon as a man had selected a spot, he settle down and make the most of it. Many tried, working diligently through the week and then laying off on Sundays to patch and wash their clothes—a chore that most abominated—to write letters, bake enough bread and beans to last through the coming week, and then go to the nearest camp to buy supplies, swap news, and, too often, relax with more drinking and gambling than one had intended on setting forth.

As the days leaped past, the disquieting knowledge came to many of them that if they had invested at home the money they had spent coming west and had worked with equal diligence to develop the outlay, they would have ended up better off. (*Jane, i left you and them boys so that we could have a place of our own.*) The realization bred several reactions. Some shoveled harder than ever: "work, *work*, WORK: *Work or perish!*" Others, and they probably were the wisest, turned to the trades they knew, storekeeping, carpentry, wagon driving, farming. Some tried to escape through excitement, gambling, drinking. But the most common reaction was a feverish restlessness. Perhaps—even though winter was coming— perhaps—even though living was desperate in the farthest canyons— perhaps they could do better somewhere else. Anyway, it would be a break in the monotony. And so they abandoned claims that were paying them $10 a day—who had come to California for that?—and off they went, borne on the tide of each vagrant rumor. Swift improvisation, a facile optimism, a willingness to take risks, rootlessness—they are traits that California still imposes on part of each new batch of immigrants. Why else did you come?

The miners had some foundation for their hopefulness. The gold regions opened during 1848 and 1849 reached from the Trinity country near Oregon south to Mariposa, an area of some 35,000 square miles. The 50,000 prospectors who were roaming the region by the fall of 1850, most of them completely inexperienced, were not enough to exhaust that much in a twinkling. Although the likelihood of a fabulous '48-style strike declined each year, the chance nevertheless did exist for the next decade, and it did materialize on occasion. To thousands of eager, avaricious men that was enough. Why work in this worn field when over yonder? . . .

Yonder might be Gold Lake or Gold Bluff. The first, a fabled body of gleaming blue water, its shores pebbled with the purest of nuggets, was born originally of yarns spun at Sutter's Fort by that ancient of days, trapper Caleb Greenwood. Later the story was given immediacy by a mental case, John Stoddard, who said he had just visited the place; it was hidden among the tangled headwaters of the Middle Fork of the Feather River, and he'd be glad to lead a party there. The excitement—who was crazy, anyway?—all but depopulated the northern camps during the summer of 1850. But at least the principal loss was limited to time. Gold Bluff was more crass. Promoters spread tales of a coastal bluff south of the Klamath River in northern California where ocean waves, operating on the cliffs like water roaring through a sluice box, had washed gold out of the rock during untold ages and had deposited it as shining sand on the beach. A company was formed to exploit the riches—one "estimate" placed the potential yield at $43 million—and stock sold by the basketful until skeptics punctured the balloon.

Not every frenzy was so barren. During the first half of the 1850's, recurrent stampedes opened hundreds of new camps where gold really did exist. As elbows began to rub in the tight ravines and along the constricted bars, it became necessary for the precipitantly gathered throngs to draw up a minimum of rules for preserving order and for distributing as equitably as possible the available ground, which, under a strict interpretation of the laws, was not legally open to anyone.

Exactly how the concept of a "claim" originated in the Sierra Nevada is unknown. During the reputedly blissful days of '48, when there was space enough for everyone, boundaries were vague, if they existed at all, and a man scratched into the crevices with his horn spoon or shoveled earth into his pan pretty much where he pleased. If someone edged onto a patch of gravel that he regarded as "his," he called a meeting of the local old-timers to testify out of personal recollection about the facts of occupation: first come first served, and, Joe, there are plenty of other places farther down the creek. Generally that settled the case. But it did not suffice when too many people wanted too little space and when the numbers and fluidity of the populace were greater than unaided memory could encompass. At that point some kind of standard acceptable to the majority of the miners had to be imposed.

"Acceptable" is one of the key words. During the critical days when the system was taking form, the supreme legal authority in California was Mexican law as modified and supported by American military governors. That being so, Mexican mining rules presumably prevailed. Few stampeders knew anything about those regulations, however, and fewer still would have consented to abide by them. This was American ground, wasn't it? Yet the only American mineral regulations that existed had been drawn up for the copper and lead mines of Wisconsin and Iowa, and were hardly relevant to the California situation. As a result the forty-niners were required to invent procedures that in their opinion were fair and workable. They did this during the course of many open-air meetings in many rough camps, and conceivably the results were better than if a blue-ribbon committee of distant jurists had tried to decide the matter from behind their law books.

With the American talent for eclecticism, the prospectors drew suggestions from many sources: the Wisconsin laws, Mexican custom, the advice of Cornish tin miners, Germanic tradition, and their own experience with organizational meetings of many kinds. Practicality was everything. No "district" (generally a district was defined geographically by reference to nearby topographic features) presumed to legislate for more than itself, but when a man moved from an established camp to one still unorganized, he carried with him a memory of what had worked before. Thus the ripples spread. During the 1850's some 500 codes were adopted in different sections of the gold fields. Though details varied erratically, basic procedures remained remarkably similar, both in California and afterward in other sections of the mineralized West to which Californians spread.

As soon as it appeared that a gold field was likely to last for a while, the inhabitants of the area met at some central spot, generally the vicinity of the first store or bar, and elected a committee of old-timers—that is, men who had at least traveled through some other mining region—and charged them with drafting a code for the camp. Having threshed out the regulations among themselves, the committee submitted the code to a second general meeting. Amendments were accepted or rejected by popular vote, and the whole was then voted into existence as the law of the district.

Because the miners wanted only the right to remove gold from the earth, none of the "constitutions" pretended to convey permanent title. A man possessed a piece of ground only as long as he occupied it. The presence of usable tools on a claim was prima facie evidence of intent to mine, but even those could not maintain a claim against jumpers for more than a limited time. Disputes were settled by various methods—camp meetings, boards of arbitration, and, later, by jury trials.

Claim sizes were carefully circumscribed by popular vote. The idea was to let each man have an equal chance at the area's potential wealth. In the early days in very rich areas, claims were occasionally as small as 10 feet square. Later, as increasing amounts of earth had to be worked to yield satisfactory returns, sizes were increased to 100 by 200 or even 100 by 300 feet. Exact dimensions necessitated clear rules about the marking of boundaries. In addition, most codes provided for the election of a recorder whose job was to enter in a ledger the date of each claim filing, its precise location, and all subsequent transfers of title.

Peonage was swiftly outlawed. A man could not outdistance his neighbors, as the most successful miners of '48 had done, by moving onto the most promising bars with gangs of Indian laborers paid for their work with food and trinkets. He could not use Negro slaves, as Thomas Jefferson Green forcibly learned in July, 1849, when he and the blacks he had brought from Texas were driven away from Rose's Bar on the Yuba River.

The *patrón* system, under which a wealthy Latin American or a trader in Hawaii equipped a group of indigents and sent them to California to mine under the supervision of a major-domo, was particularly resented and harder to check. In a sense the peons were individual entrepreneurs. They filed claims in their own names—after all, they did retain half or more of their earnings—and they were following customs normal to their own countries. The Americans, however, found the very notion of a *patrón* undemocratic and repugnant. Why should one man, who often stayed comfortably at home—and a "greaser" at that—profit from his surreptitious share in several claims? When a group of Chilean peons followed Green's blacks onto Rose's Bar and refused orders to leave, an impromptu posse hanged the major-domo, cut off another man's ears, and flogged several of the workers with bullwhips. Let the foreigners remember: one man, one claim. Some rabid racists were even beginning to say, as early as the spring of '49, that noncitizens, especially nonwhites, should be denied claims under all circumstances—but more of that shortly.

A claim owner could hire white labor at going rates if he was able to find a stampeder willing to work for wages. Few were in '49 or even '50. A man could also buy claims in addition to the one he filed for himself. (Many camps limited purchases to one, however.) Using a hired hand to develop a purchased claim could be risky. If the earth turned out to be rich, the laborer might jump the claim on the grounds that his work made him the rightful owner. Sometimes he carried the point.

The camp codes also contained, in addition to regulations about claims, a few rudimentary scraps of criminal law. Although California may have been idyllic in '48, conditions soon changed as bandits from northern Mexico, erstwhile convicts from Britain's penal colony in Australia, and discharged soldiers from the American Army began drifting through the hills, drawn by the thought of sizable quantities of gold floating through a land where organized forms of law enforcement did not exist.

Spontaneous reaction by the citizens themselves was about the only way of handling violations. Whenever a malefactor was nabbed, generally by individual initiative, he was haled before a swiftly summoned meeting of the miners of the area. Sometimes the gathering formed itself into a jury-of-the-whole to hear the evidence. More often the crowd elected from among its members a judge, jury, prosecutor, and—be it noted—attorney for the defense. Such right of appeal as existed was reserved for the audience; that is, it could express by voice vote, and in capital offenses was often asked to do so, its approval or disapproval of verdict and sentences.

Even though trials were a diversion for excitable men, working miners disliked having to drop their shovels and run off to a meeting every time an alleged criminal was brought before the bar. Before long, accordingly, the camp codes began providing for the election of a magistrate, often termed an alcalde in lip service to Mexican law, and empowered him to conduct preliminary examinations, summon juries, preside at trials, and call on a sheriff, also elected, for help in the execution of writs. Trials continued to be abrupt, however, and punishment was summary, largely because facilities for holding culprits did not exist. A man guilty of relatively minor offenses was banished from the camp. More serious wrongs, generally theft, were punished by both flogging and banishment; for some reason, 39 lashes was a favorite number. Ear croppings occurred but were rare. Hanging was inflicted for major larcenies, aggravated assaults, and murder.

In civil affairs—that is, claim adjudication—these rough codes worked well, often to the surprise of European visitors to the gold fields. Less unanimity prevails concerning their handling of crime. Banishment simply swept an unwanted person, burning now with resentment, into another camp. Nor were the convicted the only sufferers. The brutal nature of the well-attended punishments may have been one more factor, along with physical misery and acute anomie, in the coarsening of the mountain populace—a view, to be sure, which some historians decry as coming from the squeamishness of our own remote, soft, and overly intellectualized times.

Circumstances being what they were, could the miners have devised more "civilized" methods of justice? The question seems academic. Alternates weren't devised or even seriously discussed. That in itself says much about the nature of the codes. They were ad hoc affairs, government for one purpose only—to let the wheel of chance spin through the giant lottery of the Sierra foothills as equably as possible. In one respect a criminal was like a peon; he interfered with the odds and had to be removed. Where he went, or how, hardly mattered.

The most obvious flaw in this headlong immediacy was a lack of checks and balances to protect the helpless against the passions of an inflamed majority. One early, notorious example was a multiple lynching at Dry Diggings near Weber Creek in January, 1849. Five men, a mix of French and Chileans, none of whom understood English well, were accused of robbing a Mexican gambler. Each was found guilty by a camp jury-of-the-whole, stripped to the waist, and flogged bloody. While they were still too weak to stand, fresh charges of attempted robbery and murder at a place miles away were brought against three of them. Immediately the camp jury went back into session, with no thought about Dry Diggings' right of jurisdiction. This time the sentence, approved by a roar from the crowd, was for death. One spectator, a discharged soldier named E. Gould Buffum, climbed onto a stump to protest but was shouted down with threats that if he did not desist he would be hanged beside the others.

"The prisoners," Buffum continued, "were marched out, placed upon a wagon, and the ropes put round their necks. . . . Vainly they called for an interpreter, for their cries were drowned by the yells of the now enfuriated mob. A black handkerchief was bound around the eyes of each; their arms were pinioned, and at a given signal, without priest or prayer-book, the wagon was drawn from under them and they were launched into eternity."

Thereafter Dry Diggings became Hangtown, until civic shame rebelled in 1854 and the name was officially changed to Placerville.

Nativism may or may not have been involved in the Hangtown affair. It certainly triggered later encounters, however, and in those instances, too, the mountain codes provided no protection for the weaker party.

The times guaranteed nationalistic strife. Throughout the latter part of the 1840's the East had been wracked by anti-Catholic, antiforeign riots, and the stampeders brought those prejudices to California with them. Related to the animosities was the Americans' contempt for the Mexicans whom they had so recently defeated in war. During the war "greaser" had become a common term for the enemy. In California all Catholic, Spanish-speaking Latin Americans (and Frenchmen, too, at times) fell under that same pejorative, greasers. The word even embraced native Californios, although by terms of the Treaty of Guadalupe Hidalgo the Californios were, if they chose to be so, as completely American in citizenship as was the fairest Nordic of all the land.

Sharpening this xenophobia was an acute economic fear. The west coasts of Mexico, Peru, and Chile had been among the first sections to learn of the California gold discoveries. Citizens of those countries, many of them experienced miners financed by *patrónes*, hurried north in great numbers, the Mexicans of Sonora by land over Anza's old trail, and the others by ship. When Americans began arriving from the East, they found these foreigners, together with several hundred Californios, solidly established in the gold fields. Worse, the strangers seemed to have a nose for ore. It was small comfort to reflect, while watching them work, that without their example, the Americans would have floundered around much longer than they did learning the rudiments of mining technique, especially in waterless diggings.

No one knew, in 1849, how much gold existed in California. But the first-comers did know that hordes of other hopefuls were already pressing west on their tracks. Would there be enough metal to go around? Memories of the trip's agony, threats of disease, accident, and isolation, the uncertainty of being able to make the return journey (*Jane, i left* . . . Melvin Paden, be it remembered, died in California)—all those tensions gathered into a knot of fear in many a man's stomach. And the most available object on which to vent the nervousness was those gabbling foreigners.

The first step was to ask whether outlanders had any real right to own claims. Actually, since Congress had not yet made any provision for transferring mineral rights in the public domain to individual ownership, everyone, Americans included, was technically a trespasser. These legalistics did not occur to many stampeders, however, and would not have impressed them, anyway. Their army had won the land, hadn't it?

Such precedent as existed was on the questioners' side. The land law with which they were most familiar, the Preemption Act of 1841, designed to ease the passage of small farm plots from the national domain into private hands, reserved its privileges to American citizens or to those who had formally declared their intention of becoming citizens. Should not the same provision apply to mining claims? In the opinion of no less a person than Brigadier General Persifor F. Smith, it not only should but did.

In November, 1848, it will be recalled, Colonel Richard Mason had asked to be relieved as military governor of California and commander of the Army's Department of the Pacific. It so chanced that before the request reached Washington, the brass there decided to bring Mason east for routine reassignment. His western functions were split between two men. Brigadier General Persifor Smith was to take command of the Department of the Pacific; Brigadier General Bennet Riley was to become military governor of California.

Smith started west several weeks ahead of Riley. Traveling with him across Panama in January, 1849, were between 700 and 1,500 excited gold seekers—accounts vary. The hope of each one of them was to catch the first of the Pacific Mail Steamship Company vessels, the *California*, then rounding Cape Horn on its way to inaugurate mail service between Panama City, San Francisco, and Astoria, Oregon. So many passengers were far more than the ship could carry. While the distraught argonauts were absorbing that shock, rumors swept through their fever-ridden camps to the effect that Mexican miners had already taken more than $4 million from the California placers and that very little gold remained. Near-panic ensued.

When the *California* at last dropped anchor far out in Panama's shallow bay, she had aboard 75 Peruvian gold seekers who had boarded her at Callao. They declined to go ashore in order to make room for American citizens, and the captain of the ship, a man named Marshall, supported them. One of the outraged throng on the beach thereupon wrote to the editor of the *Panama Star*, a small weekly being put out by two of the stampeders, a letter that was featured on the front page. In it the writer stated that because gold had been discovered *after* the conquest, providence obviously meant the mines "for Americans only, who possess noble hearts and are willing to share with their fellow-men more than any other race of men on earth, but still they do not wish to give all. . . . We will share our interest in the gold-mines with none but American citizens."

Infected by the frenzy and upset by the suffering on the beach, General Smith added official sanction to the declaration. In an open letter to the United States consul in Panama City, he stated, quite correctly, that American law did not allow foreigners to acquire title through mere occupation to any part of the public domain of the United States. As soon as he reached California he would see to it that the trespassers were ejected. To the stampeders the implication was clear: there was no use for the Peruvians to continue, so why didn't they disembark?

A compromise evolved. The Peruvians stayed, but Captain Marshall put aboard his ship the maximum number of passengers allowed by safety regulations and then added one more for each foreigner. Overloaded by those extra 75 men, the ship crawled on north, the passengers on short rations and the crew stoking the boilers with spars, furniture, and even part of the deck in order to maintain headway against the northwest winds. In San Francisco the entire crew deserted for the gold fields. Shortly thereafter, on March 15, General Smith repeated his pronouncement against foreigners.

Later, after Walter Colton, still the alcalde of Monterey, had convinced Smith that most of the gold mined by the Latins ended in the hands of American storekeepers and whiskey vendors and after Mason had set him straight on the law—*every* digger in the mountains was a trespasser—the general backed away from his edict. News of his original statements spread swiftly, however, and his words were shouted back and forth by the stampeders to justify open attacks on all greasers. (Less was said about foreign Germans, Cornishmen, Englishmen, and Irishmen, who seemed more like Anglo-Saxons.) In April, gangs of roughnecks drove all dark-skinned miners from the diggings near Coloma. Sporadic attacks followed in other camps and were topped by a Fourth of July assault in Sacramento.

Utterly discouraged, the Californios withdrew to their ranches. The Mexicans retreated to the southern mines surrounding what was then called the great camp of the Sonoranians, today's Sonora, on a tributary of the Stanislaus River. Simultaneously scores of Chileans streamed back to San Francisco. No escape was there; the ships in the harbor had been immobolized by the desertion of their crews. So the refugees took shelter with certain of their countrymen who were camped on the north side of Yerba Buena cove while they worked as bricklayers and bakers for the expanding city. There we will meet them again, victims once more, down beside the gorgeous bay, of California's governmental vacuum.

For it was not just in the mines that near-anarchy prevailed. Everywhere—on the ranches, in the towns, at the military headquarters in Monterey—uncertainty and confusion clouded each attempt to provide for the future. Somehow those wild and grotesque forces had to be controlled. As long as Congress refused to act, the responsibility rested with the military, yet already it was doubtful that the military could stay atop the situation, as no one realized any better than did Colonel Richard Mason, waiting uneasily for the arrival of his successors.

13. A Harness for the Tiger

California's sixth military governor, General Bennet Riley, assumed office on April 13, 1849—a fitting date, the superstitious might have argued. For in addition to the tumult in the mines, he was faced, as Mason soon made clear to him, with a plethora of other crises whose solution, within the American tradition of divided executive, legislative, and judicial powers, lay far beyond the competence of a monolithic military government.

Of these issues, Mason said, none raised knottier problems than did Mexican land titles. Under the Treaty of Guadalupe Hidalgo the United States had solemnly pledged to respect them. To American land seekers, raised on the small subsistence farms of the humid East, the promise was too absurd to be considered.

What, they demanded, was so sacrosanct about a Mexican grant? Fewer than 10 percent of those in California had been in existence longer than fifteen years; more than 50 percent were less than nine years old. The owners, moreover, had not earned that land, as Melvin Paden might have said, by the sweat of their brows. Save for several hundred thousand acres in the Sacramento and lower San Joaquin valleys, the bulk of it, 12 million acres or so, had been plundered from the missions. It wasn't used efficiently, either. Long stretches fertile enough to support scores of enterprising American farm families were lightly grazed by wandering herds of runty cattle owned by a single individual—generally a greaser, at that.

The gold rush was increasing the pressures. Many men who had been lucky in the mines were returning to the valleys eager to invest their earnings in the most traditional of American ways, in land. Less fortunate men, repelled by the labor of mining and shaken by the prices they had paid in the mountains for food, saw farming as a quicker road to fortune than searching for gold. But the grants were fencing both groups away from their desires.

190

Was it right to be frustrated so? For as one immigrant truculently declared, California was American now, purchased "by the treasure of the whole nation, and by no small amount of the best blood that ever coursed or ran through American veins." No ranchero, such Americans argued, could alter that truth by merely waving his hand toward an empty valley and saying, "Mine!" on the grounds that some rascally Mexican governor had given it to him in return for practically nothing.

As noted earlier, Mason had quickly sensed the approach of this clash. Hoping to prepare guidelines for the government, he had directed his chief of staff, Lieutenant Henry W. Halleck, to draw up a report on Mexican land laws and grant procedures. In March, 1849, Halleck had published his findings. Instead of easing matters, they intensified the polarization.

The Mexican rancheros, Halleck charged, had committed many legal wrongs during the careless days following the secularization of the missions. Surveys had been haphazard; no one really knew what open land might lie illegally within some of the far-ranging boundaries. Requirements concerning the prompt building of houses and the introduction of livestock onto the granted land had often been ignored. The California *diputación*'s formal approval of each title, a necessary step under the law, had not always been obtained. The governor had not always issued signed deeds—and some of those that had been issued by Pio Pico during the opening days of the war had been wrongfully antedated. Doubt even existed that the old presidial settlement of San Francisco, located originally above the Golden Gate, had been granted a valid title. If not, then the ownership of every lot in erstwhile Yerba Buena, which the Mexicans had regarded as lying within the presidial bounds, could be disputed.

Challenges to the grants, Mason predicted, were certain to come, for as soon as a title was invalidated, the land would become part of the public domain of the United States, subject to eventual appropriation by home seekers. Knowing this, squatters were already beginning to edge onto land they thought was vulnerable. What kind of Donnybrook would result if, as the tide grew and Congress still did not act, the army tried to patrol *that* situation?

There were other dilemmas—coinage, for instance. Practically no lawful money was available for circulation. Although private individuals were seeking to fill the void by manufacturing gold slugs stamped with their reputed value, the substitute was not satisfactory. California needed bonded assayers, a government mint, a trustworthy currency. Only Congress—certainly not the military—could provide that.

And what of the mountain Indians, who were growing increasingly hostile as the miners overran their acorn grounds, chopped down their trees, fouled their fishing streams, and ordered them not to mine in their own home territory? Impromptu militia fought them savagely at Coloma in May. Murderers' Bar on the Middle Fork of the American River had been named for six Oregonians killed there in retaliation for their violation of a nearby ranchería. Farther south, horse stealing, often engineered by one-time mission Indians, was a frequent occurrence. Victims demanded help from the Army, but the Army, riddled by desertions, hadn't enough troops to send. And certainly the Army was not entitled to enter into formal peace treaties with the tribes, necessary though treaties were.

So it went—roads, bridges, navigational aids, schools, hospitals, jails, taxes, and all the other things demanded by communities growing at a more headlong rate than had ever before been experienced on any frontier in the United States. How long were the people going to stand still, waiting for Congress to act?

The San Francisco Legislative Assembly was symptomatic. A series of electoral misadventures early in 1849 had left the city with rival town councils claiming jurisdiction. Exasperated by the squabble, the voters held a special election without authorization from the military governor, abolished both councils, ordered Alcalde Thaddeus Leavenworth out of office, and placed the city's administration in the hands of a fifteen-man Legislative Assembly. Power to the people, they were saying in effect.

The step had scarcely been completed when General Persifor Smith arrived to assume command of the Army's Department of the Pacific. Although Smith had no civil authority, the Assembly, impatient to test the military—and determined also to circumvent Alcalde Leavenworth, who had appealed to Smith for help in maintaining his office—sent a committee to call on the general and explain why the city was rejecting the Mexican alcalde-*ayuntamiento* system that he was supposed to support.

Smith retorted that they could not reject it. Only Congress could authorize fundamental changes. The Assembly was therefore illegal and he would not recognize it.

If that argument held, then any convention that met without authorization to draw up some form of constitutional government for California would also be illegal and its actions void. During the winter of 1848–49, it will be remembered, several mass meetings had called for such conventions. Some delegates had been elected. But distance, bad weather, bad roads, and the reluctance of a few civic leaders to act outside legal channels had resulted in postponements. So Smith might have tiptoed around that sleeping dog by not raising the question of authority. But he had stamped hard, though it wasn't his responsibility, and his rejection of the

Assembly led that body to rear up and utter yet another call for an election of delegates to gather in Monterey in September. California would have a government responsible to its citizens, whether the Army approved or not. Now what would the general say?

Belatedly Smith decided to say nothing and let the proper officer, Bennet Riley, handle the problem on his arrival. Faced with what amounted to rebellion, Riley had no choice but to declare in his turn that the Assembly was indeed illegal. He ordered the voters of San Francisco to schedule a new election at which they would choose a new *ayuntamiento* and a new alcalde. Until that was done, he decreed, Leavenworth would remain in office.

Underneath his apparent rigidity, Riley was nevertheless shaken. As Mason had made very plain, California badly needed an area-wide civil government within the framework of the American system. If Congress remained dilatory, then the people were almost sure to follow San Francisco's lead in acting without permission. About the only way he could maintain a show of authority was to undercut the Assembly's presumptions by stepping in ahead of it and calling for a constitutional convention on his own responsibility. But how would Washington react to that? Indeed, the step might be unnecessary. Polk's lame-duck Congress might have ordered, just before its expiration in March, some kind of action, and Riley would look mighty foolish if he went out on a limb to order what had already been done. A quandary. . . .

Like most career officers, Riley didn't like quandaries. He was sixty-two years old, very erect, his round amiable face framed by curly hair and fine, fuzzy sideburns that reached almost to the corners of his smooth-shaven mouth. Several campaigns, beginning with the War of 1812 and stretching through Scott's final drive on Mexico City, had brought him a reputation for high courage, sonorous profanity, remarkable tact, and unfailing carefulness. The latter trait asserted itself now. He sent the new steamship *Edith* to Mazatlán with orders that she stay there until her captain received definite word about Congress' actions during the closing days of Polk's regime.

The ship returned at the end of May, 1849. Nothing. Riley plunged then. On June 3, he issued a proclamation calling for an election, on August 1, of delegates who would meet in Monterey early in September and draw up a constitution for either a state or a territorial government, as seemed wisest after full discussion. Upstaged thus neatly, the San Francisco Legislative Assembly tried to persuade the people to heed *its* call rather than Riley's, but could not win interest. Withering for lack of support, it went out of business, leaving San Francisco in the charge of Alcade Leavenworth and an ineffective caretaker government.

On June 4, proponents of a state rather than a territorial government for California received unexpected help. The *Panama*, another vessel of the Pacific Mail Steamship Company, nosed through the Golden Gate with two hopeful politicians among the swarms on her decks. One was Thomas Butler King, an ambitious Congressman from Georgia and the personal representative of the newly inaugurated President of the United States, Zachary Taylor. The other was Dr. William McKendree Gwin of Mississippi, a rich land speculator and war profiteer who was now in quest of political power.

King, his natural vanity swollen by the touch of presidential blessing, had been instructed by Taylor to determine whether California was truly ready for statehood. If so, then perhaps her residents could break the Congressional deadlock over slavery by deciding for themselves, at a state constitutional convention, whether involuntary servitude was to be allowed within her borders. Congress would either have to accept the decision or create an infernal row. Taylor expected acquiescence. Meantime the Californians had already started the ball rolling. A new state meant two new senatorships . . . why not, King wondered as he contemplated the situation, declare himself a resident of California and lay hold of one of them?

A similar thought had struck Dr. Gwin. He was a tall man, silver-haired at forty-four, his lean face somewhat resembling that of Andrew Jackson, whose protégé he had once been. Trained in both law and medicine, Gwin had never practiced the latter calling but liked to be addressed as Doctor. Although he had served for a time as a federal marshal in Mississippi and had been elected to a single term in the House of Representatives, major offices had eluded him. The defeat of the Democrats in '48 suggested that the drought might continue, at least in the East. But in the West. . . . As he stood on the steps of Willard's Hotel in Washington, watching Taylor's inaugural parade, he remarked to his companion, Senator Stephen A. Douglas of Illinois, that inasmuch as Congress had failed to provide a government for California, the residents would have to act for themselves. He proposed to join them, push for statehood without any intervening territorial stage, and in the process have himself elected Senator.

Let us anticipate briefly here. Still another potential candidate was riding west, young Lochinvar himself, John Charles Frémont. After his court-martial, Frémont had been employed by St. Louis businessmen, his father-in-law Senator Benton among them, to find a railroad route between Missouri and San Francisco. His reputation restored by success, the explorer would then settle in California. His wife Jessie and their small daughter Elizabeth were already journeying there via the Isthmus to meet him. By coincidence they reached San Francisco aboard the *California* (it had finally corraled a new crew) on June 4, the same day that King and Gwin landed from the *Panama*.

Frémont meanwhile had run into disaster while searching during the dead of winter for a pass through the San Juan Mountains of what is now southern Colorado. One-third of his thirty-three men died in howling blizzards. Retreating to Taos, New Mexico, the party regrouped and continued west by way of the Gila River. In southern Arizona they encountered an extraordinary caravan out of Sonora—1,200 men, women, and children, according to Jessie Frémont's recollection of her husband's tale. In spite of their numbers, the men, dressed in baggy white pantaloons and big sombreros, feared the Apaches. They begged to accompany Frémont's group for protection. The explorer agreed and also helped ferry the caravan across the Colorado River in boats improvised out of cowhides.

From the Sonorans, Frémont learned of the gold discoveries. His despair over his failures at the court-martial and in the Rockies changed to wild hope. The grant, Las Mariposas, that Larkin had bought for him from Alvarado for $3,000 was no great distance southeast of the deposits on the Tuolumne and Stanislaus rivers. Suppose Mariposas' streams also contained mineral!

Forgetting his earlier fury at Larkin for fobbing the remote place off onto him, Frémont became *patrón* for twenty-eight of the Sonoran males, grubstaking them and their families for the rest of the year in return for half of whatever gold they found. After sending them to Mariposas under one of his mountain men, Alexis Godey, Frémont picked up Jessie and Elizabeth in San Francisco and moved them to a small adobe house in Monterey. He then rode as fast as his horses could carry him out to the grant. By that time the Sonorans were bringing gold into Alexis' camp in leather sacks that held (again the figures are Jessie's) 100 pounds of gold dust and nuggets each.

The legality of Las Mariposas was suspect. It was a floating grant; Pio Pico's decree awarding it to Alvarado had designated only a general area, leaving it up to the grantee to determine the final boundaries after receiving the papers. That in itself was frowned on by Mexican law, unless unusual circumstances could be cited. The grantee, moreover, should have made his surveys within a year and then have gone through the obligatory steps of building a house and introducing livestock. Because of the hostility of the Indians, Alvarado had not met the requirements. It could be argued, therefore, that the title Larkin had purchased for Frémont was by no means valid.

(How lucky can you get? In June, 1849, before anything was known in Washington about the grant, other than Frémont's displeasure, Senator Benton had arranged for another son-in-law, William Carey Jones, to be appointed special agent of the General Land Office for examining Mexican land practices in California. Lawyer Jones, who had been Frémont's counsel during the court-martial, landed in Monterey in September, 1849. Naturally he talked to the Frémonts. He was familiar by then with Halleck's negative report on the validity of most Mexican titles. But when Jones issued his own report a few months thereafter, he said that in his opinion most grants were defensible, at least in equity. One might be tempted to cynicism, except for the fact that Benton and Jones had already indicated, in dealing with French and Spanish grants in Louisiana, Arkansas, and Missouri, a disposition to favor an easy interpretation of foreign land laws.)

No one knows how many leather sacks filled with nuggets the Sonorans brought to Frémont. More importantly, they traced the gold to its source in quartz veins that outcropped nearby. Drawing on native Mexican techniques, they introduced hard-rock mining to California, grinding the ore in clumsy *arrastres*, stone-floored pits in which the quartz was pulverized beneath huge boulders pulled in circles by weary mules. Altogether Las Mariposas yielded to Frémont, through the Sonorans, the largest single fortune ever taken from the early diggings. And if you're that rich, you must be smart. Frémont decided that he, too, would be a good Senator for California to have.

Before there could be senators, there must be a state. Thomas King and Dr. Gwin both toured the northern settlements, urging the voters to instruct their delegates to skip the territorial stage, just as Texas had done, and enter the Union with full political maturity—just as though a declaration of maturity were enough to bring it about.

As the President's representative, King was able to command a military escort headed by no less than General Persifor Smith. Unhappily, the Congressman's judgment did not match his dignity. He insisted on riding through the midday summer heat of the Central Valley until sunstroke dropped him half-dead in his tracks. Silver-maned William Gwin traveled more cautiously and more quietly, listening as much as he talked. By the time he returned to San Francisco, he was well acquainted with the problems of most immediate concern to the electorate: land titles, foreign miners, Indian unrest, and law and order.

In mid-July two of the issues—racism and order—boiled over in the chaotic city beside the bay. Many Latin Americans, it will be recalled, had sought refuge there after being driven out of the mining camps, largely by the swinging clubs and profane threats of several members of Colonel J. D. Stevenson's disbanded regiment of New York volunteers. Unhappily for the victims, still other New Yorkers were in San Francisco, where they had been commissioned by Alcalde Thaddeus Leavenworth to function as a sort of unofficial police force. Calling themselves variously the Hounds and the Regulators, these irregular patrolmen operated out of a huge tent labeled Tammany Hall. Associated with them were several newly arrived stampeders from the penal colonies of Australia. San Franciscans called the latter Sydney Ducks.

When patrolling the streets—they often began their evenings by swaggering into some restaurant and demanding food and drink for which they did not pay—the Hounds occasionally amused themselves by tormenting greasers. On Sundays they paraded through the center of town behind blaring bands. Most of San Francisco's rapidly shifting population reacted by keeping out of the way. Eventually, though, lawlessness by these protectors of the law passed endurance.

On July 14, at the close of one of their Sunday celebrations, the Hounds swarmed over to the encampment of Chileans and Peruvians on the north shore of the cove. They broke into shacks, tore down tents, robbed, raped, beat, and, in one or two instances, killed. The next day Alcalde Leavenworth, utterly disillusioned by the excesses of his constabulary, summoned a mass meeting in the plaza, now Portsmouth Square. Climbing onto the roof of the alcalde's office building, Sam Brannan urged the angry crowd to form a Law and Order party.

On the face of things, Brannan was an incongruous defender of decency, for after his apostasy from the Mormon Church he had appropriated to his own use church tithings that he had been collecting from the faithful in California and church property that had been entrusted to his care. Perhaps, as Walton Bean has suggested, his aggressive support of virtue in vigilante situations was an unconscious effort to purge away his own sense of guilt. Be that as it may, he had a compelling presence and a stirring voice. His transported listeners took up a collection for the injured Chileans and then organized a counterattack against the Hounds.

American legal procedures were carefully followed. A grand jury of twenty-four men heard evidence from the distraught Chileans and issued indictments against about twenty suspects, including the leader of the Hounds, Sam Roberts, a one-time lieutenant of Stevenson's volunteers. Citizen patrols arrested the accused and then, because San Francisco had no jail as yet, handed them for safekeeping to the *Warren*, a U.S. warship in the harbor.

As alcalde of the city, Leavenworth had the duty of presiding over the trials that followed. Leavenworth, however, was suspect. The citizens accordingly elected two men to serve as his associate judges. One was William Gwin. Prosecutors and defense attorneys were appointed, and the trials held at once. Sam Roberts and eight others were convicted. But in a jailless city what could be done with them? Repelled by the thought of flogging, Gwin argued for banishment. The recommendation was accepted, perhaps unfortunately. The culprits merely dropped out of sight for a time. Then, after seeing that retribution was neither terrible nor sure, they drifted back into the streets. The only effect of the episode was to make them more careful—for a time.

Gwin had scored, however. On August 1, fifty-seven days after his arrival in California, he was chosen one of San Francisco's delegates to the constitutional convention at Monterey. Altogether forty-eight men assembled there in early September, in Colton's stone meeting hall. Of this number exactly one-fourth were forty-niners. (Neither King, who had been ill at election time, nor Frémont, who had been too busy weighing sacks to campaign, was among them.) Eight were native Californios. One of them, Manuel Dominguez of Los Angeles, was the son of an Indian mother. Only two of them could speak English. Associated with those eight were three Anglo-American ranchers, once naturalized Mexicans, who had married Californio girls. A fourth rancher, Hugo Reid, was married to an Indian. To put it another way, the Californios, who by September, 1849, made up less than 24 percent of the area's total population, were well represented at the convention, both directly and indirectly.

Efforts were made to placate them. After Robert Semple, a one-time Bear Flagger, had been chosen presiding officer, the delegates requested that he be escorted to his chair, as a sign of amity, by Mariano Vallejo and John Sutter. It worked. Considering the wide divergence in interests between northern and southern California, and between greasers and gringos, the lack of rancor during the deliberations was remarkable.

The rancheros and traders of the south desired a territorial government, for then federal money would support most civic institutions. Statehood, by contrast, would mean heavy taxes. Inasmuch as the miners held no title to their claims, only usufructuary rights, and were adamantly opposed to any form of licensing, the levies would almost certainly fall heaviest on ranch property. Hoping to wriggle out of the dilemma, José Carrillo of Los Angeles suggested dividing California in half, the northern part to be a state, the southern to be a territory. The motion lost. Yet even this clear indication that the agricultural south was going to be dominated by the gold-mining north did not lead the southerners to bolt the meeting.

A few delegates, Gwin included, favored extending California as far east as the Rockies. The majority rejected so vast an ambition. Such a state would be hopelessly big to administer, and, besides, what about the Mormons around Great Salt Lake? They could not be included without representation at the convention, could they? After long discussion, the boundaries that still prevail were accepted.

Dueling was prohibited—fruitlessly, as we shall see. A married woman's right to own property was recognized, as it had been under Mexican law, in the hope that the liberality might attract females to predominately male California.

Aware that slavery had been the great issue blocking Congressional action concerning California, the delegates treated the question with gingerliness. Even though several Southerners were in the body, they unanimously outlawed servitude. They also voted down a provision that would have excluded free blacks from the state on the grounds that working beside a Negro, free or slave, would be degrading. The question of suffrage for blacks was left to future action by the legislature. Less restraint was shown toward Indians and half-breeds. In spite of the presence of mestizo Manuel Dominguez and the impassioned plea of Pablo de la Guerra of Santa Barbara that the Indians "were once a proud and gifted race," the indispensable builders of Spanish and Mexican California, both groups were denied the right to vote.

The debates ended on October 12, 1849. The four tables at which the delegates had been working were then hustled outside, and pine boughs were brought in to decorate the hall for a grand ball financed by the state makers as a gesture of appreciation for Monterey's hospitality. Three chandeliers, "neither of bronze nor cut-glass," reported visitor Bayard Taylor, furnished light. A Mexican orchestra of two guitars and two violins provided music. Sixty or seventy begowned and bejeweled women attended; "the dark-eyed daughters of Monterey, Los Angeles, and Santa Barbara mingled in pleasing contrast with the fairer bloom of trans-Nevadaian belles."

The next day was reserved for the signing of the constitution. Sutter wept for joy. Ships in the harbor boomed out thirty-one salutes for (Congress agreeing) the thirty-first state of the Union. The completed document was then rushed to San Francisco, to the only print shop in California.

Eight thousand copies, 6,000 in English and 2,000 in Spanish, were run off and distributed to every known settlement—new ones kept springing up nearly every day. Balloting took place at designated spots on November 13, 1849. Heavy rains held down participation, but even granting that, interest could not have been intense. Only 15 percent of the eligible voters went to the polls. They approved the constitution 12,061 to 811.

Peter Burnett, who had come down from Oregon in '48 and had played an active part in promoting the movement for civil government, was chosen governor.

The men elected to the assembly and the senate of the first legislature met in an unfinished hall in San Jose on December 15, 1849. Although at first they did not have enough paper for writing down resolutions, they settled to work with vim. Their first order of business was the election of two United States Senators—assuming always that Congress would receive them. Thomas Butler King, though nominated, was no contender. Frémont was selected on the first ballot, Gwin on the third. The pair left for the East via Panama on the first ship they could catch—and then spent months cooling their heels in the nation's capital.

In California, the legislature was so busy that it declined to adjourn even for the holiday week between Christmas and New Year's. It defined the duties of state officers, formed 27 counties and designated their seats, and established machinery for county and town governments. Just as the Californios had feared, it inaugurated the first property tax in California. It defeated attempts either to abolish or to license gambling. Because of expense it did nothing about public schools, handing over the responsibility during the first few years to religious organizations and private educators. Both groups worked hard, but the long-range effect of the neglect can be surmised from the report of the Superintendent of Public Education in 1859, after a public school system had finally started. Of the 40,530 school-age children in California, only 11,183 had received any formal education whatsoever.

Except for this neglect of education, the work of the first legislature was fully in tune with the insistent spirit of Manifest Destiny. Insofar as homogenization could be achieved by legislative action, California was to be made recognizably American—or, as Timothy Hunt, the first Protestant minister to reach San Francisco, put it, she was to shine forth as "THE MASSACHUSETTS OF THE PACIFIC."

To help speed New England's light among the Spanish-speaking, the office of state translator was created. Except where it was repugnant to the constitution of the United States or to the laws of California, the common law of England was to guide the work of the state courts. Nativist and color biases emerged nakedly. Any person having one-fourth or more Indian blood or one-half or more Negro blood was barred from giving evidence in court cases involving whites. A tax of $20 a month was imposed on foreign miners. (They would have been excluded entirely except that states could not legislate concerning the public domain.) Although the proponent of the tax bill, Thomas Jefferson Green, argued perfunctorily that the measure would raise $2.4 million in needed revenue, his primary purpose, he admitted candidly, was putting pressure on Latin Americans. He had no more compunction about injuring them, he said in public, than about crushing body lice.

Its multitudinous tasks accomplished, the legislature adjourned on April 22, 1850. Shortly afterward, one of its members, state senator John Bidwell, sailed for the East. He had charge of one of those gaudy propaganda symbols for which California has always shown a penchant, in this case a great chunk of gold-bearing quartz to be used in the Washington Monument, then under construction. He was also to lobby for the state's admission to the Union.

The slow grinding of politics had more effect than did Bidwell. After months of acrimonious debate, the Senate hammered out the famed Compromise of 1850, under which California was recognized as a free state. President Fillmore signed the bill of admission on September 9, 1850, a legal holiday in California still. Frémont and Gwin drew straws to determine which should have the short term ending March 3, 1851, and which the long, ending in March, 1855. The short fell to Frémont.

The official documents confirming admission were entrusted to John Bidwell for delivery home—fittingly enough, since he had been a leader of the first party of American settlers to cross overland to Mexican California nine years before, in 1841. (Time does march: in 1850 he was still only thirty years old.) On September 13 he left New York aboard a ship bound for Panama. Traveling with him were the wife and daughter of lawyer Elisha O. Crosby of San Jose, another member of that first legislature. Gallantly Bidwell gave the papers to the daughter, Mary Helen Crosby, for safekeeping. She slept with them under her pillow at night and carried them across the Isthmus, in bongo and on muleback, tightly bound in her umbrella. On October 18, 1850, after one of the fastest trips yet made from the East Coast, she stepped ashore with them in her hand to a wild celebration of bonfires, cannon shots, band music, serpentine parades, and endless oratory. The tiger had a harness now. Whether he would be any more manageable in it than he had been without it remained to be seen.

14. Organized Violence

The consent of the governed implies cooperation between the governed and the officials whom they elect to enact, administer, interpret, and, if necessary, change the rules of the game. For various reasons, that essential cooperation frequently collapsed in gold-rush California, to be replaced by organized violence on the part of a minority of citizens who took it upon themselves to decide, just as they had done before legal government was established, how certain brutal crises in their lives should be resolved.

The main areas wherein the most of this social violence occurred have already been suggested—land problems, the treatment of foreigners, Indian affairs, and crime. The provocations that triggered the popular uprisings were sometimes extreme. In spite of those justifications, however—and in spite of the good men and true who in nearly every instance called for a return to those concepts of fair play that are as much a part of the American heritage as are its moments of barbarism—the story adds up to some of the most distressing reading in the nation's history. On the basis of that warning, the squeamish may decide to skip this long chapter.

For the sake of convenience, let us employ subheads, as textbooks do, and group the uprisings according to the predominant trait that lifted each into fury.

Greed

Frustrations over land acquisition first erupted into violence in Sacramento. During the wet winter of 1849–50, the city absorbed thousands of derelicts: miners washed out of the hills by severe storms and immigrants who had crossed the Sierra too late in the year to continue to the gold fields. The tents and board shanties of the throngs filled every vacant lot along the existing streets and spilled helter-skelter into the outskirts beyond.

Simultaneously the city was spinning into hectic prosperity as a distribution point for merchandise bound to the northern mines. After contemplating the frantic growth, many newcomers decided to stay in Sacramento rather than continue to the foothills. But when they tried to buy lots, they discovered that the bulk of the city's real estate was controlled by a handful of men claiming to hold titles that derived from Sutter's Mexican land grant of 1839. Ubiquitous Sam Brannan, for one, owned 200 choice lots that he had bilked from the befuddled Swiss for next to nothing.

Mutterings intensified. Monopoly built on a Mexican title? To hell with such frauds. Truculently the more aggressive squatters, as the landlords called them, moved onto the lots they wanted, built flimsy fences, put up tents or plank shacks, and dared the rapacious speculators, as the squatters considered them, to start proceedings toward ejection.

There might have been violence that winter, except for an enormous yellow flood that early in January, 1850, rolled across the city, seven feet deep in places. Tents collapsed; shanties filled with mud. Rescuers in rowboats plucked invalids off mattresses floating aimlessly about and delivered them through the attic windows of a little hospital recently built by doctors Morse and Stillman. People able to move about fled to the top floors of the few two-story houses in town, to ships tied to the submerged *embarcadero* (landing place) on the riverbank, or to high ground occupied by a lumberyard where, one observer remarked dryly, wood for coffins was handy.

Nobody was discouraged. Speculators on rooftops made deals for vacant lots invisible beneath the stagnant flood. As the streets dried, more people poured in. By March, 1850, according to a letter that merchant Collis Huntington wrote home, the town's population had reached 10,000 including 600 women "and Som foure-fiths of those are Harlots." Meantime the first state legislature, meeting in San Jose, set up the forms of county and city governments, including courts. Rejoicing that they now lived in an American-style municipality, Sacramentans trooped to the polls and elected Harden Bigelow as their mayor on a platform committed to building flood-control levees along the river fronts.

As soon as he was safely ensconced in office, Bigelow declared that he would maintain existing land titles until the proper U.S. courts could rule on the validity of Sutter's grant. Emboldened by the support, Sam Brannan and other landholders secured writs of ejection against certain obstreperous squatters who had settled on their lots. Armed with these writs, a sheriff's posse began tearing down the offending shacks. A crowd gathered. Rallying a group of law-and-order citizens, Mayor Bigelow joined the posse and sought to disperse the jeering throng. A wild riot erupted. During it the city assessor and the leader of the rioters died; the mayor and several more were wounded. The next day an augmented posse went to a tavern outside the city limits to arrest some of the more active rioters. Another fracas developed. This time the sheriff and two squatters were killed; many were injured.

Sentiment swung behind the legally constituted government. The leaders of the ill-organized squatters were arrested and charged by a complaisant grand jury with murder, even though some of them had not been present during the fighting. (One had been in jail at the time.) In the squatters' view, the jury and court actions that followed were part of a conspiracy to break them. Intense excitement swept through the northern counties and into the state senate, where impassioned debates were held over a motion to condemn the actions of the grand jury and the judge of the district court.

The driving force behind this effort to make the legislature interfere with judicial organizations that it had just created was David C. Broderick. Once an abstemious saloonkeeper and capable Tammany ward heeler in New York City, Broderick had traveled west with a vow like William Gwin's: in California he would lift himself by his bootstraps into the United States Senate. Shortly after reaching San Francisco in June, 1849, he had gone into business manufacturing gold slugs for the almost coinless city. Investing his profits judiciously in real estate, he became comparatively wealthy within a few months. Aided by discharged members of Stevenson's regiment of New York Volunteers, he simultaneously developed a highly efficient, brass-knuckle political machine modeled on Tammany Hall. In January, 1850, at a special election to fill a vacancy in the state senate, this creation showed its power by rounding up 2,503 votes for Broderick as against 101 votes for all his rivals combined. Within another year Broderick was presiding officer of the senate.

During the intense debate over the resolution to condemn the district court, Broderick declared that if the bill failed to pass, he would raise an army of 5,000 men and forcibly free the Sacramento prisoners. How effective this extraordinary threat of rebellion really was cannot be determined. Most legislators favored the squatters—they had the votes—and the bill was easily whooped through, only to be vetoed by the governor. No march proved necessary, however. Lacking evidence to sustain murder charges against the accused (and cowed perhaps by the squatter feeling that was rallying behind Broderick), the prosecuting attorneys of Sacramento County suddenly entered nolle prosequis and the cases were dropped. The triumphant squatters immediately elected one of the erstwhile defendants, Charles Robinson, to the legislative assembly. But until some final decision concerning the validity of Sutter's title was handed down by the United States, no permanent solution to the tensions was possible.

In Washington, Senator William Gwin was preparing a more legal assault than rebellion on titles derived from Mexico. Let each claimant, he said, convince a board of impartial commissioners that his deed met every requirement of legitimacy. If so, then of course the United States would respect the property, as promised by the Treaty of Guadalupe Hidalgo. There were snags along the way, however. If either the claimants or the attorneys of the United States government disagreed with the decisions of the Land Commission, they could appeal to the suitable district court for reversal, and, if necessary, from there to the nation's Supreme Court. What could be fairer?

Instantly Senator Benton of Missouri was on his feet with a roar of sarcasm. Any law that might require a grantee to prove his case three times (before the Land Commission and then, if the government appealed, before a district court and possibly the Supreme Court, too), any such a law, because of the delays and expenses it enforced, amounted to "confiscation—slow, expensive, agonizing confiscation."

Benton spoke out of experience. In his younger days he had handled hundreds of grant cases throughout the southern parts of the Louisiana Purchase. He knew how easy it was, during frontier times, for a grantee to violate one or more of the technicalities of the law. Over and over he had argued that unless obvious fraud was involved, the very show of title should be accepted as prima facie evidence of legitimacy. If some covetous squatter wanted to challenge a grantee's deed, let *him* assume the burden of proof.

Trends were against the Senator, however. Suspicious of large, undeveloped holdings and committed to the nineteenth century's agrarian faith in the widespread distribution of land as one means of assuring human dignity, Congress had consistently placed the burden of proof upon the grant holders. (Gwin's bill was merely an adaptation of those earlier statutes.) In the California situation, furthermore, Benton's eloquence was tainted by his two sons-in-law. One, William Carey Jones, after reporting favorably to Congress on the validity of Mexican titles, had purchased a huge holding in southern California and of course wanted it confirmed with as little pain as possible. The other son-in-law, John Charles Frémont, had even stronger motives. The 45,000 acres he had purchased from Alvarado had not only made an overnight millionaire of him but had helped lift him out of national disgrace into a United States senatorship. For whom, exactly, was Benton pleading?

Congress shut its ears to him, and on March 3, 1851, less than three weeks after Broderick had threatened marching 5,000 men against Sacramento to free the jailed squatters, Gwin's bill became law.

So claimants were wrong until they proved themselves right! The moment the word reached California, settlers who had been leasing land from grant holders ceased paying rent and began treating the property as if they already owned it. Thousands of squatters, particularly in the northern counties, moved in beside them, hoping to obtain the plots they settled on by preemption as soon as title was invalidated and the grant became part of the public domain. They killed the cattle that "trespassed" on "their" unfenced land and sold the meat to the butcher shops in the closest towns. They fenced off owners from necessary streams and cut down their trees for firewood. They formed associations that hired lawyers to fight the grantees; a Settlers' League in Santa Clara County financed its legal battles by picking and selling the fruit of its opponents' orchards. The east coast of San Francisco Bay, occupied even before secularization by several members of the Estudillo and Peralta families, was lined by the shanties of some 1,500 squatters. By ingeniously playing on the desperation of the Peraltas, a sharper named Horace Carpentier gained the family's confidence and then fleeced them out of 19,000 lovely, bay-front, tree-shaded acres whereon he founded the city of Oakland.

The three-man Land Commission brought into being by Gwin's bill began its hearings in San Francisco on January 2, 1852. It adjourned permanently on March 1, 1856. Throughout those four years, except for the commission's brief sitting in Los Angeles during the fall of 1852, grant holders had to travel to the Bay city with their documents for their hearings. All told, 813 cases were investigated. They involved grants ranging from one to eleven leagues in size. The total area embraced in the litigation amounted to more than 12 million acres.

By and large the commission proved sympathetic to the grantees. Of the claims presented, it approved 521 and disallowed 273. The remaining 19 cases were dropped before hearings were completed, presumably because they were hopeless to start with.

Sympathy was of little help, however, in the face of delay. The commission moved like a glacier, and after that came the appeals. One hundred and thirty-two of the claimants whose titles were rejected appealed to the courts; 98 eventually won reversals. By contrast, the government's attorneys appealed 417 decisions favoring the grantees—but won only 5 reversals! The ratio is absurd enough that one wonders whether the government appeals were still another form of deliberate harassment. Be that as it may, two-thirds of the grant holders had to find money and time enough, often in the face of constant annoyance from the squatters on their property, to see their cases through the upper courts.

Even when they won they weren't finished. They had to dig into their pockets again to pay for accurate surveys of what the United States had finally agreed to let them have. This, too, took time and resulted in bitter contests—even open battles—when squatters suspected that a grantee was deliberately jiggling his lines, as some did, to absorb choice meadows, streams, or strands of timber that hadn't been part of the original allotment.

Let Las Mariposas serve as an example. It was the first claim presented to the commission (William Carey Jones served as Frémont's lawyer) and was quickly approved, though many legal requirements had not been met by either Frémont or Alvarado. The government appealed, and the District Court reversed the decision, declaring the grant invalid. Jones and Frémont promptly carried the case to the Supreme Court. It ruled in Frémont's favor just before he became the Republican nominee for the presidency of the United States. When his surveyors deliberately bent their lines (so local residents charged) in such a way as to include some of the mining towns on the land, the settlers attacked, posses tumbled out, and considerable blood was spilled before Frémont had his way. Not that it did him much good. He had poured most of his fortune back into the ground in mismanaged efforts to develop suitable milling techniques for the quartz ores his Sonora peons had found, and now he was almost bankrupt again.

Frémont being who he was, his case was handled with unusual celerity. By the time the average claimant received final patent on his land (which his family had perhaps wrested originally from the mission Indians) he had spent *seventeen years* in litigation.

Towns that were grantees-in-trust for their inhabitants experienced comparable troubles. Four years passed before Sutter's title was confirmed and the tenseness in Sacramento could be relieved. San Francisco swindlers, counting on the uncertainties surrounding the original pueblo title, brazenly appeared before the commission with forged Mexican documents purporting to convey ownership to different parts of the city. Eventually these frauds were all exposed, but for years title to nearly every building lot in the city was obscure. Encouraged by the confusion, squatters even hired professional gunmen to camp on desired lots, intending eventually to make possession amount to right. Legitimate owners grew so nervous that after buildings burned down during one of the city's periodic fires, they built fences around the hot ashes to keep intruders away.

The social costs of this scramble for land were staggering. Everyone lost—squatters, grant holders, the state. The rancheros, indeed, were ripe for ruin. The high prices they received in the mines for their cattle fired their penchant for extravagance and gambling. Credit, meanwhile, stayed tight. Because of clouded titles, real estate was not considered prime collateral, and this helped keep interest rates fantastically high— 3 percent or more per month for many years. Whenever a Californio's calculations were upset by flood, drought, property taxes, squabbles among heirs, collapsing cattle prices, or, above all, by the long battle to retain his holdings, he had no reserve on which to fall back. Great chunks of land passed into the control of moneylenders and other creditors, principally lawyers. Such parcels as happened to be near towns were often subdivided, thus extending ownership, but the majority weren't. Concentrated quickly in a few hands, these vast estates became one more incentive leading to the corporate farming of future years.

The squatters' situation was no better. They would be ejected if grant titles proved sound, and this discouraged permanent building or land improvement. Although many honest land seekers were involved during the early days of the movement, the delays and uncertainties caused most to drift away, leaving the field to a restless, shiftless, opportunistic class that hoped to batten on luck, not farming. Meantime potential agriculturists in the East heard the clamors and stayed away in droves. It has been estimated that if the grant problem had not existed, California's population in 1860 would have been more than a million rather than 380,000. The growth that did occur was for the most part industrial and urban, not agricultural, as elsewhere on the frontiers. By reducing demand for the subdivision of big ranches, this slowing of agricultural expansion also helped perpetuate monopolistic landholdings—the very ogre the first squatters had thought they were slaying.

It is too easy to blame Gwin's bill for the troubles. The real villain, aside from the law's delays, was widespread, gold-fed lust for profitable lands—unearned increment—in areas where little acreage was open for claiming in classic American ways. Since a sizable part of the populace wanted to block the confirmation of Mexican titles under any circumstances, they probably would have found ways to snarl whatever system of reviews was offered. But this is guesswork. The only thing that appears to have been confirmed beyond appeal is an old folk saying: ramming your whole fist into a cookie jar isn't always the best way to get what you want.

Prejudice

During the second week of May, 1850, a tax collector named Lorenzo A. Besançon, a New Yorker by birth despite his name, posted notices throughout Tuolumne County that on the thirteenth he would open an office in the town of Sonora for collecting the monthly tax of $20 recently imposed on all foreign miners by the legislature. It was really a humane bill, he said. Payment of the tax would soften American resentment against outsiders who were appropriating gold to which they had no right; amity thus restored, the persecution of foreigners would end.

The foreigners in Tuolumne County didn't believe any such thing. They suspected, moreover, that although the tax law read as if it applied to all foreigners, it was really zeroed in on those with the darkest skins. Anyway, $20 was too much. By 1850 incomes had dropped sharply, particularly in the dry southern mines, where a man could work only a few months a year. In those diggings $20 represented two days' work for most men, and living costs were high. The punitive drain deserved answering. Throughout the southern mines crudely lettered posters went up: "*Notice to Foreigners!* It is time to unite: Frenchmen, Chileans, Peruvians, Mexicans . . . go to the camp of Sonora next Sunday: there will we try to guarranty security for us all!"

Tree-fringed, mountain-cupped Sonora, the economic center of Mariposa, Tuolumne, and Calaveras counties, was exotic even for gold-rush California. Because the area lay at the southern end of the Sierra gold belt, it had naturally drawn a high percentage of the Mexican miners hurrying north from the province of Sonora. During the summer of 1849 their settlements became havens for Latin Americans fleeing from mobs in the northern counties—the same mobs that had sent other Latins to San Francisco and persecution by Sam Roberts' Hounds. Of these camps Sonora was the queen. Each weekend thousands of Spanish-speaking people flowed back and forth through her winding streets, eagerly attended by shopkeepers and gamblers, many of them Americans.

At first most of the town's buildings were mere open-fronted booths covered with evergreen branches and decorated with gaudy serapes and Mexican flags. Out front were rough plank tables covered with rich cloth. Some were for gambling. Others were loaded with rare dainties—cakes, pies, fresh fruit, and drinks cooled with snow brought down from the Sierra. Indians wearing scarlet headbands hawked fresh drinking water, no insignificant item where placer mines turned every creek to liquid mud.

Women, dressed for the weekends in gay shawls and white stockings, were more common than in the northern camps, for many Sonorans brought wives or companions with them. A girl of the latter class was called a man's *mujer*, his woman, and she was not a whore, as prowling Americans sometimes failed to realize. To be sure, there were prostitutes as well, Indians and also Frenchwomen brought up from San Francisco. There were other entertainments, too. On Sunday afternoons almost everyone turned out for the bullfights, and at night there was a great deal of music and singing.

In this milieu American miners and storekeepers formed a small minority. As the protesting Latins, some 5,000 of them led by two exiled French revolutionaries, began gathering on a hill overlooking the town, fear shivered through the Anglos. The few American women in the vicinity ran for shelter in William Perkins' adobe store, the stoutest building available, and the local justice of the peace rushed messengers to nearby camps, begging for help.

The balance of power changed swiftly. The Latins had marched on Sonora without a definite program, and their French leaders provided them with nothing more than incendiary slogans to shout. The gathering was so fragmented, indeed, trying to enjoy a holiday while confronting the government, that it did not even try to check the armed rescuers who, during the evening and the next morning, marched from the neighboring camps into the beleaguered town. Soon 500 or so were on hand. The gun-shy Latins—the Americans lumped them all together as Spaniards —thereupon melted away.

Hearing that the greasers were regrouping at the newly discovered, extraordinarily rich camp of Columbia four miles to the north, the Americans marched there, guns ready. All was quiet. The patriots tore down the few foreign flags they saw floating, raised the Stars and Stripes on a staff improvised from a tall pine tree, fired a salute, fined the two French leaders of the protest five dollars each for "treason," and dispersed in good humor.

Anticlimax enough. But to the foreigners, most of them Mexicans, the quick rallying of the Americans to Besançon's aid was a chill omen. By the thousands they packed up and left the mountains, some for southern California and some for Mexico. The instinctive reaction was far more effective than any number of mass meetings, for each departing miner was a lost customer. After casting up their ledgers, the storekeepers of Sonora and Stockton petitioned the legislature to repeal the tax. Realizing on their own part that the measure was producing only $30,000 a year as compared to the $2,400,000 predicted by T. J. Green, the lawmakers complied.

The light came late. The winter of 1850–51 was as dry as its predecessor had been wet, and this imposed further difficulties on mining in the south. More Mexicans departed. Those who for one reason or another chose to stay were gradually relegated to the poorer placers and quartz veins, or else eased into jobs as mule skinners, at which they excelled, or as laborers for the nascent mining and ditch companies that were springing up throughout the Sierra.

Racial antagonism remained bitter, nevertheless, as illustrated by one of Dame Shirley's letters from Rich Bar on the North Fork of the Feather River. During a wild Sunday melee in July, 1852, a "Spaniard" fatally stabbed an American. His *mujer* on his arm and a cheering throng around him, the murderer brazenly paraded the streets, waving his knife on high. The Americans hastily formed a Committee of Vigilance that dispersed the throng. The murderer disappeared. Something had to be done, however. After a night filled with bonfires and whooping, the committee arrested five leading Spaniards, accused them of fomenting the riots, confiscated their property, sentenced all to banishment, and added flogging for two. One begged for execution rather than the shame and agony of whipping. He was beaten anyway, so vigorously that Dame Shirley heard the blows through the shawl in which she muffled her ears. Facing his punishers afterward, the victim vowed revenge on all Americans he could reach. Dryly the narrator adds that he probably kept his promise.

From such situations came willing recruits for the hard-riding, lasso-swinging, professional bandits, products of social upheaval in Mexico, who followed their caudillos, or chieftains, to California in search of easy pickings, either as highwaymen in the gold fields or rustlers in the ranching country. They stirred real fear—and spasmodic reaction. Of the scores of alleged criminals lynched in the mines and near Los Angeles during the first half of the 1850's, a disproportionate percentage bore Mexican names. No doubt many were guilty. And some, it developed too late, were not.

Even in official cases of justice, there was no great need to be careful about seizing the right Mexican. In May, 1853, hysteria over a legendary badman named Joaquín Murietta reached such a pitch that the legislature appointed Harry Love, one-time Texas Ranger, as captain of a special twenty-man posse, salaries $150 a month each, devoted to running Murietta to earth. In time the hunters returned with one severed head and one severed hand preserved in separate jugs of alcohol—evidence, they said, of their notable victory over Murietta's gang during a blazing gunfight in the coastal mountains. Though skeptics doubted that the head belonged to Joaquín (quite possibly he was a mythical compound of several bandits) or the hand to his crony, Three-Fingered Jack García, the legislature paid Love the $1,000 reward authorized by the governor and added out of gratitude another $5,000. For a time, be it added, banditry in the mountains did fall off.

Except that there were no Chinese bandits (Mexican *bandidos* plucked Orientals as readily as Americans), the story of the yellow-skinned miner follows a similar pattern. As long as their numbers were small, they were largely ignored. But in 1852, the year of the gold rush's biggest influx, 20,000 of the 67,000 immigrants who reached California by sea came from China. Most were indentured by their own rapacious countrymen as cheap labor for Chinese placer mining companies. This was a bitter pill. By 1852 the richest placers had been skimmed. Individual enterprise was giving way to volume work that required both capital and a labor force working for wages. To the disappointed prospectors who were being forced by grim economics to shovel not for themselves but for some faceless corporation, cheap Asiatic labor looked like yet another threat to security.

The usual preludes to discrimination followed. Authorities were found who readily declared that the Chinese were "naturally an inferior race, both mentally and corporeally." They were given to vice, opium, personal uncleanliness, depraved diets, and heathenish superstitions. In short, they were not quite human and therefore did not have to be treated like other humans.

Once more the legislature levied, for their special pain, the antiforeign miners' tax. This time, however, the assessment was kept low enough (at first $3 a month and then $4) so that it would not bring about a wholesale exodus. For the Chinese did have their financial uses. They would pay high prices for placer claims that Americans were ready to abandon. By painstaking labor they not only stayed alive on these, but for several years they also provided, through tax payments, 25 percent of the state's revenue. So it was enough simply to torment them when they came to town, pass laws requiring them to cut off their pigtails, and, as in the case of blacks and Indians, prevent them from testifying in court against whites. Their children, too, had to attend separate schools. Routine disabilities, in short. Real violence, as we shall see, was reserved for later years.

Hatred

Between 1848 and 1870, the overall Indian population of California declined, according to the estimates of S. F. Cook of the University of California, by 48,000. Most of this excess of deaths over births resulted, as in Spanish and Mexican times, from diseases against which the tribes had developed no immunity. What is harder to render statistically is the susceptibility to disease caused by malnutrition among a hunting, food-gathering society displaced from a once intimately known environment.

In addition to disease, there was violence. Cook believes that during the decade 1851–60, at least 1,000 Indian women, a high percentage of a fairly limited group, were raped so brutally that most of them died. Between 3,000 and 4,000 Indian children were kidnapped and sold into slavery. Thousands of adult women were forced by desperation into concubinage with whites. Males were reduced to peonage through vagrancy laws that allowed drunken or merely idle Indians to be jailed, often in nothing more than a walled corral, fined, and then auctioned off at so much per day to employers who would pay the fines the Indians could not meet. Supposedly the "culprits" received some pay for themselves, but generally it was handed out in the form of cheap brandy. Los Angeles' notorious Nigger Alley, the so-called toughest street in the world, was crowded each Sunday with yelling, fighting Indians who killed each other, reports merchant Harris Newmark, at the rate of one to four per weekend. Swept into the corral by a marshal's posse, they would sleep off the drunk, then be lined up for the Monday auction, and begin the round again.

They could not protest. The courts, let us remember, were not allowed to hear Indians testify in cases involving white men.

The tribes of the coastal valleys and the Los Angeles basin, their initiative already crushed by the Spanish and Mexicans, sank deeper into apathy. Those in the Sierra and the rugged Klamath Mountains of the northwest struck back. Counterreprisals of such ferocity then engulfed them as to make that much abused, loosely used word *genocide* seem almost appropriate.

Manhandling Indians is an old story, of course, and not uniquely American, as the course of the Spanish conquistadors illustrates. In pre-conquest California, such frontier rancheros as the Vallejo brothers had carried on the tradition by making peons of meek Indians and slaughtering resistant ones. Despite laws to the contrary, many *gente de razón* purchased Indian children as slaves. But the missions and simple arithmetic had provided checks of a sort; there were a lot more Indians around than Californios. It was different after the stampeders poured in—as many during the single year of '49 as there were Indians still alive. Those Indians, moreover, were gunless and horseless and lived in scattered, small, combustible villages—easy picking, boys.

By its very nature the gold rush attracted a sizable number of hoodlums, misfits, and natural bullies. Many were from the frontiers of Texas, Missouri, and Oregon, where the title "Indian fighter" was still an accolade and a black-haired scalp was a trophy to be exhibited with pride.

Dominated personalities, they attracted to their orbit many lonely, alienated semioutcasts for whom Indian hunts provided excitement, camaraderie, and a rare feeling of accomplishment. More solid citizens, stung by Indian retaliations, also leaped for their rifles from time to time, hotly convinced that they were defending hearth and home from an implacable foe.

All that is true, but it still does not fully explain what can only be called an irrational upwelling of hate against an inconvenient race. Perhaps guilt was the unrecognized soil that fed the black roots. If you loathed something enough, you didn't have to feel sorry about all the wrongs that you and yours had been inflicting for as long as memory ran.

In 1849, when no civil government had existed in California and the army had been too sapped by desertions to heed calls for help, the miners themselves had formed posses to punish Indians who stole horses to eat or who ambushed whites in revenge for an offense against some village. There was scant monetary gain in such impromptu action, however. As soon as California declared her statehood, the men who fought her battles and those who supplied the warriors began demanding pay for their services and their merchandise.

The most famous of the early militia outfits was the Mariposa Battalion. The proximate cause of its founding was the burning, by Indians, of James Savage's trading post on the Fresno River near today's roadside stop of Coarsegold, and the killing of some of his employees. (We first met Savage in '48, trading raisins to the Indians for an equivalent amount of gold dust.) Stirred by the depredations and a scattering of other murders, the governor, at the end of 1850, called for 200 volunteers, to be commanded by Savage himself. The legislature authorized a war chest of $500,000.

At that point a conflict in jurisdictions snarled what might otherwise have been a direct approach to profitable annihilation. The federal government, having at last recognized California's existence, also recognized its duty to the Indians there and moved into the field with its worn program of land swapping. The idea, half a century or so old, was to offer a tribe whose range discommoded settlement certain rewards—annual amounts of food and clothing and also instruction in farming and handicrafts—if it would yield up the area and move somewhere else. Because tribes were regarded as "nations," these bargains were sealed by solemn treaties and had to be approved by the United States Senate.

In the old days the Indians who relinquished land had generally been transported to "reserves" provided for them somewhere in the unsettled West. Nothing except ocean lay west of California, however, and so it was deemed necessary to provide land—not too valuable, of course—somewhere within the state itself. The responsibility of delineating these reserves and then persuading the Indians to move onto them was assigned to three commissioners, Redick McKee, George Barbour, and Dr. Oliver M. Wozencraft. Their budget was $50,000.

About the time the commissioners were ready to go to work, they heard of the Mariposa Battalion. War, of course, would hinder their treaty making. Accordingly they hotfooted down to the Fresno River and prevailed on Savage to suspend operations—at full pay for the idle volunteers—until they could test their own program. They laid out their first reservation beside the Fresno River and signed their first treaty with neighboring headmen on March 19, 1851. Unhappily, a significant number of Indians, declining to be bound by arbitrarily chosen "chiefs," failed to appear for resettlement. Many of the absentees, rumor said, were renegades from several bands who had hidden out in a deep, secret mountain fastness on the upper Merced River. In order that the embryo system might not be jeopardized by this kind of defiance, the Battalion was dispatched to bring them in.

En route, wading through soft spring snow, the Indian hunters came out on a high point overlooking a view so stunning that one of them, Lafayette Bunnell, remembered afterward, "A peculiar exalted sensation seemed to fill my whole being, and I found my eyes in tears with emotion." They named the valley Yosemite—Bunnell's book would help make it a household word in California—and then, tears or not, continued their human roundup.

The scheme did not work. Many Yosemite Indians avoided the net entirely. Others either escaped while being moved toward the reserve or else ran away later. The Battalion spent most of its half year of service (but only $300,000) exploring, with varying degrees of appreciation, the fantastically tumbled Yosemite area as an incident in chasing fugitives. Meanwhile the commissioners were working rapidly. During the next ten months they interviewed 402 "chiefs" representing 139 bands and laid out 18 reservations embracing 7,488,000 acres, mostly in the great Central Valley. In awarding contracts for supplying the Indians who were supposed to flock to these reserves, they exceeded their $50,000 budget by $700,000.

Everybody protested. Like the Yosemites, thousands of Indians flatly refused to be committed by the "headmen" whom they sometimes didn't even know. Those who did submit found the reservations mismanaged and hateful. The whites on their part decided that giving more than 7 percent of California's area to the aborigines was too much. In fact, any amount was excessive. Heatedly four members of the legislative assembly's five-man committee on reservations urged the national government to return to its original "policy of removing the Indians beyond the limits of civilization"—that is, kick them entirely out of California, never mind where.

Rancher J. J. Warner of San Diego, the lone dissenter on the committee, retorted angrily, "Will it be said that . . . while our doors are open to the stranger from the uttermost parts of the earth, we have not spare room for the residence of the once sole inhabitants of our magnificent empire? . . . Has the love of gold blotted from our minds all feelings of compassion or justice?" It is well to recall that voices such as Warner's were always raised against the more flagrant injustices—but there were seldom enough of them; the cost in unpopularity was too great.

Cowed by the howls of the white settlers and angered by the excessive expenditures of the commission, the Senate rejected all eighteen treaties. This enormous breach of faith with those Indians who had kept their part of the bargain led the newly appointed Superintendent of Indian Affairs for California, Edward Fitzgerald Beale, to search for a palliative. With the permission of the War Department he instituted military reserves—these did not need Senate approval—where Indians could be taught civilized arts near an Army post. The first one he established, El Tejon, in the shaggy Tehachapi Mountains of southern California, soon had 2,500 Indians farming well enough that their first harvest yielded 50,000 bushels of grain. Beale, however, fell victim to his own sloppy accounting and to the spoils system of the Indian department. In 1854 he was replaced by Thomas J. Henley, whose main interest in extending the system northward turned out to be the lucrative swindles it made possible.

Supposedly no Indian was to be compelled to live against his will on any of the five military reservations or three supplementary farms Henley established. But that edict, too, was ignored by an angry citizenry—which brings us to the horror parts of the story, parts that could be paralleled many times over if space allowed.

In the upper Sacramento Valley, in the rimrocked canyons and on the brushy ridges east of the hamlets of Tehama and Red Bluff, lived the Yana tribe. They were desperate. Mining had reduced the salmon runs; white hunters had thinned out the deer and had turned the surviving animals so wary that they were hard to reach with a bow. Every now and then slave hunters swooped up a child or two, for indentured Indian labor was quite legal in California "with the parents' permission" until 1863. Boys brought good prices from farmers; bachelors in the cities, reported the San Francisco *Bulletin* in 1861, would pay up to "a hundred dollars for a likely young girl."

The Yanas' common revenge was to steal livestock; the thefts not only exasperated the whites but also furnished food. Sometimes they capped the raids by burning a barn or a house. In 1859 one fire they set near Tehama incinerated seven whites. Thinking that a twelve-year-old Indian boy who worked for the family was at least partly responsible, a mob seized him from the county courthouse, where he was being held for questioning, and lynched him. Meeting privately then, several local ranchers launched a campaign to raise funds for wiping out the Yanas.

Years of intermittent guerrilla thrusts followed. Striking back in 1863, Indians kidnapped three white children and killed two; one escaped. Instead of trying to ascertain guilt, the whites began a frenzied roundup of the handiest Indians available. Most of those seized were Maidu who lived across the ridges on the Feather River and almost certainly had no part in the crime. Away with them, nevertheless. Four hundred and sixty-one were forcibly herded without adequate food on a 120-mile foot march to a reservation in Round Valley. Nearly 200 of the heat-stricken victims were left sick beside the trail. Of that number 32 are known to have died. Of the rest some managed to crawl back to the mountains. Concerning those who reached the reserve, where no preparations had been made for receiving them, the records are silent.

A few months later, in 1864, the Yanas killed two white women. Again no attempt was made to locate the guilty. Children first, then white women!—that proved it; Indians were fiends. Volunteers swarmed in for a concerted sweep. Everyone was fair game, including workers in the fields and servants in the farmhouses. One girl, torn from her white defenders, was shot thirteen times through the breast. The bodies of dead laborers were stripped of what little they had. By the time the systematic attack was over, between 2,000 and 3,000 Indians of all ages and both sexes were dead. There was no Yana tribe left, except for a handful of fugitives from the Yahi subband. For forty-seven years, with incredible courage and dignity, that handful survived, tragic bit players in Theodora Kroeber's heartbreaking *Ishi in Two Worlds: A Biography of the Last Wild Indian in North America.*

The slaying of two white women at least provided an excuse. The 1860 massacre at Humboldt Bay, so reported Major G. J. Raines, commanding at Fort Humboldt, had no justification whatsoever—no recent loss of life or even of cattle. Carefully rehearsed vigilantes nevertheless fell simultaneously during the dark of Saturday night, February 25, on four different villages, including one on an island where the inhabitants were holding a dance. According to Raines, 188 men, women, and children died; other reports raise the figure above 200. "I beheld," wrote the major, who went to the scene the next day, "a spectacle of horror, of unexampled description—babes, with brains oozing out of their skulls, cut and hacked with axes, and squaws exhibiting the most frightful wounds in death which imagination can paint."

A young reporter named Francis Bret Harte was harried out of the county because of his outraged editorials. The grand jury deplored the incident, but said it could not find evidence enough to warrant indictments. The shocked Army meantime took the survivors to the nearest military reserve, not to defend the whites from revenge, the classic responsibility of the War Department, but to save the Indians.

So it went, more cases than can be listed, on through the last-gasp stand of a handful of Modocs who forted up in the lava beds of northeastern California and held off 400 soldiers equipped with howitzers, on to the final indignities of poverty, starvation, and disease. By 1900, of the 250,-000 or so Indians who had lived in California when Cabrillo first saw the lovely coastline, only 16,000 remained.

Fear

For varied reasons, a large number of the stampeders did not trust their government. Busy delving for treasure, they did nothing about this breakdown in confidence so long as their own lives or pockets were not directly menaced. But whenever threats seemed to grow personal to a significant segment of the population, that segment reacted by shoving the duly constituted authorities aside and taking matters into its own hands—by revolting, in short.

In searching for a philosophical justification of these assaults on the social fabric (the Declaration of Independence is, after all, a justification of revolt), the more thoughtful proponents of disruption found shelter beneath the umbrella of social need. Government existed to promote the well-being of the body politic. Whenever government consistently failed to meet its responsibilities, then the citizens had the right, even the obligation, to substitute more efficient measures of their own devising. The remark, indeed, became a litany.

Consider three widely spaced examples. The first, as recounted by Walter Colton, occurred in 1848. Two hoodlums who had killed and robbed a pair of miners sleeping under a tree on the road between Monterey and Stockton joined forces with three sailors who had jumped ship. During the course of looting a ranch belonging to a Mr. Reade, the new partners slew twelve people—Reade, his wife, a kinswoman, seven children, and two Indian servants. Other ranchers rose in wrath and formed a posse that caught the suspects on the coast near Santa Barbara. During the ensuing gunfight, one citizen was killed and several were wounded. One robber was shot to death; one jumped over a cliff into the sea. The other three were captured, tried on the spot by the members of the posse, convicted, and immediately hanged.

In commenting on the affray, Colton, a Protestant minister, a chaplain of the United States Navy, and alcalde of Monterey, declared, "There is a spirit in California that will rightly dispose of the murderer; it may at times be hasty, and too little observant of the law, but it reaches its object. . . . The first duty of society is to protect its members."

Three years later, after serving on Sonora's Committee of Vigilance, merchant William Perkins wrote vehemently that when "those to whom the execution of the laws is delegated [prove] incompetent . . . to protect society by the fulfillment of their duties, the People have the indisputable right to resume temporally [sic] the power of executing the laws themselves." Inasmuch as the vigilantes were "actuated by a calm sense of duty and not from passion," Perkins continued, their actions could not be classified as "Lynch Law."

Mobs, however, also used the arguments of need and expediency to justify themselves. After a thief in Calaveras County had been given a hundred lashes, had had his ears cut off, and half of his head shaved as a symbol of his depravity, an observer named Ryan commented approvingly, "There's nothing like lynch law, after all. It's so prompt and so effectual!"

The duty of the people: on that stern gallows scores of men and two women were hanged and hundreds, probably thousands, were either whipped or banished during the decade of the gold rush. (The San Francisco Chronicle for December 31, 1855, as quoted by Rodman Paul, California Gold, p. 206, says that in 1855 alone, 47 men were executed illegally in California, as against 9 legal executions.) Meanwhile vigilantes like William Perkins had very little to say about improving the system whose functions they were usurping. For instance: in July, 1850, Sheriff George Work and the judges of newly formed Sonora County managed to rescue from an impassioned mob four Mexican Indians who had been caught burning the corpses of two Americans—"which means," growled Perkins to his journal, "that in a week or a month, they will escape from jail and recommence their crimes. . . . We want a court that will try, sentence, and execute a man on the same day. By no other means will we be able to rid this country of the thousands of ruffians who now commit crimes with impunity."

When the quartet were tried, however, it was proved that they had not killed the Americans but had come on their decomposing bodies eight days after the date of death. In keeping with their own sense of propriety, they had burned the corpses after the custom of their country. The prompt acquittal that followed brought from Perkins no remarks whatsoever about the possible dangers of haste during extralegal criminal proceedings.

More documentation comes from San Francisco. On October 29, 1850, the city implicitly celebrated the American system of government during a day of official rejoicing over California's admission to the Union. (Word of that event had been received via the steamer *Oregon* on October 18, but preparing suitable parades and speeches took time.) That same night there occurred a spectacular comment on the insecurity of life in the Golden State. The river steamer *Sagamore*, bound for Sacramento, blew up as it was pulling away from its dock. Thirty or so of its 120 passengers were killed; more were injured. Most of the maimed were carried to a hospital run by a certain Peter Smith on contract with the city. Though the place was already crowded with cholera patients, space was found in the halls and other such nooks for the new influx.

Adjacent to the hospital stood a famed bordello. On the night of October 31, it caught fire, probably as the result of arson. With notable calmness the madam directed the removal of "French bedsteads, mirrors, carpets, silk curtains, hangings, toilet furniture, rich female apparel, etc. etc." To no avail. Flying sparks set the pile ablaze. They also ignited the hospital. While the madam, losing her aplomb, kicked a cut-glass chandelier apart, volunteers evacuated the patients, including the victims of the steamboat explosion, but they suffered intensely in the chill October air before other shelter could be found. "Truly," mused Daniel W. Coit, who described the episode in a letter to his wife, "the events of years in other countries transpire here in days."

For Peter Smith, there had been too many events. He gave up his contract and demanded that the city council, which had been paying him in scrip, redeem the notes in cash—$64,000. The bankrupt city declined. Smith thereupon sued and won judgment. By this action he prepared the way, perhaps unintentionally, for the greatest land fraud in San Francisco's history. The relationship between this and "law" as defined by the vigilantes will emerge shortly.

Hecticness, the feeling that life was galloping and had to be seized on the instant, was a San Francisco hallmark. The city was growing prodigiously. Its permanent population, still predominantly male, had topped 35,000. Large numbers of transients flowed through; endless orders poured in from the mines; demands for services and supplies were incessant. Although merchants occasionally miscalculated and ordered unsuitable cargoes that on arrival had to be auctioned off at a loss, most made money with extraordinary rapidity. There was little sense of a secure future, however, and one reason was the sense of imminent danger that pervaded the city as relentlessly as the sting of the sea winds.

Beginning on Christmas Eve, 1849, and continuing intermittently throughout 1850—May 4, June 14, September 17, December 14—came a series of catastrophic fires that destroyed large sections of the city. The Peter Smith conflagration, though minor in the sense that it spread through only a block or two, reinforced suspicion that these blazes were the work of looters, who pillaged exuberantly during the confusion of each major blaze. No class was any more susceptible to these disasters than were the merchants, who lost not only goods and buildings but occasionally life itself.

Concurrently they were forced to take cognizance of other threats. The city harbored a large number of criminals, many of them Australians— Sydney Ducks—who congregated on the north side of Yerba Buena cove. At first the Ducks found their principal targets near the gambling halls and bawdy houses, where they robbed unwary celebrants, generally transient miners, and also shot and stabbed each other with considerable abandon. Respectable San Franciscans clucked about the deplorable conditions and carried handguns for self-protection, but otherwise paid little attention to a situation which, after all, was largely peripheral to their immediate concern of making money.

This abnegation of social responsibility resulted in a corrupt and inefficient municipal government controlled largely by David Broderick, who reputedly sold lucrative civic offices to the highest bidders. There was great demand for the places. Boodle was easy. Swiftly expanding public services—water systems, wharf building, street grading, and so on—led to contracts that were very easily padded.

The criminal courts also produced the sour fruit of venality. Prosecutors held their places less through a knowledge of the law than through political services rendered Broderick. Their inept handling of cases— some could not even draw up proper indictments—let criminal lawyers win an appalling number of decisions on mere technicalities. If that didn't work, then one tampered with juries. This, too, was easy because of the practice of rounding up veniremen from the hangers-on outside the courts. A lawyer merely had to plant hirelings in the crowd in order to guarantee his client a hung jury. Before a new trial could be held, key witnesses in that highly mobile society had often moved on, and the case was then dropped.

No one cared very much—until, as California historian Roger Olmstead has pointed out, the criminals, growing bolder, edged out of the tenderloin and began attacking the merchants within their own stores.

The precipitating event was the brutal robbing and beating, early one February evening, 1851, of a mild, well-liked storekeeper named Jansen. Picking up the hue and cry, the newspapers poured scorn on the city police force. If it couldn't handle the situation, then the people should: "If two or three of these robbers and burglars were caught and treated to 'Lynch law' their fellows would be more careful about future depredations."

Stung, the police pounced on two handy suspects, both Australians. One was named Windred. The other was identified over his earnest denials, as James Stuart, wanted in Marysville for the murder of a sheriff. After the half-dead Jansen had peered at the pair through swollen eyes and had mumbled painfully that they were indeed his assailants—well, probably—a mob gathered outside the city hall. Prodded ahead by Sam Brannan, it attempted to seize the accused but was turned back by militia providentially on hand for a Washington Birthday parade.

Taking advantage of the moments of hesitation that followed, a twenty-seven-year-old merchant, William Tell Coleman, prevailed on the gathering to appoint a mining-camp style, ad hoc jury, judge, prosecutor, and defense attorney for handling the explosive situation. Cowed by the people's roaring approval, the city meekly surrendered jurisdiction to this revolutionary tribunal. The result, to the amazed disgust of many, was a hung jury, and the disgruntled people's court returned the prisoners to the city. Your turn. Hoping to restore their tarnished image, the authorities placed the accused in a kind of amorphous double jeopardy by trying them once again for the same crime. This time the jury returned a verdict of guilty and the judge sentenced each man to fourteen years in prison. Windred promptly escaped. Stuart, as he was still believed to be, was taken to Marysville, to be tried for the murder of the sheriff.

Although the city had proved firmer than the popular court, the merchants and newspapers were not satisfied. An unprecedented surge of civic interest in the municipal elections of April 28 resulted in a slate of reform candidates who turned Broderick's machine out of office. Overwhelmed by a fresh series of catastrophes, the victors unfortunately had little chance to prove themselves.

Late at night on May 3, 1851, only hours before the new administration took office, a new fire leaped alive in a paint store. Spreading swiftly throughout the early hours of May 4, the flames destroyed 22 blocks of the business district. This was exactly one year after the blaze of May 4, 1850, which had destroyed 300 structures. The terrified residents were convinced that the repeat holocaust was no coincidence. Ragged nerves were not eased by a rapid-fire sequence of false alarms. Soon every untoward incident assumed giant proportions. Although robberies were probably no more frequent than before, they now stirred torrents of outrage. Another nudge into unbearable tension came on June 3, when a frenzied mob trying to take a suspected arsonist from the authorities was balked in large measure by its own lack of coherence.

Knots of men gathered on nearly every corner to discuss solutions. The result, on June 10, was the formation, under the leadership of Sam Brannan, of a Committee of Vigilance whose 103 members, mostly commission merchants and sea captains (no lawyers at all), dedicated themselves to investigating all offenses against person or property in San Francisco. This was a relatively small, narrowly based group, but within hours, thanks to an extraordinary coincidence, it soared into citywide prominence.

That very evening, June 10, a Sydney Duck occasionally known as John Jenkins stole a small safe from a wharfside store and fled in a rowboat. He was seen by volunteer watchmen. They gave pursuit, captured him, and dragged him back to the Committee's headquarters. The prearranged tolling of a firebell brought 80 of the 103 new members rushing back to the spot where they had vowed vigilance. As a curious mob gathered outside, they formed a jury, convicted the captive, and sentenced him to death.* Brannan then stepped outside and asked the crowd whether it approved the verdict. It bellowed affirmation.

A guard of Vigilantes marched Jenkins through bright moonlight past the gaunt skeletons of burned buildings to Portsmouth Square, the populace streaming behind. A rope was thrown over a beam end projecting from the roof of the old adobe building that had once served Mexican Yerba Buena as a custom house. At that point David Broderick joined the city's new police captain in an effort to stay the execution. The machine boss may have hoped to regain stature by helping the new regime do its work and thus raise indirect questions about its competence. Or perhaps he was acting from principle; except when personal ambition counseled otherwise, he often fought courageously for his beliefs. But whatever his motives may have been on this moonlit night, they did not suffice. The wedge that his men and the police tried to form was driven back, and a call went up for volunteer executioners to haul on the rope.

Scores surged forward. An instinctive need to wash away through this group action their individual fears of disorientation, sickness, failure, lonesomeness, hurt, and loss; man's age-old hope for order in anarchy—

---

*During the spring, citizens of El Dorado County had petitioned the legislature to declare horse, mule, and ox stealing capital offenses. The lawmakers responded in April with a bill allowing the death penalty for grand larceny and flogging for petty larceny at the discretion of the jury. The Committee's harsh verdict for burglary was thus technically justifiable.

every hand that could reach the rope laid hold. Jenkins' heavy body, violently convulsed, soared upward. In order that everyone who wished might have a turn, the corpse was held aloft for hours by relays of straight-shouldered men finding solace in thus punishing a symbol of their own collapse.

The triumph established the committee beyond even Broderick's reach. Most of the city's ministers and every newspaper but one applauded the hanging. Opposition collapsed, and the committee went about cleansing the city according to its own lights.

During this same period, another cleansing body, a funding commission established by the new regime, was struggling to reorder the city's demoralized finances, which on May 1, 1851, were $1.5 million in arrears. The idea the commission produced went roughly like this. It would assume control, as trustee, of all city-owned land, issue bonds against the real estate, and use the bonds for consolidating and fending off the wild clutter of debts pressing on the treasury. Available land, including the burned-over city hall lot, was insufficient, however. To get more, the commission asked the legislature to transfer to the city certain state-owned lands lying beneath the shallow waters edging Yerba Buena cove.

Speculators' mouths began to salivate. Waterfront land originally granted by the old alcaldes to favored individuals was being rapidly filled in and leaping each day in value. These new lots should duplicate the rise. To make sure that the city got them, various individuals spent an alleged $80,000 bribing key members of the legislature to favor the bill. Again Broderick thundered protest but was unable to check the tide.

At that point Peter Smith bobbed up again and announced that he would not accept bonds for the $64,000 owed him. He must have cash. Other creditors, following his lead, won test cases in court. The funding commission thereupon said mournfully that it would have to auction off at public sale enough city property, waterfront lots included, to meet the demands. At the same time it implied in tortured legalese, as did the city attorney, that buyers had better watch out; titles might not be valid. Prices thereupon dropped so abysmally that the commission had to sell nearly 2,000 acres to raise the money it needed.

Broderick was one of the principal purchasers. Peter Smith, acting evidently as agent for certain merchants who wished to remain anonymous, was another. The deeds executed, the purchasers asked the court for a ruling on the titles. It said they were perfectly sound. Values skyrocketed. Obviously a raw and brazen fraud had been perpetuated, but the Vigilantes, who had pledged themselves to cleaning up the city, paid no attention. They weren't interested in that kind of crime. Besides, it is probable that at least some committee members had grubby little fingers in the pie. As Melville asked at one point in *Moby Dick:* Who does the judging when the judge is haled before the bar?

They were busy, though. Their watchmen patrolled the streets effectively during another great fire on June 14. They turned fifteen minor fry on whom they pounced over to the city for attention. They accidentally caught the real James Stuart, hanged him, and rushed a messenger to Marysville to free the innocent man awaiting execution there. Taking it upon themselves to decide which of their fellows they could get along without, they ordered fourteen men out of the state and deported fourteen others to Australia. They boarded ships entering the harbor, examined the passengers, and refused to let some of them land. After Sheriff Jack Hays, armed with a writ of habeas corpus signed by the governor, had seized two condemned men in a surprise raid on their headquarters, they retaliated by storming the city jail, recapturing the pair, and hanging them before a crowd of some 7,000 persons.

Their example swept through the state. Every city and most of the larger mining camps also formed, often under the tutelage of the San Francisco group, committees of their own.

No town needed cleansing more than did Los Angeles, overrun with resentful Sonorans chased from the mines by the tax collectors, criminals fleeing from the committees in the north, roughneck teamsters freighting goods from the harbor at San Pedro across the desert to Salt Lake City, drunken Indians, and bandits drifting in from Texas and Mexico to look over possibilities. Liquor inflamed racial animosities. Personal vendettas exploded. In the fifteen months between August, 1850, and October, 1851, the little town of slightly more than 2,000 people, children included, suffered 44 homicides with no convictions. It was hard to find a sheriff —the job was too dangerous—and personal measures of fierce savagery were sometimes substituted for the law's feeble protection. In April, 1851, as a notorious example, a justice of the peace named José María Lugo called on the Coahuilla Indians for help against a gang led by a certain Red Irving, once a Texas Ranger. The Indians obligingly trapped eleven of the bandits in a canyon and methodically slaughtered them all.

Nothing was done about any of this until 1852, when finally the robbery-murder of two cattle buyers and the mysterious slaying of popular Major General Joshua Bean led to the formation of two separate committees of vigilance. These groups arrested several suspects, conducted trials, and hanged a total of five men. One of them was later proved to have been innocent.

In spite of the obvious dangers of summary punishment, approval of vigilante activity was general throughout the state. "Property," wrote merchant Collis P. Huntington, after watching a hanging behind his home in Sacramento, "is quite safe hear to what it wos before thay wos strung up."

But was it? On November 2, 1852, a little more than a year after Huntington penned his remark, a wind-driven fire probably set by arsonists destroyed 55 blocks of central Sacramento, including Huntington's store. In Los Angeles, banditry and murder continued unabated. In 1853, says Carey McWilliams, there were more killings in California than in the rest of the United States combined, and more in Los Angeles County than in the rest of California. Thus it would seem that citizen revolutionaries were not much more effective in stemming crime than were the inept civic governments they temporarily superseded. The mere name of vigilance was not enough. Before order came to California, there would have to be a widespread readjusting of values. Whether or not this was possible while the mania for gold persisted was highly questionable.

15. The Fevers of Prosperity

Probably the world had never known a more exhilarating speculative frenzy. Each year gold production soared—$41 million in 1850, $76 million in 1851, $81 million during the fiscal year from June 30, 1852, to June 30, 1853. An ending? Not yet, surely. This was Golconda unlimited, in dollars that were much bigger then than inflation lets them seem now.

Immigration, which had dropped sharply in 1851, quickened again. In 1852, an estimated 52,000 people made the long journey overland. Among them were a significant number of forty-niners who had gone home and were now returning with their wives and children. New motives possessed many of the migrants. They either knew from experience or had heard from others of the extraordinary prices being paid for labor and for food, and they were eager to provide both.

Prosperous adventurers drove cattle and sheep along as a speculation —100,000 animals that year, gobbling up the grass beside the trail. Poor men rose to weary heights of endurance. Some trudged afoot, yanking along a single reluctant pack animal dawdling at the end of a halter rope. Or they pushed wheelbarrows. A few managed to walk the entire distance with their possessions in knapsacks on their backs, cadging food however they could. Once again rescuers went out to help laggards over the Sierra Nevada and were astonished to learn that the dry-throated, scurvy-afflicted immigrants, women in particular, craved pickles above all else. It was an almost unbelievable hegira, the ardors of the journey considered, and it accounted for less than half of the year's influx. For, as noted earlier, 67,000 people reached San Francisco Bay by ship, 20,000 of them from China.

This population increase added heavily to California's urgent need for articles of every description. In 1853, 1,028 ships entered the Golden Gate, carrying 100 million pounds of flour, 80 million feet of lumber, bales of needles, axes, iron, cheese, sugar cane, books, and whatever else fancy suggested could be sold to gold-happy miners.

Demands for speed produced those rakish greyhounds of the sea, the California clippers: thrusting concave bows, towering masses of canvas, and names to match—*Northern Light, White Squall, Sword Fish*. Space in the yawning holds sold at a dollar a cubic foot, plus 5 percent primage. At such rates a ship could earn her cost of construction on a single journey —if she was fast enough to justify the charges. The clippers were. The *Flying Cloud,* running up the coast of Chile in July, 1851, at 18 knots set records no steamship of the day could touch. Her elapsed time from New York around Cape Horn to San Francisco was 89 days, 21 hours, compared to the 6-month average of '49. In 1853, the *Northern Light* ran from San Francisco to New York in 76 days.

The lean, plunging ships were misery for anyone but a sailor. Besides, three months were too long to spend reaching Golconda. Seeking swifter, easier travel for well-heeled passengers, the Vanderbilt interests of New York put together a route across Nicaragua. Competing fiercely with them and aided by post office subsidies, the Pacific Mail Steamship Company outdid the Vanderbilts by completing in 1855, at a cost of $7.5 million, a 48-mile railroad through the swampy jungles of Panama. Now a man (and freight, too, though costs of transshipping were exorbitant) could travel from New York to San Francisco in one month. But he did face risks. Every now and then one of the Nicaragua or Panama paddle-wheel steamers went aground and broke apart. Fire was a lurking threat; in 1853, 125 persons died when the *Independence* burned off the coast of Baja California. And disease: in 1855 cholera broke out on an over-crowded Nicaragua steamer; 104 corpses, from among 650 persons, were tossed overboard before the journey was completed.

Chafing over lost time, lost materials, and lost lives, Californians began agitating for federal aid in building a transcontinental railroad. Technically, the job was possible. Expenses, however, would be so astronomical that more than one road, whether to Oregon, northern California, or southern California, was unthinkable. Where in the East should that single line begin? Where in the West should it end? From Lake Superior to New Orleans, from Puget Sound to San Diego Bay, local interests scrambled for preference. Overshadowing those struggles was the growing sectional strife between North and South; neither region wanted the other to pull California into its orbit by so potent a tie as iron rails.

Congress sought to sidestep the dilemma by authorizing the Department of War to conduct surveys through the northern and southern Rockies and the Southwest. Perhaps only one route would prove geographically possible . . . but the sketchy examinations, conducted for the most part in 1853, indicated that all the routes were feasible. True, the southernmost promised, on paper at least, to be cheapest to build and easiest to maintain because of light snowfall. Moreover, Lieutenant Robert S. Williamson, who had been probing the Sierra passes, deprecated all of them. The best ingress for rails, he said, was the San Gorgonio gap opening out of the desert into the Los Angeles Basin.

On the strength of those reports, Secretary of War Jefferson Davis recommended a southern line. But Davis was from Mississippi. San Franciscans grumbled; Northerners roared. They would not be bilked; lines commencing in the North were perfectly feasible, the Sierra could be breached . . . and so the paralysis set in again. Until the broader issues of the national fury were resolved, no transcontinental railroad would be built.

Rigidity ended at the border. Within California the gold rushers demanded the best service available and never mind the cost—even the staggering cost of importing enough track, rolling stock, and locomotives around Cape Horn for building a local railway. That notion was the brainchild of a ship captain named C. L. Wilson, who in 1853 proposed running tracks from Sacramento City up the American River to Negro Bar (later renamed Folsom) and then north along the toes of the mountains to Marysville. The mines in that area, Wilson calculated, used 162,-700 tons of freight a year. Hauling the material in wagons from the river landings to the foothills was costly. A railroad that speeded deliveries while reducing expenses was bound to prosper, or so he told potential stockholders in what he had already named the Sacramento Valley Railroad.

They believed him: wasn't anything possible in California? Assured of enough financing to start the work, Wilson hired, in the East, a lean, wiry, dreamy-eyed engineer named Theodore Dehone Judah to run the necessary surveys, and on February 12, 1855, shovelers began scratching out, along R Street in Sacramento, a bed for the first railroad west of the Missouri River.

This pioneering event, bold though it was, by no means presaged a network of iron. Because of the overwhelming power of geography—two great rivers born in the gold-rich Sierra and funneling through one superlative bay into the sea—California's freight distribution was still wedded to water, and it was on water that the spectacular transportation developments of the 1850's took place. Wilson's railroad was an adjunct to boating; after all, he was a ship captain himself.

By 1850 the little sailing schooners that had once spent a week or longer tacking through heat and mosquitoes to Sacramento and Stockton had been replaced by 50 or more steamers of varying degrees of seaworthiness. Competition brought about cutthroat fares, increasing luxury, throbbing races, and frequent wrecks. Weary of the chaos, the leading lines in 1854 formed a joint-stock monopoly called the California Steam Navigation Company. Outsiders were crushed, and fares were stabilized at levels that raised eyebrows but resulted in no drop in business. For even the most disgruntled traveler felt a stir of personal pride on boarding the queen of the company's fleet, the trim, fast *Chrysopolis*—Golden City—and sitting down to a sumptuous meal in a glittering salon decorated with murals of California scenes. Nor did excellence end with appearance. The *Chrysopolis* could speed 1,000 passengers and 700 tons of freight between Sacramento and San Francisco in six hours.

Stagelines went through a comparable evolution, with competing firms joining hands to form giant combinations. By far the most successful of the new amalgamations was the California Stage Company, created by two young men in their early twenties, James Birch and Frank Stevens. Capitalized in December, 1853, for $1 million and supported by 30 or so mail contracts, the firm was, by 1856, the biggest stageline in the United States, operating 200 vehicles over nearly 2,000 miles of road—most of it smoothed out after a fashion by the company's own men. The famed Abbot-Downing factory in Concord, New Hampshire, built specially designed, egg-shaped, hand-finished coaches for the persnickety Westerners to use on the most popular runs (mud wagons continued to serve the hinterlands), and the gleaming harnesses were then filled with blooded horses imported by steamer at costs of up to $2,000 per span.

Southern California, too, had its youthful entrepreneur, twenty-one-year-old Phineas Banning, who first opened, with ramshackle equipment and half-wild mustangs, a 22-mile run between San Pedro and Los Angeles. Within two years, he had spread north to San Luis Obispo and south to San Diego. The aggressiveness led the federal government to award Banning and a new partner, D. W. Alexander, contracts for freighting goods over the fearsome Tehachapi Mountains to Fort Tejon at the southernmost tip of the San Joaquin Valley and through the seared desert to Fort Yuma on the Colorado, quite possibly the two toughest stage and freight runs in the nation.

Even better customers than the government were the Mormons. Eager to open a corridor to the sea, Brigham Young in 1851 sent 450 colonists along the old Spanish Trail past Las Vegas to the Pacific side of Cajon Pass, where his scouts had bought from the Lugo family 35,500 acres for $77,500. Naming the colony San Bernardino, the Saints erected a sawmill in the nearby mountains, built dams and ditches for irrigating 4,000 acres, set out 50,000 grape vines, planted fruit trees and wheat, and grazed

15,000 cattle. By 1855, San Bernardino's population had trebled. Banning & Alexander provided daily stage service to Los Angeles. And each winter their massive freight wagons, loaded with sea-delivered cargo, rolled on from San Pedro over Cajon Pass to Salt Lake City, a rugged 800-mile trip that was nevertheless 300 miles shorter than the haul from the Missouri River and much less afflicted by snow. Which helps explain why Utah has always been, despite Mormon claims of self-sufficiency, a semisatrapy of California.

Local promoters were less successful in retaining control of the express companies they formed for carrying packages and gold dust between San Francisco and the mines. Invaders from the East crushed them. In 1849 Adams & Company of New York opened an office in San Francisco, followed three years later by one of the most resonant names of the West, Wells, Fargo & Company, an offshoot of American Express. Brass-knuckle competition immediately erupted. Both firms spread throughout the mountains, entered into complex carrying contracts with stage companies they could not purchase outright, and (the noisy contentions of local historians notwithstanding) ran their own vehicles whenever it so served their purposes.

As one means of building up an image of dependable dispatch, Wells, Fargo & Company used relays of pony express riders to rush copies of important news items—President Pierce's State of the Union message to Congress, for one instance—into outlying communities. If competitors wished to race them, fine. The company's superbly mounted riders nearly always won. Its reputation for competence enhanced by such feats, Wells, Fargo transported, during its first five years of existence, $58 million in gold from the mining camps to San Francisco.

More significantly, both Adams & Company and Wells, Fargo entered the banking business. In addition to storing and transporting gold for the miners, they also purchased it. Having bought it, they put it to work by lending it at interest rates that soared, on occasion, as high as 60 percent a year.

This development was the result of a provision in the California constitution that prohibited the state from chartering banks, lest they issue inflationary amounts of undependable paper currency, as had happened in the East. Yet banks there had to be. Since neither chartering nor regulatory provisions existed, anyone who was able to lay hands on a sack of gold could enter the business if he wished. Many people did, often as a sideline to other pursuits, as in the case of the express companies. Excessive competition led shadier firms to questionable political tie-ins for the sake of government business, and the underpinnings of all of them were so shaky that any contraction in business was certain to produce explosive repercussions, as will become evident. Gold-rushing Californians simply would not scramble with caution, a state of mind still detectable.

The fever raged even in the supposedly phlegmatic fields of agriculture. Although ship captain Barney Green was unable, in 1850, to sell 1,000 fruit trees that he imported as a speculation—no one, reported his agent, Howard C. Gardiner, would "await the slow process of growth" —goals, if not moods, changed as soon as it became evident that the miners were going to be around for a while. Miles of fruit and vegetable farms, watered by deep wells, sprang up in the Santa Clara Valley, conveniently located at the southern tip of San Francisco Bay. By the middle of the decade, the Los Angeles area was exporting to the north an annual half-million gallons of sweet wine and fiery brandy produced from the hardy stock of mission grapes originally cultivated by the Franciscan fathers. Drier varieties grew profusely in the Sonoma Valley, partly as a result of the pioneering work of Mariano and Salvador Vallejo.

Haste overpowered quality. Green, spoiled, poorly cleaned grapes were dumped indiscriminately with ripe fruit into the vats; the wine was stored in whatever barrels were handy, regardless of what they had contained before; and the product was moved to the insatiable market without proper aging. To add a touch of distinction—and to stretch out volume—quantities of vintage wine were imported from abroad and added to the local product. California wines in those days were not widely respected.

Barley, less susceptible than wheat to dew-spread rust, flourished in the coastal valleys and was in profitable demand as a supplemental feed for legions of hard-worked horses and mules. Farther inland, wheat offered temptations to men in a hurry, especially squatters. Capital requirements were negligible. Plowing was easy; there were few trees to remove and no sod to break. (California's native grasses were annuals and did not develop tough, matted root systems.) A farmer simply waited for the first winter rains to soften the ground, then harrowed, planted, and, before fertility was drained from the earth by excessive demands, saw his efforts rewarded by heavy-headed stands of grain sometimes 8 feet tall. Harvests came during the dry season. The flinty kernels produced by the hot, dry climate of the Central Valley could be stored for months without shelter and shipped long distances without spoilage.

There were problems, of course. Insects were voracious, spring rains undependable. By state law a farmer had no recourse against trespassing cattle unless he himself surrounded his fields with stout fences, and in a treeless country this meant high costs for importing the necessary posts and rails. (Barbed wire had not yet been invented.) Even so, by the middle of the 1850's California was raising enough wheat and grinding enough flour to be self-supporting in those items. In 1860, the crop reached 5.9 million bushels—a fair increase when one recalls that ten years earlier production, most of it from the farms of John Sutter, had amounted to a meager 17,000 bushels.

To the bedazzled rancheros of southern California, cattle were the road to gold. During the earliest days of the rush, drovers who hit the mines at the right moment realized up to $500 an animal. Prices quickly tumbled to $16 to $20, but even that was a gratifying increase over the $1 to $2 that traders had paid for a hide during the Mexican regime. Long trail herds wound north, sometimes along the old mission road near the coast, sometimes over the Tehachapi Mountains into the Central Valley. The trips were tedious, beset by mosquitoes, Indians, rustlers, heat, thirst, and exhaustion. Lame animals often had to be abandoned. In places forests of wild mustard grew taller than a man on horseback; steers disappeared among the thick stalks like animated needles burrowing into haystacks.

In spite of losses, the drives were profitable and brought the Californios temptations that few could withstand. They bedecked themselves in silver braid, their women in satin and lace, their horses in gold-plated bridles. They built 30-room houses and employed extra scores of Indian and Mexican retainers. They entertained lavishly, gambled extravagantly at cards, and imported thoroughbred horses for the sake of prestige races on which they bet thousands of dollars. Jewish peddlers, traveling from Los Angeles to the outlying ranches with wagonloads of allurements, often sold not just the merchandise at a single transaction but horse, harness, and wagon as well.

To keep coin jingling in their pockets, the rancheros sold each year's calf crop as soon as the animals were big enough to travel. They neglected to improve the scrawny breed, and they were too swaddled in euphoria to grasp the implications of the enormous trail herds that began to appear from as far away as Texas and Missouri. Sheep, too, moved west in huge, dusty flocks. Despite heavy consumption, the state's livestock population soared fantastically, cattle from 300,000 in 1848 to 1.25 million a decade later; sheep from 17,500 in 1850 to 1 million in 1860.

Meantime radical innovations were altering the character of the mines responsible for this all-pervading Midas touch. By 1853 most of the rich, shallow placers had been carelessly skimmed. Intent on recovering what had been wasted by the first stampeders, the new miners began improving techniques. The common method for washing gold became the sluice, a series of wooden troughs fitted end to end until their length reached 200 feet or more. There was space enough now for boisterous heads of water to roil the gravel thoroughly and thus separate still higher percentages of gold from the dross. The metal settled behind rows of parallel ribs, called riffles, placed in the bottom of the sluice. To keep the metal there until clean-up time, the miners smeared mercury where eddies were formed by the riffles; the quicksilver captured the settling gold and held it in the form of amalgam.

Once again the luck of geography played a major part in success. The Sierra Nevada furnished ample water and timber for the work—but first the raw material had to be delivered to the mines in usable form. Sawmills sprang up everywhere. Water companies built thousands of miles of ditches and cliff-hung flumes in order to transport the almost priceless fluid from canyon-locked streams to sluices in remote, dry, unbelievably rich gulches.

All this paled beside the amazing fact of mercury. At the time of the American conquest, Mexicans had been in the process of opening one of the great quicksilver mines of the world, New Almaden, a few miles south of San Jose. British interests wrested the property from its Mexican owners; after complex and odorous litigation revolving around land-grant titles, Americans took the property from the British. Meanwhile hundreds of Mexican laborers kept probing deeper into the murky red depths. The cinnabar ore they blasted loose was loaded into 200-pound leather sacks and carried on human back over a steep path, an *escalara*, that spiraled upward around a dark shaft. On the surface the load was dumped into furnaces whose mephitic vapors brought lingering death from mercury poisoning to unknown numbers of workers. Scant time was wasted on safety measures, however. The demand from the hills was insatiable, and by 1852 New Almaden was pouring out such amounts of ore that the price of a flask of quicksilver dropped from $100 to $47. In the opinion of one government inspector, J. Ross Browne, this fortuitous flood of reasonably priced mercury was the key factor in making possible the full exploitation of California's golden trove.

Mercury quickened the search for new sources of gold. Temporary dams, rushed to completion during the summers, diverted rivers from their sources so that miners could scrape the gravel from the stream bottoms. Cliffs of gravel left high on the hillsides by the changing courses of ancient rivers were battered down by powerful jets of water from hydraulic hoses. Hard-rock miners delved into quartz veins, crushed the ore in stamp mills and ground it still finer in *arrastres*, hoping that the pulverizing would loosen the gold enough for the quicksilver to lay hold.

The individual miner working his own small claim began to vanish from the streams. The new methods demanded a consolidation of many holdings, a pooling of labor, an enlistment of capital. Curiously, the otherwise reckless banks of San Francisco and Sacramento were reluctant to enter the field. Riverbed mining was chancy. The bared bottom might be all but plated with bullion—or it might be profitless. There was no sound way of predicting; a company simply drew in its collective breath, poured thousands of dollars into a dam and diversion canal, and hoped for the best—hoped, too, that early rains would not trigger dam-destroying floods before the cleanup was finished. Meantime quartz mining was proving equally illusory. Unquestionably there was gold in many of the deep veins, but mechanical and chemical problems impeded full recovery. Tantalized by high assays, many a company poured every dollar it could scratch together into a weird assortment of machines and processes that promised to solve the enigma but didn't. Burned by the failures, banks by and large stayed away from both quartz and riverbed mining.

The solution was the formation of joint-stock associations by miners who had cash to spare and by local merchants who wanted to keep their ephemeral towns alive a little longer. Men unable to afford stock slid down the social scale to positions as hired laborers. Inexorably the poor man's gold rush, which Walter Colton had predicted would at last bring true democracy to the nation, was turning into a corporate exercise.

In San Francisco, the commercial heart of the state, few cared who produced the gold as long as it kept flowing. Nearly every ounce produced in the state changed hands at least once, and nearly every change brought stimulus to the residents of the Bay city. As a result, nearly 17 percent of California's population congregated in that one urban center —some 50,000 people by the end of 1853. Sugar factories refined cane from Hawaii, leather workers made boots and belting, iron fabricators turned out pipe and castings of every description. Though gutted by fire six times in eighteen months, the city rebuilt more lavishly after each conflagration, importing Douglas fir from Puget Sound, redwood from California's north coast, granite from China, sandstone from Australia. Anyone who could hold a hammer was assured a job.

Buildings were tall, narrow, and protected by iron doors and iron shutters. As early as 1854 streets were lighted with gas produced from coal shipped in from Washington state and were paved with noisy cobblestones, heavy planks, or asphaltum dug from oil seeps near Santa Barbara. Crescent-shaped Yerba Buena cove was turned into a fat peninsula by a busy little steam engine running on temporary tracks and hauling sand enough from the hills to raise 40 square blocks of land above the line of high tide. Beyond the water's edge, balanced on a forest of pilings, stretched row upon row of docks, each lined for about half its distance with warehouses, grog shops, and dark stores hawking cheap clothing to wide-eyed newcomers.

The theater and allied institutions flourished. A three-mile plank road led to the ruins of Mission San Francisco de Asís, near which stood a raucous circus, a zoo of sorts, an amusement park, beer gardens, and a race track. In the heart of the city ornate theaters offered fare that ranged from Shakespeare to sensational Lola Montez, one-time mistress of King Ludwig I of Bavaria. Lola's spider dance, wherein she pretended to shake insects from her abbreviated clothing and stamp on them, enthralled the city.

For a time California also enthralled Lola. She married Pat Hull, the editor of a newspaper in the mining camp of Grass Valley, and settled down to domesticity with her new husband and a pet bear. Something went wrong. Pat shot the bear and departed. Lola also went her way, but not without leaving a legacy. She was one of the many coaches of a versatile eight-year-old gamine named Lotta Crabtree, who learned to dance, it is said, on an anvil in a blacksmith shop. Whether dressed in miniature top hat and green coattails to tap out Irish jigs, in crinoline to sing sentimental songs, or in Spanish costume while playing a guitar, pixie Lotta, shrewdly managed by her cold-eyed mother, was the toast of every hill town in California.

Soberer institutions filled quieter social needs. Each camp had its newspaper. There were twelve in San Francisco, including German, French, and Spanish journals and a literary weekly, the *Golden Era*, that published the early efforts of Bret Harte and, somewhat later, Mark Twain. Bookstores abounded—San Francisco is still the most bookish town on the West Coast—and a public library was opened in March, 1853. Nearly everyone belonged to a fraternal order or lyceum. Churches and missionary societies labored diligently, passing out free Bibles, espousing temperance causes, and trying without marked success to convert the Chinese. Perhaps their greatest service was fostering education. Almost invariably the first teachers in both the supply cities and the mountain camps were priests, ministers, or ministers' wives. (There were no public high schools in California until 1856.) The state's first institutions of higher learning, the University of California among them, grew out of private colleges founded by churchmen.

Such pursuits lent a deceptively familiar gloss to San Francisco. One newly arrived wife wrote home that the ships in the harbor, the clothes of the women, the signs on the buildings—Adams & Company for one —and the singing at church reminded her of Boston. She was kidding herself. In 1853 San Francisco was nothing like Boston. Half of her 50,000 residents were foreign—Germans, French, Irish, Spanish Americans, Chinese. Only 8,000 were women, only 3,000 children. Because women were rare they were independent and readily divorced their husbands when better replacements appeared.

Living customs reflected the bents of this predominantly male population. In 1853 there were 537 establishments that sold liquor, 66 restaurants, and 160 hotels and lodging houses, many of which also provided meals. "Eating out" is still a San Francisco trait. Ice was imported from the glaciers of Alaska, oranges and lemons from Sicily. (By this time William Wolfskill, one of the openers of the Old Spanish Trail from New Mexico, had planted from mission stock an orange grove where the Los Angeles Union Station now stands, but the pithy, seed-filled fruit was not popular.) Laundry, which in the early days had been sent to Hawaii, fell into the hands of a heterogeneous collection of Chinese males and Irish, Indian, and Latin American females. Because water delivered to buildings inside the city was expensive, these launderers trooped with their baskets to a pond in the suburbs and there noisily pounded the soiled linen clean with stones, sticks, and strong yellow soap.

(All of which calls to mind the two-mile *zanja* that brought water from the Los Angeles River to open roadside ditches for distribution throughout the pueblo. "From sunrise to evening," sniffed the Los Angeles *Star* on June 16, 1855, "groups of females from snowy white to sooty can be seen at the daily avocation of washing clothes, through nearly the entire length of the water canals—and very few of them . . . take care to prevent the filthy rinsings from running back into the streams. A stranger would be very apt to suppose that our water canals were built for the purpose of carrying off garbage and foul matter that is continually accumulating . . . instead of being the source from which a large portion of the inhabitants are supplied with water for domestic purposes.")

Energy such as pervaded San Francisco generates its own blind momentum. Portents were ignored. In 1853–54, gold production abruptly dropped by $14 million. Most people shrugged. It was a temporary setback, they assured each other, occasioned in part by light rainfall that handicapped washing operations. Just wait, things would soon be better. Concurrently immigration slumped and departures increased. The state's net gain for 1854 was 24,000, for 1855 only 6,000. But immigration had picked up before; surely it would again. Although a third of the city's business houses stood empty, builders went right on erecting new establishments with unabated zeal.

Explanations for the contraction eluded even so shrewd an observer as William T. Sherman, who had watched the beginnings of the rush as a member of Colonel Mason's staff and was now back in San Francisco as a private citizen in charge of a branch bank recently opened by Lucas, Turner & Company of St. Louis. "California," Sherman wrote home, "is a perfect paradox, a mystery." Wages were high, crops good, activity ceaseless. Yet steamer revenues were slacking off, cattle raisers, farmers, and merchants were failing. Strange, strange. Such ups and downs—

again Sherman used the word that explained nothing—were a "complete mystery."

From the vantage point of hindsight, it is clear that there was no mystery at all. The madness was burning out, and a painful period of convalescence, complicated by fresh outbreaks of vigilante protest, loomed ahead.

16.   Ride the Whirlwind

One California legend has David Colbert Broderick passionately declaring that in order to reach Washington as a United States Senator he would gladly cross a thousand corpses "and every corpse a friend!" Hyperbole. Still, he was obsessed. For the sake of his ambition he did manipulate, with bleak cynicism, the gigantic storms of ideological hatred, political corruption, and social irresponsibility that he found rending the state during his upward march. Corpses did result. Eventually one of them would be Broderick's own.

Yet he had convictions. As president of the California senate and a leader of the Free Soil wing of the Democratic party, he urged the case of the squatters against the holders of ill-defined land grants. He argued eloquently for such slim civil rights as the Californians of his era were willing to accord Negroes. He won acclaim as a parliamentarian, and in 1852 he felt strong enough to contend for the seat in the U.S. Senate briefly occupied by John C. Frémont.

The result was humiliation. A fellow Democrat, Senator William Gwin, easily slapped him down and elevated instead a man of good voice but meager attainments, John B. Weller, a one-time Congressman from Ohio with avowed pro-Southern, pro-slavery leanings. The shock of defeat unsettled Broderick, who normally was careful of his Irish temper. Shortly after the crushing, he plowed into a saloon fistfight with a Southern strutter and received facial cuts that left him permanently scarred. Three weeks later he and a hotheaded Virginian dueled with revolvers, each man advancing on the other, firing as he came. When Broderick's gun jammed, he held steady, recovered, and stalked on. Amazingly, the only physical damage was puncture wounds that Broderick received when his pocket watch shattered under the impact of one of his adversary's bullets.

These political rows mirrored the fissures that were splitting the Democratic party throughout the nation. They also hinted at Broderick's desperation. Franklin Pierce's election, which had turned the Whigs out of power in Washington, guaranteed that Gwin, who held Weller under his thumb, would dispense all federal patronage in California. Not a crumb would come Broderick's way.

It was like the jammed gun in the duel. He panicked briefly, recovered, and drove on. Ignoring those who urged him to restore party unity by reaching an accommodation with the victors, he set about exploiting the rift. No matter how state and nation were wracked, he would ride the whirlwind to power.

Two more antithetical contenders than William Gwin and David Broderick can scarcely be imagined. At the beginning of 1852, California's senior Senator was forty-seven years old, tall, suave, and well educated, his lean, handsome, beardless face topped by a striking mane of prematurely white hair. Married to a woman of great social charm, he moved with ease among the power wielders of Washington.

Broderick was thirty-two, his pugnacious jowls circled by a ruff of red whiskers. Though he never drank, he was more at home in saloons than in drawing rooms. A bachelor, he was awkward in the presence of women. He preferred to spend his leisure time alone, reading omniverously to compensate for his lack of formal education.

In spite of his puritanical streaks, he drew wild enthusiasm from the ebullient fire fighters of San Francisco—Broderick had formed the first engine company in San Francisco—and their support was the basis of his political power. Starting afresh on those foundations, he set about expanding his municipal machine into a statewide organization capable of toppling Gwin's and Weller's federally oiled bandwagon.

Swiftly the machine gathered momentum, fueled by a mass of sweetheart contracts for buying a theater building from one of Broderick's closest friends and remodeling it as an inadequate city hall, for paving streets, building municipal docks, laying out gas lines and waterworks. Kickbacks made city offices valuable. Though firm evidence on the charge was never produced, Broderick was widely believed to sell the lushest places to the highest bidder. He did not pocket the pelf himself but put it in a war chest devoted to maintaining the principles of the Free Soil wing of the party—and to overturning William Gwin.

That was the second whirlwind—massive corruption. Broderick did not create it. San Francisco's civic irresponsibility being what it was in those days of the golden harvest, the situation would have existed without him. But he saw its uses and, ignoring the lessons of the vigilante lashback of 1851, took his chances. His crassness, which completely disrupted the course of California politics, shook the entire state.

In those days Senators were elected by the state legislature. Having put a razor-thin majority of his followers into the body that convened in January, 1854, Broderick sought to have the lawmakers pass a bill allowing for the immediate election of California's next U.S. Senator—even though Gwin's seat would not fall open until 1855. The very effrontery of the plan, along with strident charges of bribery and intimidation, defeated his efforts. By the thinnest of margins normality prevailed; elections would be held on schedule. In order to win Gwin's seat Broderick would have to purge the rebels and place enough of his committed followers in the legislature of 1855 to make sure that this time the lines held. Gwin, eager for reelection, would of course do his best to defeat the drive.

As usual there was no subtlety in Broderick's strategy. He hoped to pocket the party's nominating convention, and thus its nominees, by forcibly excluding rival candidates from the annual meeting, scheduled to be held that summer (1855) in Sacramento's sparkling new First Baptist Church building.* Just before the body met, a crowd of his supporters rushed in through the back doors in an attempt to occupy every seat. The Gwinites anticipated the move. Simultaneously their swarms burst in through the front doors. Both groups nominated chairmen who were thrust onto the platform by flying wedges of men soaked with perspiration from Sacramento's July heat. Obscenities, fistfights, and brandished pistols climaxed in near-panic when an accidentally discharged derringer caused some of the more timid delegates to leap through the stained-glass windows in a dash for safety.

Long after dark the tumult subsided. The next day the rival wings held separate conventions and nominated separate slates of candidates. The result was paralysis. In 1855 and again in 1856 neither Broderick nor Gwin could muster enough votes in the divided legislature to be elected. Neither would give way to a compromise candidate. To the mounting anger of the state's citizens, California for the next two years had only a single Senator in Washington, Gwin's errand boy, John B. Weller.

Other shocks kept erupting. One was provided by Honest Harry Meiggs, a popular developer of the North Beach section of San Francisco. Meiggs seemed like the fulfillment of the California dream. He looked rich. He erected his own sawmill in Mendocino County for supplying redwood to his bustling lumberyard in San Francisco. He graded streets and built a wharf for attracting business to North Beach. As a member

---

*After wandering from San Jose to Vallejo to Benicia, the legislature early in 1854 finally placed the state capital in Sacramento, strategically located halfway between San Francisco and the mines. Thereafter party conventions generally met in the same city.

of the city council, he helped allocate many a rich municipal contract.

He had bet on the wrong horse, however. The city expanded south and west rather than north, and as business turned sluggish in 1854, Meiggs found himself floundering in debt. For a time he staved off ruin by forging some $800,000 in city warrants. (They were worth, as collateral for loans, only about half that figure.) Then, when suspicious bankers began to stalk him, Honest Harry chartered a ship and fled with his family to South America.

Stunned taxpayers launched investigations that unearthed dark evidence of the laxness, incompetence, extravagance, and political favoritism that permeated the city government. While this blow was being absorbed, the ship *Oregon* arrived on February 17, 1855, with news that the economic doldrums afflicting the nation had brought about the failure of the potent St. Louis banking firm of Page, Bacon & Company. A wild run immediately engulfed the bank's San Francisco branch and then spread to the rest of the city's financial institutions. Among those that collapsed was the state's largest business firm, Adams & Company.

Corruption fed on its death. The bank shut its doors while it still had considerable money on hand. Bankruptcy receivers of dubious honesty were appointed, and eventually the firm's surviving assets landed in the hands of Palmer, Cook & Company, official depository for most state and municipal tax receipts. Joseph Palmer, the company's president, was Broderick's close friend and, reputedly, his paymaster when legislative votes needed buying. His firm's engrossment of Adams & Company's assets looked to many like a raw return for favors rendered.

And still the shocks mounted. The tottering city government, also bankrupt, declared that of the $2.1 million in depreciated warrants that it had issued in lieu of the cash it did not have, $1.75 million worth were tainted with fraud and would not be honored, though by that time they were diffused throughout the northern part of the state. Almost simultaneously the state supreme court ruled that since California law specified a popular vote on all bond issues in excess of $300,000, several millions that had been floated without such approval would have to be repudiated.

Partial refunding would eventually be worked out, but for months the state's business community reeled with dismay. Frayed nerves demanded scapegoats. Politicians!—*they* were at the bottom of this mess. They won their elections by stuffing ballot boxes, lining up "repeaters" who voted more than once, and using "shoulder-strikers" to frighten unfriendly voters from the polls.

The result of the widespread disgust was a stampede away from both wings of the Democratic organization to the new American party, called the Know-Nothings because its members, organized in secret cells, commonly denied knowledge of the group's workings. Drawing brief strength from nativist and religious animosities, the Know-Nothing group shot into national prominence in the mid-1850's. In the California elections of September, 1855, they gained control of all branches of the state government. Their most significant victors, so far as this account is concerned, were two disaffected Democrats, J. Neely Johnson, who became governor at the age of twenty-eight, and David S. Terry, thirty-three, a Stockton lawyer who was elected to the California supreme court.

Before the new administration was inaugurated, a fresh series of scandals swept San Francisco. During certain primary elections in August, rival ward heelers clashed in a shootout at the corner of Kearny and Pine streets. Two men were seriously wounded. Among the participants whom the police arrested was James P. Casey, a Free Soil Democrat who had been one of Broderick's musclemen at the disorderly convention in Sacramento's First Baptist Church. During the September elections Casey, still under indictment for assault, was chosen supervisor of the 12th ward. Rumors flew through the city that his triumph was the result of an ingenious new mechanism, the Double Improved Back Action Ballot Box, invented by one Yankee Sullivan, a prizefighter, stout Broderick henchman, and official watcher of the 12th ward polls.

During Casey's trial in November, testimony revealed that some years before he had served eighteen months in New York's Sing Sing prison for larceny. Although San Francisco newspapers made a great deal of the exposure, it had little bearing on the charge of assault. Freed on a plea of self-defense (evidently the opposition really had started the shooting), Casey settled down to his not very onerous duties as city supervisor. Meantime one of his victims in the August affray, Gwinite John Bagley, found recompense by being appointed to an equally undemanding position in the United States custom house.

During prosperous times such antics would have raised no more than grumbles. Now, however, discontent was coalescing. Leading the protests was the *Daily Evening Bulletin*, a tiny, intemperate four-page newspaper, each page 10 by 15 inches in size. Editor and the entire staff of the *Bulletin* was James King of William, aged thirty-three.

As a youth James King had worked on a newspaper and in a bank in Washington, D.C. He had a flair for publicity. Because there were many James Kings in Washington, he added "of William" (his father's Christian name) to his legal signature and thereafter was remembered. Moving west, he tried mining and then opened a bank. Injudicious loans to a Sierra ditch company and to San Francisco real estate promoters put him in hot water. He carried more sound accounts than poor ones, however, and so Adams & Company agreed to bail him out, absorb his business, and put him to work as an upper-echelon officer at a salary of $1,000 a month.

When Adams & Company failed and Palmer, Cook & Company took over its remaining funds, King was frozen out. For months he and his family lived on his brother's charity. Completely embittered, he launched on October 8, 1855, his undersized, vitriolic newspaper. A crusading zeal for reform and a black desire for personal vengeance were equally mixed in the scurrilous exposures that he now unleashed for the edification of distraught San Francisco.

His primary targets were the leading officers of Palmer, Cook & Company, and David C. Broderick, "the most conspicuous of all . . . as high over all his compeers as was Satan among the fallen angels." So it went for six weeks, along with routine attacks on gambling and prostitution, until suddenly, on November 17, 1855, he found a new field for vituperation in the spectacular murder of U.S. Marshal William H. Richardson by a gambler named Charles Cora.

Women were involved. Cora consorted with a notorious, New Orleans-born, fabulously rich operator of a chain of whorehouses, Arabella Ryan, or, as she called herself, Belle Cora. When the Coras and Richardsons chanced to sit in adjacent seats at the theater one night, the gambler, who knew the marshal, attempted public demonstrations of friendship. Hotly embarrassed, Mrs. Richardson evidently needled her husband afterward. The next evening the marshal took on a bigger load of whiskey than he should have, found Cora, fell into an altercation, and was shot down on the street for his pains.

Cora was jailed amid intense excitement. The impassioned Belle hired as defense attorneys for her paramour the most expensive legal talent in California, including two future U.S. Senators, James McDougall and Edward Baker, the latter recently arrived from Illinois, where he had been an intimate friend of Abraham Lincoln.

Before the legal hearings could begin, James King of William, like other newspaper editors before and since, tried the case in his columns. The very connotation of words was used in lieu of evidence. "Marshal" sounded honorable; "gambler," "pimp," and "prostitute" did not. Righteously King cried out that the city wanted no vigilante activity, but . . . : "One bad man on the jury will be sufficient to prevent an agreement. . . . If the jury which tries Cora is packed, either *hang the sheriff* or drive him out of town. . . . If Billy Mulligan [the keeper of the jail] lets his friend Cora escape, *hang Billy Mulligan* or drive him to banishment." For good measure he added what many people knew but didn't dare say openly:

Sheriff David Scannell and Warden Billy Mulligan were members of Broderick's machine. Circulation soared. King increased the *Bulletin*'s page size and hired extra help.

Cora's trial resulted in a hung jury; four members voted for murder, six for manslaughter, two for acquittal. No evidence of packing was ever produced. Those two apparently voted their beliefs: Richardson had been the aggressor and Cora had fired in self-defense. The *Bulletin* did not see it that way, however. "Rejoice ye thieves and harlots!" King cried in his issue of January 17, 1856. "Rejoice with exceeding gladness. . . . The money of the gambler and prostitute has succeeded and Cora has another respite."

Cora was returned to jail to await another trial. King resumed castigating Palmer Cook & Company, Broderick, their associates, and also assorted members of Gwin's "Chivalry" wing of the Democratic party. The recipients of this unremitting flagellation found it tiresome and, so some people later contended, began looking for a way to dispose of the editor.

Opportunity came Tuesday, May 14, 1856, when King repeated the worn charge that Supervisor Casey was a jailbird from Sing Sing. Infuriated by the "revelation," Casey accosted King in a crowded street, ordered him to defend himself, and when the editor made a gesture toward his coat, shot him through the left side of the chest.

King staggered into a nearby store and collapsed. Do-gooders sprinting in all directions brought back a cluster of doctors—twenty or so, the accounts aver. Hampered by curious onlookers, they laid the victim on a counter and then fell into a dispute. Some thought that an artery had been severed and that before surgery could be attempted the flow of blood should be stopped by a temporary plug. Others, doubting damage to an artery, recommended an immediate operation. The pluggers won, and an unsterilized sponge was thrust into the bleeding hole.

Casey meantime had been jailed. A mob led by the editor's brother, Thomas King, gathered outside the building and howled for vengeance. Militia summoned by Mayor James Van Ness checked an effort to storm the jail, but the balking led to demands for a new Committee of Vigilance. The next morning, Wednesday, William Tell Coleman, leader of the 1851 group, agreed to head a new organization if his executive board was allowed to conduct its meetings in absolute secrecy and if its decisions were accorded absolute obedience by the membership.

Mobilization followed with such rapid precision as to suggest that plans for just such a contingency may have already been laid. During the next 24 hours hundreds of men were enrolled, grouped into companies, and armed with rifles and ammunition taken from the armories of the state militia, many of whose members left their colors to join the vigilantes. Alarmed by the swift growth of this extralegal army, Mayor Van Ness called for help on Governor Johnson and on the newly appointed general of the state militia, William Tecumseh Sherman.

Sherman had already scouted the jail and was discouraged. Built against the side of Telegraph Hill, it was overlooked in such wise by the rising ground and by several nearby houses that it would be next to indefensible against armed attack—unless troopers occupied the houses first, and Sherman had no authority to order so radical a move. He knew, moreover, that he could not count on the rank and file of his men. With such prospects in mind, he walked through the serene, moonlit night of Friday, May 17, to the International Hotel to meet the governor, "a young man, very pleasing in his manner," who had just arrived from Sacramento.

Toward midnight the general, the governor, and a few others called on Coleman at vigilante headquarters. What followed depends on whose memoirs you accept. Johnson and Sherman offered personal guarantees of speedy trial for Casey and said that the vigilantes could station ten of their own men in the jail to make sure that the accused did not escape through collusion with the sheriff. In return for these concessions, Coleman promised, or so the officials thought, that the vigilantes would not take the law into their own hands. According to Coleman, however, the vigilantes maintained full freedom of action and promised only that they would notify the governor if and when they decided to storm the jail.

The notice was given Sunday morning. Sharing none of Sherman's hesitations about the sanctity of private property, armed commandos occupied every house that overlooked the jail. Mounting a white horse, Coleman led 2,500 marchers (Sherman's figure) along the street to their goal. Dividing smartly, this force formed a lane through which loaded cannon were run up to the gates. A committee called on Scannell and demanded not only Casey but, for good measure, Cora as well. For the sake of the record the sheriff entered a protest but delivered the pair without resistance.

While the governor of the state, the general of the militia, and the mayor of California's largest city watched helplessly from a rooftop, the captives were placed in a carriage and driven between silent files of armed citizens back to vigilante headquarters. "San Francisco," Sherman wrote, "is now governed by an irresponsible organization claiming to be armed with absolute power by the people."

The secret trials began on Monday. Evidently they were conducted with decorum and fairness, even though the attorneys for the accused were members of the committee's executive board. Meanwhile King, his wound infected by the sponge plug, was sinking rapidly. Toward noon on Tuesday, May 20, the tolling of a bell announced his death. While crepe appeared as if by magic on buildings throughout the city, the trials of the accused went on.

Both were found guilty and sentenced to death by hanging. Under the supervision of executioner Sterling Hopkins, gallows were erected in front of vigilante headquarters. Cannon and armed squads were stationed where they could block attempts at rescue. On Thursday, May 22, while King's enormous funeral cortege filed toward the cemetery, an equally impressive crowd watched the hangings. Practice does help. Mechanically at least, Hopkins' show was a great improvement over the clumsy executions of '51.

Johnson and Sherman had hoped that as soon as the rogues were dispatched, the vigilantes would disband. Not so. Their strategy was to sweep the city with so relentless a show of power that thereafter honesty would prevail at all elections and that chastened servants of the people would henceforth attend to their duties, not to their pockets. After declaring that the regular courts would continue to handle ordinary crimes, especially "crimes of passion," the vigilantes began a swift roundup of suspected political malefactors. Some were exonerated at secret trials; many were deported; still greater numbers fled in terror. A large percentage were Broderick supporters.

Most newspapers and ministers of the gospel joined the bulk of the populace in approving these actions. Dissidents were subjected to blunt pressures. Merchants, who as a class provided the vigilante leadership, withdrew their advertising from the city's only critical journal, the *Herald*. When the Reverend W. A. Scott of the Calvary Presbyterian Church insisted that vigilantism was un-American and that the people should remember *"there is a constitutional way to change or amend our laws, and to remove unfaithful officers"* (Scott's italics), he was hanged in effigy. In spite of the warnings, however, objections persisted. These resulted, toward the end of May, in the formation of a "law-and-order" party that was able to stiffen the bewildered young governor's determination to fight back.

Plans were drawn with care. Johnson and Sherman obtained from General John Ellis Wool, commander of the Army of the Pacific, a promise of arms from the federal arsenal at Benicia. Next, David Terry of the California supreme court issued a writ of habeas corpus for Billy Mulligan, then being held by the vigilantes. When the vigilantes failed to surrender Billy, Sheriff Scannell telegraphed Sacramento that the defiance "cannot be put down without exercising the Military power of the State." Governor Johnson thereupon ordered Sherman to enroll as many militiamen as needed from more loyal sections of the state and issued a proclamation declaring San Francisco to be in a state of insurrection.

At that point Wool stunned the law-and-order group by reversing his stand and refusing to deliver arms without direct permission from the President of the United States. Militiamen did not respond as rapidly as expected. Coincidentally a group of moderate businessmen offered themselves to Johnson as peacemakers.

After damning Wool as a barefaced liar in collusion with the enemy, Justice Terry, a 200-pound, 6-foot 2-inch Texan, persuaded Johnson to turn down the mediation offer and continue his collision course. Crippled by lack of armament and men and dejected by Terry's radicalism, Sherman resigned from the militia, to be replaced as general by a fire-breathing Southerner, Volney E. Howard.

Howard rounded up 113 rifles, loaded them aboard a chartered schooner and started them toward a waiting militia officer in San Francisco, R. P. Ashe. A vigilante vessel, in an act of open piracy, intercepted the ship and confiscated the guns, but released the three men who had been in charge of the weapons. The mildness displeased Coleman. He ordered the arrest of the trio's leader, a noisy swaggerer named Rube Maloney.

It so happened that Terry, Ashe, and a few others were with Maloney when Sterling Hopkins' vigilante police endeavored to take the man into custody. During the scuffle Justice Terry drew a bowie knife and dealt Hopkins a severe wound in the neck. Infuriated, reinforced vigilante squads seized Justice Terry, captured all the state armories in the city, confiscated the few weapons they found, and tossed into jail for the night sixty-eight militiamen who chanced to be on the premises.

Governor Johnson reported this armed rebellion to the President of the United States and appealed for help. The Attorney General turned him down: there had been no offenses against federal property. Besides, the appeal ought to have come from the legislature. Mere sound. The real, unstated reason was Bleeding Kansas, where the town of Lawrence had just been sacked in the opening struggles between North and South. For President Pierce those outbreaks and their ominous implications were trouble enough. Let California handle her own isolated, internal quarrels.

It took time for the reply to reach the coast. In the interim it seemed very possible to the vigilantes that an open clash with the federal government might develop. They surrounded their headquarters with a wall of sandbags guarded by cannon—thereafter the building was called Fort Gunnybags—and the wilder of them began urging California to secede from the Union in favor of that old chimera, a Pacific Republic.

Terry was a defiant prisoner. In a letter to his wife, which she gave to the *Herald* for publication, he declared, "I was educated to believe that

it is the duty of every American to support the Constitution of his country . . . to regard it as a sacred instrument . . . & if necessary to die in its
defense. . . . So My Darling dont fear that I will falter." Even Broderick
worked for him. Politically they were enemies, but Broderick had just
been haled before the committee, grilled remorselessly, and then turned
loose, presumably in the expectation that the experience, along with the
deportation of several of his henchmen, would leave him chastened. Instead he began contributing $200 a week to three northern papers that
were willing to speak out on Terry's behalf.

As the weeks dragged by—seven altogether—the leaders of the vigilantes grew increasingly agitated. If Hopkins died, the rank and file, 6,000
strong by now, would demand Terry's execution. Yet what repercussions
might follow the slaying of a justice of the state supreme court?

Fortunately, Hopkins lived. Meeting in secret, the executive committee found Terry guilty of assault—and then voted to turn him loose.
Fearing popular wrath, they spirited the judge and his wife aboard a U.S.
sloop of war in the harbor. As a distraction they then tried two men
accused of "crimes of passion" of the very sort they had announced they
would not review, found them guilty of murder (rightly so, it would
appear), and hanged them in front of an enormous concourse of spectators. On August 18, 1856, after a massive parade through flag-hung
streets, they disbanded.

There was an aftermath. Leaders of the group formed a "People's
Reform Party" and for several years secretly examined the slate of
municipal nominees offered by the city's various political parties. They
placed their stamp of approval on cleanly men, occasionally advanced
choices of their own, and then watched the polls to prevent subversion
of the popular will. They did not elect all their candidates. But they
certainly had an impact. Taxes dropped, contracts were opened to public
scrutiny, officials attended to their business. For the next decade San
Francisco was reputed to be one of the best-governed cities in the United
States.

Throughout these tumultuous times, David Broderick remained obsessed with his yearnings for a United States Senatorship. His party's
defeat by the Know-Nothings actually raised his hopes, for the American
party's unexpected rise to power, coupled with the second failure of the
legislature to fill California's vacant Senate seat, jarred the Democrats
into working for unity.

In April, 1856 (just before the vigilante uprising began), Gwin and
Broderick met secretly to examine the rewards of peace. According to
rumors never wholly proved, the deal they worked out went like this. At

the next party caucus they would calm the fevers of factionalism and then labor hand in hand to replace the Know-Nothings with a thoroughly Democratic legislature. When this legislature convened in January, 1857, it would put Gwin back into the Senate seat he had left vacant in March, 1855. Inasmuch as two years of that term had already passed, he would hold office four years only. To restore the prestige he lost by accepting this truncated span, he would be allowed to name, with no opposition from Broderick's Free Soilers, the Democratic party's two nominees for the House of Representatives in Washington.

On his part Gwin agreed not to oppose Broderick's efforts to capture the Senate seat currently held by John B. Weller. That term, due to begin in March, 1857, would run a full six years. By promising not to support Weller, who wanted reelection, Gwin was in effect abandoning a faithful, if somewhat inept, protégé.

The legislative election turned out to be a shoo-in. The Know-Nothing party collapsed as abysmally in California as it did in the rest of the nation. Though blackballing by the People's Reform group defeated most of Broderick's candidates in San Francisco, he led the Democratic resurgence in the rest of the state, where disapproval of vigilantism had been strong. When the new legislature convened in Sacramento in 1857, he was ready to reach at last for the elusive prize.

Because two Senate seats were to be filled, several aspirants appeared. Only four had any real chance, Broderick, Gwin, the incumbent Weller, and former Congressman Milton S. Latham, collector of the custom house and wealthy enough to mount a formidable campaign. Broderick confounded them all with cynical and consummate skill.

Normally the short senatorial term would have been filled first. Broderick's strategy was to ram through a motion that would reverse the order of the elections. He succeeded by hinting to Weller's managers (the Senator himself had foolishly stayed in Washington) that if they supported the motion and he was elected to the six-year term, he would consider backing Weller for the short term. Unaware of the secret Gwin-Broderick agreement for mutual back-scratching, Weller's men swung into line and the motion passed. From then on Broderick paid Weller no heed.

Though puzzled by Broderick's motives for switching schedules, Gwin kept his promise to offer no opposition, and the boss of San Francisco soared to victory. Senator at last! And now to make himself invincible! During the balloting for the second seat, he managed the votes of his followers in such a way that neither Gwin nor Latham could command a majority. Realizing that they would have to kneel to him for election, they came around.

Latham arrived first. What was the price? Broderick's answer was ready: the dispensation of *all* federal patronage in California. Political emasculation!—Latham refused. But William Gwin, whose wife was the most ambitious hostess in Washington, crept in disguise shortly after midnight on Monday morning, January 12, through the back door of Broderick's hotel in Sacramento and signed papers of capitulation. Broderick snapped his fingers, and on Tuesday Gwin was elected.

New York fired a salute of 100 guns when her native son, trained at Tammany, arrived in the harbor on his way to Washington. It was the last triumph David Broderick would experience. For, as he soon learned, a California meat-ax was not an effective weapon against the practiced rapiers of the national capital.

The new president of the United States, James Buchanan, and William Gwin were personal friends. Buchanan's political drift was toward the South. Moreover, Gwin's promise to yield patronage rights to Broderick did not bind either the President or California's two representatives in the lower house—and they were Gwin's men. Although Gwin scrupulously refrained from recommending a single appointment to either the President or the members of the Cabinet, his wishes reached the proper places. To the incredulous dismay of Broderick's followers, waiting expectantly in California for their rewards, every plum went to a Chivalry supporter. Thanks partly to that and partly to Weller's active campaigning in California, pro-Southerners regained control of the state machine.

Ineffectual, ignored, and embittered, Broderick found an issue in the so-called Lecompton constitution, favored by Buchanan, that would let Kansas enter the Union as a slave state. Bolting the majority of his party, he joined Senator Stephen A. Douglas of Illinois in vigorously attacking the document. The California legislature responded by passing a resolution ordering him to support it. Buchanan, outraged by the revolt, threatened to read both obstructionists out of the party if they did not toe the line. As he had done before, guns jammed, Broderick kept right on going. Hurrying to California, he mortally split the Democratic party there by organizing an anti-Lecompton wing.

His timing was disastrous. The state was having trouble enough without political dissension. Although the annual value of both the wheat crop and manufactured items was now almost equal to the yearly output of gold, the figures were deceptive. Gold production had dropped to $44 million a year, little more than half of what it had been during the rainbow year of 1852–53. Wages had skidded to $3 a day, considerably more than the $1 paid coal miners in the East but barely adequate for covering the high cost of living in the West.

Physical isolation remained a fearful handicap to economic progress.

Although Gwin and Broderick had both urged Congress to help build a transcontinental railroad (meanwhile quarreling snappishly about details), the most they had gained was federal sponsorship of two wagon roads, one through present Wyoming, the other in the Southwest. When at last subsidies were granted John Butterfield for operating stagecoach and mail service between the Mississippi Valley and the Pacific Coast, he was ordered by the pro-Southern postmaster general to use the arduous southern route through the deserts into Los Angeles. In spite of first-class equipment, sleek horses, and able organization, service to northern California over this circuitous route took almost as long as a crossing of the Isthmus, and San Franciscans remained disgusted with federal conniving.

Southern California suffered worst of all. Excessive importations of cattle eroded the price of livestock. Severe drought in 1855–56 tightened the pinch, and many a ranchero, glum in his silver-mounted saddle, found himself surrendering great chunks of land in order to meet tax and mortgage payments and the bills of lawyers defending his grant claims before the land commission.

Racial animosities seethed. Rumors of Mexican rebellion boiled up periodically. At their Holy Week fiestas, early-day chicanos took to burning effigies not of Judas Iscariot but of symbolic gringos.

Politicians were corrupt; crime went unchecked. Scoundrels fleeing detection by the San Francisco vigilantes sought haven in Los Angeles. In 1857 the small, disorganized gangs of Mexican outlaws roaming the region were given cohesion by Juan Flores, a twenty-one-year-old escapee from San Quentin prison. To meet the threat, Yankee merchants, Californio ranchers, and a body of tough Texas settlers from the El Monte district formed a 120-man vigilante posse that for eleven exhausting days swept every canyon in the mountains in the northern part of Los Angeles County. They captured seventy or so alleged *bandidos* and hanged seventeen, Flores included. Later some of the victims were shown to have had only the most casual of connections with the gang.

From San Luis Obispo southward, discontented citizens grew increasingly vocal about leaving northern California and setting up a separate territory. Inadequate law enforcement was only one complaint. More galling were inequities in taxation and political representation. Because property was the basis of state revenue, the "cow counties" each year paid far greater sums into the treasury than did the more populous north, yet were allotted so few representatives that they could not protest effectively. Slavery sympathizers, seeing a possible way of adding territory to the cause, abetted the movement, and in 1859 the legislature passed a bill that would allow the division of the state—provided that Congress, distracted by far more ominous moves toward national separation, ever got around to approving the split. Congress didn't. Otherwise there almost certainly would have been two states instead of the one that at times still wars angrily within itself.

Depression, isolation, lawlessness, dissension—to Broderick all those ills were of less moment than reasserting himself politically. Choosing the gubernatorial election of 1859 as the field of battle, he proposed one of his shadows, John Curry, for the governorship and persuaded his followers to adopt a platform roundly condemning the admission of Kansas to the Union under the pro-slavery Lecompton constitution. Gwin's regular Democrats gladly accepted the challenge, nominated Broderick's enemy, Milton Latham, as governor, and passed a thunderous resolution in favor of the Lecompton measure.

Lip service thus paid to ideology, the Lecompton issue sank to a subordinate spot in the campaign. It was David Terry who set the tone—personal denunciation. His term as a supreme court justice was due to expire that year (he had been elected originally as a Know-Nothing), and he appealed to the regular Democratic caucus to nominate him for reelection. The delegates preferred someone else. Terry nevertheless delivered an emotional speech thanking them for their consideration and then, ardent Southerner that he was, launched a blistering attack on Broderick as a spiritless dupe not of Senator Stephen A. Douglas but of Frederick Douglass, an ex-slave who was a leader of the abolitionist movement in the East.

Shocked by this pummeling from a man whom he had spent hundreds of dollars defending during the weeks when Terry had been a captive of the vigilantes, Broderick exploded in a public dining room and heaped scurrilous insults on the judge's head. A Terry supporter who overheard the outburst challenged him to a duel but was put off with the remark that until the election was over, Broderick had more important things than Terry's pride to worry about.

Both Senators took to the hustings in ostensible support of their gubernatorial candidates but actually used the public platforms for lambasting each other mercilessly. Sensing that the tide was running against his splinter party, Broderick grew desperate. Declaring that his purpose was "to arraign before you two great criminals, Milton S. Latham and William M. Gwin . . . dripping with corruption," he revealed the details of the patronage deal whereby Gwin had been elected. The exposure damned him, too, but never mind that. His opponents had crawled to him for his favors, and in his fury he wanted the world to know who had been their master.

Bored by the mudslinging, the voters did not respond. Too late Broderick returned to the issue he himself had chosen: Was slavery to be extended? As a whole, California was opposed. Unhappily for Broderick, however, the electorate had grown even more opposed to him. They crushed him at the polls, electing Latham over Curry by a 2 to 1 margin.

While the defeated campaigner was still distraught and exhausted, Terry challenged him to a duel over the insults in the public dining room. They met at dawn, September 13, 1859, in an open field a few miles south of San Francisco. The news had leaked, and seventy-one spectators were on hand for the show. Broderick's bullet, fired too hastily, plowed into the ground. Terry's pierced the Senator's chest. He fell and a few hours later died in a farmhouse overlooking the ocean that he had traveled so far to reach only ten years before.

Edward Baker, friend of Lincoln, defender of Cora, paid for his briefly successful defense by the richest whore in California—Edward Baker, Senator-to-be from Oregon and slain hero of Ball's Bluff in the irrepressible conflict shaping up between North and South—Edward Baker delivered Broderick's funeral eulogy. Sound of trumpets—or strumpets, if you will. What had died on the field of honor was a symbol of as wild, hopeful, lax, self-serving, extravagant, disastrous, creative, and exciting a decade as America had ever known.

The taint had grown offensive. When the legislature of 1860 accepted the resignation of the new governor—Latham served exactly five days—and then elected him Senator in Broderick's stead, revulsion crystallized. Once again the voters turned the Democrats out of power, replacing them with Republicans led by a Sacramento merchant named Leland Stanford.

For a time it seemed that the frenzies might be subsiding. California, however, has always been too rich for her own good. Even then an unbelievable new bonanza, attended by new outbreaks of uncontrollable fever, was being unearthed on the desert side of the Sierra.

part four

MORE STATELY PLUNDER

17. Still Bigger Bonanzas

As happened elsewhere in the nation, industrial capitalism fell like a thunderbolt on California. Unexpected new pools of money and labor to manipulate, new technologies to exploit; expanded markets for agriculture, fresh methods for absorbing imperial domains of land and water—to men of a special blend of vision, daring, ingenuity, and rapaciousness, the years that followed the gold-rush decade were far more challenging than even that first wild scramble for riches had been.

Not by coincidence, it is a story that began almost simultaneously with the Civil War, a catastrophe that out on the West Coast sometimes seemed like one more stroke of California's outrageous luck.

The national agony did send some shock waves westward, of course. Many Southern sympathizers, following the lead of General Albert Sidney Johnston, a Texan who commanded the Army's Department of the Pacific, resigned from whatever they were doing and returned east to offer their services to the Confederacy. A greater number—between 15,000 and 17,000 men—enlisted in the Union Army and then found themselves bored stiff patrolling the Overland Trail against Indian raids or garrisoning miserable forts in Arizona and New Mexico.

Within the state Home Guards organized themselves after the pattern of the Vigilantes of 1856 and took position to fend off boogers: a possible attack on San Francisco harbor by either Confederate raiders or an English naval expedition seeking to capitalize on the nation's travail. A few reckless Southerners outfitted a sailing ship to prey on vessels carrying bullion, but were apprehended by a Navy patrol before they could leave San Francisco Bay. Here and there hotheads whispered busily over that stalest of West Coast conspiracies, an independent Republic of the Pacific. Otherwise emotionalism was limited to duels, fiery newspaper editorials that triggered occasional press-smashing raids by offended readers, massive Fourth of July parades, and lavish contributions to the Sanitary Fund, a Union-wide charitable organization formed for bringing medical aid to Northern soldiers.

Seeking an ideological explanation for this relative calm in a state where sectional antagonisms ran high, the Los Angeles *Star* declared that California's primary duty was to remain aloof from the conflict, providing "shelter for all who may flee to her from the storm." And indeed more men came west to escape the fighting than went east to join it. Remoteness, too, fostered noninvolvement. Towering over all other causes, however, was the overwhelming urge of self-interest.

The depression of the late 1850's had ended, and opportunities were proliferating. With so much at home, why worry about sadnesses abroad? As a sign both of the times and of the state's truculent independence, the legislature disdained the federal government's Legal Tender Act of 1862, which declared greenbacks to be lawful money throughout the nation, and decreed that gold alone would continue to be the basis of California's currency. As long as business boomed, the nation's financial needs were not going to interfere with the heated flow of local capital into local enterprises.

Chief fuel of the economic upsurge was a wide vein of metal on the barren slopes of Mount Davidson, just east of the California border. Plunging down Mount Davidson's slopes toward the emigrant trail along the Carson River were two steep, tan ravines. One was called Six-Mile Canyon, the other Gold Canyon. As early as 1849 both had shown traces of gold. During the subsequent decade an ever-changing handful of men had kept following the tantalizing gleams higher and higher up the arid hillsides. Watching this activity with vulture-like interest was a ne'er-do-well named Henry Comstock, frequently called Old Pancake.

In 1859 both ravines suddenly yielded richer amounts of gold than had yet appeared on the eastern side of the Sierra Nevada. Comstock was instantly on hand. He filed one claim in Gold Canyon and blustered his way into part ownership of another, called the Ophir, in nearby Six-Mile Canyon. His weapon: an undocumented assertion that he and his crony, Manny Penrod, controlled the water rights essential to success. Call Henry a premonitory symbol. His technique was crude, but he had the fundamental idea: brass so confident as to hesitate at nothing.

After giving one share each to Comstock and Penrod, the discoverers of the claim, Peter O'Riley and Pat McLaughlin, sold two more shares. Soon the six owners were producing, from primitive rockers, up to $1,000 a day. They would have done even better, they thought, except for a heavy sand with a bluish cast to it that settled behind the riffles of their rockers, defied segregation, and added so much extraneous matter to the gold dust that it reduced the price to a meager $11 an ounce. Even so, the returns started a small stampede among the miners in the two canyons and the ranchers in the lower valleys. Comstock undertook to be the local guide and made so much noise about "his" mine that the original discoverers were forgotten and the great vein came to be known as the Comstock Lode. In comparable fashion the ramshackle settlement that sprang up nearby, Virginia City, took its name from the antics of one of Comstock's boozy companions, "Old Virginny" Fennimore.

The prospectors pounded, shoveled, washed, scraped out their rockers, and cursed the heavy sand. What was it? Who cared? They were too busy to worry about that. Thus it was an outsider, not a claim owner, who first wondered about the actual composition of the vein's material. Were its full values being recovered?

Somehow—contemporary records are discrepant—somehow selected samples of Comstock ore reached an assayer in the California quartz mining town of Nevada City on the western slope of the Sierra Nevada. Results were astounding—$1,595 per ton in gold and, marvelous to say, a dazzling $3,196 in silver. Sand indeed!

Although assayers were supposed to treat their diagnoses as confidentially as physicians do, this was too sensational to keep bottled. Small groups saddled up and hurried across the Sierra to buy as many claims on Mount Davidson as possible before the Comstockers realized what they had.

Among those in the van was George Hearst. He had come overland from his Missouri home in 1850, nearly dying of cholera along the way, and in recent years had been trying with mediocre success to develop quartz mines around Nevada City and its twin settlement, Grass Valley. By selling a mine he owned and borrowing more money from friends, Hearst was able to acquire a one-sixth interest in the Ophir. With the mine's other new owners (the original claimants sold for sums ranging from $3,500 for O'Riley to $11,000 for Comstock, and $40,000 for hold-out McLaughlin) he ran a deep cut through the property and extracted several tons of ore too complex to yield to placer washing. Loading the best 38 tons of material aboard a hundred or more pack mules, the jubilant miners delivered the freight to a small smelter in San Francisco.

The net for each man was $91,000. While his partners delved deeper into the treasure trove, Hearst used part of his share to make his first visit home since 1850. There he met a piquant little Dresden-doll schoolteacher, Phoebe Apperson, who at eighteen was less than half his age. After stubborn hesitations she married him, and on April 29, 1863, in San Francisco, the middle-aged husband welcomed his first and only child, William Randolph Hearst. As for himself, George became California's second millionaire (assuming Frémont to have been, very briefly, the first), a United States Senator, and one of the awesome names of American mining history, for his newly found Midas touch soon spread throughout the West—to the Ontario mine at Park City, Utah, Anaconda in Montana, the fantastic Homestake in the Black Hills of South Dakota.

To California's restless miners, the Nevada strikes sounded like '49 all over again. The men needed encouragement, for the past years had not been good. Even partnership placer diggings had given way to deep quartz shafts and powerful hydraulic operations. The ordinary miner either labored at day wages for one of those companies or else wandered the hills in search of recalcitrant veins he'd have to sell to richer men for development. But now, just beyond the Sierra. . . .

A frenzied rush gathered headway during the fall of 1859, dwindled under the impact of snow, and then, prodded by the electric gossipings of a new telegraph line, reached stampede proportions during the spring of 1860.* Soon the alkali and sagebrush hills around Mount Davidson were plastered with 17,000 claims. Some were the cynical underpinnings of stock promotion schemes. Far more, however, were the result of ignorance.

There was nothing like the Comstock Lode anywhere in California. Over there a wide scattering of separate veins had produced, through eons of decomposition and erosion, a multitude of shallow placer diggings. On Mount Davidson, by contrast, mineralization was confined to a single giant fissure a little more than two miles long and from a dozen to a hundred or more feet wide, slanting an unguessable distance into the unfriendly earth.

The massiveness of the vein, its strange internal structure, and the admixture of silver sulfurets with its gold ores created unfamiliar problems in mining, milling, law, and money raising. How prevent disastrous cave-ins of crumbly rock in a fissure far wider than had ever before been encountered in the United States? How lift ore from great depths? How extract the minerals once the ore had been obtained? How determine, in

---

*This slack-wired, tree-hung line was the creation of Frederick and Albert Bee. Spurred by promises of state bounties to the first company that made connections with an eastern line, the Bees began work at Placerville in 1858 and reached the Carson Valley in the spring of 1860. When Congress in June of that same year authorized a transcontinental telegraph line, the California stub refurbished its sloppy Sierra crossing and sped on across the desert to join its eastern counterpart at Salt Lake City in October, 1861. The splicing of the wires placed Virginia City, San Francisco, and Los Angeles in instant communication with the East—and at the same time brought sudden technological unemployment to the storied riders of the 19-month-old Pony Express.

the maze of underground shoots, spurs, dips, and angles, when one mine was trespassing on ground belonging to another? Above all, how find capital enough, during the costly stages of opening the mines, to pay for the talent and the huge works demanded by this oversized bonanza?

Fortunately for the mine owners, California's hectic ten-year tussle with the gold of the Sierra had provided springboards from which an overnight leap into full industrialism could be made. The first big technical breakthrough concerned timbering. By December, 1860, the Ophir mine had reached a depth of 180 feet and was in bonanza ore. It was friable ore, however, as unstable as sand under enormous pressures in a vein whose width varied, at that point, from 45 to 65 feet. Standard procedures simply would not hold the mass, as fatal collapses in neighboring mines amply warned.

Their own ingenuity baffled, the managers of the Ophir began scouring the quartz mines of California for clues. Soon they heard of a young German-trained engineer, Philip Deidesheimer, superintendent of a small property in El Dorado County, who reputedly had developed radical ideas about underground procedures. They hustled him over to Mount Davidson, where he swiftly developed a unique system of "square sets," too technical to describe here, that in a stroke solved the Comstock's timbering problems for the rest of its life.

It was Deidesheimer, too, who persuaded the Ophir management that the only economical way to reach still deeper into the steaming earth was to develop, with the aid of San Francisco foundries, heavier machinery than had yet been built on the coast. Other mines followed suit; inventions proliferated. In 1864, for example, A. S. Hallidie produced a new kind of wire rope for speeding gargantuan hoists through the long shafts. Later, in 1873, after watching the cruel struggles of delivery horses on the steepest of San Francisco's hilly streets, Hallidie devised a way of putting his cable into an underground slot, powering it with big steam plants, and using it to move the city's still-famed cable cars up slopes that other modes of transportation could not handle.

Equally revolutionary developments in milling were brought about by Almarin B. Paul, a friend of George Hearst's. Like Hearst, Paul was in the van of the Comstock rush, but instead of staying he gathered up several sacks of representative ore, packed them to Nevada City, and spent the winter experimenting. On the basis of his findings, he drew up plans for a mill and used these to win contracts from several embryo Nevada mines on a promise to begin crushing ore for them within 60 days. He then raised capital for building the mill by showing the contracts to San Francisco financiers. Amazingly, he erected his buildings and installed machinery within the specified time. Drawing on the experience of other California technicians and recruiting the help of Mexican millmen, he steadily improved his "Washoe Pan Process" (while competitors were still floundering with "secret" brews containing such ingredients as tobacco juice and sagebrush tea) until his methods became standard not only on the Comstock but wherever similar ores occurred anywhere in the world. Without California's background both this breakthrough and Deidesheimer's square sets probably would have been long delayed, with severe losses in unrecovered mineral as a consequence.

Lawyers responded with equal ingenuity to the demands of the giant fissure. The basis of the problem was the Comstock's puzzling geology. Between the fissure's wide walls, isolated from each other by intrusions of clay and barren porphyry, were many apparently distinct veins. Some were enormously rich. Hence the question: Were they truly separate entities? Or did they merely seem separate because of irrelevant geologic faultings that had occurred after the formation of the main "ledge," to use Nevada jargon?

The point was crucial. No matter how close the offshoots might be to the main lode, if they could be proved to be separate, they could be mined by separate companies. The mountain's wealth would then be distributed much more widely—but at a cost, perhaps, of too many units for economical operation. If, however, the spurs were attached to the main lode, they belonged to whatever company owned the contiguous section of the parent fissure. Such concentrations would lead to efficiency in operations but would put great power into very few hands.

Without waiting for a scientific resolution of the questions, hastily formed corporations began trying to muscle in on each other, much as Henry Comstock had muscled in on Peter O'Riley and Pat McLaughlin. The result was a chaos of lawsuits—the Ophir alone was involved in 37 court actions—that burdened the Comstock with legal costs estimated at $10 million.

Chief proponent of the theory that the Comstock consisted of many ledges, or lodes, was David S. Terry, who had fled to Nevada to escape the opprobrium brought on by his killing of David Broderick. His most persistent opponent, defender of the one-ledge theory, was William M. Stewart, a forty-niner and product of Yale University. A hulking giant, 6 feet 4 inches tall, with a luxuriant black beard that swept to his chest, Stewart had more brass in his constitution, Mark Twain once remarked, than the Colossus of Rhodes. Over and over he thundered at confused juries and befuddled, often corrupt, judges that appearances were deceptive; the Comstock was a single vein no matter what Terry proclaimed. Stewart's successes came frequently enough that he earned $100,000 a year in fees and, as soon as Nevada became a state in 1864, a seat in the United States Senate. What's more, science eventually proved him right; the Comstock was a single lode.

While these legal battles were going on, the contentious mines and mills were clamoring for more capital than individual financiers or individual institutions could provide. The shortages led to what was, for California, a new method of financing—the opening, early in 1861, of the Pacific Coast's first stock exchange, where cash could be traded for "feet," or shares, in the Comstock operations. The novelty bred fresh fevers beside the bay. During 1863 alone, nearly 3,000 Nevada mining companies invited California participation.

Obviously the majority of these holdings lay in the sagebrush far beyond the confines of the main lode. Gullible investors, bemused by memories of California's widespread mineral, were slow to realize this, however, and with lemming-like madness poured money into the sterile desert—and into the pockets of unscrupulous promoters. It was a merry jig. For money did circulate, mountains of equipment were sent across the mountains, wagonloads of bullion did come back. The ripples spread. Bathed in prosperity, breathless San Francisco rushed into a new real estate boom that during 1864 added 1,000 buildings to the downtown section alone.

Like most speculative frenzies, this one kept soaring while dark clouds were gathering. At depths of 500 to 600 feet, and while masses of known ore still awaited extraction and milling, the shrewder Comstock engineers began to suspect that for many of the mines only borrasca (barren ground) lay ahead. Insiders began unloading their stock. The tremors eventually reached the public; prices broke sharply. Between the beginning of April and the end of September, 1864, shares in the Ophir fell from $1,580 to $300; in the Gould & Curry from $4,550 to $900. Panic swept the city, trade stagnated, construction fell off, long-faced plungers scrambled to avert ruin. Yet, as often happens, one man's disaster was another's opportunity. In the readjustment that followed the collapse, two new developments transpired, one quiet and healthy, the other flamboyant and of almost incalculable harm.

First the quiet change. California engineers who had taught the rudiments of industrial mining and milling to the Comstock had in turn learned from their continuing experiments there. During the latter part of the decade, when the lode's production slipped to half of what it had been in 1864, some of these engineers returned to the Sierra quartz mines with a new confidence and an improved expertise. Resolutely they built more efficient mills and started driving their underground workings toward unprecedented depths—salvation for California's ailing gold industry.*

The precipitator of flamboyance was William C. Ralston, a cheery, short-bearded, sparse-haired thirty-eight-year-old banker with Periclean dreams of turning San Francisco into the Athens of the West—if he could find the money. Born beside the busy Ohio River in 1826, Ralston's principal school had been the steamboats of the turbulent Mississippi drainage and the demimonde of New Orleans. He started for California in 1849 but for five punishing years marked time in Panama as a successful shipping agent. In 1854 he moved on to San Francisco and began assiduously exploiting the contacts he had developed on the Isthmus. Within ten years he had made himself well enough known so that in 1864 he was able to persuade several of northern California's leading businessmen to join him in incorporating, under the state's newly liberalized banking laws, the Bank of California, capital $2 million. Darius O. Mills of Sacramento, one of the state's most respected bankers, agreed to act as figurehead president, if Ralston, as cashier, did the work.

Work he did, with a recklessness that turned some of his associates stark white behind their long beards. Almost immediately the Nevada depression bequeathed to the Bank of California dangerous amounts of questionable Comstock paper. What could be salvaged? Deciding that aggression was the best approach to the problem, Ralston sent to Virginia City as his personal representative William Sharon, an obscure, dapper, slight-framed, bed-hopping real estate dealer with a razor-sharp mind.

By that time, late 1864, the "one-ledge" structure of the Comstock had been pretty well settled, thanks in large measure to the testimony of Yale's eminent geologist, Benjamin Silliman, Jr. As a result, ownership of the giant fissure was limited to a relatively few mines stretched end to end along the vein's two-mile course. Most of these few did not have mills of their own, but instead employed a multitude of competing custom mills, scattered around wherever water was available.

As Sharon studied the situation, his breath caught. The Comstock's wealth was not only concentrated in a few heavily capitalized companies, but also flowed out through tight bottlenecks—those shaky mills and limited supply routes. The vulnerability suggested daring raids to acquire control of the vein's entire output—if new ore bodies existed somewhere in the steamy depths.

---

*Two notable examples. The Kennedy mine of Jackson, Amador County, which kept digging away until 1942, eventually reached a vertical depth of 6,000 feet while turning out roughly $45 million. The Empire of Grass Valley descended 7,000 feet and by the time it closed in 1956 had yielded perhaps $80 million. The operators have not chosen to release exact data.

Sharon, who'd had no formal training in either geology or mining, decided that the ore was there, an opinion not supported by most experts. But there were practical miners around Virginia City who had faith—all prospectors have faith—and Sharon chose to listen to them, perhaps because he had the lure of almost incredible opportunity to predispose him. Let there be ore. . . .

He mesmerized Ralston, who opened a branch bank in Virginia City, named Sharon its manager, and authorized loans at half the existing rate of interest. Joyous mine managers and mill owners flocked in for operating funds, spent the money on marginal ores, returned for additional loans—and found Sharon icily insisting on either immediate repayment or foreclosure.

The multitudinous little mills proved particularly susceptible. By 1867 Sharon had gained control of seventeen of them and was urging consolidation in a single mighty unit. Because Comstock production was showing only tremulous signs of reviving, the bank directors threw up their hands in protest, but after a sharp confrontation, during which Ralston supported him to the hilt, Sharon carried his point. Out of the victory came the potent Union Mill and Mining Company, to which all Comstock mines sensitive to bank pressures—and that was most of them—were required to ship such ores as they were producing.

To obtain ample water for the mill, Sharon had to locate it in the Carson Valley, 13 steep miles from Virginia City—expensive miles for wagons. A railroad would do better, and would also tighten the bank's hold. After bludgeoning the nearby counties, all of them dependent on the Comstock for their well-being, into passing bond issues for the benefit of the road, Sharon in 1869 laid out what was then the crookedest line in the world—a continuous sequence of wheel-torturing curves, deep cuts, and six tunnels lined with zinc as protection against fires set by locomotive sparks. Eventually 52 trains were traveling the line each day, hauling ore down and timber and cordwood up. Nor was that the end of ambition. The tracks also extended from the mill southwest to Carson City, the state capital, and from Virginia City northward to Reno and a junction with the new transcontinental. Meantime the King of the Comstock was also busy setting up a monopolistic water company to supply Virginia City and a lumber company that swooshed its timbers out of the Sierra down steep, V-shaped, water-filled flumes.

There was just one flaw in the imperial plan. When fresh ore was found at depths of 1,000 feet or so, just as Sharon had predicted it would be, it was not spread evenly throughout the vein but was embedded here and there in the borrasca like random raisins in a boardinghouse pudding. Rich raisins! As matters transpired, the bulk of the Comstock's $300

million yield came from half a dozen or so mines perched through sheer
luck above the right places. Though Sharon put spies everywhere underground, he found that he could not sniff out all the bonanzas in time to
forestall rival raiders.

His principal contenders were Alvinza Hayward and John P. Jones,
the latter of whom incurred extra enmity by contesting with Sharon, at
fantastic cost per vote, for a seat in the United States Senate; and those
fabled silver barons of Nevada, John Mackay, James Fair, James Flood,
and William O'Brien, who found the biggest bonanza of all in the Consolidated Virginia, producer of $105 million, three-quarters of which
reached the stockholders in dividends.

The discovery of bonanzas like that meant also the building of rival
mills, the founding of competitive banks and lumber companies. Such
prizes led to titanic struggles to control, through stock acquisitions, properties that *might* develop, even briefly, into rich producers. Prices rose
and dipped like swallows, with attendant temptations for plungers. Between battles, the fevers were maintained by secret deals between mills
and mines to hide the real values of ores and by slyly spread rumors of
borrasca or bonanza that drove stock quotations up or down at the will
of the manipulators.

It was a precarious kind of prosperity, but for Ralston it was enough.
He flooded his own profits and the bank's into his beloved city and on
into the state, building silk and woolen mills, a carriage factory, irrigating
canals, a dry dock for ship repairs, ornate theaters, and the fabulous
Palace Hotel. Seeing him spread himself so and hearing the jingle of
silver from beyond the mountains, a large segment of the populace concluded that the Comstock had no bounds. A fresh mania for speculation
seized sweaty miners and cool brokers' clerks who should have known
better, housewives and housemaids, Chinese coolies, storekeepers, manufacturers, farmers, all experiencing again, vicariously through stock certificates, a taste of the excitement that had lured so many of them west
in the first place.

The clichés of gullibility. Though several made fortunes, thousands
were impoverished. Scores of millions of dollars were diverted from
other, more essential industries at a time when depression was rolling
ever closer from the stricken cities of the East. But before counting the
full costs of that (and the gains; after all, Comstock money built much of
San Francisco), it is well to look at some of the other thrusts toward
monopoly that the spirit of the times, combined with the temptations of
California's peculiar geography, made almost inevitable.

18. The Transportation Trap

In the summer of 1860, Theodore Judah returned, intensely excited, to California from yet another lobbying session in Washington, D.C. National sentiment for a Pacific railroad, eagerly manipulated by Midwestern promoters, had at last gathered enough momentum, he assured himself, so that the necessary funding bill would roll through the next session of Congress in spite of Southern opposition. Judah's goal now was to pull together several San Francisco capitalists into a firm that would be named in the bill as the official builder of the line's western end. His first step in gaining attention, he decided, would be the running of a "survey" to prove that rails could economically cross the central Sierra Nevada, a matter questioned even by some Californians.

He was obsessed. The Sacramento Valley Railroad, which had brought him to California in the first place, had been halted by the depression of 1856 at Folsom (originally Negro Bar), 22 miles from the state capital. Since then the frustrated engineer had alternated between surveying routes for other would-be short-line railroads in the Sacramento area and traveling to Washington to lobby for a transcontinental. Like many zealots, he was hard to warm to—self-centered, pompous, opinionated, and humorless, veering between toplofty idealism and crass expediency. He was also capable, tireless, and stuffed with essential information on transcontinental railroad problems.

Back in California once more, he joined forces with another advocate of Sierra rails, Daniel W. Strong, an amiable druggist of the hydraulic mining town of Dutch Flat, high above the canyoned North Fork of the American River. On horseback the two men thrust from Dutch Flat into the mountains north of Lake Tahoe. It was not a first trip for either of them, but this time they found, through Strong's skillful guidance, what Judah agreed was the key to the project—a long, timbered ridge that would let a locomotive climb along manageable grades to the mountain's crest at Donner Summit, 7,042 above sea level. Triumphantly, the promoters then set about meeting California's not very rigid requirements concerning the incorporation of railroad companies.

Papers could be filed as soon as ten or more investors agreed to buy stock to the amount of $1,000 per mile along the proposed line. Since Judah estimated the distance from navigable water on the Sacramento River to the Nevada border at 115 miles, the two men could launch what they named the Central Pacific Railroad as soon as they had found subscribers for 1,150 shares of $100 stock.* Inasmuch as only 10 percent of the stock's face value had to be paid in cash at the time of pledging, the search ought not be difficult.

By scouring the mining camps of the area, they obtained pledges for 465 shares. Hoping that these would act as decoys for the remaining 650, Judah hurried to San Francisco. There he sought out the bankers who had gained control of his original creation, the Sacramento Valley Railroad, and made his pitch: for an initial investment of only a few thousand dollars, they could become his partners in a company that would soon bridge the continent. Service to the nation, glory for themselves. . . .

They rejected him out of hand. Crazy Judah! His horseback reconnaissance didn't tell a thing about the true costs of either building the road or maintaining it afterward during the snow-heaped winters. Anyway, Congressional approval was still uncertain. The San Franciscans were more interested in developing what they already held in the palm of their hands, the growing wagon traffic to the Comstock, which crossed the Sierra south of Lake Tahoe on a road that had been built in 1857. Freight came to the highway over their little Sacramento Valley line— 22 miles that in 1860 would net them $500,000. Service, glory . . . thanks, but they'd settle for present profit. And if Judah tried to promote a transcontinental whose western end would break their monopoly they'd fight him to a standstill. It was no idle threat. San Francisco's powerful shipping interests, which had no desire to see competition arrive by land, would stand behind them to the end.

Undeterred, Judah shifted his efforts to Sacramento. He had learned from his first experience. When a small audience gathered in the St. Charles Hotel to listen to him, he concentrated not on long-range national visions but on immediate local advantages. As a precursor to the railroad, he said, his company would construct a new wagon road over Donner Summit to Virginia City. He knew the mountains. He knew that this road could be made shorter and easier than anything else available.

---

*The actual distance to the border turned out to be 140 miles, an error that probably resulted from Judah's ingrained optimism and not from deception.

Freighters would flock to it. The tolls they paid would create a reserve for railroad work. Of equal importance, the railway company would have a supply road ready for moving heavy equipment into its grading and track-laying camps. And then, after rails were across the mountains and the roadbed was streaking up the Humboldt Valley toward Great Salt Lake . . . gentlemen, the opportunity of a lifetime!

Listening in the audience was Collis Huntington, a burly six-footer, son of a Connecticut tinker, who in partnership with spindly Mark Hopkins owned a flourishing Sacramento hardware store. He calculated quietly. If he and four friends each subscribed to 150 shares, they could give Judah another 150 as payment for his preliminary work and still be able to outvote him and the shareholders in the mountains. Control for $1,500 down!

Along with himself Huntington signed up his partner, Mark Hopkins; Charles Crocker, the fat owner of a local drygoods store; Leland Stanford, a wholesale grocer; and James Bailey, a jeweler. A scattering of other businessmen, including Charles Crocker's brother, E. B. Crocker, a lawyer, pledged themselves to smaller amounts.

Reputedly James Bailey was the most prosperous of the group, which was not saying a great deal. A more important member was Leland Stanford. Titular head of the state's new Republican party, which Huntington had helped found, Stanford stood a very good chance of being elected the next governor of California. Obviously such a triumph could mean a great deal to the new company if and when it sought state and county aid to supplement federal grants.

And so the Central Pacific Railroad Company was incorporated—Stanford, president; Huntington, vice-president; Hopkins, treasurer. Judah was given a salary of $100 a month, plus his stock, and told to get into the mountains and make a real survey this time, one that would produce a reliable estimate of costs.

Results were chilling. To maintain grades up that "easy" ridge to the summit, the infant company would have to excavate scores of deep cuts, drill 18 tunnels, pile up innumerable fills and trestles. Costs would soar to at least $13 million, nearly $93,000 a mile for 140 miles, which was far more than any subsidy bill yet considered by Congress had proposed allowing.

Oddly, the outbreak of the Civil War gave them hope. With Southern obstructionists gone from Congress, with the North in desperate need of the West's outpouring of precious metals for creating credit abroad—surely a generous railroad bill would be forthcoming. Besides, the Comstock madness was on the associates, as they were called. By Stanford's own admission years later, the mineral strikes beyond the mountains had stampeded them into a belief that "we could afford to build the road with the prospect of the further development of Nevada."

They attacked vigorously. They launched the Donner Pass wagon road. They saw Stanford elected governor. They raised Judah's salary to $150 a month, provided him with a satchelful of newly printed stock certificates, and sent him to Washington. There he was to join Midwest promoters in pushing for the sort of bill they wanted.

During prior visits to the nation's capital Judah had developed many contacts. Now he had, in addition, the support of California's victorious Republicans. In what today would be considered an unconscionable conflict of interests, he had himself appointed clerk of both the Senate and the House committees on the Pacific railroad. He doled out, to recipients now unknown, Central Pacific stock with a face, but not actual, value of $66,000. The promoters of various Kansas, Iowa, and Missouri companies also dispersed sheaves of certificates. Clerk Judah, among others, received $25,000 worth for his help, all of which prompted Congressman Justin Morrill of Vermont to observe sarcastically that there seemed to be far more interest in generating subsidies for short lines at either end of the transcontinental than in building the main road.

Naturally there was. Local lines in regions filling rapidly with miners (Nevada) and farmers (western Iowa, western Missouri, Kansas, and Nebraska) would be profitable much sooner than a long line through the wastelands in between. Congress, however, was wary of doling out federal largess to local stubs. Thus the transcontinental was used by private interest groups for carrying their own little projects to success. It is not the first time that great goals have been reached by devious paths.

Although the bill that President Lincoln signed into law on July 2, 1862, did designate the Central Pacific as the company to build the western end of the route, financial provisions were below expectations. Land grants—6,400 acres for each completed mile of track—would not produce cash for many years, if ever. (In 1941, for example, some of the granted land in Nevada was still being offered for as little as 91 cents an acre.) Government loans of $16,000 to $48,000 per mile, depending on the difficulties of the terrain, took the form of 30-year bonds that the company had to turn into cash in the open market. Because of doubts about the railroad's feasibility and competition from other industrial enterprises, these bonds seldom sold at par. Worse, under the Legal Tender Act of 1862, a buyer could pay in greenbacks, themselves sorely depreciated (at one point during the war greenbacks were worth only 37 cents on the dollar), whereas labor and materials in California had to be paid for in gold, a painful squeeze. Finally, the government bonds constituted a first mortgage on all railroad property and income. As a result the company's own bonds would amount to a second mortgage and could be sold only at drastic discounts.

To overcome these handicaps, the Californians resorted to various expedients. They persuaded the state geologist to support their contention that the Sierra Nevada began, geologically at least, at Arcade Creek in the flatlands, a ruling that would let them draw mountain loans of $48,000 per mile several miles before they reached the foothills. Then, instead of having the Central Pacific build the line itself, they awarded the first construction contract—the bridging of the American River and the grading and tracking of 18 miles of roadbed—to a specially formed organization called Charles Crocker & Company.

The device appeared honorable enough. On accepting the contract, Charles resigned from the railroad's board of directors (but was replaced by his brother, E. B. Crocker). His bid was reasonable—$400,000 for the bridge and tracklaying. Comparable work in the area had cost the Sacramento Valley Railroad nearly double that sum. Moreover, to hold down the outflow of cash, of which the Central Pacific had little, Charles agreed to accept $150,000 worth of railroad stock and bonds in part payment of the $400,000 called for in the contract. Very considerate, in view of the straits the Central Pacific was in—but it opened the way to mischief. For when the first financial crunch was over, the promoters would be able to form a secret partnership with Crocker, pay themselves in railroad securities, and thus keep a grip on most of the CP stock—a bonanza if ever the paper rose in value.

Meanwhile, however, prospects were bleak. No federal loans would be available until after the company had proved its stability by completing 40 miles of track. How could funds be raised for surmounting this hurdle? While Governor Stanford pushed for state and county aid, the other directors of the Central Pacific launched a campaign to sell stock to the public. At that point the San Francisco bankers made good their threat to Judah. Enlisting the support of ocean shippers, wagon freighters, teamsters, stagecoach operators, and the banking and supply houses that dealt with them all, they raised fogs of doubt and slander. It almost worked. Although Sacramentans subscribed to nearly 10,000 shares of railroad stock—10 percent down, or less than $100,000 in desperately needed cash—the Central Pacific's brokers in San Francisco were able to sell, during 22 days of effort, only 14 shares, a gain to the company of $140!

Fortunately for the Central Pacific, the rank and file of voters were not as susceptible as investors to that kind of attack. They wanted a railroad. At a series of elections in Sacramento, Placer, and San Francisco counties they voted to exchange a total of $1.15 million in county bonds for company stock. The state legislature, wooed by Governor Stanford, approved a $15 million bond issue. But again there were frustrations. Acting through friends in the various counties, the railroad's San Francisco opponents launched taxpayer suits challenging the constitutionality of the measures and kept the funds immobilized when they were most needed. Although the railroad eventually obtained all but $200,000 of the county bonds ($950,000 worth eventually yielded $650,000 in gold) they had to compromise the state case, accepting in lieu of an uncertain $15 million a surer guarantee of interest payments on $1.5 worth of 7 percent company paper—in effect an outright gift by the state of $105,000 a year over a 20-year period.

During this time Judah grew increasingly intransigent. He objected to the sloppy work Crocker was doing in an effort to pare costs; he turned high-minded about the trickiness of moving the Sierra's base into the flatlands. Beneath the sulks lay wounded pride. The overfed merchants to whom he was yoked—all towered over him physically—owned enough stock to outvote him at every turn, so that his dream was now beyond his control. Because he had been unable to put money into the Donner Pass wagonway, he had been given no interest in that project, though he had suggested it in the first place. Didn't he count anymore?

Completely embittered, he lined up enough strength to put the next series of grading contracts into the hands of outsiders. It was a costly victory. Closing ranks, Huntington and the others forced a showdown. Either Judah could buy them out for $100,000 each, or they would pay him $100,000 in company bonds for his interest in the road. Judah tried to hang on. Although San Francisco was the home of the Central Pacific's most determined enemies, he sought to raise the necessary money there, failed, and started for New York. While crossing Panama he was stricken fatally with yellow fever. Back in Sacramento his opponents dabbed the tears from their eyes, removed Judah's supporters, Strong and Bailey, from the road's directorate, and, in complete amity now, turned to the urgent tasks ahead, not the least of which was patching up the mess that Judah's outsiders had made of their grading contracts.

In the East, Huntington borrowed, persuaded, connived, cajoled, and somehow erected a huge, inverted pyramid of credit on the tiniest of bases. Together with the adroit directors of the Union Pacific, he helped push through Congress in 1864 an act liberalizing the government's commitment to the road. Land grants were doubled. More importantly, the bonds that the government turned over to the railroads as loans were reduced to second mortgages, a change that stimulated the sale of the companies' own bonds. Of more immediate help, the bill reduced from 40 miles to 20 miles the amount of track that had to be completed before the railroads could draw their first payments.

As the Central Pacific inched upward during the latter part of 1865, new concepts about its future took shape. The exorbitant costs of building in the mountains and the unexpected shrinkage of the Comstock boom indicated that Nevada traffic alone would not bring solvency. To forestall ruin the associates would have to compete vigorously with the Union Pacific for a larger share of such business as existed or could be developed between the Sierra Nevada and the Rockies.

Green River, Wyoming, thus became the builders' goal. A junction there with the Union Pacific would put more than half of the line's total trackage in the Central Pacific's control. This would give the Californians a paramount voice in determining rate schedules for all transcontinental traffic, including the flood of merchandise anticipated from the Orient. California would dominate the Mormon settlements of Utah and the new mines of southern Idaho and western Montana. Even more alluring were the coal fields of eastern Utah and western Wyoming, for California, rich in most resources, had little coal and presumably would import enormous tonnages. Finally, by sitting astride northern Nevada and Utah, the CP could forestall any notion its rival might develop about skirting its flanks and entering California through gentle Beckwourth Pass, north of Donner and 1,800 feet lower, a path used today by the Western Pacific.*

Even those gains weren't the main lure. For by this time the associates had realized that if they continued using railroad stock in part payment of the construction bills rendered by Charles Crocker & Company, reorganized in 1867 as the Contract & Finance Company, they could retain mastery of the finished line. (Eventually they even bought back the shares issued to outsiders during the early struggles to raise money.) If, on completion of the transcontinental, its earning capacity seemed bright— Green River, here we come!—then its stock could be watered almost at will and offered to the public at such high prices that losses suffered during construction would be almost irrelevant.

The great obstacle was the Union Pacific. Its promoters had generated a similar stock scheme in Crédit Mobilier and were as frantic as the Central Pacific to raise values by dominating the line that would result from their "cooperative" efforts. Hence their rabid construction race, perhaps the most familiar tale, except for the California gold rush, of the nation's westward surge.

The odds at the end of 1865 seemed to favor the western line. The

---

*Judah's flailing rhetoric notwithstanding, Donner Summit is not the best railpass over the Sierra Nevada. But the Big Four (as Huntington, Stanford, Charles Crocker, and Hopkins became known after E. B. Crocker's death) snapped at his bait for the sake of the ephemeral Comstock traffic and thus committed central California to an uneconomical line.

slow-starting Union Pacific had laid only 40 miles of track across land as flat as a table. The Central Pacific had meantime pushed 50 miles into the mountains and nearly 2,000 feet upward. Crocker had almost 1,000 teams and 10,000 men at work, nearly three-fourths of them Chinese—docile swarms that with only hand tools and small carts moved almost incredible amounts of earth from massive cuts into equally impressive fills.

Tunnels were bottlenecks, but thanks to the Donner wagon road, already the most popular highway to Virginia City, Crocker was able to advance far ahead of tracks' end, set up camps, and put his drillers to work. In order to keep rails and other fabricated materials moving steadily to this dogged army, Huntington at one point had 23 ships at sea on the stormy voyage around Cape Horn.

Then, in 1866, the Union Pacific spurted. Construction experts released by the ending of the Civil War hired thousands of discharged Irish soldiers and in 182 working days laid 247 miles of track up Nebraska's Platte Valley. Then, to the further discomfiture of the Central Pacific, came the unusually severe winter of 1866–67. Forty-four separate blizzards roared across the Sierra. Avalanches roared continuously; twenty Chinese died in one of them. In despair Crocker moved thousands of his men into the Nevada desert, where storms did not howl so endlessly, and put them to work there. This entailed sledding 40 miles of rail, three dismantled locomotives, and twenty work cars across the summit to them—thanks again to the wagon road. Reluctantly Stanford authorized covering 37 miles of track with snowsheds, a project that eventually involved scattering 30 sawmills throughout the nearby forests and cluttering the already crowded construction tracks with snorting lumber trains.

Right while costs were soaring, the associates were faced with the alarming possibility that competitive lines might enter California from north or south and undercut the value of their trouble-beset property. In 1864, Congress had chartered the Northern Pacific, designed to reach from Lake Superior to Puget Sound. There was talk, too, of a Union Pacific branch line along the Oregon Trail to the Columbia River. Although neither the NP nor the UP had started actual work on these projects, prospects were hopeful enough that a firm called the California & Oregon had won a promise of land grants from the federal government and was inching northward through the Sacramento Valley toward a possible connection with one or the other of the rivals.

A graver threat existed in the south. In 1866, Congress had given the Atlantic & Pacific land grant subsidies (but no bond loans) for pushing through the Southwest to a point on the Colorado River near present Needles, California. Like the Northern Pacific, the A&P had not got started. In 1868, however, one of the formidable figures of American railroading, Thomas A. Scott, vice-president of the expanding Pennsylvania system, began toying with the idea of helping yet another ambitious road, the Kansas Pacific, take over the moribund A&P charter and do the work. Stirred by this heady vision, a group of San Franciscans had incorporated the Southern Pacific. Supported by the prospect of generous land grants from the public domain, they proposed following the coast to San Diego and then veering westward to meet Scott's tracklayers.

In Huntington's opinion, both rival overlands would be built some day. Worse, both would be able to haul freight at cheaper rates than could the Central Pacific, plagued by the steep grades and bludgeoning snows of Donner Pass. The only way to counter the threat—and, as a corollary, the only way to make sure that Central Pacific stock sold well when it finally was offered to the public—was to dictate the terms under which their opponents' traffic could enter California. That in turn meant controlling every short line capable of reaching toward the state's borders.

As a supplement to this dominion the associates would need to control, as nearly as possible, docking facilities in San Francisco Bay, sole ocean inlet to what was in those days the only flourishing part of the state. This mastery could best be achieved, the schemers decided, by obtaining from the state 6,620 strategic acres of waterfront land just south of the city and from the federal government a grant to Goat Island, once called Yerba Buena Island, midway between San Francisco and Oakland. They would build their own harbor on Goat Island and connect it to Oakland, where they would buy bay-front land from private owners, by means of a giant causeway. And finally they would end riverboat competition by purchasing the California Steam Navigation Company.

All California buttoned in their pockets—but meanwhile the race to Green River was heating up. Hoping to slow the Union Pacific by legal sophistries, Huntington somehow persuaded Orville Browning, pliant Secretary of the Interior, to approve the Central Pacific's proposed route east of Salt Lake while disapproving the Union Pacific's—even though both planned to use the same canyon gateways through the Wasatch Mountains! In order for the scheme to work, the Central Pacific would have to outspeed the Union Pacific to within striking distance of the canyons. Huntington thundered behests at Charles Crocker, underscoring the words with heavy strokes of his pen. "Let out another link. . . . *Work on as though Heaven was before you and Hell was behind you.*" Obediently Crocker, a relentless dynamo in spite of his enormous bulk, scattered 15,000 men, mostly Chinese, across the Nevada deserts.

The scheme was too vast for the associates' grasp. Seeing the tips of the tentacles, thoughtful Californians took fright. An impassioned San Francisco typesetter-journalist named Henry George cried out that the chief product of a monopolistic railroad in California would be a further inflation of land values; in order to obtain farms or city house lots, ordinary agriculturists and laborers would have to pay higher rents than ever to the capitalists who even then were absorbing the state's most desirable real estate. John Bidwell, sage of Chico and recently a one-term Congressman, warned that experience with Central Pacific trains already running showed how rapacious the Big Four would be once their network covered the state. Seeing themselves ringed with iron, San Francisco financiers and wholesale distributors raised strenuous protests in Sacramento and Washington, where their representatives were strengthened by Midwest Congressmen friendly to the Union Pacific.

Assaulted thus, the Central Pacific watched many of its dreamed-of prizes melt like sea fog. Although the associates did obtain a large slice of the Oakland waterfront, their request for 6,620 acres south of San Francisco was whittled by the state down to 60. The Congressional act that would have given them Goat Island was rejected entirely. The aggressive directors of the Union Pacific upset Huntington's approved-route scheme—it had been bold rather than clever—and pushed on through the strategic canyons to a junction with the Central Pacific at Promontory, in northern Utah.

Significant victories offset these losses, however. The associates spun a web almost completely around San Francisco Bay. Some lines—the California Pacific between Benicia, Sacramento, and Marysville for one —they forced into their orbit with ruthless legal and financial manipulations. Others they paid for at figures that made them gag. The vital short line from San Francisco to San Jose, for instance, cost them $3.25 million in gold (in installments) at a time when their treasury was staggering under the extravagances of their Green River frenzy. They had to pay heavily, too, for the California Steam Navigation Company. But the bay area was theirs. Now for the state.

They acquired the California & Oregon and continued its slow thrust north past bonanza wheat ranches rich with traffic in grain. They bought the Southern Pacific and moved it south 45 miles or so from San Jose to the hamlet of Gilroy. There a momentous decision faced them. As originally chartered, the Southern Pacific was to run south near the coast to Los Angeles and San Diego, receiving as its reward for each mile of completed track 12,480 acres of land from the public domain. Because of old Mexican grants, however, little public land was available along that route. Accordingly the company, smiling its golden smile, prevailed on the Congress of the United States and on the legislature of California to ignore the protests of the coastal counties and let it shift its assigned route southeast from Gilroy into the western part of the land-rich San Joaquin Valley. It would meet the Central Pacific, currently building south along the east side of the valley at Goshen Junction, near present-day Visalia. (Actually, the SP stretch between Gilroy and Goshen Junction was never wholly laid, with tragic results, as we shall see when we come to the bloody story of Mussel Slough.) From Goshen Junction on over Tehachapi Pass to Mojave and then to Needles, the original destination, everything would be Southern Pacific.

Gaining these rights was much. More was to come. Tom Scott of the Pennsylvania system had switched his attentions from the moribund Atlantic & Pacific charter to a new line farther south, the Texas & Pacific. This line he proposed to run through Yuma to San Diego. Citizens of that little coastal village—there were only 2,500 of them in 1872—were ecstatic, visualizing themselves as the coming masters of southern California.

The Southern Pacific's original charter entitled it to strike the border at Needles only. While retaining that right (someone might yet revive the A&P), the Big Four obtained from Congress permission to build a "branch" line from Mojave through *or near* Los Angeles to meet Tom Scott at Yuma. By "meet" the associates meant block. If they succeeded, they would kill San Diego's aspirations, a pleasant prospect, since they did not want any other California harbor competing with the northern bay that they already held in their vise.

Confident of their chartered strength, the Big Four notified the citizens of Los Angeles that the Southern Pacific would by-pass their town unless the county presented them with as much money as California law allowed—5 percent of Los Angeles County's assessed valuation. The sum, $602,000, amounted to less than the cost of the tunnel the builders would have to drive through the San Fernando Mountains north of the city— the fourth longest tunnel, at the time, in the United States. Dollars were not the main consideration, however. The SP demanded, in part payment of the total, the $252,000 worth of stock that the city and county of Los Angeles owned in a diminutive short line, the Los Angeles & San Pedro, that Phineas Banning had recently built between the city and the old hide-loading wharves due south. If the voters agreed, the SP would control, at whatever rates it chose to exact, all freight moving by sea into the Los Angeles area. So much for competition from *that* harbor, poor though San Pedro's facilities were at the time.

Tom Scott responded instantly. Hurrying west, he offered to build a branch line from San Diego to Los Angeles for a mere $377,000, if Los Angeles voters would give *him* that many bonds. During the fall of 1872 a fevered three-way electoral campaign developed between those who favored the SP and direct connections with San Francisco, those who liked Scott and the Texas & Pacific, and the rural barley growers who sold feed to legions of freight horses and wanted no railroad at all. There were fireworks, parades, band music, lavish publicity brochures, and ringing oratory. Tempers heated. The town's leading physician, Dr. John S. Griffin, laid open the head of banker Isaias Hellman with his cane and then, as Hellman's private doctor, promptly patched him up.

Scott hadn't a chance. All he offered were branch-line connections through San Diego with New Orleans. The Southern Pacific offered what the cow counties really wanted, direct routes through the San Joaquin Valley to San Francisco, the Comstock, whose mines were reviving, and the Midwest. Its advocates carried the contest handily. Although the nationwide financial panic that developed shortly thereafter slowed construction somewhat, Crocker's 2,000 Chinese managed, during the next four years, to spiral an extraordinarily complex line over the shaggy Tehachapis and under the San Fernandos. The golden spike, symbolic of completion, was driven on September 6, 1876. A month later the first carload of California oranges rolled toward Donner Summit and the East.

Other laborers were meantime pushing SP tracks eastward from Los Angeles through the seared bottomlands of the Imperial Valley toward Yuma. Although the Texas & Pacific, crippled by the financial depression of the seventies, was still 1,000 miles from the California border, Scott set up barriers. To reach the only feasible bridge site over the Colorado River, the Southern Pacific would have to cross a corner of the Fort Yuma military reservation. Only a special act of Congress could grant the necessary right of way, and Scott's lobbyists, fully as effective as Huntington's, saw to it that the act was not forthcoming.

Crocker fumed helplessly—until a revolt of Nez Percé Indians in the distant Northwest caused troops to be pulled out of Fort Yuma to assist in the campaigns. Seizing the opportunity, the builder stealthily gathered men and materials. They leaped forward at the beginning of darkness one October night and spanned the river. Before the handful of guards remaining in the fort were fully aware of what was happening, a flag-bedecked locomotive crossed brazenly into Arizona.

Even the *Alta California* of San Francisco was amused by the lawlessness. Under a headline reading "The Iron Horse Has Snorted in the Ear of National Authority," it asked editorially, "Now what are you going to do about it, Uncle Samuel? . . . Will you set us back to the days of Forty-Nine, when we crossed the river in a basket covered with the skin of a dead mule? . . . Uncle, what will you do?"

Uncle, mollified by Huntington, sawed the air but did nothing. It was the end of San Diego's aspirations to outstrip Los Angeles—and the beginning of the end for the Texas & Pacific, for shortly thereafter the SP began driving implacably toward New Orleans. California in their pockets! Stock prices assured! For the Big Four, three of whom were erecting imperial mansions on Nob Hill overlooking San Francisco Bay, it was a heady triumph, wrested from imminent disaster. But it was not what the rest of California had envisioned when they had begun agitating, along with Theodore Judah, for railroads to connect their cruelly isolated state to the rest of the nation.

Strangulation . . . it was a term, many thought in growing anger, that could be applied with equal accuracy to still other gigantic monopolies they saw rising around them.

19. Mastering the Land

To fortune hunters, the very diversity of the 800-mile reach of the state was a stimulation. Fog-shrouded redwood forests on the northwest coast, sunken deserts in the southeast that might be transformed by water from the Colorado River (Oliver Wozencraft, former Indian agent, had suggested that as early as 1853), deep harbors, mountain canyons singing with cascades, tawny plains without a tree or rock to hinder plowing—surely those 101 million ill-explored acres contained wealth enough to outdo the expectations of Forty-Nine itself. If only the keys could be found!

Individual enthusiasts proclaimed their visions. One prime mover was Count Agostin Haraszthy, who as a young man had become involved in a revolution and forced to flee to the New World from his wine-producing estate in Hungary. After living for a time in New York and Wisconsin, Haraszthy had traveled to San Diego, searching for grape lands. Politics distracted him, and as a reward for his services to Senator William Gwin, he was appointed in 1854 to the directorship of the new federal mint in San Francisco.

During his brief regime, $135,000 worth of gold bullion disappeared. Although Haraszthy avoided indictment by persuading investigators that the shortage had been occasioned by fine bits of molten metal flying off through a flue during refining, he lost his job. Nothing dismayed, he bought land in the Sonoma Valley from a fellow grape enthusiast, Mariano Vallejo, and hired enough Chinese labor to plant 85,000 vines, the beginnings of the famed Buena Vista vineyards, showplace of early California.

Most of the vines under cultivation at that time were offshoots of old mission stock. Haraszthy, grimacing sourly, was convinced that the state could do better. He filled local farm journals with articles on viticulture. In 1859 he helped lobby through the legislature a bill exempting young vines from taxation. Two years later the lawmakers named him to a committee charged with preparing a report on better methods of wine production. Interpreting the instructions broadly, Haraszthy sailed to Europe. There he bounced from vineyard to winery, snipping, sniffing, tasting, talking. Aided by his son Arpad, he selected and packed for shipment home between 100,000 and 200,000 cuttings (accounts vary) from hundreds of famous stocks.

This was too much exuberance for the newly elected Republican legislature. When Haraszthy, a stalwart Democrat, presented his expense account of $12,000, the lawmakers rejected it. Despite the rebuff, the Hungarian distributed free of charge throughout the Bay area such cuttings as had survived the long journey from Europe. He borrowed money from William Ralston for expanding Buena Vista and building a mansion as grand as those he had known in Budapest. Memorable among its festivities were the balls he presided over in conjunction with the double wedding, on June 1, 1863, of his two sons with two of Mariano Vallejo's daughters.

The lavishness did not last. Ralston began to pinch. Unable to wriggle free, the dashing Hungarian, father-in-law of two of the land's vanishing Californios, was forced to sell his estate to a Yankee concern known as the Buena Vista Viticultural Society. In the end, though, he had the last word. The state that now produces four out of every five bottles of wine sold in America has chosen to pass over other candidates, Vallejo included, and enthrone Agostin Haraszthy in its folklore, and at many a Sonoma festival, as "the father of the California wine industry."

Not every enthusiasm was equally productive. At about the time that Haraszthy was touring Europe for cuttings, a naturalized Frenchman named Louis Prévost was filling the farm journals with accounts of the silk he had produced on his farm near San Jose. Bemused by his statistics, the legislature in 1864 offered bounties to whoever would set out specified numbers of young mulberry trees and raise silkworms that, after feeding on the leaves, would spin cocoons of rich, raw thread.

Yielding like Haraszthy to his own exuberance, Prévost formed the California Silk Center Association, bought 8,500 acres of a one-time Mexican grant in southern California (the site of present Riverside), and prepared to raise silk on a sultanic scale. Others followed suit, but the zest was for speculation, not production. Farmers eager to reap bounties planted mulberry saplings as close together as the teeth of a comb. Demand for worm eggs ballooned the price to $10 an ounce and led to such frenzied overproduction that in 1869, 100 million eggs were dumped on the market. Realizing belatedly that it had paid out $250,000 in return for very little silk, the legislature called off the program. Prices collapsed, and that road to instant riches turned suddenly gray.

Grapes and silk were single-shot efforts. A far more comprehensive attempt to understand and thus master the giant land was the famed California Survey, charged by a legislative act of April 21, 1860, with conducting "an accurate and complete geological, mineralogical, and botanical survey" of the state. This staggering task—just what *did* the ambiguous instructions mean?—was entrusted to Josiah D. Whitney.

Forty-one years old at the time of his appointment, Whitney had rounded out a Yale scientific education with study in Paris and Berlin. After service as assistant state geologist of copper-rich Michigan and, later, as state chemist of Iowa, where lead was the magic mineral, he had published a treatise entitled *The Metallic Wealth of the United States.*

The very sound of the words enthralled Californians. Surely a geologist who could write such a tome was a practical man and would search like a bloodhound for exploitable ore bodies, rich farm soils, and ungrazed meadows of nutrient grass. Nor would it hurt if the Survey's pronouncements were delivered with the sort of Haraszthy-like enthusiasm that would make capital easier to raise. To show the importance that the state attached to the work, the legislators allotted Whitney a munificent first-year budget of $20,000 and gave him a salary equal to that of the governor, $6,000.

They misread their man. Of shorter than average height and with a rigidly square-cut beard adorning his larger than average head, the geologist looked pugnacious and was. He had a touchy sense of professional integrity, and during his years in the Lake Superior copper fields he had learned to detest speculators. Choosing to interpret his directive as authorizing a quest for pure knowledge, he recruited a cadre of bright young Easterners from prestige colleges—Californians had expected at least some of the plums—and sent them off on the kind of ideal reconnaissances that textbooks urged.

When the Survey's first publication turned out to be a report on fossils, Whitney's employers exploded. Angrily the San Francisco *Bulletin* railed that the business community "wants to know not what manner of monsters peopled the shores during the pre-Adamite epoch, but . . . what secrets are locked in [the state's] adamantine caskets." Whitney retorted undiplomatically that he had no intention of reducing himself to the status of a mere prospector. Infuriated, the legislators halved the Survey's appropriations, Whitney's salary included, and ordered the director to confine his work to practical concerns. Stubbornly Whitney went right on with the scientific investigations he had launched, producing funds when necessary out of his own pockets.

At that point, in April, 1864, there appeared from Yale University a scientist of the stamp that Californians wanted. He was Benjamin Silliman, Jr., tall, big-nosed, hearty, and vigorous. In addition to teaching, Silliman also acted from time to time as a consultant for commercial firms. His most sensational triumph had been his geologic work in connection with the 1859 discoveries of petroleum in western Pennsylvania. Impressed by the results, Thomas A. Scott of the Pennsylvania Railroad (he had not yet begun to think seriously of transcontinental tracks) had hired Silliman to go to California during 1864 and examine certain gold properties near the Colorado River.

On reaching the state the geologist found himself besieged by entrepreneurs wanting advice. Dizzied by the attention, he accepted consulting jobs that in ten months brought him $75,000 in fees. (His salary as a full professor at Yale was $2,765 a year.) Inevitably his examinations, many of them involving long jostlings in the saddle, and his reports, mostly scribbled at white heat in grubby wayside hotels, were superficial. No matter. Whenever he saw the least sign of hope, he turned out the kind of prose that helped sell stock—stock in companies in which he was sometimes given an interest.

As he coursed about, he was approached by an oil firm that had acquired leases to scattered lands along the Santa Barbara Channel in the hope that the numerous asphaltum seeps in the vicinity indicated oil. An affirmative determination could result in great profit, for the whales whose oil then filled most of the nation's lamps were diminishing in numbers. To be nearer the remaining pods, whalers were shifting their bases from New England to California. Fleets berthed at San Francisco combed the Arctic every summer, sometimes catastrophically; in 1871, ice would swallow 33 vessels in a single crunching disaster. Although the intense activity kept the try-pots full, prices were rising as the prospect of shortages increased.

The Pennsylvania discoveries that Silliman helped initiate had resulted in the first satisfactory substitute—a thin, pale oil easily refined into a liquid, called kerosene, that burned in lamps with a clear, almost sootless flame. On learning of the development, a few alert California whale-oil distributors began wondering whether a comparable product could be drawn from the oily-smelling tar seeps that surfaced in black patches throughout the state, principally in the south. Prospectors possessing only the scantiest knowledge of what to do began digging shallow wells and running tunnels into likely mountainsides. Among the most persistent of them was George S. Gilbert, a one-time whale-oil merchant from Brooklyn, who centered his activities at the lower end of the ruggedly beautiful Ojai Valley, a few miles inland from the coastal town of San Buenaventura, today's Ventura. During his experiments Gilbert nearly

blew himself sky high, but his activities and those of a handful of neighbors led to the formation of an oil company that yearned to make the most
of this promising new business.

The California Survey pooh-poohed the excitement. A detachment of
its men, led by William H. Brewer, took a cursory look at a few of the
seeps near the Santa Barbara Channel, and Whitney sent samples east for
analysis. His conclusion was that California asphaltum, thick with carbon, would not produce an economical illuminating oil.

Dejected but unconvinced, the promoters turned to Silliman. With his
usual feverish energy the Yale geologist galloped through the Ojai prospects and visited others near Los Angeles and in the Santa Clara Valley
of the south. He then wrote an ecstatic report. The petroleum fields of
California, he declared, were fully as promising as those he had unearthed
in Pennsylvania.

Thomas Scott responded instantly. Through agent Levi Parsons of San
Francisco he bought and leased some 450,000 acres in choice localities
from Los Angeles County northward to the vicinity of Cape Mendocino.* Chunks of this land were sold to hastily formed oil companies
both in California and in the East. Drillers and equipment were rushed
from Pennsylvania across Panama to the West Coast, and an eager public
was invited to participate, through the purchase of stock, in this newest
of California's exotic treasures. On his return east, Silliman, who had
been given an interest in certain of the companies, furthered the cause
by lecturing discreetly to small audiences, illustrating his points by burning a thin, colorless oil that Levi Parsons sent him from California. The
flame it produced was clear, steady, smokeless.

Legislators who had recently renewed Whitney's contracts, albeit on
a limited basis, bayed at the geologist's heels. Why hadn't the California
Survey promoted during four years of expensive work this resource that
Silliman had waved into being within days?

Resentful of the implication that his Survey was inadequate and
offended by what he considered Silliman's prostitution of science to the
services of shady materialism, Whitney retorted furiously. If incompetence—or worse—existed, he snapped, the flaw was Silliman's. For in
spite of the Yale professor's clear, bright flame, neither Whitney nor his

---

*A man of dubious distinction was Levi Parsons. Seeing a chance to capitalize on the mess
that San Francisco's municipal government had made of the city's harbor, he and several
other speculators had formed a private corporation for taking over the waterfront. The
People's party, child of the Vigilantes of 1856, bitterly opposed the grab, as did outlying
communities fearful of strangulation by a San Francisco water monopoly. To break the
deadlock, the state assumed, through a harbor commission, the administration of the entire
bay, a rare intrusion, at the time, of state power into local commercial affairs. Deprived of
the harbor, Parsons was eager to find another plum.

principal assistant, William Brewer, believed for a minute that California asphaltum would produce a satisfactory illuminating oil.

Their doubts were given cruel and sudden support by Stephen Peckham, a twenty-six-year-old chemist employed by one of the newly formed oil companies. The tarry liquid with which Peckham worked in California simply would not yield the kind of liquid Silliman was burning before admiring audiences in the East. Curious, the young chemist began a patient tracking of faint spoor that led him to believe the geologist was being victimized by salted samples of selected California oil mixed with Eastern kerosene purchased at a general store in San Buenaventura. If fraud was involved, as it seemed to be, the most likely motive was to stimulate stock sales. But there the trail frayed out. Though suspicion swirled around three or four promoters, including Levi Parsons, no firm proof of guilt was publicly revealed.

Inflated stock prices collapsed abruptly. One distraught investor shot himself, and several sued Silliman for misrepresentation. Victory seemed to be Whitney's. Strangely, however, the speculative spirit in California was not sobered by the oil fiasco, and attacks on the Survey mounted rather than diminished.

What, growled impatient exploiters, had Whitney accomplished? To be sure, his men had produced some handsome topographic maps, including detailed charts of the new state park, Yosemite. They had cleared up a few abstruse geological puzzles and had brought the High Sierra to public attention, partly through their discovery that the highest peak in the United States outside Alaska was a soaring uplift, 14,495 feet in elevation, that they named Mount Whitney for their boss. As events would show, the Survey also provided a unique training school for many of the scientists who under federal aegis would later delineate the entire West. It was even responsible, indirectly, for one of the most readable local-color books of the time, Clarence King's *Mountaineering in the Sierra Nevada*. But how much money had it put into men's pockets?

In 1868 the survey was killed. All that Whitney could rescue from the debacle was reimbursement for personal expenditures and a reluctant underwriting of a few publications.

Most of the leading scientists in the United States decried the short-sightedness, yet in one respect—to jump briefly ahead of our narrative—time justified not Whitney but his opponents. Fortified by a willing faith in Silliman's glowing prose, persistent drillers kept pecking away at the edges of the tar seeps. In 1867, Scott's able young driller, Thomas R. Bard, brought in California's first meager, short-lived "gusher" in the Upper Ojai Valley; though profitless in the long run, that, too, helped keep faith alive. Meanwhile refiners were struggling to produce a kerosene that, in the words of Bard's biographer, W. H. Hutchinson, would not "char the lamp wicks and smoke the chimneys, nor stink like the back door to hell itself." Eventually both groups succeeded. In time, too, technology would justify another of Silliman's predictions, seemingly far-fetched when he made it, that the chief use of California's sooty, carbon-filled oil would turn out to be fuel for an almost coalless state. Whitney, suspicious of promoters and envious of rivals, foresaw none of this—an easy sneer to make from the vantage point of hindsight.

And so men groped with the stubborn land, seeking patterns that would work. In the end neither surveys, bounties, nor salted samples provided nearly as much stimulus for adaptations as did a series of natural disasters.

First came the floods of 1861–62. The Central Valley turned into a lake more than 200 miles long and 40 miles wide. Steamers followed wagon roads to avoid the angry, snag-filled river channels. Leland Stanford, returning to his Sacramento home after his inauguration as governor, disembarked from his rowboat through a second-story window. After the waters receded, the city embarked on a painful program of straightening the river channels and raising the entire downtown section an average of 9 feet. A resident of San Buenaventura wrote of listening to a sound he had never heard before—the sodden crash of falling adobe buildings. Waves of water roaring out of the San Gabriel Mountains slashed new channels through orchards and buried vineyards in sand. But at least, chirped one Pollyanna, the shortage of firewood in the Los Angeles Basin was relieved by the tangle of uprooted trees tumbled out of the canyons onto the plains.

During the deluge an estimated 200,000 cattle and untold numbers of sheep drowned. That was just the beginning. The land dried . . . dried. Grass vanished throughout 1863–64. By the time the consecutive blows of flood and drought were over, the state's cattle population had dropped by one-half. From Monterey to San Diego those Californios who had survived earlier droughts, land-grant litigation, and their own extravagance were compelled (with only a few exceptions) to surrender their ranchos to tax collectors and mortgage holders.

Much of the alienated acreage went to sheepmen. Sheep had proved better able than cattle to survive drought. Besides, the blockade of the South's cotton and the Union armies' demand for wool had skyrocketed prices. During the 1860's the number of sheep in California soared from 1 million to 2.75 million, and since the quality of the animals rose with their numbers, the wool clip increased fivefold during the same period. James Irvine, aided by squabbles among the heirs of certain grantees, began welding together as a sheep farm the three huge Mexican grants that later became Orange County's most famous estate, site now of the flourishing city and college campus that bears Irvine's name. His occasional associates, the two Flint brothers and Llewelyn Bixby, acquired in the same vicinity and in Monterey County eight ranchos totaling more than 300,000 acres. At shearing time the once-indolent, now dispossessed offspring of the Dons put silver bridles and hand-tooled saddles on their blooded horses and rode out to the dusty pens to work for day wages beside the Indians and mestizos who had once been their peons.

The purchasers of other beset ranchos found their profits in subdividing. The end of the Civil War and the imminent completion of the transcontinental railroad brought about a surge of immigration, particularly Southerners fleeing the ravages of reconstruction. Most of those people wanted farms. If the country's new theory of land distribution, as embodied in the Homestead Act of 1862, had worked as intended in California (and in other arid sections of the West), a large portion of the newcomers would have settled on 160-acre plots of the public domain. After living on their chosen farms for five years while making certain improvements, they would have received free title from the government. But land in California's treeless, sun-stricken Central Valley, which contained most of the state's available agricultural land, looked too obstinate to be worthwhile even as a gift. The bulk of the immigrants pressed on to sections where irrigation seemed easier.

Early comers to the foothills, notably in the Placerville area, converted miners' ditches into irrigating canals and nursed pear and apple trees into lush production. Others leased or bought orchards, vineyards, and wheat and barley farms in the developed areas around Sacramento, Stockton, and the short valleys opening into San Francisco Bay. The demand pushed up prices, and then the surge swung south toward Los Angeles County.

Two contemporaneous triumphs there quickened the pace. In 1869 Phineas Banning completed his twenty-mile railroad between Los Angeles and the San Pedro-Wilmington roadstead, where produce could be loaded aboard steamers. At the same time, hard-twisted desert freighters like Remi Nadeau pushed their wagons through the sand traps of the Mojave Desert and made the new silver mines of Cerro Gordo, high in the hot Inyo Mountains east of Owens Valley, tributary to Banning's road. Hundreds of miners, to say nothing of the straining freight teams, demanded food. So you'd better get your farm now, boys, while prices are right.

The rough Transverse Ranges, northern boundary of the Los Angeles lowlands, produced three streams susceptible to diversion—the Los Angeles, San Gabriel, and Santa Ana rivers. (Before a multitude of wells sucked away their sources, these streams really did flow water the year around.) Other water collected in ciénagas, or marshy places, along the toes of the hills and could be tapped by shallow artesian wells. These were the areas that speculators subdivided and sought to sell to the newcomers.

The career of scarred old Abel Stearns—Horseface, they had called him during his hide-trading days—furnished a spectacular example. After marrying into the Bandini family, Stearns had acquired scores of thousands of acres and tens of thousands of scrawny longhorn cattle from his improvident relatives and neighbors. The gold rush made him briefly rich, and then the drought shattered him. He lost 30,000 animals and his creditors closed in.

Another hide trader whom we have met, Alfred Robinson, came to his rescue, not altogether philanthropically, by forming a six-man trust made up of himself, Stearns, and four San Francisco capitalists. Among the latter was that man of all seasons, Sam Brannan. Stearns deeded to the Robinson Trust, as it was called, 177,796 acres that had escaped foreclosure. In return he received $50,000 for liquidating his debts, plus a promise of a share in the proceeds from subdividing.

Functioning eagerly on the Trust's behalf was the California Immigrant Union, a quasi-official bureau of the state formed in 1869 for inducing settlers to come to the Coast. The Union published promotional booklets and maintained agents not only in the East but in northern Europe as well. Immigrants who were lured by the propaganda to the Union's San Francisco headquarters found themselves in the agreeable clutches of carefully trained salesmen passing out brochures concerning real estate available for purchase throughout the state. Not by pure chance many of these salesmen focused on the lands of the Robinson Trust.

Southward, the Trust was developing procedures destined to become very familiar during California's next century of real estate booming. Its workers laid out towns with carefully contrived names. They erected signs purporting to show where churches, schools, community centers, hotels, and the like would soon spring into being. Salesmen meanwhile were meeting every incoming stagecoach and steamer and were haunting the campgrounds where wagon trains corraled.

Not every town that showed on the maps grew into maturity. Savana, wrote one traveler, never held more than weather-faded signs and a lone coyote "gazing despondently . . . upon the debris of an abandoned sheep camp." But enough of the Trust's settlements succeeded so that its officers grossed $2 million before dissolving. Stearns did not enjoy his full share. On August 23, 1871, just as he saw himself started back on the road to riches, he died in a San Francisco hotel of a heart attack.

Buying land was only the first of a settler's expenses. His new holding also had to be fenced, watered, plowed, and planted. Many people sought to dilute the risks either by sharing the labor, as the Mormons had done at San Bernardino, or, more frequently, by dividing the cost of hiring to have it done. In 1857 vintner John Froehling of San Francisco helped persuade several German Jews interested in grape culture to buy shares, at $750 each, in what he called the Los Angeles Vineyard Society. An agent employed by the group purchased 1,165 acres on the Santa Ana River southeast of the village of Los Angeles, and then used cheap Mexican labor to dig an irrigation ditch, plant vines, and erect a tight, live fence of brush around the tract. The shareholders named the creation Anaheim—*Ana* from the stream and *heim* from the German word for home—and settled on 20-acre tracts distributed by lot. Although frustrations were frequent, they were soon selling to Froehling enough grapes to make 120,000 gallons of wine and brandy a year. A century later, Anaheim could boast an even headier producer of fantasies than wine—Disneyland.

Thus the pattern went: settlements of like-minded people carefully prepared in advance. Wineless Presbyterians clustered at Westminster, a creation of the Robinson Trust; Methodists founded Compton; Indianans, after many vicissitudes, launched Pasadena. An energetic promoter named John W. North (he had already founded Northfield, Minnesota) formed the Southern California Colony Association, sold shares, bought the lands of Prévost's defunct Silk Center Association, dug yet another ditch out of the Santa Ana River, and laid out Riverside. There, on the site of Prévost's dismal failure, two of North's settlers, Mr. and Mrs. Luther Calvin Tibbetts, planted three Brazilian navel orange trees sent them by a friend in the U.S. Department of Agriculture. A horse trampled one tree, but from the other two came the buds that within a decade transformed the pithy, sour, mission stock into a new kind of California gold. Naval oranges, which ripen during winter, were soon followed by Valencias, harvested in the summer, so that the citrus crops developed into an almost continuous bonanza.

A far different and, for many years, a far more important kind of agricultural gold was wheat. Expansion of acreage, swift during the gold-rush decade, became feverish during the late 1860's and early 1870's. Crop failures in Europe boosted prices in Liverpool extravagantly, while in California a return of "normal" weather led farmers to forget the earlier blows of flood and drought. Their hunger for increased productivity at top prices stimulated mechanical improvements, and those in turn added still more acres to the leaping spiral of growth.

The first thrust for land was in the Sacramento Valley, where winter rainfall was more dependable than it was farther south. Title to most of those broad plains stemmed from Mexican grants, and so there was no need to devise ways for circumventing the 160-acre maximum that the government had set as the amount of land that an ordinary man could acquire from the public domain. All that a would-be soil miner needed was credit and determination. Dr. Hugh Glenn, educated originally in a Missouri medical college, was one spectacular example. By pyramiding his earnings as a California freighter and poker player, Glenn acquired 55,000 acres fronting a 20-mile stretch of the Sacramento River, the largest-producing wheat ranch at one time in the United States. And just north of Glenn in Tehama County, sixteen other men owned a total of 365,000 acres—figures that could be matched in all the other valley counties.

It was not possible to till that much soil with old-style walking plows. Inventors soon produced the gang plow—a wheel-mounted beam holding six or more evenly spaced, deep-biting shares, the whole pulled by eight horses or mules—all of which gulped more capital than the average farmer could scratch together. Nor was a solitary gang plow enough for the soil miners. After the first rains had softened the soil, Glenn would start *100* eight-mule teams in echelon, plowing a strip several hundred feet wide around one of his 20,000-acre fields. Intricate machines pulled by more batteries of horses then pulverized the clods and planted and covered the seed in a single operation.

In the spring a misty greenness of breathtaking beauty suffused the land. Soon it yellowed. Hordes of wildlife moved in, supposing that nature had prepared a special feast. Battles raged. For a time the state offered bounties for ground squirrel and gopher scalps taken in lots of 50 to the nearest justice of the peace, but so many picayune frauds developed that the program had to be abandoned. The ranchers themselves organized rabbit drives, 300 to 400 men marching in a wide line, sometimes to band music, as they drove the terrified creatures through a funnel-like wire fence leading to a pen. There thousands of shrieking animals were clubbed to death and either left to rot or sent to San Francisco, where fat carcasses sold at $1.50 a dozen.

"Goose herders" made regular rounds of the fields, firing into the gorging flocks. Hugh Glenn employed twenty or more guards each season and spent $13,000 a year buying ammunition for them. Some men even soldered two double-barreled shotguns together, triggered four charges at once, and, with luck, reputedly knocked down as many as 100 birds at a blast. Ambitious herders eked out their pay by plucking feathers, which sold at 50 cents a pound for mattress stuffing, or by sending the bodies to city restaurants.

Harvest brought a new invasion of monster machines. First came the horse-drawn "header," so called because its long, whirling blades clipped off, in a swathe 20 or more feet wide, just the heavy yellow heads of the grain. Belts fed these heads into special wagons that hauled the grain to the thresher. After fear of fire in the dry fields had been overcome, so that steam power could be utilized, threshers grew unbelievably. Glenn's "Monitor," its ravenous maw fed by 21 header wagons, filled 3,000 hundred-pound sacks a day, but was so ponderous that 50 mules were required to move it from field to field.

No Robert Frost glamour bathed the work. These were industrial operations in which utility alone counted. Here and there on the stifling flats stood a lonesome house, unpainted, unsoftened by lawn or tree. The migrant workers—whatever newly arrived immigrants from Europe, or Indians, Mexicans, and Chinese could be rounded up by labor contractors —ate sullenly in the heat, amid clouds of flies at long tables covered with stained oilcloth. In the fields they took out their fury on the fractious animals, tied their trouser legs and sleeves against the swarms of black gnats, put flour sacks over their heads to filter the dust and pulverized horse manure, drew their pay, drank deep, and moved with their hangovers to the next stand. Behind them hung palls of smoke, for the stubble they left would not rot into mulch if plowed under in that dry climate and so was disposed of by burning.

Because most of the wheat was marketed in England, it was put into sacks, for shippers believed that loose grain would shift dangerously in a vessel's hold. Big wagons drawn either by horses or, later, by waddling, steam-powered road machines carried the bulging sacks to the nearest steamboat landing or railroad siding. At tidewater the cargo was picked up by sailing vessels, for coal was too expensive for the long trip around the Horn.

There, at dockside, the farmers found themselves gripped by another of California's massive monopolists, Isaac Friedlander—literally massive, for he stood 6 feet 7 inches tall and weighed 300 pounds. A forty-niner from South Carolina, Friedlander had grown wealthy during gold-rush days by building California's first substantial flour mill. He raised wheat, too, about 10,000 acres' worth, but his genius lay in assembling, under his personal control, two essentials for marketing—sacks, of which the Californians used millions each year, and ships.

An intricate information system let Friedlander estimate with remarkable precision the needs of each year's harvest, so that he could order without waste the requisite number of sacks and charter, from all over the world, the right number of vessels—steps facilitated by the unlimited credit granted him by William Ralston's Bank of California. The Grain King's smooth-flowing operations unquestionably helped stabilize a new, speculative, ill-organized commerce. He met every contract obligation with scrupulous honesty, yet insisted on maximum profits for himself. Although big shippers could wring concessions from him, small ones were at his mercy. He set transportation costs to suit himself, and high prices for grain in Liverpool seldom trickled back undiminished to the little farms in the enormous valleys.

Friedlander was involved, too, in the spread of wheat growing into the San Joaquin Valley. Patterns there differed from those in the Sacramento Valley. For one thing, much more of the San Joaquin land lay in the public domain, and obtaining enough of it for bonanza wheat farms—160 acres just would not support the operations—involved finagling with public officials on a nationwide scale. Furthermore, supplemental water was often needed to bring a San Joaquin crop to maturity. The amounts of moisture that could be readily diverted from the streams were limited, however, and this brought conflicting interests into play, for clearly the man who controlled the water also controlled the land.

On the west side of the valley, where streams were few, a titanic struggle for control shaped up between a speculator named William S. Chapman and the extraordinary livestock firm of Miller and Lux. Son of a German butcher, Henry Miller (his name was Heinrich Kreiser before he Anglicized it) had reached New York City in 1847, aged nineteen. He worked for a while as a butcher's helper, then was swept by the gold rush to San Francisco. There he resumed his trade, touring neighborhood farms for good buys and holding the animals near his slaughterhouse until they were needed. Before long it occurred to him that he could make more money speculating in cattle than in butchering them. Joining forces with a tall, polished Alsatian named Charles Lux, he began buying increasing numbers of livestock. This soon involved purchasing ranches on which to run the animals.

By applying adroit pressures the partners picked up at bargain rates from Mexican owners several ranchos along the parched western rim of the San Joaquin Valley. These were small, though, compared to the swamplands they acquired from Sacramento. In 1852 the federal government had allowed the different states to sell the overflow lands within their borders for $1.25 an acre, a sum that was canceled if the purchaser swore he had spent an equivalent amount on dikes and drainage canals. Since state officials were careless about what buyers said, it was easy for

Miller and Lux to scoop up, at the cost of small bribes, large amounts of government real estate. One block of this swampland lay southwest of present Bakersfield in the southern San Joaquin Valley, where the Kern River lost itself in vast tule marshes dotted with islands of waving grass. (The partners did do some reclamation work there.) Another block of swampland, contiguous to some of the grants they had purchased, ran for 40 miles along the west bank of the San Joaquin River, northward from, roughly, the hamlet of Mendota.

Just north of this San Joaquin domain lay some of the holdings of William S. Chapman. Chapman had amassed that land by means of land scrip issued through the federal government. There were two kinds, military bounty scrip and scrip issued to the different states to help them finance agricultural colleges.

Ever since the Revolutionary War, Congress had been giving soldiers land scrip as a bounty for enlistment. Since many recipients did not want to move west in person to enjoy their reward, Congress had finally made the bounty scrip transferable, and its holders were generally willing to sell it at a rate of a dollar an acre on down. The other scrip represented donations of federal land to the different states under the Morrill Land Grant College Act of 1862. States without public land within their borders in 1862 were allowed to select acreage in sparsely settled regions of the North and then sell the land at whatever it would bring. Working through brokers and financed by several San Francisco Germans, including Isaac Friedlander, Chapman gathered up scrip enough to give him control of approximately a million acres, more land, for a time, than was owned by any other individual in the United States.

Some of Chapman's property lay near present Fresno. More, as stated above, bordered the San Joaquin River north (downstream) of the Miller and Lux holdings. Although Chapman planted several thousand acres to wheat, he differed from Miller and Lux in that he had no intention of using the bulk of his land for his own enterprises. Instead he wanted to resell sizable chunks to wheat farmers who were being attracted south by rising prices, favorable weather, and the approach of the Central Pacific and Southern Pacific railroads. Later, when he realized that grape growers were venturing into the Fresno area to dry raisins—a crop that still bulks large in the region—he became eager to sell smaller plots to them, too, through a subdivision called the Central Colony.

The crisp fires of drought always burned near. To increase the attractiveness of his land, Chapman tried to lay hold of two embryo irrigation systems. One, in the Fresno area, was the brainchild of goat-bearded Moses Church. The other, a staggering project for the time, had been envisioned by John Bensley, a freewheeling San Francisco entrepreneur, for carrying water from the mouth of Fresno Slough, by which the Kings River enters the San Joaquin, northward along the valley's west side— a giant ditch 70 feet wide at the top, 48 at the bottom, and 6 feet deep.

The project overwhelmed its creator. In 1871, Chapman, Friedlander, and Ralston took it over, retaining Bensley as supervisor of construction. In order to obtain a right of way through 40 miles of Miller and Lux land, the San Joaquin and Kings River Canal & Irrigation Company, as it was called, gave the cattlemen $20,000 and an interest in the firm.

A thousand men and hundreds of horses went to work under the searing sun. Meantime depression was crawling across the land. In serious trouble at the Bank of California, Ralston withdrew his support. Desperately the company tried to sell the ditch to the state. The legislature refused, though what was being offered was, in essence, the beginning of the huge California Water Plan that the government would sponsor nearly three-quarters of a century later.

When the crash came, Miller and Lux picked up the unfinished canal for one-third of what the others had spent on it. They acquired much of Chapman's land as well, and then finished the ditch, which they valued at $1 million. Altogether they now held 100 miles of west valley land, plus strips on the east bank of the river as well. One can only guess at the long-range effects of this monstrous acquisition. Though Chapman was widely execrated as a monopolist, he at least would have distributed the land among as many buyers as he could find. Years passed, however, before Miller and Lux relinquished a foot of it. The wheat and hay they raised with their water went almost entirely into their own cattle, and, later, into enormous herds of sheep.

Chapman had no better luck at Fresno, where he tried to induce immigration by selling small farms at reasonable prices and by pushing such new crops as alfalfa for dairy cows. But he needed more water than he had, and in struggling to gain control of Moses Church's Fresno Canal Company he at last overreached and went into bankruptcy.

These battles among titans merely disgusted the rank and file of Californians. They felt hemmed in and frustrated by corrupt politicians, stock jobbers, a monolithic railroad system, a stony shipping king, land and water barons who had absorbed public lands intended for all, and Chinese coolies imported, as the workers saw it, to take their jobs at cut rates. Voices began to cry for reform. How it could best be achieved, no one really knew, but as generally happens in times of distress, there was no end of suggestions.

20. Boil and Bubble

During the 1870's throughout the nation, times were hard. Farms, banks, and commercial houses tottered. Unemployment soared; unprecedented violence marked labor's clash with capital. To these general aches California added her own specialties, wrought by geographic remoteness and capricious weather, by the growth of long-tentacled monopolies and the volatile nature of a polyglot population composed largely of adventurers.

Even men not ruled by opportunism were dismayed. Like James Lord Bryce of England, who toured the West while gathering material for his classic *The American Commonwealth*, they believed that California "is in many respects the most striking [state] in the whole Union, and has more than any other the character of a great country, capable of standing alone in the world." But the potentials eluded the reach of the ordinary citizen, and the discrepancy between dream and reality created furies. In their anguish the dispossessed rushed toward panaceas and finally, in a burst of passion, tried to re-create Utopia by overhauling their entire government.

One of the most eloquent criers for change was Henry George. He was a small man, about 5 feet tall, and knew misery well. Born in Philadelphia in 1839, he had left school at the age of thirteen to earn his living sometimes as a printer's helper, sometimes as a common sailor. In 1858 he reached California, prospected briefly, and then, marrying, haunted the newspaper composing rooms for work. Layoffs were frequent; during one of them he was reduced to panhandling on the streets of San Francisco. All this while he kept studying, seeking an explanation for the stark conjunctions of poverty and wealth that he saw in every city. He also began writing, rising to reportorial jobs on a sequence of journals.

In bustling Oakland the sight of unused land being held for an increase in prices gave him an answer to the question that tormented him, and in 1871 he poured his anger into a pamphlet entitled *Our Land and Land*

Policy. Greed for unearned increment—*there* was the cause of California's troubles. It spawned two classes of men who regarded agriculture not as a way of life but as a speculation. One deplorable group, in George's eyes, was the marginal operators, often renters. Eager to make their fortunes by hitting a high market with a single crop, they spread their limited resources over more land than they could handle, living meantime in graceless shacks, buying on credit, and hiring labor for the shortest possible time.

The other type was the absentee landlord. Holder of vast acreages, he lived in style in San Francisco. Part of his holding he might lease, if convenient, to sharecroppers. Part he might farm on his own account, hiring contractors to do the plowing and harvesting. Or he might just let the ground lie idle, for his true goal was a rise in real estate values. Lurking in the background, a powerful factor in perpetuating the system, was the railroad, whose land grants in California alone totaled nearly 11.5 million acres.

(Statistics on California's agricultural situation are slippery. For instance, in 1870 there were 23,602 farms of less than 500 acres each, which sounds like a sturdy base for a goodly number of self-sufficient yeomen. *But* the state also held 122 other farms of 70,000 acres or more each. To put it another way, 122 owners controlled, in total, more acreage than did their 23,602 fellows combined. These figures do not count railroad land. Reformers insisted that without the railroad and those other 122 monopolists standing in the way, California would have attracted tens of thousands of additional farm families, with a consequent boost to the whole state's economy.)

Whatever the system, the worker was the victim. "Over our ill-kept, shadeless, dusty roads . . . plod the tramps, with blankets on back—the laborers of the California farmer—looking for work, in its season, or toiling back to the city when the plowing is ended or the wheat crop is gathered."

The answer? George struggled toward it throughout the decade. The results were incorporated in a book, *Progress and Poverty*, that he first published at his own expense in San Francisco in 1879. From there it swept the world, one of the best-selling economic treatises of all time.

Why, George demanded in its pages, should a man be rewarded for simply owning land for resale or rent on a rising market? The way to end the unfairness and redistribute the wealth was to absorb all unearned increment by means of a single tax on land. No other form of governmental revenue would be necessary. By abolishing land monopoly the single tax would, in addition, "raise wages, increase the earnings of capital, extirpate pauperism, abolish poverty, afford free scope to human powers, purify government, and carry civilization to yet nobler heights."

What more could be asked of any program?

The vision, however rosy, was too long-range for most of California's hard-pressed small farmers. They wanted relief in a hurry. To get it they turned toward the beckoning roads of cooperative associations and legislative action. Results were disastrous.

The Farmers Union and its successor, the Grange, were the leaders in the agitation. The latter, founded in Washington, D.C., in 1867, boasted 104 local chapters in California a mere six years later. Bursting with confidence, the Westerners decided to crack Isaac Friedlander's monopolies by chartering their own vessels and buying their own wheat sacks. But confidence was no substitute for know-how. Friedlander broke the sack attack by cutting prices and watching his one-time opponents come scrambling to him for bargains. As for shipping, his enemies in their exuberance chartered too many vessels and went broke paying for them. Their plans to hold their wheat off the market until prices rose went awry when quotations slumped instead. Standing amid the wreckage of their hastily executed plans, the farmers chewed unhappily on the mocking thought that no matter how much they hated the extortions of the Grain King, they'd have done better by staying with him.

Legislative action fared as poorly. Much of it was directed at the Central Pacific Railroad. Of all California's disappointments at the time, that was the greatest. Its completion, enthusiasts had once declared, would draw through San Francisco harbor vast amounts of Oriental traffic bound for New York and even England. Within a decade, westward immigration would boost the Bay area's population to more than a million. Commerce would flourish; real estate values—that lust again!—would leap.

None of the predictions came close to fulfillment. The simultaneous completion of the Suez Canal pulled Asiatic traffic that way. Immigration lagged. Real estate values, overinflated in expectation of the boom, sagged dismally. Meantime Eastern factories poured in manufactured woolens and fabricated iron at lower rates than Californians could meet. Industry faltered rather than quickened.

Despite these dull results, the railroad did nothing to brighten its image. As it pushed tracks north and south into the Central Valley, it demanded subsidies from the towns it approached. Whenever aid was refused, it created a rival town nearby and built the tracks there. It imposed, especially on short hauls, the maximum rate allowed by California law—then gave secret rebates to quantity shippers of grain and cattle. Working hand in glove with Eastern roads, the Big Four carried merchandise from New York to San Francisco at lower rates than from

San Francisco to Reno, a discrimination that helped fill transcontinental freight cars but boosted outside competition at the expense of California industry. The West, in short, was still regarded as a colony—supplier of raw material, buyer of finished goods.

Taxes were another sore point. Like other large property owners, the railroad persuaded county assessors to place low values on its holdings. When protests arose, the Central Pacific lawyers retorted that the line operated under federal charter and was not subject to local interference. If defiant county supervisors did raise bills, the railroad refused to pay and dared the rural gnats to try taking the cases into court.

Throughout the seventies, the Grange and the San Francisco Chamber of Commerce (the CP had recently moved its headquarters to the Bay city) sought redress through political action. Once again failure was complete. After Newton Booth had been elected governor in 1871 on an antirailroad platform, he developed senatorial ambitions, campaigned for a willing legislature, won, and in Washington turned into a friend of the railroad—a magical transformation that likewise stole across Congressman John Luttrell. By contributing to the campaign expenses of both Republicans and Democrats, by doling out free passes to travel-loving legislators and their families, by paying "legal fees" for unspecified services, and by suggesting that wealthy shippers show appreciation for rebates by putting pressure on their representatives, the road guaranteed friendly smiles not only in Sacramento but, as far as it chose, in every county courthouse in the state.

Then, too, there was the tactic of losing small battles in order to win big ones. After defeating in 1876 a bill that would have cut freight rates by almost one-half and passenger fares by one-third, the railroad diplomatically allowed the passage of an act calling for the creation of a three-man commission charged with collecting information that might lead to future regulatory measures. It then crippled the commission by refusing to open its books, and there was no law to force compliance. Fair enough, Charles Crocker insisted. The demagogues were violating the rights of private property, and "any man would throw a bucket of water on a fire that attacked his house."

In addition to these general grievances, the farmers and rural towns of the Sacramento Valley had a private complaint, hydraulic mining. Newly developed flexible pipe, reinforced hoses, and cannon-like nozzles called Little Giants were enabling men to use jets of water for blasting down gravel cliffs hundreds of feet high. These tremendous spouts could (and once did) kill a mule at 200 feet. When one of them struck a gravel bank, a corona of mud, sand, and cobblestones flared like a soiled sunburst. In order to handle the masses of earth that tumbled under the roaring impact, workers equipped with newly invented power drills sank outlet shafts into bedrock near the base of the cliffs awaiting disintegration. At the bottoms of the shafts, long tunnels reached out into canyons big enough to hold any amount of debris. Sluice boxes designed to pick up infinitesimal particles of gold lined the tunnels and often extended hundreds of feet beyond. At the final lip of the trough, a cascade of mud and sand poured unheeded into the gorges.

Spring runoff distributed this material throughout the river channels. Coarse gravel raised streambeds in the mountains as much as a hundred feet. On the plains the lighter sand, a brown-white slime known as slickens, spread out in desolate flats 20 feet thick, smothering orchards and wheatlands. The levees protecting the twin cities of Marysville and Yuba City from the Feather and Yuba rivers were raised repeatedly—and were not enough. On the night of January 19, 1875, the dikes protecting Marysville crumbled. Frame houses floated from their foundations, one child died, stores and homes were filled with slime. Months were needed to dig out again.

A battle of injunctions against waste dumping began. Unfortunately for themselves, the farmers were not well organized. A small group would take a case against a specific mine into a county court and win. But, like the levees, that was not enough. The mine owners, mostly San Francisco capitalists, formed an industry-wide group known as the Hydraulic Miners' Association, hired the best legal talent available, and appealed each case—a costly process for the disorganized complainants. Technicalities seemed to rule the decisions. One favorite: mining had been going on in the area since 1849. How was it possible to prove that any particular operator was responsible for the slickens complained of? And on that basis the state supreme court reversed the decision of the county judges. Wealth, the frustrated farmers growled, was the real key to justice.

In spite of such plaints, no one truly hated wealth, particularly if it came suddenly and effortlessly. Even among farmers the mania for gambling in Nevada mining stock grew steadily wilder. Stock quotations gyrated as unpredictably as the white ball in a roulette wheel, largely because of the manipulations of insiders. Yet even the insiders could be victimized by their own frenzies. William Ralston, for instance. During the early seventies he poured millions of his own money and, without authorization, another million of his bank's money into imaginative projects, some already mentioned: the San Joaquin and Kings River Canal and Irrigation Company, a hydraulic mine, silk and woolen mills, a carriage factory, a dry dock, and, most especially, into the ornate, $7 million Palace Hotel of San Francisco. Overextended and lured on, probably, by crafty little William Sharon, Ralston decided on a desperate gamble: he would gain control of the Ophir mine in the hope that its depths held a continuance of the bonanza ore recently unearthed in the neighboring Consolidated Virginia.

His plunge into the market sent Ophir stock booming. To get the last certificates he needed, he paid a certain Elias Baldwin—thereafter Lucky Baldwin—an exorbitant figure for Baldwin's holdings. The transaction had scarcely been completed when word spread that there was no more rich ore in the Ophir. Prices in the stock of all Comstock mines plummeted, a book value loss of $60 million. Suspicions about Ralston's solvency triggered a run on the Bank of California, and on August 26, 1875, its doors closed.

The next day Sharon joined the rest of the bank directors in demanding Ralston's resignation. Stunned by the knowledge that he could no longer count on the support of the man he had made and whom he regarded as his best friend, the shorn banker walked through the unseasonably hot afternoon to a public beach for his daily swim in San Francisco Bay. This time he ventured farther than usual into the combers rolling through the Golden Gate. When a boat fished him from the water, he was unconscious. He died shortly after being taken ashore.

In time his bank reopened. And Sharon, as all San Francisco soon learned, ended up with both the Palace Hotel and Ralston's ornate mansion, Belmont, on the peninsula south of the city.

Conceivably Ralston's death was not suicide. There was no such doubt concerning William Workman. One of the leaders of the pioneering trip from New Mexico to Los Angeles in 1841, Workman had risen to prominence first as a rancher, then as a businessman. In 1871 he joined forces with his son-in-law, Francis P. F. Temple, to found a bank in Los Angeles. Poorly managed at best and overcommitted by Temple's fanning of the local real-estate fires, the institution was forced to suspend operations during the statewide panic following the temporary closing of the Bank of California. Hoping to recoup, the proprietors appealed for aid to Lucky Baldwin, who had recently bought the Rancho Santa Anita. (The Santa Anita racetrack stands today on part of the property.) Baldwin sent $210,000 in gold to the partners—at high monthly interest— then foreclosed when this did not bring stability. On May 17, 1876, Workman, most of whose ranches passed into Baldwin's hands, shot himself through the head. Gloom spread throughout the south, and Los Angeles' first real estate boom sagged to a gray end.

More shocks followed. During the winter of 1876–77, a drought almost as severe as the one of 1863–64 killed hundreds of thousands of sheep and sent a migration of surviving owners northward into Oregon. Grain harvests were cut in half; hundreds of men were thrown out of work in the hydraulic mines. In January of that same disastrous winter, the Consolidated Virginia Mine ran out of ore and stopped dividend payments. Another stock market crash cost California investors $100 million and left them shivering with the knowledge that this time there would be no revival. The great days of the Comstock were forever ended, as were those of the silver mines of Cerro Gordo, farther south.

The depths of the national depression, plumbed in the East in 1875, reached California a year later. Some 30,000 unemployed workers poured into San Francisco, there to live on meager charities and sporadic public works. Bitterness, needing a scapegoat, found it in the Chinese.

The animosity, born during gold-rush days, had turned white hot during the next decade when the Central Pacific had imported thousands of Orientals to work on the railroad. Most were young men recruited by Chinese labor contractors from the poverty-stricken agricultural districts of Kwangtung Province, near Canton. The recruiters advanced passage money—to be repaid, plus 5 percent interest per month, out of the worker's first earnings—and packed the exploited as tight as the bristles of a brush aboard vessels of the Pacific Mail Steamship Company. After 40 miserable days they landed at San Francisco, were loaded into wagons, and started toward Chinatown. White hoodlums, one shocked minister wrote, "follow the Chinamen through the street, howling and screaming. . . . They catch hold of his cue, and pull him from the wagon. They throw brickbats and missiles. . . ." Yet there seemed to be more hope in California than in Kwangtung, and the forlorn immigrants kept coming. During the worst of the times a group of compassionate San Franciscans met the ships and shielded the new arrivals until they could reach the city's spreading Chinese ghetto and contact a representative of the famed Six Companies for help in adjusting.

In 1868 the Burlingame Treaty with China removed the last barriers to the influx. Shortly thereafter the completion of the Central Pacific dumped 12,000 or more Asiatics into the labor markets of the state. Wheat growers welcomed them. So did fruit farmers. For they were cheaper than slaves. There was no initial investment, and no upkeep costs during off seasons. And since they worked for lower wages than whites would, they released money for irrigation projects and machinery. This boosted production and thus increased many a Californian's conviction that only by linking low-cost labor with intensive, high-cost methods could the state's farm products compete with Eastern offerings in distant markets.

Other employers than agriculturists took advantage of the human bargains. Soon Chinese factory hands were manufacturing most of the cigars (cigarettes were not smoked then) and work clothing produced in the state. Even worse from the white view, the industrious Asiatics developed their own trades. They excelled at abalone fishing, raised vegetables, ran laundries, were popular as houseboys. Vendors in blue cotton blouses, carrying their wares in baskets hung from either end of a flexible pole, hawked their products through the principal towns. They clung together, and in spite of restrictions often prospered.

As the depression intensified, alarmists began warning of the yellow peril, 400 million strong, waiting to pounce from beyond the Pacific. Books appeared under such ominous titles as *Short and True History of the Taking of California and Oregon by the Chinese in the Year A.D. 1899*. And what one fears, one degrades. The Asiatics were demeaned as ignorant, filthy, and immoral, carriers of leprosy and kidnappers of small girls for the purposes of prostitution. The legislature regularly passed edicts designed to slow immigration, and these were just as regularly struck down by the U.S. Supreme Court as contrary to federal law. Fuzzy-whiskered Frank Pixley, sometime attorney general of the state, declared while serving as regent of the University of California, "I believe the Chinese have no souls to save, and if they have they are not worth saving." Employers hired them anyway, no matter what souls they had, and so the acid of class antagonism was heaped onto the furies of racism.

The inevitable eruption of senseless violence came in Los Angeles on the evening of October 24, 1871. When a policeman sought to break up a crowd of armed Orientals who were quarreling, evidently, over the possession of a woman—in California there was, statistically, only one Chinese female to every eighteen or twenty men—he was mortally wounded by a pistol shot. A mob of several hundred Mexicans and Americans gathered swiftly, vowing revenge. They pumped bullets ineffectively for a while at the thick-walled adobe building in which the Chinese had barricaded themselves, then cut a hole through the roof and fired through it into the crowded room beneath. Simultaneously others battered down the doors of adjoining buildings, looting and dragging out the Chinese they found inside.

Accounts vary as to whether the municipal police acted with the mob, stayed aloof, or tried to break up the rioting. Conceivably some did one thing, some another. More certainly, the county sheriff, James Burns, and a few stalwart citizens led by real-estate salesman Robert Widney rescued several of the persecuted at considerable danger to themselves. Despite their efforts, however, four men were pinioned to the tall side of a freight wagon and shot and stabbed to death. Some were gunned down as they ran. At least six were hanged from convenient awnings before armed deputies finally gained control. During "the horrible feast of indiscriminate death," to use the words of the Los Angeles *Star*, between nineteen and twenty-two Chinese died. (Some corpses, it seems, may have been spirited away.) The nation was shocked, and the shame-faced government paid without protest the indemnities demanded by China. But only a handful of the rioters received minor sentences for the evening's work.

Except for San Francisco's prior training in vigilantism, her experience might have been worse. On the evening of July 23, 1877, several thousand men met on a sandy vacant lot beside the new city hall, then under construction, to shout their sympathy for striking railroad workers in the East. Afterward, a part of the excited gathering spun off toward Chinatown. Police dispersed them but not before windows had been smashed and a few buildings set afire. On leaving, the rioters howled threats of returning in strength to finish the job.

Fearing a pogrom that would spread fire and looting throughout the city, several property owners persuaded William Coleman, leader of earlier vigilante groups, to form a new Committee of Safety. He was backed by real muscle—a war chest of several thousand dollars plus three U.S. warships sent at the governor's request into San Francisco Harbor from the Mare Island Naval Yard. Volunteer vigilantes—estimates of their numbers ranged from "more" than 1,000 to 6,500—swarmed to Coleman's banners. Their mood led him to decide against distributing the firearms he had been collecting and to arm the brigades with pick handles instead.

The showdown came on the night of July 25. An enormous mob marched to the waterfront to burn the wharves of the Pacific Mail Steamship Company, whose vessels had landed 22,000 Orientals during the preceding year. Coleman's pick wielders charged, and a wild melee followed. Four men died, and a lumberyard adjoining the wharves disappeared in towering flames. The dock itself was saved, however, and the rioters were so thoroughly overwhelmed that shortly thereafter the Committee of Safety felt justified in withdrawing.

Another sign of mounting frustration was the Workingmen's Trade and Labor Union of San Francisco, founded less than a month after the rioting. Its leader was Denis Kearney, a stocky, bull-voiced, self-educated Irish orphan who had lost his draying business as a result of injudicious gambling in the stock of the Comstock mines. Night after night Kearney harangued crowds of unemployed on the vacant lot beside the city hall, with the result that his followers became known as Sand-lotters. His two main ploys, each productive of frenzied cheering, were maledictions heaped on wealth achieved through monopoly or stock jobbery, and a reiterated slogan, "The Chinese Must Go!" His frequent arrests on charges of disturbing the peace merely increased his popularity.

The group swelled so rapidly that within six weeks it was reorganized as the Workingmen's party of California. (It had no official connection with the Workingmen's party of the United States, soon to be rechristened the Socialist Labor party.) During the early months of 1878 the infant organization astounded Democrats and Republicans alike by capturing several municipal offices. Its next goal, the victors crowed, was the state capital.

Most California newspapers opposed the rising power. Not so the opportunistic San Francisco *Chronicle*. Launched in 1865 by the De Young brothers, Michael and Charles, it had achieved gaudy prominence by means of small theatrical scoops, lurid exposures of sexual misdeeds in high places, and unrestrained attacks on whatever the editors chose to regard as political wrongdoing. In addition to circulation, these stories brought on twelve libel suits in six years. Editor Charles de Young, a small man weighing about 140 pounds, was whipped once with a cane and on another occasion was clubbed with a pistol. Once when he and a rival editor were being booked for disturbing the peace, they drew their guns and resumed their dispute inside the city jail itself—bloodlessly, thanks to quick intervention by the startled police.

The *Chronicle*'s fervid support of Kearney led to rumors that its reporters were writing his speeches. In addition, the paper backed demands emanating from the rural counties that a convention be summoned for writing a new constitution that would force a remodeling of the railroad's rate structure, equalize taxation, and remedy the ills of land monopoly. Charles de Young's motives in picking up these crusades may have gone deeper than mere circulation. For if Workingmen dominated the convention, De Young, through his hold on the new party, might become the next political boss of California. Or so the speculations ran.

Dismayed by the state's deep economic distress and assaulted by both the farmers and the workers, the legislature authorized the constitutional convention. June 19, 1878, was set as the day for electing delegates. Fearful of the radical Workingmen, Republicans and Democrats agreed to close ranks and sponsor conservative representatives under the label Non-Partisan. Their cause was helped by dissension within the Workingmen's party. When the returns were in, the Non-Partisans held 78 seats, the Workingmen only 51. Another 23 were divided among Republicans, Democrats, and independents who had refused to wear the Non-Partisan label.

For 157 days the delegates met, wrangled, and slowly hammered out compromises. The document that resulted established an elective three-man Railroad Commission to regulate rates and check discriminatory practices. It created a State Board of Equalization to assess railroad property and equalize tax rates throughout the different counties. An eight-hour day was decreed for public works. An emotional section spelled out restrictions on "aliens, who are, or may become . . . dangerous or detrimental"—that is, the Chinese. Nothing was said about hydraulic mining on the grounds that it was not a statewide issue.

Businessmen opposed the wordy document as a confiscatory and socialistic abomination. The Workingmen's party denounced it as timid and conservative. Few newspapers other than the *Chronicle* supported it. The farmers, though, felt that the Railroad Commission and the State Board of Equalization would cure their deepest grievances. Their votes carried ratification by a margin of 77,959 to 67,134. When the victory was announced, celebrants poured into the streets of the Central Valley towns, leading the Marysville *Appeal* to sneer, "Every dung hill and barnyard . . . contributed to a midnight serenade, as the air vibrated with cat calls and the bawling of jackasses." Sour grapes. The document the victors cheered, now heavily amended, is still California's constitution.

The first election of state and local officials under the new constitution was to be held September 3, 1879. Sensing that the divided Workingmen's party was not going to be the power that he had hoped, Charles de Young, boasting of the *Chronicle*'s share in achieving ratification, called through the columns of his newspaper for the formation of a New Constitution party. This led to a violent break with Kearney, who refused to endorse De Young's candidate for mayor of San Francisco. Instead Kearney tapped as the Workingmen's nominee a strapping, red-haired, red-bearded Baptist minister, the Reverend Isaac S. Kalloch, pastor of the city's ornate new 3,000-seat Metropolitan Temple.

Reacting typically, De Young sent reporters snooping along Kalloch's back trail. On August 20 they came up with a juicy tale charging the minister, now dubbed the Sorrel Stallion, with adultery in Boston. Faced with an overflowing congregation two days later, Kalloch confessed the escapade, which had occurred 28 years earlier, when he had been nineteen. To the delight of his audience, he then unleashed from the pulpit a blistering attack on the De Young brothers, calling them among other things "infamous hybrids, whelps of sin and shame . . . assassins, ghouls, hyenas of society."

Charles de Young, who could not take what he had dished out, had himself driven in a closed carriage to the side door of the Temple and sent a note to Kalloch, saying that a lady wished to speak to him. When the minister approached, De Young shot him twice and ordered the driver to flee. The bolting carriage overturned. Bystanders dragged the assailant out and were beating him cheerfully when the police arrived and snatched him away to jail. Kalloch was taken to the hospital. There, after several days of suspense, he rallied. De Young was thereupon released on bail.

Sympathy resulted in Kalloch's being elected mayor by a margin of 519 votes over the *Chronicle*'s candidate.* Outside the city resentment fastened on the joint nominee of the New Constitution party and the Democrats, Dr. Hugh Glenn, the gargantuan wheat grower of the Sacramento Valley. He was thoroughly crushed by the Republican candidate, George C. Perkins, backed by the railroad. And so the earthquake of reform ended up producing a mouse.

Only two changes of consequence occurred during the next decade. In 1882, the United States government, uneasy over labor agitation everywhere, declared a ten-year moratorium on Chinese immigration. In 1884, a federal, not a California, court used injunctions to end stream pollution by hydraulic mining companies, some of whom recouped part of their losses by turning sections of their 7,000-mile ditch system into irrigation canals and selling water to the farmers they had once despised.

Otherwise, nothing. Mayor Kalloch ended up quarreling so bitterly with his board of supervisors that the city government was paralyzed. The Southern Pacific continued its ways unchecked, even in the face of enormous unpopularity incurred by the murderous clash at Mussel Slough, an affray that calls for some explanation.

Mussel Slough, now named Lucerne Valley, lay westward of Goshen Junction in the San Joaquin Valley. Goshen was the point where the Southern Pacific, moving southeast from San Jose, was designed to join the Central Pacific, moving south through the eastern part of the San Joaquin Valley from the vicinity of Stockton. The valley land to the west of Goshen was good wheat country, easily irrigated in the spring by overflow from the Kings River. In the late 1860's and early 1870's, many settlers, the majority of them from the rough frontier areas of Texas, took up homesteads in Mussel Slough under the careless assumption that the land was open.

They might have been more circumspect. As noted earlier, the Southern Pacific had been designed originally to run south through the coastal counties. The road's land grant would be largely meaningless there, however, because most of the coastal region was privately held. On ac-

---

*There was a postscript. After Kalloch's election, the *Chronicle* continued its scandalous attacks on him. On April 23, 1880, the minister's outraged son entered the newspaper office and killed Charles de Young. After two drawn-out trials filled with charges of perjury young Kalloch was acquitted on a plea of self-defense. All of which led Lord Bryce to sniff, in *The American Commonwealth*, that the episode was, of course, quite typical of primitive societies such as prevailed in Albania, Corsica, and California.

quiring the SP the Big Four had accordingly shifted its route into the San Joaquin Valley so that they could lay hold of more of the public domain. To enemies this looked like naked opportunism, and they clamored that a juggling of the original charter invalidated the land grant. After five years of vacillation, the Secretary of the Interior ruled in the railroad's favor. Men whose property would be affected by the decree prepared to challenge it in the courts.

They soon had another grievance. The Big Four decided not to waste funds finishing the line through the desolate hills bordering the San Joaquin's western rim. (The Central Pacific connection via Goshen and Stockton was enough to link Los Angeles and the Bay area.) They did, however, push a 40-mile stub along the abandoned route, from Goshen west through fertile Mussel Slough. On the strength of that they claimed ownership of a checkerboard of mile-square sections in a 20-mile belt on either side of the new track.

If the contention held, many a Mussel Slough settler would be trans- formed overnight into a squatter on railroad land, and be subject to eviction. Naturally they shouted "Foul!" The road's charter specified that the entire line should have been completed by July 18, 1878. Those terms had not been met, and the entire grant, the farmers insisted, was subject to forfeit.

The railroad countered by submitting to the settlers on its presumed holdings bills that were far higher than its standard charge of $2.50 an acre for ordinary, unimproved farmlands. The Mussel Slough lands, of course, were not ordinary. Besides, the squatters, as the railroad viewed them, had been using the ground without rent for several years. Now they should either pay up or get out.

To the infuriated farmers this was one more example of the corpora- tion's bad faith. They formed a vigilante committee, dressed themselves as Indians, and burned the houses of a few newcomers who indirectly accepted the railroad's title by purchasing land from it. On its part the railroad won a court decision confirming the 40-mile grant. The settlers set about collecting money for an appeal to the Supreme Court, but before the papers were filed the railroad forced the issue. Two men, probably hired for the purpose, bought land occupied by defiant settlers, obtained writs of eviction, and went out with the local marshal to take possession. The result was a gunfight, May 11, 1880, in which the two "purchasers" and six settlers died.

Five Mussel Slough firebrands were fined $300 each and sentenced to eight months in jail for their parts in the bloodletting. On their return home—in wagons, not on the train—they were greeted by 3,000 cheering valley residents. But the railroad kept the land on either side of the stub.

Further evidence of the Southern Pacific's venality emerged during an 1883 lawsuit brought against the Big Four by Ellen Colton, widow of one of the Big Four's trusted employees. Some 600 letters exchanged between David Colton and Collis Huntington became part of the trial transcript. In their correspondence the men had openly discussed the necessity, cost, and methods of "influencing" certain judges, legislators, and Congressmen. When the letters became public property, newspapers throughout the United States pounced eagerly, printing long extracts to prove the brazenness of corporate graft. For years the letters would rise to haunt the magnates, but it brought no discernible change in their practices.

It had been the hope of many voters that the Railroad Commission authorized by the new constitution would oversee rate schedules firmly and equitably. Most of the commissioners, however, proved as unable as other government agents to withstand temptation. Of the original trio, lawyer Charles Beerstecher, once a vocal member of the Workingmen's party, left office a wealthy man, though his salary was only $4,000 a year. Joseph Cone, a Sacramento Valley wheat grower, resold a ranch he had recently bought (the Gerke Ranch, part of the old Peter Lassen land grant) to the treasurer of the railroad for a clear profit of $100,000. Somehow the land floated away from the ostensible purchaser into the hands of Leland Stanford, whose workers set out 3 million vines on it, thus creating for the railroad president the largest vineyard, at the time, in the United States.

Though no such circumstantial evidence roosted on the shoulders of the third commissioner, George Stoneman, he was untrained in bookkeeping and totally unable to understand the railroad's intricate auditing system—nor were there any provisions in the laws that would let him hire expert help. Subsequent commissioners proved no better qualified, and the railroad's rate practices remained as they had been. Matters were further complicated in 1884 when the Big Four incorporated, under the lenient laws of Kentucky, a holding company called the Southern Pacific Company and placed under its umbrella all of their proliferating rail lines and steamship firms. Useful information was now doubly hard for the public to come by.

The story of the State Board of Equalization was comparable. Because the language creating it specifically mentioned railroads, the lawyers of the Southern Pacific contended that the measure was discriminatory and hence unconstitutional under the Fourteenth Amendment. Justice Stephen Field of the U.S. Supreme Court, presiding over the California Circuit Court, as was customary in those days, agreed and in a series of complex decisions decreed for the railroad. It may have been pure coincidence that Field was an intimate friend of Stanford's, but many Californians did not think so. Doubts availed nothing, however. For years the railroad paid only those tax bills, generally worked out as compromises with the resentful counties, that it chose to notice.

Land monopoly also continued unchecked. A convenient new tool was government surveyor John Benson, who awarded surveying contracts to himself and, when measuring public lands for private corporations, managed to make the number of acres in a square mile, 640, expand under the magnifying eye of his instrument to as much, in some instances, as 1,400. Charles Conrad, a special agent of the U.S. General Land Office, gathered evidence enough to have Benson indicted—but Conrad was abruptly removed from office because of pressures exerted by Senator John P. Jones of Nevada and Leland Stanford of California, and the case against Benson was dropped.

Then there was the group of San Francisco capitalists who contracted to sell 50,000 acres of redwood land near Humboldt Bay to Scottish investors—and afterward set about getting the land. Their device was to use dummy entrymen under the Timber and Stone Act of 1878, which allowed a citizen to buy up to 160 acres of timberland at $2.50 an acre (a single redwood log delivered at a mill was worth more than that) if he swore he had no contract to resell his acquisition. The law itself created fraud, for operations among the redwoods, which generally grew in rough country, required more expensive machinery than could be paid for by the trees of 160 acres. In order to get more, grafters worked openly throughout the redwood coast and among the giant pines of the western Sierra Nevada.

The San Franciscans mentioned above advertised in the newspapers for entrymen. They accosted farmers and sailors in the streets of the little town of Eureka. They prepared the necessary papers for whoever agreed, at a price of about $25, to act as a dummy, took the hirelings in batches to the land office, where the clerks had been bribed to notice nothing, and stood at their elbows as the entrymen purchased, with syndicate money, the acreage described in the documents. The syndicate employees then made out bills of sale to the land without bothering to leave the office, where oaths had just been sworn that no sale was contemplated. Thus, at a cost of about $150,000, the capitalists absorbed 57,000 acres of trees estimated to be worth $11 million. Again government agents obtained indictments but the cases never came to trial.

In such a milieu politics smelled no better. The Republican sweep during the election following ratification of the new constitution had left the Democrats demoralized, particularly in San Francisco. To a minor ward boss named Christopher A. Buckley, this seemed like opportunity.

Born in Ireland and raised in New York City, Buckley had arrived in

San Francisco in 1862, aged seventeen. He left his first job as conductor on a horse-drawn streetcar to become a bartender in a saloon frequented by Republican precinct captains. In his new school he drank himself blind—literally—but the handicap sharpened his other senses. He learned to recognize people by their footsteps; he unfailingly remembered names and birthdays; he was genial and ready to lend a hand whenever needed. Soon Blind Chris was the most popular man in his district, but he saw no real future in a victorious organization controlled by men bent on maintaining their position. So he switched to the Democratic party, pushed past its discouraged ward bosses into a position of leadership, and began the work of rebuilding.

He succeeded wonderfully, first in San Francisco, then in the state. He bled payments from all of the Bay city's municipal employees, even schoolteachers. By controlling the election of the county supervisors, who granted franchises and set rates, he reached his fingers deep into the pockets of San Francisco's utility companies. By playing off the Senatorial ambitions of mining magnate George Hearst against those of Leland Stanford, he formed combinations that let him call the tune in most state elections. In return he saw to it that between 1882 and 1890 not a single piece of effective antirailroad legislation emerged from Sacramento.

The public, in brief, was being roundly damned, a particular bitterness to those who had hoped for so much from the new constitution. But they had spoken out then, and as the century drew toward its end, they began to again, this time with a better understanding of the kind of tactics that were necessary for success.

part five

THE BIG SHIFT

21. The Sound of the Boom

Although only a few of the near-sighted residents of San Francisco noticed the trend at the time, Southern California—it is appropriate now to use the capital S—had recovered quickly from the depression of the 1870's. When the new decade opened, the area was ready to jump headlong into the most extended period of sustained growth ever experienced by any equally compact region of the United States.

A few small straws heralded the hurricane. Transportation facilities, for instance, were steadily expanding. Prodded ahead by Phineas Banning, the U.S. Army Engineering Corps constructed long jetties in San Pedro Bay in such wise that they forced the tides to scour out deeper channels for coal and lumber ships. Promptly the amounts of seaborne freight moving in and out of the little Wilmington harbor that served Los Angeles soared from 81,000 tons in 1879 to 285,000 tons in 1882. Meantime the Southern Pacific pushed its tracks through Houston, Texas, to New Orleans and by adding a steamship line from Louisiana to New York City enabled Eastern manufacturers to ship goods to the West Coast under a single bill of lading.

The tendency of birds of a feather to flock together to the Los Angeles Basin resumed as soon as hard times softened. In 1882, to pick a single example from many, sixty Methodists rented a railroad car, equipped it with their own bedding and a community stove, hitched it to a freight train, and rolled west to found Long Beach.

Real estate developers grew increasingly sophisticated, none more so than George Chaffey (often spelled Chaffee), promoter of the twin settlements of Etiwanda and Ontario in the western part of the San Gabriel Valley. Born in Ontario, Canada, in 1848, and self-educated as an engineer, Chaffey had made a modest fortune before he was thirty by inventing a new ship's propeller and by designing vessels for plying the Great

Lakes. In 1880, he and his family traveled west to visit his father, recently moved to Riverside, the American home, it will be remembered, of the American navel orange.

Enthralled by the transformations that could be wrought through irrigation, Chaffey decided that he could parley his engineering talents into truly great profits by somehow linking water development to land sales. Persuading his brother William and certain other Great Lakes capitalists to support him, he purchased several thousand acres from the old Cucamonga Rancho, added more from the Southern Pacific, and set about waving his magic wand.

Straightway he found himself in the legal briar patch of water rights. The state constitution of 1849 (and by implication, that of 1879) stated that unless specific decrees forbade, the common law of England was to rule all court decisions. English common law sanctioned riparian water rights. That is, the owner of land bordering a stream could use its waters but could not divert them. Miners, however, did divert the Sierra streams at will, and the Supreme Court of the United States, in commenting on a decision of a California tribunal, declared, in the words of Justice Stephen Field, that "the regulations and customs of miners . . . constituted the law governing property in the mines and in water on the public mineral lands." Thus the doctrine of appropriation for beneficial use was also sanctioned by California law.

Which of the contradictory concepts should prevail? The problem came to a head in a bitter controversy between the giant Miller and Lux Land and Cattle Company and the aggressive Kern River Land and Cattle Company controlled by three San Francisco capitalists, Lloyd Tevis, James Ben Ali Haggin (his father was a Turk), and William B. Carr. In 1875, the Tevis-Haggin-Carr group laid claim to a sizable portion of the water in the Kern River near Bakersfield in the southern San Joaquin Valley and began digging a canal to irrigate 13,000 acres lying some 30 miles away. Miller and Lux immediately filed suit. The appropriation, they said, would interfere disastrously with their riparian rights, for it would dry up 200,000 acres of swampland that they had reclaimed farther down the stream.

The suit, dragging on appeal through court after court, put Chaffey in a quandary. Some of the land he had purchased lay along San Antonio Creek, plunging down the side of 10,000-foot Old Baldy, high peak of the San Gabriel Mountains. Along with that land, Chaffey had bought water rights in the creek. But rights to do what? If the court of final appeal held in the *Lux* v. *Haggin* controversy that riparian doctrine prevailed, established communities on lower San Antonio Creek, notably Pomona, could block diversion of the water he owned to his proposed colonies. How could he prepare for that contingency?

Aided by newspaperman L. M. Holt, Chaffey hit on a dazzlingly simple solution. He chartered, under the laws of California, a mutual water company to hold the riparian rights he had acquired with his land. To each purchaser of a 10-acre plot in his holdings he transferred 10 shares of water stock in the company. Thus each stockholder owned a share of the mutual company's riparian rights, and under that umbrella the organization diverted water as far as need be to reach the limits of its jurisdiction—first in Etiwanda colony, named for a Great Lakes Indian chief, and then bigger Ontario, named for Chaffey's natal province. Tricky, yes, and in time Chaffey's use of mutual water companies to boom land sales would grow trickier still. But the device did offer a method for turning the riparian rules of English common law into a system more relevant to California's needs. Before the decade was out, 57 companies would follow Chaffey's lead.

A digression here. In 1885, by a vote of 4 to 3, the California Supreme Court, in the wordiest decision ever handed down by that tribunal, held in favor of Miller and Lux as against Carr, Haggin, and Tevis, and thus confirmed the doctrine of riparian rights. No stream diversion! The angry farmers of the Central Valley, prodded into action by William Carr, demanded legislation to cancel the decision. Again Carr proved to be Johnny-on-the-spot. At a party he encountered Governor George Stoneman, mellow with strong drink, and prevailed on him to sign papers calling the lawmakers into special session.

The result was the Wright Act of 1887, which allowed 50 or more neighboring landowners to incorporate an irrigation district under the laws of the state. District engineers could draw up plans for an irrigation system, and if two-thirds of the area voters agreed, the district could then issue bonds to pay for the works.

The rush of incorporation that followed was more enthusiastic than wise. Internal squabbles set voters at sword point. Farmers who did not understand financing or corporate management overbonded themselves and dumped huge quantities of paper onto a market chilled by the depression of 1893. Sales were further slowed when big landowners challenged the constitutionality of the act.

Although the U.S. Supreme Court upheld the measure in 1897, the damage had been done. Of the first 52 districts created under the original act, only 9 survived. By contrast, Chaffey-style mutual companies irrigated 90 percent of California during the decades bracketing the turn of the century. *But* . . . the Wright Act, after constant amendment by the legislature, eventually provided the organizational framework for the gargantuan water diversions of later years. So even tipsy governors, it would seem, have their uses.

The demand for land, including Chaffey's, was intensified during 1882–83, by the thrust of yet another transcontinental railroad, the Atchison, Topeka, and Santa Fe, across New Mexico and Arizona to Needles, California, on the banks of the Colorado River. No hopes jumped higher than those in diminutive San Diego. Eastern rail connections! Deprived once by Collis Huntington's defeat of Tom Scott, the handful of residents were determined not to be forestalled again. Leading citizens incorporated the California Southern, wheedled a construction loan from the Santa Fe in exchange for a fat land subsidy south of their village, and started building north to meet the new transcontinental at San Bernardino, southern gateway to strategic Cajon Pass.

The Southern Pacific retorted by thrusting its tracks westward from Mojave to Needles. No trespassing: California was SP property. But this time the Santa Fe had a lever. It had run a line southward to the Mexican port of Guaymas on the Gulf of California and threatened to use the harbor as a way of reaching San Francisco by sea. Jay Gould, sitting in the center of the financial spider web in New York City, also applied pressure for his own purposes, and Huntington, plagued by financial reverses, had to yield. The Southern Pacific sold its Needles-Mojave branch to the Santa Fe for $7.2 million and leased trackage rights from Mojave to Oakland for $1,200 per mile per year. The monolith had been cracked at last.

Although San Francisco was the Santa Fe's main goal, the road's directors did not ignore the eager southland. Tracklayers surmounted rugged Cajon Pass in 1885 and hooked onto the flood-battered California Southern at San Bernardino. That same year Santa Fe trains reached Los Angeles.

Competition was immediate and intense—strident advertising campaigns, guided excursions, and rate wars that for a year dropped the cost of a ticket from the Mississippi Valley to the coast to roughly $25. (Earlier it had been $125, and for a day or two in March, 1887, it sagged to an unbelievable $1.) Why travel to the Mediterranean, boomers said, when the same glamour was available at cut rates in one's own native land?

Scores of thousands of people started westward, eyes wide and guards down. So many locomotives were diverted to passenger trains that freight was stranded in the East and suddenly the Coast found itself plagued by a shortage of essential goods. Who cared? Real estate promoters ran to meet the newcomers with outspread arms. To draw prospects away from the blandishments of established communities, salesmen in new developments—there were between 60 and 100 of these instant cities —hired brass bands, offered free barbecues of oxen roasted whole, and employed balloonists, always called "Professors," to risk their necks at $400 to $500 an ascent.

To prove the stability of their towns many promoters erected resort hotels showy with peaked roofs, bay windows, and wide verandas framed with fretted woodwork. Separately and in conjunction with local chambers of commerce, these hostelries worked overtime in thinking up ways to advertise the delights of Southern California. It was, for instance, a hotel manager, Charles Frederick Holder of Pasadena's Raymond, who joined with members of the elite Valley Hunt Club to launch, on New Year's Day, 1889, one of the great publicity gimmicks of all time, the famed Tournament of Roses.

Zenith of opulence was San Diego's Hotel del Coronado, erected by two Midwestern capitalists, E. S. Babcock and H. L. Story, as a come-on for the scrubland they had purchased on what was then called San Diego Peninsula. Month after month hired spellbinders standing beside the rising walls auctioned off residence lots at gratifying figures. After the hotel had been completed in 1888, tourists were lured by a mammoth cage filled with chattering monkeys, a lawn dotted with large turtles for children to ride, and ads that chanted the charms of the entire locality: "There is not any malaria, hay fever, loss of appetite, or langor in the air; nor any thunder, lightning, mad dogs, cyclones, heated terms, or cold snaps."

Success was next to unbelievable. San Diego's population in 1884 was estimated at 5,000. In 1888, 32,000 were tramping through the streets, buying chunks of real estate mostly on credit, and reselling them within weeks at more profit than they were likely to have made at home in years. Buyers throughout the south were so eager that they paid up to $500 for a place in line outside the office of each hot new subdivision.

Northern California was dumfounded. For decades its residents had mocked the cow counties; now it tried to imitate them. Deciding that oranges were the secret of success, developers in the Sacramento Valley planted groves near the foothills, where winter temperatures were warmer than in the valley bottom, and held fruit fairs where meretricious displays of imported oranges were heaped under waving palm and banana fronds. The depths to which jealousy descended appeared in advertising copy promoting two subdivisions near Oroville: Palermo, boomed as the Riverside of the Sacramento Valley; Thermalito, self-hailed as the Pasadena of the north. To no avail. Mere names could not evoke the southland myth of Mediterranean romance. A cold snap killed the incipient groves, and the wind ran out of the northern promotions with scarcely a sigh.

A collapse soon followed in the south. Obviously the same land could not keep changing hands indefinitely at constantly accelerating prices. As demands for credit soared, lenders grew cautious. In the spring of 1888, Isaias Hellman announced that the Farmers and Merchants Bank of Los Angeles would advance no more money for speculative purposes. Others fell in line, and suddenly the fever broke. Trains from the East began arriving empty and returning full. Dozens of paper towns stood empty; a surprising number of unoccupied hotels burned down, presumably for their insurance.

A powerful residue remained, nonetheless. The 1890 census showed that despite a massive exodus of disillusioned, the population of both San Diego and Los Angeles had more than quadrupled during the feverish decade. The reason was clear, the faithful assured themselves. The opportunities afforded by Southern California's benign climate, fertile soil, new rail connections, and beckoning sea remained as great as ever.

To tout these advantages in a more systematic way than had been done before, a group of Los Angeles businessmen formed, late in 1888, an aggressive new Chamber of Commerce charged with recapturing the area's lost momentum. The organization worked with fervent effectiveness. Although the rate of Los Angeles' growth did slump by more than one-half during the nationwide depression that closed out the century, enough new settlers arrived to boost population above the magic 100,000 mark. Regardless of what toplofty San Franciscans might say (there were 343,000 of them in 1900), Los Angeles was a village no longer, but, numerically at least, a full-fledged city.

The growth was paralleled throughout the southland, and not all of the newcomers were health seekers or retired Midwest farmers. Somehow they had to make a living. One favorite pursuit among those with money enough to see them through the tight years of beginning was citrus ranching. They too worked fervently and successfully. They solved their fluctuating labor needs by hiring, at rock-bottom wages, immigrants from Japan, who were just then beginning to replace the excluded Chinese. Plagued by a destructive pest called cushion scale that clung in soft, waxy masses to their orange trees, they called for help on the Department of Agriculture. The answer was an early-day ecological triumph. Albert Koebele of the Department discovered in 1891 that Australian ladybird beetles (more commonly called ladybugs) fed ravenously on the pest. He imported jars full, released the insects in key groves, and watched them multiply beyond belief. Within eighteen months cushion scale in California was under control. Equally gratifying to the industry were marketing developments wrought by the potent California Fruit Growers Exchange. Organized in 1905, the Exchange systematized the packing and distribution of citrus products under one of the most successful merchandising labels ever coined—Sunkist.

The demand for irrigated farmland created new speculative booms and brought George Chaffey back into as fantastic an adventure as can be imagined, even in Southern California. He had sold his Etiwanda and Ontario holdings at top prices in 1886 and, entranced by the challenges of irrigation, had gone to Australia to try his hand where conditions were really hard. The effort failed, more because of transportation and marketing difficulties than because of construction flaws, and twelve years of work evaporated into nothingness. In 1898 he returned to Southern California, stone broke and looking for a way to recoup.

The region was in the grip of another drought. Desperate, Chaffey's former colonists at Ontario offered him $500 a month to help them develop new sources of ground water by means of tunnels and wells. Succeeding bountifully, he diverted the excess moisture that he produced onto a nearby tract, felt the jingle of new money in his pockets, and, restless always, began looking for a challenge to match those that had frustrated him in Australia.

Early in 1900, opportunity appeared in the form of big-boned, heavy-jowled Charles Robinson Rockwood of a firm called the California Development Company. This organization, Rockwood said, had a desert reclamation scheme afoot and would like Chaffey's advice—and some of his money, if he thought well enough of the plan to invest.

Interested in spite of warning voices, Chaffey went with Rockwood to the southeast corner of the state. There an enormous trough slants for 180 miles through the desert, from San Gorgonio Pass, the eastern exit from the Los Angeles Basin, to the vicinity of the Colorado River delta. The central position of this trough, called the Salton Sink, lies 273 feet below sea level, so that both ends slope toward the middle. To the west are the rugged Peninsular Mountains, a formidable barrier on the way to San Diego. Eastward, lower mountains, almost denuded of vegetation and collared with continually shifting sand dunes, separate the trough from the Colorado River.

Inasmuch as the river was higher than the trough, it was theoretically possible to move water westward by gravity—an attractive economy—and use it for irrigating many hundreds of thousands of acres. Land prices would leap; the promoters would grow rich. Chaffey's part in the project would be building the necessary canals.

He spent six weeks investigating the geography, soil, and climate.

Together they formed a remarkable tripod for speculative agriculture. The lay of the land appeared to be entirely in his favor. He could easily tap the west bank of the river in the vicinity of Yuma and avoid the sandhills by curving his canal south into Mexico. There he would meet an ancient overflow channel called Alamo and use it—a ready-built ditch —for transporting the water to the southern end of the trough. The fact that the river, laden with silt, frequently choked its own channels and then cut new ones like the Alamo did not worry him, even though the deep alluvial soil in the trough provided mute evidence that river water had been there before.

Except where alkali had intruded, that deep soil was incredibly fertile. Moreover, the climate was right. Summer's pile-driver heat would be hard on men but as wonderful as a glasshouse for forcing plants to maturity. Very little rain fell to interfere with harvests. Wind would be taxing, but trees could be planted as barriers against drifting sand. The frost-free growing season was 300 days long. In effect this would double a farm's acreage, for the land would produce two crops a year, whereas the ordinary farm had to be content with one. The Southern Pacific's main line to New Orleans lay nearby, and so it would be easy to rush choice winter fruits and vegetables to the snowbound East in time to command premium prices.

Without investigating the company as thoroughly as he had the trough, Chaffey on April 3, 1900, signed a contract to build the canals. He was eager to plunge straightway to work. The company demurred. It wanted to attract buyers first, for it lacked resources and needed to raise capital by selling land and water stock at the outset. Even this hope, as Chaffey soon discovered, was precarious. Although the company claimed 20,000 acre feet of Colorado River water, it owned relatively little land over which to spread this immense outpouring. Worse, about the only plan Rockwood had for acquiring more acreage, most of which lay in the public domain, was to hire dummy entrymen to take up 320-acre desert claims and then surreptitiously transfer title to the California Development Company in a local variant of an old American skin game.

Outraged by the fussiness rather than by the dubious ethics, Chaffey forced a reorganization that put him in charge of operations. His key for absorbing more acres than fraudulent land entries would readily provide was an interlocking set of eight mutual water companies like those he had developed nearly twenty years before for watering Etiwanda and Ontario.

In an inspired publicity stroke he got rid of the sterile desert connotations clinging to the region by renaming the southern part of the trough the Imperial Valley. He then blanketed the valley with the eight mutual water companies. Each of these companies bought from the California Development Company one share of water stock for every acre inside the mutual company's boundaries. This stock was then transferred to a holding organization, the Imperial Land Company, staffed entirely by the promoters of California Development.

Prospective settlers took care of getting their own land. They could obtain it from the government by using scrip or by filing homestead claims. They could buy it from the checkerboard land-grant acres owned by the Southern Pacific Railroad or from the skimpy holdings of the California Development Company. But of course the key was water. To obtain water for their new land, the settlers purchased stock in whatever mutual company served their area. This meant dealing through the Imperial Land Company, which controlled every share of stock in the eight mutuals.

Cost of water stock averaged $22 a share—$3,520 for a farm of 160 acres. Imperial Land was most obliging about selling this stock on credit, taking as security a mortgage on the purchaser's land. If the buyer failed to meet payments, and it was virtually certain that during the difficult days of pioneering many would fail, the Imperial Land Company could foreclose and thus acquire acreage to sell on a rising market.

The complex scheme had other charms as well. One was the neat separation it wrought between Imperial Land and the heavily indebted California Development Company. Under Chaffey's plan, the promoters could not only absorb land without creditors immediately attaching it, but they could also resell it later on without accounting for the proceeds. Imperial Land, moreover, had no responsibility for maintaining either the canal from the Colorado River or the multitude of distribution ditches. Those burdens belonged to California Development and the eight mutual water companies.

The scheme's neatness, together with Chaffey's reputation as an irrigator, enabled California Development to raise enough money to build a preliminary ditch. Chaffey spaded up the first earth in November, 1900. Before the thick red water began flowing down the Alamo channel, the first settlers arrived to begin a long battle with heat, wind, sand, brackish domestic water imported in drums, and a total dearth of wood for fires, fences, or homes. But the soil was as rich as Chaffey had foreseen. As soon as water arrived—it touched the valley in May, 1901—crops sprang alive.

As Rockwood had anticipated, land prices skyrocketed. The Southern Pacific built a spur track as far as Calexico-Mexicali, Siamese twin villages astride the international border, and ran special excursions for the inpouring farmers. The mutual companies laced the valley with lateral canals as fast as they could lay hold of funds. By 1904, less than three years after the boom began, 7,000 people had braved one of the most inhospitable areas of the United States to claim 100,000 acres on which they grossed, that year, $700,000—without having yet hit on what would turn out to be the valley's great money crops, melons, long-staple cotton, and winter lettuce.

And Chaffey controlled the company! Consumed with jealousy, Rockwood and his cohorts somehow managed to buy him out. Conceivably he did not resist strenuously, for several tough problems were beginning to appear.

One, as far as the promoters were concerned, was the United States Reclamation Service, later the Bureau of Reclamation, which had been founded in 1902 to build irrigation works for watering arid lands. As gung-ho as most new bureaus are, the Reclamation Service wanted to add the Imperial Valley to its sweeping plans for the lower Colorado River. Rockwood's crew, backed by the valley farmers, resisted. The act creating the Bureau stated that no individual or corporation could use water provided by the government on more than 160 acres. Peanuts! Although some of the valley settlers intended to farm, most were interested in creating attractive green spots that they could sell at resounding profits. A mere 160 acres would not resound sufficiently. When an agent of the Reclamation Service sought to apply pressure by challenging the right of the California Development Company to take a whopping 20,000 acre feet of water out of a supposedly navigable river, the infuriated farmers tarred and feathered him and ran him out of the valley. They'd do things their own way, thanks.

They might better have listened. Although the Imperial Land Company was waxing fat, the California Development Company was too near bankruptcy to maintain properly the scratchy little preliminary canal that Chaffey had built. In 1904 silt plugged the upper end of the canal. Water deliveries shrank; the farmers began to howl. As an emergency measure the company directors cut a new opening in the riverbank south of the border and used it to take water through a "temporary" ditch that connected with the original canal below the barricade of silt. But they neglected, parsimoniously, to put in any sort of headgate to control possible high water.

The California Development Company had become a liability to its owners. Eager to be rid of it so that they could concentrate on the Imperial Land Company, Rockwood sold the water firm to the Southern Pacific for $200,000. E. H. Harriman, who had succeeded Collis Huntington as president of the railroad, wasn't exactly suckered into a bad bargain. He had his eye on land south of the border to which the California

Development Company delivered half its water in exchange for right of way. Improving the canal, which the railroad was in a position to do, would improve the speculative possibilities of those Mexican lands, 876,-000 acres of them owned by an agreeable syndicate in Los Angeles.

Immediately luck ran sour. A series of floods swept down the Colorado and Gila rivers. The unguarded break below the border yawned wide. Pouring through, the entire river plunged into its ancient overflow channel, the Alamo, and then flooded in syrupy waves on to the Salton Sink. In passing it chewed away parts of the towns of Mexicali and Calexico, forced the railroad to move its tracks five times to higher ground, gouged monstrous gullies through hard-won land, and filled the farmhouses with terror. If the flood continued, all of the trough that lay below sea level would be inundated.

Theodore Roosevelt declined to let the government intervene. The break was in Mexico, the promoters' own folly was responsible, and, anyway, welfare work of that sort was not deemed, in those days, to be the government's responsibility. Let the Southern Pacific take care of itself.

For two years the river defeated the railroad's every attempt to close the gap. The body of water in the Sink—now called Salton Sea—spread until it was 35 miles long, up to 15 miles wide, and 40 feet deep. In a final climactic effort to halt the spreading disaster, the engineers of the Southern Pacific called in 2,000 Indian laborers from southern Arizona and northern Mexico, managed to build a trestle over the swirling waters in the break, rounded up every freight car that the company owned, borrowed more, arranged trains like relays of pony-express riders, and in fifteen days dumped 3,000 carloads of gravel and boulders into the gap. Grudgingly the river returned to its normal channel. Knowing that the long fight had cost the Southern Pacific close to $2 million, but unaware as yet that the railroad had bought California Development and hence was open to damage suits arising from the flood, the farmers loudly cheered Harriman as the selfless savior of their valley.

Uneasiness remained, however. The silted river kept threatening new breaks. Moreover, as the valley's population grew and cultivated land expanded, by 1910, to 200,000 acres, impatience grew with a canal that had to turn over half its water inside Mexico. It seemed, too, that the Southern Pacific was more interested in that alien half than in the American side of the valley. In order to gain a controlling voice in water affairs, valley residents in 1911 formed, under the Wright Act, the Imperial Irrigation District and voted $10.5 million in bonds to buy the canal and the distribution and drainage systems from the railroad and the mutual water companies. The Southern Pacific's share was $3 million. Since the railroad had already managed to collect $700,000 from the government for its flood control work, the $2 million spent battling the river had not turned out so painfully after all.

No irrigation system could be dependable until the river was controlled. According to surveys by the Bureau of Reclamation, the best way to accomplish this was to build a fantastically expensive high dam upstream in Boulder Canyon, Nevada. Not even a farming district as rich as Imperial Valley could justify that outlay of funds, and the rest of the nation was reluctant to have the government undertake the work for the benefit of one small section. So the dream might have stayed just that if the unparalleled growth of Los Angeles had not forced a new consideration of the problem . . . but, for the time being, that is moving us too far ahead of our story.

As usual, California luck had taken a hand in speeding the development of the southland. In November, 1892, three men untrained in petroleum geology began digging an exploratory shaft inside the Los Angeles city limits, near the Second Street park. Leader of the trio was Edward E. Doheny, a down-at-the-heels metal prospector from the Rocky Mountains. His partners were Sam Cannon and C. A. Canfield. Lacking funds for anything better, they began work with ordinary picks and shovels, and a hand windlass for lifting earth. As the shaft deepened, a heavy oil began exuding from its walls. The workers scooped up the fluid, sold it for fuel, and bought a primitive drilling rig. They hit—not much, but it started a rush. Soon 300 wells were scattered about the locality, many in residential backyards or on lots from which houses had been removed. It was a noisy, dirty, disruptive, and exciting time. During 1894 and 1895 the clutter turned out 729,000 barrels of black gold, a major factor in lifting statewide production (the rest mostly from Ventura County) to an 1895 total of 1.2 million barrels. The populace grew so hysterical over prospects that merchants drew customers by giving away a share of oil-company stock with each purchase of $3 or more—trading stamps with a vengeance. Not until 1907, after 3,000 wells had been punched down inside the city limits did Los Angeles tighten controls. Thereafter drilling within the city almost ceased.

Because all California oil was difficult to refine into acceptable kerosene, the greater part of the new production was used to fire boilers in breweries, steamships, cement plants, and the big beet-sugar refineries springing up in the Parajo and Salinas valleys near Monterey. During cold winters no inconsiderable amount went into smudge pots to protect citrus orchards from frost damage. But the big breakthrough came in October, 1894, when a Santa Fe locomotive, equipped with burners developed by the Union Oil Company (an amalgamation of Ventura County producers) ran tests on Southern Pacific tracks in Ventura County to compare costs with those of trains activated by imported coal. The saving was 25 percent and obviously could be increased by technical improvements. Now, if the oilmen could guarantee a dependable flow of supplies. . . .

They could. Along with a multitude of other lace-booted prospector-engineers, Doheny and Canfield helped bring in the huge Kern River, McKittrick, and Coalinga fields in the southern part of the San Joaquin Valley. The Lakeview gusher in the San Joaquin spewed out, during the 18 months following its eruption in March, 1910, 9 million barrels, nearly 30 times the production of the entire state in 1890. Comparable strikes were made throughout the Los Angeles Basin. Production, which in 1900 had staggered even boosters by reaching 4.3 million barrels, soared in 1910 to 77 million. Pipelines laced the southern part of the state and ran northward to immense refineries beside San Francisco Bay. Until 1927 and intermittently thereafter, California would be the nation's leading producer of petroleum.

Even though Santa Fe and Southern Pacific locomotives gulped down 8 million barrels of oil between 1902 and 1906, the overall production was scarcely dented. Of necessity oil exports became a significant part of the new economy. New uses appeared as well. California oil had a high octane rating, fine for a highly volatile distillate called gasoline. Farmers began using it in irrigation pumps and tractors. Housewives in the warm parts of California liked it in stoves. There was no wood or coal to carry, no ashes to dump; the flame sprang up at a touch, and no lingering heat troubled the user afterward. Then, too, certain reckless experimenters began rattling down the dusty roads in strange, odorous, self-propelled little vehicles called automobiles; the drivers bought gasoline by the can at the handiest general store and, risking self-immolation, poured it themselves into the tanks. By 1910 there were almost 20,000 of the contraptions in Los Angeles County alone. Visionary oilmen, thinking that there might be a future in this new transportation medium, began making adjustments in their refineries.

The effects of this explosion of black energy in a region otherwise almost devoid of power sources can hardly be exaggerated. Petroleum extraction, refining, and distribution, together with the development of related industries, quickly concentrated tens of millions of dollars in the Los Angeles area. This in turn attracted first-class talent, spurred educational expansion—and intensified speculative fevers. Almost surely it helps explain the surprising 1900 census revelation that whereas industrial production in San Francisco had sagged 2 percent during the preceding decade, in Los Angeles it had jumped 115 percent. Just as surely, the exporting of the flood of oil was among the motives behind another fantastic development of the period—the creation, on Los Angeles County's ill-favored coastline, of a man-made harbor capable of competing with the superlative natural advantages of San Francisco Bay.

A bit of geography here. After passing Santa Monica and cliff-girt Point Fermin, the coastline bends abruptly east and then north before resuming its southeasterly trend. The scallop that results forms shallow San Pedro Bay, described in the 1830's by hide trader Richard Henry Dana as the worst harbor he had ever seen.

At the end of the last century a chain of sandbars bearing such ominous names as Dead Man's and Rattlesnake islands paralleled the bay's northern curve. Slicing the mud flats between the sandbars and the shore was a shallow channel leading to the docks that Phineas Banning had built in the 1850's at his town of Wilmington. Tide scouring induced by Army-built jetties mentioned early in this chapter served to deepen the channel somewhat, but ocean ships were increasing in size. By the end of the 1880's larger vessels were again having to anchor outside the approaches and lighter their cargoes into the inner "harbor." Expense and inconvenience were such that some shipments were being diverted to San Diego and sent north from there over the Santa Fe.

Nervous Angelenos began bombarding Congress for help with three essential improvements: the dredging of a deep channel; the excavation of inner basins large enough for ships to turn around in; and the construction of a breakwater to protect the outer harbor from southwesterly gales. As if in expectation of success, a new organization suddenly appeared—the Terminal Railroad. In 1891 this short line purchased a piece of Terminal Island, nee Rattlesnake, and ran tracks from Los Angeles out onto its new acquisition.*

The implications were immediately apparent to Collis Huntington of the Southern Pacific. If San Pedro Bay were turned into a deep-water harbor served by two railroads, the Southern Pacific would no longer monopolize the distribution of all seaborne traffic landed in California. Therefore, he decreed, San Pedro was not to be developed. Instead, the government should spend its money building a harbor at Santa Monica. It was Huntington's intent to control this new harbor.

As the opening move of his campaign, he had his chief engineer, Wil-

---

*Gossip buzzed, correctly, that the Terminal Railroad was fronting for the Union Pacific, which hoped to reach California by striking southwest from Salt Lake City. The completion of that line in 1905 obviously gave a boost to the economy of Southern California. So, too, did the Southern Pacific's "Coast Line" from the Bay area south through San Luis Obispo, Santa Barbara, and Ventura to Los Angeles, completed in 1901.

liam Hood, wire the Commerce Committee of the U.S. Senate, chaired by Huntington's good friend Senator William P. Frye of Maine, that the rocky bottom of San Pedro Bay precluded satisfactory pile-driving for piers; the railroad was therefore shifting operations to Santa Monica. Simultaneously Huntington purchased from another friend, Senator John P. Jones of Nevada, a quarter interest in a ranch that Jones owned atop the tall palisades bordering the Santa Monica coast. Assured now that no competing railroad could reach the narrow beach, the Southern Pacific spent $1 million building a deep-water wharf 1,500 feet long and 130 feet wide at the new location. Obviously, Huntington said, Santa Monica was the port of the future and as such merited the government's undivided attention.

A fierce tug of war erupted between real estate speculators who wanted Los Angeles to spread west toward Santa Monica and those who wanted it to grow south toward the San Pedro-Wilmington area. Charges and countercharges resounded in the municipal council, the state legislature, the federal Congress. Whipsawed thus, Congress appointed investigative boards that reported regularly in favor of San Pedro. Just as regularly the Senate's Commerce and Rivers and Harbors committees reported in favor of Santa Monica. When a final blue-ribbon group of Army engineers flatly recommended San Pedro, another Huntington friend, Secretary of War Russell Alger, buttoned up the report in his office and disgorged it only when compelled by direct orders from President McKinley. On April 26, 1899, the first stones for the new breakwater were dumped into the bay while the supporters of San Pedro rejoiced at a windy picnic atop Point Fermin.

Victory was not complete, however. The Southern Pacific, which still owned the bulk of the bay's waterfront and most of its warehouses and dock facilities, blocked any improvements to the inner harbor that might benefit someone else. Deciding that municipal ownership was the only solution to the continuing impasse, Los Angeles lawyers searched the land records, found an imperfection in the railroad's title, sued, and wrested away 1,000 acres. Theoretically these reverted to the state, but the legislature obligingly assigned them to the city. Next, in 1906, the city council annexed a narrow shoestring of land running due south to the contiguous waterfront villages of San Pedro and Wilmington. The town voters then agreed to consolidation with the reaching metropolis, and once-landlocked Los Angeles now extended to the sea.

Prodded in part by the oil companies, whose drillers were making strike after strike in the Los Angeles Basin, the city embarked on a program of harbor improvements that so far have cost about $130 million. Nearby Long Beach, rich with royalties from tidelands oil, has spent an equal amount extending facilities within her range. As a fillip the federal government has added another $50 million, partly for the sake of installations for the United States Navy. The result is the busiest harbor on the Pacific Coast.

As much as anything else that extraordinary mushrooming typifies the spirit of boomland. Few natural advantages existed to make anyone suppose that a harbor of worldwide importance would grow up behind the inadequate clay bulwarks of Point Fermin. But neither was there any apparent geographic reason to account for so overwhelming a megalopolis as Los Angeles. City and harbor both happened because energetic men, mixing vision, opportunism, and magnificent hope, were determined that they should.

The confidence of unbridled technology: the attitudes it bred were not unique to California, of course, but in few other places would its twentieth-century advent be attended with such extravagances in physical and cultural change.

22. New Brooms

Even in quixotic San Francisco, one would hardly expect Adolph Heinrich Joseph Sutro to be a hero of the people. He was balding, massive, and well fed, his beak-nosed face adorned with a curly mustache and fuzzy muttonchop whiskers. He spoke with a heavy German accent. His outstanding achievement, a four-mile tunnel to drain and ventilate the mines of Virginia City, Nevada, had been finished too late to revolutionize Comstock mining as much as he had predicted. Even so he made a fortune and invested the proceeds profitably in San Francisco real estate. By 1890 he was reputed to own one-twelfth of the city.

He was willing to share his prosperity. In exchange for an admission fee of 10 cents, a visitor could stroll through the formal gardens, dotted with plaster statues, that surrounded his turreted mansion, perched on the tall bluffs that overlooked Seal Rock, outside the Golden Gate. More energetic souls could rent bathing suits for 25 cents each and swim under the glass roof of a bathhouse that held six big pools of warmed sea water. Nearby was his famous Cliff House restaurant.

He called the agglomerate Sutro Heights. On mild Sundays as many as 25,000 San Franciscans came to stare and play. To reach their destination, which lay six miles due west of the city, they rode a steam train that chugged past Golden Gate Park, its sand dunes just then being anchored down by dour John McLaren. The fare was 20 cents—too much, Sutro decided, for clerks who earned, on the average, $12 a week. Accordingly he helped finance a rival electric line on the understanding that it would carry passengers to Sutro Heights for 5 cents.

Alas for civic-mindedness—or, as cynics said, for a neat come-on gimmick. In 1893 the Southern Pacific's Market Street Railroad laid hold of the electric line and boosted fares. Although Sutro appealed directly to Collis Huntington for fulfillment of the original bargain, Huntington refused. To the delight of all San Francisco, Sutro thereupon declared war on the mighty SP.

Once again depression was stalking the land. Partly because of that, the city was going through another of its spasms of reform. Needing a villain to pummel for their political and economic woes, the residents once again fixed on the Southern Pacific. To understand both the fury and the curious nature of the attacks, one needs to examine not only the railroad's oppressive policies, but the nature of the city itself.

To the San Franciscans of the 1890's, all California was divided into two parts—their city, crowded onto 7 square miles at the end of a sandy peninsula, and another 158,690 square miles of hinterlands. One-fourth of California's entire population lived within San Francisco's borders. Her voters elected more Congressmen and state legislators than did any other district in the state. There was no comparable financial, shipping, or manufacturing center within a thousand miles. When anyone west of the Continental Divide spoke of going to "the city," no doubt existed as to his destination, the presence of Sacramento, Oakland, Stockton, Los Angeles, and San Diego notwithstanding—and while you're at it throw in Seattle, Portland, Boise, Salt Lake City, and Tucson to boot. So why bother naming the obvious?

Although the city's vistas were superb and the sea air bracing, architecture was not prepossessing. Most of the buildings were low, unimaginative, and wooden, adorned with endless rows of bay windows to catch the fleeting sunlight. But the spirit of the place—there was the difference! It was cosmopolitan, sophisticated, fun-loving. Bookstores abounded, the theater flourished, even the opera was well attended. Restaurants were world famous. An easy tolerance of drinking, gambling, and prostitution dated back to gold-rush times. Bars outnumbered grocery stores; the cocktail is, reputedly, a San Francisco invention.

There were more Catholic, foreign-born residents, particularly Irish and Italians, than in any other Western city. Labor unions took a strong and early hold beside the Bay. At first they did not concern themselves officially with politics, partly because of the failure of Denis Kearney's Workingmen's party to achieve lasting results within the system. Under the pressure of the reform movement, however, that aloofness would disappear.

The political rebellion began in 1891. The year before, Chris Buckley, the blind boss of the Democrats, had showered sufficient Southern Pacific gold onto the legislators so that they had returned Republican Leland Stanford to the U.S. Senate—this in return for Stanford's promise to work for the reelection of Democratic Senator George Hearst in 1893. When a grand jury began asking sharp questions, Buckley decided to take

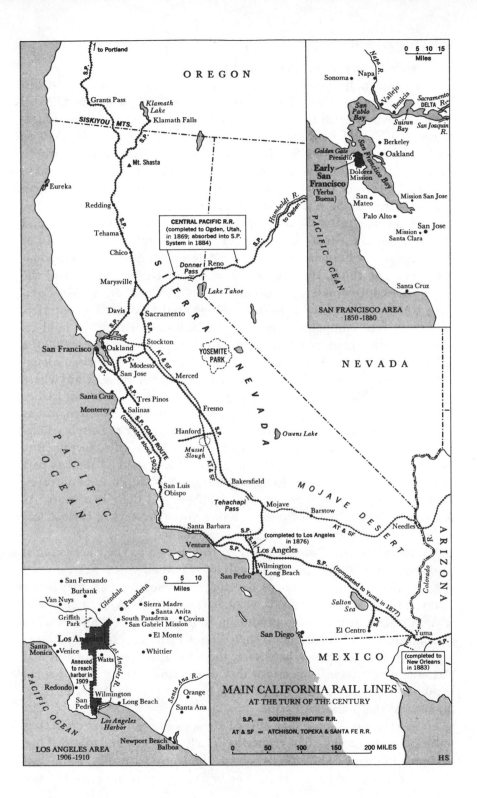

to Portland

OREGON

S.P.

Grants Pass

Klamath
Lake

SISKIYOU MTS.

Klamath Falls

S.P.

Eureka

▲ Mt. Shasta

Redding

S.P.

Humboldt R.
to Ogden

Tehama

CENTRAL PACIFIC R.R.
(completed to Ogden, Utah,
in 1869; absorbed into S.P.
System in 1884)

S.P.

Chico

Donner
Pass

Reno

Marysville

Lake Tahoe

Davis

Sacramento

San Francisco

Oakland

S.P.

AT & SF

Stockton

Modesto

S.P.

San Jose

Merced

YOSEMITE
PARK

NEVADA

S
I
E
R
R
A

N
E
V
A
D
A

Santa Cruz

Monterey

Tres Pinos

Salinas

S.P. COAST ROUTE
(completed about 1902)

Fresno

Hanford

Owens Lake

Mussel
Slough

AT & SF

San Luis
Obispo

Bakersfield

Tehachapi
Pass

Mojave

Barstow

M O J A V E   D E S E R T

AT & SF

Needles

Colorado R.

ARIZONA

Santa Barbara

S.P.

(completed to Los Angeles
in 1876)

Ventura

S.P.

S.P.

Los Angeles

Wilmington
Long Beach

San Pedro

S.P.

(completed to Yuma in 1877)

Salton
Sea

El Centro

S.P.

Yuma

San Diego

MEXICO

(completed to
New Orleans
in 1883)

PACIFIC
OCEAN

SAN FRANCISCO AREA
1850–1880

Napa R.

Sonoma

Napa

Vallejo

Benicia

Sacramento
DELTA R.

San
Pablo
Bay

Suisun
Bay

San Joaquin
R.

Berkeley

Oakland

Golden Gate
Presidio

San Francisco Bay

Early
San
Francisco
(Yerba
Buena)

Dolores
Mission

San
Mateo

Mission San Jose

Palo Alto

San Jose

Mission
Santa Clara

PACIFIC OCEAN

Santa Cruz

0   5 10 15
Miles

LOS ANGELES AREA
1906–1910

San Fernando

Burbank

Van Nuys

Glendale

Pasadena

Sierra Madre

Griffith
Park

Santa Anita

South Pasadena

Covina

San Gabriel Mission

Los Ar

El Monte

Santa
Monica

Venice

Whittier

Annexed
to reach
harbor in
1909

Watts

Los Angeles R.

Redondo

Wilmington

Long Beach

San
Pedro

Santa Ana R.

Orange

Santa Ana

Los Angeles
Harbor

PACIFIC OCEAN

Newport Beach

Balboa

0   5   10
Miles

MAIN CALIFORNIA RAIL LINES
AT THE TURN OF THE CENTURY

S.P. = SOUTHERN PACIFIC R.R.

AT & SF = ATCHISON, TOPEKA & SANTA FE R.R.

0   50   100   150   200 MILES

HS

an extended vacation in Canada and Europe.

Collis Huntington smiled benignly upon this housecleaning. His dis-
like for Stanford had boiled into active ill will in 1885, when the railroad
president had first seized the seat in the United States Senate that Huntington felt should have gone to his friend Aaron Sargent. In 1890 he
found revenge in taking Stanford's place as president of the Southern
Pacific. Never again, Huntington intoned, would the railroad be used to
further the private ambitions of any self-seeking individual. Henceforth
the Southern Pacific was out of politics.

For a time thereafter the smell of corruption was less noticeable around
the city's polling places. The railroad nonetheless remained as odious as
ever to most San Franciscans. In their minds it was killing them economically. For one thing, the Southern Pacific, the Union Pacific, and the
other transcontinentals were paying the Pacific Mail Steamship Company and the railroad across Panama to keep up their rates. This interference with free competition enabled the Southern Pacific to hold its
charges on cross-country freight artificially high. Yet even that wasn't the
worst. The Southern Pacific was also undermining San Francisco's long-
held position as *the* distributing center for merchandise sent anywhere
in California, Nevada, southern Oregon, and parts of Utah and Idaho.

Once all westbound freight had gone straight to San Francisco, just as
most sea freight did. There it had been reassembled by the city's wholesalers and sent by them to the interior towns—Marysville, Sacramento,
Stockton, Fresno—often over the same rails it had used on the last part
of its western journey. This seemingly unnecessary duplication of travel,
paid for at high rates, irritated inland jobbers and their customers. As
markets increased, they began demanding direct delivery of carload lots
at the same rates given San Francisco merchants.

Naturally the San Franciscans tried to hang on to their accustomed
business, and they were potent enough to make their voices heard—until
the peculiarities of California's developing commerce began to work
against them. The canned goods, wool, barley, citrus, beans, lumber, and
wine (already California was producing 80 percent of the domestic wine
consumed in the United States) that Western producers sent east were
bulkier than the dry goods, hardware, and other manufactured items that
Easterners sent west. This meant that westbound freight trains hauled
many an empty car whose hollow rattle brought pain to the traffic coor-
dinators of the Southern Pacific.

To fill this waste space they offered attractive rates to Eastern dealers
willing to compete with San Francisco in California's inland towns. Thus
Sacramento's and Stockton's wholesale trade rose steadily while San
Francisco struggled to stay even. The bay city's manufacturers also lost

out. Labor costs on the Coast were high, and techniques laggard. As Eastern freight rates to the valley towns sank, it became possible for, say, a Chicago hatter to sell headgear in Fresno cheaper than a San Francisco manufacturer could. The unkindest cut of all came when Los Angeles jobbers, helped by competitive rates occasioned by the appearance of the Santa Fe, began invading the southern San Joaquin Valley. Was San Francisco going to wither away on her hilltops? Why, even Oakland was beginning to look like a threat.

After long discussions, San Francisco's worried merchants decided that the best way to solve the crisis was to force the railroad to give them better rates. To this end they formed, in October, 1891, the Traffic Association of California. To justify the name they appealed to the businessmen of the interior for support. They were rebuffed. Why should a Stockton merchant return to dependence on San Francisco? As a result, 97 percent of the Association members were San Francisco manufacturers, wholesalers, and financiers.

In announcing the formation of the Association, the group declared that their sole intent was to negotiate as a unit with the Southern Pacific. Actually, they did not negotiate for an instant. Like Sutro, they declared war.

Their first attack, begun early in 1892, was to set up water competition. Through agents, they leased 24 clipper ships to sail around the Horn. Learning a few months later that the transcontinentals had fallen to squabbling with each other and had ended the subsidy to the Panama Railroad, they leaped to form their own steamship company and deal directly with the Isthmus lines.

Though imaginative and courageous, the moves were too ill-timed to succeed. Because of the depression, business everywhere was slumping. As volume sagged, the merchants discovered that maintaining the assault was costing more than they were saving through the reduced rates they squeezed from the railroad. Reluctantly they gave up the leased clippers and steamers, hoping that fear of renewal would help keep the SP in line —which, to an extent, it did.

Far more effective was the belated emergence of the San Francisco and San Joaquin Valley Railroad, designed by the Traffic Association to move goods into the southern valley at the lowest possible rate. Initially the merchants had not been able to support both it and the ocean attack, but after their foray into shipping had collapsed, the drive to build the railroad intensified.

The men who lifted it off the drawing board were Claus Spreckels and his sons John and Adolph, wealthy sugar refiners, who in January, 1895, subscribed to $700,000 worth of stock. Although the Spreckels trio did not say so aloud, they probably intended from the outset to recapture their investment by selling the railroad to the Santa Fe, which was still running precariously into Oakland over tracks leased from the Southern Pacific. First, though, there had to be something concrete to offer.

An emotional campaign to sell additional stock was launched in San Francisco. As sobersided Stuart Daggett remarked in his account of the affair, ". . . there has probably never been a commercial enterprise on the Pacific Coast so advertised and praised and predicted about. . . ." Clubs, including one of blacks, were formed so that small savers could group together to buy a single share. The San Francisco *Examiner*, then being personally managed by young William Randolph Hearst, ran subscription blanks in each daily paper. The main appeal was not to profit so much as to local patriotism. Save San Francisco by slaying the Southern Pacific! Money flooded in. Within a month of the opening of the campaign tracklayers started south from Stockton. Another line was projected northward from Stockton to Richmond, so that the San Joaquin Valley Railroad would also have a toehold beside the bay.

As in the case of the short-lived ship campaigns, the residents of the San Joaquin Valley, suspicious of San Francisco's motives, did not succumb to the frenzy. Their coolness, however, implied no love for the Southern Pacific. They too despised the mighty corporation. It classified their goods in ways known only to itself, set arbitrary freight charges according to those classifications, and then changed the schedules without notice. Short-haul rates were exorbitant. Large shippers were given secret advantages over small ones, but in return had to open their books to railroad auditors who wanted to make sure that the generosity was not leading to excess profits. There was no use appealing to the state Railroad Commission. It hadn't staff enough to investigate every charge, and, besides, the majority of its members generally owed their election to campaign funds provided by the railroad.

Farmers chafed under similar handicaps. As for labor, its grievances culminated in the fierce Pullman strike of 1894. Although violence was not as widespread in California as in the East, dynamite exploded, militia and strikers clashed, men died—and, for the workers, only failure resulted. Meanwhile business continued to stagnate, unemployment soared. Throughout the state, and particularly in San Francisco, the Southern Pacific was excoriated as the breeder of every ill.

Such, then, was the popular state of mind when Adolph Sutro prepared to do battle with the giant corporation over the question of a nickel streetcar fare.

Coincidence as well as antirailroad sentiment favored him. The 30-year bonds that the federal government had loaned the Central Pacific (by then a relatively small segment of the Southern Pacific system) were falling due. During those 30 years, the railroad had made only perfunctory gestures toward repayment, so that the principal and interest due the government amounted to almost $59 million. Insisting that the Central Pacific, as distinct from the Southern Pacific, could not pay, Huntington prevailed on friends in Congress to introduce a series of bills that would allow the CP to refund its debt with an issue of new bonds bearing a trivial 2 percent interest and maturing a century later.

Westerners roared protest. This was too easy. Besides, they feared that the railroad would use the new bonds as an excuse to raise rates at the very time they were fighting to lower them. Throughout 1894, San Franciscans gathered in huge mass meetings, with Sutro generally acting as chairman, to thunder approval of resolutions condemning the railroad. One example: "This monopoly has spread a black cloud over the surface of the state. . . . It has seduced and drawn into its service many prominent men, whose Americanism and integrity were not equal to their brains. It has antagonized the people, minimized immigration, choked enterprise . . . controlled legislation, executive action, and the administration of justice." Simultaneously, the San Francisco *Examiner* collected 194,663 signatures to a petition urging the defeat of the funding bills. Hearst sent his most acidulous reporter, Ambrose Bierce, and a slashing cartoonist, Homer Davenport, to Washington to cover the hearings in Congress. They followed Huntington like terriers, yapping mercilessly at his heels with scandalous stories and sketches.

Seeking to capitalize on the discontent, the Populist party of California prevailed on multimillionaire Sutro to run as the poor man's choice for mayor of San Francisco. Belatedly alarmed, the SP five days before the election dropped the streetcar fare to Sutro Heights back to a nickel. No use. Sutro swept into office and continued his attacks with undiminished vigor. At his own expense he sent every Congressman tirades against Huntington; the envelopes containing the blasts bore on their faces, in huge red print, such sentiments as "OH! WHAT A HOG!" He formally requested the legislature of Kentucky, where the Southern Pacific Company maintained its nominal headquarters, to abrogate the railroad's charter and thus "rid us of this horrible monster which is devouring our substance, and which is debauching our people, and by its devilish instincts and criminal methods is every day more firmly grasping us in its tentacles."*

The Kentuckians ignored the outcry. Not so Congress. In January,

*It is perhaps relevant to note here that both Sutro's health and his sanity began to fail during his two-year term in office. He died in 1898.

1897, it decisively defeated the refunding bill. Both the governor of California and Mayor James D. Phelan of San Francisco, who had succeeded Sutro, proclaimed legal holidays of rejoicing. But what, really, had they won?

Westerners had expected that if refunding were disallowed, the government would foreclose on the Central Pacific and then either operate the road itself or sell it at auction to some kindlier corporation. Both notions were naïve. The Southern Pacific, leaser of the Central Pacific, could not be held liable for the CP's debt unless it chose—a matter that most Californians either could not or would not grasp. Yet how much sense did it make from a practical standpoint for the government to seize and then try to operate a mere part of a tightly integrated system, even assuming that Washington was prepared to go into the railroad business, which it wasn't? As for a foreclosure sale, Huntington could form a syndicate and buy back his erstwhile property debt-free!

No, foreclosure was not the answer. Reasonable refunding was. As soon as Huntington was convinced that terms of his own dictating were not to be had, he yielded to quiet pressures from President McKinley of the United States and worked out a settlement whereby the Southern Pacific undertook to pay the Central Pacific's debts. Like it or not, California still had the Octopus, under the same old management, to contend with.

Quietly the railroad waited for the storms to subside. Soon affairs began to roll its way. In December, 1898, the directors of the San Joaquin Valley Railroad sold the line to the Santa Fe. Their excuse: many small stockholders, losing their emotional highs, were selling their certificates. To keep the Southern Pacific from absorbing these and gaining control, the Spreckels trio, at high profit to themselves, surrendered the Valley line to the Santa Fe. In the way that railroads of the era had, the Santa Fe then entered into quiet traffic arrangements with the Southern Pacific. As prosperity returned to the nation at the close of the century, freight rates were adjusted upwards. Still, the battle had not been a complete failure. Freight costs had dropped for a while; San Francisco's merchants and bankers had maintained, at considerable cost, their commercial dominance of the state.

The struggle for civic virtue was equally short-lived. Mayor James D. Phelan, an Irish Catholic Democrat, did produce a new charter granting increased power to the mayor's office at the expense of the board of supervisors (in effect the city council), an organization that had proved itself eminently corruptible. He broadened civil service, cut utility rates, and began studies for a municipally owned municipal water system. But when he tried to take the middle ground during a furious strike in the fall of 1901, he was so battered from both sides that his regime toppled and a new political party, the creature of one venal man, took over the running of San Francisco.

The man was Abraham Ruef, a small, dapper, abstemious lawyer and real estate speculator consumed with ambition to become a United States Senator. On first entering politics, Ruef had cast his lot with the Republican machine and under the tutelage of its bosses had become the most adept manipulator of votes in the city. Overconfident, he attempted to oust his tutors and to gain control of San Francisco's Republican organization, but was easily put back in his place by the bosses.

While he was rubbing his bruises, the labor trouble mentioned earlier swept the Bay area. Beginning with a walkout of teamsters, the strike soon involved sailors, dock workers, and warehousemen as well—15,000 men all told. Employers, eager to use the occasion for breaking the unions, demanded that Mayor Phelan request Governor Henry Gage for state militia to be used in restoring order. To their fury, Phelan refused. But when rioting broke out in September, Phelan sent in police and special officers to protect strikebreakers. The move resulted in the beating of several picketers, and now labor was outraged.

In October, Governor Gage, reputedly a tool of the Southern Pacific, forced a settlement that resulted in victory for the employers. Victory through political maneuvering . . . militants among the embittered losers demanded that the unions reassess their hands-off policy toward politics. The traditional argument in opposition was the internal bickering caused by political involvement. But if abstention gave victory to the employers, so the malcontents argued, that was worse. The result was a rebellion against the stand-patters and the formation, in San Francisco, of a naïve but vigorous Union Labor party.

Abraham Ruef watched the birth pangs of the new party with interest. Might he be able to lift himself into the Senatorship he wanted by nurturing this awkward child into strength? Secretly, without severing his connections with the Republican party, he went to work to gain control of the laborites.

His great stroke was selecting as candidate for mayor colorful Eugene Schmitz, a popular orchestra leader who, though a member of a musician's union, had taken no part in labor uprising and so was not unduly offensive to business interests. Under Ruef's expert direction, Schmitz conducted a low-keyed campaign that capitalized effectively on the voters' disaffection with both the Republican and the Democratic machines. When the three-way race was over, Schmitz was mayor.

Subsequent elections gave Ruef control not only of the mayor's office but of the board of supervisors as well. If he could continue extending the Union Labor party's strength out into the state, surely the Senatorship he yearned for would be his. Meanwhile, however, he did not let his ambitions for the future interfere with opportunities for present plunder.

The city's notorious French restaurants were one obvious target. They were a peculiar mixture. A man could take his family to the elegant, expensive, downstairs dining room in any one of them without stirring a whisper. Upstairs, where the elegance extended from small supper alcoves to adjoining bedrooms, a man did not take his family. To keep trade flowing on both levels, the restauranteurs needed regular renewal of their liquor licenses—fine wines were an attraction both upstairs and down—and freedom from police raids. Hiring Abe Ruef as attorney and giving him a big enough fee to split with the appropriate commissioners, all of them appointees of Mayor Schmitz, was the surest way of guaranteeing serenity.

More profitable payoffs resulted from San Francisco's renewed growth. The Alaska gold rush, the Spanish-American war, and the Philippine insurrection that followed it boomed the harbor. Westward immigration stepped up again. As the city expanded, building contractors, competing telephone companies, the privately owned Spring Valley Water Company, the Pacific Gas and Electric Company, and the newly formed United Railroads of San Francisco eagerly sought municipal favors.

None was more egregious than the United Railroads, creation of paunchy, pale-eyed Patrick Calhoun, grandson of John Calhoun. Core of Calhoun's system was the Market Street Railway, once controlled by the Southern Pacific. Major changes had taken place in the giant corporation. Collis Huntington had died in 1900. Shortly thereafter his principal heirs, his widow Arabella and his nephew Henry E. Huntington (later they would marry and reunite the fortune), had sold most of their railroad stock, not including the Market Street system, to E. H. Harriman of the Union Pacific. Next, Henry Huntington had unloaded the Market Street property onto an Eastern syndicate headed by Calhoun and had gone south to start an interurban system in the Los Angeles Basin, where we will meet him again.

Calhoun journeyed to California to swoop the rest of San Francisco's traction companies into a single heavily overcapitalized company, the United Railroads. He planned to standardize this heterogeneous mass by means of overhead trolleys for delivering electricity, even though a majority of San Franciscans preferred underground conduits as being safer and less unsightly.

Attorney for the United Railroads of San Francisco was Abraham

Ruef. Because tension concerning United's proposed franchise for over-head wires was high, Ruef was able to extract a fee of $200,000 from Calhoun's lawyer, Tirey L. Ford, to be divided among himself, Schmitz, and the franchise-awarding supervisors.

Leader of the opposition to Calhoun was Fremont Older, the tall, lean editor of the San Francisco *Bulletin*. Convinced that the city administration was totally corrupt, Older had put reporters on Schmitz's and Ruef's trails but had been unable to produce concrete evidence. Despairing, he went to Washington to ask President Theodore Roosevelt for help. From the sympathetic President he obtained access to two potent government agents, special detective William J. Burns and prosecutor Francis J. Heney.

Older knew Heney. He was a roughneck young Californian who, between drinking bouts and work in Idaho mining camps, had managed to earn a law degree in San Francisco. Later he killed a man in Arizona —self-defense, the jury agreed—and also became known as the territory's most successful attorney general. In 1903 he and Burns had been employed by the U.S. Department of Justice to root out timber fraud cases in northern California and Oregon. Among those they put behind bars was U.S. Senator John H. Mitchell of Oregon. To such a pair even Abe Ruef might not seem out of reach.

Heney agreed to serve his native city without charge if San Francisco reformers would raise a fund of $100,000 to meet the heavy expenses that would be entailed in gathering evidence and conducting the trials. Burns, too, professed willingness, though his circumstances were such that he would need a salary. Returning west in high hope, Older contacted former mayor James D. Phelan and millionaire Rudolph Spreckels, youngest son of the sugar-refining, railroad-building family. Infuriated by Calhoun's arrogant determination to drape the city with trolley wires, the two men agreed to finance the graft investigation and subsequent prosecution.

Their plans were interrupted by the roughest jolt imaginable. At 5:12 A.M., April 18, 1906, just as the mist above the hills was shimmering under the first sunlight, the San Andreas earthquake fault slipped a few feet. To the accompaniment of an indescribable roar, San Francisco's gray streets buckled and cracked. Streetcar tracks twisted; electric wires writhed and crackled. Brick buildings cascaded onto horses and draymen making their early rounds. After a moment's hush there was a deeper shock, then another. From a hundred broken gas pipes flames began to leap. Dazed firemen ran to their posts, then discovered that water mains were ruptured. Dynamite was the only weapon left, and soon a crescendo of explosions was added to the roar of the flames.

For three days and two nights the conflagration raged. Rescuers clawing at the rubble unearthed 452 bodies. Nearly 500 square blocks containing 28,000 buildings were devastated, leaving 250,000 people homeless. Swarms of refugees fled south, their hastily gathered possessions piled in carts, buggies, automobiles, even wheelbarrows. Others huddled hungry and thirsty on the beaches and in the parks.

Looters prowled openly, even stripping the bodies of the dead until soldiers from the Presidio took over with orders to shoot whenever necessary. Oakland, only slightly damaged by the shocks, loaded ferries with milk and clothing. Los Angeles and other cities sent trainloads. Though the Southern Pacific was already taxed by its flood control work in the Imperial Valley, E. H. Harriman ordered the railroad to focus every available resource on aiding the stricken city. Mayor Schmitz, every account agrees, rose to the challenge, inspiring the bewildered people, coordinating relief efforts, and appointing able committees, Ruef prominent among the members, to launch the work of rebuilding.

Unhappily, exaltation brought about by emergencies does not last, and there are other ways of looting a city than filching goods from broken counters. Pleading that the earthquake had destroyed all underground conduits, the United Railroads won the trolley franchise it wanted. Companies involved in municipal rehabilitation clamored for and received special privileges. Feeling unassailable and richer than ever, Ruef led a big block of Republican delegates to the September meeting of the party's nominating convention at Santa Cruz. There he delivered, for $20,000, enough votes to secure the gubernatorial nomination for James Gillett, the choice of the Southern Pacific. Subsequently Gillett was winner at the statewide general election and went to Sacramento with—this is a broad statement but defensible—the most venal, incompetent, and disorderly legislature in California's history.

Gillett's nomination put the Southern Pacific's chief counsel, William Herrin, in Ruef's debt, and it began to look as if a Senatorship might not be out of reach. Shortly after his return to San Francisco, however, Ruef was stunned by a subpoena to appear before the newly convened grand jury. The one honest man in the city's administration, District Attorney William Langdon, had appointed Francis Heney as his special prosecutor, and the crackdown on graft began.

Despite intricate delaying tactics—Ruef was a bold and skillful lawyer —Schmitz and he were indicted for extorting bribes from several French restaurants. This was petty vice, however, as common as soot in most cities, and the small victory by no means satisfied prosecutor Heney. A disciple of that urban moralist Lincoln Steffens, Heney believed that bribe takers were mere opportunists and that lasting reform could not be achieved until an example had been made of such high-placed bribe givers as Patrick Calhoun, William Herrin, even E. H. Harriman himself.

The fixation led to questionable tactics. Prodded ahead by the prosecution, a businessman whom Schmitz had discharged from a lucrative post and another who feared exposure concerning past offenses offered bribes to supervisors Thomas Lonegrin and Edward Walsh. Detective William Burns, who watched the transactions through convenient peepholes, promptly arrested the receivers. Under promises of immunity, the rattled pair talked enough to implicate every member of the board of supervisors. Heney and Burns rounded them up and used their panic to wring from them confessions connecting Ruef and Schmitz with bigger quarry than the French restauranteurs. On hearing the evidence, the grand jury returned no less than 65 additional indictments against Ruef.

The errant boss was imprisoned not in the county jail but in a private home that, coincidentally enough, had once belonged to Mayor Schmitz. There he was subjected to psychological pressures that eventually broke him, and in return for a promise of immunity, he agreed to tell all—or so Heney thought. It may be, however, that Ruef in reality outsmarted the prosecutor.

On the basis of Ruef's tales Calhoun and several other well-known businessmen (but not Herrin or Harriman) were indicted. They marshaled formidable arrays of legal talent. Their trials, dramatically reconstructed in Walton Bean's *Boss Ruef's San Francisco*, were long, complex, and filled with shocks. Witnesses were suborned. A bomb destroyed the home of one supervisor, presumably to remind him not to talk too freely. Libel suits greeted some of the more lurid newspaper accounts. In connection with one of these, Fremont Older was seized on a spurious warrant and whisked by stony-faced gunmen as far away as Santa Barbara, all the while trembling for his life until rescued by a sheriff bearing a writ of habeas corpus obtained by telephone.

Prospective jurors—literally thousands of them—were dogged by detectives looking for exploitable flaws in their characters. One victim, his past scornfully revealed by Heney during a challenge, brooded over the disgrace for several weeks, then returned to the courtroom and shot the prosecutor through the head. Heney did not die, but his attacker did— by his own hand in the county jail. The chief of police was pilloried by both the prosecution and the newspapers for negligence in allowing the self-inflicted death to occur. Some days afterward, the police chief's dead body was found floating in the Bay, another suicide, or so it seemed.

Throughout the trials Ruef cheerfully admitted that he had received money from the accused and that he had passed part of it on to Schmitz and the supervisors. But to Heney's dismay he persistently said that the payments he received were honest legal fees and that no one had ever mentioned bribery—which, of course, all of the participants were too sophisticated to do.

Without Ruef's cooperation, convictions were impossible. Utterly exasperated, Heney revoked his promises of immunity and put Ruef on trial. During the preliminary sparring he was shot, as stated above, and the handling of the case devolved on his chief assistant, stocky, round-faced, eloquent Hiram Johnson, occasional attorney for the San Francisco Teamster's Union. Johnson won Ruef's conviction, and the boss was sentenced to fourteen years in San Quentin prison.

As soon as Heney had recovered from his wound, he doggedly haled Patrick Calhoun before the bar. Revulsion met the new effort. By that time the trials had been dragging on for more than two years, and San Francisco, engrossed in rebuilding, was bored with them. The business community, moreover, resented these unremitting attacks on men of their own class who, so the argument ran, had merely hired Ruef to help them through the brambles. On top of that, Calhoun had just crushed a strike of the city's streetcar workers and the Employers' Association was cheering him to the rafters. Why didn't Heney let a good man alone?

Labor, too, was angry. Ruef and Schmitz had given the workers, through the Union Labor party, a heady taste of political victory. Now it looked to many of the buffeted losers in the streetcar strike as if the graft trials, aimed mostly at leaders of the Labor party, were being used as one more weapon in the employers' drive to turn San Francisco into an open-shop town—this in spite of the fact that their *bête noir*, Patrick Calhoun, was also under fire.

Thus beset, Heney decided to carry his case to the voters in 1909 by campaigning for election as district attorney in place of William Langdon, who was retiring. The result was a disastrous defeat at the hands of Charles Fickert, nominee of both the Republicans and the Union Labor party. Interpreting his victory as a mandate to end the prosecution, Fickert dropped the cases still pending. The few men who had been convicted, Schmitz among them, were later freed by the state supreme court on very shaky technicalities. Only Ruef stayed behind bars. This seemed so grossly unfair to Fremont Older, the initiator of the prosecutions, that he began a long and ultimately successful campaign to obtain a full pardon for his one-time quarry!

Despite these ironic endings, the hope for reform remained very much alive in California. Prime movers in the continuing drive were Illinois-born, European-educated Chester H. Rowell, editor of his uncle's Fresno *Morning Republican*, and Edward A. Dickson, a reporter for the Los Angeles *Express*. They first met in Sacramento while covering the deplorable antics of the legislature of 1907. Completely disgusted, they began discussing ways of cleaning house.

They were not radicals. They believed that unsullied business was the solid rock underlying America's greatness. Trouble came when businessmen turned traitor to their own class and formed unholy alliances with corrupt politicians. Restoration, they believed further, could best be achieved through true democracy. The machinery of government must be placed in the hands of the people, who could then make their wills known by means of such direct legislative measures as the initiative, referendum, recall, direct primaries rather than machine-controlled conventions, and the popular rather than legislative election of U.S. Senators.

Good Government groups espousing these measures had already taken root in Los Angeles—the first city in the world, believe it or not, to adopt the initiative and referendum and the first to use the recall against an errant official. Building on those foundations and drawing further inspiration from Robert M. La Follette's Wisconsin Progressives, Dickson, Rowell, and a handful of supporters inaugurated the statewide League of Lincoln-Roosevelt Republican Clubs. After achieving some success in scattered municipal elections, they determined to strike for the governorship in 1910. Their reluctant candidate was Hiram Johnson, the lawyer who had sent Ruef to prison.

Once committed, Johnson campaigned tirelessly, using a red Locomobile to cover 20,000 miles of dusty road, since he would not ride the train. He harped endlessly on a single theme: Kick the Southern Pacific out of politics. As election time drew near, he became pessimistic. Theodore Bell, the Democratic candidate, was more widely known than Johnson and equally dedicated to reform. Labor, moreover, was suspicious of these middle-class exponents of Good Government—the Goo-Goos, as scoffers termed them. Were there enough Republican votes in California to offset these handicaps?

Luck, if that's the word for disaster, helped decide the issue. Los Angeles in 1910 was torn by labor strife. On October 1, a massive charge of dynamite shattered the building of the antilabor Los Angeles *Times*, killed twenty workers, and injured seventeen. Because Republican Johnson was incorrectly believed to be antilabor, the reaction in the southland swung many Democrats and independents to his banner. So, too, did the blundering of Walter F. X. Parker, the Southern California boss of the Southern Pacific. Though Parker could scarcely stomach either gubernatorial candidate, he decided, to Bell's horror, that this year he could swallow Democrats more easily than Republicans. By throwing his support to Bell, he sent still more votes to Johnson. Thus, although Johnson lost most of the northern counties, he carried the south and the rural areas of the Central Valley by a big enough margin to win the election.

Safely installed in Sacramento, the new governor shocked some of his more conservative southern supporters by pushing through the legislature the most thoroughgoing set of reform measures, many of them favorable to labor, that California had yet experienced. He did not kick the Southern Pacific entirely out of politics. Any corporation dependent on the public will must maintain its lobbies. But they need not be corrupt lobbies. And that sort of venality is what irascible, unlikable, rigidly honest Hiram Johnson, soon to identify himself with the nationwide Progressive party, did kick out of the state government. Considering California's headlong growth and insatiable demand for gigantic public works and franchises of every kind, it was no mean accomplishment.

23.   Water's Dreadful Price

Henry E. Huntington and the Los Angeles Chamber of Commerce awakened to the changing pattern of American folk migration at about the same time. Until 1900 or so, the Chamber assumed that most people moving west were farmers seeking virgin soil to tame and then resell at a profit. To hurry the movement along, the Chamber's pitchmen accompanied roving trains called "California on Wheels" throughout the nation, showing to millions of gawkers great mounds of oranges, grapes, walnuts, and other exotic produce. Out of the mails, meanwhile, tumbled endless brochures lauding the ease of irrigation, the beneficence of the climate, and the productivity of the soil.

The ballyhoo drew enough farmers that by the end of the new century's first decade, Los Angeles was the richest agricultural county in the nation. Yet even while this influx was under way, a very different kind of migration was gathering momentum. Though composed of rural folk, it was actually part of a nationwide rebellion against the agrarian system.

Life on prairie farms and in small Midwestern villages was cold in winter, searing hot in summer, and at all seasons lonely, drab, and monotonous. The possibility of escape arrived when mechanization began taking over more of the chores. Simultaneously the rise of industrial cities seemed to offer farm children not only excitement and gaiety but fortune as well. From fields everywhere in the vast Mississippi Valley young men and women swarmed toward the beckoning lights.

Many of their parents, as Robert Fogelson pointed out in *The Fragmented Metropolis*, were also discontented—and had money enough to react, for in 1896 farm prices had at last begun a slow, steady rise. But what did prosperity mean if one could look forward only to a continuation of the old routines?

According to promotional literature aimed originally at winter tourists, a different life abloom with health awaited in Southern California, where snow, glimpsed only through fragrant orange blossoms, came no closer than the mountaintops. Why limit such joys to vacations? Thousands of Midwestern agriculturists and rural businessmen sold their farms and stores and moved west, not to make money but to enjoy, on their savings, what remained of their lives. With them came more thousands who needed supplemental income from light work. Thus the surge in beekeeping: Southern California became the nation's leading producer of honey. Less sweet was the effect on white-collar labor. Part-time clerks and repairmen kept wages for services at dismally low levels.

Realizing belatedly that here was an unexpected source of population, the Los Angeles Chamber of Commerce softened its emphasis on agriculture and began speaking of self-fulfillment. The lure caught many hesitant Midwesterners at the critical moment of decision. Results were phenomenal. During the first half-dozen years of the new century the population of Los Angeles city alone jumped from 100,000 to 250,000.

It was a different population from that in San Francisco. The number of foreign-born, mostly natives of England and Canada, was small. There were relatively few Catholics, but no dearth of Protestant churches— more per capita in Los Angeles than in any other city in the nation. Farm-oriented, the newcomers tended to be highly suspicious of the ferment brought about by urbanization—restless labor, ghettos crowded with strange-tongued immigrants, dirt, turmoil, and systematized vice. Well aware that to such unsophisticated voters the word "reform" meant moral rather than political purification, Hiram Johnson accepted as his candidate for the lieutenant-governorship in 1910 a man he privately detested, A. J. Wallace, president of the Anti-Saloon League of California.

How could rural attitudes like those be grafted onto city living? Almost instinctively, subdividers found a solution: they would connect quiet country suburbs to downtown Los Angeles by means of a new technological development, the electrified interurban railway. As an adjunct to that, promoters either formed new mutual companies to provide water or prevailed on existing firms to extend their pipelines. Other utilities were lured by subsidies that the recipient agreed to return to the developer if and when population in the new subdivision reached a high enough point to make operations profitable.

The pattern was still largely inchoate in 1901, when Henry E. Huntington arrived, rich with the proceeds of the Southern Pacific stock that he had sold to E. H. Harriman. Grasping quickly how strong the new migratory trend was, he set about meeting it on its own terms. Like other promoters, he formed a land company to select potential residential sites with care and promote them assiduously. He, too, operated water companies when necessary, even at a loss. Unlike the other developers, however, he did not limit his vision of transportation to one or two undercapitalized stub lines serving predetermined sites. Instead he amalgamated several shoestring roads into the potent Pacific Electric Railway Company and proceeded to lace tracks throughout the Los Angeles Basin from Santa Monica to San Bernardino, from Pasadena to the beaches at Balboa. Throughout this broad area, it is worth remarking, there were no natural barriers—compare San Francisco, for instance—to impede the way.

He built his own power company to provide energy. To quiet the resentment of the Southern Pacific he worked out an agreement with Harriman whereby freight distribution in the Los Angeles Basin fell to the transcontinental, which also built electric lines, while Huntington concentrated on short-haul passenger traffic. Soon his big red cars were as familiar to the southland as the orange groves through which they swayed and clattered. People used them in swarms not only for commuting but for excursions of every kind, from picnics beside the ocean to picking the poppies that flared on the hillsides back of Altadena.

There were so many branch lines into sparsely settled areas that the system as a whole was no great moneymaker. That was not Huntington's point, however. He used his web of tracks to determine which areas appealed to his riders, or could be made to appeal, and then focused real estate promotion there. For it was in the manipulation of property values that big money lay.

Whenever he or other developers laid out a subdivision, they fit it to the desires of the new influx—neat rectangular blocks where row upon row of tidy houses could be set amid trim lawns brightened with hydrangeas and Cecil Brunner roses. Physical homogeneity became racial as well; property deeds in most of the suburbs contained restrictions about who could or could not move in.

To San Franciscans it added up to overgrown Dullsville. For the newcomers themselves it was a Midwestern Eden stripped of farming's rigors but not of its Christian ethics, all within range of big-city conveniences, thanks to Henry Huntington's hurrying red cars. These, not the automobile, were the true implementers of the Los Angeles sprawl that still baffles visitors from the East.

The new suburbanites, proud of their thirsty lawns and exotic shrubs, were insistent on ample water. So, too, were the county's prosperous farms and incipient industries—this in an area where the average annual rainfall was half the amount that supported grass, crops, and people in the Midwest. For a time, topography forestalled crisis. The rugged mountains north of the Basin drained much more moisture from winter clouds than fell on the lowlands. In addition to producing the little streams that had been diverted to irrigate the original colony settlements, this water percolated slowly into the deep, porous soil at the foot of the slopes. As George Chaffey and others had demonstrated, these natural reservoirs could be tapped with free-flowing artesian wells.

As more and more wells were drilled, the water table dropped. Natural flow ceased. Sensing danger, water companies in the eastern end of the San Gabriel Valley went high into the adjacent mountains and built two storage reservoirs destined to become major southland recreational attractions, Big Bear and Arrowhead lakes. California's first national forest, the San Gabriel Reserve, was established in 1892 to protect the watersheds supplying Los Angeles. Conservation alone was not the solution, however. As demands increased, the new magic of electricity let pumps reach deeper and deeper into the underground catch basins, until by the first decade of the new century 1,500 wells were sucking away at a constantly diminishing supply. If population growth were to continue—and in those days no Californian questioned its desirability—water would have to be imported from some source outside the arid southland.

The visionary who located a potential supply was Fred Eaton. A native of Los Angeles, he had worked first for the private water company that supplied the region. Later, he became city engineer and eventually, 1899–1901, the mayor.

Eaton was also an outdoorsman. One of his favorite fishing and hunting haunts was the Owens River, which runs southward beside the abrupt eastern scarp of the Sierra Nevada. The northern end of the river, cradled in Long Valley, is 8,000 feet above sea level. The southern end is Owens Valley, between 3,000 and 4,000 feet in elevation. Owens Valley has no outlet. In those days the river, fed by side streams from the Sierra, emptied into saline Owens Lake, 100 square miles in area and deep enough so that ore from the Cerro Gordo silver mines was ferried across it for several years in an 85-foot steamer.

The history of Owens Valley is violent—a minor mineral rush during the 1860's that resulted in savage Indian warfare and then, in 1872, the most severe earthquake, from the standpoint of released energy, in California annals. It was also a lonely land, trapped between mountains and desert; there was no railroad closer than Mojave, more than 100 miles away. But the alluvial soils were fertile, the growing season was long, and abundant water could be easily diverted to the bottom lands north of Owens Lake. By 1900, some 40,000 acres of irrigated hay fields were scattered along the 44-mile stretch between the little towns of Lone Pine and Bishop. Population numbered about 5,000.

About 1893, engineer Fred Eaton looked over the heads of those people at the river flowing wastefully into the desert lake. He knew that the Wright Irrigation Act of 1887 had made water diversion legal. None of the legislators voting for the act had envisioned moving mountain water to distant cities . . . but why not? True, there would be bleak mountains to tunnel through and precipitous canyons to cross with massive inverted siphons, but the drop between Owens Valley and the Los Angeles Basin was sufficient to make the project theoretically feasible. In addition there was a superb reservoir site in unpopulated Long Valley near the northern sources of the river. Enough spring runoff could be stored there to maintain steady flow throughout the year. Even after the valley farmers had been allotted their claims, thousands of acre feet would remain for sale to the city of Los Angeles and to the farmers of the San Fernando and San Gabriel valleys, 230 miles away. . . . A chimera. No such aqueduct existed on earth. Nor was there money enough in Southern California to build one—not in those days of economic depression.

In 1899, Eaton was elected mayor. That was the period when reform groups were arguing that the best way to reduce political corruption was to remove private enterprise from public business. Although the Los Angeles Water Company was more honest than most utility firms, it was cautious about extending service to outlying areas, and so the impatient city decided to take over the company. Squabbles about price filled most of Eaton's term as mayor, but in 1902 the sale was consummated for $2 million. As head of the project the city retained the private company's chief official, William Mulholland.

An immigrant from Ireland, Mulholland had reached Los Angeles in 1877, aged twenty-two and destitute. Settling down as ditch tender for the water company, he improved himself by nighttime study and rose to be the firm's chief engineer. As engineer he often listened with amusement to Fred Eaton's grandiose talk of bringing Owens River water to the city, but as the drought of the early 1900's lengthened he ceased smiling. Expanding farms blocked Mulholland from developing nearby sources of water, and the city was growing faster than he had believed possible. Finally, in 1903 he entered into serious discussions with Eaton about the gigantic problems facing the dream.

Two troublesome coincidences occurred that same year. Henry E. Huntington, Harrison Gray Otis (publisher of the Los Angeles *Times*), and a handful of other local financiers formed a syndicate that paid $50,000 for a three-year option on 16,500 acres of land in the San Fernando Valley near the spot that Eaton recommended as the outlet for the aqueduct. Conceivably the speculators had somehow obtained inside information concerning the water plans. Or, as modern historians are inclined to believe, they may have been prompted only by Huntington's plan to run a streetcar line in that direction.

The other coincidence involved the newly formed U.S. Reclamation Service, whose engineers began looking over the Long Valley reservoir site in 1903. Although consideration by no means guaranteed performance, the residents of Owens Valley jumped to the conclusion that their area was destined to be the scene of a major government irrigation project.

Learning of the government plans, Eaton and several city officials secretly entrained for Washington. There they convinced President Theodore Roosevelt that the needs of Los Angeles were greater than those of the remote valley. Roosevelt halted whatever plans, if any, the Service had for the area. Next Eaton, who on his own hook had already acquired some land and water rights in the Owens Valley, began buying more, on commission, as agent for the city.

His position was precarious. The municipal government had appropriated no money for the work and had given him no open authorization to act, lest speculators rush in and raise prices. Pretending that he was a rancher, he covertly committed Los Angeles to upwards of $1 million. He also acquired for himself, through the Eaton Land and Cattle Company, most of Long Valley. Although he knew the aqueduct was to precede the building of the reservoir, he assumed that a storage dam would soon follow and that he could sell the essential site to the city for enough money to recompense himself for the bold plan he had devised.

During this period Mulholland made his estimate of costs—$23.5 million for what would be, on completion, the world's then biggest aqueduct. This was so much money that the first approach to the voters was cautious—a proposed $1.5 million bond issue to pay for the Owens Valley land that Eaton had contracted for and to provide exact engineering studies for the canals.

The Los Angeles *Times*, whose publisher, Harrison Otis, was a member of the syndicate that held options of the San Fernando land near the aqueduct's assumed outlet, broke the story on July 29, 1905. This scoop brought sharp reaction from the rival Los Angeles *Examiner*, whose publisher, Edwin T. Earl, lived next door to Otis and waged unremitting personal and professional feuds with him.

Los Angeles, Earl's editorial writers charged, did not face a critical water shortage. The recent institution of water metering and court injunctions against the pumping of certain wells in the San Fernando Valley were underhanded devices to frighten the voters. Mulholland was incompetent; Eaton was a grafter. The whole expensive project was being foisted off on the city for the enrichment of a few robber barons, notably Earl's archenemy, Harrison Otis.*

---

*Southern California's current dispute with the north over water has led to a resurrection of Earl's whiskery charges, although the truth seems to be that the original syndicate was not crooked, merely lucky.

The sound and the fury had no effect on the voters. They wanted to keep their lawns green and bring in still more people. Meanwhile, precipitation figures showed that a drought did exist. By an overwhelming margin of 14 to 1 the city approved the bond issue.

Resorting to geographic sleight of hand, the federal government next declared that the sandy wastes along the upper part of the aqueduct right of way lay within the bounds of the nearest national forest, a move that prevented homesteading by speculators. At that point the long drought began to break, but the voters remained so enthralled with the idea of unfailing water—the transplanted river would provide for 2 million people, Mulholland said—that in 1907 they gave him, by a margin of 10 to 1, the $23.5 million he wanted. The next year, 5,000 men went to work on a project outranked in magnitude, Los Angeles boosters declared, only by the Panama Canal, also under construction during that time. Five years later the work was finished, and celebrants rattled out from the city in 15,000 dusty automobiles to watch the first glistening cascade pour down a concrete chute in the San Fernando foothills.

Henry Huntington's syndicate also rejoiced. Land prices jumped, and opponents of the project pointed accusing fingers at irrigating ditches that were immediately run from the San Fernando reservoir to rich valley farms. Told you so—the water wasn't for the city at all, an argument that overlooked the fact that the aqueduct had been built primarily as a safeguard against the future and that in the meantime the city would be foolish not to sell the surplus for whatever it would bring.

Throughout the construction years, the residents of Owens Valley had regarded the water diversion with mixed feelings. Since the aqueduct's intake was only 12 miles north of the midway hamlet of Independence, farms farther upstream—more than half of those in the valley—were not affected. Those owners who had sold to Eaton were chagrined, however, to think that they had been duped, as they saw it, into parting with their land at lower prices than they might have received in open bargaining. Many were irritated by the collapse of the Reclamation project. There was irony, too, in learning that water that might have been used near home was instead fructifying fields in the San Fernando Valley.

Still, there was balm. Hundreds of Owens Valley workers found good jobs on the aqueduct. Voracious demands for material to complete the cement-lined canal, the steel-encased siphons, and the 142 tunnels led the Southern Pacific to push a branch-line railroad from Mojave north through the valley and on to the Nevada mining towns of Tonopah and Goldfield. When the line was finished, valley farmers could easily ship produce both to the mines and to Los Angeles. The needs for power on the project led Mulholland to build small hydroelectric plants beside the streams tumbling out of the Sierra, and after the aqueduct was completed, the electricity generated at those facilities was sold at low rates entirely within the valley. Thanks to such benefits, objections were muted at first.

Trouble came when the city turned its attentions to the Long Valley Reservoir. Again greed was the cause of discord. Eaton asked $1 million for the land his cattle company owned there. Mulholland, snapping that the price was outrageous, advised the city not to pay so much, and the long friendship between the two men ended in rancor. Shortly thereafter two brothers appropriately named Wilfred W. and Mark Q. Watterson entered the fray. In addition to controlling the five banks that served Owens Valley, the Wattersons owned or held mortgages on land scattered from Owens Lake north into Long Valley. Under their leadership the farmers insisted that the city build for the valley the kind of dam and storage system they had hoped for from the Reclamation Service. Believing—or at least saying—that the proposals were neither safe nor practical, Mulholland persuaded the city to refuse. Such were the seeds of disaster.

In 1920, when postwar Los Angeles was booming full speed again, a cycle of normal rainfall ended and drought returned. Because no storage existed in Long Valley, the city in 1923 decided that it must purchase additional land and water near the town of Bishop. Simultaneously plans were made to build a reservoir in San Francisquito Canyon, a rugged gorge near the head of the Santa Clara Valley, some 30 miles north of Los Angeles.

No one paid much attention to the dam, but the purchasing program in Owens Valley stirred violent reaction. The more vocal farmers protested that they were being bulldozed out of their homes by an insensate urban monster that had no right, other than strength, to seize water that nature had given to them. If the rape succeeded, they cried to the state, a fruitful land would become a desert, business in the towns would stagnate, and a self-reliant people would be cut adrift.

If it weren't for the shadow of the Wattersons, one could be more sympathetic. True, Los Angeles was stubborn. But so were the valley people. Led by the banking brothers, they formed pools to jack up prices to 10 times assessed valuation. When the ranks broke and some men sold —the city paid an average of $145 an acre, though $100 had been the going price before the program began—local newspapers accused Los Angeles of pressure tactics but seldom offered specific examples. Seeking pressure of their own, valley residents besought the legislature to pass a bill that would force the city to pay "reparations" for vaguely defined damages to their economy. That failing, they resorted, under the leadership of Mark

Watterson, to the age-old American device of using violence to call attention to their plight. Nine times between May 21, 1924, and July 16, 1927, they dynamited critical sections of the aqueduct.

Six of the blasts occurred in two months—from May 14 to July 16, 1927. Conceivably desperation attended the stepped-up terrorism. The Wattersons were on the edge of bankruptcy, and only a quick sale of high-priced land would save them. But the blasts failed to bring the city to terms, and in August their five banks failed. On closing their doors, the brothers blamed the "destructive operations" of the Los Angeles water hogs. State bank examiners soon showed, however, that the pair had embezzled $460,000 from their depositors. They were sentenced to San Quentin, yet in many minds they still remain martyrs of the vain struggle with the urban dragon.

The Watterson fiasco was not the only collapse. Mulholland had placed the new dam in San Francisquito Canyon on insecure footing. At midnight, March 12, 1928, great slabs of it toppled and a wave 140 feet high swept down the gorge, obliterating a new powerhouse nearby. Reaching the Santa Clara Valley, the flood spread wide. Sheriff's deputies, alerted by telephone, raced through the towns of Piru, Fillmore, and Santa Paula, shouting warnings. Terrified people scrambled through the darkness for safety as roads, bridges, farmhouses, farm animals, and village homes vanished behind them in a maelstrom of debris. Not everyone escaped. The Ventura County coroner later stated that 319 corpses were dug from the debris; 101 persons were reported missing. Although property damage was a relatively mild $13 million or so, the death toll from the San Francisquito flood—Little San Francisco, grim coincidence—made the terrible night second only to the 1906 earthquake and fire in the tale of California disasters.

The catastrophe stunned the citizens of Los Angeles into a realization of what their water was costing. Contrition replaced stubbornness. Although suspicions were openly voiced that Owens Valley dynamiters had caused the collapse, which is highly unlikely, Mulholland made no effort to use that as an excuse. "Don't blame anyone else . . . ," he told the coroner's jury, and the words must have been hard to get out. "If there is an error in human judgment, I was that human." A citizens' committee from the devastated Santa Clara Valley met with representatives of Los Angeles to work out schedules of restitution and repair, and succeeded so well that not a single case went to court, though fast-buck lawyers from as far away as Stockton came swarming in to stir up trouble.

The spirit of adjustment extended to the Owens Valley, whose citizens had been chastened on their part by the debacle wrought by the Wattersons. Land purchases were completed amicably; indeed, they were the straw of hope for many men who faced ruin because of the bank failures. Among them was Fred Eaton, whose cattle company owed the Watterson receivers $200,000. He went bankrupt. Los Angeles, which might have squeezed hard then, instead paid him the full appraisal price of $650,000 for his Long Valley lands, site today of California's favorite fishing hole, Crowley Reservoir.

In further efforts toward conciliation, Los Angeles helped push the state highway department into building a paved road into the valley. It promoted recreational advantages so well that Owens Valley soon became one of Southern California's favorite vacation spots. Resentment and a vague sense of futility still linger, nevertheless. Owens Valley did not—does not—control her own destiny. Megalopolis had won.

San Francisco's simultaneous thrust for mountain water also brought into the open other antagonistic philosophies born of headlong urbanization. Characteristically, the clash in the north was more sophisticated than that in the south, for it involved a concept that seldom occurred to people with rural backgrounds—unsullied nature as an antidote for the ills of industrial progress. Prime spokesman for this wilderness cult was California's hallowed prophet of the High Sierra, John Muir.

Born in Scotland in 1838, Muir had grown up on a frontier farm in Wisconsin. Unsoured by its rigors and unimpressed by the agricultural notion that only tamed nature was good, he grew into an exuberant lover of wildness. Belatedly entering the University of Wisconsin at the age of twenty-two, he spent two exciting years studying geology, biology, botany, and, best of all from his standpoint, America's leading transcendentalist writers, Emerson and Thoreau, whose works showed him the bridge between the humanities and natural science: along with dust and stars, man was, if he would only realize it, part and parcel of a beneficent cosmos.

After field excursions in the East, including a long hike from Indianapolis to the Gulf of Mexico, he sailed for California, arriving in March, 1868. An exhilarating walk through masses of wild flowers in the San Joaquin Valley brought him to Yosemite. There he encountered a hitherto untried experiment in land use for the public good.

Four years before his arrival, Congress, acting largely at the behest of landscape architect Frederick Law Olmstead, had granted to the state of California the Mariposa Grove of giant sequoia trees and "the Cleft, or Gorge in the granite peak of the Sierra Nevada Mountain, known as the Yosemite Valley." These acquisitions, the bill directed, were to be used solely "for public pleasuring, resort, and recreation."

At the time of Muir's arrival there was little public pleasuring. The railroad had not yet penetrated the San Joaquin Valley, and visitors bound for the new state park had to take a river boat to Stockton, ride a stage for two days to Merced, and then endure a saddle for the final 50 roadless miles. But at least there was a hotelkeeper at the end of the trail, eccentric James M. Hutchings, a one-time magazine publisher who had grown so entranced with the Cleft or Gorge that he had left his San Francisco home and with his own hands had built a small wooden hotel near the foot of Yosemite Falls. Because the hostelry's inner walls consisted of muslin, guests who were not careful with their lamps sometimes produced, Hutchings admitted, "unintentional shadow pictures." But it was shelter from the weather, and mountain appetites made the food taste good.

A brief visit left Muir as entranced with the Sierra as Hutchings was. In order to return he took over a flock of sheep from a rough Irish herder and the next summer moved the animals to the high Tuolumne country northeast of Yosemite Valley. It was the beginning of a lifelong hate affair with almost the only living creature Muir disliked—"hoofed locusts," he called sheep. Even lambs wrought no softening—those "wrinkled duplicates of their mongrel, misarranged parents . . . born to wretchedness and unmitigated degradation."

After a summer of that he switched gladly to a jack-of-all-trades job in the little sawmill Hutchings had built in the valley. When work was slack, he acted as guide for artists and young geologists from the University of California. Or, preferably, he took solitary rambles far and wide, sleeping wherever night overtook him as he studied the flora, fauna, and geology of the stupendous High Sierra. In 1871 he published his first article, the beginning of an unceasing effort "to baptize [my fellow sinners] in the beauty of God's mountains." Because his fervor struck a yearning response from urban readers who felt increasingly cut away from America's frontier experience with an untrodden earth, Eastern editors were soon competing for his work.

The beauties of God's mountains were under attack. In the foothills and around Lake Tahoe, lumberjacks were driving deep into the forests, felling giant sequoias and sugar pines without thought for the future and then transporting the logs to the sawmills over ox-roads, narrow-gauge railways, or spectacular flumes built in utter disregard of damage to the countryside.

High in the alpine meadows were Muir's despised sheep. Actually, the trouble wasn't with the herds so much as with the way they were managed. Owners seldom accompanied the flocks to the mountains. After lambing season in March, when the broad floor of the San Joaquin Valley was beginning to dry to a dusty brown, they entrusted the animals, in bands of 2,000 or so each, to a herder—generally a Basque, Portuguese, or Mexican but sometimes a down-at-the-heel Irishman or American—and ordered the worker not to return until fall, when the sheep were roly-poly fat from mountain grass and heavy with new wool.

Off to the high country they went, smelly, noisy, half-starved from winter, churning the soil to dust. Unless the animals were closely herded, they were difficult to control, so the weary men and overworked dogs kept them in tight masses. The browse they didn't eat, they trampled. Beset by rival flocks, they overcrowded the best meadows. To clear away underbrush for easier travel and to let in sunlight for better grass, the herders set fires that more often than not raced away unchecked through dozens of miles of forest.

By that time, the late 1880's, many scientific organizations were pointing out to the managers of the public domain the close interrelationship between forest cover and stream flow. If trees, brush, and humus disappeared, melting snow flushed unrestrained off the hills, and by late summer little water remained to percolate into the dwindling creeks. It was the duty of the government, therefore, to protect the forests for the public weal.

The campaign enlisted enthusiastic support in the San Joaquin Valley, where streams flowing westward out of the Sierra fed a multitude of irrigation ditches. Leaders of the demand that exploitation be checked were George W. Stewart, editor of a small-town newspaper, the Visalia *Delta*, and Daniel Zumwalt, a land agent of the Southern Pacific, to whom assurances of ample water were a big selling point. There was nothing modest about the two men's original proposal. They urged the federal government to "reserve" from any kind of commercial entry an immense forest tract reaching from Yosemite Valley to the southern end of the tree belt in Kern County.

The area, larger than Rhode Island and Connecticut combined, proved too big a bite to start with. Shifting tactics abruptly, Stewart, Zumwalt, and their fellow conservationists joined a move to save from advancing lumbermen two notable stands of redwood trees, to be called, if Congress agreed, General Grant National Park and Sequoia National Park. The language in the bill designed to save the groves was frankly patterned after that in the act that had established the nation's first national park, Yellowstone, in 1872.

Not by coincidence, Muir was simultaneously engaged in a similar project farther north. In 1889 he had taken an influential editor, Robert Underwood Johnson of *Century* magazine, camping in the wild Tuolumne country above Yosemite. There he showed Johnson the sheep-denuded slopes and pointed out that as a result the magnificent waterfalls of Yosemite Valley were reduced by summer to mere dribbles. To Muir the matter was not one of practicality, as it was to Stewart and Zumwalt, but of aesthetics. Natural beauty, he argued, was as essential to man's well-being as any amount of sheep's wool.

Johnson agreed, and the two opened a campaign to have Congress place a protective 1,500-square-mile federal reserve entirely around Yosemite Valley State Park. Helped by the Southern Pacific's interest in stimulating tourist traffic, they won their battle, as did Stewart and Zumwalt. In September, 1890, Congress created Sequoia National Park, General Grant National Park (later incorporated into King's Canyon National Park), and Yosemite National Park. As in Yellowstone, the job of patrolling the new pleasuring grounds, principally against trespassing sheepherders and lumbermen, fell to the United States Army.

Other steps followed swiftly. In March, 1891, Congress passed legislation that allowed the President of the United States to set aside forest reserves, later National Forests, where resources could be utilized only under government supervision. As part of that program, the 4-million-acre Sierra Reserve, first advocated by Stewart and Zumwalt, was established in 1893—and later divided into five separate units for ease in administration.

Exulting in the nation's new awareness of its natural jewels, Muir in 1892 joined 26 other California wilderness lovers in incorporating the militant Sierra Club. Its stated purpose was "to explore, enjoy, and render accessible the mountain regions of the Pacific Coast"—accessibility was eventually eschewed as an ideal when it became evident that people in automobiles could be as destructive as sheep—and "to enlist the support and cooperation of the people and the government in preserving the forests and other natural features of the Sierra Nevada."

An initial project was to persuade the state to return the Cleft or Gorge known as Yosemite Valley to the federal government so that it could be managed as a part of the National Park. Thanks again to the help of the Southern Pacific, this triumph over bureaucratic inertia was achieved in 1905. Well before then, however, the Sierra Club had found itself embroiled in a controversy that split its membership into antagonistic factions and stirred angry recriminations from one end of the nation to the other.

Like Los Angeles, San Francisco was nearing the limits of her local water supply. As early as 1882, engineers had pointed out that ample replenishment, together with a superlative reservoir site, existed in the granite-walled Hetch Hetchy gorge of the Tuolumne River, a few miles north of Yosemite Valley. Even though the establishment of the National Park had closed the area to entry, Mayor James D. Phelan of San Fran-

358 THE BIG SHIFT

cisco felt, in 1901, that the city's need justified asking the Secretary of the Interior for the right to use the gorge as a municipal reservoir site.

The secretary refused. This heartened William S. Tevis, son of Lloyd Tevis. Young Tevis and other promoters had gained control of extensive water rights near Lake Tahoe, and they proposed to Boss Ruef and his hungry supervisors that the city buy the holdings for $10.5 million, $1 million of which would be remitted to Ruef and his henchmen for their services in putting the deal across. The graft trials led to a hasty dropping of that notion—and also created a strong popular prejudice against further private offerings of water. Meantime the devastating fire of 1906 had intensified demands for an enlarged system. Because Hetch Hetchy seemed the best solution available, a new application was forwarded to Washington in 1908. This time the grant was allowed.

Wilderness lovers, marshaled by Muir, leaped to arms. Ostensibly the issue was the integrity of a National Park. Actually, the conflict reached far deeper—the material needs of civilization set against a growing belief that civilization might not prove worthwhile if it destroyed the natural world from which man himself had come. The ideological ax split both the Sierra Club and the country's vigorous young conservation movement in twain. On one side were the preservationists, who saw nature's aesthetic values as higher than all else—even, implied Senator Marcus Smith of Arizona, than "the wail of a hungry baby." On the other side were the advocates of controlled, beneficial use of all national resources for the greatest good of the greatest number of people.

The rub lay in the taint of economics. Hetch Hetchy water would be cheaper than anything else available. The argument roused Muir's full talents for sarcasm and eloquence. His opponents were "devotees of ravaging commercialism . . . [who] instead of lifting their eyes to the God of the Mountains, lift them to the Almighty Dollar. . . . Dam Hetch Hetchy! As well dam for water-tanks the people's cathedrals and churches, for no holier temple has ever been consecrated by the hearts of men."

The uproar, which grew more intense the farther east one went, bewildered most San Franciscans. Didn't those people understand? What had California been built on, other than the free development of the state's superb natural resources? Were those resources now to be locked beyond reach so that a few lovers of solitude could enjoy a scenic view to the detriment of the taxpayers of an entire city?

Union labor, envisioning many jobs, naturally favored the project. Perhaps more telling, as conservationist Roderick Nash has suggested, was the support of Congressman William Kent, whose home district, Marin County, lay north across the Golden Gate from San Francisco. An ardent outdoorsman and an admirer of Muir's work, Kent in 1907 had donated to the federal government a magnificent stand of Marin County redwood trees with the request that the grove be known as Muir Woods National Monument, as it still is. Yet when the showdown over Hetch Hetchy came in Congress in 1913, it was Kent who chided Muir with having lived alone in the wilds for so long that he had lost all sense of social responsibility. Muir's followers, Kent added, were fuzzy-minded idealists who were being used as tools by private power interests bent on forestalling the municipal ownership of the electrical energy that would be generated at Hetch Hetchy.

Such words from a man whose motives were beyond reproach helped persuade Congress to deny Muir's attack and confirm the grant of Hetch Hetchy to the city. After spending more than two decades and more than $100 million, workers completed a massive dam in the gorge, added subsidiary reservoirs nearby, and constructed a 155-mile aqueduct that bored through the Mount Diablo Mountains in a 25-mile tunnel, the world's longest at the time of its building. Meantime private power interests were placated by being sold municipal electricity at low rates.

Once again megalopolis had won. Unlike the Owens Valley controversy, however, this victory did not answer a question—could rural values withstand urban demands?—so much as it made concrete doubts that ever since have refused to go away.

What, exactly, is the spiritual price of industrial civilization?

24. The Creakings of the Gravy Train

The word made flesh, so far as Southern California boosterism was concerned, was Harrison Gray ("Bray," one enemy sneered) Otis, publisher of the Los Angeles *Times*. A native of Ohio, he was twice wounded in the Civil War. For a time he served as the Washington editor of a veterans' magazine, then moved to Santa Barbara in 1876. After four years on a newspaper there and two more as a government agent in Alaska, he shifted to Los Angeles, where he bought an interest in the *Times.*

In 1886 he acquired full control, only to have the boom of the 1880's collapse beneath his whitening goatee. Belligerently, as if reacting to a personal affront, he set about strong-arming prosperity back to Southern California and the *Times*. His approach was as blunt as one of his own headlines. "Los Angeles," he shouted at audience after audience of mesmerized businessmen, "wants no dudes, loafers and paupers, people who have no means and trust to luck, cheap politicians, failures, bummers, scrubs. . . . We need workers! hustlers! Men of brains, brawn, and guts! Men who have a little capital and a great deal of energy—first class men!"

In pursuit of those men Otis helped found the Los Angeles Chamber of Commerce in 1888. To give the new hustlers room in which to operate, he promoted the harbor at San Pedro. Swallowing his objections to the municipal ownership of utilities, he backed the city's efforts to transport Owens Valley water and power to Los Angeles—and, as a corollary, to his lands in the San Fernando Valley. Most of all he resisted the unionizing of labor, declaring in trumpet tones that freedom from strikes meant steady jobs for workers, increased profits for employers, and a general trickle-down-from-above prosperity for the great middle class that was the backbone of American civilization.

The bias showed itself early. In 1890, he announced without prior negotiation a 20 percent cut in printers' wages, locked out his employees when they sputtered, and replaced them with scabs. He was a founder and supporter of the Merchants and Manufacturers Association, which saw to it that bank loans and orders were withdrawn from firms that dared deal with union officials. With Henry E. Huntington and other capitalists, he underwrote the Los Angeles branch of the Citizens Alliance, formed to enlist public opinion against organized labor. He supported advertising campaigns featuring the economic opportunities of Southern California, with the sly hope, it is charged, that an influx of workers would help hold down wages.

His shield and buckler were tens of thousands of immigrants from the Midwest, who had brought with them a country-bred conviction that unions were another product of the wicked cities. It was a time, moreover, of economic inflation. Shrinking dollars alarmed people on fixed incomes—there were many in Southern California—and they regarded higher wages as one more item leading toward higher costs of living. Otis was their voice, and they applauded him to the rafters.

The *Times*'s bellowing intemperance infuriated not only the unions in Los Angeles but also the stronger ones in San Francisco, for the leaders there feared that the imposition of citywide open shops in the south would encourage union-busting activities in the north. Inevitably, then, when brewery, streetcar, and structural ironworkers launched a series of walkouts in Los Angeles in 1910, financial aid and trained organizers flowed down from the Bay to help them along their thorny path.

Attention soon centered on the ironworkers' strike. Labor's enemy in that contest was not a local group, but the mighty National Erectors' Association, supported by United States Steel. Only in Chicago and San Francisco had workers been able to hold their ground against the giant. If Los Angeles succeeded, the morale of labor everywhere would be strengthened. Otis poured out vitriol, demanding that the city council pass legislation in aid of the beleaguered employers. The councilmen wrung their hands. Most were insurgent Republicans, heirs of a turn-of-the-century Good Government League that had later entered into an alliance with the new statewide Progressive party that was running Hiram Johnson for the governorship. Otis scorned the mixture as "Goo-Goos." His stated reason was their undermining of Republican regulars. The Goo-Goos charged him with more insidious motives: he still resented, they said, a successful recall drive that the Good Government League had conducted in 1904 against a councilman who had awarded the *Times* an unjustifiably rich contract for municipal printing.

As a measure of Progressive opinion of Otis, consider this oft-quoted outburst by Hiram Johnson when he was campaigning in Los Angeles during the troubled days of 1910. Although San Francisco in the time of Ruef had drunk the dregs of infamy, the would-be governor shouted at his stunned audience, there was in the north "nothing so vile, nothing so low, nothing so debased, nothing so infamous . . . as Harrison Gray Otis. There he sits in senile dementia with gangrene heart and rotting brain, grimacing at every reform, chattering impotently at all things that are decent . . . disgraceful, depraved, corrupt, crooked, and putrescent."

It is a commentary, therefore, on Los Angeles' animosity toward union labor that in spite of such feelings the Progressive council yielded to Otis' demands and passed the nation's most stringent antipicketing ordinance. As wholesale arrests began, repercussion rolled east to the ironworkers' headquarters at Indianapolis, where John J. McNamara, the union's national secretary, responded with a foolish idea.

During recent years McNamara had been trying to bolster morale by having his brother James McNamara and a saboteur named Ortie McManigal blow up nonunion construction projects in various parts of the country. Deciding that a hearty explosion would bring the sweetness of fear to the breast of Harrison Gray Otis—an extraordinary psychological miscalculation—Secretary McNamara directed brother James and Ortie to blow up the *Times* building.

James also made a mistake. He nestled his suitcase full of giant powder against a wall of the proscribed structure shortly after midnight on October 1, 1910, at a time when a crew of workers was inside preparing the day's morning edition for the press. The explosion tumbled the stone building like an earthquake, killed twenty men, and injured seventeen.

The city was outraged. Jumping to conclusions, Otis and the Merchants and Manufacturers Association blamed the union for this "crime of the century." Local labor leaders, unaware of the facts, retorted waspishly that Otis was guilty: the true cause of the blast was a leaky gas main that the publisher had neglected to repair. Wasted breath. On Christmas Eve, Secretary John McNamara personally set off yet another explosion at the Llewelyn Iron Works and brought more fingers pointing at the union, though once again direct evidence was lacking.

As special agent for investigating the *Times* disaster, the city employed William J. Burns, the detective who had helped the federal government break up Senator Mitchell's timber frauds in Oregon and afterward had produced evidence for the San Francisco graft trials. Earlier investigations had already put Burns on the trail of Ortie McManigal. He gathered more threads in Los Angeles, followed Ortie to Detroit, and pounced. Promised immunity, McManigal blurted out a confession implicating the McNamaras. Burns seized the brothers and with complete disregard for normal extradition procedures brought them to Los Angeles for trial.

Labor throughout the United States cried, "Frame-up!" The annual May Day parade of the Los Angeles Socialist party turned into a massive anti-Otis demonstration. The American Federation of Labor paid Clarence Darrow $50,000 to conduct the McNamaras' defense and added $200,000 more to cover expenses. Socialist Job Harriman, running once again for the mayor of the city, based his campaign on the injustice of the case.

The very real possibility that Harriman might be elected panicked Otis and the regular Republicans. By warning confused conservatives and Goo-Goos alike that a Socialist regime would make bonds for completing the Owens Valley aqueduct impossible to sell, they solidified party ranks. Even so, Harriman might have won except for an extraordinary deal arranged by Clarence Darrow and journalist Lincoln Steffens, who was covering the trials.

Details were never revealed by the participants. Apparently, however, the course of the trial, which had opened in October, 1911, led Darrow to believe that confession was his clients' only hope of avoiding the death penalty. Steffens on his part seems to have hoped that if justice were tempered with mercy, the antagonists in all the state's labor disputes could then sit down at a conference table and work out a program for industrial peace. Be that as it may, three weeks before the municipal elections, the McNamaras suddenly stood up before their judge and changed their plea to guilty.

Little mercy followed. James McNamara, who had planted the fatal dynamite, was sentenced to life imprisonment, his brother John to 15 years. Disillusioned voters deserted Harriman in such droves that he was soundly defeated. No industrial peace conferences were called, and labor's hope of bringing the closed shop to burgeoning Los Angeles was thoroughly shattered.

If the violence of the McNamaras brought no gain to labor, neither did the curious nonviolence of the new Industrial Workers of the World, who proclaimed class warfare yet used tactics of passive resistance in their confrontations with California authorities. A small group led by totally committed organizers, the I.W.W. concentrated its Western efforts on the down-and-outers of the vanished frontier, the generally uneducated, sometimes mentally retarded miners, lumberjacks, and agricultural tramps who drifted forlornly toward whatever temporary job opportunities held out hope of another meal, another bottle of cheap red wine.

In California, itinerant fruit and vegetable pickers were the chief target of the Wobblies, a derisive nickname said to have been coined by Harrison Otis. It is hard to know how many migrants there were, even though the census listed 54,000—25,826 European immigrants and native Americans, 22,811 Japanese, 2,091 Chinese (race riots and bans on immigration had ended their once dominant position in the fields), plus a sprinkling of Mexicans, Hindus, and American Indians. Unquestionably the figures are incomplete. For one thing, the throng was too restless to be numbered accurately. For another, many of the whites traveled with their families. All participated in the work—the children in particular were adept fruit pickers—but not all were listed as laborers. So it is likely that the migrant throng numbered more than 100,000 hapless souls.

They served a small part of California's 88,197 farms. Beware the word. "Farm" generally raises a picture of a self-contained homestead supporting the rosy-cheeked family of its independent owner. In theory, American land laws fostered just such an agrarian ideal. But, as we have seen, theory seldom worked in California, where a hodgepodge of old Mexican grants, large railroad holdings, and sprawling conglomerations pieced together through fraud had always militated against homesteading. In 1910, a mere 310 individuals and companies owned 4 million acres—enough, according to theory, to support 25,000 independent farm families. Of about 25 million acres suitable for farming in California, only 11 million were actually cultivated. The rest were being held idle, under low taxes, until water development and population pressures allowed subdivision at high prices.

To put it another way: of California's 88,197 farms 3,407 were supervised by professional managers. These were the factories in the fields, to borrow Carey McWilliams' angry term. Although in 1910 they constituted less than 4 percent of the arithmetical number of farms in the state, they produced more than 20 percent of its agricultural income. This sharply reduced the take available to the other 96 percent and produced a still greater list toward bigness. Defeated by the high costs of machinery, transportation, water, and interest, more and more marginal operators sold out to their sinewy neighbors and with their families dropped down into the ranks either of tenancy or of migrant labor.

A more wretched, restless group can scarcely be imagined. As the summer turned hot, they emerged from their hovels—shanty towns at the edges of the rural villages or tenements in the cities—and began a forlorn drift from crop to crop. One lure was California's great variety of produce. The harvests were ready at different times, according to type and climate, and so it was possible to keep working from 30 to 35 weeks —assuming that a man reached a waiting employer ahead of his competitors—and thus earn $500 to $600 a year. There was, in a general way, a division of labor. The Japanese tended to gravitate toward sugar beets and berries, the Mexicans to the southern citrus groves and the new cotton fields of the Imperial Valley, the Europeans to grapes, peas, and artichokes, the Americans to the orchards and canneries.

The growers insisted that they paid higher wages, by roughly 40 percent, than did the farm employers of, say, the North Atlantic states. True. But the hired hand in the East generally worked the year around in one place, sat down to eat with the family that employed him, and felt some sense of individual accomplishment. In California the harvesters swarmed through like locusts, picking frantically at piece rates from sunup to sundown. Accommodations were rudimentary. Why, the growers demanded, should they spend money on houses and toilets that would be used only a few weeks a year by people too crude and ignorant to appreciate what was done for them anyhow? So as soon as a field was empty, on the wanderers went—until winter, when they were supposed to vanish entirely.

Such was the group that the Industrial Workers of the World sought to unionize. Their concentration was on the whites, not because of racism —I.W.W. philosophy embraced all workers everywhere—but because the next-largest group, the Japanese, were clannish and had formed their own associations for dealing with employers.

Since little could be accomplished in the fields, the organizers made their pitch during the winter on the street corners and around the saloons of the towns where the idle were wont to congregate. At these strategic open-air spots, leading Wobblies delivered revolutionary harangues. But they did not act like revolutionists. Though insisting on their right to free speech, they offered no resistance when arrested for violating ordinances against street gatherings. They just kept coming. As fast as one speaker was dragged off to jail, another took his place.

In jail they sang revolutionary songs, shouted slogans down the corridors, beat on the floors and bars with anything that would make a racket. Brought to trial, they resorted to whatever tactics would clog the courts and raise costs for the taxpayers. They were not doing all this for free speech as a matter of principle. It was a tactic. They wanted to raise their prestige among the workers by proving that even the downtrodden could challenge authority. That achieved, they would be in a better position to win members, or so they hoped.

During the winter of 1910–11, Fresno, largest town in the San Joaquin Valley, was the I.W.W.'s chief California target. Leader there was Frank Little, tall, stringy, half-Indian, blind in one eye: seven years later vigilantes in Butte, Montana, would hang him from a railroad bridge.

Violence also greeted Little's efforts in Fresno. After he had filled the jail with obstreperous Free-Speechers from all parts of the West, the exasperated police one icy night turned on their fire hoses under 150 pounds of pressure and battered the prisoners into sodden silence. Mobs beat known Wobblies on the streets and burned down their tent camp outside the city limits. And still they came, until in March, 1911, the weary city gave in, released the protesters still in jail, and allowed street meetings in designated areas. Unquestionably it was a victory. But the migrant farm workers, sunk in the apathy of hopelessness, remained unconvinced that this was a solution to their problems and in the summer shuffled back to the fields unorganized.

San Diego was an even greater anticlimax. In 1912 the city sheltered about 50,000 sun-seekers. There was little industry and only a small winter influx of hibernating farm workers—"not worth a whoop in Hell from a rebel's point of view," wrote ballad composer Joe Hill, whose 1915 conviction for murder in Salt Lake City would become an international cause célèbre. Harrison Gray Otis nonetheless stirred a whoop from the rebels by making a ringing speech in the city that urged San Diegans to tolerate no nonsense from any radical. Roused to righteousness by this outside advice, the city council passed an ordinance that forbade gatherings on E Street between Fifth and Sixth, long a favorite haunt for anyone with a message on his chest.

Instantly the Wobblies poured in. By the middle of February, 150 Free-Speechers were in jail. Armed vigilantes surrounded a freight train bringing another 140 from Los Angeles, kept the men penned in a cattle corral overnight, and the next dawn marched them afoot to the county line. There, one of them wrote later, "We were forced to kiss the flag and then run a gauntlet of 106 men, every one of which was striking at us as hard as they could with their pick ax handles. They broke one man's leg, and everyone was beaten black and blue."

Such activities—one leader had the letters I.W.W. burned into his back with a lighted cigar—led Governor Hiram Johnson to appoint an investigating committee. Its report was a scathing denunciation of the police and citizen vigilantes. Another moral victory for the Wobblies. But it did not bring a single agricultural laborer into the union.

Another Pyrrhic victory, darkened with death, occurred the next year on the hop ranch of Ralph Durst, near the town of Wheatland in the Sacramento Valley. Hoping to hold down wages through competition, Durst advertised for more pickers than he needed. They flooded in— 2,800 men, women, and children speaking 27 different languages. There were hobos, small farmers from the foothills seeking extra money, unemployed from the cities, families out for a "country vacation." They found that if they wanted privacy they had to rent tents from Durst for $2.75 a week; otherwise they slept on straw piles. Daytime temperatures reached 105 degrees. Water was a mile from the fields; the only liquid delivered to the workers, at a price, was a sour drink made from citric acid by Durst's cousin Jim. Eight toilets black with flies served the entire camp. Wages ran from a dollar a day on down.

Outrage gave the handful of Wobblies in the crowd an opening. Led by Blackie Ford, they sponsored a mass meeting on Sunday, August 3, 1913. Alarmed by the gathering yet making no effort to contact the workers, Durst demanded that Yuba County authorities disperse the crowd. As nervous deputies sought to arrest Ford, one of their members fired a warning shot over the heads of the people. A riot erupted. During it four people died: two workers, a deputy sheriff, and the district attorney of the county.

The terrified itinerants, Jack London reported, fled from the scene as if from an earthquake. Sleuths hired from the William J. Burns Detective Agency took to the trail of the radicals and soon brought back for trial in Marysville, seat of Yuba County, both Blackie Ford and a mentally retarded companion, Herman Suhr. No evidence was produced to show that either man had participated in or had even urged the killings. They were nevertheless convicted of second-degree murder on the grounds that they were responsible for summoning the protest meeting and hence for the deaths.

Rancher Durst, who had summoned the posse, received no legal attention whatsoever.

The trials of the accused, held during the early months of 1914, brought the plight of the itinerants before the eyes of the nation. Hoping to benefit from the widespread sympathy, a man named Charles Kelley recruited from among the 35,000 winter unemployed in San Francisco an army of 1,500 to march on Sacramento and demand relief from the legislature. They were met by a drenching rain and 800 special deputies armed with pick handles. Under the combined assault, Kelley's army dissolved, but not before the nation had heard their protest.

Heeding the outcries, Governor Hiram Johnson appointed a Commission on Housing and Immigration to investigate the conditions of the migrant laborer. So that, too, could be claimed by the I.W.W. as a victory. But was it, really?

Johnson was known as a friend of labor. The measures that he had pushed through his first legislature, that of 1911, had been described by Theodore Roosevelt as "the most comprehensive program of constructive legislation ever passed at a single session of any American legislature"—an overstatement designed in part to flatter Johnson, by then a power in the nationwide Progressive movement. Two years later, in 1913, the California legislature strode even farther along the liberal path. The reforms were largely political, however—the initiative, referendum, and recall, women's suffrage, a stronger railroad commission, and so on. Social and economic measures had been limited, in the main, to mild conservation and workmen's compensation acts and to minimum wages (except in agriculture) for women and children.

The Wheatland tragedy and Kelley's army demanded more. Unfortunately for themselves, however, the I.W.W. strategists alienated the brief sympathy they had won by trying to force a pardon for Blackie Ford and Herman Suhr through threats of a statewide tie-up of the hop harvest. The pressure merely made Johnson obdurate. There was no pardon, and the Commission on Housing and Immigration was twisted into a device for undercutting the radicals by complying with minor demands. Liberals nodded approval and the public was soothed, but in the fields very little happened. Thus that moral victory, bought in part with blood, ended as hollow as the others.

Oriental laborers were meantime suffering under special disabilities. Behind the attacks lay California's long ingrained antipathy toward "the yellow peril." As soon as the Japanese influx began early in the twentieth century, rural newspapers began sputtering with copy much like that stirred first by the Chinese—demands for school segregation, charges of sexual immorality, worries about strange diseases, warnings that America's agrarian ideals were being destroyed.

This time, however, there were few riots. Japan, recent victor over Russia, had muscle enough to make even local authorities circumspect. Instead, starched legality became the method of attack. By means of a "Gentleman's Agreement," U.S. diplomats persuaded Japan not to allow additional laborers to immigrate to this country. There was a loophole, however. Men already here could bring over parents, wives, children. These newcomers—there was a spate of proxy marriages to "picture brides"—also went to work in the fields. Forming their own aggressive labor unions, they wrested higher wages from employers. Pooling their savings, they began to buy valley lands susceptible to intensive farming and turned rice and potato raising into two of California's most profitable pursuits.

Their success bred envy not just among white laborers but also among small farmers who found themselves outbid for land. Employers, eager for more tractable workers, turned toward Mexico while joining the hue and cry against Asiatics. Heeding the uproar, the state legislature in 1913 declared that persons ineligible for United States citizenship—any Oriental—could not own land in California or lease it for more than three years.

The Japanese evaded the provisions by transferring title to dummy corporations ostensibly controlled by Americans or to their American-born children who, as automatic citizens of the United States, were beyond reach of the restriction. To angry Californians, enough was enough. In 1924, they persuaded Congress to close this country's doors entirely to Japanese immigration. It was less easy to remove the seeds of guilt and fear that seventeen years later would explode, under the shock of Pearl Harbor, into hysteria.

The ugliness that we see in hindsight was not apparent to most Californians of the time. They felt they had reason for satisfaction. The recession of 1912–13 was fading, and optimism glowed again, much of it revolving around the imminent completion of the Panama Canal. To celebrate this newest link with the markets of the world, the port cities of San Diego and San Francisco prepared competing fairs calculated to draw attention from everywhere.

San Francisco's Panama-Pacific International Exposition was official, by authority of Congress. San Diego's was self-generated, thanks largely to sugar millionaire John D. Spreckels, whom we met earlier building the so-called People's Railroad into the San Joaquin Valley as part of San Francisco's attack on the Southern Pacific.

After moving to San Diego, Spreckels acquired newspapers, the Coronado Hotel, a streetcar system, and a water company that bejeweled the surrounding hills with reservoirs. He promoted the spectacular railroad, completed in 1919, that winds along the Baja California border, through shaggy mountains and across breathtaking abysses, to Yuma, where it gives San Diego her only direct rail connection with the East. To show his faith in these investments and in the city's gentle climate, lovely setting, and superlative harbor, Spreckels promised to underwrite a Panama-California Exposition even in the face of San Francisco's giant competition.

The site was charming Balboa Park. The fair buildings were designed to serve later—they still do—as the cultural core of the city. Architecture was a handsome rendering in tan stucco of Spanish baroque and Spanish colonial styles. The exposition's overall theme, carried out with sparkling brilliance, was water's magic powers in the desert.

Irony served as background. The fair glittered its way through a severe drought. By December, 1915, the situation was so desperate that the city called for help on a locally famous native son, Charles Mallory Hatfield, who had invented on his father's farm near San Diego an "evaporator" that he filled with secret chemicals for coaxing moisture from the clouds during rainy seasons when no rain fell.

Perhaps the contraption was a chemical brother of the sodium iodide cloud seeders of a more recent date. Anyway, it had worked with such success at different locations in Southern California that the San Diego city council risked offering Hatfield $10,000 for replenishing their empty reservoirs. He succeeded too well, creating a 16-inch deluge that not only filled the reservoirs but washed out highways and railroad bridges and forced a temporary closing of the fair that was devoted to extolling water's fairy powers. On the grounds that they had asked for a normal rain, not a flood, the councilmen declined to pay the magician.

San Francisco's Pannama-Pacific International Exposition, far more overwhelming in size than San Diego's, was also a gesture of civic confidence, a way of proving that the city had risen phoenix-like from the ashes of 1906. Even while rebuilding, the voters had authorized millions of dollars for the effort. In 1912, after Congress had finally bestowed its accolade (and more money), workers began filling a watery 635-acre site on the northern tip of the peninsula, just inside the Golden Gate. Bedazzlement: a brilliantly illuminated Tower of Jewels 432 feet high, a vast colonnaded Palace of Fine Arts curving around an illuminated lagoon, exhibition halls large enough to tire even a Californian, and a strident amusement area seven blocks long. In less than nine months nearly 20 million visitors trooped in to stare, admire, and feel the vitality of the re-created city.

Part of that vitality was the result of a far sharper stimulation than the Panama Canal. World War I had broken out in Europe. Agents from both sides of Armageddon swept through the state, buying food in the Central Valley and oil and gasoline from the refineries on the east shore of the Bay. The harbor bustled—until the longshoremen went on strike for a bigger share of the prosperity.

To many employers the episode seemed a golden opportunity to break San Francisco's long honeymoon with the closed shop. People in general resented the union's interference with the progress of their rapidly accelerating gravy train. As an indication of their mood, 2,000 of them poured into the civic auditorium in response to a call from the San Francisco Chamber of Commerce. There they formed a vigilante-style Law and Order Committee to protect property from sabotage.

Other functions soon absorbed the group. President Wilson asked the nation to show, by means of widespread Preparedness Day parades on July 22, 1916, its fitness for war if need arose. By and large labor opposed the demonstrations as a step that might lead toward America's entry into the conflict. San Francisco employers seized on the objections as a way to discredit their opponents. Decrying pacifism as lack of patriotism, members of the Law and Order Committee assumed prominent roles in organizing the parade. Not a single labor union agreed to participate, and the great demonstration, designed to prove American unity to the world, became in San Francisco a symbol of disunity.

Warnings that violence would result if the parade marched were telephoned to municipal officers and some newspapers. The ceremony proceeded nonetheless. As the long column was passing the corner of Steuart and Market streets, a massive curbside explosion drowned the cheering. Ten people died; fifty or more were injured. The city was horrified. Thousands poured into the civic auditorium to demand immediate apprehension of the guilty.

Suspicion centered on known radicals. Thomas J. Mooney, who had recently fomented an unsuccessful wildcat strike among streetcar workers, his wife Rena, a young radical named Warren Billings, who had just completed a prison term for the illegal transportation of dynamite, and two lesser fry were swept with a fine disregard for legal niceties into a hastily engineered net. During the excitement the longshoremen's strike faded into futility.

On the flimsiest of testimony, some of it almost certainly perjured, Mooney was sentenced to death and Billings to life imprisonment. (The others were acquitted.) Labor shouted, "Frame-up!" Crowds demonstrated outside American embassies as far away as St. Petersburg, Russia. At the insistence of President Wilson, Mooney's death sentence was commuted to life imprisonment. Most Californians, however, remembering that the McNamaras really had blown up the *Times* building in Los Angeles, stayed stubbornly behind the prosecution. If the two men had not caused the explosion, who had? And why? Two decades passed before an influential body of public opinion swung to a belief that San Francisco's notorious vigilante spirit, working this time through the district attorney's office, had allowed a travesty on justice to take place merely to discredit labor. That divide crossed, the two men were finally pardoned in 1939.

Seen from broader perspective, the Mooney-Billings affair was just one more incident in a nationwide swing to conservatism. Quickening the trend was a fear of radicalism brought on by the success of the Russian Revolution. Caught by the hysteria, the California legislature followed the lead of other states in passing criminal syndicalism laws that imposed severe penalties on anyone advocating "unlawful acts of force or violence" to effect changes in either politics or "industrial ownership or control." The Los Angeles police department formed a "Red Squad" that energetically employed the new law as a club to drive the I.W.W. out of the southern part of the state. San Francisco enthusiastically embraced "the American Plan," a new name for the open shop, and throughout the postwar decade unionism had little effect even in the Bay area.

Social and political conservatism also prevailed. Although a "wet" state alcoholically speaking, California joined the stampede to ratify the Eighteenth Amendment to the Constitution—and then enthusiastically ignored its prohibitions. Panicked at first by the new law, the state's multimillion-dollar wine-grape industry soon found that like other California shocks this too was a blessing of sorts; homeowners throughout the nation bought so many trainloads of grapes for fermenting wine in their own basements that coastal vineyards were hard put to meet the demand.

The tune of the state was sounded meantime by three arch-Republican newspapers, the Los Angeles *Times,* run since 1917 by Otis' son-in-law, Harry Chandler; Joseph Knowland's Oakland *Tribune;* and George Cameron's San Francisco *Chronicle.* Voters followed their advice with sheeplike exactness. During the decade of the 1920's, Republican candidates in California won 92 percent of all elective offices. With reason America's favorite humorist, cowboy Will Rogers, moaned, "I am a member of no organized political party. I am a California Democrat."

Why derail the gravy train? For most residents, California was more prosperous than ever. Between 1920 and 1930 population climbed by 2.25 million. San Francisco numbered 634,000 residents, the Bay area 1.3 million. Los Angeles, however, was the phenomenon. No other American metropolis has ever matched the twenty-year growth rate she experienced between 1910 and 1930—a quadrupling of population from 319,000 to 1.24 million. County population kept pace, rising to 2.2 million.

Appropriately, most of the growth resulted from the world's first folk movement by automobile. Largely because of mild temperatures and long months of clear weather, Southern California had already embraced the internal combustion engine with passionate intensity. As soon as highway construction began to boom, Los Angeles set about making herself the hub of the longest spokes she could manage, just as she had created, in defiance of nature's niggardliness, a harbor and a water system huge enoug': to satisfying her overweening ambitions.

Offended that the first transcontinental road should be aimed toward San Francisco, busy Angelenos hurried to Nevada and Utah to set up billboards directing traffic their way. When San Diego in 1916 sponsored a direct road from the East through Imperial Valley, paving the worst of the sand dunes with planks, Los Angeles retorted by making her road through San Gorgonio Pass so much better that neither tourists nor truckers hesitated over which way to go. During that same period the city, acting through the state's highway department, threw concrete chains around the southern San Joaquin Valley by spiraling the awesome Ridge Route across the Tehachapi Mountains. Success was instantaneous, for the project, stupendous for its time, undercut the railroad run through Mojave by 50 miles.

Car registrations soared steadily. By the middle of the 1920's, when the nation as a whole had 1 automobile for each 7 people, California had 1 for 4—and Los Angeles 1 for 2.25. The sprawling city seemed (at the time;

doubts came later) to be particularly suited to the new mode of transportation. Its geographic area, like its population, quadrupled between
1910 and 1930, mostly because Los Angeles had ample water and her
small neighbors had not. Through annexation of thirsty petitioners, the
city ballooned her size from 100 square miles to 441. Within the perimeter
lay huge squares of empty land that had escaped subdivision by being
inconveniently far from the big red streetcars or by embracing hillier
country than the trolleys could manage. The automobile changed that,
completing the dispersal begun by the trams.

Downtown traffic congestion led a man named A. W. Ross to move as
far west on Wilshire Boulevard as the La Brea Tar Pits. There he created
an auto-oriented shopping center named, with true California assurance,
"Miracle Mile." Soon Wilshire was the busiest motorway on earth, and
the fact that a spot of greenery then called Westlake (now MacArthur)
Park interrupted its asphalt course was to many drivers an abomination.
In 1934 the park was bisected. Call the wound symptomatic. Urban
development was changing direction. Following the Los Angeles pattern,
cities would diffuse rather than concentrate, and there was no time on the
way out to pause, even for greenness.

Diffusion, mobility, and rapid growth brought to the residents of Los
Angeles and other cities of the southland a gnawing sense of personal
isolation. The result, some sociologists believe, was a frantic quest for
community through state picnics, religious cults, mystic involvements.
Meantime business somehow had to catch the attention of these floating
wisps. Billboards and lighted signs proliferated; hard-sell commercial
architecture featured such eye catchers as ice cream parlors housed in
overgrown concrete milk bottles, refreshment stands built and colored
like giant oranges, restaurants shaped like derby hats.

The maze afforded such endless fodder to satirists that solid accomplishments were overlooked. During this same period, modern architecture, adapting to the bright skies and mild climate, began to find expression in the work of Richard Neutra and Bertram Goodhue, designer of
perhaps the best civic building constructed in California in the 1920's, the
Los Angeles Public Library. The Pasadena Playhouse flourished as a
training ground for actors. The Los Angeles Symphony took shape,
presenting many of its concerts outdoors in the 22,000-seat Hollywood
Bowl. Henry E. Huntington repaid some of his family's debt to the state
by creating on his San Marino estate the magnificent Huntington Art
Gallery, Library, and Botanical Gardens, opened to the public in 1927.
By the end of the decade the southland, so generally berated as the
incomprehensible citadel of kooks and conservatism, was ready to challenge the supremacy of San Francisco's elegant but somewhat compla-

cent musical and theatrical offerings, galleries, and museums.

Commerically there was no question where leadership lay. San Francisco, to be sure, remained the financial heart of the West, in large part because of Amadeo Giannini's building of the Bank of America into the largest institution of its kind in the world. Otherwise, the southland's business activity was preeminent. By 1924 the man-made harbor at San Pedro was the busiest on the coast. In 1929, Los Angeles County's 4,908 manufacturing establishments turned out products worth $1.32 billion, whereas the 3,903 plants in the San Francisco-Oakland area brought in a lesser $1.17 billion. When automobile and tire companies began opening Western branch plants, the majority sought Los Angeles, not because of the open shop, as the Chamber of Commerce still insisted, but because of the convenient conjunction of large labor pools (whether unionized or not), ample water, plenty of electricity, growing markets, and well-developed transportation facilities of all kinds, not the least, for the tire companies, being the truck routes to the new cotton fields of the San Joaquin Valley.

Three indigenous industries helped carry the graph ever higher: aviation, motion pictures, and petroleum. The land's beneficent climate had much to do with wooing the first two. Because of dependable weather, the nation's first international air show was held at Dominguez Field near Long Beach on January 10, 1910. The excitement spurred the opening of several small plane factories in a variety of makeshift buildings, including an abandoned church. The First World War added unexpected stimulus. San Diego became a major training ground, and in 1917 an astounding 212 planes massed over the city in celebration of the armistice. In 1922, a one-time army flier, T. C. Ryan, established the country's first scheduled air passenger service; it ran between Los Angeles and San Diego. Five years later Charles Lindbergh electrified the world by flying from New York to Paris in one of Ryan's San Diego-built planes.

The movies reached Hollywood, then a small village devoted to growing vegetables for Los Angeles, at about the same time that aviation reached Dominguez Field. The original camera crankers were in flight from the process servers of Edison's monopolistic film company in the East. Burrowing out of sight in Hollywood, they discovered unexpected bonuses: a greater number of clear days for shooting and a wider variety of scenic backgrounds than were available in New Jersey. Even so, they were cautious, and development at first was imitative. Not until Europeans and Easterners had shown the dramatic possibilities of "feature-length" productions did Hollywood leap aboard the bandwagon. Once there, it quickly took over the reins, marshaled funds in New York, fostered the rube-dazzling star system, and within a decade had created a fantasy world of almost immeasurable force and profit.

Expensive cinema palaces, their lofty ceilings atwinkle with lights, became a civic necessity throughout the land, nowhere more so than in California. Tourists swarmed to Hollywood to take sightseeing tours past the homes of the famous, dropping hundreds of millions of dollars en route. The svelte figures of leading ladies helped swing the national diet from meat, bread, and potatoes to lettuce, celery, tomatoes, and orange juice, with corresponding adjustments in the state's agriculture. A craze to imitate the casual clothing of the stars at play made Los Angeles the country's leading manufacturer of sportswear. Resorts like Palm Springs owed their success to the favors of these new arbiters of taste. And all this centered, paradoxically, in moralistic Los Angeles, whose rural-born millions read of the movie colony's high jinks and shocking scandals with delicious shivers of self-righteousness.

These things were much, but towering above them, both in dollars and in corruption, was the petroleum industry. Between 1917 and 1929, fifteen new fields were opened in the San Joaquin Valley, Ventura County, and the Los Angeles Basin. At some of the areas, notably Signal Hill back of Long Beach, derricks were packed so tightly together that their legs interlocked, and a wildly inefficient race began to suck more fluid from the ground than a neighbor could. The state's production leaped from 103 million barrels in 1920 to 263 million in 1923. The tax money that resulted upgraded schools, hospitals, libraries, and county highways. But the dazzling profits also presented temptations.

The most notorious scandal involved Albert B. Fall, President Harding's Secretary of the Interior from New Mexico. As a protection for the Navy during the war, the government had established two reserves on land underlaid, so geologists believed, with huge pools of oil. One reserve, Teapot Dome, was in Wyoming, beyond our concern. The other was Elk Hills in the San Joaquin Valley.

Elk Hills attracted the eye of Edward Doheny, who had struck the first oil within the Los Angeles city limits and later had helped open sections of the San Joaquin. In Mexico he had made more millions. As he aged he grew wispy, until he looked something like a movie stereotype of a New England storekeeper. He lived simply, gave liberal sums to the University of Southern California, and dabbled in politics. He headed the state's delegation to the Democratic National Convention when it met in San Francisco in 1920, and was offered to that body as a potential nominee for the vice-presidency. His attorney was Woodrow Wilson's gangling son-in-law and Secretary of the Treasury, William Gibbs McAdoo.

Doheny hardly needed more money. Still, if he could tap Elk Hills the way Harry Sinclair was tapping Teapot Dome. . . . It so happened that about then Secretary Fall, whom Doheny had known during harder times in New Mexico, needed a little loan for buying a cattle ranch. Doheny sent his son around with a suitcase stuffed with $100,000 in cash. A casual favor to an old friend, he later told Congress; $100,000 meant no more to him, he said, than $25 to the average man. But possibly it meant more to Fall. He executed a secret lease of Elk Hills to his pal.

The California story became public property during the Teapot Dome investigations. Fall, a broken man by the time the trials were over, went to prison, the first U.S. Cabinet officer to do so. Doheny lost his Elk Hills lease but was acquitted of bribery. The disgusted populace thereupon turned its shafts on luckless McAdoo, who had known nothing of the shenanigans. In 1924, McAdoo, a California resident since 1922, was seeking the Democratic nomination for the presidency of the United States. Unhappily for him, it was widely known that he had done legal work for Doheny. Although the connection was honest, it destroyed him. Every time his name was mentioned at the nominating convention, bellows of "Oil! Oil! Oil!" rained down from the balconies. After 103 ballots, he lost the nomination to John W. Davis.

To tens of thousands of California investors, more painful scandals than Doheny's were those involving the Julian Petroleum Company, a stock fraud that in 1927 cost the gullible public $150 million, and the Richfield Oil Company, which went into receivership after losing $56 million as the result of embezzlement and gross inefficiency. In both cases the tarry touch of dishonesty smeared public officials and revered civic leaders. There were suicides, trials, jail sentences, and, worst of all, shaken public confidence. And still the toll continued with the crash of three leading building and loan and mortgage associations. No other American city, according to historian John Caughey, ever suffered so many bankruptcies caused by fraud as did Los Angeles at the close of the 1920's.

It had been a wild, overcharged ride through continually inflated prosperity. But the cooling off had come, and now the state, along with the rest of the nation, was headed for real trouble.

part six

INTO NOW

25. Double Helpings of the Same

Twice-told delusions: Like the forty-niners, the immigrants who stampeded into Southern California throughout the 1920's found that they had pursued a yearning for self-fulfillment into strangeness. It wasn't just a difference of place. The whole ambience of the southland was as unnatural to them as the gouged placer diggings had been to their predecessors. Here, in a desert remade by technology, was their dream village. But with terrible speed, water pipes, electricity, and gasoline spun the village out beyond comprehension, obliterating the sense of individual ties that had helped give meaning to the towns from which the immigrants had fled. And so they wandered, psychologically at least, looking for fresh anchors. The forty-niners could have told them about that, too.

Appearances of stability abounded. In return for a properly executed mortgage, a man could snuggle down in his stuccoed, single-family, lawn-girt dwelling, take pride in a new car that let him visit startling extremes of scenery within a single weekend, and all the while feel bolstered in his new freedom by his savings account and by payments coming in from the farm or business he had sold in the Midwest. At the outset these things and sunshine had seemed enough. But there is always a better gold strike just over the hill. Thousands of hustlers dinned opportunity at them—oil stocks, real estate, and extra-big interest payments in the newest building and loan associations. Like gold-rushers, the newcomers swarmed into the new fields and, as we have seen, most returned from the adventure with only burned hands to show.

On top of those shocks came the waves of the nationwide depression of the 1930's. Incomes from home dried up. Banks failed, wiping out savings accounts. Mortgage holders foreclosed. With devastating abruptness skilled laborers, genteel white-collar workers, and retired elderly found themselves reduced to living on relief payments of $16.20 a month.

Where now were the anchors in Eden?

The state's own income producers offered no help. California's agricultural earnings dropped from $750 million in 1929 to $327 million in 1932; freight car loadings fell by half; oil companies producing 875,000 barrels a day could sell only 675,000. Drastic cutbacks became inevitable. But because California had always been touted as the land of opportunity, unemployed from elsewhere instinctively drifted that way, hoping that at least the vaunted climate would prove kindly to a shelterless man in threadbare clothing. By 1934, some 1.25 million destitute—about 20 percent of the state's population—were living on public relief.

An impoverished forty-niner had been able to blame hard luck for his failure—or, more satisfyingly, the Mexicans who were skimming away gold that belonged to Americans. But where did one fix blame for the failings of a trusted economic system? Abstract talk of overproduction, overspeculation, and national frivolity was not a satisfactory purge for the emotions. One needed scapegoats. Out with the old leaders, in with the new! And down with the Red Menace, a favorite villain of William Randolph Hearst, whose newspaper chain blanketed the state.

As in most other parts of the country, Republicans sat astride the local government. In 1930 California's registered Republicans outnumbered Democrats 3 to 1. As governor they elected an amiable but shallow political trouper, "Sunny" Jim Rolph, former mayor of San Francisco. His lieutenant governor was Frank Merriam, an aging standpatter from Long Beach, a fixture in the state legislature. And so the roll went. Both of California's United States Senators and ten of its eleven Congressmen were Republicans. Republicans held 37 of 40 seats in the state senate, 74 of 80 in the assembly. Such bones as fell to the Democrats merely produced furious intraparty strife that made the vast Republican monolith harder than ever to crack—or so it seemed.

The national agony changed that. Within less than two years the Republican preponderance shrank from 3 to 1 to 3 to 2. And even Republicans liked the New Deal promises. That intransigent loner, Senator Hiram Johnson, announced his support of Roosevelt, as did most of the state's leading newspapers. In 1932, FDR's unprecedented triumph helped carry long-frustrated William Gibbs McAdoo to Washington as California's second Democratic Senator in 35 years.

Sages all predicted continued Democratic triumphs when the contests for the state's main office were held in 1934. Even the rattled Republicans seemed determined to help in their own defeat. To take just one example: although state revenues were tumbling disastrously, Governor Rolph vetoed a state income tax on the rich in favor of a general sales tax on everybody. Because the levy included food transactions, it bore most onerously on multitudes who could barely afford to eat. The reaction was inevitable—out with the rascals!

Confidence was further shaken by raging class warfare in the fields. After the withdrawal of the Japanese, the growers in the state's huge, fertile valleys had turned increasingly to Mexican and Filipino labor. The first group, reputedly docile and inured to heat, dust, and aridity, was particularly favored among the sugar beets and in the expanding cotton fields of the southern San Joaquin Valley. In 1900 there had been only 8,000 Mexicans in California—an erstwhile Mexican province! But in 1920 there were 121,000 and ten years later 368,000.*

Most came because they were enticed. As harvest time neared, Spanish-speaking labor contractors went south across the border to poverty pockets in Mexico. By glowing use of that most magic of *norteamericano* words, "dollar," they signed on batches of workers who were then moved north in bands, like sheep. At first the workers were trucked to the fields by the employers. This was so miserable an experience that the exploited escaped it as soon as possible with that dream of all poor people, an automobile. These traveling wrecks, propelled mostly by a series of sporadic inner explosions, let wives and children accompany the men to the labor camps. The conditions they found were as wretched as always—substandard wages, rows of hovels devoid of conveniences, and a deliberate segregation from nearby towns and other workers, lest discontent prompt efforts at combination. The growers pled necessity. Water, taxes, machinery, spraying, and other operational costs were fixed. Only by paring harvest costs, they said, could California's all-important agricultural industry withstand the fierce nationwide competition brought on by the Great Panic.

As soon as the harvest was over, the migrants were told to move on. Although some returned to Mexico, most could not. Those glowing dollars had proved illusory. Such money as had survived the demands of daily living had been sent, for the most part, to needy relatives at home. Now the indigent must find some way of surviving until the next harvest.

Battered caravans drifted south over the Ridge Route into the Los Angeles Basin. There the migrants sought out the ragtag collection of huts and odorous outhouses, surrounded by collapsed automobiles, that served as home for Mexicans who worked in nearby citrus groves, vineyards, and packing plants. Screened behind trees or isolated beyond the railroad tracks, these *colonias* were true settlements. The thousands of children born in them were by law American citizens. Yet to most Californians they were morally as well as physically invisible. Community

*Between 1920 and 1930 the number of Filipinos in the state rose from 2,700 to 30,500.

services—sewers, water, garbage collection, police and fire protection, and, most vital of all, schools—reached the *colonias* slowly if at all.

Even in the heart of Los Angeles the picture was comparable. Thousands of Mexicans crowded into "courts," collections of flimsy rooms, mostly unfloored, built around cramped plazas and served by communal water faucets and communal outdoor toilets. One favorite spot, until it was usurped by those marvels of Americana, a freeway and Dodger Stadium, was Chavez Ravine. This harshly eroded gulch and others within clear view of the city hall's heavy tower had been left untouched during the city's headlong expansion toward more delectable suburbs. Poor people, mostly Mexicans, flocked in and hung flimsy shacks on the precarious slopes. In those strange villages within the monster village, more thousands of Americans were born, learning their own variety of English as best they could, wearing cheap imitations of American clothing, and struggling desperately to adapt to a civilization that did not want them except as cheap labor on construction projects or, briefly, at harvest time in the Valley.

Public relief provided sustenance during periods of unemployment. But as relief rolls swelled, beset taxpayers raised objections to caring for tens of thousands of foreigners while Americans were out of work. In February, 1931, Los Angeles authorities began rounding up aliens and sending them back across the border by the trainload. It was an exercise in futility. Some of the ejected, finding poverty in California less crushing than in Mexico, sneaked back. Labor contractors went after more, used them, and then kicked them onto the highways again, to repeat the process.

Such a stew was bound to boil over. Late in the 1920's, the reputedly docile Mexicans of the Imperial Valley struck twice for higher wages and better living conditions. Both attempts were crushed. Discontent kept showing itself nonetheless as the growers, pinched by falling profits, tried to slice wages still more. *¡Basta!*—enough! Of the 84 agricultural strikes that occurred throughout the United States during 1930–32, 44 took place in California.

The void among the workers was leadership. The I.W.W. had been eliminated, and because of racial animosities and the failure of the field workers to stay in one place, the American Federation of Labor was not really interested. Into the gap came the Communists, forming in 1933 the Cannery and Agricultural Workers' Union. Passions flamed instantly. Reds in the heartland! The Hearst papers and the Los Angeles *Times* worked themselves into frenzies, a righteousness given smug confirmation by the discovery, dramatically recorded in John Steinbeck's novel

In Dubious Battle, that the organizers were battling for power rather than for the workers.

The new union launched 24 strikes involving 37,000 workers and $200 million worth of pears, grapes, peas, celery, and cotton. The biggest walkout was at Corcoran in the San Joaquin Valley, where the union rented a 40-acre field, set up a camp for the strikers, and tried to halt the entire cotton harvest. They failed. Eleven ranchers indicted for killing three workers during an attack on a union meeting were acquitted; strike-breakers were imported from Mexico; pickets were manhandled by armed deputies. After 24 days the union accepted a mediated settlement that on paper looked like a gain but actually proved little since nonunion men remained in the fields after the peace.

As the union stepped up its activitites, the growers responded by forming the Associated Farmers of California, Incorporated. The State Chamber of Commerce and the State Farm Bureau lent their blessings. The California Packing Company (a huge canning firm), the Bank of America, and the Pacific Gas and Electric Company provided funds. Whenever a strike erupted, volunteer deputies, mostly members of the American Legion, offered their services and were armed with newly lathed pick handles. Officials of the Associated Farmers were often allowed by the county sheriffs to take over the direction of tactics. The State Highway Patrol countenanced and sometimes supported armed guards running truckloads of produce through the strikers' picket lines. Fiery crosses burned at night on hillsides above the workers' camps. Their meetings were disrupted by tear gas shells lobbed out of the darkness. In the farm towns fundamentalist preachers fervently linked Satan and Communism. Excited mobs, reviving the vigilantism of earlier times, joyously beat dark-skinned wanderers on the streets or upset food trucks sent to the camps by city sympathizers.

Wages did go up—a little. State investigating committees did glance at the camps and cluck. But momentum was with the growers. By means of wholesale arrests for vagrancy and a dusting off of the old Criminal Syndicalism laws, they broke the leaders of the Cannery and Agricultural Union. Dust bowl migrants swarming into the valley in search of jobs completed the disorganization. Though 1936 saw desperation strikes by Mexican workers in the citrus groves of Orange County and in the lettuce fields of the Salinas Valley, the situation remained as it always had been —in the control of the growers and their organizations.

Strikers on the waterfront fared better. Emboldened by a provision in the National Industrial Recovery Act that allowed workers to form unions of their own choice for collective bargaining with employers, laborers led by Australian-born Harry Bridges formed the International Long-shoremen's Union. Its primary goal in 1934 was to elbow aside the employer-dominated union that supervised hiring through a system (so the workers believed) of favoritism, bootlicking, and discrimination against men who would not toe the bosses' line.

When employers refused recognition, the new union on May 9, 1934, called a strike that tied up every port on the Pacific Coast from San Diego to Seattle. Determined not to let San Francisco return to the closed-shop situation of the early 1900's, the employers and the San Francisco Chamber of Commerce dug in for a protracted battle. No yielding to Communists!—for that charge swiftly became a city as well as a rural slogan.

The impasse was a grievous blow to an already stunned economy. Unable to ship their products, manufacturing plants in the cities, lumber-mills on the redwood coast, and oil refineries in the Los Angeles Basin either shut down or curtailed operations, putting more unemployed into the bread lines. Farmers and canners eyeing bumper crops wondered what they would do if normal shipments by water proved impossible.

Trying to force a solution, the employers on July 5, 1934, prevailed on the city to marshal 1,000 policemen as an escort for strikebreakers. They were met by 5,000 pickets. Stones flew; trucks were overturned and burned; scabs and strikers were beaten. Then the shooting began, from both sides. By nightfall two strikers were dead and a hundred or so men were wounded.

The rioting was checked by Frank Merriam. He was governor then, as a result of Rolph's death in June, and he aspired to a four-year term in his own right. Thus his reaction to the San Francisco strike was wholly political. Although the mayor of the city did not ask for troops, Merriam sent them in, bayonets fixed.

Labor protested by calling a general strike on July 19. Eerie silence fell across the normally bustling streets as 150,000 workers left their jobs.

Hoping to forestall public hostility, strategists among the strikers allowed the delivery of essential items to hospitals, orphanages, and the like, and permitted nineteen restaurants to open for men who normally ate out. The gesture backfired, for the operation went forward under big signs that amounted to licenses by the union. To many citizens this taking over of civic processes seemed intolerable arrogance. They cheered militiamen who tore the permits off restaurant doors and from the sides of delivery trucks. As popular disgust soared, the union leaders fell to quarreling among themselves. Within four days the general strike collapsed, and to the employers Merriam was the man of the hour.

The sullen dockworkers stayed out until October. By then the whole state was chafing, and federal mediators were able to force on the employers reformed hiring procedures and recognition of the new union. There was little rejoicing, however. The whirlwinds of distress were sweeping masses of oddly assorted dissidents into one of the strangest political confrontations that California has ever known.

Precipitator of the uproar was Upton Sinclair, born in Baltimore in 1878 and educated at both the City College of New York and Columbia. He was a crack tennis player, a vegetarian, a teetotaler, and a volcano of words. At first Sinclair spent his extraordinary fluency on stories for the popular pulp magazines of the era, but soon switched to attacks against the capitalistic system, which in his mind was the cause of democracy's ills. In 1906 he published a powerful novel, *The Jungle*, in the hope that it would awaken the country to the plight of new immigrants in the Chicago stockyards. Instead, his graphic descriptions of the filthy industry nauseated his middle-class readers into demanding the country's first pure-food legislation. When no comparable legislation emerged for the workers, the newly prosperous author remarked sourly that although he had aimed for the nation's heart, he had hit its stomach.

In 1916 he settled in Southern California. While continuing his flood of muckraking novels, notably *Oil!*, he campaigned at different times on the Socialist ticket for a seat in the House of Representatives, in the United States Senate, and in the governor's mansion at Sacramento. California business interests considered him contemptible but not worrisome. They did not change their opinion when he announced, in 1933, that he was leaving the Socialist party and registering as a Democrat so that he could run the following year on that ticket for the governorship.

Typically, he embellished the announcement with yet another book— his forty-seventh or forty-eighth—entitled *I, Governor of California and How I Ended Poverty: A True Story of the Future*. In it Sinclair proposed a socialistic system of production for use, not profit. To raise money (Rolph's treasury surplus of $24 million in 1930 had shrunk by 1934 to a deficit of $65 million), the state would replace the general sales tax with a stiff, graduated income tax and heavy levies on corporations, banks, and insurance companies. A 10 percent penalty would be imposed—shades of Henry George!—on unused land.

With this revenue, the state would buy idle land on which to establish farm colonies for the unemployed. The state would also take over unused canneries, garment factories, lumbermills, and the like. Products turned out by those establishments would be bartered for colony food by means of scrip. On top of that, all persons over sixty would receive a pension of $50 a month. When questions were raised about such problems as distribution, credit, and competition from capitalistic concerns, Sinclair answered vaguely. After all, it never behooves a radical to be too explicit.

His utopian seeds fell on fertile ground. The nadir of the depression reached California during the campaign. Yearning for light in the darkness, tens of thousands of voters had embraced the New Deal, only to find that California's old-line Democrats, snapping and quarreling over patronage resulting from the national victories in 1932, had nothing to offer in local affairs.

Into this vacuum came Upton Sinclair's EPIC plan—"End Poverty in California." Despairing people, their life savings gone, immersed themselves in the plan with the same fervor that had led many into ecstatic acceptance of the Four Square Gospel of Sister Aimee McPherson or the thundering fundamentalism of the Reverend Robert Shuler. Salvation! The response, particularly south of the Tehachapi Mountains, dumfounded regular party leaders, eight of whom leaped into the lists to snatch the nomination from the presumptuous reach of this Socialistic intruder.

It was no use. Sinclair grew daily stronger. When party regulars shut their pocketbooks, he financed his campaign by selling scores of thousands of copies of *I, Governor* and by printing a weekly newspaper, Upton Sinclair's *EPIC News*, which boasted a circulation of 1.4 million copies. In place of party organization, there were EPIC clubs—more than 2,000 of them as the primaries drew near. They sufficed. Sinclair and his candidate for lieutenant governor, Sheridan Downey—inevitably they were tagged Uppie and Downie—rolled up more votes than all their opponents combined.

The state Democratic organization buttoned securely in his pocket, Sinclair rushed east for a conference with Franklin Roosevelt and emerged declaring that the President would soon endorse him. The assumption proved overly optimistic. FDR, skirting gingerly around EPIC socialism, stayed silent. But California labor declared in Sinclair's favor, the number of EPIC clubs swelled toward 3,000, and for the first time in the century Democratic registrations passed Republican.

Terrified Republicans poured money into the battle. Strategy was entrusted—this had never before happened in the United States—to professional publicists, the high-pressure, trailblazing firm of Clem Whitaker and Leona Baxter. Under their direction the state was plastered with anti-Sinclair billboards, a then-unique use of that automobile-oriented medium. Sinclair's books were combed for quotations—and they abounded—that could be made to sound scornful of religion, puritanical morals, and the American way of business. Radios dinned out the scurrilous findings. Movie producers and newspapers faked horrifying "documentaries" about undesirables already flooding west to milk the EPIC cow. To blunt Sinclair's something-for-nothing appeals, Merriam went him one better by endorsing Dr. Frank Townsend's $200-a-month pension for all residents over sixty years of age.

Unprecedented numbers trooped to the polls in November, 1934. Those who could stomach neither Merriam nor Sinclair turned to a third-party candidate, Raymond Haight. The rest searched their consciences in secret, returned to traditional modes, and in spite of heavy Democratic registration seated Republican candidates in most state offices, including the governorship.

It was not a victory for the publicists. They had channeled anti-EPIC sentiment, but they had not created it. What had welled up, in Democrats and Republicans alike, was an expression of faith in California's ingrained patterns of progress, as made visible at the time of the election in vast public work programs devoted to typical California objectives—moving automobiles and moving water. Within that framework, Merriam seemed familiar. Sinclair did not.

Aided by federal money, San Francisco was at last breaking her geographic barriers by thrusting magnificent bridges—the biggest in the world at the time, a bore to keep saying, but that's the way it was—east across the Bay to Oakland and north across the Golden Gate to Marin County. A midway pier of the Oakland span was Goat Island, originally called Yerba Buena by the Spanish. The debris produced by the roadmakers in tunneling through Yerba Buena's hills was hauled to the island's north shore and used to create what was named Treasure Island. On that man-made expanse the Bay area held, in 1939, another lavish exposition to commemorate the opening of the bridges—a gesture to the world as exuberant as the Panama-Pacific Exposition had been 23 years before. The earthquake of economic disaster, the people were saying, could no more halt the city than the physical quake of 1906 had.

More stupendous than the bridges were the projects devoted to appropriating water from the Colorado and Sacramento rivers for the sake of urban and agricultural developments far removed from the streams themselves. There were several of these, intricately linked, but the one that thrilled the nation with renewed faith in America's technological prowess was mighty Hoover Dam, its concrete bulk plugging desolate Black Canyon between Nevada and Arizona.

This giant growth sprang from seeds first planted by the relatively minute Imperial Valley Irrigation District. Formed in 1911, as already noted, the District's original purpose had been the buying of the badly managed canals of the California Development Company, by then a subsidiary of the Southern Pacific Railroad. As soon as the Valley farmers had their hands on the system, they grew ambitious. Why not remove the alternate threats of flood and drought that hung over the canals by persuading the federal government to tame the unruly, silt-laden Colorado with a dam located somewhere upstream? Then, for good measure, let the government build them a new cement-lined canal through the sand dunes on the American side of the border and thus rid them of the complications that beset the old canal's course within Mexican territory.

The notions were not pure fancy. Engineers of the Federal Bureau of Reclamation had long since stated that it was theoretically possible to control the lower Colorado River by means of a high dam in either Boulder or Black canyon, far above the intakes of the Imperial Valley canals. But who was to pay? The dam that choked either one of those inhospitable canyons would have to be far larger than any other structure on earth. Why should the taxpayers of all the nation assume such a bill for the sake of wetting one corner of California? Not until craggy Phil Swing, longtime lawyer for the Imperial Irrigation District, was elected to Congress in 1920 did anyone even venture proposing the absurdity to Congress.

Swing's initial legislative act authorizing the dam sent tremors throughout the West. The Colorado River was the single greatest resource of a vast, semiarid region. One foreign nation (Mexico) and seven states (Wyoming, Colorado, Utah, New Mexico, Nevada, Arizona, and California) embraced long stretches of either the main stream or its principal tributaries. By law, water diversion anywhere along the river would create rights that would have to be observed for all time by other potential users. If California began siphoning away substantial quantities of water, developments elsewhere might be forever checked. That was enough to bring all seven of the states up fighting.

To stop the squabbling, Secretary of Commerce Herbert Hoover persuaded the states concerned to meet in Santa Fe in November, 1922, and work out a division of the available flow, with some left over in case Mexico asserted her rights. When Arizona was not granted as much as she felt she deserved, her representatives withdrew in a huff. The others completed the compact anyway, granting Arizona what they considered just, and now each state knew the maximum amount of water she could divert from the river.

The agreement brought Swing's bill no nearer to passage. Arizona politicians in league with private power companies that dreaded competition from publicly generated electricity quickly buried the proposal. Imperial Valley simply did not have muscle enough to support such grandiose pretensions.

At that point, 1923, a powerful ally appeared. William Mulholland, head of the Los Angeles Water Department (this was before the disaster in San Francisquito Canyon), had been eyeing with amazement his city's leaping growth. After drawing a few projection curves, he told the equally astonished yet happy officials of the municipal government that very shortly the still-embattled Owens Valley aqueduct would not be able to meet demands. To forestall water famine, Los Angeles should lay claim to a goodly portion of the river flow recently allotted California under the six-state compact. That in turn would mean supporting Imperial Valley's fight for a control dam, because the city's project would also depend on the mighty structure—its flood protection, its water storage capacity, and, above all, its electricity, vital for pumping the waters of the man-made river across the desert mountains to Los Angeles.

Was the wild scheme possible? Surveyors flocked into the wastelands. After studying more than 50 aqueduct routes, they picked one whose intake would leave the Colorado near a place called Parker, 150 miles below the sites being considered for the control dam. Assured that the water could be transported, the city next laid claim to 1.1 million acre feet of the river's annual flow, nearly 4 times the amount carried by the Owens Valley aqueduct. And now to create an administrative unit for handling the monstrous project. After endless polishing, municipal attorneys succeeded in drafting legal guidelines for what they called the Metropolitan Water District of Southern California. If Sacramento approved, this District, which spread across Los Angeles and ten neighboring cities, would be empowered to finance, build, and maintain the reservoirs, canals, transmission lines, filtering plants, and so on needed to turn paper plans into concrete reality.

The nation's giant utility lobby, which was simultaneously trying to checkmate the proposed dams of the Tennessee Valley Authority, fought the Southern California plans both in Sacramento and in Washington. Sheer weight of numbers brought Los Angeles victory in the state legislature, and in 1927 the Metropolitan Water District was formally sanctioned. In Washington the fight was harder, even though that formidable Western warrior, Senator Hiram Johnson, had joined Congressman Swing in pushing for the dam.

Ultimately the balance was tipped by the election of a Californian, Herbert Hoover, as President of the United States. In December, 1928, well before the depression had made public work projects popular, the Bureau of Reclamation was authorized to spend nearly $50 million building Hoover Dam in Black Canyon. (Boulder Dam is a misnomer resulting from the pleasanter-sounding name of the alternative site.) Another $76 million was earmarked for running a huge cement-lined canal into Imperial Valley and then on north into Coachella Valley. A $126 million oak from Imperial Valley's little acorn! For the first time, the United States was made acutely aware of the weight that Southern California could pack, once it had decided to act.

Work on Hoover Dam began September, 1930, as the depression was deepening. One year later, on September 29, 1931, when the economic outlook was really bleak, voters of the Metropolitan Water District authorized, by a margin of 5 to 1, the spending of $220 million—more than 4 times the cost of the Hoover Dam—for building the complex elements of their own project. The first part of the system, spatially, was Parker Dam, for creating Lake Havasu. Arizona, hoping to remind the country that she too had stakes in the river, sent out the militia to halt the work. The farce lasted only a day or two, and the work roared on. From Havasu a massive aqueduct ran 242 miles west. Along the way were 92 miles of tunnel, pump lifts of 1,700 feet, and 29 miles of inverted siphons for crossing 144 canyons of varying extent. The discharge point was the huge reservoir of Lake Mathews, south of Riverside. From there a maze of laterals laced the southland.

A $220 million folly, concocted mostly for the benefit of the fat landlords of the Imperial Valley? There were those who said so, only to be chanted down by the faithful. The project was already providing 11,000 jobs, wasn't it, and as soon as water began flowing west again, so would people. The California shibboleth: water equals growth equals prosperity. It had always been true in the past, hadn't it?

The $76 million Imperial and Coachella Valley canals produced less fanfare. For one thing, the project brought about a massive evasion of United States law. The Newlands Act of 1902, which had established the Reclamation Service, stated that no one man or company could obtain government-developed water for more than 160 acres—or 320 acres for married couples in community-property states like California.

Congressman Swing was well aware of this law and of his constituents' hatred for it. Years earlier, the pioneer settlers of the Imperial Valley had tarred and feathered a representative of the Reclamation Service whom they suspected of wanting to impose the restriction on them. Their discovery that they could improve their water system only with government help had not changed their hostility. All during the Congressional push for the project, Swing had been careful not to mention limitations. As soon as the law had passed, he began dropping around to see influential people. Let's be reasonable: those Valley farms, many of them far larger than 320 acres—as they had to be to carry the costs of machinery and water—had been wrested from the desert when there had been no thought of limits. Would it be fair to penalize the owners now?

In February, 1933, a week before the Hoover administration left office, the Secretary of the Interior, Dr. Ray Lyman Wilbur, also a Californian, decided that Swing had a point and that as far as the Imperial Valley was concerned the laws of the United States could be ignored. The normal acreage limitation, he stated by letter, "does not apply to lands now

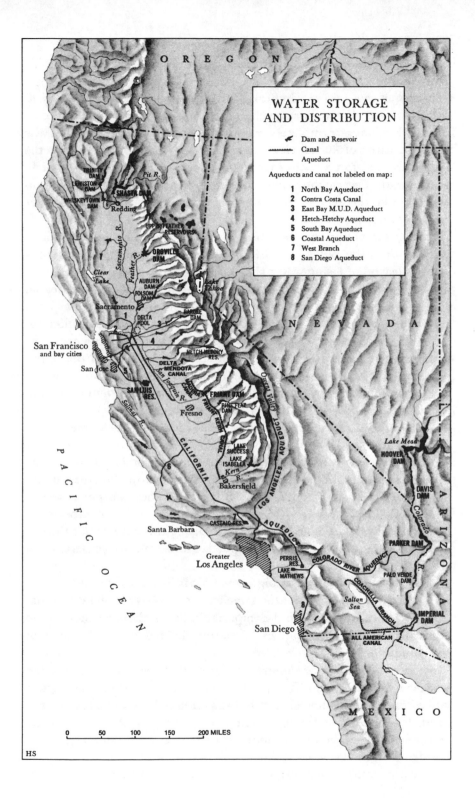

WATER STORAGE
AND DISTRIBUTION

🜞 Dam and Resevoir
~~~~~~ Canal
――――― Aqueduct

Aqueducts and canal not labeled on map:

1 North Bay Aqueduct
2 Contra Costa Canal
3 East Bay M.U.D. Aqueduct
4 Hetch-Hetchy Aqueduct
5 South Bay Aqueduct
6 Coastal Aqueduct
7 West Branch
8 San Diego Aqueduct

OREGON

NEVADA

ARIZONA

MEXICO

PACIFIC OCEAN

CALIFORNIA

TRINITY DAM
LEWISTON DAM
WHISKEYTOWN DAM
Redding
SHASTA DAM
Pit R.
Sacramento R.
UPPER FEATHER RESERVOIRS
OROVILLE DAM
Clear Lake
Feather R.
AUBURN DAM
FOLSOM DAM
Sacramento
DELTA POOL
PARDEE DAM
Lake Tahoe
San Francisco
and bay cities
San Jose
HETCH HETCHY RES.
DELTA MENDOTA CANAL
SAN LUIS RES.
San Joaquin R.
CALIF. FRIANT KERN CANAL
FRIANT DAM
Fresno
PINE FLAT DAM
LAKE SUCCESS
LAKE ISABELLA
Kern R.
Bakersfield
Salinas R.
Owens Valley
LOS ANGELES AQUEDUCT
Lake Mead
HOOVER DAM
DAVIS DAM
Colorado R.
PARKER DAM
PALO VERDE DAM
CASTAIC RES.
Santa Barbara
Greater
Los Angeles
PERRIS RES.
LAKE MATHEWS
COLORADO RIVER AQUEDUCT
COACHELLA BRANCH
Salton Sea
IMPERIAL DAM
San Diego
ALL AMERICAN CANAL

0   50   100   150   200 MILES

HS

cultivated or having a present water right."

Ought not sauce for the Imperial Valley be sauce for the San Joaquin Valley as well? Water shortages had grown serious there, too. The San Joaquin River was completely exploited. Out beyond the tips of the canals upwards of 40,000 electrically pumped wells were sucking the level of ancient ground water reservoirs lower and lower. In the north, meantime, the Sacramento Valley each year received a surplus of precipitation. Could not some of that water be transferred to the larger, drier San Joaquin?

Though the notion was almost as old as the state, it was not pushed seriously until the 1920's. Opposition came immediately from northern counties fearful of losing water rights, utility firms whose hydroelectric plants hummed in every Sierra canyon, and big ranchers who feared acreage limitations if the federal government financed the work.

The depression softened resistance. Partly in hope of providing jobs, the state in 1933 offered the voters a complex plan for implementing the water transfer by means of two enormous dams—Shasta on the upper Sacramento River and Friant on the San Joaquin—plus 273 miles of canals that would be kept flowing where necessary by mammoth pumping plants. The cost was estimated at $170 million.

Los Angeles County, burdened by her own water developments, opposed the plan as actively as any rancher. The need for employment prevailed, however, and at a statewide election the voters authorized the project by a slim 33,000 margin. Promptly Sacramento offered $170 million in water bonds to the nation's financiers. They did not respond. Undismayed—it seems probable that the reaction had been expected—the authorities then put the bonds in storage and turned to the Bureau of Reclamation. In 1935 the Bureau agreed to undertake the project, using federal funds.

This was exactly what the big growers had feared. Grimly they declared that they would expect the same exemptions from federal law that had been granted ranchers in the Imperial Valley. Otherwise they would be unfairly chained to a one-horse statute devised before the days of mechanization.

Just as grimly, the new Congress retorted that the days of exemption were over. Water subsidized by public taxes was intended for the greatest good of the greatest number, not for a favored few—truly a few, critics added, for 34 corporate landlords (not sturdy yeomen) owned, in the southern San Joaquin Valley alone, 750,000 acres. Why should they be subsidized by the general public?

While this impasse was shaping up, the labor in the fields went on as usual, but with a new cast. As early as 1933 "flivver immigrants" who had gone broke on a multitude of small farms in Oklahoma, Texas, and Arkansas had started rattling west in search of work. In 1935 drought on the plains swelled the flow to a torrent. Appalled by the growing burden on their welfare agencies, Los Angeles officials stationed patrols at the border crossings in an ultimately futile effort to halt the influx. The growers, however, welcomed the newcomers. The sudden surplus of labor enabled them to shunt aside the Mexicans, whose strikes were growing troublesome, and draw instead on this desperate, disorganized throng.

An old pattern. To keep wages down, employers advertised for more hands than they needed. The camps stayed as atrocious as ever. Lucky people crowded fifteen-deep into one-room shacks. The rest lived under bridges or in hovels patched together from cardboard and gunnysacks. They drank from the same irrigation ditches in which they washed. They had no way to dispose of their filth. Disease skittered. Children, many suffering from malnutrition, received only scattered weeks of education in overcrowded schools. A very old story. But this time the exploited were native Americans, and the truth struck home at last in the angry polemics of Carey McWilliams, in John Steinbeck's searing *Grapes of Wrath*, and in Dorothea Lange's stark photographs.

Protest generated investigations, but before the slow mills of the government had ground out anything more than chaff, the advent of the Second World War completed what the New Deal had not wholly accomplished; it shook away the last tendrils of the depression. After Hitler's breaching of France's Maginot Line, Roosevelt called on American aircraft plants to produce 50,000 planes a year, with obvious impact on the factories of Southern California. A simultaneous drive to produce Liberty ships for Britain and her allies reinvigorated San Francisco Bay. Petroleum, chemical, textile, machine tool, and similar factories, together with the state's burgeoning military camps, added to the call for workers.

Tens of thousands of Okies and Arkies fled from the fields to new jobs in the cities. Short-handed, California's corporate farmers turned again to Mexico for help. By promising good wages and decent living conditions—a bargain never wholly kept—growers in all Western states gained from the Mexican government license to import seasonal laborers who at the end of the harvest were to be returned free of cost to their homes. These transportation bills led the employers to cry out so dolorously that the federal government agreed to help pay the bill—this at a time when farm prices were skyrocketing to unprecedented levels.

No one noticed this additional windfall to the state's most favored industry. Japan's attack on Pearl Harbor thoroughly stunned the West.

Fear shivered through the land. What defenseless city would be the next victim? Improvised blackouts dimmed patterns of lights that otherwise might lead bombers to strategic targets. Volunteer air-raid wardens scanned the skies; hastily mobilized defense units prepared for chaos. As the hysteria mounted, suspicious eyes turned on the 112,000 or so Japanese, two-thirds of them American citizens, who lived along the Pacific Coast.

False reports of Japanese fifth-column activities in Hawaii sprang out of nowhere and flashed through the cities. The ease with which California power lines and harbor installations might be sabotaged led to panicked conclusions that sabotage was already planned. Racial prejudices as old as the gold rush mushroomed again. All Orientals were treacherous, sly, disloyal. For the safety of the war effort they must be contained.

No one succumbed to the jitters more completely than did Lieutenant General John L. DeWitt, head of the Western Defense Command. In the excitement he ignored the Army's presumption that the Japanese Americans in Hawaii were as trustworthy as any other citizens. He attributed the lack of sabotage in California to the Orientals' crafty waiting for a proper moment to let loose a concerted blast. On February 14, 1942, after conferences with Mayor Fletcher Bowron of Los Angeles and Earl Warren, then attorney general of California, he formally requested that he be allowed to remove from the vicinity of the coast all persons of Japanese ancestry.

Five days later President Roosevelt issued—and the Supreme Court subsequently upheld—the necessary order. As if to confirm its rightness a lone submarine surfaced near Santa Barbara on February 23 and fired a few ineffective shells at some oil storage tanks. A prelude to invasion! —or perhaps, some cynics whispered, the United States Navy was playing games in order to stimulate war work. Alarms mounted. A night or two after the submarine episode, nervous watchers spotted in the sky above Los Angeles, or thought they did, objects that have never been conclusively identified. Antiaircraft guns cut loose with a dazzling display that brought millions of gawkers stampeding onto their front porches. To the echo of that din, some 93,000 California Japanese were removed from their homes—it has been estimated that they lost $365 million through the forced sale of their possessions—and were taken with others from Washington and Oregon to inland "relocation centers" snugly surrounded by barbed wire. The majority remained in those camps until 1946.

Young Mexicans in the spreading barrios of East Los Angeles also became the scapegoats of fervor. Gregarious by nature, yet shut away by racial prejudice from the normal entertainment centers of the city, these *pachucos*, as they were called, asserted themselves by banding together in groups that Anglos described as "gangs." Like hippies of a more recent date, the *pachucos* used bizarre dress to emphasize their alienation. Their jackets had abnormally long skirts and exaggerated shoulders; the trousers, tight at the ankles, rose nearly to the wearer's armpits. Belligerent Anglos called these outfits "zoot suits" and chose to regard them as symbols of un-Americanism. Early in June, 1943, hundreds of off-duty military personnel, followed by yelling civilians, stormed along the edges of the Mexican section of Los Angeles, beating every zoot suiter they could catch. This small-scale civil war was not interrupted until diplomats reminded Army and Navy officers and the Los Angeles newspapers that Mexico was an ally, fighting the Axis in defense of the same freedoms that Americans professed to cherish. Belatedly then, MP's and municipal police moved in to restore order.

Such backlashes were perhaps inevitable. Almost overnight California, home of Hiram Johnson and long a center of isolationism, had to be remade into a major military camp and staging area for troops bound for the far side of the world. Military procurement produced incredible economic fevers. The value of goods produced in California factories jumped from $2.8 billion in 1939 to $10.14 billion in 1944. During the same period agricultural output swelled from $625 million to $1.74 billion —enough to make California far and away the leading agricultural state of the nation. During a single year, over 500,000 immigrants, many of them blacks, poured into the state, clamoring for shelter, services, schools, doctors, food, sewers. In such flux how could there be stability?

By the luck of timing, the Metropolitan Water District of Southern California was ready. Swiftly it sent Colorado River water to thirsty new industries and growing towns everywhere south of the Tehachapi Mountains. Even San Diego, hopeful at one time of developing independent supplies through an extension of the All-American Canal, had to surrender to the demands of war and embrace the spreading octopus. Thanks to the momentum generated during those years, the Metropolitan Water District now sprawls across 120 communities inhabited by more than 10 million people.

Demographic patterns were shattered and re-formed overnight. By the droves, men left service industries for factories; women learned to drive trucks and use rivet guns; the state's gold-mining industry, still the producer of $50 million a year, was shut down in order to divert its skilled labor to more essential work—and for golden California that was irony indeed.

For the sake of steel plates for ships, Henry Kaiser built the state's first

396 <small>INTO NOW</small>

steel mill, east of Los Angeles. Such Bay area hamlets as Richmond and Vallejo—poor Mariano Vallejo hadn't been able to make much of the latter place a century earlier—increased their populations from 20,000 to 100,000 each in three years. Hillsides were scabbed with tacky houses slapped down in sterile rows. Flatlands were crowded with trailers. Block-long lines of buyers queued up outside supermarkets in whose service yards discarded crates were tossed in piles higher than the roofs.

How describe the indescribable? Seeking means, an anonymous reporter for the San Francisco *Chronicle* in 1943, hit on the only possible metaphor. "The second gold rush," he wrote, "has hit the West Coast."

Just so. Ninety-four years gone by, populations swollen, contexts totally different, and yet here it was again: the get-rich-quick hopes, the recklessness, intolerance, ingenuity, accomplishment, anomie, yearning, triumph, endurance, waste—all of it rerun on an infinitely more massive scale. Even during the intensities of war, the parallel was startling enough to make thoughtful men wonder what the adjustments would be like this time, once the second heat had begun to cool.

26. The Juggernauts

Caretaker of the new prosperity was Governor Earl Warren, a master tactician who had learned to conjure up political advantage from a situation that most campaigners considered a handicap—the California voter's lack of loyalty to the party whose label he wore.

This disdain of partisanship sprang from many roots. By the nature of things, immigrants tended to be more independent than stay-at-homes, and of course the Coast was full of immigrants. History, too, favored maverick tendencies. While attacking the Southern Pacific Railroad shortly after the turn of the century, the voters had also attacked the political structure that sheltered the railroad. Direct primaries replaced the nominating conventions that the railroad had once sought to rule through alliances with venal bosses. In order to "free" candidates still more, they were allowed to enter any party's primary without stating on the ballot what their own affiliations were, a process carried toward its ultimate by Hiram Johnson, who in 1934 and again in 1940 won automatic election to the United States Senate by persuading both Republicans and Democrats to name him as their candidate. Voters meantime were encouraged to short-cut the legislative process in Sacramento by means of initiative and referendum measures. Thus neither party labels nor party platforms seemed necessary for the attainment of goals.

Earl Warren, nominally a Republican, learned these lessons well. In 1938, when the state was electing its first Democratic governor since the 1890's, he won a triple nomination—Republican, Progressive, and Democratic—as the state's attorney general. In war-shocked 1942, when the incumbent governor, Culbert Olson, made an issue of partisanship, Warren retorted with a call for unity: "I am, as you know, a Republican. But I shall make no appeal to blind partisanship, or follow any other divisive tactics." It was the kind of pragmatism that Californians, busy with war contracts, wanted to hear. In the November election, 57 of the state's 58 counties voted by decisive margins for the ruggedly handsome contender.

Amazingly, Warren was able to maintain his Olympian detachment after the war. The economic shocks of adjustment to peace, freely predicted by most observers, did not seriously hurt the state. Although thousands of released workers went home late in 1945, they soon turned west again in search of the sunshine, scenery, and casual life styles they had learned to like. Discharged servicemen who had tasted the same amenities during training camp days joined the flood.

These inheritors of prosperity were, for the most part, young people eager to start the families that war had delayed. They wanted homes, cars, household appliances, clothing, and sports equipment of all kinds. Jobs were abundant. For in spite of the high hopes that had attended the organization of the United Nations in San Francisco in 1945, true peace had not arrived. Russia awoke latent fears by exploding her own atom bomb in 1949; the Korean "police action" erupted in 1950; Sputnik's astounding appearance in 1957 launched a massive space race; and shortly thereafter came the slowly accelerating involvement in Vietnam. Defense contracts poured out of Washington. California, thanks to factories and research facilities already in existence, received the greater part. So everyone seemed to be eating cake those years, unless you looked sharply at the inner cores of some of the cities or out in the fields of the agrifactories.

Under such circumstance a genial man with a firm sense of direction was bound to be popular. In 1946, Warren was reelected governor by winning both the Republican and the Democratic primaries. Two years later, curiously enough, he failed to carry California when running as Dewey's vice-presidential candidate, but in 1950 he returned to form by becoming the only governor in the state's history to be elected to a third term. In the process he crushed the Democratic nominee, James Roosevelt, by more than a million votes.

The trend continued after Warren had gone to Washington in 1953 as Chief Justice of the Supreme Court. His successor, Goodwin Knight, trod carefully along the trail Warren had blazed, and Republicans could probably have dominated state politics indefinitely if their moderate and conservative factions had not locked horns in 1958.

After complex wheeling and dealing, the conservatives won, nominating for the governorship Senator William Knowland. Knowland promptly guaranteed statewide divisiveness by advocating a return to the long-moribund open shop. Having precipitated turmoil, the candidate then inexplicably stayed in Washington, leaving all but two weeks of the campaign to his wife, an undiplomatic woman given to such oratorical profundities as this: her husband's goal in his crusade was to keep California from becoming another helpless satrapy in Walter Reuther's political empire.

Gleefully the Democrats picked up the baton of nonpartisanship that the Republicans had dropped. They had a popular, Warren-style candidate ready—Edmund G. Brown, the attorney general. To make sure no one missed the parallel, Brown declared that he would continue the middle-of-the-road policies laid down by such notable Progressives (and Republicans) as Hiram Johnson and Earl Warren. With a sigh of relief, prosperous California chose him instead of Knowland and then nodded approvingly as a Democratic legislature ended cross-filing forever.

Keep things rolling—that was the ticket Californians wanted, especially in the traditional fields of water manipulation, agriculture, improved transportation, continued population growth to ensure rising land values, freewheeling exploitation of natural resources, and (less traditionally) a massive expansion of facilities for higher education. Roll these things did, faster and faster. Why not? For so much more was possible, now that the war-born technology for doing more was available.

When protests arose, they were rolled down, too, at least for a while. After all, you can't just drop the big-growth dreams of a century and start over again.

Can you?

Think big for prosperity. In 1945, Earl Warren appointed a State Water Resources Board to study the "control, conservation, protection, and distribution of the water of California"—*all* California. From such pedestrian phrases sprang a giant. The Board absorbed a bagful of other agencies that dealt with water, was renamed the Department of Water Resources, and from its new heights handed down, in 1957, the mind-staggering California Water Plan. If its proposals were accepted in full, the state would be committed to moving practically all of the north's "surplus" water (an undefined term) southward into dryness. Completion was scheduled for the year 2020. Costs were estimated at $11.8 billion.

Opponents roared. Water projects were already proliferating everywhere. Los Angeles had pushed the Owens Valley aqueduct north into the Mono Lake area and now was increasing flows still more by building a second aqueduct parallel to the first. San Francisco and the cities along the east shore of the Bay were also double-tracking their probes into the Sierra Nevada. The Bureau of Reclamation was pouring more than $1 billion into the Central Valley Project, a considerable expansion over the $170 million first contemplated by the state. Much of the Bureau's outlay was spent damming the Trinity River in the far north, so that its waters could be taken under part of the Klamath Mountains into the Sacramento system for use in the south.* Wasn't all that enough?

There were regional complaints as well. Many big growers in the San Joaquin Valley feared that new irrigation projects of the scope implied in the plan would result in overproduction of specialty crops and consequent drops in price. The Metropolitan Water District of Southern California, already loaded with water payments, asked for firmer guarantees about deliveries, cost amortization, and the like. Northern California grew stridently emotional, fearing that a transfer of still more water beyond the Tehachapi Mountains would cripple her own potentials for growth and result in Los Angeles' thrusting ahead to dominate the state government. Finally, a handful of environmentalists began asking what was then a strange question: What would these massive tamperings with nature do to ecological systems?

Equally vehement voices were raised in the plan's favor. Residents of the lower Sacramento Valley called up memories of the Christmas Eve flood of 1955 when the rampaging Feather River had killed 55 people and had caused widespread property loss in Marysville and Yuba City. No such disaster would have occurred if the key element of the California Water Plan, a gargantuan dam near Oroville, its crest 770 feet high and a mile long, had been in existence at the time. Wasn't that worth considering?

Adverse legal decisions simultaneously brought second thoughts to many farmers of the San Joaquin Valley. For years they had been battling in the courts and in Congress to have the Bureau of Reclamation's 160-acre limitation on federal water deliveries set aside. Final defeat came in 1958, when the United States Supreme Court sustained the law. To ease the shock of transition, growers who had been buying federal water during the trials were granted a breathing spell. They could continue using government water for ten more years if they agreed to sell their holdings in excess of 160 acres at the end of that time—a requirement,

*The Central Valley Project works like this. Friant Dam intercepts the San Joaquin River north of Fresno. Some of the displaced water is diverted to farms northwest of the dam; a greater portion goes through a 160-mile canal to the southern part of the valley near Bakersfield.

The looted San Joaquin is replenished by water released into the Sacramento River from the great reservoir behind Shasta Dam above Redding and Folsom Dam on the American River above the city of Sacramento. This regulated water runs into the tangled Delta formed by the confluence of the Sacramento and San Joaquin rivers east of Carquinez Strait. From this huge natural reservoir it is pumped into a giant canal that delivers it to the San Joaquin River below Friant Dam. (A northern arm of the canal delivers part of the Delta water to the industrial cities south of Carquinez Strait.) And so the San Joaquin flows as usual to claimants farther downstream, a dexterous rob-Peter-to-help-Paul switch that brought hundreds of thousands of new acres into cultivation in the heat-blistered southern reaches of the great Central Valley.

incidentally, that is still not being enforced. The law also allowed the growers to buy outside water for their "excess" acreage. But what water was available—except that brought from the north by a state project free of federal limitations?

Yet another agricultural consideration favored the state plan. Crushed by ad valorem taxes on their lands, fruit growers, dairy farmers, and truck gardeners in Santa Clara County south of San Francisco Bay and in Los Angeles County, once the richest agricultural region in the nation, were selling out to subdividers and freeway builders at a rate of 375 acres per day. Many of these displaced farmers wanted to start again in a new location. The only raw land they could afford was in the dry southwestern reaches of the San Joaquin Valley—squarely in the path of the proposed state aqueduct. So they, too, began putting pressure on their legislators.

But mostly there was momentum. The census of 1960 would show that during the preceding decade the Los Angeles-Long Beach metropolitan area had grown in a single decade by 54 percent, San Diego by 85 percent. Since that sort of expansion had been going on for half a century no one was awed by predictions that in 1980 there would be 10 million people in Los Angeles County alone. In fact, many Southern Californians had geared their lives to an assumption of unbroken growth.

Ownership of single-family dwelling units, most of them very modest, was more widespread south of the Tehachapis than in any other urban area in the United States. Paying obeisance to the life values represented by this property filled an incredible number of leisure hours. Owners puttered endlessly to improve landscaping, build patios, add extra rooms, or roof carports, telling themselves that they were increasing the value of the place. What they were really counting on was a growing demand for houses in their neighborhoods. That meant that eventually the investor could sell at a far higher price than he had paid. He would then use the unearned increment as down payment on another home, generally in one of the new suburbs, where the subdivider and his contractors were also living on unearned increment—on down payments against the future.

There was a chain-letter effect to this. To keep the movement rolling, population growth had to be unceasing, or the last ones in would be caught short. So it was something of a shock for those who paid attention to such matters to learn, in 1952, that one essential leg of the scaffold, unfailing water, might be in jeopardy.

In 1922, it will be recalled, the states embracing the watershed of the Colorado River had divided up what engineers said was the stream's average annual flow. Time proved the figures overly optimistic. The river seldom delivered as much water to the states of the lower basin as they had assumed. When Mexico began asking for part of what had been reserved for her, there was embarrassment. When Arizona, which had refused to sign the original compact, entered suit in the United States Supreme Court to establish rights to more than the other states had originally allotted her, there was consternation.

After lengthy preliminary hearings, the overburdened high court appointed a Special Referee, Samuel Rifkind, to finish the hearings and make recommendations. The case opened in San Francisco in 1954 and lasted 26 months. Although Rifkind's recommendations and the court's final rulings would not be announced until the early 1960's, it was evident to thoughtful observers that Southern California stood to lose as much as 1 million acre feet of water per year. This loss would be more apparent than real until Arizona started diverting the water allotted her. Meantime, however, shouldn't California face reality by developing her own northern supplies?

Heeding the expansionists, Governor Brown set about overcoming the state Water Plan's opponents. First he and his advisers pared the complex elements of the $11.8 billion project to irreducible basics—the huge dam near Oroville and a 444-mile aqueduct, spotted where necessary with unbelievable pumps, for thrusting Sacramento water through the new agricultural lands of the western San Joaquin Valley and over the Tehachapi Mountains into Southern California. Costs of this minimum were estimated at $1.75 billion, to be raised in installments by the sale of bonds bearing 5 percent interest.

Balloting on the bond issue was scheduled for November, 1960. For months, voters were assailed with arguments. The San Francisco *Chronicle*, leader of opposition in the north, described the plan as a new Octopus that would make the Southern Pacific of the bad old days look anemic. Brown countered by writing letters to the *Chronicle*'s editor. These were dutifully published in the paper's letters column and then answered with an acerbic questioning of every estimate the governor made.

Finally, four days before the voting and after long quarrels among themselves about the plan's viability, the directors of the Metropolitan Water District of Southern California signed a contract with the state that involved cash payments in advance for water deliveries scheduled to begin in the early 1970's. In spite of this psychological boost, 2.8 million people voted against the bonds. Nearly 3 million favored them, however, and soon thereafter the huge earthmovers began to roll. If all went well, the rest of the $11.8 billion project would follow before 2020.

Beginnings were favorable. In 1964, the Oroville Dam, still only 25 percent complete, drew crows of vindication from its supporters by stopping a flood that otherwise might have been as deadly as the one nine years earlier. Meanwhile the growth and prosperity on which the work was predicated continued undiminished. In 1962 alone, the fourteen counties of Southern California received a net inflow of 256,000 immigrants, plus a native-born increase of 411,000. In order to house the throng, contractors in 1963 hammered together 292,000 new residential units. Mortgage payments were no problem. In 1966, the defense and aerospace contracts awarded to California factories and research agencies reached an all-time high.

Newly affluent wage earners washed more cars, installed more bathrooms, operated more dishwashers and garbage disposal units than ever before, so that the average daily consumption of water in Los Angeles rose from 134 gallons per person in 1930 to more than 170 in 1960, the last year for which figures were available. Spectacular suburbs, as contrived in their charms as a Disneyland mountain, were built around man-made lakes artfully scalloped to offer home buyers miles of shoreline lots. To check seepage, prevent erosion, and keep the places from smelling like swamps, the water was circulated through expensive pumps and the lakebeds were lined with special waterproofing materials. Simulated driftwood and rock outcroppings completed the illusion; though costs were fantastic, customers swarmed in, hoping to buy along with clear air, water recreation, and security (most water villages had guarded gates) a taste of the sort of prestige they had never known before.

The proliferation of suburbs, whether tracts or carefully controlled instant villages, involved a proliferation of freeways. Predictably, the opening of each new stretch of expressway stimulated more tract building, more water consumption, and then more highways—a frenetic spiral, for new industries also needed room and began to follow the freeways into the countryside. And industry gulps more water than people do; the production of a single barrel of beer, for example, consumes 13 barrels of water.

So on the face of things, the water manipulators had reason to praise their own foresight. But then, as had happened in the case of earlier booms, soft spots appeared. After 1966, procurement cutbacks shook the aerospace and defense industries. Unemployment crept upward. Inflation made mockery of cost estimates, while at the same time investors grew reluctant to buy the 5 percent bonds that were supposed to finance the water works.

As the economic picture darkened, increasing numbers of doubters began questioning the entire philosophy of growth. What had it brought? The mushrooming cities were strangling in smog and waste. Crime rates soared. Minority groups that had expected a larger share of the new prosperity than they were receiving seethed with frustration. Though educational facilities expanded endlessly, students remained unconvinced that quality was keeping pace with quantity. And if one sought escape in the country, he found beaches and mountain slopes overrun with motorized litterbugs.

Had the time come to rearrange priorities?

In December, 1967, the U.S. Army's Board of Engineers helped precipitate the heretical question—heretical at least in California—by revealing plans for a dam, Dos Rios, on the Eel River in the northern part of the state that would be almost as big as the Oroville Dam on the Feather River. Conceived originally as a flood control project, Dos Rios had grown under the Aladdin fingers of the engineers into a multipurpose genie that would, if it materialized, also whisk Eel River water through a 21-mile tunnel into the Sacramento system. Costs were pegged at $400 million. Of this sum the state need pay only $153 million for the tunnel, a lush windfall, since the California Water Plan envisioned the state's eventually undertaking the full project on its own hook.

Eel River is a long way from anywhere. Few people noticed what was afoot—other than local cattlemen led by thirty-five-year-old Richard Wilson, whose Round Valley range lands would be flooded by the project. To Wilson, inundation did not pose as sore a financial threat as it did to some of his neighbors, for he had money enough so that he could move wherever he chose. That was not the point, however. He and his wife had fled from Pasadena to Round Valley in the hope of escaping the very pressures the water juggernaut was helping to create. Now it was on their backs again. And this time, Wilson was convinced, the upheaval would turn out to be no true bargain even for the state. Grimly he prepared to fight.

Adroitly he gathered allies. Some were nature lovers who, like John Muir before them, were constitutionally opposed to the destruction of any lovely landscape. Others chimed in with the new concept of environmental ethics: didn't unspoiled land have its own claim to consideration, just as people did? Still others rallied on behalf of the local Indians, descendants of tribelets who on being shoved aside by land-hungry pioneers a century earlier had been promised permanent homes in Round Valley. Only 350 still lived on or near the reservation, and there had been a day in California when a promise to 350 Indians wouldn't have meant a thing. Now, however, some whites were saying that honor, too, has its claims.

Though welcoming their clamor, Wilson, a hard-headed businessman, went on gathering statistics from consulting engineers and university professors. Armed with bales of figures that shredded the Army's arithmetic, he bulled his way up through Sacramento's red tape until he reached Norman B. Livermore, Jr., Secretary of Resources for the State of California. From there he moved on to Brown's successor, Governor Ronald Reagan. On May 13, 1969, the two officials, declaring Dos Rios to be premature, called a halt to the project.

The repercussions were more staggering, probably, than Wilson had anticipated. For the first time in California history, a major water project had been derailed. A thrill ran like burning powder through environmentalists. Why not stop the entire California Water Plan in its tracks?

The state's financial embarrassment provided an opening. Although the cost of completing the initial stages of the Plan had been estimated at $1.75 billion, actual outlays were approaching $2.8 billion, a crisis rendered doubly acute by the refusal of investors to buy the last $600 million of the 5 percent bonds that had been authorized as funding. For a time the treasury had kept ahead of the bill collectors by diverting tideland oil revenues into the yawning maw, but that kind of bookkeeping would no longer suffice. Somehow the bonds had to be made attractive. To that end a proposition authorizing an increase in interest rate to 7 percent was placed on the ballot for June, 1970.

Budget watchers picked up their cudgels. This extra interest burden, they cried, was unjustifiable on the grounds of supposed benefits either to the corporate farmers of the San Joaquin Valley or to the residential ant heaps of Los Angeles and San Diego counties. Rather than hurry along at increased costs, why not slow down? Growth rates were dropping drastically—from an annual 4 percent population increase in 1958 to 2.1 percent in 1967. Arizona's projects were lagging, and years would pass before she started drawing on her allotments of Colorado River water. Shouldn't Southern California use the breathing spell for studying alternate sources of water—the recycling of wastes, the use of nuclear energy to desalinate ocean water, the harnessing of the huge geothermal basin under Imperial Valley, where steam wells could perhaps be utilized for providing both electric power and heat enough to purify the Valley's corrosive underground waters? If any or all of these substitutes worked out, then the bloated Water Plan could be cut down to manageable size.

Environmentalists went further. What Los Angeles needed, they said, was not more water to bring in more people, but breathable air. Supplies of that were running out, too. Already the city's smog was threatening to destroy a million ponderosa pines in the San Bernardino Mountains, and down in the lowlands, when temperature inversions sent pollutants above acceptable levels, schoolchildren were required to stop active outdoor play. Were these the vaunted amenities of Southern California living?

Northward, the project's approach to the 738,000-acre Sacramento Delta aroused even greater emotionalism. It was an incredibly lush and productive area, its farms laboriously reclaimed from myriad islands once thick with reeds and willows. Wildlife still abounded. Recreationists delighted in winding their houseboats through the tranquil channels. But how much tampering could the area tolerate?

Before the day of dams, annual wet-season floods had swept stagnation out of the Delta and had also repulsed damaging salt water that during dry times kept inching inland with the tides through Carquinez Strait—a balancing act that extended deep into San Francisco Bay. The spread of farming throughout the Central Valley increased the need for this yearly laundering, because soil salts released by irrigation drained inexorably, along with the residues of chemical fertilizers and pesticides, into the Delta's great pool. Yet the new dams on the upper streams were taming the annual floods.

Worried by the deteriorating quality of the Delta's water, project engineers of both the Bureau of Reclamation and the California Department of Water Resources decided not to let the carefully regulated Sacramento River contaminate itself by entering the Delta, as it had been doing for eons. Instead they would control matters scientifically and hence efficiently. They would dump practically the entire river into a canal 30 feet deep, 400 feet wide at its surface, and 43 miles long and use this for taking the water *around* the Delta to the huge pumping plants near Tracy, where it would be elevated high enough to start its long journey south.

During this end run water would be released into the starved Delta at ten carefully selected control points. This action, the engineers said, would hold contamination in the Delta to acceptable levels and at the same time would resist intrusion of ocean water. Because both state and federal agencies were involved (each had developed its own dams on the upper Sacramento drainage system, and their waters were inextricably mixed) they would share the costs—another financial windfall for the state's Department of Water Resources. So naturally everyone should be pleased.

The Delta farmers were not. They knew that nature's way had worked; they weren't sure about man's. Besides, they demanded skeptically, whose hand would be on the vital release valves in case of another severe drought in Los Angeles? Their objections were mild, however, compared to the din that went up in San Francisco and its neighboring cities. The Delta Peripheral Canal, alarmists cried, would destroy the Bay itself.

There was more than a little irony in the sudden anguish. Since 1849 the Bay cities had been treating one of America's superlative scenic and economic resources with careless contempt. Fills for San Francisco's towering financial district, for warehouses and refineries, for highways, housing tracts, airports, and, incredibly, endless garbage dumps, had reduced the Bay's original area from 700 square miles to roughly 400. Into this remnant, human sewage and industrial effluents were dumped almost without check. Why bother? Each day the shifting tides and the currents set by the Central Valley's vast river system swished the stuff out of sight and smell through the Golden Gate. But the Peripheral Canal, if built, would limit the currents to whatever was set swirling by the release valves. Even with the aid of the tides those might not be enough—or so said the engineers of yet another federal bureau, the U.S. Geologic Service. And if that warning proved true, the Cassandras said, then San Francisco Bay could quite conceivably end its life as a fetid mess of human rot.

Project engineers denied the likelihood. William Gianelli, head of the state Department of Water Resources, scorned the handwringers as "Chicken Little evironmentalists." Crusty John Jensen of the Metropolitan Water District of Southern California snorted that of course he was interested in improving ecology—in getting the desert to bloom like a rose. Governor Reagan, who had helped kill the unbuilt Dos Rios project as premature, declared that it would be total folly to stop, through an emotional attack on interest rates, a statewide project that was nearly 90 percent complete. What gain to the environment was there, he demanded, "in crops that fail or towns that die because the faucet is turned off?"

But mostly it was history that carried the day. If slowdowns really were occurring in the state's growth, then (proponents argued) a stimulus was needed, and always before, water had helped provide the boost. Trooping to the polls, the voters agreed to burden themselves with higher interest rates (but not yet with the cost of the canal) for the sake of a prosperous future. Yet opponents still struggled. In March, 1971, the Sierra Club and a handful of other allies sought court rulings that would restrain construction until the Department of Water Resources had complied with environmental law by making a complete study of the project's ecological impacts. The plea was denied. In the fall the great pumps throbbed, and $3 billion worth of water began flowing southward.

And then there was the automobile, its cultural preeminence typified by an anecdote that would be hard to believe anywhere else. The time was the long weekend that followed the San Fernando Valley earthquake of February 9, 1971. In addition to killing 51 persons, the predawn temblor had spilled chaotic masses of shattered concrete overpasses onto the main freeway arteries leading north. Foreseeing hopeless traffic snarls, the chief information officer of the California Highway Police took to the air and begged citizens to stay home. But it was a weekend! Appalled by his own absurdity, the petitioner finished lamely over the radio, for all to hear, "We realize no one will pay attention to us. . . . It's part of the nature of Californians to travel"—particularly at high speeds between white lanes, earthquake or not.

Heeding the penchant, the state in 1959 had committed itself to a program of coordinated freeway construction almost as staggering as the water project: 12,500 miles of multilane concrete to be laid down in 20 years at an estimated cost of $10 billion, this in addition to federal programs. Czar of the works, with sole authority over the selection of routes, was the California Highway Commission, which listened mostly to the advice of its own children, the engineers of the Department of Highways. The Department's touchstone, naturally enough, was the engineering ideal of pushing its gray swaths forward in as straight a line as possible, no matter what might stand in the way.

Revolts began in San Francisco. Offended at losing their views of the Bay to a stilt-legged, double-decked behemoth designed to follow the full arc of the shoreline, concerned citizens raised such a clamor that the expressway was stopped cold, stub ends hanging unconnected in space. Residents of Malibu on the coast above Los Angeles also kept a freeway from spoiling the scenery in that area. Widespread indignation brought about the rerouting of another monstrosity that otherwise would have ravaged a prime strip of redwood forest in Prairie Creek State Park.

Nor were aesthetics the only reason for protest. "If I can deny an area transportation," one state senator exulted openly, "I can beat the subdividers." Other legislators carried the sociological ball even farther, pointing out that the Highway Department's goal of placing a freeway within four miles of every residential area in Los Angeles and Orange counties would eventually uproot enough families to populate a city the size of Sacramento. Were expressways worth that kind of suffering?

City councilmen joined the attack, using as a weapon a law that let them prohibit the closing of streets, an inevitability in the case of intracity freeways. Thus allied, municipal and state lawmakers in 1971 managed to whittle down the freeway mileages scheduled for the Bay area and Southern California by 125 miles—out of thousands of miles still on the drawing boards. Though planners in the Division of Highways growled privately that the guerrilla warfare was shooting an integrated system into patchwork, they were shaken enough that they now sat through public hearings on highway location without exhibiting their old-time condescension of "O.K., go ahead and gripe and then we'll do things our way."

Skirmishes against smog brought other victories. Strange though it seems today, the chief components of the eye-stinging smudge were unrecognized for several years. When the first pall spread across Los Angeles during the closing years of World War II, coughing citizens blamed practically everything except their own automobiles. The city council banned backyard incinerators, and the county supervisors cracked down on factories, particularly power plants burning crude oil full of sulfur—yet let the Department of Light and Power go on advertising the joys of the electric home. Finally, about 1950, Professor Arie J. Haagen-Smit of Cal Tech isolated the villain—photochemical pollutants formed by the action of sunlight on the emissions of the gasoline engine.

The evidence finally led, after considerable foot dragging, to laws requiring that antismog devices be installed on all new cars sold in the metropolitan areas. The contraptions worked, by no means perfectly in the case of oxides of nitrogen, but well enough so that scientists from throughout the smog-burdened world took to visiting Los Angeles to learn from the Southern California experience. But do you really shoot down a god? In 1962 San Francisco tried to reduce her traffic congestion by launching a rapid transit system underneath the Bay to the Contra Costa cities. Even while the work was under way car owners began agitating for a second trans-Bay bridge capable of carrying another 75,000 cars a day into the city! As for Los Angeles and San Diego, years of study of similar systems brought no action whatsoever, partly because no one could agree on travel corridors but mostly because drivers and those who batten on drivers simply did not want restrictions on their mobility.

The first head-on battle was joined at the polls in November, 1970. As in the attack on the Water Plan, money provided the opening wedge. By law, all revenues raised from state taxes on gasoline had to be spent on highway construction. As a result, funds available for alternate modes of transportation stayed picayune. Hoping to rectify the balance, freeway opponents succeeded in placing on the ballot a proposition that would allow gasoline tax revenues to be used for smog research and rapid transit developments.

The so-called Highway Lobby—an informal alliance of oil companies, banks with oil company accounts, cement manufacturers, steel fabricators, trucking organizations, the Southern California Automobile Club, and on and on—came up swinging. While proponents of the measure were spending $22,721 advocating passage, the lobby poured out $333,445 urging defeat.

The nay-sayers, aided by the automobile's historic momentum in California, won easily. This time, however, there was a postscript. Angered by the revelation of campaign expenditures and increasingly aware of the needs of minority groups who could not afford as many cars as their affluent fellow citizens, the legislature in 1971 at last created a special sales tax on gasoline that could be used for studies of rapid transit. So something might happen after all, though disillusioned observers were not yet quite ready to hold their breath while waiting.

Bitter struggles in the fields of outdoor recreation and conservation followed much the same pattern. Here again people pressures, heightened by mobility, were the underlying problem. By the end of the 1960's campgrounds maintained by the state were requiring reservations almost a year in advance for popular holiday weekends. When the clot of visitors in Yosemite National Park reached 2.5 million persons a year, harried officials discussed banning automobiles entirely from the valley floor. Neon signs glared unrestrained out across much of Lake Tahoe, and sewage drainage began to bring the green tinges of eutrophication to its famed blue waters.

Neither season nor place raised barriers. Dune buggies equipped with oversized tires for traction prowled beaches and deserts. Winter weekends brought Mammoth Mountain on the eastern slope of the Sierra Nevada the heaviest concentration of skiers in the world. During summer so many hikers ascended Mount Whitney (2,000 on long weekends), the highest peak in the conterminous United States, that the Forest Service had to send up chemical outhouses by helicopter and use special mule trains for removing litter. In 1969 the state's fish hatcheries planted 46.5 million trout weighing 1,770 tons and still could not keep up with the demands of 2.2 million licensed anglers. Motorboats roared on the Colorado River; sailboats skimmed in and out of dozens of marinas carved deep into the coastline.

This recreational stampede produced two movements—a search for additional space to accommodate the throngs and, at the same time, a stubborn effort to defend areas threatened by commercial developments. The careers of both endeavors turned out to be familiar, victories in small skirmishes followed by gritty compromises or outright defeats in major encounters.

High hopes attended the drive to acquire new land. After long controversy, California won from the federal government ownership of a narrow strip of her oil-bearing coastal tidelands and used part of the subsequent revenue from oil leases for improving beaches and parks. The voters in 1964 added another $150 million for purchasing and developing additional facilities. Simultaneously Washington undertook to establish, with state cooperation, two new national parks, one at Point Reyes a short distance above San Francisco, the other in the redwood forests farther north.

In spite of blockades thrown up by recalcitrant property owners, the government by 1962 had pieced together enough acreage to dedicate Point Reyes National Seashore. In the redwoods, however, the patterns of history brought about tougher going.

In 1850, the year California became a state, a 2-million-acre strip of coastal redwoods (not to be confused with their equally overwhelming cousins of the Sierra slopes) spread from Monterey Bay north to the Oregon line. By 1920 the southern end of the line was mostly gone, but in the three rugged counties of the northwest—Mendocino, Humboldt, and Del Norte—a million emerald acres remained, much held by private owners who had acquired it through fraud and were now sitting tight in anticipation of rising prices.

Environmentalists glimpsed the specter. In 1920, a group of them formed the Save-the-Redwoods League and sought donations for the purchase of notable groves. By 1960, when the agitation for a national park was gathering steam, the League, aided by other concerned organizations, had salvaged and turned over to public administration about 70,000 acres. During that same 40-year period, the saws of the lumbermen chewed through something like 500,000 acres

The towering stands of Douglas fir in the mountains behind the redwood belt suffered even more, mostly during the postwar housing boom of the late 1940's when the number of fly-by-night "popgun" mills in Humboldt County alone jumped from 6 to 214. Sentiment, however, centered on the ancient redwoods, partly because fir lands can be more readily reforested—if proper procedures are followed.

If the pace of cutting continued—and pace was increasing if anything —the redwood industry would be out of business by the end of the century. Yet when the government would have speeded the process slightly by offering current market prices for 90,000 or so acres of remaining forest, the owners cried out against socialism and the destruction of the region's economy—without admitting that tourism might produce as many jobs for the region as the threatened mills. To no avail conservationists charged that the lumbermen's real interest was the future value of irreplaceable logs. Aided by the momentums of the past—and by Governor Reagan—the mill owners squeezed the size of the park to a few attenuated segments totaling 56,000 acres, some of it already under state protection. Once again California history had run true to form.

And so the cycle went, hope for change upset by the reassertion of long-established patterns. When plans for a dam on Sespe Creek northwest of Los Angeles threatened the nesting grounds of the endangered California condor, nature lovers killed the project. Disney's successors where checked, at least for a time, from going ahead with plans for a mountain fantasyland that would lure millions of visitors and a super-highway into the Mineral King region adjacent to Sequoia National Park. A leader in that battle, the Sierra Club, also stood in the forefront of the national drive for a wilderness preservation system—and then faced an ironic dilemma when hordes of vacationists, many of the club's 140,000 members included, trampled up the trails in a rush to see the salvaged wonders. Meantime urban sprawl was fought by a 1965 law that granted tax breaks to farmers who promised to keep their agricultural lands intact for a specified number of years.

Commercial exploitation had lost none of its vigor, however, as became evident in the years following the oil spill off the Santa Barbara coast in the early weeks of 1969. The ocean bed in that vicinity was dangerously porous; as early in 1792 explorer George Vancouver had noted iridescent oil slicks caused, as we know today, by underwater seeps. Nevertheless the federal government neglected to impose on drilling outside the California three-mile limit the stringent controls that the state recommended. A well on one of the ponderous platforms that warted the ocean surface sprang a leak. Before control was regained half a million barrels of thick crude oil had spread across 800 square miles of water and had fouled 40 miles of beach, bringing gooey death to several thousand birds.

The company concerned spread straw on the grimy sand to soak up the oil, settled numerous suits for damage, financed studies to show that marine life in the area had not suffered permanent damage—and asked the federal government for permission to go on as before. Critics immediately compared the attitude to that of the lumbermen in the redwood forests. Why such a hurry to cash in? Before long, America was going to have to find some substitute for her dwindling supplies of petroleum anyway, so why risk further damage in an effort to drain relatively negligible amounts of oil from demonstrably fragile ground? Why not turn the offshore fields into a reserve to be tapped only if real emergencies arose before alternate energy sources could be developed?

The answer was clear, of course, and had been clear ever since the days of '49. Free access to California's natural resources, whether gold or trees or oil or land, was the stimulus, boosters insisted, that had made the state the most prosperous in the Union. Was that to be ended by the bleeding hearts?

True, it was the federal, not the state, government that had yielded to the oil lobby. But the state's own feelings emerged clearly enough during the legislative session of 1970. Environmental bills rained on the lawmakers—it was the year of the fad, skeptics scoffed—only to be steered into hostile committees, where they expired. In legislative matters, the chastened amateurs soon realized, enthusiasm alone was not enough.

To give themselves muscle, they decided to concentrate. Even before the year of the oil spill, several special interest groups had formed an alliance called the California Planning and Conservation League and had sent to Sacramento the country's only full-time professional conservation lobbyist. In 1971 he was instructed not to ride off in several directions at once. Instead, the League directors declared, they would focus in 1971 on an issue of statewide significance, yet one not too broad to be feasible— a state planning board with authority enough to restrain the haphazard developments, both residential and industrial, that were gobbling up the coastal regions and compressing millions of recreationists into a sorely limited number of state parks.

The juggernaut scarcely twitched. Calling for help on local boards of supervisors jealous of losing power and on citizens fearful of one more spongy Big Brother bureaucracy intruding in their affairs, the ancient alliance of real estate speculators and land developers easily smothered the bill.

Where next? There had been too much protest for the victors to be complacent and too much commitment for the losers to surrender. Everywhere there were headshakings, everywhere searching reviews, not just in traditional fields of property rights but also, as the next chapter will indicate, in an area where many Californians had always been rigid, the explosive field of human rights.

27. Protest!

A current cliché has it that California is the sounding board of the future. In support of the generality, local seers point toward the unprecedented upheavals in agriculture, race relations, and student affairs that stunned the Western state during the 1960's and then spread like the ground rolls of an earthquake to the rest of the country.

As the decade opened, however, prospects for radical change seemed dim, particularly in the field of farm labor. One estimate states that during the preceding century there had been 500 agricultural strikes in California and all had been crushed. No union of farm workers had ever survived, partly because national labor legislation excluded farm workers from provisions concerning collective bargaining, welfare, and minimum wages, even while the government was subsidizing the employers with federally developed water and with cash bounties for reduced crop production.

Still more harmful, from the workers' standpoint, was Public Law 78. Passed as an emergency measure during the Korean War, this act allowed growers throughout the Southwest to import each year from Mexico workers to help with plant thinning, pruning, and harvesting. Each winter, the braceros, as they were called, were sent home. A new force was recruited the following spring.

California growers employed about 60,000 braceros a year. So long as that pool of cheap labor existed to be used as potential strikebreakers, local workers saw little hope in unionization. Nonetheless, two groups decided to risk the bleak prospects. The first, formed in 1959, was the Agricultural Workers Organizing Committee (AWOC), an affiliate of the newly amalgamated AFL-CIO. Three years later came a grass-roots organization, the National Farm Workers Association, created by one of the few authentic folk heroes (or horned devils, depending on your stance) of the state's recent history, Cesar Chavez.

414

Chavez knew the workers' story well. After his father had lost his small farm near Yuma, Arizona, during the depression—Cesar was ten then—the family had hit the road as migrants. By the time the boy gave up on formal education in the seventh grade, he had lost count of how many schools he had attended. Reminiscing in *Ramparts* magazine, July, 1966, he set the number at 67. Most biographers settle for about 40.

Eventually the family settled in a barrio in San Jose. (*Barrio* means "neighborhood" but is sometimes misused as a synonym for a Mexican-American ghetto.) Cesar, however, kept knocking around the fields until he was twenty-four. That year, 1950, he joined the Community Service Organization, a Mexican-founded group dedicated to helping barrio dwellers by means of credit unions, cooperative buying, group insurance, classes in civic rights and responsibilities, and so on. The young man proved to be an effective worker, but the conventional, urban ideals of the organization grew irksome to him. After the CSO had declined to step into the quagmires of unionism, particularly among the farm workers, he left. It was 1962. He was married and had eight children.

To be near his wife's family, who would help with a meal or two if need be, Cesar and Helen Chavez moved to the San Joaquin town of Delano, population 13,000. The four-room house they rented had to serve both as a home for ten people and as an office for the union he dreamed of founding, the National Farm Workers Association. For months on end they seldom had enough to eat. Most of the money they scratched together in the fields went to buy mimeograph supplies, postage, and gasoline so that Chavez and a few devoted followers could attend organizational meetings throughout the valley.

His greatest resources were intangible: a total commitment, endless patience, a mystic feeling for powerful symbols, and an accurate sense of timing. With his cousin Manuel Chavez he designed a banner that stirred Mexican Americans deeply—a blocky, black Aztec eagle in a white circle set against a flaming red background. As for his timing, he knew that dissatisfaction with the bracero program was gaining more force than the growers could contain. Their recruiting programs hurt the poor villages of northern Mexico by enticing able-bodied men away from their families. Small shopkeepers in Southwestern agricultural towns lost trade because braceros took their little savings home. Police were kept busy rounding up illegal immigrants who followed the braceros across the border. Bracero competition filled city streets with men who might otherwise have found work in the fields, so that nonagricultural wages dropped and welfare costs rose. But worst of all was the effect on American citizens who knew no other trade than field work.

In the early 1960's, according to the California Department of Employment, there were about 180,000 of these nonimported casual farm workers in the state. The majority were Mexican Americans, but there were also Filipinos, Japanese, Puerto Ricans, a few Indians, some Anglos, even Arabs. About a third of this work force migrated from the cities during the harvest season. The rest, some 120,000, had settled for the sake of relief payments, which demanded permanent addresses, in rural slums outside the farming towns.

Conditions had not changed a great deal since the day of the Indian peon. True, hourly wages for agricultural work remained higher in California than in the rest of the United States. True, piecework bonuses during picking time enabled adept harvesters to earn good wages for a few weeks. But the average field hands worked less than half as many hours per year as did unskilled factory employees. Their annual income averaged less than $3,000, and when the dull times of winter closed in, nothing but the grayness of despair loomed ahead. Such minor civic services as garbage collection and untainted drinking water seldom reached the rural barrios. Children attended schools whose harried teachers knew little Spanish and less about their pupils' cultural needs. Infant mortality was high, life expectancy short.

In 1964 one basic element of the situation changed abruptly. Yielding to pressure from many sides, Congress ended the bracero program. From then on, those growers who concentrated on specialty crops that demanded quantities of hand labor—rose grafting, lettuce, berry, celery, citrus, and grape raising—were going to have to find irrigators, pruners, sprayers, and pickers among citizen applicants. Nor could worker demands, reasonable or otherwise, be turned aside any longer by the simple threat of alien importations.

Confrontations came quickly. In the spring of 1965, grape pickers in the desert-surrounded Coachella Valley won wage increases. The small victory led Larry Itliong, the Filipino head of the local Agricultural Workers Organizing Committee, to take an enormous risk. He demanded similar concessions from ten producers of wine grapes in the San Joaquin Valley. Only ten, but they were giants: the Di Gorgio Corporation (S&W canned foods), Schenley, Incorporated, the Christian Brothers wineries, Gallo, Paul Masson, and others.

The employers refused to negotiate. On September 8, 1965, several hundred AWOC members left the fields. Most, like Itliong, were Filipinos. In the old ploy of setting race against race, the growers retaliated by hiring Mexican Americans as replacements.

Itliong went to Chavez. Would the three-year-old National Farm Workers Association support the strike?

It was a risky decision. Chavez, knowing the fears and inherent conservatism of his people, had been moving slowly. He had inaugurated a credit union and a death benefit insurance plan for NFWA members and had won lawsuits against growers whose labor camps did not meet state standards. Those gains and his eloquence had brought the union about 2,000 family memberships (there were generally two or three workers in a family) paying dues of $3.50 a month. In May he had won a strike against a handful of rose growers in the Delano area, and that had encouraged his group enormously. Defeat now would be ruinous.

But did not the struggle have to come?

He put the question to a gathering of about 1,000 members in the meeting hall of the Roman Catholic Church in Delano. Not by chance, the date was September 16, Mexican Independence Day. On one wall was the Association's huge Aztec flag, framed by portraits of Mexican heroes. A band played the Mexican national anthem. When Chavez made his motion, the crowd roared back, *"Huelga!"* "Strike" is the literal translation. But that day the word took on, with the black eagle, a broader meaning. *Huelga!*—the aspirations of a people.

The reverberations reached across the continent, for if this strike worked, farm laborers everywhere in the United States might be organized at last and brought under the legal NRLA umbrella that covered other workers. Catholic priests, Protestant ministers, and Jewish rabbis came to Delano to help. So did a sprinkling of long-haired youths and girls in blue jeans who not long since had participated in civil rights activities in the Deep South and, more recently, in the turmoils at the Berkeley campus of the University of California. In December, Walter Reuther visited Delano and pledged AFL-CIO support to the extent of $5,000 a month. Protection against flank attacks came when the independent Teamsters' Union, an old enemy of the AFL-CIO, agreed to keep its recruiters out of the fields if Chavez and Itliong would make no move to line up truckers and workers in the packing sheds, where the Teamsters claimed jurisdiction. It was, as we shall see, an agreement destined to bear bitter fruit.

In spite of so much support, the strike in the fields did not get off the ground. Concerted action against great might was too new to be grasped by thousands of workers inexperienced in union matters. Strike pay— and Chavez lived on it along with his men—was $5 a week. When winter came, then what? Men who needed the good wages of harvest time to tide them over the empty months listened to the blandishments of strikebreakers and went into the fields under the protection of police escorts. Others, including members of Itliong's and Chavez's unions, were frightened by scare talk. If the strike lasted, the braceros might come back, and those who had participated in the walkouts might never be hired again.

This Chavez, this wild man—who could tell where he was taking them?

As the strike faltered, Chavez conjured up another symbol, transforming the grape itself from a synonym for joy into a sign of suffering. Nationwide pleas called on sympathizers to join a massive boycott against the products of his opponents. Liberals in the East joined pickets outside stores; TV cameras and newspaper stories spread the tale. In March, 1966, more sympathy was generated when a handful of faithful marched afoot to Sacramento to plead their cause to the governor and were met by 10,000 cheering well-wishers. Stockholders in Schenley, Incorporated, Di Gorgio, and other publicly held corporations began to fear that adverse publicity was costing more than increased wages might.

One by one they capitulated. In return for a promise that strikes would not be called at harvest time, they signed contracts that raised wages and conferred small fringe benefits. At the humble union hall in Delano there was tumultuous rejoicing. Never before had farm workers in America won such a victory.

Big though the triumph looked in Delano, a contract with ten growers, even giants, scarcely dented California's $4 billion agribusiness. Success needed repetition. To streamline operations the two victorious groups amalgamated into a single union, the United Farm Workers Organizing Committee, Chavez director and Itliong assistant director, that maintained AFL-CIO affiliation. To quiet talk that most workers did not want to be represented by this hybrid, the union leaders promoted secret elections at the Di Gorgio and Goldberg fields near Arvin, Delano, and Borrego. The voters spoke clearly: a total of 294 decried all unions, 331 said they would prefer the Teamsters, and 1,098 chose the new UFWOC. Assured then that a majority of the field hands were behind them, Chavez and Itliong trained the UFWOC's new guns on the next biggest target in the Delano area, the Giumarra Vineyards, producer of more table grapes than any other grower in the world. And there they ran into an emotionalism as profound as that motivating their own members.

The Giumarras, father and son, spoke for independents throughout the state. These were not impersonal corporations. The parents or grandparents of many of the landholders had come to the San Joaquin Valley as poor immigrants from Italy, Yugoslavia, Armenia. By bitter thrift they had saved enough to buy their first sun-stricken acres from early speculators, and by bitter effort had made the land productive. They were jealous of it and still worked, many of them, in the hot earth from dawn to dark. They did not want power-hungry union bosses, as the enemy looked to them, taking advantage of the blows that every rancher sooner or later suffered from the unpredictable weather and the capricious marketplace. They felt that in appealing to distant bleeding hearts who did not understand the farmers' side of the story, the boycott had been grossly unfair. They resented the influx of outsiders, and many of them probably believed their own words when they charged that the true source of the valley's labor trouble lay far off, in Moscow.

In June, 1967, when the UFWOC asked the Giumarras by registered letter for a meeting to discuss worker election concerning union representation, the company did not reply. On August 3 the strike began.

Once more pickets proved unable to halt the influx of strikebreakers. Accordingly Chavez resorted again to a boycott, asking users everywhere not to buy Giumarra grapes. Neighboring growers then allowed the Giumarras to use their labels, with the result that the strike and boycott were extended to employers throughout the southern San Joaquin and on into the Coachella Valley.

What words can capture it—this nationwide reaction caused by a handful of people in the hot interior of a distant state? Conscience was mixed in it, of course, and memories of *The Grapes of Wrath*, a book that hadn't concerned itself with actual grapes at all. There were carryovers of emotion from the civil rights movement in the South. Senator Robert Kennedy lent his powerful blessings after visiting Delano during hearings conducted by a Senate Subcommittee on Migrant Labor. But mostly there was Chavez. He himself was a symbol now; liberals saw him as mystic, nonviolent, long-suffering, ennobled by dedication. Stirred so, significant numbers of people, mostly outside of California, simply stopped eating grapes.

In the Valley, however, progress seemed slow. The union bought 40 acres of poor land west of Delano—"To have a piece of ground is to have roots in the community," the union paper wrote, quoting the Mexican revolutionary Zapata—and on it built a modest union hall, painted pink. They drilled a well of good water, erected a gas station (these were migrants, remember), and established a spruce medical clinic in a trailer. Very nice. But the strike was slow. The young men, hearing of the accomplishments of violence elsewhere, grew impatient. Ugly clashes broke out between pickets and strikebreakers; there was a rash of mysterious fires in the packing sheds.

To reinforce his plea for nonviolence—or to stage a grandstand play, as some charged, for few are neutral about Chavez—Cesar in the spring of 1968 began a 25-day Lenten fast. The impact on his people was profound. Violence ceased. Scores of men and women maintained vigils outside his home and held prayer sessions in the new union hall. At the end of the time, Robert Kennedy arrived to break the first bread with Chavez, before an enormous throng, many weeping. Later, in June, during the intense California Democratic primary campaign between

Kennedy and Eugene McCarthy, Chavez sent recruiters into the city barrios to round up votes for his supporter. The chicanos' unusually heavy turnout may have been the margin of victory for Kennedy. Not that it mattered in the end, for during his victory celebration in the Ambassador Hotel in Los Angeles Kennedy was slain by an assassin's bullet.

Sullenness replaced exuberance. Painfully the strike dragged on through 1969, with Chavez sick and bedridden most of the time. It was a bad year for the growers, too. Economic recession, an unusually heavy grape crop, and the persistent boycott combined to produce a disastrous drop in prices. In June, 1970, the Coachella Valley growers began to surrender, as did smaller operators in the San Joaquin. The big break came in mid-July, when John Giumarra, Jr., asked Chavez to meet with him after midnight in the Stardust Motel in Delano. Three days later the strike was over. The UFWOC, in return for a promise not to strike during harvest time, had won better wages, a union hiring hall to replace labor contractors, and the first health insurance program ever accorded American farm workers.

Again rejoicing filled the valley, and again the leaders realized that they had advanced only a step, for the grape growers farther north and the producers of scores of other specialty crops throughout California had been shocked into more truculent defiance than ever. The endless road . . . Chavez and Itliong, very weary now, prepared to move against the melon growers of the Imperial Valley, the lettuce, berry, and vegetable raisers of the Salinas Valley.

The growers had anticipated their move. Abruptly 200 of them announced that they preferred a stable union to the radical UFWOC. Accordingly, they said, they were letting the Teamsters represent their field workers.

Chavez and Itliong were stunned. Harking back to the 1966 hands-off arrangement with the Teamsters, they denounced the rival union's act as a stab in the back and demanded that the "sweetheart contracts" be abrogated. The Teamsters refused. Chavez retorted with a demonstration of UFWOC power. At his request more than 5,000 lettuce and berry pickers walked out of the fields. It was the biggest agricultural strike in American history.

The Teamsters fought back. They ran their trucks through the UFWOC picket lines; they set up pickets of their own. At that, outroar erupted everywhere. On September 2, 1970, the unions of the California Labor Federation, many of whom had longstanding alliances with the Teamsters, voted unanimously at their state convention to support Chavez and sent his union $10,000. George Meany, national president of the AFL-CIO, broke his longstanding vow of nonrecognition and met with Teamster officials for the first time since the rift between the unions in 1955. It was more pressure than the Teamsters could withstand, and they let Meany announce that the 1966 California division of spheres of influence between the contending groups would be maintained.

The growers refused to accept any peace that strengthened the UF-WOC. Insisting that their contracts with the Teamsters were valid, they demanded a return to the original agreement. When they refused even to meet with Chavez, he ordered his pickets out again and asked the country to support yet another boycott, this time on lettuce. Response was apathetic. National attention spans are short-lived at best, and besides, the brawl seemed like a grubby jurisdictional dispute rather than a battle of ideals.

Pushing their luck, the growers in the Salinas Valley next obtained an antipicketing injunction against the UFWOC on the grounds that this was not a legitimate strike. Chavez personally defied the order and early in December, 1970, was jailed for the first time in his life.

Belatedly an old truth came home to the growers: few things succeed so well as martyrdom. Silent crowds carrying lighted candles maintained night-long vigils outside the jail. The widows of Martin Luther King and of Robert Kennedy flew west to visit the prisoner. Headlines flamed, and that pressure, too, became irresistible. On Christmas Eve, Cesar Chavez was freed.

The strike dragged on. But already it was evident that the true turning point had been reached that July night in 1969 when John Giumarra, Jr., had entered a stereotyped motel room in drab Delano to talk terms to this ill-educated, dark-skinned child of dispossessed migrants. No longer was there any real doubt that all American farm labor would eventually be unionized.

A hollow victory? Some thought so. More and more small farmers either were being displaced by suburbs or were selling out to their neighbors and moving into the cities. In 1945, as a result of the stimulus of World War II, there had been 139,000 farms in California. By 1970 the number had dropped to 57,000. Moreover, 3,124 of the remaining owners held more than 70 percent of the state's arable land.

Those were the farms that hired appreciable amounts of labor. But they were also the ones that were swinging more and more rapidly toward mechanization, even though the change meant developing special strains of crops—tomatoes and head lettuce, for instance—with shape and firmness adapted to mechanical harvesting. Thousands of men, in short, were going to find themselves unemployed whether they were unionized or not.

Chavez had realized this. His epochal contract with the growers of table grapes contained provisions for a fund that would help grape pickers learn new jobs in the event of automation. A triviality, some said. Grape pickers were a small element of what might become a serious problem of technological unemployment. But offsetting that apparent insignificance was a new declaration of dignity. Always before, casual farm laborers had been used as needed and then discarded, like dry ballpoint pens. But now, for the first time, there was concern, written for all to read. A man was not disposable, even when the machines came.

It was an electrifying idea. It flowed with the ever-shifting migrants into the barrios of Los Angeles, it jumped west to the Mexican-American communities in Texas and beyond, it became incorporated almost instantly into the rage for self-realization that was welling up among disadvantaged people everywhere.

Los Angeles is a compartmented city. Tens of thousands of its white residents and white visitors never set foot in the huge Negro section of Watts in the southern part of the metropolis, or in the equally huge Chicano barrio to the east. Out of sight, out of mind. Struggling for civic identity that would conjure up images of grace when someone said *Los Angeles,* local leaders embraced the nation's cultural boom of the early 1960's and at a cost of $54 million created two dazzling complexes, the Music Center on a hilltop overlooking the ponderous mall of the civic center and the Los Angeles County Art Museum out on Wilshire Boulevard near the La Brea Tar Pits.

Though the two clusters stood six miles apart they were clearly related. Each consisted of a triad of buildings dominated on the west by a colonnaded pavilion. Each made dazzling use of water in reflecting pools and fountains, as if to celebrate the city's triumph over aridity. In the accelerating rearrangement of urban patterns, each served as a magnet for soaring new skyscrapers. *Los Angeles* they indeed said, proudly and unmistakably, to the affluent part of the metropolis. To the two major subcompartments of the city, however, they meant scarcely a thing.

There was historic reason. Los Angeles (and what is said here of the city is applicable to the county) was an energetic white community of considerable size before any appreciable number of nonwhites appeared. Of those belated arrivals, the Mexicans had a short head start in time, but the pull of World War II on Southern blacks soon equalized the flow. Although in 1970 persons with Spanish surnames retained a numerical lead in the state as a whole (there are about 3.1 million of them), in Los Angeles blacks were ahead, accounting for 17 percent of the city's population as compared to the Mexican Americans' 14 percent.

This influx came too swiftly to be assimilated, even if the old-timers in the city had wished assimilation or even integration. They didn't. Their reasons were common to those of fellow whites throughout the United States and need no listing here, except for a passing reminder that racial prejudices had always been virulent in California and in the small Midwestern towns from which so many Southern Californians hailed.

The colored newcomers contributed to the separateness. Strange to the land, poor, uprooted, uncertain, and, in the case of the Mexicans, set aside by language, they clung together for reassurance. So it was easy to shunt them off into tight ethnic clusters, the Negroes in the southern section of the city, the Mexican Americans in the east, where once the *colonias* of the farm workers had been located.

Those areas, filled with single-family dwellings shaded by palm trees, did not look like Eastern tenement slums. The erosion of poverty and overcrowding was on them, nevertheless. Unemployment was high, especially among teen-agers. Few could afford cars, yet public transportation to hiring centers was inadequate. The segregated schools—de facto segregation maintained by a gerrymandering of district boundaries— were substandard. Police-community relations were tense. In the black sections, family conditions were chaotic; illegitimate births were frequent; fathers were demeaned by their inability to find work.

Worst of all, perhaps, was the pervading sense of helplessness. Here were extensive communities—cities within the city—and yet the citizens had little to say about their destinies, few responsible ears to turn to in their distress. Control came from outside, from The Man, a vaguely defined, unapproachable entity that most whites would have spoken of as "Them."

Both groups, chicanos and blacks, had expected more. The latter in particular had found hope in the spread of the civil rights movement, not least in California's Rumford Act of 1963, which declared against discrimination in the sale or renting of real estate. They were badly jarred, therefore, when the California Real Estate Association placed on the next year's ballot an initiative measure, Proposition 14, that would not only repeal the Rumford Act but would forbid any governmental infringement whatsoever on a person's right to sell or rent his real property "as he in his absolute discretion chooses." The measure passed by an overwhelming margin. Although the U.S. Supreme Court would soon declare the act unconstitutional, the blacks regarded the vote as a clear statement by the white majority that they were inferior. (It should be noted that the Mexican sections of Los Angeles also supported, though by smaller margins, the "Right To Sell" proposal.)

The answering flare-up came in a section called Watts on the hot smoggy night of August 11, 1965. When police halted and sought to arrest a young car driver who had been drinking, a crowd gathered. Obscenities rapped out, then pushing, and suddenly rioters were swarming through the streets, smashing, burning, looting.

On August 13, after the terror had spread across 43 square miles of the city, the Chief of Police called for help, and 14,000 armed troops of the National Guard moved into Watts. Guerrilla war began then, snipers on rooftops and in alleys, the troops in their armored cars. When quiet finally came on August 17, under a heavy pall of smoke from the still-burning ghetto, $140 million in property had been destroyed and 34 people were dead, 31 of them Negroes. Another 1,032 were wounded or hurt, and 3,952 were arrested, 3,162 of them black.

Watts was a signal to the United States that nonviolence was finished, as Hunter's Point near San Francisco, Detroit, Chicago, Washington, and other communities would learn. Black militancy became a tactic. Huey Newton and Bobby Seale founded the Black Panthers in Oakland. Blacks seeking to alter university admission policies, hiring practices, and curriculum content kept San Francisco State College in turmoil for nearly two years. Shoot-outs with law enforcement officers became increasingly spectacular, notably the kidnap-killing of a San Rafael judge during an escape attempt by three convicts accused of murdering a prison guard—an episode that resulted in the arrest, on a charge of gun smuggling, of fiery Angela Davis, discharged black professor from UCLA. With all this came a rejection of the old goal of adapting to white culture and a substitution of the new ideal of separatism: Black is beautiful.

None of this was lost on the Mexican-American community. In some ways they were different from the blacks, who they felt received more than a fair share of such government-created jobs as were available. They did not have the indignities of slavery to look back on, but they did remember that California, once Mexican, had been torn from their homeland by force. Their family ties had suffered less than those of the blacks; the front porches of the barrio homes were generally filled with aunts, cousins, grandparents, and children. But they knew poverty, too, the frustrations of schools that ignored their history and language, and the heavy hand of the police.

For years they had been considered docile. Cesar Chavez's work in the fields helped change that, for he gave them pride and the black eagle as a sign of solidarity. A radical group calling themselves Brown Berets began speaking up for chicano power and for separatism: Bronze is beautiful. Protesting the Anglo orientation of their classes, 15,000 high school students struck on March 18, 1968, and paraded through the Los

Angeles streets under such signs as "EDUCATION, NOT CONTEMPT," "TEACHERS, SI, BIGOTS, NO!" When thirteen of the strike leaders were tried, convicted, and placed on three-year probation, chicanos seized the downtown office of the Board of Education and staged a week-long sit-in.

In time, the barrios, too, knew death. Toward the end of August, 1970, five years after the Watts riot, chicano leaders staged a massive street parade to protest what they believed was an unjustly high proportion of Spanish surnames on Vietnam casualty lists. Youths along the fringes of the march began scuffling with the police. Suddenly glass was crashing, looters were running, shots were banging. Among the casualties was Reuben Salazar, popular columnist for the Los Angeles *Times* and news commentator for a Spanish-language television station. He had been killed by a tear-gas projectile, strong enough to pierce walls, that was fired without apparent provocation through the open door of a café where he was sitting.

The rage spread to the Indians. For years the government had been sending young men and women to trade schools in various metropolitan centers in the expectation that they would first adapt to and then be assimilated by the urban whites. As a result of the program, California's Indian population had risen from its low of 16,000 to about 80,000—45,000 in Los Angeles County and 35,000 in the Bay area. Size did not indicate success, however. Many trainees, declining to be "melted down" in the great American melting pot, returned to their reservations. Others, finding pride in the new pride of the black and brown racial groups, also sought the uplift of separatism. Delegations appeared before the State Board of Education to demand fuller and fairer treatment of Indian matters in school textbooks. An Indian Historical Society took shape in San Francisco and published its own journal.

To dramatize the plight of their people and to remind whites that once the land had been theirs, a militant group of men, women, and children moved into the abandoned federal prison on Alcatraz Island in San Francisco Bay. Pointedly they offered to give $24 worth of baubles for the island, which they said they wished to turn into an Indian cultural center. For months they camped there in desolate circumstances. Finally, after most had drifted away in discouragement, U.S. authorities removed the rest. The country was not yet ready, at least under the terms of confrontation, to grant the Indians a symbolic rallying place.

And students. It was difficult for most elders to conceive of the beneficiaries of America's vaunted educational system as disadvantaged. And yet sociologist Paul Goodman had written, "At present in the United States, students—middle class youth—are the major exploited class. . . . [Their] labor is needed and they are accordingly subjected to tight scheduling, speedup and other factory exploitative methods."

Big-think: during the decade of the 1950's California's school-age population, the maturing products of the postwar baby boom, increased twice as fast as did the adult group. To meet the glut a master plan for higher education was devised—this was the era, too, of the California Water Plan and the freeway expansion program—and projections were laid out for a carefully structured educational hierarchy of some 80 junior colleges (now generally called city or community colleges), 21 state colleges, and 8 branch campuses of the University of California. Nerve center of the university ganglia would remain at prestigious Berkeley.

Throughout California new buildings mushroomed. Research, cultural, and athletic facilities were elaborate, faculties were renowned, costs were astronomical—and growing numbers of students were dissatisfied. These dissidents, most of them products of a narrow affluence that had meant so much to their parents, scorned the sprawling system, as Goodman did, as a methodical, uninspired knowledge factory whose programs were geared to furthering the goals of an increasingly restrictive, materialistic society.

The restlessness came to an angry focus at Berkeley during the fall of 1964 in what was labeled the Free Speech Movement. A university rule, regarded as archaic by many, prohibited on-campus recruitment for political purposes. Such activity, accordingly, was carried on in a busy but ambiguous area at one edge of the campus—ambiguous because, by chance, the ownership of a strip of ground 26 feet wide in that well-traveled section was not clearly defined: did title rest with the city or the university?

It was an explosive time. Many students had just returned from participating in civil rights activities in Mississippi and Alabama. Fired with enthusiasm, they were determined to carry on their work by organizing marches and sit-ins against discriminatory practices in the Bay area. Further excitement was generated by the approach of the November elections. Lyndon Johnson, running for the presidency as a peace candidate against Barry Goldwater, and Proposition 14 to repeal the Rumford Fair Housing Act were both on the ballot. So student politicians and their nonstudent associates were busy as school opened. To some people, many of whom resented their long hair, bizarre clothing, and unwashed aura, they were far too busy. A university supported by taxpayers of all political hues, the argument ran, had no business sheltering potentially disruptive activists.

The university, discovering that it owned the 26-foot strip where most of the organizing tables were located, clamped down. Objections from the students involved were immediate and vehement. The fact that a slight move would take them away from university jurisdiction was dismissed as irrelevant. A great university devoted to the ideals of truth, so the organizers said, should take political stands. Certainly it could not legitimately abrogate the students' fundamental right to free and unrestricted speech, on campus or off.

Involved negotiations got nowhere. On October 1, 1964, several young people sought to clog activities at Sproul Hall, the university's administrative center. One trespassing nonstudent was arrested and hustled into a police car. Bystanders promptly lay down in the road in front of the vehicle. A great crowd gathered, and for 32 hours the arresting officer and his prisoner were immobilized, although police reinforcements hovered about in readiness for a call that, perhaps fortunately, never came.

Compromise produced an uneasy truce that broke at 3:00 A.M. December 2, when 800 students invaded Sproul Hall and sat down wherever there was space, with full intent of bringing university affairs to a halt. This time the police were called. Exasperated by the mockery of the sit-ins, they dragged the dissenters out of the building with what the students afterward said was unnecessary roughness. Meeting in full regal majesty for the first time, the faculty passed resolutions that, in general, supported the Free Speech Movement while condemning the use of outside police.

Shocked conservative voters rallied behind the banners of the Republican contender for the governorship, Ronald Reagan, who promised an end to the flagrant permissiveness of state-supported institutions. In November, 1966, Reagan was elected.* (A white backlash against Negro restiveness was also involved in the victory.) Student radicals, feeling very grim now, found a new issue on December 2, 1966, exactly two years after the Sproul Hall sit-ins. Navy recruiters were allowed to set up a table in the lobby of the Student Union building, but a similar privilege was refused to an outside antidraft organization. The Union building filled swiftly with shoving, shouting protestors, police appeared again, and the next day there was an angry strike by 8,000 students—out of a campus population of some 27,000.

Many puzzled Californians tried to tell themselves that all this was just another, if excessive, case of student high jinks. The explanation was far too simplistic, as the President's Commission on Campus Unrest pointed

---

*Yet with characteristic California inconsistency, the electors two years later chose a liberal Democrat, Alan Cranston, as U.S. Senator over his reactionary, student-baiting Republican opponent, Max Rafferty, State Superintendent of Public Instruction.

out some years later when it said, "What happened at Berkeley had altered the character of American student activism in a fundamental way." Not that youth's alienation from society was either new or limited to the United States. Nor was civil disobedience novel—the use, for example, of sit-ins in defiance of local ordinances. Factory workers had employed the technique at least as early as the 1930's, and civil rights demonstrators had elaborated on it some years later. What was germinal was for a hitherto indulgently regarded minority group to apply the weapon unexpectedly and devastatingly to a sacrosanct institution that had sought to hold itself aloof from society's turmoils even while serving the ends of that society. Like the riot at Watts, the Berkeley sit-ins were an announcement to the country that passivity was over. The universities were to be called to account, and the means of forcing answers were now at hand.

Almost inevitably violence was the next development, a step taken at Columbia in 1968. The terror promptly jumped back to California. Two men died in Berkeley during a clash with police over a piece of unused university land that student activists and allied hippies wanted to dedicate as a People's Park. Bombs exploded with varying degrees of effectiveness on several campuses. Private universities, Stanford in particular, suffered along with the public institutions. Mingled with these overt attacks were startling, and to many conservatives, deliberately defiant expressions of "counterculture"—drugs, open obscenity in underground papers, outlandish clothing and hair styles, rock music, easygoing sexuality, and the like.

Bewildered elders asked what on earth the young rebels wanted. Actually, except in the case of extreme radicals who wished to destroy all existing institutions so that society could be entirely restructured, the answers were clear.

Self-determination was one thing. Like the barrios of the Mexican Americans and the ghettos of Watts, student communities were governed from outside. It wasn't just a matter of bed hours, though paternalistic dormitory rules were challenged and changed. Rather, it was a profound question about the future. What should a young man's or young woman's expectations be, regardless of background, and how should the university prepare them for those expectations? Teaching methods, course content, and the diversion of university talent to research projects that simply furthered (in the eyes of the protestors) old patterns of racial injustice, resource exploitation, pollution, and acquisitive materialism all came under attack. Above all, the new activists despised the war in Vietnam.

The crescendo came in 1970. On February 25, the Santa Barbara campus of the University of California was aroused by an inflammatory talk delivered by one of the lawyers who had helped defend the "Chicago Seven" against charges that they had deliberately conspired to disrupt the 1968 Democratic National Convention in Chicago. That night a riot as aimless-seeming as the wild outbreak in Watts churned through Isla Vista, a chaotic, ill-managed bedroom community adjacent to the university campus. During the uproar a branch of the Bank of America, execrated as an exponent of all capitalistic wrongdoings, was burned to the ground. Two months later, on April 16, university officials refused permission for Jerry Rubin, one of the Chicago Seven, to speak on the campus. Student response was another Isla Vista riot. Although the rebuilt bank building survived the attack, one youth was killed and several were hurt.

Throughout the state tempers ran high. Thus there were particular dreads in California when the extension of the Vietnam war into Cambodia early in May triggered bloody protests at Kent State University in Ohio and Jackson State College in Mississippi. As student strikes erupted across the land, Governor Reagan sought to forestall confrontations in California by closing every university and college campus in the sprawling state system.

In June, Isla Vista's uneasy quiet was broken again when Santa Barbara police sought to arrest several persons who had been indicted for the destruction of the bank during the February uprisings. New riots thereupon swept Isla Vista for five days. Reinforcements poured in from the sheriffs' offices in Los Angeles and San Luis Obispo. More than 600 young people were arrested to the tune of bitter recriminations about excessive police brutality.

A tense and weary state prepared for deadlier demonstrations when classes resumed in the fall. Amazingly, as proved true in the rest of the country, the outbreaks did not come.

Why? No one was sure. It seemed, though, that the students were weary, too, and more interested in developing their own "things," whether studying enough chemistry to fight pollution or withdrawing to communes to live their own kinds of life, than they were in butting their heads any longer against the monolith. If change was to be wrought, it evidently would have to be done within the system, a prospect brightened by the extension of the vote to eighteen-year-olds.

The quiet extended to other areas. Cutbacks in the space program and in military expenditures had severely hurt the aerospace and aircraft industries to which so much of California's economic well-being was tied. Concurrently, the census of 1970 revealed a startling slowdown in growth rates both from immigration and from births. Whereas demographers had predicted in 1960 that 25 million people would be living in

California within ten more years, the actual count showed 20 million—
a shrinkage that extended to the universities, which in the fall of 1971
reported, for the first time ever, a slight decrease in enrollment.

What did it mean? Were the momentums of twelve decades of exploitative history running down at last? Had overcrowding, underemploy-
ment, smog, and tumult finally tarnished the state's fabled allure? Or was
this lull temporary, as the President's Commission on Population
Growth implied when it predicted, at the opening of 1972, that in thirty
more years California's population would equal that of the next two
largest states, New York and Texas, combined?

Again no one could be sure. But obviously the exponents of master
plans for water, highways, education, power plants, airports, and what-
not had badly overestimated the needs of at least the immediate future.
Abruptly this brought a relaxing in the hitherto unremitting pressures
for the state and its major businesses to provide expanded services in
anticipation of an everlasting inflow of people.

Strangeness! After twelve decades of gearing life to automatic growth,
this pause was, to some, dismaying. To others it was exciting—an unexpected boon of time in which to reflect and anticipate, to weigh the
dynamics of a vibrant past against the challenges and the hopedfor qualities of the future.

What qualities? There was no real agreement. California was far too
varied for consensus. But everyone wondered, each according to his own
lights.

Afterword

Facing the Future

Since the first publication of this book fifteen years ago, the dynamics of change have remained California's one constant. And nowhere—not in agriculture, water manipulation, manufacturing, urban living, recreation, or in environmental warfare—does it show up more markedly than in the state's ever-shifting population.

Statistically, the scene can be summed up this way. In the United States as a whole, blacks, Native Americans, and Third World peoples constitute about 20 percent of the population. In California the percentage is at least thirteen points higher. The exact figure is elusive because of the impossibility of counting illegal immigrants, known officially as undocumented aliens.

After years of struggling with the problem of illegal immigration, Congress passed, in 1986, a compromise bill that granted residency status to undocumented aliens who can prove they have lived in the United States continuously since January 1, 1982. Farm workers received even more generous terms. In addition, all who can meet the residency requirements will be allowed to apply for full citizenship after five years.

It has been estimated that at least one million Hispanics will gain residency rights. Moreover, most of them are young people whose birthrates are high enough to offset whatever exclusions result from the act . . . if any. For though the Immigration Service vowed to seal the border, many knowledgeable people—for example, Richard Rothstein, head of the Los Angeles branch of the Amalgamated Clothing and Textile Workers Union—doubted that the border can be closed. Poverty in Mexico, they say, is so dire that the flow will inevitably find leaks, many of them leading, as in the past, straight into California. Moreover, Rothstein declares, California garment makers, construction firms, restaurants, and hotels depend heavily on these illegals to fill sweatshop jobs Americans won't touch.

Adding to the flood are Asiatics. In 1965 Congress replaced a system of immigration quotas based on countries of origin with flat figures. One hundred and seventy thousand persons a year can enter this country from nations lying outside the Western Hemisphere; 120,000 more, Hispanics included, can enter legally from the Western Hemisphere. During the ten years immediately following the act, half of the newcomers from the Eastern Hemisphere were Orientals, the bulk of them educated, ambitious Filipinos and Koreans. Later, in 1972, the United States opened its door to refugees—the so-called "boat people" fleeing from the turmoils of Indonesia. Forty percent of all migrant Asians have chosen to settle in either the Los Angeles or San Francisco areas, many moving there after trying other parts of the U.S. because of the support systems provided by fellow nationalists already living in the Golden State.

Again, let's resort to statistics. Forecasters (the Wells Fargo bank's analysis "California 2000"; the Palo Alto–based Center for Continuing Study of the California Economy; the California Assembly's Office of Research) agree in predicting that California's population will reach and probably pass the thirty-three million mark during the early years of the twenty-first century. Of that awesome number, about 40 percent will be whites, 40 percent will be Hispanics, 10 percent will be Asians, 8 percent will be blacks, and the rest will be a scattering from everywhere. For instance, more than one hundred different languages are currently spoken in Los Angeles County. Whites no longer will be a majority race in California, but they probably will remain the most potent voting block because of longer experience in the ways of American political organization.

Education in a Multilingual State

Awareness of the state's growing diversity led to an initiative on the 1986 ballot designed to make English California's official language. If it passed, all government business, except for emergency fire, police, and health services, and all instructions in the state's schools would be carried on in English only. Proponents of the bill argued that a common language would bring unity to a rapidly fragmenting society and would speed the entry of school children into the mainstream of American culture. Many Latino and Chinese opponents (supported by many liberal whites) retorted that the aliens were anxious to learn English, but wanted to maintain their own heritages as well. The truth was, they said, the proposition, number 63 on the ballot, was essentially racist, belittling all who spoke in different tongues.

The debate aroused memories of the furor that had raged during the 1970s over the busing of school children from district to district in order to end segregation that resulted not from legal action by any government agency but from the *de facto* segregation of residential districts. Opposition was instantaneous and widespread.

The Chinese of San Francisco objected furiously to having their children carted off to distant schools, while the voters across the Bay in Richmond ejected the liberal school board that had allowed blacks to be introduced into their lower middle-class but predominantly white schools. Los Angeles voters ended the judicial career of Albert Gitelson, the superior court judge who in 1970 ordered that city to institute busing—an order upheld in 1976 by the state supreme court.

So many white families fled to the suburbs to escape the order that the proportion of white children in the Los Angeles schools dropped from about 56 percent in 1970 to 24 percent in 1980. That same year California voters overwhelmingly approved a constitutional amendment limiting busing to cases of *de jure* segregation. This, in effect, dismantled the whole program. By then, however, the point hardly mattered in Los Angeles. The white flight to the suburbs continued. (It had begun, incidentally, before the busing uproar, but the school problem accelerated it.) By 1986 only 20 percent of the pupils in the huge district, second largest in the nation, were white. Under those circumstances no busing program would have worked.

The question of racial prejudice carried over into the debate about bilingual schools. Would it affect voting patterns in 1986? A poll conducted by the *Los Angeles Times* indicated that, though California was more tolerant racially than most states, prejudice against Mexicans was more widespread than against blacks. But evidently California's Hispanics did not read Proposition 63 as a harmfully intolerant document. They were familiar with bilingual schools designed to help children of foreign parents keep pace with their English-speaking peers. Each year for ten years roughly half a million California pupils had attended such schools. Even so, large numbers of Latino and Oriental voters joined white California conservatives in piling up a heavy majority in favor of making English alone the state's official tongue. Turnout at the election, to be sure, was unusually light, and this may have affected the outcome. Still, you just can't tell from the color of their skins which way voters are going to jump.

A problem less emotional but more serious than language was school construction. For reasons not wholly clear, public school enrollment declined by about 900,000 between 1973 and 1983. (Private school enrollment increased by more than 100,000 during the same period.) Meanwhile, California's national ranking in the amount of money spent per pupil declined from sixth place to thirty-first.

A turnaround came in 1983 when the state, prodded ahead by an aggressive, newly elected superintendent of education, Bil Honig, raised teachers' salaries, made it easier for school boards to fire incompetent teachers, and encouraged longer school days and longer terms. At the same time, the children of increasing numbers of fertile immigrant families began knocking on the schoolhouse doors. Surprised administrators projected 600,000 more pupils by 1990.

Will response be too little and too late? On November 12, 1986, smiling officials of the Los Angeles school district broke ground for a new elementary school in the South Gate section—the first new school in the nation's second largest city in twenty years. When completed in 1988, it will provide space for 800 grade-schoolers. Other new and expanded schools currently on the drawing boards in Los Angeles will provide room for 21,000 more pupils by 1991—but by then, it is predicted, 82,000 will be clamoring for admission. Although the state's voters approved, in 1986, an $800 million bond issue as the first step in a $5 billion construction program, California's 1,160 school districts clearly have problems ahead of them.

The Hydraulic Empire

Readers will recall that during the 1960s California voters, led by Governor Edmund G. Brown, Sr., launched the mammoth State Water Project for shifting northern rivers south into the San Joaquin Valley and on over the Tehachapi Mountains into the Los Angeles Basin. After an energetic beginning, the program had languished for want of investors to buy its 5 percent bonds. When the Department of Water Resources proposed to make the bonds more attractive by raising interest to 7 percent, a storm of protest broke out. Much of the anger was directed at a so-called peripheral canal, forty-three miles long and four hundred feet wide, that would carry a large part of the Sacramento River around the marvelously unique delta that opens into San Francisco Bay.

The projected canal, which would not be built until after the first stage of the State Water Project had been completed, raised a tangle of questions. the Bureau of Reclamation's Central Valley Project was already pumping water out of the delta for transport to San Joaquin Valley farmers. Until the Peripheral Canal was built, the state project would also draw water from the delta. Why this competition? Well, farmers in theory could irrigate no more than 160 acres with cheap, federally produced Bureau of Reclamation water. The valley's huge corporate farmers did not like the restriction and hence had supported the State Project, which would sell them, at state-subsidized rates, all the water they wanted. Southern California could also buy state project water, but not federal water, through the Metropolitan Water District, and its support had helped carry the day for the state plan. (See pages 402–7 above.)

By not letting water "developed" in the north enter the delta and then drift off through San Francisco Bay into the ocean—that is, by making an end run with the Peripheral Canal—the state project could augment the flow of its south-bound California Aqueduct by an estimated 700,000 acre feet—a real treasure, since Arizona was on the point of finally utilizing its share of the Colorado River, which Californians had been using for years just as though it really belonged to them.

But what would the removal of that much water do to the ecology of the delta? Northern California environmentalists, who had opposed the State Water Plan from the beginning, feared the worst. So why not end the threat *now* by defeating the bond-interest proposal and thus stopping the entire project in its tracks? The effort failed, as we have seen, and in 1980 the legislature predictably passed a bill authorizing the project's next stage, the Peripheral Canal. The bill also outlined the complex technical steps that, state engineers said, would preserve the integrity of the delta.

Outraged environmentalists disbelieved the promises, distrusted the water hustlers, and saw no reason why the taxpayers of the entire state should further the growth ambitions of gargantuan Los Angeles while at the same time satisfying the greed of a handful of corporate agribusinesses. By collecting far more than the required number of signatures, they put on the June 1982 ballot a referendum calling for the rejection of the proposal. By then inflation had elevated the costs of the project so astronomically that even southern California voted against it. In northern California the margin of defeat was an almost unbelievable nine to one.

During this period, however, agribusiness won a sizable victory of its own. West of Fresno lay 600,000 parched acres where, in 1952, a handful of corporate farmers had formed the Westlands Water District. Their long-range aim was a fruitful contract with the Bureau of Reclamation's Central Valley project. "Long" turned out to be sixteen years.

It so happened that ten corporate landlords owned approximately 260,000 acres in Westlands. When the reclamation service ordered those owners and a few others not quite so fat to sell their holdings in excess of 160 acres (320 in the case of family ownership) or else buy higher-priced state water, the owners complied. But . . . the purchasers turned the operation of the many plots over to syndicates managed by relatives or associates of the original holders, so that in effect most of Westlands was still run by the same people. Small farmers who had been anticipating a piece of the action found themselves excluded as effectively as ever.

Protest flared so intensely that the Department of the Interior ordered a review of all reclamation projects in the West. It might have been better to let sleeping dogs lie. Agribusiness pointed to Cesar Chavez's United Farm Workers Union. In 1975 Governor Edmund G. "Jerry" Brown, Jr., and his secretary of agriculture, Rose Elizabeth Bird, created an Agricultural Labor Relations Board whose policies and wage scales, combined with inflation, had raised labor costs so high that growers had been forced to turn more and more to elaborate mechanization. The massive machines, the farmers said, could not be operated economically on 160 or even 320 acres. Heeding their cries, the Bureau of Reclamation decided that, although corporations would still be limited to the 160-acre rule, a family could receive federal water for as much as 960 acres. Economists have calculated that subsidies connected with federal water delivered to high-cost regions like Westlands amount to an annual $2,200 per acre—a $2 million-dollar taxpayer's gift to each holder of 960 acres. Mom-and-pop farms? Oh, sure, run by computers from a boardroom high in some San Francisco financial tower.

Obviously no sturdy, self-sustaining yeoman of the kind envisioned by Thomas Jefferson—and by the proponents of the original 1902 reclamation law—could break into that millionaires' club. Nor would they be allowed to try. After maneuverings whose description would glaze the eyes of even a corporate reader, Congress in effect abolished the whole concept of the 160-acre, single-family farm. (The *average* size of a California farm has risen from 260 acres in 1950 to roughly 500 in 1986.) "Think Big" seemed to have triumphed again.

Seemed. But bigness brought its own problems with it. Partly as a consequence of inflation, California's more than two hundred crops produced, in 1980, close to $15 billion, by far the greatest return from any industry in the state. Barring another burst of inflation, however, that handsome sum is not likely to be realized again. The defeat of the Peripheral Canal, the escalating costs of big construction projects, foreign competition, and shrinking income resulting from the nationwide farm depression make attempts to develop extensive new sources of water unrealistic.

Irrigation itself adds to the problems. Intensive cultivation depletes the soil, requiring the heavy use of expensive chemical fertilizers. Salt accumulations have to be battled with extensive drains or even more costly desalination plants. The humidity in heavily watered fields fosters an exuberant growth of pests. Each year California farmers use more than ninety thousand tons of pesticides in battlng insects. That, too, creates hazards. Groundwater supplies are polluted (chemical fertilizers add their bit), and farm workers suffer a greater incidence of health afflictions than does any other group of laborers in the state. Bird life in Kesterson Wildlife Refuge has been gruesomely endangered by selenium compounds in waste water draining out of Westlands.

Once arrogantly wasteful in their use of water, battered Californians are now beginning to feel frugal and hence cooperative. One dazzling result of this came in November 1986, when Sacramento and Washington agreed to operate the parallel State Water Project and the federal Central Valley Project as a single unit. As soon as a contract is worked out, which will take some time, more water can be moved into the delta, to its great benefit. Also, more can be pumped out, to be distributed through the linked networks to wherever it is needed. At the time of this writing, comparable success had not yet attended a proposal whereby the Metropolitan Water District of southern California will pay for the cost of lining canals and ditches in Imperial Valley with concrete and participate in other conservation measures in return for a part of the water saved. Optimists, however, believe that this, too, will come to pass and that because of such steps it will be possible to stave off major water crises for some time to come.

City Lights

In spite of the economic dominance of agriculture, the broad fields of the valleys show few signs of human habitation, for 95 percent of California's people are crowded into clusters defined by the Census Bureau as cities. Most live in southern California—upwards of twelve million metropolitan dwellers in the Los Angeles area and the counties adjacent to it, plus another two million in San Diego County. Another six and a half million have grouped themselves around San Francisco Bay and in the lower Sacramento Valley. The remaining 20 percent are scattered thinly through the deserts, mountains, inland valleys, and northern forests.

California's prosperous middle-class, urban residents are energetic in their work, yet highly informal in their life styles, devoted to both spectator and participatory sports, happier outdoors than in, committed to health regimes, and willing to support an extraordinary number of museums, art galleries, theaters, orchestras of all kinds (the recording business has passed film-making in profitability), and even bookstores. San Francisco, long noted for its live-and-let-live spirit, contains the largest community of homosexual men and lesbian women in the United States. When an initiative forbidding the hiring of gay schoolteachers was placed on the ballot in 1978, nearly half of the city's population, many attired in bizarre costumes, turned out to take part in, or watch, an enormous parade of protest. A large majority of voters from throughout the state joined them in defeating the measure, as they did eight years later in rejecting a bill that would have placed severe constraints on victims of the sexually oriented disease AIDS (acquired immune deficiency syndrome).

Ridiculing California cities for their unconventional amusements, evangelical excesses, neon jungles, nudist beaches, and far-out clothing has long been a favorite pastime among visiting journalists. The image may be changing. When a scoffer jibed that Californians spend so much time working on their bodies that the fat collects on their minds, an outsider, Hillary Johnson, fired a return salvo in *Vogue* magazine. Los Angeles, she wrote (as happily quoted by popular columnist Jack Smith of the *Los Angeles Times*), "is a fantasy island where people can hope to reinvent themselves in mid-life. A more potent lure is hard to imagine." All around, she continued, "is a nearly palpable sense of anything is possible here." Not least among the events fortifying Miss Johnson's enthusiasm was Los Angeles's hosting of the Olympic Games in 1984 and, for the first time ever by any city, making a profit on them, the money to be used for furthering youth sports programs.

Preserving this sense of well-being absorbs a considerable amount of civic energy. One notable example came in response to soaring property taxes, which are based on assessed valuations. In 1970, the average home in southern California sold at the national median of $32,000. Then came inflation. The national median jumped to $74,000. But in southern California, crowded with baby boomers who had reached the age of wanting homes of their own and job hunters drawn by one of the periodic surges in the aerospace industry, the median price of an ordinary home squirted up to $118,000. Taxes soared commensurately.

Riding high on the property owner's anger, a one-time realtor, Paul Gann, and Howard Jarvis, a hoarse-voiced, small-time politician who was director of the Apartment Owners Association of Los Angeles, easily collected enough signatures to place the since-famed Proposition 13 on the ballot of June 1978. If passed, it would limit property taxes to 1 percent of a property's assessed value, as determined in 1975. Assessments, furthermore, could rise by no more than 2 percent a year. Although Governor Jerry Brown and most of the state's political establishment pointed out that the measure would deprive school districts and city and county governments of $7 billion in revenues, the voters approved the measure by a two-thirds majority. Two years later another initiative sponsored by Paul Gann limited annual increases in government spending to a rate no greater than the rate of inflation combined, complexly, with the rate of population growth.

Property taxes plummeted—57 percent in some areas. The biggest benefits went to the owners of commercial property; Standard Oil of California, for example, saved $47 million a year. Retailers claimed business was stimulated by a flow of cash that otherwise would have gone into government coffers. By contrast, schools cut down on extracurricular activities and still had to be financed primarily by the state, with an inevitable loss in autonomy. Libraries, parks, and recreation departments became penurious, in spite of help from enthusiastic volunteer workers.

One unexpected outcome was a partial reshaping of California cities. To help compensate for lost property tax revenues, metropolitan governments began imposing heavy fees for sewer hookups and building permits. This prompted persons who might have built homes in the suburbs to turn instead to patching up old houses in decaying downtown districts, to the great distress of the construction industry. Then there was the escape clause in Proposition 13 that allowed property to be reassessed at full current value whenever it was sold. Rather than face so staggering a jump in taxes on moving into a new home, people became more willing to stay where they were. This in turn led them to take a greater interest in protecting the amenities of their neighborhoods.

The majority of their complaints revolved around problems created by growth—too much traffic in residential areas, high-rise apartments and office buildings that shut out sunlight, the bulldozing of trees to widen streets, and the destruction of fine old-style California bungalows in order to crowd in ticky-tacky condominiums. The town of Petaluma, north of San Francisco, began the revolt with a 1973 ordinance rstricting to five hundred the new residential units that could be built within its limits during a single year, a step upheld in 1976 by the United

States Supreme Court. In 1974, burgeoning San Jose, smothered by smog, ended its growth-oriented advertising, elected Janet Gray Hayes, a crusading conservationist, as mayor, and prohibited the building of new tracts until the developers funded additional schoolrooms. San Diego forbade view-killing high-rises along the coast (compare Honolulu), while Sacramento, the Santa Barbara suburb of Goleta, Pleasanton and Livermore in the hills behind Oakland, Santa Cruz, and a dozen other communities sought to control headlong expansion by limiting water and sewer hookups, by establishing high ratios of open space to structures, and so on.

Los Angeles tried its own variation of these ameliorations. An old put down of the city sneered at it as forty suburbs in search of a city. And, in truth, Los Angeles is a lot of towns gathered up like eggs in a basket—about 180 of them. Neighborhood bonds are stronger than city bonds; an activist is more likely to define himself as living in San Pedro, Eagle Rock, or Canoga Park than Los Angeles. About three hundred community watchdog associations have sprung into being, ready to invade city council meetings with their shouts and placards, to file lawsuits, and to form coalitions with each other for the sake of more muscle. One such group calls itself Not Yet New York—just as San Diegans like to use Not Yet Los Angeles as a battle cry.

The most significant victory came in 1986, when the affluent West Side district and prosperous sections of the San Fernando Valley decided to finesse cumbersome zoning rules and keep high-density apartment houses, office complexes, and traffic-bringing shopping malls out of sensitive areas by means of a ballot initiative known as Proposition U. Appalled developers and conservative politicians decried the replacement of zoning provisions with government by initiative. Some soothsayers said the measure would drive high-rises back into the central city and create worse traffic gridlocks there. Others predicted commercial developments would follow jobs and customers farther out into the suburbs and add to Los Angeles's already almost unmanageable sprawl.

Paying no heed to the arguments, a thumping majority of voters pushed the initiative through. What its ultimate effect will be can't yet be said. However, a sobered city council has taken out of its files and dusted off a long-neglected proposal to divide the city into thirty-five planning districts wherein community residents will at last have recognized voices in determining how to keep their city livable.

Fantasy island, of course, has its dark fringes. The Federal Clean Air Act some years ago set standards it said had to be met by December 1987. A year before the deadline the South Coast Air Quality Management Board, which oversees Los Angeles, Orange, Riverside, and San Bernardino counties, the smoggiest in the nation, announced it would be unable to meet the requirements. Sacramento, Ventura, and Fresno counties were not in much better shape. The specter of sanctions loomed—unfairly, perhaps, because the penalties were designed to punish districts that weren't really trying to clean up their acts. But what of districts that were trying but failing?

One problem is that federal standards were imposed as if the situation they addressed were static. It is not. Population steadily climbs. According to the Automobile Club of Southern California, there will be three million more people in the area it serves by the year 2000. That means hundreds of thousands of new cars and who knows how many more factory boilers, heaters, refineries, and coastal oil wells? Even if laggard air quality control boards do come up with quick fixes, which is unlikely, they will be overtaken regardless.

There is another complication. Streets and highways are steadily deteriorating. Planned freeways haven't been built because of escalating costs. California, again according to the Auto Club, ranks last among the nation's states in per capita spending on roads. The Club recommends, accordingly, that the California Transit Authority spend $20.5 billion over the next fifteen years on building new freeways, a cost not likely to sit well anywhere outside the highway lobby.

The Auto Club's recommendation does not mention that early in 1986 work began on Los Angeles's long-delayed subway system—a tiny beginning on a segment 4.4 miles long, with the rest in doubt because of funds and environmental problems. But it is a start toward facing the problems of both traffic and smog, as is San Diego's light-rail connection with neighboring Tijuana, Mexico, a city of close to 800,000 people. Yet these alternatives to autos probably seem too trivial to the potent Auto Club to bear mention.

Then there is the dilemma of trash. You put your garbage, junk mail, plastics, lawn trimmings, and left-over dabs of toxic paints, varnishes, and spot removers into bags and cans, set them beside the curb on specified days, and they disappear as if by magic—an annual *thirty-six million tons* of the stuff. In 1984 the collections were being hauled off to 481 landfill sites throughout California. By the time you read this only about three hundred will be left with room in them for more trash. After 1993, it is predicted, Los Angeles and the cities that ring San Francisco Bay will have no landfill available unless they build new sites or extend old ones. But places within reasonable driving distance are not easy to find; people object to the passage of heavy garbage trucks, and to having rats and human scavengers as neighbors. Plans to scatter thirty-four huge incinerators throughout the state, ten of them in the heavily populated San Gabriel Valley east of Los Angeles, and to use the burning trash to produce electricity, have also been resisted. Citizens fear that poisonous dioxin gases will be spewed out during the incineration. Meanwhile, band-aids are suggested: compacters to reduce volume, recycling, and drives to make packaging less bulky.

And then there is the human dilemma—the homeless; the chronically unemployed, especially black and Hispanic teenagers; the high school dropouts (the California rate of 19 percent is well above the national average); the children born each year to unwed mothers (18 percent among whites, 57 percent among blacks). The number of Californians living below the poverty line exceeds the combined total populations of Utah and Nevada. The spread between the top group of earners and the bottom group steadily widens, a growing drain on welfare services. Automation hurts workers in heavy industries; computers, whose development is closely associated with California, offers little to the unskilled—except for components that can be assembled by female immigrants working at home for sweatshop wages.

Crime is a constant, suppurating sore. In 1982 police records showed that nearly a million and a half adults and a quarter of a million juveniles were arrested for one cause or another. There were 2,788 murders, 12,529 forcible rapes, half a million burglaries, and 164,530 thefts of automoblies. Hundreds of youth gangs, mostly composed of minorities, carried on a guerrilla warfare with each other and with the police in the poorer sections of major cities. California's overcrowded prison population numbered 33,453.

Alarmed by statistics such as these, the state's voters in 1982 decisively defeated an initiative that would have required the registration, with the police, of handguns—even though handguns were the weapon most commonly used in the commission of serious crimes. Ten years earlier angry voters had also reinstated, by a 67.5 percent majority, the death penalty. When it seemed that three of the justices of the California Supreme Court were granting new trials to an undue number of persons sentenced to death by lower courts, the voters removed them from office. Those summarily dismissed were Chief Justice Rose Bird, the only woman on the bench; Cruz Reyonoso, the only Hispanic; and Joseph Grodin, a liberal.

Governor George Deukmejian promptly named the court's leading conservative, Malcolm M. Lucas, a former law partner of his, to replace Rose Bird. On announcing the appointment, Deukmejian spoke of "the great need to restore public confidence in and respect for [California's] highest court." Whether shifting the philosophy of the bench farther to the right will reduce the political turmoil in which the court has been enmeshed for the past decade and will help restore its national prestige remains, at this writing, to be seen.

Big Is Better? Small Is Beautiful?

Despite the statistics of despair, despite the fact that San Francisco is the suicide capital of the United States, California still glows in the public mind as the land of new beginnings. Growth feeds on itself. Dollars blossom. By 1980, wholesale and retail trade employed 2.3 million persons. Services—health, recreation, hotels and motels, motion pictures and television production, computer data processing, and a host of other endeavors—hired still more, 2.4 million.

Meanwhile, southern California had grown so experienced in handling defense items that, when the aerospace industry underwent one of its periodic resurgences during the early 1980s, the area received an annual $40 billion worth of new contracts for developing ultrasophisticated strategic bombers and varieties of deadly missiles that could be fired from sea, land, or air. An intricate net of subcontracting links an enormous number of seemingly unrelated firms—photographic equipment, electrical devices, cardboard containers—to the main pursuit. The massive Boeing plant in Seattle, Washington, subcontracts 25 percent of its work in southern California.

Northern California dominates the electronics industry. During World War II several electronics firms gathered in the Stanford Industrial Park south of Palo Alto. Out of the ferment that arose from joining federal funding, university research, and private entrepreneurship came the magic silicon chip. From it sprang a computer and microprocessing industry whose peak, in spite of a current slump resulting from overproduction, is not yet in sight.

Consider, as an example of new opportunities, Steven P. Jobs, age 21, and Stephen D. Wozniak, 26. In the 1970s they set out to design and develop a small personal computer that anyone could use at home or in business. They named it Apple because, they said, an apple represented the clean simplicity they were seeking. They raised $1,350 by selling a used calculator and an old Volkswagon van, and began work in Jobs's garage. Soon money was pouring in. They introduced new models (the Macintosh is a tasty variety of apple) and expanded operations worldwide. Within six years after incorporation, Apple Computer had sold a million systems for upward of a billion dollars and was employing 4,000 workers. During that same period another 1,500 computer, data processing, and, more recently, genetic splicing firms crowded into what was called Silicon Valley, a thirty-mile strip between San Francisco and San Jose. From there the industry spread to other centers throughout the industrial world.

Older industries have expanded on a comparable scale. Shipping, for instance. California long eyed the Orient as a potentially huge trade bonanza—and it now is. In 1982 trade with Asia accounted for 69 percent of California's $34.5 billion international commerce; another 5 percent went to Australia and New Zealand. Most of this passes through two port areas, San Francisco–Oakland and Long Beach–San Pedro, the latter the largest manmade harbor in the world. The biggest trading partner is Japan, which in 1982 received about $7 billion worth of electrical equipment, machinery, processed food, chemicals, and the like. It sent back about $13 billion worth of automobiles, television sets, plywood products, and art objects. No wonder a Japanese firm opened, in 1986, an imposing ultramodern, fifty-story office and management tower at the intersection of Figueroa Street with Wilshire Boulevard in Los Angeles. As the head of the tower development company remarked, southern California "has a special orientation toward the Pacific rim."

As they have been doing for more than a century, tourists as well as goods traveled into (and out of) California.* Californians joined them in droves to enjoy the state's recreational advantages. In 1980, ninety million people visited California's state and national parks. More millions went through the national monuments, national forests, and the far-flung lands administered by the Bureau of Land Management, principally in the state's deserts. Overcrowding of favorite sites has led to proposals that three additional sites in the desert be elevated to national park status—expanded Death Valley and Joshua Tree National monuments and a brand new Mojave Desert National Park in between the other two.

Urban attractions vied in popularity with country ones. San Diego could hardly function without tourist dollars. Disneyland, Hollywood (where few movies are made now), the Pasadena Rose Parade, and San Francisco's stunning Bay bridges draw sightseers from practically every country in the world. Conventions went far in bringing to the state, in 1982, $27 billion worth of travel-related revenues—and yet the California Office of tourism spent only $580,000 to lure in visitors as compared to New York's advertising output of $12 million.

No spot was inaccessible. Rugged, fat-tired three and four-wheeled scooters chewed up once quiet terrain—power trips insensitive to the landscape. Four-wheel-drive vehicles and multitudes of motorcycles scoured the desert, thoughtlessly destroying irreplaceable Indian itaglios. Kayaks and neoprene rafts coursed what few Sierra streams remained undammed. Not one towering wall in Yosemite remained unscaled, but at least climbers ceased driving pitons into the rock for holding their ropes and instead thrust ingenious, removable chock blocks into handy cracks. In 1969, Hoyle Schwitzer of Torrence attached a free sail to a Malibu surfboard and created a single-person sailing vessel, called a windsurfer, that allowed adventurers to test, standing upright on that thin board, any lake, harbor, or stretch of open ocean they wished. By 1980 he was selling his windsurfers worldwide. Simultaneously, Francis Rogallo fitted graceful, mothlike wings to a light, portable frame and created the hang glider. Soarers came down from spiraling on high thermals to declare they had been close enough to hawks to watch their eyes blink.

The expansive feeling that anything went led inevitably to attempts to maximize profits by subjecting nature to man's desire. Fill the air with noxious fumes, push oil wells farther and farther into the sea, poison the ground with pesticides and herbicides, dam the rivers, pour sewage into the harbors (in 1985 Los Angeles, after ignoring several warnings, paid heavy fines for doing just that), shred forest for lumber, carve up hills and city neighborhoods for freeways. Jungles of bill-

---

*Between 1974 and 1980, more Californians moved to Arizona and other sunbelt states than came from those regions. The deficit was more than counterbalanced by inflow from the northeastern and central states, to say nothing of immigrants from Mexico, Central America, and Asia.

boards and wires, unsightly used-car dumps, din of trucks, snarl of chain saws, blare of automobile horns—for years people seemed not to mind, for here was proof that opportunity had been seized, jobs opened up.

But the protective strain was also strong in California and has been since the days of John Muir. Dogged by environmental groups, the federal government has set aside millions of acres of California land as roadless wilderness areas into which no motor vehicles can intrude. Fifty-one nature reserves and national wildlife refuges protect threatened and endangered species of plant, bird, and animal life. The California Nature Conservancy, drawing on contributions by tens of thousands of members, has purchased other sensitive spots. Self-appointed watchdog groups strive to defend rivers from would-be dam builders, to restore Mono Lake, whose level has been sharply reduced by the concrete tentacles of the Los Angeles Department of Water and Power, to halt off-shore oil leases, and block the Forest Service's 1984 plan to increase timber cutting by as much as 75 percent. In 1986 voters easily passed a ballot initiative that imposed strict controls on dumping toxic wastes that might in any way percolate into groundwater supplies.

Perhaps the most significant environmental measure of recent times came in 1972, when conservationists placed on the November ballot an initiative calling for a coastal planning commission charged with drawing up a plan for regulating all future development along the shore line between Oregon and Mexico. Governor Reagan, who was philosophically opposed to governmental interference with private initiative, led the state's construction firms, building trade unions, real estate agents, savings and loan associations, the oil industry, and owners of coastal property in a lavishly financed attack on the measure. Nevertheless, it carried by a 55 percent margin.

Four years of planning resulted in the California Coastal Zone Conservation Act. This created a permanent commission with authority to review every new project that might affect the integrity of the coast. In places, that line is deemed to extend as much as five miles inland. The study of each proposal has poured as many as fifty thousand documents a year onto the backs of the commission, its counsels, and administrative assistants. Reaction to its decisions have varied, as might be expected, from applause to denunciation.

When the time came to appoint the members of the commission, Jerry Brown, a liberal Democrat, was governor. Though he was a poor administrator, evasive at times, and given to changing his stance according to his reading of public moods, he was also innovative and imaginative. He felt the world in general and California in particular was entering an ''era of limits.'' His philosophic idol was E. F. Schumacher of England, author of *Small Is Beautiful* and proponent of the idea that trying to increase supplies to meet demands rather than reducing demands to fit supplies is the way to ruin.

Naturally, Brown appointed to the coastal commission and to other government agencies people whose beliefs coincided with his. One result was that a subsidiary of Dun and Bradstreet branded the state as a highly unfavorable spot for locating a new industry.

Reactions were intense and oversimplified: ''small is beautiful'' environmentalists against growth-oriented, nature-bashing industrialists and developers. But perhaps another way is emerging—cooperative endeavor. At the time of writing, the militant Environmental Defense Fund and Los Angeles's once inflexible Metropolitan Water District are gingerly discussing a breathtaking proposal for solving one of California's most persistent problems, moving water south without offending the north.

The plan envisions drawing water out of the Delta during wet years, when levels in that marvelous funnel would not be reduced to the ecological danger point. The extracted water would be moved south and stored in a huge aquifer (a natural underground reservoir) until needed during dry periods, when, for the sake of the Delta, no water would be transported south.

The aquifer in question is the Chino Basin, some twenty-five to thirty miles east of the Los Angeles Civic Center. Already a source of residential, industrial, and agricultural water for a rapidly growing area, the Basin is showing signs of becoming polluted by agricultural waste and toxic dumping. The solution now under consideration envisions an expensive research program, jointly financed by the water district and the Environmental Defense Fund. The aim would be learning how to halt the pollution at its source by working out, with the polluters, more environmentally acceptable ways of carrying on their businesses. The underground reservoir will then be relatively clean, the Delta will be safe, and water will move into the growing southland without another acrimonious dispute.

Will the plan work? Will it even be tried? Can the principle be extended to other fields? At this point prediction is too risky to be attempted. But at least it does sound like a new beginning.

five kinds of mammals who left their bones in the dark pitch of the La Brea Tar Pits no longer survive in North America. Many have vanished entirely from the earth.

Man, whatever the place of his origin, proved more resilient. It is not likely that his adaptations were conscious, panicked, or hurried. Probably the groups who inhabited the slowly drying Great Basin and Southwest had already experimented, between feasts on mammoth meat, with other foods: seeds, pine nuts, rabbits, the small deer of the brushlands, lizards, locusts, and even the larvae of certain flies that collected in masses in the sedge around the shrinking lakes. As big-game grew scarce, reliance on these substitutes increased until at last the methods of obtaining and preparing them seemed as old as time. The new life styles that accompanied the changes were codified meanwhile by a fresh corpus of myth and ritual handed down from generation to generation until this mode seemed part of eternity. It is so with all evolving cultures, including our own.

As has already been suggested, the first groups to arrive in California may have been hunters whose origins are lost in dimness. Or, possibly, the land really was inhospitable to nomadic man after the shift from a hunting to a food-gathering culture had begun. Whenever the migration developed, it was not so concerted. The wide diversity of tongues spoken within historic times—more than a hundred dialects of six basic language stocks—suggests a varied tribal overlay for a period from many starting points, until at last the area sustained more native Americans than any other region north of tropical Mexico—as many, according to such noted anthropologists as S. F. Cook and A. L. Kroeber, as 125,000 persons. Villages appeared in every part of the state—take except the High Sierras—and even its delicious meadows became refuges, then as now, for dwellers in the Central Valley who were eager to escape the heat of the rainless summers.

The magnet during the centuries was California's profusion of food. Successive runs of salmon ruled the northern rivers, including the Sacramento system, throughout most of the summer. The coast furnished an abundance of shellfish. A variety of seeds, among them acorns and mesquite beans, grew in the valleys and on the hillsides. Between harvests these could be stored in big baskets on platforms out of reach of rodents. Ground into flour with stones and the acorn meal leached of its bitter tannic acid with hot water, they were boiled into mush or baked into cakes. Meat came from fishing and small game that could be killed with curved throwing-sticks. There were numerous bear, elk, and deer. Though hard to stalk now, and kill with the weapons available, these furnished both variety and challenge.

Bibliography

For convenience the listing that follows is broken into divisions. First come general, regional, and special studies. These are followed by groupings arranged chronologically. There is some arbitrariness in the divisions, for obviously many books and even articles will overlap in their subject matter from one grouping into another.

The publication date appended to each title is that of the edition used rather than the date of first publication, though of course the two often coincided. The names of the three periodicals most frequently consulted are abbreviated: *CHSQ* for *California Historical Society Quarterly; PHR* for *Pacific Historical Review; SCQ* for *Southern California Quarterly* and its predecessor, *Historical Society of Southern California Quarterly.*

General Histories

BANCROFT, HUBERT HOWE. *History of California.* 7 vols. San Francisco, 1884–90.
BEAN, WALTON. *California: An Interpretive History.* New York, 1968.
CAUGHEY, JOHN. *California.* Englewood Cliffs, N.J., 1970.
CLELAND, ROBERT G. *California in Our Time.* New York, 1947.
———. *From Wilderness to Empire.* New York, 1944.
DURRENBERGER, ROBERT W. *California: The Last Frontier.* New York, 1969.
HITTELL, THEODORE H. *History of California.* 4 vols. San Francisco, 1885–97.
HUTCHINSON, W. H. *California.* Palo Alto, Calif., 1969.
McWILLIAMS, CAREY. *California: The Great Exception.* New York, 1949.
MORGAN, NEIL. *The Pacific States.* New York, 1967.
POMEROY, EARL. *The Pacific Slope.* New York, 1965.
ROLLE, ANDREW. *California: A History.* New York, 1963.
STONE, IRVING. *Men to Match My Mountains.* New York, 1956.

Regional Histories

AUSTIN, MARY. *The Land of Little Rain.* Boston, 1903.
CLELAND, ROBERT G., and ROBERT V. HINE. *The Irvine Ranch.* San Marino, Calif., 1962.

ELDREDGE, ZOETH S. *The Beginnings of San Francisco.* 2 vols. San Francisco, 1912.

FARQUHAR, FRANCIS P. *History of the Sierra Nevada.* Berkeley and Los Angeles, 1965.

FOGELSON, ROBERT M. *The Fragmented Metropolis, Los Angeles, 1850–1930.* Cambridge, Mass., 1967.

HITTELL, JOHN S. *A History of San Francisco.* San Francisco, 1878.

KINNAIRD, LAWRENCE. *History of Greater San Francisco Bay Region.* 3 vols. New York, 1966.

LEE, W. STORRS. *The Sierra.* New York, 1961.

LEWIS, OSCAR. *San Francisco, Mission to Metropolis.* Berkeley, 1966.

McGOWAN, JOSEPH A. *History of the Sacramento Valley.* 3 vols. New York, 1961.

McWILLIAMS, CAREY. *Southern California Country.* New York, 1964.

MUIR, JOHN. *The Mountains of California.* New York, 1894.

RAND, CHRISTOPHER. *Los Angeles: The Ultimate City.* New York, 1967.

REISENBERG, FELIX, JR. *Golden Gate: The Story of San Francisco Harbor.* New York, 1940.

ROBINSON, W. W. *Los Angeles: A Profile.* Norman, Okla., 1968.

SMITH, WALLACE. *Garden of the Sun* [San Joaquin Valley]. Los Angeles, 1953.

Miscellaneous Special Studies

California, A Guide to the Golden State. New York, 1967.

COOK, S. F. *The Conflict Between the California Indian and White Civilization.* 3 vols. Berkeley and Los Angeles, 1943.

COOPER, ERWIN. *Aqueduct Empire.* Glendale, Calif., 1968.

DASMANN, RAYMOND E. *The Destruction of California.* New York, 1965.

DAVIS, W. J. *History of Political Conventions in California 1849–1892.* Sacramento, 1892.

DELMATIER, ROYCE D., CLARENCE F. McINTOSH, and EARL G. WATERS, (eds.). *The Rumble of California Politics, 1848–1970.* New York, 1970.

DURRENBERGER, ROBERT W. *Patterns on the Land.* Palo Alto, Calif., 1965.

GOETZMANN, WILLIAM H. *Exploration and Empire.* New York, 1966.

GREEVER, WILLIAM S. *The Bonanza West.* Norman, Okla., 1963.

HAMMOND, GEORGE P. (ed.). *The Larkin Papers.* 10 vols. Berkeley and Los Angeles, 1951–68.

HARTMAN, DAVID N. *California and Man.* Dubuque, Iowa, 1964.

HEIZER, ROBERT F., and ALAN F. ALMQUIST. *The Other Californians.* Berkeley and Los Angeles, 1971.

HILL, GLADWIN. *The Dancing Bear.* Cleveland, Ohio, 1968.

——*History of Sacramento County* (pub. by Thompson and West). Sacramento, 1880.

HUTCHINSON, CLAUDE V. (ed.). *California Agriculture.* Berkeley, 1946.

LANTIS, DAVIS W., RODNEY STEINER, and ARTHUR KARINEN. *California, Land of Contrast.* Belmont, Calif., 1963.

McWILLIAMS, CAREY. *Factories in the Fields.* Boston, 1939.

——. *North from Mexico.* New York, 1968.

MELENDY, H. BRETT. "One Hundred Years of the Redwood Lumber Industry, 1850–1950." Unpublished Ph.D. dissertation, Stanford, 1952.

PARSONS, JAMES J. "The Uniqueness of California," *American Quarterly*, VII (1955)
PITT, LEONARD. *The Decline of the Californios*. Berkeley and Los Angeles, 1970.
ROBINSON, W. W. *Land in California*. Berkeley and Los Angeles, 1948.
VORSPAN, MAX, and LLOYD P. GARTNER. *History of the Jews of Los Angeles*. San Marino, Calif., 1970.
WATKINS, T. H. *Gold and Silver in the West*. Palo Alto, Calif. 1971.

Anthologies of Various Sorts

CAUGHEY, JOHN W., and LAREE CAUGHEY. *California Heritage*. Itasca, Ill., 1971.
HALE, DENNIS, and JONATHAN EISEN. *The California Dream*. New York, 1968.
KIRSCH, ROBERT, and WILLIAM S. MURPHY. *West of the West*. New York, 1967.
PITT, LEONARD. *California Controversies*. Glenview, Ill., 1968.

The Indians and Spanish California

AINSWORTH, KATHERINE, and EDWARD M. AINSWORTH. *In The Shade of The Juniper Tree* [life of Serra]. New York, 1970.
BOLTON, H. E. "The Mission as a Frontier Institution . . .," *American Historical Review*, Oct., 1917.
———. *Outposts of Empire* [Anza's expeditions]. New York, 1931.
———. *The Spanish Borderlands*. New Haven, 1921.
BRANDON, WILLIAM. "The California Indian World," *The Indian Historian*, Summer, 1969.
CHAPMAN, CHARLES E. *A History of California: The Spanish Period*. New York, 1921.
COLLEY, CHARLES. "The Missionization of the Coast Miwok Indians," *CHSQ*, June, 1970.
DENTON, V. L. *The Far West Coast*. Toronto, 1942.
DUNNE, PETER M. *Pioneer Jesuits of Northern Mexico*. Berkeley and Los Angeles, 1944.
ENGLEHARDT, ZEPHYRIN. *The Missions and Missionaries of California*. 4 vols. San Francisco, 1908–15.
FARB, PETER. *Man's Rise to Civilization*. New York, 1968.
FIREMAN, JANET, and MANUEL P. SERVIN. "Miguel Costansó, California's Forgotten Founder," *CHSQ*, March, 1970.
GOLDER, FRANK A. *Russian Expansion in the Pacific*. Cleveland, 1914.
GRANT, CAMPBELL. *The Rock Paintings of the Chumash*. Berkeley and Los Angeles, 1965.
GUEST, FLORIAN. "The Establishment of the Villa de Branciforte," *CHSQ*, March, 1962.
HASELDEN, R. B. "Is the Drake Plate of Brass Genuine?" *CHSQ*, Sept., 1937.
HEIZER, ROBERT F. "The California Indians," *CHSQ*, March, 1962.
——— and M. A. WHIPPLE (eds.). *The California Indians*. Berkeley and Los Angeles, 1953.
KROEBER, A. L. *Handbook of the Indians of California*. Washington, D.C., 1925.
———. "The Nature of the Land-Holding Groups in Aboriginal California," in *Aboriginal California*. Berkeley and Los Angeles, 1966.

PALÓU, FRANCISCO. *Life of Fray Junípero Serra* (trans. by Maynard Gieger). Washington, D.C., 1955.

Publications of the Academy of Pacific Coast History. (Contains accounts by Portolá and Costansó.) Berkeley, 1911.

RICHMAN, IRVING B. *California under Spain and Mexico, 1535–1847.* New York, 1911.

SIMPSON, LESLIE B. (ed.). *Journal of José Longinos Martínez.* San Francisco, 1961.

———. (ed.). *The Letters of José Señan, OFM, 1796–1823.* San Francisco, 1962.

UNDERHILL, RUTH. *The Indians of Southern California.* Washington, D.C. (n.d.).

WILBUR, MARGUERITE E. (ed.). *Vancouver in California, 1792–1794.* Los Angeles, 1953.

The First Outsiders

BEECHEY, Frederick. *Narrative of a Voyage to the Pacific* . . . London, 1831.

BLAKE, ANSON S. "The Hudson's Bay Company in San Francisco," *CHSQ,* June–Sept., 1940.

BYNUM, LINDLEY. *Journal of a Voyage* . . . *in 1804 by William Shaler.* Claremont, Calif., 1935.

CHEVIGNY, HECTOR. *Lord of Alaska: Baranov and the Russian Adventure.* New York, 1951.

———. *Lost Empire* [Rezanov]. New York, 1937.

CLELAND, ROBERT G. *This Reckless Breed of Men* [Southwestern fur trappers]. New York, 1950.

COUGHLIN, MAGDALIN. "Boston Smugglers on the Coast," *CHSQ,* June, 1967.

DAKIN, SUSANNA B. *The Lives of William Hartnell.* Stanford, 1949.

———. *A Scotch Paisano: Hugo Reid's Life in California, 1832–1853.* Berkeley and Los Angeles, 1939.

DANA, RICHARD HENRY. *Two Years Before the Mast* (ed. by John H. Kemble). Los Angeles, 1964.

DAVIS, WILLIAM HEATH. *Seventy-Five Years in California* (ed. by Harold Small). San Francisco, 1967.

DU HAUT-CILLY, A. "Account of California in the Years 1827–28," *CHSQ,* June–Sept., 1929.

ELLISON, WILLIAM H., and FRANCIS PRICE (eds.). *The Life and Adventures in California of Don Agustin Janssens.* San Marino, Calif., 1953.

EWERS, JOHN C. (ed.). *Narrative of the Adventures of Zenas Leonard.* Norman, Okla., 1959.

FORBES, ALEXANDER. *California: A History of Upper and Lower California.* London, 1839.

GEIGER, MAYNARD, OFM. *Mission Santa Barbara.* Santa Barbara, 1965.

GIBSON, JAMES R. "Russians in California," *Pacific Northwest Quarterly,* Oct., 1969.

HANSON, WOODROW JAMES. *The Search for Authority in California.* Oakland, Calif., 1960.

HILL, JOSEPH J. "Ewing Young in the Fur Trade of the American Southwest," *Oregon Historical Quarterly,* March, 1923.

HUTCHINSON, C. ALAN. *Frontier Settlement in Mexican California.* New Haven, 1969.

JAMES, GEORGE WHARTON. *In and Out of the Old Missions of California.* Boston, 1913.

McCARTHY, FRANCIS. *The History of Mission San José, California, 1797–1837.* Fresno, Calif., 1958.

McCRACKEN, HAROLD. *Hunters of the Stormy Sea.* New York, 1959.

MALONEY, ALICE. "The Hudson's Bay Company in California," *Oregon Historical Quarterly,* 1936.

MORGAN, DALE L. *Jedediah Smith and the Opening of the West.* Indianapolis and New York, 1953.

NIDEVER, GEORGE. *Life and Adventures* (ed. by William H. Ellison). Berkeley, 1937.

OGDEN, ADELE. "Alfred Robinson, New England Merchant," *CHSQ,* Sept., 1944.

———. "Boston Hide Droughers Along the California Shore," *CHSQ,* Dec., 1929.

———. *The California Sea Otter Trade.* Berkeley, 1941.

———. "Hides and Tallow: McCulloch, Hartnell & Company, 1822–1828," *CHSQ,* Sept., 1927.

———. "New England Traders in Spanish and Mexican California," in *Greater America.* Berkeley and Los Angeles, 1945.

PATTIE, JAMES O. *Personal Narrative.* Philadelphia, 1962.

ROBINSON, ALFRED. *Life in California.* New York, 1846.

RUSCHENBERGER, W. S. W. *Sketches in California,* 1836 (ed. by John H. Kemble). Los Angeles, 1953.

SERVIN, MANUEL P. "The Secularization of the California Missions: A Reappraisal," *SCQ,* June, 1965.

SIMPSON, GEORGE, SIR. *Narrative of a Journey Round the World.* 2 vols. London, 1849.

SMITH, ALSON J. *Men Against the Mountains* [Jedediah Smith]. New York, 1965.

TAYS, GEORGE. "Mariano Guadalupe Vallejo and Sonoma," *CHSQ,* 6 installments, beginning June, 1937.

———. "Revolutionary California." Unpublished Ph.D. dissertation, University of California, Berkeley, 1932.

WATSON, W. S. *West Wind, the Life Story of Joseph Reddeford Walker.* Los Angeles, 1934.

WEBB, EDITH BUCKLIN. *Life in the Old Missions.* Los Angeles, 1952.

American Infiltration and Conquest

BIDWELL, JOHN. *A Journey to California in 1841* (ed. by Francis P. Farquhar). Berkeley, 1964.

BROOKE, GEORGE B. "The Vest Pocket War of Commodore Jones," *PHR,* 1962.

BRYANT, EDWIN. *What I Saw in California . . . in 1846–47.* New York, 1849.

BURGESS, SHERWOOD D. "Lumbering in Hispanic California," *CHSQ,* Sept., 1962.

CAMP, CHARLES L. (ed.). *George C. Yount and His Chronicles of the West.* Denver, Colo., 1966.

——— (ed.). *James L. Clyman, Frontiersman.* Portland, Ore., 1960.

COLTON, WALTER. *Three Years in California.* New York, 1850.

DE VOTO, BERNARD. *The Year of Decision, 1846.* Boston, 1943.

DILLON, RICHARD. *Fool's Gold: A Biography of John Sutter.* New York, 1967.

DRURY, CLIFFORD M. "Walter Colton, Chaplain and Alcalde," *CHSQ,* June, 1956.

FREMONT, JOHN CHARLES. "The Conquest of California," *Century Magazine,* April, 1891.

————. *Memoirs of My Life.* New York, 1887.

————. *Narratives of Exploration and Adventure* (ed. by Allan Nevins). New York, 1956.

GRAEBNER, NORMAN A. *Empire on the Pacific.* New York, 1955.

GRIVAS, THEODORE. *Military Government in California, 1846–1850.* Glendale, Calif., 1963.

GUDDE, ERWIN G. *Sutter's Own Story.* New York, 1936.

HANSEN, WOODROW J. "Robert Semple, Pioneer, Promoter, Politician," *CHSQ,* Sept., 1962.

HASTINGS, LANSFORD. *The Emigrants' Guide to California and Oregon.* Princeton, 1932.

HAWGOOD, JOHN A. (ed.). *First and Last Consul* [mostly Larkin letters]. San Marino, Calif., 1962.

————. "John Augustus Sutter: A Reappraisal," *Arizona and the West,* Winter, 1962.

————. "John C. Fremont and the Bear Flag Revolt: A Reappraisal," *SCQ,* June, 1962.

————. "The Pattern of Yankee Infiltration in Mexican Alta California," *PHR,* Feb., 1958.

HINE, ROBERT V. *Edward Kern and American Expansion.* New Haven, 1962.

HUNT, ROCKWELL. *John Bidwell, Prince of California Pioneers.* Caldwell, Idaho, 1942.

HUSSEY, JOHN A. "New Light on the Original Bear Flag," *CHSQ,* Sept., 1952.

IDE, WILLIAM B. *Who Conquered California?* Claremont, Calif., 1880.

LYMAN, GEORGE D. *Dr. John Marsh, Pioneer.* New York, 1930.

MELDRUM, GEORGE WESTON. "The History of the Treatment of Minority Groups in California, 1830–60." Ph.D. dissertation, Stanford University, 1948.

MERK, FREDERICK. *Manifest Destiny and Mission in American History.* New York, 1963.

MORGAN, DALE L. *Overland in 1846* . . . [diaries, letters, etc.]. 2 vols. Georgetown, Calif., 1963.

NASITIR, A. P. "International Rivalry for California . . .," *CHSQ,* March, 1967.

NEVINS, ALLAN. *Fremont, Pathmarker of the West.* 2 vols. New York, 1932.

NUNIS, DOYCE B. *The Trials of Isaac Graham.* Los Angeles, 1967.

PARKER, ROBERT J. "Thomas Larkin, Anglo-American Businessman in Mexican California," in *Greater America.* Berkeley and Los Angeles, 1945.

PHILLIPS, CATHERINE. *Jessie Benton Fremont.* San Francisco, 1935.

PREUSS, CHARLES. *Exploring with Fremont.* Norman, Okla., 1958.

REVERE, JOSEPH. *A Tour of Duty in California* . . . New York, 1849.

STEWART, GEORGE R. *The California Trail.* New York, 1962.

————. *Ordeal By Hunger: The Story of the Donner Party.* New York, 1960.

UNDERHILL, REUBEN L. *From Cowhides to Golden Fleece* [Thomas O. Larkin]. Stanford, 1939.

ZOLLINGER, JAMES PETER. *Sutter, the Man and His Empire.* New York, 1939.

The Gold Rush Decade

ALLEN, R. H. "The Spanish Land-Grant System . . .," *Agricultural History*, July, 1935.

AUDUBON, JOHN W. *Audubon's Western Journal* (ed. by Frank H. Hodder). Cleveland, 1906.

BAILEY, PAUL. *Sam Brannan and the California Mormons*. Los Angeles, 1953.

BAKER, HUGH S. "The Book Trade in California, 1849–1859," *CHSQ*, 4 installments, 1951.

BANCROFT, HUBERT HOWE. *California Inter Pocula*. San Francisco, 1888.

———. *Popular Tribunals*. 2 vols. San Francisco, 1887.

BANNING, WILLIAM, and GEORGE H. BANNING. *Six Horses*. New York, 1930.

BENSEN, WILLIAM. "The Stone and Kelsey Massacre on the Shores of Clear Lake in 1849," *CHSQ*, Sept., 1932.

BORTHWICK, J. D. *Three Years in California*. Edinburgh, 1857.

BROWNE, LINA FERGUSSON. *J. Ross Browne* . . . Albuquerque, N.M., 1969.

BRUFF, J. GOLDSBOROUGH. *Gold Rush* [journals, etc.] (ed. by Georgia W. Read and Ruth P. Gaines). 2 vols. New York, 1944.

BRYAN, BERRYMAN. "Reminiscences of California, 1849–1852," *CHSQ*, March, 1932.

BUCHANAN, A. R. *David S. Terry of California, Dueling Judge*. San Marino, Calif., 1956.

BUCK, FRANKLIN. *A Yankee Trader in the Gold Rush*. Boston, 1930.

BUFFUM, E. GOULD. *Six Months in the Gold Mines* (ed. by John W. Caughey). Los Angeles, 1959.

BUNNELL, L. H. *The Discovery of the Yosemite*. Chicago, 1880.

BURNETT, PETER H. *Recollections and Opinions of an Old Timer*. New York, 1880.

CAUGHEY, JOHN W. *Gold Is the Cornerstone*. Berkeley, 1948.

———. "Their Majesties, the Mob." *PHR*, July, 1957.

CLAPPE, LOUISE A. K. S. [Dame Shirley]. *The Shirley Letters from the California Mines*. New York, 1949.

CLARKE, DWIGHT L. *William Tecumseh Sherman, Gold Rush Banker*. San Francisco, 1969.

COLEMAN, WILLIAM T. "San Francisco Vigilance Committees," *Century Magazine*, Nov., 1891.

DAVIS, STEPHEN CHAPIN. *California Gold Rush Merchant* (ed. by B. B. Richards). San Marino, Calif., 1956.

DELANO, ALONZO. *Life on the Plains and Among the Diggings*. New York, 1936.

DILLON, RICHARD. "The Black Knight of Zayante," *The American West*, July, 1970.

———. "J. Ross Browne and the Corruptible West," *The American West*, Spring, 1965.

———. "Rejoice Ye Thieves and Harlots!" *CHSQ*, June, 1958.

DWINELLE, JOHN. *Colonial History of San Francisco*. San Francisco, 1863.

EGAN, FEROL. *The El Dorado Trail*. New York, 1970.

ELLISON, JOSEPH. *California and the Nation, 1850–1869.* Berkeley, 1927.

ELLISON, WILLIAM H. "Memoirs of Hon. William M. Gwin," *CHSQ,* 4 installments, 1940.

———. *A Self-Governing Dominion: California, 1849–1860.*

FRANKLIN, WILLIAM E. "Peter Burnett and the Provisional Government Movement," *CHSQ,* June, 1961.

FREDMAN, L. L. "Broderick: A Reassessment," *PHR,* Feb., 1961.

GATES, PAUL W. "Adjudication of Spanish-Mexican Land Claims . . .," *Huntington Library Quarterly,* May, 1958.

———. *California Ranchos and Farms, 1846–1862.* Madison, Wis., 1967.

———. "California's Embattled Settlers," *CHSQ,* June, 1962.

———. "Pre-Henry George Land Warfare in California," *CHSQ,* June, 1967.

GROGH, GEORGE W. *Gold Fever.* New York, 1966.

GUINN, JAMES M. "The Sonoran Migration," Hist. Soc. of Southern California, *Annual Publications,* vol. 8 (1909–11).

HAINE, DR. J. J. F. "Memoir: A Belgian in the Gold Rush," *CHSQ,* June, 1959.

HAMMOND, GEORGE (ed.). *Digging for Gold—Without a Shovel.* Denver, Colo., 1967.

HANCHETT, WILLIAM. "The Question of Religion and the Taming of California, 1849–1854," *CHSQ,* March–June, 1953.

HARGIS, DONALD. "The Issues in the Gwin-Broderick Debates of 1859," *CHSQ,* Dec., 1953.

HELPER, HINTON. *Land of Gold.* Baltimore, 1855.

HITTELL, JOHN S. *The Resources of California.* San Francisco, 1863.

HOLLIDAY, J. S. "The California Gold Rush Reconsidered," *Probing the American West.* Sante Fe, N.M., 1963.

JACKSON, JOSEPH HENRY. *Anybody's Gold.* New York, 1941.

KEMBLE, JOHN HASKELL. *The Panama Route, 1848–1869.* Berkeley and Los Angeles, 1943.

KROEBER, THEODORA. *Ishi in Two Worlds.* Berkeley and Los Angeles, 1961.

LEWIS, OSCAR. *Sea Routes to the Gold Fields.* New York, 1949.

MANLY, WILLIAM LEWIS. *Death Valley in '49.* Los Angeles, 1949.

MARRYAT, FRANK. *Mountains and Molehills.* Philadelphia and New York, 1962.

MOREFIELD, RICHARD. "Mexicans in the California Mines," *CHSQ,* March, 1956.

MORGAN, DALE L. (ed.). *In Pursuit of the Golden Dream.* Stoughton, Mass., 1970.

——— (ed.). *The Overland Diary of James A. Pritchard.* Denver, Colo., 1959.

——— (ed.). *Three Years in California . . . Life at Sonora, 1849–1852.* Berkeley and Los Angeles, 1964

MORSE, JOHN F. *The First History of Sacramento City.* Sacramento, 1945.

OLMSTEAD, ROGER. "San Francisco and the Vigilante Style," *The American West,* Jan.–March, 1970.

PAGE, ELIZABETH. *Wagons West.* New York, 1930.

PAUL, RODMAN. *California Gold.* Cambridge, Mass., 1947.

———. *The California Gold Discovery.* Georgetown, Calif., 1966.

———. *Mining Frontiers of the Far West.* New York, 1963.

_____. "The Origins of the Chinese Issue in California," *Mississippi Valley Historical Review*, Sept., 1938.

PITT, LEONARD. "The Beginnings of Nativism in California," *PHR*, Feb., 1961.

POMFRET, JOHN E. (ed.). *California Gold Rush Voyages*. San Marino, Calif., 1954.

POTTER, DAVID M. (ed.). *The Trail to California*. New Haven, 1945.

RICE, William B. *The Los Angeles Star, 1851–1864*. Berkeley, 1947.

ROYCE, JOSIAH. *California from the Conquest in 1846 to the Second Vigilance Committee*. New York, 1949.

ROYCE, SARAH ELEANOR. *A Frontier Lady* (ed. by Ralph H. Gabriel). New Haven, 1932.

SCHERER, J. A. B. *The Lion of the Vigilantes* [W. T. Coleman]. Indianapolis, 1939.

SCOTT, REVA. *Sam Brannan and the Golden Fleece*. New York, 1944.

SHERMAN, WILLIAM TECUMSEH. *Memoirs*. Vol. 1. New York, 1875.

SOULÉ, FRANK, JOHN GIHON, and JAMES NESBIT. *The Annals of San Francisco*. New York, 1855.

STEWART, GEORGE R. *Committee of Vigilance . . . 1851*. Boston, 1964.

STILLMAN, J. B. D. *Seeking the Golden Fleece*. San Francisco, 1877.

TAYLOR, BAYARD. *El Dorado*. New York, 1949.

THOMAS, LATELY. *Between Two Empires* [William Gwin]. Boston, 1969.

WAGNER, JACK R. *The Gold Mines of California*. Berkeley, 1970.

WAITE, EDWIN G. "The Discovery of Gold in California," *Century Magazine*, Feb., 1891.

WARREN, AUGUSTA B. "Judge Robert Thompson," *CHSQ*, Sept., 1951.

WILLIAMS, DAVID. *David C. Broderick: A Political Portrait*. San Marino, Calif., 1969.

WINTHER, O. O. *Express and Stagecoach Days in California. . . .* Stanford, 1946.

WISTER, ISAAC JONES. *Autobiography*. Philadelphia, 1914.

WRIGHT, DORIS M. "The Making of Cosmopolitan California, 1848–1870," *CHSQ*, Dec., 1940, March, 1941.

WRIGHT, LOUIS B. *Culture on the Moving Frontier*. New York, 1961.

From the Gold Rush to the End of the Century

BARKER, CHARLES A. *Henry George*. New York, 1955.

BARSNESS, RICHARD. "Iron Horses and an Inner Harbor at San Pedro Bay, 1867–1890," *PHR*, 1965.

BAUER, JOHN E. *The Health Seekers of Southern California, 1870–1900*. San Marino, Calif., 1959.

BELL, HORACE. *Reminiscences of a Ranger*. Santa Barbara, 1927.

BLOSS, ROY S. *The Pony Express: The Great Gamble*. Berkeley, 1959.

BREWER, WILLIAM G. *Up and Down California in 1860–64*. (ed. by Francis P. Farquhar). Berkeley, 1949.

BROWN, J. L. *The Mussel Slough Tragedy*. Fresno, 1958.

BRYCE, JAMES. *The American Commonwealth*. Vol. II. London, 1891.

CALLOW, ALEXANDER, JR., "San Francisco's Blind Boss," *PHR*, Aug., 1956.

CHIU, PING. *Chinese Labor in California, 1850–1880*. Madison, Wis., 1963.

CLARK, GEORGE T. *Leland Stanford.* Palo Alto, 1931.

CLARKE, GORDON W. "A Significant Memorial to Mussel Slough," *PHR*, Aug., 1956.

COHEN, A. A. *An Address on the Railroad Evil and Its Remedy.* San Francisco, 1879.

DAGGETT, STUART. *Chapters in the History of the Southern Pacific.* New York, 1922.

DOBIE, EDITH. *The Political Career of Stephen Mallory White.* Stanford, 1927.

DUFAULT, DAVID V. "The Chinese in the Mining Camps of California," *CHSQ,* June, 1959.

DUMKE, GLENN S. *The Boom of the Eighties in Southern California.* San Marino, Calif., 1944.

DUNHAM, HAROLD G. *Government Handout.* New York, 1970.

Fresno County Centennial Almanac. Fresno, 1956.

GATES, PAUL. "California's Agricultural College Lands," *PHR*, May, 1961.

GEORGE, HENRY. *Our Land and Land Policy, National and State.* San Francisco, 1871.

_____. *Progress and Poverty.* New York, 1926.

_____. "What the Railroad Will Bring Us," *The American West*, July, 1968.

GRISWOLD, WESLEY S. *A Work of Giants.* New York, 1962.

HAFEN, LEROY. *The Overland Mail, 1849–69.* Cleveland, 1926.

HUTCHINSON, W. H. *Oil, Land, and Politics.* 2 vols. Norman, Okla., 1965.

JOHNSON, KENNETH. "California's Constitution of 1879," *CHSQ,* June, 1970.

JONES, LAMAR B. "Labor and Management in California Agriculture," *Labor History*, Winter, 1970.

KAUER, RALPH. "The Workingmen's Party of California," *PHR*, Sept., 1944.

KELLEY, ROBERT L. "Forgotten Giant: The Hydraulic Gold Mining Industry in California," *PHR*, Nov., 1954.

_____. *Gold vs. Grain.* Glendale, Calif., 1959.

_____. "The Mining Debris Controversy in the Sacramento Valley," *PHR*, Nov., 1956.

KERSCHNER, FREDERICK D., JR. "George Chaffey and the Irrigation Frontier," *Agricultural History*, Oct., 1953.

LAVENDER, DAVID. *The Great Persuader* [Collis Huntington]. New York, 1970.

LEWIS, OSCAR. *Bay Window Bohemia.* New York, 1956.

_____. *The Big Four.* New York, 1935.

_____. *The Silver Kings.* New York, 1947.

LOMAS, CHARLES. "Kearney and George," *Speech Monographs*, Mar., 1961.

LYMAN, GEORGE D. *Ralston's Ring.* New York, 1937.

_____. *The Saga of the Comstock.* New York, 1934.

MCCAGUE, JAMES. *Moguls and Iron Men.* New York, 1964.

MCKEE, IRVING. "Notable Memorials to Mussel Slough," *PHR*, Feb., 1948.

_____. "The Shooting of Charles de Young," *PHR*, Aug., 1947.

MILLS, JAMES. "A Loving Look at the Hotel del [Coronado]," *San Diego Magazine*, April, 1969.

MILLS, MINNIE TIBBETS. "Luther Calvin Tibbetts . . .," *SCQ,* Dec., 1943.

MOORHEAD, DUDLEY T. "Sectionalism and the California Constitution," *PHR*, Sept., 1943.

NADEAU, REMI A. *City-Makers, 1868–1876.* New York, 1948.

NASH, GERALD D. "Henry George Reexamined," *Agricultural History,* July, 1959.

———. "Problems and Projections . . . California Land Policy," *Arizona and the West,* Winter, 1960.

NEWHALL, RUTH W. *The Newhall Ranch.* San Marino, Calif., 1958.

NEWMARK, HARRIS. *Sixty Years in Southern California, 1853–1913* (ed. by W. W. Robinson). Los Angeles, 1970.

NORDHOFF, CHARLES. *California: For Health, Pleasure, and Residence.* New York, 1872.

PAUL, RODMAN. "The Great California Grain War," *PHR,* Nov., 1958.

———. "The Wheat Trade between California and the United Kingdom," *Mississippi Valley Historical Review,* Dec., 1958.

PERCY, R. G. "The First Oil Development in California," *California Historian,* Dec., 1959.

QUIETT, GLEN CHESNEY. *They Built the West: An Epic of Rails and Cities.* New York, 1934.

SAXTON, ALEXANDER. "The Army of Canton in the High Sierra," *PHR,* May, 1966.

———. "San Francisco Labor . . .," *PHR,* Nov., 1965.

STEWART, ROBERT E., JR., and MARY FRANCES STEWART. *Adolph Sutro: A Biography.* Berkeley, 1962.

STIMSON, MARSHALL. "A Short History of Los Angeles Harbor." *SCQ,* March, 1945.

SWANBERG, W. A. *Citizen Hearst.* New York, 1961.

SWISHER, CARL B. *Motivation and Political Technique in the California Constitutional Convention, 1878–1879.* Claremont, Calif., 1930.

———. *Stephen J. Field.* Washington, 1930.

TAYLOR, PAUL S. "Foundations of California Rural Society," *CHSQ,* 1945.

———. "Water, Land, and People in the Great Valley," *The American West,* March, 1968.

TWAIN, MARK. *Roughing It.* New York, 1962.

WEINSTEIN, ROBERT A. "The Million-Dollar Mud Flat" [Los Angeles Harbor], *The American West,* Jan., 1969.

WHEAT, CARL I. "A Sketch of the Life of Theodore Judah," *CHSQ,* Sept., 1925.

WHITE GERALD T. "California's Other Mineral," *PHR,* May, 1970.

———. *Formative Years in the Far West* [Standard Oil Company of California]. New York, 1962.

———. *Scientists in Conflict: The Beginnings of the Oil Industry in California.* San Marino, Calif., 1968.

WILLARD, CHARLES D. *The Free Harbor Contest in Los Angeles.* Los Angeles, 1899.

WINTHER, OSCAR O. "The Colonial System of Southern California," *Agricultural History,* July, 1953.

———. "The Rise of Metropolitan Los Angeles," *Huntington Library Quarterly,* Aug., 1947.

———. "The Use of Climate as a Means of Promoting Migration to Southern California," *Mississippi Valley Historical Review,* 1946.

WRIGHT, WILLIAM [Dan de Quille]. *The Big Bonanza.* New York, 1947.

The Twentieth Century

BEAN, WALTON. *Boss Ruef's San Francisco.* Berkeley and Los Angeles, 1952.

BOESEN, VICTOR. "Oh, Say Can You Breathe?" *West Magazine,* May 31, 1970.

BOYARSKY, NANCY, and WILLIAM BOYARSKY. "The Highway Game," *West Magazine,* Feb. 7, 1971.

BRONSON, WILLIAM. *The Earth Shook, the Sky Burned.* New York, 1959.

————. *How to Kill a Golden State.* New York, 1968.

California Farm Labor Problems. Report of the California State Senate Fact Finding Committee on Labor and Welfare Sacramento, 1961.

CLAYTON, JAMES L. "Defense Spending: The Key to California's Growth," *Western Political Quarterly,* June, 1962.

CLODIUS, ALBERT HOWARD. "The Quest for Good Government in Los Angeles, 1890–1910." Ph.D. dissertation, Claremont Graduate School, 1953.

CONOT, ROBERT. *Rivers of Blood, Years of Darkness* [Watts Riot]. New York, 1968.

DE ROOS, ROBERT W. *The Thirsty Land.* Stanford, 1948.

DREYFUSS, JOHN. "The High Cost of Smog . . .," Los Angeles *Times,* Pt. II, Jan. 6, 1972, p. 1.

DUBOFSKY, MELVYN. *We Shall Be All: A History of the I.W.W.* Chicago, 1969.

DUNNE, JOHN GREGORY. "To Die Standing: Cesar Chavez and the Chicanos," *The Atlantic,* June, 1971.

FROST, RICHARD H. *The Mooney Case.* Stanford, 1968.

GREENWOOD, LEONARD. "Farm Labor Troubles: Some Still Seek a Peaceful Solution," Los Angeles *Times,* Sec. G, Nov. 17, 1968.

HARTMIRE, WAYNE C. "The Delano Grape Strike," Report of the California Migrant Ministry, Los Angeles, February, 1969.

HERBERT, RAY. "More Water than Needed for 50 Years," Los Angeles *Times,* Sec. C, Oct. 25, 1970.

————. "Mounting Pressure by Public Slows Highway Construction," Los Angeles *Times,* Dec. 12, 1971, p. 1.

HOSMER, HELEN. "Triumph and Failure in the Imperial Valley," in *The Grand Colorado* (ed. by T. H. Watkins). Palo Alto, 1960.

JONES, HOLWAY. *John Muir and the Sierra Club.* San Francisco, 1965.

KIRSCHBAUM, LAWRENCE. "A Report on the California Water Controversy," *West Magazine,* July 19, 1971.

LARSEN, Charles E. "The Epic Campaign of 1934," *PHR,* May, 1958.

LILLARD, RICHARD G. *Eden in Jeopardy.* New York, 1966.

MCKEE, IRVING. "The Background and Early Career of Hiram Warren Johnson," *PHR,* Feb., 1950.

MEERS, JOHN R. "The California Wine and Grape Industry and Prohibition," *CHSQ,* Mar., 1967.

The Migratory Farm Labor Problem in the U.S. Report of the Committee on Labor and Public Welfare, U.S. Senate. Washington, 1968.

MORGAN, NEIL. *The California Syndrome.* New York, 1969.

————. *Westward Tilt.* New York, 1963.

MOWRY, GEORGE E. *The California Progressives.* Berkeley and Los Angeles, 1951.

NADEAU, REMI A. *The Water-Seekers*. New York, 1950.

NASH, RODERICK. *Wilderness and the American Mind*. New Haven, 1967.

OLIN, SPENCER, JR. "Hiram Johnson . . . and the Election of 1910," *CHSQ*, Sept., 1966.

OUTLAND, CHARLES F. *Man-Made Disaster: The Story of the St. Francis Dam*. Glendale, Calif., 1963.

RAPOPORT, ROGER. "The Fox and the Grapes" [Chavez], *West Magazine*, Nov. 23, 1969.

REGISTER, RICHARD. "Rage, Rage Against the Dying of the Light" [smog], *West Magazine*, June 13, 1971.

The Report of the President's Commission on Campus Unrest. Washington, 1970.

RICHARDSON, Elmo. "The Struggle for the Valley: California's Hetch Hetchy Controversy," *CHSQ*, Dec., 1959.

ROBINSON, W. W. "The Southern California Real Estate Boom of the 1920's," *SCQ*, March, 1942.

RUNDELL, WALTER, JR. "Steinbeck's Image of the West," *The American West*, Spring, 1964.

SHOVER, JOHN L. "Progressives and the Working Class Vote in California," *Labor History*, Fall, 1965.

STEFFENS, LINCOLN. *Autobiography*. 2 vols. New York, 1931.

STEINBECK, JOHN. *The Grapes of Wrath*. New York, 1939.

STEINER, STAN. *La Raza: The Mexican-American*. New York, 1970.

STRONG, DOUGLAS. "The Sierra Forest Reserve," *CHSQ*, 1967.

TAYLOR, PAUL S. *An American Exodus*. New York, 1969.

———. "The Desert Shall Rejoice . . .," in *The Grand Colorado* (ed. by T. H. Watkins). Palo Alto, Calif., 1969.

———. "Reclamation," *The American West*, July, 1970.

TOSI, UMBERT. "Everybody Loves Yosemite," *West Magazine*, Sept. 20, 1970.

WATERS, FRANK. *The Colorado*. New York, 1946.

WATKINS, T. H. "Crisis on the Eel," Sierra Club *Bulletin*, April, 1969.

———. "Making an Empire to Order," *The Grand Colorado*. Palo Alto, Calif., 1969.

———. "The New Romans," in *The Water Hustlers*. Sierra Club, 1971.

WHITTEN, WOODROW C. "The Wheatland Episode," *PHR*, Feb., 1948.

Wolfe, Linnie M. *Son of the Wilderness: The Life of John Muir*. New York, 1945.

Afterword

BEAN, WALTON and JAMES J. RAWLS. *California: An Interpretive History*, 4th ed. New York, 1983.

BERNARD RICH and BRADLEY P. RICE, eds. *Sunbelt Cities*. Austin, Texas, 1983.

FAY, JAMES S., ANNE G. LIPOW, and STEPHANIE W. FAY. *California Almanac, 1984–1985*. Novato, Calif., 1984.

FITZGERALD, FRANCES. "The Castro," *New Yorker*, July 21, 1986.

JACKSON, WES, WENDELL BERRY, and BRUCE COLMAN, eds. *Meeting the Expectations of the Land*. San Francisco, 1984.

JURMAIN, CLAUDIA and JAMES J. RAWLS, eds. *California: A Place, a People, a Dream*. San Francisco and Oakland, 1986.

KAHRL, WILLIAM. *Water and Power*. Berkeley, Calif., 1982.

LINDSEY, ROBERT. "Los Angeles," *New York Times Magazine*, July 22, 1984.

STEINHARDT, PETER. "Trashing California," *California Magazine*, July 1984.

———. "The Bay Water's Downhill Course," *California Magazine*, September 1984.

WOLLENBERG, CHARLES. "A Usable History for a Multicultural State." *California History*, Summer 1985.

WORSTER, DONALD. *Rivers of Empire*. New York, 1985.

The *Los Angeles Times* was also frequently consulted, particularly concerning issues voted on in the election of November 1986.

Index

461